Quintus of Smyrna's *Posthomerica*

Quintus of Smyrna's *Posthomerica*

Writing Homer Under Rome

Edited by Silvio Bär, Emma Greensmith
and Leyla Ozbek

EDINBURGH
University Press

Edinburgh University Press is one of the leading university presses in the UK. We publish academic books and journals in our selected subject areas across the humanities and social sciences, combining cutting-edge scholarship with high editorial and production values to produce academic works of lasting importance. For more information visit our website: edinburghuniversitypress.com

Edinburgh University Press Ltd
The Tun – Holyrood Road, 12(2f) Jackson's Entry, Edinburgh EH8 8PJ

Typeset in 11/13 Bembo Std by
IDSUK (DataConnection) Ltd

A CIP record for this book is available from the British Library

ISBN 978 1 4744 9358 1 (hardback)
ISBN 978 1 4744 9360 4 (webready PDF)
ISBN 978 1 4744 9361 1 (epub)

Contents

List of Contributors   viii

1 Introduction: Going to Rome, Returning to Troy   1
   Silvio Bär, Emma Greensmith and Leyla Ozbek

Part I: Contexts and Poetics

2 Temporality and Temper: Time, Narrative and Heroism in
   Quintus of Smyrna   17
   Simon Goldhill

3 Poetry, Performance and Quintus' *Posthomerica*   38
   Katerina Carvounis

4 A-Sexual Epic? Consummation and Closure in the *Posthomerica*   57
   Emma Greensmith

5 Images of Life and Death: Visualising the Heroic Body in
   Quintus Smyrnaeus' *Posthomerica*   75
   A. Sophie Schoess

Part II: Religion, Gods and Destiny

6 A Non-Homeric Fate in Quintus of Smyrna's *Posthomerica*?
   Representation, Function, Problems   97
   Calum A. Maciver

7   Disempowering the Gods   118
    Katia Barbaresco

8   Animal and Human Sacrifice in Quintus of Smyrna   138
    Jan N. Bremmer

Part III: Between Narratology and Lexicology

9   A Narratological Study of the Role of the Fates in the *Posthomerica*   161
    Eirini Argyrouli

10 Wielding Words: Neoptolemus as a Speaker of Words
    in Quintus' *Posthomerica*   175
    Tine Scheijnen

11 Stepping out of Place: σχέτλιος in Quintus of Smyrna's *Posthomerica*   194
    Jordan Maly-Preuss

12 Renewing Homer with Homer: The Use of Epithets in
    Quintus of Smyrna's *Posthomerica*   214
    Alessia Ferreccio

13 Polychronic Intertextuality in Quintus of Smyrna's *Posthomerica*   229
    Vincent Tomasso

Part IV: The Struggle with the Literary Past

14 The Dissolution of Troy: Homeric Narratology in the *Posthomerica*   247
    Fran Middleton

15 'Why So Serious?' The Ambivalence of Joy and Laughter in
    the *Iliad*, *Odyssey* and *Posthomerica*   267
    Arnold Bärtschi

16 Reshaping the Nature of Heroes: Heracles, Philoctetes and
    the Bow in Quintus Smyrnaeus' *Posthomerica*   287
    Leyla Ozbek

17 Quintus and the Epic Cycle   298
    Giampiero Scafoglio

Part V: Re-Readings and Re-Workings

18 Philological Editor and Protestant Pedagogue: How Lorenz Rhodoman
    (1545–1606) Worked on the *Posthomerica* of Quintus Smyrnaeus 321
    Thomas Gärtner

19 Too Homeric to Be True: John Tzetzes' Reception of Quintus
    of Smyrna and the Importance of Plausibility   351
    Valeria F. Lovato

20 A Postmodern Quintus? Theories of Fan Fiction and the *Posthomerica*   373
    Stephan Renker

Bibliography   386
Index of Passages Cited   420
General Index   429

Contributors

Eirini Argyrouli studied Classics at the National and Kapodistrian University of Athens and at the University of Amsterdam. She is an independent researcher and she is interested in narratology, late antique epic and lyric poetry.

Silvio Bär is Professor of Classics at the University of Oslo. His research areas and interests include Greek hexameter poetry (especially of the imperial period), tragedy, lyric, the novel, mythology, rhetoric, the Second Sophistic, intertextuality, transtextuality, diachronic narratology, and the reception of antiquity in English literature and popular culture. He has published widely on Quintus of Smyrna's *Posthomerica*, on the genre 'epyllion', and on the character of Herakles in Greek epic and beyond.

Katia Barbaresco is a PhD student in Ancient Heritage Studies at the Ca' Foscari University of Venice. She spent part of her academic education in the UK (2017 at the University of Reading, 2019–20 at King's College London). Her PhD project is a commentary to the third *logos* of Quintus Smyrnaeus' *Posthomerica*, with a focus on the death and funeral of Achilles. Her main research area of interest lies in Greek epic poetry from its oral origins to the imperial poems. She is a member of the Aletheia research group of Ca' Foscari and collaborates with Classici Contro.

Arnold Bärtschi obtained his BA at the University of Basel (2012), his MA (2014) as well as his PhD (2018) at the Ruhr University Bochum with a dissertation on 'Titanen, Giganten und Riesen im antiken Epos' (published 2019). He was a research assistant of Prof. Dr Manuel Baumbach (2014–19) and currently works as 'Studienrat' and operational director of Classical Philology at the Ruhr University Bochum (since 2019). His main research includes epic poetry, adaption of literary theory in Classical Philology and reception of antiquity in modern media, especially in comics. He is a member of the 'Gesellschaft für Comicforschung'.

Jan N. Bremmer is Emeritus Professor of Religious Studies at the University of Groningen. His recent books include *Initiation into the Mysteries of the Ancient World* (2014), *Maidens, Magic and Martyrs in Early Christianity* (2017), *The World of Greek Religion and Mythology* (2019), *Greek Religion* (2021²), *Becoming a Man in Ancient Greece and Rome: Myths and Rituals of Initiation* (2021) and, as co-editor, *Marginality, Media, and Mutations of Religious Authority in the History of Christianity* (2019), *The Protevangelium of James* (2020) and *The Apostles Peter, Paul, John, Thomas and Philip with Their Companions in Late Antiquity* (2021).

Katerina Carvounis is Assistant Professor in Ancient Greek Literature at the National and Kapodistrian University of Athens and was previously a British Academy Postdoctoral Research Fellow at the Faculty of Classics, Cambridge, and a Fellow of Murray Edwards College, Cambridge. Her main research interests include the Greek epic tradition and later Greek poetry, and she has published widely in these areas. Among her recent publications is *A Commentary on Quintus of Smyrna, Posthomerica 14* (Oxford University Press).

Alessia Ferreccio is a PhD in Greek and Latin Philology and secondary school teacher of Ancient Greek and Latin. She has worked on Greek lexicography and ancient Greek scholarship and grammar (Montanari's *GI. Dizionario Greco-Italiano, Words in Progress* and *LGGA-Lexicon of Greek Grammarians of Antiquity* projects). Her main research interests concern late Greek epic, especially Quintus of Smyrna. She published *Commento al II libro dei Posthomerica di Quinto Smirneo* (2014) and *Gli epiteti degli dèi nei Posthomerica di Quinto Smirneo* (2018). She is on the editorial board of the *Rivista di Filologia e di Istruzione Classica* and of *Trends in Classics: Journal of Classical Studies.*

Thomas Gärtner is Außerplanmäßiger Professor of Classics and Medieval Latin at the University of Cologne and has worked as a lecturer at several German universities. His research interests focus on Latin poetry of all periods from the Augustan Age onward, as well as Neo-Ancient Greek from the Humanist period, especially Lorenz Rhodoman and Michael Neander's school of poets in Ilfeld.

Simon Goldhill is Professor of Greek at the University of Cambridge, Foreign Secretary of the British Academy and a Fellow of King's College, Cambridge. He has published very widely on Greek literature and culture. His books have been translated into ten languages and won three international prizes. His most recent books are *Preposterous Poetics: The Politics and Aesthetics* *of Form in Late Antiquity* and *The Christian Invention of Time: Temporality and the Literature of Late Antiquity*, both published by Cambridge University Press.

Emma Greensmith is Associate Professor of Classical Languages and Literature at the University of Oxford and a Fellow of St John's College. She specialises in imperial Greek literature, and is particularly interested in epic, poetics and religion. Her recent book, *The Resurrection of Homer in Imperial Greek Epic: Quintus Smyrnaeus' Posthomerica and the Poetics of Impersonation* (2020) offers a new reading of the role of epic and the reception of Homer in Greco-Roman culture. She has also written recent articles on Nonnus, Gregory of Nazianzus and the Sibylline Oracles, and is editing a new *Cambridge Companion to Ancient Greek Epic*.

Valeria F. Lovato is a Swiss National Science Foundation postdoctoral fellow at the Centre for Medieval Literature (University of Southern Denmark), with a project on Isaac Comnenus Porphyrogenitus. Her research also encompasses the reception of Homeric epics in Byzantium and in Renaissance Europe, a topic on which she has published extensively. Her current book projects include an edited volume on Isaac Comnenus and a monograph investigating the interplay between classicising learning and self-fashioning in John Tzetzes and Eustathios of Thessalonike.

Calum A. Maciver is Senior Lecturer in Classics at the University of Edinburgh. He has published on Greek and Latin poetry of the imperial period, as well as the Greek novel and Lucian.

Jordan Maly-Preuss is a DPhil student in Classical Languages and Literature at the University of Oxford (Merton College). She is an alumna of the Ertegun Graduate Scholarship Programme in the Humanities and currently holds a Stonehouse Foundation/Faculty of Classics scholarship. Her present research focuses on the diachronic development of ancient Greek epic poetics, with a special interest in classical, Hellenistic and late antique reanalyses of archaic formular idioms.

Fran Middleton is a specialist in poetry of the high and later Roman Empire.

Leyla Ozbek is Research Fellow of Greek Language and Literature at the Scuola Normale Superiore of Pisa. She studied as an undergraduate at the Scuola Normale Superiore and at the University of Pisa, working on fragmentary plays of Sophocles. She obtained her PhD in Classics at the Scuola Normale with a dissertation on Quintus' *Posthomerica* Book 9, now forthcoming for publication. She has been an annual visiting scholar at University College London and at the University of Zurich. In 2015–16 she was Research Associate at the University of Cambridge on the AHRC-funded project 'Greek Epic of the Roman Empire: A Cultural History'. Her research interests are Greek epic and culture of the imperial period, Greek tragedy and fragments, papyrology and the study of ancient manuscript transmission.

Stephan Renker is DAAD Lecturer at the German Department of Shanghai International Studies University. He studied Classics, German and English at the University of Bamberg and at Carleton College (Northfield, MN). His doctorate on Quintus Smyrnaeus is from the University of Hamburg. He has also published on Virgil and Pseudo-Oppian.

Giampiero Scafoglio obtained his PhD at the University of Naples 'Federico II' and his Habilitation (HDR) at the University of Nantes. He is Professor of Latin Language and Literature at the University of Nice (Université Côte d'Azur) and Research Coordinator at the CNRS. He works on Homer, the Greek epic cycle, Roman tragedy, Virgil, late antique poetry, the Homeric presence in the literature of the imperial age and classical reception in Italian culture. Among his publications: *Noctes Vergilianae* (2010) and *Ajax: Un héros qui vient de loin* (2017). Since 2019, he has been a member of the 'Conseil National des Universités' (on the nomination of the French Minister of University and Research).

Tine Scheijnen is a postdoctoral researcher at Ghent University (Belgium), where she obtained her PhD in 2016. Her research interests lie in the field of ancient, late antique and medieval Troy literature and heroism. She has published widely on Quintus of Smyrna, including a 2018 monograph on *Quintus of Smyrna's Posthomerica: A Study of Heroic Characterization and Heroism* (Brill), and is co-editor of *Greek and Latin Poetry of Late Antiquity: Form, Tradition and Context* (forthcoming with CUP). She currently explores the reception and evolutions of heroic characterisation in Middle English Troy romances.

A. Sophie Schoess is Associate Lecturer in Classics at the University of St Andrews. Her research interests include late antique epic poetry, the relationship between image and text in the ancient world and the reception of classical myth from late antiquity through modernity. Her doctoral thesis (University of Oxford, 2018) traced the reception of Ariadne's myth in literature and the visual arts from antiquity through the Renaissance. Her current research focuses on Christian interpretations and appropriations of classical myth in late antiquity and the Middle Ages.

Vincent Tomasso is an Assistant Professor of Classical Studies at Trinity College in Hartford, CT. His publications have focused on reception in two areas: in ancient Greece, especially in epic of the imperial period, as well as in the modern world, in film, television and comics. His articles on these subjects have appeared in edited volumes and in journals like the *American Journal of Philology, Classical Receptions Journal* and *The Classical Journal*.

CHAPTER I

Introduction: Going to Rome, Returning to Troy

Silvio Bär, Emma Greensmith and Leyla Ozbek

Τὰ μεθ' Ὅμηρον – 'The Events after Homer'! This was the flamboy-
ant announcement that attracted almost all inhabitants from the city of
Smyrna to the theatre on a late Spring afternoon in the early 180s CE. Expectations were high. But when the poet – a man in his early thirties about whom
almost no one had heard before – started reciting, everyone was dumbstruck.
The vivid portrayal of the battle of the Amazons and Achilles' belated love for
Penthesilea, composed in the best Homeric style, was deeply moving. Some of
the more gullible in the audience were convinced that this was indeed a genuinely Homeric poem, whereas other, sharper listeners noticed that many of the
words and phrases used were clearly un-Homeric. However, everyone agreed
that after so many rhetorical competitions, time was ripe for something new.

The poet in question was a schoolteacher who came from an upper-middle-
class family from Smyrna, a city in Asia Minor which at that time belonged to
the Roman Empire. His parents had given him the name 'Quintus' because
they had hoped that with a Roman name, their son was going to have a career
in the administration of the capital. However, he had instead chosen the profes-
sion of a teacher and an epicist. He disappeared from the record later; probably
he went on tour with his songs, and at some point he settled down and married.
He had a son called Dorotheus, who also tried his luck as an epicist, but never
became quite as proficient as his father. There were rumours that Dorotheus
joined a Christian sect later in life and that he even had religious visions; at least
this is how they explained why he wrote an esoteric account of a divine revelation in which he twice mentioned his father by name.

This biographical sketch of the Greek epic poet Quintus of Smyrna is
entirely fictional. However, almost every piece of information is, in one way
or another, based on assumptions and speculations that scholars have made

ever since the *Posthomerica* (*PH*) was rediscovered in the second half of the fifteenth century.[1] Just to enumerate some of the most notorious moot points: in the so-called *Visio Dorothei* (probably early fourth century CE), a poet called Κόϊντος/Κύϊντος is mentioned as Dorotheus' father, but his identification with Quintus of Smyrna is purely hypothetical;[2] the first secure attestation of Quintus' name stems from the twelfth century CE.[3] Along similar lines, the dating of Quintus and his poem to the late second (or third) century CE relies on rather weak evidence.[4] Likewise, Quintus' supposed provenance from the city of Smyrna is solely based on a biographic interpretation of the narrator's Call to the Muses depicted at *PH* 12.306–13.[5] Furthermore, Quintus' connection to the cultural milieu as outlined above is a matter of disagreement between scholars: Quintus belongs to the same period as the Second Sophistic and its intellectual setting, which focuses on the glorification and revival of classical rhetoric in old Attic prose, and scholars have therefore frequently debated about whether – and if so, how – the author of a Homericising epic could be viewed in this context.[6] Finally, similar uncertainties concern the question of whether the *PH* may actually have been publicly recited – or whether it was enjoyed by readers privately, independently and in silence.[7]

In what follows, we provide a brief synopsis of scholarship on Quintus and the *PH*. In view of the fact that comprehensive surveys exist about the state of the field of Quintus studies in the centuries and decades before (and right after) the turn of the millennium,[8] a few general strokes shall suffice here. In a second step, we will discuss in some more detail how and why scholarship has

[1] A similar (but completely unironic) attempt at reconstructing Quintus' biography is offered by Appel (1994b).

[2] The identification of Dorotheus as the son of 'our' Quintus stems from the editors of the *editio princeps* of the *Visio Dorothei* in their introduction (Hurst, Reverdin and Rudhardt 1984: 46–9). However, this identification has been challenged – most prominently by Francis Vian already shortly after the publication of the *editio princeps* (Vian 1985), and repeatedly by Gianfranco Agosti (Agosti 2015: 90–1; see also Agosti 1989: *passim* and Agosti 2017: 235, n112). For discussions of the issue by Quintus scholars, see James and Lee (2000: 7–9); Baumbach and Bär (2007b: 4–7); Bär (2009: 18–22); Carvounis (2019: xxvi–xxvii). The problem is tightly connected to the question of dating (see note 4).

[3] John Tzetzes, *Posthomerica* lines 10, 13, 282, 522, 584, 597; Eustathius of Thessaloniki, introduction to the *Iliad*, A468 (136.4), B814 (352.2), θ501 (1608.1), λ546 (1698.48), λ592 (1702.11).

[4] For discussions of Quintus' dating, see most recently James and Lee (2000: 1–9); Baumbach and Bär (2007b: 2–4); Bär (2009: 14–23); Scheijnen (2018: 1–4); Tsomis (2018b: 13–16); Carvounis (2019: xx–xxxiii), all with references to earlier discussions.

[5] See especially Bär (2007); Maciver (2012a: 33–8); Greensmith (2018); Greensmith (2020: 157–88).

[6] See below with note 24.

[7] See Keydell (1963: 1279) and Appel (1994b). Further, see also the chapter by Carvounis in this volume.

[8] See especially Baumbach and Bär (2007b: 15–23); Bär (2009: 23–36); Tsomis (2018b: 9–28). Further, see Schmidt (1999: 139–43) and Baumbach and Bär (2010: 786–9) on literary reception.

been continued since then; we will look at the different scholarly trajectories that have been pursued in the course of the past twenty years, and taking it from there, we will then lay the foundation for this volume and its novel focus.

The history of scholarship begins with the rediscovery of the *PH* by the Byzantine exile scholar Basilius Bessarion (1403–72) in the monastery of San Nicola di Casole (Otranto, Italy) between the years 1453 and 1462.[9] Thereafter, the *PH* was slowly but gradually disseminated in Western Europe: in the 1470s, Angelo Poliziano (1454–94) quoted from it several times in his commentary on Statius' *Silvae*;[10] in 1505, the *editio princeps* was released by the Aldine Press; and in 1539, the first Latin translation (by Joost Welare, printed in Antwerp) was published.[11] Further, Joseph Scaliger (1540–1609) is known to have produced a large number of notes and conjectures on the text of the *PH*,[12] and Conrad Gesner (1516–65) read the entire poem and made continuous annotations into his copy.[13] A critical edition – yet still based on the erroneous text of the Aldine – was produced by Lorenz Rhodoman (1546–1606), and published in 1604,[14] whereas the first critical edition that was constituted through a collation of manuscripts stems from Thomas Christian Tychsen (1758–1834), and was published in 1807.[15] However, Tychsen's edition was soon to be replaced by that of Hermann Köchly (1815–76) in 1850, which also contained the first full-scale commentary on the *PH* (in Latin). Today, the standard critical edition is that by Francis Vian from the 1960s (with a French translation and annotations).[16]

In the twentieth century, scholarship on the *PH* was, for one, characterised by a generally negative attitude towards what was conceived to be the uninspired imitation of a would-be Homerist: Quintus was largely regarded as a poetic 'latecomer' who 'slavishly' imitated Homer on a large scale, but with only mediocre success.[17] For another, the scholarly discourse was dominated

---

[9] See James and Lee (2000: 1–4). On the history of the text's manuscript transmission, see in great detail Vian (1959b), and Tsomis (2018b: 37–8) for a useful synopsis.

[10] See Vian (1997: 985–7). On Poliziano's commentary, see also Mengelkoch (2010).

[11] On early editions and translations, see Vian (1959a: 7–9) and Baumbach and Bär (2007b: 17–20).

[12] See Galán Vioque (2015).

[13] See Baumbach and Bär (2010: 785).

[14] On Rhodoman, who was also a prolific poet writing in Ancient Greek, see e.g. Weise (2019: 12–19) and the chapter by Gärtner in this volume.

[15] Francis Vian rightly deemed Tychsen's work 'the most important contribution to the manuscript history' of the *PH* ('la contribution la plus importante à l'histoire des manuscrits de QS', Vian 1959b: 15).

[16] Vian (1963, -66, -69).

[17] For an overview and discussion of this negative attitude, see Schmidt (1999: 139–43); Baumbach and Bär (2007b: 23–5); Bär (2009: 33–6). A particularly misguided condemnation of the *PH* was voiced by Lloyd-Jones (1969).

by the *quaestio Latina* – that is, the question of whether Quintus knew and used Latin sources (in particular Vergil's *Aeneid*). This question led to a running debate between Rudolf Keydell, who argued in favour of Latin influence on the *PH*, and Francis Vian, who argued against it.[18] Yet it was only from the mid-1980s onward that steadier and more varied research trends gained momentum,[19] relating to various important aspects of the *PH* such as, for example, the narrative structure of the poem,[20] Quintus' allusive techniques and his sophisticated use (and adaptation) of Homeric *hapax legomena*.[21] In 2000, then, Alan W. James and Kevin Lee published their full-scale commentary on *PH* Book 5, shortly followed by Giuseppe Pompella's new textual edition and Manolis Papathomopoulos' concordance, as well as a reprint of Vian's classical edition.[22]

However, the momentous point in the history of scholarship originated in the world-first conference on Quintus and the *PH* in Autumn 2006, organised by Manuel Baumbach and Silvio Bär at the University of Zurich (Switzerland), flagged under the programmatic title 'Quintus Smyrnaeus – ein kaiserzeitlicher Sophist im homerischen Gewand'. Almost all Quintus scholars in the whole world – which at that time, admittedly, was a small number – participated in this conference in order to discuss their ongoing work on the *PH* and, most importantly, to map the future of what was going to emerge not only as a highly rewarding, but also as an unexpectedly timely research trend. First and foremost, the conference initiated a discussion that had long been overdue, namely, the contextualisation of the *PH* in its broader cultural and intellectual milieu. As the title of the conference indicates, the organisers chose the Second Sophistic as their main point of reference – so much so that they labelled Quintus, somewhat hyperbolically, as a sophist proper. In the published proceedings which followed the conference, the author-centred conference title was then shifted towards a more work-centred approach: the resultant volume was entitled *Quintus Smyrnaeus: Transforming Homer in Second Sophistic Epic*.[23]

However, the application of the term and the concept of the Second Sophistic to the study of an imperial epic poem was not only welcomed, but it

---

[18] See Keydell (1949/50; 1954; 1961: 279–82) vs Vian (1959a: 95–101; 1963: XXXIV). On the further history of the debate, see Gärtner (2005: 30–7), with detailed references, and James (2007: 145–9). More recent discussions of the *quaestio Latina* include Gärtner (2005); James (2007); Gärtner (2013); Bär (forthcoming a).

[19] See Baumbach and Bär (2007b: 22–3) for a more detailed overview.

[20] Schmiel (1986); Schubert (1996); Schenk (1997); Schmidt (1999).

[21] Chrysafis (1985); Giangrande (1986); Appel (1994a).

[22] James and Lee (2000); Pompella (2002); Papathomopoulos (2002). Vian's (1963, -66, -69) edition was reprinted in 2003.

[23] For the initial discussion regarding Quintus and the Second Sophistic, see Baumbach and Bär (2007b: 8–15) in their introduction.

was also met with resistance. On the one hand, Silvio Bär argued that the *PH* could be understood as a response to revisionist tendencies against Homer that were popular in the Second Sophistic (as seen in works such as Philostratus' *Heroicus* and Dio Chrysostom's *Trojan Oration*); seen from this angle, the intellectual milieu of the Second Sophistic offered a frame for understanding why a poet would compose a Homericising epic in this setting. Calum Maciver, on the other hand, suggested that the horizon of the Second Sophistic should be restricted to its core (i.e. Atticising prose rhetoric) and that the interpretation of the *PH* be uncoupled from its wider cultural context and that it instead be understood solely in terms of a Homeric continuation, influenced mainly by poetry.[24] This dispute ultimately fed back into a wider debate of principle about the actual 'existence' of the Second Sophistic. In this debate, Tim Whitmarsh took an extreme view by condemning the Second Sophistic as 'a modern fantasy projected back on to the ancient world' in his introduction to a compilation of essays collected under the heading *Beyond the Second Sophistic*.[25]

The Zurich conference then 'popularised' the *PH* further as an object of research particularly among junior scholars – a trend that eventually led to the publication of numerous important and groundbreaking publications. Most notably, commentaries on (parts of) Books 1, 2, 7, 9, 10, 13 and 14 have been published since the initiation of this 'boom'.[26] Furthermore, several PhD theses and thesis-based monographs have contributed significantly to a more holistic understanding of the *PH* and a further broadening of the research perspectives. Vincent Tomasso discusses the self-construction of Quintus as a poetic 'latecomer' and Quintus' strategies in constructing and reconstructing his poetic past.[27] In a similar vein, Calum A. Maciver looks at Quintus' Janus-faced nature of being – and simultaneously not being – Homer, whereby he analyses the poem's texture in Alexandrian and in Stoic terms.[28] Bellini Boyten and Tine Scheijnen both offer comprehensive analyses and discussions of epic heroism in the *PH* in dialogue with the Homeric epics, with a focus on characters such as Penthesilea, Achilles, Memnon, Neoptolemus, Nestor and Odysseus. Thus, the path has also been paved towards studying the *PH* in terms of diachronic

---

[24] See Bär (2009: 85–91; 2010) vs Maciver (2012a: 17–18; 2012b). Avlamis (2019), in turn, attempts to find a middle ground.

[25] Whitmarsh (2013: 3). Whitmarsh's publication was enthusiastically reviewed by Maciver (2014).

[26] Bär (2009) on Book 1.1–219; Campagnolo (2010/11) and Ferreccio (2014) on Book 2; Tsomis (2018a) on Book 7; Ozbek (forthcoming) on Book 9.333–546; Tsomis (2018b) on Book 10; Renker (2020) on Book 13; Carvounis (2014) on Book 14. Before the 'boom', only two commentaries (apart from the annotations that accompany the editions by Köchly 1850 and Vian 1963, -66, -69) existed: Lee and James (2000) on Book 5; Campbell (1981) on Book 12.

[27] Tomasso (2010).

[28] Maciver (2012a).

narratology and narratological character analysis.[29] Arnold Bärtschi, then, devotes a major part of his study on epic giants to the *PH*; *inter alia*, his analyses advance our understanding of how Quintus uses similes and comparisons, and they also provide new insights into the hitherto understudied Hesiodic side of the epic.[30] Finally, in the most recent monograph on the *PH*, Emma Greensmith offers an entirely fresh reading of the poem by regarding Quintus as a central figure in the history of epic and Homeric reception and by framing the poetics of the *PH* as a 'poetics of the interval'.[31]

In addition to these trailblazing commentaries and monographs, mention must also be made of four new translations. Ursula Gärtner's German translation (informed by the principle of 'documentary translation' that Wolfgang Schadewaldt applied to his translations of the *Odyssey* (1958) and the *Iliad* (1975)) is the first German translation of the *PH* since the mediocre nineteenth-century attempts by Christian Friedrich Platz and Johann Jacob Christian Donner.[32] Furthermore, a new Italian translation was produced by a team of junior scholars under the direction of Emanuele Lelli (replacing the little-known translation by Giuseppe Pompella published between 1979 and 1993), while the Russian translation by Andrej Petrovich Bolshakov is, to the best of our knowledge, the first ever translation of the *PH* in this language.[33] Finally, the obsolete English blank verse version in the Loeb series by Arthur S. Way was, at last, replaced by a complete retranslation in prose by Neil Hopkinson.[34] As a reviewer rightly noted, this retranslation is 'an improvement on Way' as 'Hopkinson has chosen to make his rendering more accessible to readers of the early twenty-first century by using prose (. . .) and by translating into smooth English that is not overly showy'.[35]

The increased interest in the *PH* as an object of research can – and must – also be viewed in the wider context of a general upswing in research on later (i.e. imperial) Greek epic. First and foremost, the 'Quintus trend' has been moving in parallel with a corresponding 'Nonnus trend' for some while, as is evidenced by a series of Nonnus conferences called 'Nonnus of Panopolis in Context' that took place in the years 2011 (Rethymno), 2013 (Vienna), 2015 (Warsaw) and 2018 (Ghent). The proceedings of the first two conferences have been published,[36]

---

[29] Boyten (2010); Scheijnen (2018). On the application of diachronic narratology to the study of ancient epic in general, see Bär and Maravela (2019) and Reitz and Finkmann (2019).

[30] Bärtschi (2019: 185–354).

[31] Greensmith (2020).

[32] Gärtner (2010); Platz (1857/58); Donner (1866/67).

[33] Lelli *et al.* (2013); Pompella (1979, -87, -93); Bolshakov (2016).

[34] Way (1913); Hopkinson (2018).

[35] Tomasso (2019: 25).

[36] Spanoudakis (2014), proceedings from the Rethymno conference (2011); Bannert and Kröll (2018), proceedings from the Vienna conference (2013).

as have several further edited volumes and monographs.[37] Amongst these, the *Brill's Companion to Nonnus of Panopolis*, edited by Domenico Accorinti, must be singled out: this volume contains thirty-two chapters covering many aspects of Nonnus, his poetry and his milieu, running to a total of almost nine hundred pages. The 'giant' size of this companion can be read as standing metaphorically for the mammoth size of Nonnus' *Dionysiaca*, and simultaneously, it also ties up with the impressive increase in research that was provoked by the 'boom' on 'later' Greek epic in a wider sense.[38]

Like the Quintus conference in 2006, recent work on Nonnus aims to contextualise the poet and his work within a broader cultural, religious and intellectual framework. It is therefore important that these research trends are not viewed in isolation, but in parallel, and in dialogue. Furthermore, the work on these two 'big' epicists has been complemented by major break-throughs in the study of imperial Greek 'epylliasts', such as Laura Miguélez-Cavero's commentary on Triphiodorus' *Sack of Troy* and Cosetta Cadau's study on Colluthus' *Rapture of Helen* indicate.[39] In addition to these studies on individual epic poems, there has also been a positive trend towards a more holistic view of imperial Greek epic, as is demonstrated by an essay collection edited by Richard Hunter and Katerina Carvounis, a comprehensive investigation of Nonnus and his contemporaries by Laura Miguélez-Cavero (where it is demonstrated that the idea of a 'School of Nonnus' cannot be maintained, but that the epic production at and before Nonnus' time must nevertheless have been immense),[40] and, finally, at an international conference on 'Imperial Greek Epic and Cultural History' (organised by Tim Whitmarsh and Emily Kneebone) at the University of Cambridge in 2013.

This conference paved the way for the major collaborative AHRC-funded research project on *Greek Epic of the Roman Empire: A Cultural History* (2014–17; PI: Tim Whitmarsh), which sought to provide the first systematic analysis, in cultural terms, of the corpus of Greek epic poetry composed between the first and the sixth centuries CE. Quintus became a major figure in this project: two of the project members, Emma Greensmith and Leyla Ozbek, were focusing their research on the *PH*. As a result of these shared interests, and the growing interest in the *PH* and imperial Greek epic across classical studies, the project hosted a one-day conference on Quintus in 2016, organised

---

[37] Shorrock (2001); Shorrock (2011); Accorinti (2016); Verhelst (2017); Geisz (2018); Kröll (2020).

[38] The relation of Nonnus to imperial Greek poetry, including Quintus, is explored by Maciver (2016) in the companion.

[39] Miguélez-Cavero (2013); Cadau (2015). Further, see also the unpublished PhD thesis by Gilka (2017) on Colluthus and Dracontius.

[40] Hunter and Carvounis (2008); Miguélez-Cavero (2008). See also the earlier anthology of selected imperial Greek poems and passages by Hopkinson (1994).

by Emma Greensmith and Leyla Ozbek.[41] The event gathered some of the most important and active scholars on this author at every stage of their career, from postgraduate students to full-time professors. Its aim was not only to present different works in progress on the *PH*, but also to provide an overall view of the paths taken by research on Quintus, of the questions opened in the past which still needed to be fulfilled, and, above all, of the new prospects, approaches and methodologies opened by the recent surge of studies on the *PH* and on Greek epic of the imperial period in general.

This conference, then, aimed to collate and capitalise on the rapid developments in research on Quintus which had taken place in the decade since the seminal 2006 conference in Zurich. During this time, as can be seen from our summary of scholarship above, two main directions of study had emerged, deriving from two methodologically different approaches. One moved vertically along a diachronic line of analysis, addressing specific textual and literary issues, such as close intertextual comparisons with Homer and the subsequent epic tradition (especially the Alexandrian tradition). The other one moved along a horizontal path of synchronic approach to the text, contextualising it against its historical and cultural background, dealing with specific contextual frameworks such as Stoicism and the poem's wider philosophical texture, or – continuing the debate started by the Zurich conference and its proceedings – the Second Sophistic and the poem's other sociocultural ramifications. These important and dominant paths were, however, not the only two ways of addressing Quintus' work. Scholars have also started to ask new questions and to look for new approaches in order to shed light on this text, which, together with other works of the same period, is being increasingly recognised as an invaluable dossier of evidence for the cultural politics of imperial and late antiquity.

Given this lively context, the idea on which the 2016 Cambridge conference was based was to understand from where recent research on Quintus has come, and where it could go, through the opening (or the strengthening) of new fields of study based on different approaches and different methodologies developed within the last period, sometimes merging together different disciplines and fields of research (such as textual criticism, history of ancient literature and culture, sociocultural history, history of philosophy or history of ancient rhetoric). In this single day of intense discussion about Quintus, many new and productive results emerged. Therefore, the two organisers, along with Silvio Bär, who participated as a speaker, decided to use the conference as a launchpad for a new book: a volume which would include some of the contributions presented during the conference (expanded and modified according

---

[41] 'Writing Homer Under Rome: Quintus of Smyrna's *Posthomerica*', St John's College, University of Cambridge, 16 April 2016.

to the discussion sparked on that day), together with chapters commissioned from other scholars working on Quintus from different perspectives.

From a methodological point of view, this volume aims to tie up the diachronic and synchronic strands of research on the *PH* mentioned above, but at the same time it aims to broaden out this picture considerably. We provide a more theoretically grounded intersection of literary criticism and cultural studies and draw on a wider range of approaches and hermeneutical methods in order to consider in more unity pressing issues within the text. In so doing, we aim to focus on the poem's cultural history from a wider perspective and its literary inheritance beyond the epic tradition alone. The creative and scholarly reception of the *PH*, as well as the cultural and intellectual conditions and implications of the text's reception history, are also addressed. In other words, we aim to collect, continue and develop recent scholarly approaches to the *PH* by bringing into focus some of the most significant and under-exploited areas of this provocative text and its intertextuality, its literary and cultural interactions, and its reception.

One of the crucial aspects of our volume is to analyse Quintus' epic in the light of different approaches which historically come from different disciplines and are usually applied in separate fields of study. Addressing the *PH* from various angles and looking at it through different lenses will help to understand a text which is inherently multifaceted because of its Homeric nature and imperial dating, and its position within the epic, poetic and broader literary and cultural tradition of the late antique period. We would like to propose, for the first time in the history of scholarship, a theoretical reflection upon the question of 'why' a text like the *PH* may have been written and become popular, and which analytic tools can help us to better understand the poem within its own time as well as in its 'afterlife'. The more we engage with different aspects of the *PH*, the more we enlarge our knowledge about a work that is a *unicum* within the literary tradition, as well as our knowledge about the historic, social and cultural tradition – more largely, the *forma mentis* – of a chronologic and geographic area which appears to be a fundamental turning point in antiquity: the Greek part of the Roman Empire during the first centuries of the Christian era.

In the light of all of these considerations, we intend this volume – again, for the first time in Quintus scholarship – to be aimed at the broadest audience possible. The book is first and foremost intended for a wide scholarly audience within Classics: both for professional scholars and advanced students, with interests in, for example, literary studies, ancient history, cultural studies. However, since all quotes from Greek and Latin are translated into English, it can also be used by undergraduates in other, classically related subjects (such as modern literature, history, religious studies and philosophy) and interested non-classicists around the world.

Finally, some comments on the structure and contents of the volume. A striking structural feature of the *PH* itself is its sequential, 'episodic' structure. Thus, with the exception of two simultaneously occurring scenes,[42] the action unfolds in a straightforward, linear manner: from hero to hero, battle to battle, the story moves with each book closer to the predetermined fall of Troy, and beyond it.[43] This distinctly un-Aristotelian type of epic storytelling,[44] traditionally considered to be a detriment of the poem, has now been recognised as a rich and provocative narrative texture, which powerfully deviates from 'classical' epic plotting.[45] However, a crucial point arises from this acknowledged aspect of Quintus' craft: 'what happens' in the *PH* is extremely, distinctively clear. Unlike other imperial Greek or Roman epics such as Ovid's *Metamorphoses* and Nonnus' *Dionysiaca*, which flaunt bendy, topsy-turvy, intertwined tales that spurt out from, and melt into, one another (so much so that Nonnus' epic warranted summaries – the *periochae* – now placed at the start of each of the forty-eight books),[46] the Posthomeric plot does not require extensive synopses or precis. Therefore, in fitting imitation of this feature of our central text, we shall not provide lengthy introductory summaries of each chapter here. Instead, we shall establish the central questions which drive each section and which connect the chapters within them.

As we have discussed, an integrated understanding of the *Posthomerica* lies at the core of this volume's vision. The book is therefore divided into five sections, each of which seeks to probe the poem using a particular and elaborate mode of reading. Part I, 'Contexts and Poetics', offers close readings of some of the most charged poetic moments of the epic and explores their sociocultural purchase: temporality and ethical positioning (Goldhill), internal songs and imperial poetic contests (Carvounis), erotic episodes and late antique sexuality (Greensmith), as well as depictions of the body and visual art and literature (Schoess). Part II, 'Religion, Gods and Destiny', continues this combined textual and contextual approach, applying it to a central and contentious issue of the poem: its attitude towards religion and Fate, a topic which is also crucial to assessing the work's contemporary philosophical tenor. The first two chapters here address directly Quintus' complex approach to Fate (Maciver) and to the traditional Homeric pantheon (Barbaresco). The third chapter (Bremmer) looks at an area of the epic's religious dynamics which has

---

[42] The voyages to Skyros and Lemnos in *PH* 7.169–345 and 9.353–445.

[43] For different readings of the poem's structure, see Appel (1994b); Schenk (1997); Maciver (2012a); Scheijnen (2016a); Greensmith (2020).

[44] Cf. Aristotle's criticism of the unconcentrated, chronographic plot arrangements of the Epic Cycle poems (*Poet.* 1459a–b).

[45] See e.g. Maciver (2012a: 20–4) and Greensmith (2020: 235–8).

[46] These were either composed by the poet himself or (more likely) a later hand: see e.g. Ludwich (1911); Zuenelli (2016); Middleton (2018).

never before been considered: its frequent depiction of sacrifice, both animal and human, which is an archaic/Homeric feature of the poem, but one
which achieves new significance in this covertly imperial reworking. Part III,
'Between Narratology and Lexicology', displays the benefits of combining
contextualised readings of the *PH* with different theoretical approaches. The
first contribution here leads on directly from the previous section: Argyrouli
offers another, alternative account of the role of Fate in the epic, using a narratological method to complement Maciver's literary-cultural approach. The
following chapters then provide zoomed-in analyses of various aspects of the
epic's narrative structure and linguistic techniques: heroic speech (Scheijnen),
epithets both singular and collective (Maly-Preuss traces one key term across
the poem, while Ferreccio considers Quintus' epithet system as a whole), and,
finally, modes of literary imitation (Tomasso).

These first three sections thus offer a series of connected readings of the
epic across a horizontal axis (its intratextual movements, and its engagement
with cultural tenets of its own imperial time), while the final two parts move
to consider the poem vertically. In other words, they propel us first backwards and then forwards in time. Part IV, 'The Struggle with the Literary
Past', reflects on how Quintus interacts with the ghosts and heritage of the
vast literary tradition which he has inherited, through the legacy of the fall of
Troy (Middleton), the weight of the overarching Homeric tradition, open for
satirising as well as reverence (Bärtschi), heroic narratives and natures (Ozbek)
and older accounts of the Trojan saga, via the poem's notorious relationship
with those other 'other Homers', the authors of the Epic Cycle (Scafoglio).
Part V, 'Re-Readings and Re-Workings', offers the other side of the story of
appropriation and reception, revealing how the *PH* itself has been adapted and
interpreted by later readers, critics and authors, tracing its 'afterlife' in Byzantine (Lovato), early modern (Gärtner) and postmodern (Renker) imaginations.

A driving characteristic of all of these sections is their deep interconnec-
tivity. Not only do all of the chapters within each part share common ideas
and approaches, but there are also many important pairings to be made across
the different sections.[47] Goldhill's chapter on temporality and ethics speaks
deeply to Maciver's discussion of Stoic and Neopythagorean philosophy, and
to Middleton's account of *lusis* as both the denouement of the story (the fall
of Troy) and the Neoplatonising release of souls. Scheijnen's analysis of heroic
speech patterns finds a strong interlocutor in Ozbek's study of Philoctetes'
heroic nature and his paradigmatic weapon. Greensmith and Schoess both
examine major scenes of the *PH* which also feature in the Epic Cycle, like the
death of the Amazon Queen Penthesilea – a topic that is also given extensive

---

[47] The examples given above are in addition to the previously mentioned dialogue between
Argyrouli's chapter on the role of Fate in Part III and Part II on religion and the gods.

treatment in Scafoglio's chapter on Quintus and the Cyclic poems. Finally, Tomasso's intertextual account of Quintus' imitative practice is taken in a new direction by Renker's treatment of the *PH* in the light of Derridean theories of literary dependence and postmodern concepts of fan fiction. As a result of such cross-connections, the volume can be used by the reader in multiple different ways; each chapter has been designed to be comprehensible in its own right as a stand-alone piece, but the contributions also consciously form part of the wider ethos of the whole book: a dialogue which rewards complete reading.

Whilst this is unapologetically a book 'about' Quintus, the range of works discussed (literary and visual, ancient and modern) is designedly broad: the *PH* provides the road map for a vast journey through the epic tradition, imperial Greek literature and post-classical receptions. In addition to frequent and varied discussion of Homer (not only the most fundamental model for Quintus, but also a complex and surprising one) and of the Epic Cycle, the individual chapters also treat authors as distinct as Hesiod (Goldhill) and John Tzetzes (Lovato); Aristophanes (Greensmith) and Apollonius (Ozbek and Maly-Preuss); Nonnus (Carvounis, Goldhill, Greensmith and others) and the Greek novel (Bremmer). There is also a strong focus on the Latin tradition: both culturally, in terms of how Quintus negotiates his identity as Greek poet writing in the 'shadow' of Rome, and intertextually, expanding beyond the previously mentioned *quaestio Latina*, and suggesting many connections between the *PH* and Latin poetry, most prominently the *Aeneid*. In this emphasis, we seek to demonstrate further, and with specific focus on the *PH,* the rich and varied dialogue between Greek and Latin literary production in late antiquity: interactions between the two systems which were obscured for too long by uncertainty over levels of bilingualism in the Greek world, but are now rightly being brought back to life.[48]

We shall have succeeded in this approach if the readers of Quintus – be they deeply familiar with the poem, or brand new to it – emerge with a stronger sense of the vast and varied landscape of his epic: the breadth of its literary, cultural and narrative engagements, and the range of critical and theoretical methods which can be productively employed to unlock them. If it is now truly an outdated trope to decry critical neglect of imperial Greek epic, and unnecessary to repeat well-worn justifications of Quintus' poetic qualities, because such battles have been fought long ago, then this volume aims above all to engage with the *PH* on its own terms: to honour it, celebrate it and move forwards with it. We have tried to show the benefits of taking Quintus entirely seriously from the beginning: asking textual and cultural questions

---

[48] See e.g. Verhelst and Scheijnen (forthcoming); Carvounis, Papaioannou and Scafoglio (forthcoming); Mullen and Elder (2019), which build from e.g. Adams, Janse and Swain (2002); Adams (2003); Mullen and James (2012).

about his epic which are as deep, wide-ranging and important as we would for any work with a more long-standing seat at the table of celebrated canonical poems. As the chapters here demonstrate, both individually and collectively, Quintus rewards such enlarged thinking. The *PH* excites, and continues to excite, because it so resolutely resists its own simplicity: once we look harder at its 'straightforward' narrative structure, 'unknown' context and (seemingly) traditional literary style, we find how the text challenges any easy answers, and opens up further questions with each new reading. If, therefore, as Simon Goldhill writes in his chapter, 'Quintus marks a juncture in the slow transformation of thinking', as displayed by the 'epigonal, interstitial status of [his] story', then this volume offers a further expansion of the interval of scholarship on the *PH*: a demonstration, that is, of how much can be done with this poem, and how much there is still to do. Whatever new developments now emerge within imperial Greek epic studies, in all the new directions that it is poised to take, Quintus will be present at the centre of it. He has so much to tell us, about literary tradition, imitation, innovation; and about Greekness, empire and cultural change – a rich and riveting story which, like his own narrative, is destined to continue.

FORMATTING, STYLE AND CRITICAL EDITIONS

As editors we have aimed for a certain level of consistency throughout the volume. Nevertheless, to provide our authors with the scope to express their views as desired, we have allowed some freedom in the presentation of the ancient languages and transliterations. In most cases, contributors employ the standard critical texts as defined by the current scholarly consensus. For the *PH* itself, Vian's edition constitutes the textual basis in all chapters of this volume unless otherwise indicated.

PART I

Contexts and Poetics

CHAPTER 2

Temporality and Temper: Time, Narrative and Heroism in Quintus of Smyrna

Simon Goldhill

In antiquity, epic is fundamental to the conceptual shaping of time. In the broadest terms, we can outline at least three dominant, interrelated, routes through which epic temporality is articulated. The first could be called foundational. Epic provides the model for how the narrative of the past grounds the present. In Hesiod's *Theogony* and *Works and Days* genealogy expresses structure.[1] The form of things is explored and explained by the narrative of how Zeus's power came into being and became established. When Zeus marries Themis – established order – their children are the Horai – the seasons: regulated time is born. Sacrifice, gendered family life, agriculture – the interlinked basis of man's productivity – are provided with a story of origin that also embodies the ideological structures that underpin the normative values of working the land and maintaining the household.[2] The map in which humans are to place themselves is given its contours by its genealogical temporality, and the present is structured by the explanatory narrative of how it came to be thus, and by the equally normative patterning of the *Days* with its notion of *dikē* between men, and between men and gods, as expressed in the *Works* which define the continuing present of human existence.

The *Iliad* and the *Odyssey* remained the necessary starting point for Greek history – and Homer's epics are foundational not merely because they functioned as an educational, social and literary origin, through which values and self-understanding continued to be formulated in ancient Greek-speaking

---

[1] The influence of Vernant (1974; 1985: 19–47) on the discussion of Hesiod's genealogies is pervasive.

[2] See also Arthur (1982); Zeitlin (1996: 53–86); Strauss Clay (2003). References here and below are exemplary rather than exhaustive.

communities, but also and more specifically because of the model of memorialisation they perform. Homer's texts are well aware of the abyss of time and the struggle of humans to transcend their own passing. Achilles' search for *kleos aphthiton*, 'immortal glory' can only be achieved at the cost of a brief life: what is it worth dying for is a fundamental question of the *Iliad*.[3] The poet and the hero are locked together in the making of *kleos* that will last across time. It is not by chance that Alexander the Great is said to have travelled with a copy of the *Iliad* under his pillow: how humans relate to time through the hope-laden construction of a self-monument is given culturally privileged expression in the *Iliad*. Odysseus in the *Odyssey* is offered immortality by Calypso. On Calypso's island, he is without works and his days are all the same. It is this changeless world with its promise of living forever that he rejects to begin his arduous journey back to Ithaca. God's time and human time structure the defining difference between mortals and immortals. The time of a household – the generations of men – is what Odysseus fights to uphold.

For Virgil in the *Aeneid*, written after historiography has recalibrated the writing of time,[4] the foundational is now also necessarily political and imperial.[5] The story of Rome's beginnings is a story *for* the powers that be. The vision in the underworld is a prediction of history to come, a teleology of power. Virgil too uses the narration of the past to explain how things must be what they are. It is a prospect that promises its own unendingness: *His ego nec metas rerum nec tempora pono; imperium sine fine dedi* – Jupiter promises 'For the Romans I place no boundaries on things, no time: power without limit I grant' (*Aen.* 1.278–9). It is wilfully, knowingly and brilliantly against such a tradition that Ovid's *Metamorphoses* sets its swirls of narratives of change, a poem without end (*perpetuum . . . carmen, Met.* 1.4), where even and especially the origins (*coeptis, Met.* 1.2) are ceaselessly open to transformation (*mutastis, Met.* 1.2): another form of unendingness.[6] Epic's narratives of the past establish a genealogical, teleological, monumentalising, pattern of time: foundational temporality.

The second model of how epic conceptualises time could be called narratological. Epic repeatedly *thematises* the narrative of time. Virgil's Aeneas spends six books delaying his arrival in Italy telling his own backstory to Dido in Carthage, and falling in love. The more he talks and stares, the less he travels towards his end. The teleology of epic requires blockages to take shape. Lucan's angry and violent despair in his *Pharsalia* is aimed at the collapse of the Republic at the hands of Julius Caesar.[7] Lucan's account of the civil war

---

[3] Lynn-George (1988); Redfield (1975); Nagy (1979).
[4] Lianeri (2011); Grethlein and Krebs (2012); Goldhill (2002); Hartog (2011); Hartog (2020); Goldhill (2020).
[5] Hardie (1986).
[6] Hardie, Barchiesi and Hinds (1997); Brown (2005); Feldherr (2010).
[7] Henderson (1987); Masters (1992) are seminal.

is constantly trying to prevent or defer Caesar's inevitable crossing of the Rubicon. His narrative is pulled apart by its desire to stop its own ineluctable and disastrous conclusion. Lucan is designedly rewriting a long epic tradition. The *Iliad* itself is an epic of delay. The anticipated but not reached climaxes of the death of Achilles and the destruction of Troy, along with Phoenix's story of Meleager's misjudged stalling, have been well analysed by critics as narrative strategies of prolepsis and analepsis that reflect on the narrative's own deferrals.[8] Epic narrative displays and manipulates its own temporal unfurling, as an integral function of the thematics of each poem.

The third strategy could be termed poetic. Epic poets are well aware of the poetic tradition in which they work, and this tradition is being constantly re-established by the work of the poets. When Milton begins *Paradise Lost* with 'Of Man's first . . .' it is a knowing redrafting of the first word of the *Odyssey*, *andra*, as reprised in the opening phrase of the *Aeneid*, *arma virumque*, turned into a theological generalisation, marked as a self-conscious beginning about the origin of sin by the very word 'first' in the first line: a poetics of supersessionism as much as a poetics of literary debt. The history of the genre of epic (and the history of poetry more generally) is enacted in the composition of each epic: it performs its own history, and thus sets itself in time and with a backward glance across time.

These three conceptualisations of time – foundational, narratological, poetic – are intricately interconnected, as the example of Milton immediately shows: as much as he is engaging self-reflexively and actively with the inherited language of epic, Milton is also telling of the very foundations of the human race and their relation to time; and he is playing with the narrative of time when he asks the Muse to sing of the 'the fruit of that forbidden tree' – the fruit which is both what grows on the tree (Eve's apple), and the consequences of it, the whole narrative of humanity to come – a poetics of typology as much as causality, a theologically informed narrative of what time is for humans. It is indeed in the combination of these different vectors that epic temporality takes shape.

Now, each of these three opening formulations of epic's temporality could be greatly expanded and nuanced, of course, but enough has been said in these brief comments, I hope, to provide a basis for my discussion of Quintus of Smyrna, whose *Posthomerica* offers a remarkable example of how an epic constructs its temporality, and for whom these three aspects of temporality will provide an essential roadmap. Quintus' epic inhabits the 'in-between' space of Homer's *Iliad* and *Odyssey*, and it is the temporality of this space that he establishes. This chapter will explore how this interplay of narrative and temporality goes hand in hand with a particular recalibration of heroic agency, in and

---

[8] Schein (1984); de Jong (²2004a); Lynn-George (1988); Stanley (1993); Rabel (1997); Louden (2006).

against the constructed tradition of epic. We will look first at how waiting – the thematisation of delay – becomes integral to the narrative of the *Posthomerica;* second, we will look at how similes in particular construct description as a strategy of narrative deferral; and third we will consider how this narrativisation of delay becomes itself part of the *Posthomerica*'s engagement with the foundational ethics of epic heroism. How is the heroic temper informed by the epic discourse of temporality?

THE NARRATIVE AND TEMPORALITY OF WAITING

Let us begin, as one must, with the beginning – the framing of the fourteen-book epic. The poem begins with a temporal marker: εὖθ᾽, 'when . . .'. As Silvio Bär and Calum Maciver and now Emma Greensmith have discussed most productively, not only is it unparalleled to begin an epic with a connective, implying not so much a start as a continuation with a previous work, but also the line specifically and carefully reminds us of the first and last line of the *Iliad* in our manuscripts.[9] Εὖθ᾽ ὑπὸ Πηλείωνι δάμη θεοείκελος Ἕκτωρ, 'When god-like Hector was tamed by the son of Peleus', recalls the patronymic naming of Achilles in line 1 of the *Iliad* (although the actual form of the patronymic is closer to Aristoxenus' alternative opening of the *Iliad*), and the verb *damē*, 'tamed' echoes the final adjective of the *Iliad*, *hippodameio*, 'tamer of horses', applied to Hector. These opening lines continue with the frightened Trojans waiting (ἔμιμνον, 3), as 'they recalled all those earlier heroes (μνησάμενοι προτέρων, 9) whose spirit he had cast off (ἴαψεν, 9) as he rushed by the outflow of Idaean Scamander' (9–10). 'Recalled . . . earlier heroes' marks the self-conscious placement within poetic tradition, as the poet reminds us of the *Iliad* he is continuing: μνησάμενοι (a verb emphatically repeated six lines later), 'recalled', 'remembered' is particularly poised. Here is an epic opening without the expected invocation of the Muses, but which repeats the verb associated both with the mother of the Muses (*Mnēmosunē*), and with the memorialising function of epic: poetic memory takes the place of the Muse. The opening – waiting and remembering – thus invokes and performs its oblique relation to the language of tradition: remembering/memorialising (looking back and anticipating) and waiting (looking back and anticipating) are intimately intertwined. So, indeed, Quintus immediately looks back to the beginning of the war and the poetic tradition: they recalled 'how Achilles had conquered Hector and dragged him round the city, and had killed others from the very first moment (ὁππότε δὴ τὰ πρῶτα, 14) he had brought destruction to Troy from the tireless sea' (12–14). The whole narrative of the war till

---

[9] Bär (2007); Maciver (2012a: 27–33, 130–2); Greensmith (2020: 1–2, 86, 146, 205, 208, 308).

this moment is encapsulated – remembered – in the briefest of analepses, back to the beginning, beyond the *Iliad*, at this beginning ('the very first') – that is, precisely not the 'first' of Homer, who made 'the very first' of the *Iliad* the argument between lords Agamemnon and Achilles (*Il.* 1.6: ἐξ οὗ δὴ τὰ πρῶτα). A different first, a different beginning . . . The *Posthomerica*'s narrative is located between the *Iliad* and the *Odyssey* but it constructs its sense of a beginning through and beyond the *Iliad*.

The repetitive recapitulation that follows re-emphasises the poetic analepsis: 'Those who remembered (μνησθέντες) these events were waiting (ἔμιμνον – as they are waiting ἔμιμνον (3)) in the city' (15). Recalling the past keeps the Trojans behind the walls (it is only in poetic memory that Trojans remain). And the narrator's voice immediately imagines the future (from the beginning to the end . . .). 'Around them painful grief fluttered, as if Troy was burning with grievous fire already.' ἤδη, 'already' announces the future to come under the sign of the 'as if'. The proem thus dramatises its narrative as a continuation, while resisting the anticipated invocation of a Muse by recalling the mother of the Muses in the verb 'recall': poetic tradition is both redrafted and celebrated, as the proem plays with its status as a beginning. Similarly, like an *Iliad* in a nutshell,[10] the narrative swoops from the proclaimed starting point ('the very first') to its imagined conclusion ('burning Troy') in a bare four lines. Here is a dense poetic texture of epic temporality.

But there is more. The narrative continues, 'And then from the streams of the broad-flowing Thermodon came (ἦλθε) Penthesileia . . .' (18–19). The continuation of the *Iliad* in the Cyclic epics is included in a few manuscripts of Homer. Instead of the usual last word of the *Iliad*, *hippodameio*, 'horse-taming', these alternative texts read ἦλθε δ'Ἀμάζων, 'there came an Amazon'. It is as if the proem takes place within a space opened by the two readings. Hector's death (line 1) is separated from the arrival of the Amazon (line 18) by an expansion that includes *in nuce* the whole narrative from the arrival of Achilles to the fall of Troy. The *Posthomerica* will continue the *Iliad* but delays the expected arrival of the Amazon to look back and forwards, and to remind us of the poetics of memory. The simile which enters the narrative so soon ('as when in a thicket cows do not want to face a grim lion, but in terror cower crowded together in the dense foliage, so the Trojans in the city were terrified of that mighty man', 4–8), recalls the many times that Achilles is described as 'like a lion' in Homer and the Cyclic epics, here crowded into a single image, a simile, that is, that contains a network of associations from other epics, over time. It takes us immediately elsewhere, to a Homeric scene of rural violence, holding the narrative back. The Trojans are indeed waiting. The proem's opening is also programmatic for the poem's narrative of exhaustion, as both sides wait

---

[10] See Squire (2011).

and wait (ἔμιμνον . . . ἔμιμνον) for the end of the war, each action, it seems, expanded and slowed by the detour of a simile, a perspective of elsewhere.

Waiting indeed becomes the keynote of Quintus' poetics of delay.[11] The speed of the coming end is dramatised as a desire. Antenor, Priam's son, prays from within Troy that Zeus should keep Neoptolemus away from their city, but that if it is Zeus's will to destroy Troy, he should 'Do it immediately! Do not furnish suffering for us for a long time!' (9.23). Zeus hears his prayer: 'Part he quickly fulfilled, part he was not going to fulfil' (9.25): for he did indeed let the city be destroyed, but did not keep Neoptolemus away. (Earlier, the gods had been enjoying the drawn-out length of the battle (2.490–4), like sports commentators hoping the superb match will not end.) But, as the narrative of repeatedly inconclusive battling – which Antenor prays against – struggles towards its transformative moment in the decision to revert to the trick-ery of the horse, the Trojans, waiting since the prologue, discuss the war's progress in terms of waiting. Poulydamas, who in the *Iliad* unsuccessfully warned Hector not to cross into the Greek camp, tries to find a solution for the unending war. 'The Greeks', he summarises, 'are waiting here (*menontes*) and are strong' (10.12). So, he suggests, 'we should wait (*menōmen*) inside our well-built towers and last it out (*dērioōntes*) day and night' (10.14). Perhaps 'the Greeks will lose heart if they wait (*menontes*) here, seated without fame (*aklees*)' (10.16) (as Odysseus in the *Odyssey* or Achilles in the *Iliad* sat crying on the beach, unable to seek *kleos*). The threefold repetition of *menein* sums up the siege so far as the narrative of a lasting stand-off: the Greeks 'wait', so the Trojans should 'wait' inside – accepting the condition announced in the prologue of the epic – in the hope that the Greeks will recognise that mere staying is a contradiction of the epic pursuit of *kleos*. There is no *kleos* in just waiting, in dead time.

Poulydamas, born the same night as Hector, in the *Iliad* is a figure against whom Hector's tragic heroic trajectory is articulated: Poulydamas is the seer Hector has to shout down as he advances towards his death.[12] It is with this model that Quintus is working. Indeed, Poulydamas here is replaying an ear-lier intervention in the *Posthomerica*. In Book 2, after the death of Penthesileia, the Trojans are debating what to do. Priam has suggested that they wait for Memnon and his troops (whose story will indeed dominate Book 2). Pou-lydamas is not opposed to this: *outi megairō mimnein*, he declares: 'I do not begrudge waiting' for Memnon (2.45), but a better plan, he proposes, is not to 'keep waiting (*menontes*) and get killed by the Greeks' (2.52) but to give back Helen and her possessions to win peace. In the awkward silence that follows his proposal, Paris responds aggressively with a bitter accusation of cowardice.

[11] The contrast with Triphiodorus' haste is marked: see Maciver (2020); Goldhill (2020: 75–81).
[12] Clark (2007); Redfield (1975: 143–52); Dickson (1995: 133–9).

In his eyes, waiting is a denial of heroic virtue where men fight for *kleos*. 'You wait seated in the halls!' he commands with scorn: *mimne!* (2.73).

Poulydamas, thus, is the figure who articulates waiting as a policy and a problem. Aeneas, however, like Paris (or Hector in the *Iliad*), is having none of it. For him – as he replies to Poulydamas – waiting is suffering (10.28), waiting will involve slow starving (10.31–40); consequently, he concludes, 'It is better to die nobly, quickly protecting our homeland, than to perish miserably, waiting (*menontes*)' (10.43–4). This speech is run through with reminders of Diomedes' overcommitted bravery in the *Iliad*; Cassandra's mocking prophecies in Euripides' *Trojan Women*; the crew's foolish decision to eat the cattle of the Sun in the *Odyssey*. These echoes give a black undertow to his heroism. And yet Aeneas is the one Trojan who will escape the consequences of his bravado here, the one who will flee the sack to found Rome, the one Trojan who will not remain.[13] Aeneas' rhetoric picks up and dismisses Poulydamas' attempt to make *menein* a lasting state of affairs. For him, *menein* is to refuse the heroic injunction to deeds of valour. Better, as Antenor prayed, a quick conclusion.

Aeneas indeed leaves the city to fight and has an *aristeia* in the following book, attacking the Greeks with vehemence. This reveals another common sense of *menein* in the battle narrative. Aeneas comes up against Neoptolemus, which is the turning point of the battle. Neoptolemus forces him back but only a small distance, because Aeneas would not brook fleeing, but 'boldly withstood (*menein*) the dread fight' (11.236).[14] But his bravery is in vain. The Trojans turn and 'no longer withstood (*emimnon*) the sharp edge of the conflict' (11.298). They retreat to the walls, where 'they waited (*mimnon*), avoiding death and pitiless fate' (11.159) – as if by Book 11 nothing has changed from the proem: the book ends (11.501) πόνος δ'ἄπρηκτος ὀρώρει, 'Their toil was useless': nothing has been achieved.[15] By contrast, now it is Calchas, excited by Odysseus' plan of the Wooden Horse, who shouts to the Greeks, 'Let us no longer wait!' (*mēketi mimnōmen*, 11.59). Earlier after the death of Achilles, when Diomedes wanted to rush back to fighting (he is, from the *Iliad*, the archetype of such zealousness), Ajax commands the Greeks to wait (*menein*, 4.98) until after suitable funeral games (which will lead to his own suicide): another delay in the narrative/war, marked by the injunction to wait. Neoptolemus is quick to reject Calchas' support for Odysseus' trickery on similar grounds to Aeneas: brave men fight openly (11.67–72). But Neoptolemus is

---

[13] For the cultural politics here, see Hadjittofi (2007); Ozbek (2018).

[14] For *menein* with *tutthon* for both space and time, see Ap. Rh. 4.1257 with Mimn. 2.3–4 noted by Sider (2020: 297 *ad* 8).

[15] Itself an echo of the (false) threat in *Iliad* 2.121 of a *polemos aprēktos* – a war without a successful ending. See Middleton's chapter in this volume for more on this passage.

persuaded to take his time, to conceal himself.[16] It proves a winning strategy. The 'new warrior' – *Neo(s) Ptolem(istēs)* – has to learn that it is not *aptolemos* – 'unwarlike' (9.283) – to fight in another way. Calchas' encouragement not to wait requires a different sense of bravery. He hastens the end of waiting.

As the end approaches, 'waiting' thus becomes a bone of contention. Poulydamas is prepared for the narrative to be unending: while the siege lasts, the Trojans live. Let's wait. For Aeneas, waiting inside is cowardice and a slow death, while standing firm in battle – the same verb, *menein* – is the mark of a hero. For Calchas, now 'not waiting' marks the promised success of the Greek expedition, some closure. The fall of Troy for which we have been waiting since the prologue's announcement of it will finally come. Now despite Aeneas, all the Trojans can do is wait. As they did in the prologue.

Waiting marks the end too. The epic begins as a continuation, and ends with the longest storm of the ancient epic tradition.[17] Storms in epic usually dramatically change the course of a narrative and send the hero away from his aim: they start epic journeys. Yet the *Posthomerica* ends with the storm and the ships scattered on the sea. The *nostoi* (the songs of the return of heroes already mentioned in the *Odyssey*) will not be part of this narrative. Quintus takes one of the most familiar devices of epic plotting and leaves it without consequence or narrative fulfilment.[18] There is another narrative to come – a continuation to this continuation. The end of the *Posthomerica* is not quite yet the beginning of the *Odyssey*. Just as Aeneas' escape from Troy is not quite the beginning of the *Aeneid*, but offers also a perspective from Troy (*Iliothen*) to the empire of Quintus' own day – another story. Quintus turns the closure of his epic into a question of continuation, not just by the prolepsis familiar from the *Iliad* and the *Odyssey* (where the fall of Troy and the departure of Odysseus are anticipated but not achieved),[19] but by ending his epic with a device traditionally designed to start the narrative with a new direction, but which here just blows itself out, as we wait, still, for the *Odyssey* to come. The very appearance of Helen, on her way to the ships at last, is described in the language of sailors in a shipwreck: an apparent end, marked by desire ('So she appeared to them in their hopes', 14.62), that anticipates further disastrous events. What the capture of Troy will portend for its victorious heroes remains an open, continuing story.

The sense of epic as a continuous song – which is an idea fully part of what in shorthand we call Hellenistic poetics, from the prologue of Callimachus' *Aitia* with its denigration of 'one continuous song' to Ovid's reworking of such an idea in the prologue to the *Metamorphoses* with his *perpetuum*

---

[16] On Neoptolemus in the *Posthomerica*, see Boyten (2007); Scheijnen (2015); Scheijnen (2018: 156–226).

[17] Carvounis (2019: 216–23).

[18] Greensmith (2020: 335–41).

[19] See Schmitz (2007b) on Quintus' analepses and prolepses.

carmen – is further instantiated in Nestor's song at the funeral games of Achilles
(4.117–70).[20] As ever, the device of the performed song within the frame of
the epic is a moment where poetics are programmatically on display. Nestor's
song begins not with the arrival of Achilles on the shores of Troy (nor with
Aulis, as does the anonymous singer who reprises the story of the war after the
sack of Troy (14.121–42)), but with the beauty of Thetis and the subsequent
marriage of Thetis and Peleus, that is, with the beginnings of the story (told
in retrospect with the most allusive of brevity) in the dangerous desirability
of the sea nymph and her marriage, from which came both Achilles and,
thanks to the golden apple of Eris, the Trojan War. The Graces' dance and the
Muses' song, the traditional accompaniments of Thetis' marriage, here make
an appearance (141), recorded by Nestor in the epic, a song which thrilled the
natural world of the mountains, rivers and beasts (141–2) – a pastoral pathetic
fallacy in passing – and which delighted 'the immortal (*aphthitos*) air, and the
very lovely caves of Cheiron and the gods themselves' (142–3). This is a typically dense, transitional phrase of Quintus. 'The air' (αἴθηρ) seems to continue
the pathetic fallacy, although it expands such thinking beyond its usual framework on to a more cosmological scale; yet the air is called *aphthitos*, 'immortal',
'unfading', the adjective most associated with the aim for glory of the Homeric
Achilles. In a song which hymns Achilles and his achievements, at the very
moment when the Muses' performance is represented, unfading lastingness
is predicated of the air, the place where words are borne uselessly away. The
cave of Cheiron is where the marriage of Thetis and Peleus is consummated
in earlier accounts, and where Achilles is later educated by the centaur – in
the briefest of phrases, that is, the conceiving and childhood of Achilles – and
the concluding invocation of the gods themselves evokes the wedding party
and the epithalamium of the divinities, the celebration familiar in art and literature from the François Vase onwards. The opening of the representation of
Nestor's song is notably indirect and allusive. A few words to open an expan-
sive temporal perspective.

Nestor goes on, however, to list Achilles' achievements in more detail
(145–70), though also with the briefest of description for each. These are
summed up at the start as the *aphthita erga* (146) of noble Achilles, his 'immortal deeds'. The repetition of *aphthitos* is marked, now in its usual usage. Deeds
as lasting as the ether? Nestor starts with the sacks of cities on the voyage to
Troy, runs through the *aristeia* of the *Iliad* including the deaths of Lycaon
and Hector, moves through the killing of Penthesileia from the first book of
Quintus, and ends with a hope for the arrival of Neoptolemus his son – which
will indeed take place shortly in Book 7. The familiarity of this narrative is
explicitly underlined: 'He sung his song to the Argives who already knew the

---

[20] On Callimachus in Quintus, see Greensmith (2018; 2020: 160–7).

story themselves' (162–3): this is the poetic tradition, we know. Nestor's song starts at the beginning of the story, brings it up to the present via the *Iliad* and the *Posthomerica* itself, and anticipates the future. It performs the whole continuous story, displaying in the song within the song a summary version of the complete narrative of which the *Posthomerica* is claiming to be a part. Nestor is – programmatically – *palaiōn istori muthōn*, 'an expert in the stories of old' (8.480): he knows the mythic tradition. Where Aristotle can praise Homer's *Iliad* precisely because it does not attempt to tell the whole story of the Trojan War but has a tight thematic and temporal focus, Quintus insists on the broad, continuous temporal frame. The interval between the *Iliad* and the *Odyssey* is strategically interwoven with its preceding tales back before the *Iliad*, as if the *Iliad* and the *Posthomerica* are both slices from the same banquet.

Or rather, Nestor is represented as performing his song in this way in reported speech, while Quintus' poem still remains located between Homer's iconic poems. That is, on the one hand Quintus repeatedly displays a well-ordered mythic world in chronological order, where the beginnings and ends of stories are carefully placed. Thus, just as we go back to the marriage of Thetis here, so when Eurypylus is rampaging through the Greeks in Book 8, Antiphus escapes death, 'because he was destined to perish wretchedly at the hands of the man-slaying Cyclops later' (8.125–6). When Homer in *Odyssey* 2 tells us that Aegyptius' son Antiphus had been eaten by the Cyclops, it is an internal reference to the retrospective tale of Odysseus to come in Book 9. Here in Quintus the reference (with its conscious nod towards Homer) anticipates, as *husteron*, 'later' precisely indicates, the narrative of the *Odyssey* to come after the end of the *Posthomerica*. He escapes death *because* (οὕνεκ') of the narrative we know to be coming, because of the poetic tradition: events are determined by what we know is to happen. There is a strong sense of an ordered chronological, linear, ineluctable narrative, in which the *Posthomerica* takes its place. On the other hand, the very difference between the scale of Nestor's chronology and Quintus' in the *Posthomerica* displays the effort of repressing the epigonal, interstitial status of Quintus' story, placed between, and bounded by the *Iliad* and the *Odyssey*. As Greensmith insists and analyses superbly, the *Posthomerica* inhabits an interval, and is distinguished by the poetics of the interval.[21]

THE NARRATIVE AND TEMPORALITY OF DESCRIBING

In Homer – and thus for the epic tradition – there is a dynamic conceptual opposition between *khronos* and *kleos*. As Fränkel influentially argued – and has been tellingly nuanced by Bakker – in Homeric epic, *khronos* is brought into

[21] Greensmith (2020: 6–7).

visibility 'only at moments in which heroic action or the progression of the narrative is stalled, and so the possibility to build *kleos* temporarily blocked':[22]

> The antithetical relation between *khronos* and *kleos* sheds light on the instances of *khronos* that do occur in Homer. These denote Fränkel's 'empty time' only when we view *khronos* in our perspective of temporality. But in connection with *kleos*, the time in which 'nothing happens' becomes precisely *khronos* as factor that is averse to *kleos*, the dimension in which people just age and can do nothing to make up for it.[23]

For the *Posthomerica*, the 'empty time' of waiting dominates the epic. It is not that 'nothing happens', or that we see sitting in one's tent as an act of aggressive withdrawal; rather, it is that each stirring act of battle, each victory, each death, contributes nothing to the advance of the war or the approach of the end. In the *Iliad*, Hector's death anticipates the fall of Troy: in the *Posthomerica*, although Hector's death opens the epic, there are still twelve books of exhausted and inconclusive fighting before the trickery of the horse makes the fall of Troy possible. In Book 11 the Trojans are waiting as they do in Book 1. In this way, Quintus changes the relation between action, masculinity and the teleology of its narratives. Triumphs are temporary; boasts empty; suffering to be borne stoically; the story goes on; Quintus' redrafting of the agency of heroic masculinity, to which we will shortly return, goes hand in hand with his redrafting of the temporality of epic narrative.

The temporality of delay, in this way, is explicitly thematised; but it is also performed by the narrative strategies of Quintus' epic. The battle repeatedly pauses for truces, scenes of mourning and burial, or for the arrival of a new warrior on either side. Mourning in particular, which marks the closure of the *Iliad* in multiple ways, and which slows narrative into a ritual of loss and backward-looking memory, occurs at points throughout the *Posthomerica*: mourning does not end the narrative, but repeatedly enfolds memory and loss into its progress. But perhaps most strikingly, Quintus again and again uses ecphrasis and simile to hold events waiting until description has run its course.[24] Since Victor Shklovsky declared *Tristam Shandy* to be 'the most typical novel', because it most evidently demonstrated the ability of literary narrative to manipulate time, the manipulation of temporal frames has become a standard prospect of literary critical analysis.[25] Such formal analysis often distinguishes between narrative and description, between, that is, the advance of the story line (on the one hand) and the delay of the narrative through description

---

[22] Bakker (2002: 28); see Fränkel (1960).
[23] Bakker (2002: 28).
[24] Baumbach (2007: 118).
[25] Lemon, Lee and Reis (1965) for the texts; Steiner (2016).

(on the other). Such a stark opposition of *diēgēsis* and *ecphrasis* has been rightly criticised from multiple perspectives, but the role of similes and ecphrastic description in the narrative of Quintus is a central issue of any account of the *Posthomerica*, both because of the frequency with which they occur, and because of their repeated turn from battle to rural life.[26]

Consider, for a first example, the madness of Ajax (5.360–92). Ajax in his anger and shame at losing the arms of Achilles is about either to set the ships alight or to cut Odysseus limb from limb (μελεϊστί, 5.358, which is what Priam fears Achilles has done to Hector (*Il.* 24.409) and what the Cyclops does to Odysseus' men (*Od.* 9.291)), when Athena again changes the course of the action (marked by the pivotal counterfactual, as so often, *ei mē* . . .).[27] She drives Ajax mad. The description of his madness runs for nearly thirty lines (364–93). It begins with a long simile: 'he went like a terrible storm . . .'. This storm with its hurricanes brings terror to sailors (though Ajax as yet has no witnesses). The simile ends, 'so he went where his limbs bore him' (370) – which immediately turns into a further simile, 'He ran around like a shameless wild animal . . .' (371), who throws himself against hunters and dogs alike. This simile also transforms swiftly into a third: 'So he rushed ruthlessly and his black heart seethed like a cauldron . . .' (379–80). This too turns into a fourth simile: 'He raged like the limitless sea' which multiplies into 'or a tempest, or the swift force of tireless fire, when . . .' (386–7). Finally the description ends, 'So Ajax was pierced in his heart with pain and raged bitterly. Plenteous foam flowed from his mouth, and a roar rose in his jaws' (390–3). That is, the narrative of madness consists of basic terms of movement – he went out; he went where his limbs took him; he ran around – and a brief generic description of symptoms – pain, frothing mouth, a roar. Otherwise, simile tumbles into simile, the last of which multiplies its sense of chaos with alternative likenesses. The beast who froths at the mouth describes the movement – but not the frothing – of Ajax (373); the cauldron seethes above a burning fire; a burning fire races over a dry hillside, as simile runs into simile over thirty lines – in a far more intricate, extensive and confused manner than even the occasional build-up of multiple similes in Homer. Rather than focus on the madness itself, our gaze is constantly drawn this way and that towards another scene of rural disturbance, storms, hunters, fires, cauldrons. The narrative is drawn here and there, distracted, offering only the barest direct representation of the madness. The scene of distraction is made up of distraction.

[26] The extensive recent discussion of ecphrasis/description (including Goldhill (2007)) recognises Fowler (1991) as a crucial start; on ecphrasis in Quintus, see Baumbach (2007). On Quintus' similes, see Maciver (2012a: 125–92); Greensmith (2020: 138–53).

[27] On counterfactuals in Quintus, see Greensmith (2020: 308–24), with Prendergast (2019).

The fight over the dead body of Machaon gives a further example of this striking technique of Quintus.[28] In Homeric narrative, there are, of course, many warriors who are given brief epitaphic descriptions at the moment of their death in battle, recalling their city of origin or parentage. In *Posthomerica* 6, Podalirius kills one Lassus, an otherwise unknown figure. His mother, we are told, is a nymph Pronoe (there are several nymphs called Pronoe, it seems). This Pronoe bore Lassus near the river Nymphaeus by a cave (470). So far so Homeric; but the cave then receives fully twenty lines of description. It is a remarkable cave, with crystal water flowing and stone bowls, and statues of Pans and nymphs and looms and distaffs (476–82). It has two ways up and down, one for humans and one for gods, which descends to Hades (484–90). There is a slightly more spooky, less artistically knowing version of such a cave on the headland of Acherousia described by Apollonius of Rhodes (2.727–51), from where the river of Hades pours out; but this cave of Quintus has most obviously been fashioned with an eye to the Cave of the Nymphs in the *Odyssey*, with its two openings for humans and divinities, a cave always open to allegorical understanding. The long description of this cave in Quintus is followed with the markedly understated summary: 'A large crowd perished of those fighting on both sides around Machaon himself and the famous son of Aglaea' (492–3). The cave takes us far away from the battle, and has at first sight no relevance to the battle. It is only where this unknown Lassus was born, and no significance for his death is drawn out, nor is any motivation suggested for the length of the description. In this sense, the description is, as the formalist analysis would have it, a resolute and extended delay to the narrative, and the disjunction between the description and the battle scene is stark. Yet the ecphrasis makes the cave something to look at in wonder (471, 475, 482–3, 491) and talk about (471), an abyss into which gods can stare (491) while humans fear to tread (488–9).[29] It takes our gaze elsewhere and distinguishes it from the gaze of a god, where the underworld is concerned. In a life and death struggle over a dead body it may at very least offer an interpretative challenge to step away to a place where the descent to Hades is visible for the gods, and where the latest corpse was born to a divine nymph. But what is perhaps most insistent in this narrative technique is the delay itself, the staying of the action.

In a similar fashion, Ajax, son of Oileus, stabs Scylaeus in the shoulder, but does not kill him (10.147–50). Instead, we are told at much greater length (10.151–66) how he returned to Lycia by himself after the sack of Troy, and was questioned by the women of the town about their husbands and children, and then stoned to death by them, but his tomb, near that of Bellerophon, is a heroic shrine, and his fated day therefore came later (ὕστερον, 165 – again

---

[28] See Maciver (2012a: 188–92); Schmitz (2007a: 70).
[29] Kauffman (2018: 638) calls such descriptions 'touristic'.

marking carefully the chronological order), and he has everlasting *timē* as a hero. The hoped-for end of fighting – honour – comes, but only after a time and a different form of narrative of *kleos*, as he tells of the stories of the women's men's deaths. He does not die in this battle, but the story of his death still has a place, performing thus the announced continuity of his *timē*. Homer may proclaim the tomb of one of his dead warriors 'for future generations to know', but here we anticipate the tomb of a warrior only wounded, whose death and burial are yet to come, elsewhere. The delay in battle is also the delay in the warrior's progress to his death. The story of Lassus takes us back to the site of his birth, the story of Scylaeus forwards to the site of his death, both remarkable sights in other lands. The delay of Scylaeus' death is narrated as a delay in the action, but it reaches its fated final spot nonetheless. The epitaph's stay of the battle narrative's progression is enacted by a temporal expansion into the past and into the future.

Again and again, as the similes and epitaphs and ecphrases build up within the epic, the dynamic drive of the battle narrative is made to hesitate and change direction towards a world of rural conflict – a term I use to join the fights of beasts, beasts and hunters, and the force of natural phenomenon on the human environment – storms and the like – which dominate the content of the similes. Now, Calum Maciver has done a sterling job in turning back the negative judgements of Quintus' use of similes which previous scholarship had relished making.[30] Homer's similes have been well examined at least for how their content constructs both significant networks of meaning within the epic and an ideological world of value. Similarly, the engagement with Homer's narrative technique in Hellenistic and Roman epic has been analysed for its sophisticated intertextuality. Building on such analyses, Maciver has provided a good foundation for approaching Quintus' similes and ecphrases both intratextually as responding to each other across his epic, and intertextually, in a constant engagement with Homer in particular: reading Quintus reading Homer, as Maciver puts it – an analysis extended incisively by Greensmith.[31] In particular, Maciver analyses Quintus' long description of the shield of Achilles as the test case for such intertextuality. Homer's account in *Iliad* 18 of the weapons Hephaestus made for Achilles is the *locus classicus* of the form of ecphrasis in antiquity, and founds a series of set-piece descriptions as a defining *topos* of epic. Quintus' most evident reformulation of the Homeric shield of Achilles – the introduction of the mountain of virtue – we will soon see to underline a particular ethics of action in the poem.

Maciver does not go on to treat the other two ecphrases – the shield of Heracles carried by Eurypylus[32] and the bow of Heracles carried by Philoctetes –

---

[30] Maciver (2012a: 125–92).
[31] Maciver (2012a: 125–92); Greensmith (2020: 138–53).
[32] On which see Baumbach (2007: 129–41).

in the same detail, although it would be productive to show how Eurypylus' shield with its depiction of the labours of Heracles epitomises the violent
extremes of that most violently extreme of heroes, and is carried by a hero who
will – like all such figures in the epic – be destroyed; while Philoctetes, another,
different heir of Heracles, has on his belt images of animals struggling, but on his
quiver mythic scenes where either trickery is central to the conflict – Hermes
killing many-eyed Argus; Perseus sneaking up on the Gorgon Medusa – or
where there is a warning about transgression of the bounds of order – Phaethon
crashing to earth; or where the two themes come together – Prometheus. This
ecphrasis significantly introduces the *aristeia* of Philoctetes, where he kills Paris
and taunts Aeneas – and Philoctetes is a hero who will survive to make his
return. It is customary by now to note how in both Homer and Quintus the
use of the more everyday world of rural conflict to gloss the battles of heroes
is to normalise the outstanding – to provide a frame of familiar normativity
to gauge and frame the excellence and transgression – extremes both – of the
heroes. The very repetition of so many similes in Quintus, however, seems also
to mark the struggle of the poet to articulate precisely the boundaries and limits
of normativity. Ajax is described by fully twenty-four similes, Neoptolemus by
twenty-three. The question of 'what exactly is he like?' is posed by this repeated
narcissism of small differences. If Quintus seeks to recalibrate the emotional
and ethical economy of heroic action, this obsessional patterning of likenesses is
designed to draw and redraw how these heroes are to fit into the way of things,
how the nature of these fighting men is framed by the conflicts in nature.

INHABITING TIME

Time itself makes a brief appearance in the *Posthomerica* as a character. Zeus rides
a chariot drawn by the four Winds, a chariot which 'immortal Time (*Aiōn*)
with unwearying hands made out of indestructible adamantine' (12.194–5).
Time is distinguished by four alpha-privatives, 'immortal' (*ambrotos*), 'unwearying' (*akamatos*), 'indestructible' (*ateireos*), 'adamantine' (*adamantos*). That which
the passing of time brings about for humans – mortality, tiredness, destruction,
taming (time is traditionally *pandamatōr*, 'all taming') – Time as a god embodies in reverse. *Aiōn* becomes a divine figure to conjure with from the later
Hellenistic period, and by Nonnus is major figure for epic.[33] In Nonnus, the
representation of *Aiōn* is closely linked to the celestial bodies, as here, and also
to astrology as a predictive science.[34] So in Quintus, the four seasons, born to

---

[33] On Aion, see Degani (1961); Foucher (1996); Levi (1944); Nock (1934); Zuntz (1992); on Aion
in Nonnus, see Goldhill (forthcoming).
[34] On the importance of astrology, especially in Stoicism, see Volk (2009); Green and Volk (2011);
Barton (1994a; 1994b); Cramer (1954); and for later material the important Hegedus (2007).

the sun and moon, assistants to Hera, divide time (*aiōn*) into four portions (*moirai*) (10.342), and 'speak all that destructive Fate (*Aisa*) designs in her destructive mind'. This divine apparatus of articulating Fate's plan comes immediately after Oenone has turned Paris away – she is the only one who could have cured his wound – at which the narrator comments, 'Fool! She did not recognise her own destructive lot (*moron*). For the Dooms (*Kēres*) were going to follow her instantly after he died. For that's what Fate (*Aisa*) from Zeus had spun' (10.329–30). The vocative *nēpios/ē* is familiar from Homer, as is the recognition of the enactment of a fated story – the *Iliad* announces from the beginning that its narrative is the fulfilment of Zeus's plan – but Quintus uses such language obsessively.[35]

Every single book has a statement that its narrative is fated. 'Fate', *Aisa*, and the *Kēres*, 'Dooms', *Moirai*, 'Portions' (each term is often translated in English as 'fate'), act as characters in the story. The gods do not know what *Aisa* has planned (11.272–5); the *Kēres* stand and laugh at the hopes of man (8.11); *Aisa* plays the role of history in the historiographers, or the poet in tradition, and makes those without *kleos* famous, and makes the exalted of no account; and turns good to bad, and bad to good in the transformations of human life (13.473–77), just as the *Moirai* make life for mortals gentle or painful, as they wish (9.414–22).[36] The vague expressions of *tuchē*, 'chance', 'fortune' that are typical expressions of the vagaries of narrative in the novels of empire literature become in the hands of Quintus a full, complex and personified panoply of divine figures surrounding and directing human experience. The model is established in Book 1. Penethesileia arrives pursued by the Erinyes (1.29). Her day of fighting is marked out immediately as destined for death, and fate (*Aisa*) from god (1.104). This prophecy is picked up with the narrator's address of her as *nēpiē* (134), and with reminders of her necessary, fated, predicted death that are repeated no fewer than twelve times in the opening book.[37] Fate sounds out like a death knell through the epic. On the one hand, this sense that everything is already predetermined by Fate contributes to the narrative of exhausted waiting. Where the embassy to Achilles in Book 9 of the *Iliad* can imagine Achilles rejecting his chosen fate of an early death and immortal glory – and dramatise a complex pattern of persuasion and decision-making – in the *Posthomerica* there are no such choices to be made. Oenone may be a fool for not realising what her decision portends, but there is no suggestion that another route was a possible choice. At each step of Paris' last day (10.209), the narrator emphasises what Fate had decreed (10.220; 10.265–7; 10.269; 10.331). On the other hand,

---

[35] On *nēpios*, see Schmitz (2007a: 68), who terms it 'tragic irony'; on fate in Quintus I have learned especially from Maciver (2012a: 101–23, 162–3) and Gärtner (2007; 2014). See also the chapters by Maciver and Argyrouli in this volume.

[36] Full lists in Gärtner (2007).

[37] 172; 204; 273; 310; 374–5; 390; 493; 566; 586; 591; 610; 651.

there is also a moral narrative suggested in these narratives of destruction.[38] The first books of the epic have a repeated narrative pattern in which not only are great heroes of the *Iliad* systematically killed off, along with the greatest defenders of Troy, but also they are each killed after – and with the suggestion of *because* – they boast of their own grandeur. So after Penthesileia is introduced in her beauty and strength, and the Trojans rejoice in her arrival, she immediately announces her promise to kill Achilles and torch the ships, on which the narrator comments 'Fool! She did not know at all how much Achilles of the ash spear was superior in battle which wastes men' (1.96–7). Andromache, Hector's wife, goes on to reflect at length on Penthesileia's misplaced arrogance (1.100–14). Penthesileia's fight with Achilles is similarly framed with boasts and dismissal, fulfilled in the ease with which she is dispatched by Achilles. Memnon in Book 2 suffers a similar fate, though it is only when Eris tips the scales against him that the previously close fight swiftly ends with his slaughter. In Book 3 Achilles himself is destroyed by Apollo, after boasting he will strike Apollo and after ignoring the god's commands. In Book 4 the games lead not, as in the funeral games of Patroclus in the *Iliad*, to elaborately displayed gestures of reconciliation, but to the conflict of Book 5 where Ajax, angered by his loss of the armour of Achilles, and maddened by Athena, kills himself. The greatest of the Greeks and the greatest of their enemies perish. So too, at the end of Book 1, does the most disgraceful of the Greeks, Thersites. When he speaks against his leaders in the *Iliad* he is beaten by Odysseus and his tears raise appreciation among the watching Greeks. Here when he speaks out, Achilles simply kills him with a punch. The too low along with the too high are punished, and removed from the narrative. The final image of the rapist Ajax being slowly crushed in agony in the sea as he continues to rail against the gods is a suitable culmination of this narrative's resistance to extreme behaviour.[39]

Alongside the removal of the greatest and most disgraceful, there is a systematic evaluation of the motivations for extreme behaviour, and a rejection of it. Nestor's son is killed, but Nestor 'was not greatly crushed in his spirit. For it is a sign of the wise man to bear pain in the soul bravely, and not in any way to abandon oneself to grief' (3.8–9). This maxim – its roots seem clearly based in Hellenistic philosophy schools and in Stoicism in particular[40] – can be compared to the response to the death of Patroclus by Achilles in the *Iliad*, where the hero's grief is seen as too intense by even his goddess mother – and leads to the sacrifice of Trojans at the tomb and the explosion of Achilles' wrath against the Trojans. At the other extreme, Oenone's jealousy will not allow her to save Paris, and then her grief – observed with surprised awe by all around – leads her to immolate herself on her former husband's pyre. Such

---

[38] As argued persuasively by Maciver (2012a).
[39] Carvounis (2007: 148–154).
[40] Maciver (2012a: especially 70–3; 105–10) argues for Quintus' Stoicism.

repeated warnings against extreme behaviour and emotions culminate in one of the most surprising scenes in the epic, where the ghost of Achilles appears to his son Neoptolemus (14.179–227). Achilles enjoins his son to virtue (ἀρετή), as his own shield had carried an image of *aretē*.[41] He consoles him in his grief. But also demands that he should always take the middle road (14.201–3):

καὶ ἐν φρεσὶ πευκαλίμῃσι
μήτ᾽ ἐπὶ πήματι πάγχυ δαΐζεο θυμὸν ἀνίῃ,
μήτ᾽ ἐσθλῷ μέγα χαῖρε

In your wise mind
Neither completely ravage your spirit with pain at a disaster
Nor greatly rejoice at success.

This from Achilles, celebrated for his rage and violent response to any setback or triumph.[42] An Achilles of the middle road? Indeed, with scant regard for his own traditional representation, Achilles goes on to praise showing 'a kindly heart' (νόος ἤπιος, 204, remembering Briseis' memory of Patroclus (*Il.* 19.381–2)) towards one's dear companions (for whose death he prayed in *Iliad* 1), and towards one's children and wife (barely mentioned in the *Iliad*). Because death is all around, he concludes, always be gentle (μείλιχος, 209). Glaucus in the *Iliad*, observing the many routes to death, concluded that fighting for glory was thus the only proper response. It would be hard to imagine a more vivid demonstration of a recalibration of the martial ethics and emotional economy of the *Iliad*. The demand with which Achilles finishes – the sacrifice of Polyxena, because he is still even more angry about Briseis – comes as a shocking reversal of the very values he encourages in his son – reinforcing the sense that there is a fundamental difference between the generations. Neoptolemus is a great warrior, but his behaviour is tempered – he kills Priam not as a sacrilege but as a necessary act, even welcomed by Priam – and conforms quickly, thanks to an intervention from Zeus, to the idea that the trickery of the Trojan Horse will be required, despite his initial wish to fight straight and hard to win.[43]

This sense that heroism now needs to be redefined to escape extremes is mirrored in Quintus' most direct statement of poetic principle, which is nonetheless paradigmatically indirect, and comes as late as Book 12.[44] In Book 12,

---

[41] Maciver (2007) reprised with further context in Maciver (2012a).

[42] On Achilles, see Scheijnen (2018), who builds on Boyten (2010).

[43] See Boyten (2007); Scheijnen (2015); Scheijnen (2018: 156–226).

[44] One of the most discussed passages of Quintus in recent criticism: see Greensmith (2018) picked up in Greensmith (2020: 158–60) looking back to Bär (2007: 40–52); Maciver (2012a: 33–8); Maciver (2012b: 53–69); Campbell (1981: 100–5).

he finally appeals to the Muses for inspiration to list the Greeks who went into the horse (a less extensive burden than the Homeric catalogue of all the Greeks before Troy, it might be thought). He was inspired, he explains (12.306–11), by the Muses when he was young and tending celebrated sheep around Smyrna. As several scholars have outlined, this combines echoes of Hesiodic and Calli-machean scenes of poetic investiture with a topography associated with Homer: he is setting himself within the poetic tradition (and the adjective *perikluta*, 'celebrated', is rightly taken by Maciver to refer to the poetics of *kleos* and the poetic tradition it informs).[45] The narrator concludes that he was taught in a garden and 'on a mountain neither too low nor greatly high', οὔρεί τ'οὔτε λίην χθαμαλῷ οὔθ' ὑψόθι πολλῷ (12.313). This phrase has been convincingly understood as a programmatic statement of poetic style.[46] The claim to be on a mountain neither too high nor too low – the space of the in-between – goes, however, beyond a definition of linguistic register into the heart of the moral and narrative structuring of the epic. Quintus redrafts normative responses to the violence of war through a late antique philosophical lens, and for this the narrative of the interval between the *Iliad* and the *Odyssey* is fundamental, allowing the gradual removal of the most aggressive heroes of the war, while maintaining a focus on virtue and military success. War is never less than disturbingly fierce and bloody in the *Posthomerica*,[47] but the praised human response to it is noticeably different from that of Homer's heroes.

It is in this light that the tale of Philoctetes makes sense (9.333–546). Odysseus and Diomedes go to fetch the great hero from Lemnos where he is suffering in agony from his wound. Philoctetes has his inescapable arrows to ward off his enemies – and every reason to hate those who deserted him on the island. The plot of Sophocles' play is most familiar to us, but we also have Dio Chrysostom's account of Euripides' and Aeschylus' versions too. In Quintus, though, after he describes with some relish the horror of the wound and the desolate condition of the beast-like man – in terms that recall the vivid staging of Sophocles – as Odysseus and Diomedes approach, Athena simply dissolves his anger in a single line: 'He would quickly have achieved what his bold spirit desired, if Athena had not melted away his grievous anger' (9.403–4). Philoctetes is not overwhelmed by his disruptive heroic emotions.[48] As he later tells Agamemnon, in terms that anticipate Achilles' advice to his son, 'it is right . . . sometimes to be fearsome, sometimes gentle (ἤπιος)' (9.522) – the reverse of the Sophoclean hero's unbending commit-ment to his extreme emotion. The grammar of the pivotal counterfactual is repeatedly used in Quintus, to mark not just alternative routes that the

[45] Maciver (2012c).
[46] Hopkinson (1994) *ad loc.*
[47] Kauffman (2018).
[48] See Greensmith (2020: 318–19).

narrative has not taken (all narratives make and display their choices and Homer uses these pivotal counterfactuals often enough), but also and more specifically, as here, to emphasise the poet's aggressive redesign of the poetic tradition – in and against the dictates of the tradition, the fate to which all characters bend.[49] Philoctetes listens to their explanation that it was the Fates that caused his trouble, not any humans – the sort of argument that Sophocles' Philoctetes would have no truck with – and 'immediately he easily stayed the mental force (θυμός) of his painful wrath: he had been exceptionally angry before because of all the torments he had suffered'. *To paroithe*, 'before' indicates not just Philoctetes' previous feelings, but also the previous representations of those feelings within the poetic tradition that Quintus is transforming so starkly: what once was so bitterly painful and excessive is now melted away. Athena is the figure behind the transformation, but after the speech of Odysseus, it is Philoctetes himself who 'easily stayed' his violent emotions in a display of admirable self-control. *Rhēidiōs*, 'easily' is a word that Homer often uses for a god's effortless labour, and may hint back here to Athena's intervention; it primarily spells out, however, the normative agenda of praised resistance to extreme feelings. But it also indicates here the role of the poet as the authority or god of the narrative, the figure who drives, causes, makes things happen. It is easy for the poet to change the moral purchase of the narrative, so that the famously angry Philoctetes isn't angry any more (although, as Sophocles' *Philoctetes* dramatises, Philoctetes will ever go to Troy, be cured and sack the city, whatever narrative turns it takes to get him there). Quintus is a poet who is fully aware of his role as author in the strong sense, the figure who makes (up) the story. The counterfactual *ei mē*, 'if . . . not' is the mark of the author as the avatar of fate, or the mediator between the outcome of fate and the route that brings fate about. That is, the self-consciousness of literary tradition and the paraded manipulation of literary tradition construct a particular positioning for the poet's voice as a self-aware manipulator of the narrative, its connections, causations and events. It is the poet as much as any notion of fate that constructs the *ei mē* of this story. It is not that 'Sophocles *Philoctetes* seems not to have a strong influence on Quintus' telling of the same story', as Maciver suggests,[50] but rather that the tragic, irresolvable commitment to passionate self-expression that Sophocles' hero displays is systematically redrafted to a new normative agenda. Philoctetes embodies a new emotional economy of heroism, on neither too high nor too low a plane.

The emphatic, repeated insistence that the narrative is fated, including the suggestion of a celestial if not a fully astrological determinism, combined with

---

[49] On counterfactuals in Quintus, see Greensmith (2020: 308–24).
[50] Maciver (2012a: 120, n139); so too James (2004: 318).

an insistence on a controlled emotional engagement with even severe suffering, and a resistance to extremes of heroic violence, suggest an underlying
philosophical awareness for the narrative of the *Posthomerica*, and especially a
Stoic tenor.[51] Stoicism is the *lingua franca* of the Roman Empire's elite, educated
readership, and such philosophical awareness is evident in much imperial writing. But in the *Posthomerica* this philosophical suggestiveness, such as it is, is best
seen as part of Quintus' foundational epic perspective. Quintus' narrative of the
in-between makes every story part of a continuous, interlocking, retrospective
and prospective series of stories, in and for which the achievements of heroic
masculinity are to be reconceptualised, the heroic temper tempered. The temporality of the in-between poses a question of how it is to be inhabited, what is
heroic agency or a heroic ethos now in Quintus' fate-filled narrative.

For Homer's heroes, waiting is a time of denied action, a refusal or denial
of the pursuit of *kleos*. In the *Posthomerica*, we hear such rhetoric in the language of Paris and Aeneas when waiting is suggested as a policy. But, for all
the epic killing and striving, by Book 11 the heroes are indeed still waiting,
as they were in Book 1. It is not yet fated that a turn in the narrative should
shift the mode of action. In this world, where fate is emphasised again and
again as determinative, the potential for transformative heroic agency is recalibrated. With this recalibration, come a shift in ethos – towards patience,
control, a rejection of rage, a resistance to the transcendence of norms that
defines heroic action in the Homeric or tragic expectation. It is perhaps worth
recalling that the Christian invention of time in late antiquity makes waiting a
keystone of an ethical life.[52] For Christians, waiting for the Second Coming is
an imperative, and with it comes an ideal of continuous prayer, humbleness,
asceticism and a turn towards the promise of an afterlife that stands in sharp
contradistinction to the ideology of Homeric epic. Monastic life is ideally dedicated to *khronos*, ordered, routinised sameness, a rejection of the heroic crisis
of *kairos*, of the competitive pursuit of human fame. Scholars have wondered,
despite the lack of salient evidence, whether Quintus speaks to the Christianity taking shape in the empire around him.[53] I am not arguing for any such
direct engagement. Rather, we might see, within the glacial shifts of value,
that Quintus marks a juncture in the slow transformation of thinking about
time and agency, that takes us from Alexander, with Homer under his pillow,
conquering the world, to the monk poring over his bible, or locked in prayer
before a crucifix, denying the significance of this world.[54]

[51] Essential to Maciver (2012a).
[52] Goldhill (forthcoming).
[53] Greensmith (2020: 16–20).
[54] Thanks to Calum Maciver for comments on this chapter, and to the Cambridge Imperial
Greek Epic Project where these ideas were first aired. This chapter has been formulated in and
through many long and stimulating conversations with Emma Greensmith.

CHAPTER 3

Poetry, Performance and Quintus' *Posthomerica*

Katerina Carvounis

Efforts to situate Quintus in a literary, historical and cultural context within the Roman Empire tend to get hindered by the absence of references to, and links with, contemporary events and by the dearth of epic *comparanda*: Nonnus' *Dionysiaca* and the (Orphic) *Argonautica* belong to a different date, while the poems of Triphiodorus, Colluthus and Musaeus are considerably shorter epyllia, and other hexameter works survive in (often very) fragmentary shape. As a result, the *Posthomerica* (henceforth *PH*) is often set against the Homeric epics and Apollonius' *Argonautica* in diachronic explorations of Greek narrative poetry from the archaic to the Hellenistic and into the imperial period. There are, however, isolated scenes in the *PH* which help, to some extent, contextualise this epic, as they contain references pointing to possible influences to which Quintus and his work lay open: the ecphrasis of Achilles' shield in *PH* 5 and the battle among the gods in *PH* 12 are among such scenes; they both begin with a close echo of their Homeric models but also contain 'un-Homeric' elements pointing to later influences upon this epic.[1]

In this chapter, I shall focus on a scene from the funeral games in honour of Achilles in *PH* 4. This is an extended episode, where, like the ecphrasis and the theomachy mentioned above, Quintus strikingly departs from his corresponding Homeric model. Nestor's performance at the beginning of these games will be shown to be characteristic of Quintus' engagement with the earlier tradition and especially the Homeric epics, while also reflecting contemporary poetic performances.

---

[1] For the *theomachia* in *PH* 12, see Carvounis (2008); for recent discussions on Achilles' shield in *PH* 5, see Baumbach (2007); Maciver (2012a: 66–79); Mazza (2014).

THE FUNERAL GAMES IN *PH* 4

PH 4 comes as a respite following the successive deaths of Ares' daughter Penthesileia (*PH* 1), Eos' son Memnon (*PH* 2) and Thetis' son Achilles (*PH* 3).[2] Following Achilles' funeral, Diomedes suggests the Greeks immediately surround Troy with renewed energy to show that Achilles' death has not affected their determination; Ajax, however, advises them to wait for Thetis by the ships, as she has already informed him about her intention to hold games around her son's tomb. No sooner has Diomedes agreed than Thetis appears from the sea and urges the Greeks to begin.

Funeral games for Achilles in the epic tradition are briefly related by Agamemnon's shade in *Od.* 24.85–92, where it is stated that Thetis asked the gods for prizes, which she set up for the best of the Achaeans (*Od.* 24.85–6 ~ 24.91–2).[3] The games in Achilles' honour were also part of the *Aethiopis*, although the surviving information does not mention Thetis in conjunction with the games. The most important model for funeral games in the epic tradition is the account of the games for Patroclus in *Iliad* 23; this is not, however, an occasion where Quintus, this most 'Homerising' poet, has stayed close to the Homeric model. Willis perhaps goes too far when he states that from among the funeral games in the epic tradition, '[o]ne contest at least, that in the *Posthomerica* of Quintus Smyrnaeus, bears little or no resemblance to the games for Patroclus'.[4] Homer remains an important model, but there are, indeed, striking differences between the Iliadic and the Posthomeric games in terms of content, structure and function.[5]

Prizes in the *Iliad* – both for the winner and for the other contestant(s) – are listed at the beginning of each event, whereas in Quintus' version they are reserved on nearly all occasions for the victor alone; they are named and explained after every contest and they are almost always relevant to Achilles.[6] There are also more events in Quintu' games: to the Iliadic events have been

---

[2] For an excellent introduction to *PH* 4 (with emphasis on its structure and place within the whole epic), see Vian (1963: 129–35).

[3] With *Od.* 24.85–6, 91–2 cf. *PH* 4.93–4, 4.101, 4.115–16: see Vian (1963: 139, n4 = *N.C.*, p. 175).

[4] Willis (1941: 392).

[5] As König (2005: 237) aptly puts it, 'Quintus modernizes the Homeric games by presenting many more events than we find in *Iliad* 23, including even a contest of rhetoric (of the kind we hear about in many Imperial-period inscriptions), as if to bring his games in line with contemporary agonistic programmes, in a way which contributes to the impression that his poem has taken us into a new world which the heavy sense of closure within the final books of the *Iliad* can only hint at.'

[6] Willis (1941: 409–17) argues that in the pre-Homeric tradition there was one prize for the winner only, and that Quintus is following such a pre-Homeric source when allocating a prize to the winner for each contest rather than for every contestant.

added Nestor's performance (4.118–80), the long jump (4.465–71), the pancratium (4.479–99) and the horse race (4.545–88),[7] while the Iliadic armed combat (Il. 23.798–825) is not part of the Posthomeric games. Vian has shown that the sequence of events in Quintus' account is not arbitrary and that it points to a careful symmetry in the structure of the games: after Nestor's unrivalled victory, the lesser Ajax defeats Teucer, and there follows a draw between Ajax and Diomedes; after Idomeneus' unrivalled victory, there is a draw between Epeius and Acamas, and then Teucer defeats the lesser Ajax; after Ajax's unrivalled victory, there follows Agapenor's victory over anonymous contestants and then Euryalus' victory over anonymous contestants; and after Ajax's unrivalled victory, there follows Menelaus' victory and Agamemnon's victory too.[8] Finally, Ajax's towering role over and above all the other Greeks becomes evident in the course of these funeral games, which look forward to the imminent ὅπλων κρίσις in PH 5 and also offer a retrospective glance upon the main events of the war through Nestor's song and the brief digressions on the origin of each prize.[9]

The following two points that emerge from a close reading of the games in PH 4 and in Iliad 23 are indicative of the overall relationship between the two epics. (1) Speech and authority: an opinion expressed by a speaker in the Iliad is received as a fact in the narrator's voice in the PH. So, for instance, Epeius' admission in Iliad 23 of his deficiency on the battlefield is, in PH 4, stated by the narrator when Epeius is introduced in the boxing match;[10] likewise, Antilochus' point in Iliad 23 that the gods honour older men is closely echoed by Phoenix when he acknowledges Idomeneus' uncontested victory in the Posthomeric games.[11] (2) Sequel and repetition: the PH is openly and carefully set up as a sequel to the Iliad while also being a self-contained narrative with material that occasionally overlaps with that of the Iliad.[12] For example, whereas different pieces of the armour of Asteropaeus and Sarpedon are awarded in

---

[7] As Vian (1963: 130, n1) points out, the long jump is part of the Phaeacian games in Od. 8.103, 128, and several Homeric similes are familiar with the horse race: cf. Il. 15.679, Od. 5.371.

[8] Vian (1963: 131).

[9] Vian (1963: 132).

[10] Il. 23.670–1, ἦ οὐχ ἅλις, ὅττι μάχης ἐπιδεύομαι; οὐδ᾽ ἄρα πως ἦν / ἐν πάντεσσ᾽ ἔργοισι δαήμονα φῶτα γενέσθαι ('Is it not enough that I fall short of battle? It is not possible to be a skilled man in all works'); cf. PH 4.326–8, ἀλλ᾽ οὔ οἵ τις ἐτόλμαεν ἐγγὺς ἱκέσθαι / εἵνεκα πυγμαχίης· πολέμου δ᾽ οὐ πάγχυ δαήμων / ἔπλετο λευγαλέου, ὁπότ᾽ Ἄρεος ἔσσυτο δῆρις ('Yet nobody dared to go near him for a boxing match; but he was not very skilful in baneful warfare, when a battle was set in motion by Ares'). All translations in this chapter are my own unless otherwise acknowledged.

[11] Il. 23.787–8, ὡς ἔτι καὶ νῦν / ἀθάνατοι τιμῶσι παλαιοτέρους ἀνθρώπους; ('So even now, do the immortals honour older men?'), cf. PH 4.296 (sc. θεοὶ) ἀναιμωτὶ προγενέστερον ἄνδρα τίοντες ('[The gods] honouring an older man without the shedding of blood').

[12] For this distinctive aspect of the PH in the literary tradition, see Carvounis (2019: xxxix–xlii).

each epic,[13] the silver mixing-bowl that had been given as ransom for Lycaon is a prize awarded both in the Iliadic and in the Posthomeric games.[14]

NESTOR'S PERFORMANCE AND ITS HOMERIC MODELS

The games in *PH* 4 open with a performance by Nestor, which is prefaced by the statement that he did not desire to exert himself in boxing or wrestling because of his advanced age (*PH* 4.119–21).[15] This statement draws on Achilles' address to Nestor in *Iliad* 23.618–23, where he gave the aged king the fifth unclaimed prize of the chariot race.[16] The performance itself, however, in *PH* 4 is a departure from the tradition of games established in *Iliad* 23. Ancient variants for two Homeric *hapax legomena* might suggest a contest in eloquence at the end of Patroclus' funerary games when Achilles set up as prizes a spear and a cauldron after the archery contest: *Il.* 23.886, καί ῥ' ἥμονες ἄνδρες ἀνέσταν ('and the men who threw the javelin got up'). The noun ἥμονες (ἵημι) is 'an absolute *hapax*'[17] and would imply that the men who get up (Agamemnon and Meriones) do so to compete in the throwing of a javelin. The contest, however, does not take place, as Achilles tells Agamemnon that it is well known how much the latter excels in strength and ἥμασιν ('throw', *Il.* 23.891: also a *hapax*), and he suggests that Agamemnon take the prize and leave the spear for Meriones. The ancient variants ῥήμονες (*Il.* 23.886) and ῥήμασιν (*Il.* 23.891) would introduce a contest in speaking here;[18] Plutarch (*Mor.* 674d–675d) supports this suggestion and argues that poetry has been an old contest (ὅτι παλαιὸν ἦν ἀγώνισμα τὸ τῆς ποιητικῆς), while he also

---

[13] Asteropaeus' helmet, spears and girdle in *PH* 4.587–8 are an addition to his breastplate that was awarded in the *Iliad* (cf. 23.560–1), and Sarpedon's chariot in *PH* 4.288–90 complements his spear, shield and helmet awarded in the *Iliad* (cf. 23.798–800).

[14] In *PH* 4.381–96 there are two such bowls shared between the boxers Epeius and Acamas.

[15] I was able to consult the important work by Appel (1993) only after I had completed my own research on this chapter, and I would like to thank Ms V. Manolopoulou for translating for me part of this work (pp. 66ff.), which dealt with Nestor's performance in particular. Of special interest is Appel's suggestion (70–1) that for the funeral games for Achilles Quintus may be drawing on his own experiences, together with the material cited for games in the imperial period in the area near Smyrna.

[16] Vian (1963: 140, n4). Cf. *Il.* 23.621–3: οὐ γὰρ πύξ γε μαχήσεαι, οὐδὲ παλαίσεις, / οὐδ' ἔτ' ἀκοντιστὺν ἐδύσεαι, οὐδὲ πόδεσσι / θεύσεαι· ἤδη γὰρ χαλεπὸν κατὰ γῆρας ἐπείγει ('for you would not fight with [your] fists nor would you wrestle nor enter a javelin contest, nor would you run with [your] feet; for already grievous old age is weighing upon [you]').

[17] Richardson (1993: 270) on *Il.* 23.886.

[18] Richardson (ibid.) argues that this would be 'out of place here', and one could also add that there is no reason why Agamemnon's victory in that area should be unanimously accepted and why no further detail should be given about such a contest.

mentions Pelias' funeral games, where his son Acastus had organised a contest in poetry.[19]

A firm association between funeral games and poetic contests is made in Hes. *Op.* 654–9, where the poet mentions his victory at the games in Chalcis that Amphidamas' sons set up for their father; Hesiod carried home a tripod, which he set up to the Muses of Helicon.[20] Isocrates begins his *Evagoras* with a reference to the way Nicocles, Evagoras' son, honoured his father's tomb with offerings, dances, music and athletic contests (Isoc. 9.1). Isocrates then juxtaposes the difficulty of praising a man's virtue in prose (9.8, ἀνδρὸς ἀρετὴν διὰ λόγων ἐγκωμιάζειν) with the use of poetry and concludes that he will, nevertheless, try to see if it is possible to eulogise in prose no worse than those who have offered encomia in song and verse (9.11).[21] In the later Greek tradition, the athletic games on the Isle of the Blessed (Thanatusia) in Lucian's *True Histories* include a poetic contest as the last event: Hesiod wins the contest, although Homer was better (*VH* 2.22).[22] In these parallels, however, the topic of the poetic contest is not necessarily relevant to the deceased. On the other hand, funerals of important Romans included eulogies by a grown-up son of the deceased, which would thus move the crowd to sympathy (Polyb. 6.53–4). At Caesar's death a passage from a tragedy by Pacuvius was recited and, instead of a eulogy, a herald was asked to recite a decree of the senate in which divine and human honours had been voted to Caesar (Suet. *Caes.* 84). Moreover, Vespasian's funerals allowed for competition in singing and pantomime which imitated the manner of the deceased (Suet. *Vesp.* 19).[23] But no funerary games are mentioned in these contexts.

A later parallel in the extant literary tradition for poetry relating to the deceased as part of a competition in a funerary context is found in Nonnus'

[19] Acesander's work on Libya is then invoked for those who cast doubts on the validity of this story, and in an excerpt that follows it is mentioned that there is an offering in the Delphic treasury of the Sicyonians by Aristomache of Erythraea, who was twice winner in the Isthmian games with an epic poem (Plut. *Mor.* 674d–675d). Augustus' new Actian games (Strab. 7.7.6) also contained a combination of athletic games and music or poetic competitions: see Willis (1941: 404).

[20] West (1978: 320) on *Op.* 654 mentions that '[i]t was not only the heroes of epic who were honoured with funeral games (Achilles in the *Aethiopis*, cf. *Od.* 24.85–92; Patroclus in *Il.* 23; Amarynceus, ib. 629ff.; cf. 22.162–4). Many great men and brave warriors were similarly honoured in historical times.'

[21] Hardie (1983: 92). Isoc. 9.11, Ὅμως δὲ καίπερ τοσοῦτον πλεονεκτούσης τῆς ποιήσεως, οὐκ ὀκνητέον, ἀλλ᾽ ἀποπειρατέον τῶν λόγων ἐστίν, εἰ καὶ τοῦτο δυνήσονται, τοὺς ἀγαθοὺς ἄνδρας εὐλογεῖν μηδὲν χεῖρον τῶν ἐν ταῖς ᾠδαῖς καὶ τοῖς μέτροις ἐγκωμιαζόντων ('However, although poetry has so great advantages, one should not shrink but make trial of words, if they can do that too, to speak well of brave men no worse than those who praise in song and verse').

[22] Luc. *VH* 2.22, ποιητῶν δὲ τῇ μὲν ἀληθείᾳ πάρα πολὺ ἐκράτει Ὅμηρος, ἐνίκησεν δὲ ὅμως Ἡσίοδος ('from the poets, in truth, Homer prevailed by far, but Hesiod won').

[23] Gerbeau and Vian (1992: 78).

Dionysiaca. In the funerary games included in D. 19 there are contests in poetry and pantomime in honour of Staphylus, and athletic games are held for Opheltes in D. 37, which are closely modelled to the Homeric games (with Nonnus even keeping the same order of events as in *Iliad* 23, omitting only the *hoplomachia*).[24] The poetic contest in D. 19 takes place between the Athenian Erechtheus, who sings of Demeter and Celeus and links the content of his song to the deceased (D. 19.80–99), and Oeagrus, father of Orpheus, who sings a two-verse *syncrisis* between Apollo and Dionysus: Apollo resurrected his beloved Hyacinth, whereas Dionysus will confer immortality upon Staphylus (D. 19.104–5). Unlike Nestor's performance in *PH* 4 (see below), there is clear emphasis in D. 19 on music and on the singers as musicians (19.74, φορμίγγων ἐλατῆρες, 'strikers of the lyre'; 19.81, κιθάρην ἐλέλιζεν, 'he made the lyre quiver'; 19.97–8, ἀμφὶ δὲ ῥυθμῷ / πάντες ὁμοῦ θέλγοντο, 'everyone was enchanted with the rhythm all around'); yet the audience's reaction at the end of each performance is similar in both cases, for before the ceremonial has ended, the people break out into loud acclamations: D. 19.106–15, οὔ πω κῶμος ἔληγεν, ἐπεφθέγξαντο δὲ λαοί / εὐφήμοις ἐπέεσσιν ὁμογλώσσων ἀπὸ λαιμῶν, 'the song had no sooner finished than the people called out with fair-sounding words from throats speaking the same tongue' (cf. *PH* 4.171–2, Ἀργεῖοι δ' ἄρα πᾶσιν ἐπευφήμησαν ἔπεσσιν / αὐτή τ' ἀργυρόπεζα Θέτις, 'the Argives then applauded at all the words and so did silver-footed Thetis herself').

Nestor's performance as a whole is divided into three sections, with each section drawing on a different topic from earlier events described either within this epic or beyond.[25] The Homeric poems offer models for performances of heroic deeds within epic (when Achilles, for example, sings of κλέα ἀνδρῶν in *Il.* 9.186ff. and Demodocus sings of a quarrel between Odysseus and Achilles in *Od.* 8.73: κλέα ἀνδρῶν), as well as for heroes relating deeds already covered within the same epic, when Odysseus, for instance, offers a linear summary of his adventures to Penelope in *Od.* 23.310–43, which is the longest instance of indirect speech in the Homeric epics.[26]

Nestor starts with a brief praise of Thetis, which sums up her pre-eminence among the other sea goddesses (4.129–30, ὡς πάσῃσι μετέπρεπεν εἰναλίῃσιν /

---

[24] See Gerbeau and Vian (1992: 74).

[25] The following discussion focuses on the Homeric epics as Quintus' main models for Nestor's performance; it would be interesting also to examine Nestor's role as narrator elsewhere in the literary tradition and especially Ovid's *Metamorphoses* 12.

[26] This is the third time that Odysseus relates his adventures in the course of the *Odyssey*, following his detailed account in Alcinous' court (*Odyssey* 9–12), and his brief reference to the account he gave in Aeolia upon Aeolus' request: *Od.* 10.14–16, ἐξερέεινεν ἕκαστα, / Ἴλιον Ἀργείων τε νέας καὶ νόστον Ἀχαιῶν / καὶ μὲν ἐγὼ τῷ πάντα κατὰ μοῖραν κατέλεξα ('he questioned me about everything, both Troy and the ships of the Argives and the return of the Achaeans; and I related to him everything in order'): see de Jong (2001: 562–3) on *Od.* 23.310–41. See also Goldhill (1991: 49).

εἵνεκ᾽ εὐφροσύνης καὶ εἴδεος, 'how she was distinguished among all the sea god-desses because of her good mind and beautiful appearance'); he then describes in detail the wedding of Peleus and Thetis (see below, pp. 46–9), and finally sings of Achilles' achievements during the Trojan War. In this last section, however, he does not start from the beginning but chooses a specific point in his narrative, as the phrase ἔνθεν ἑλών (4.148) indicates. This phrase memorably signals Demodocus' starting point in his third song in *Odyssey* 8, about the construction of the Trojan Horse and Odysseus' role therein (*Od.* 8.500), thus underlining a correspondence between Nestor's tripartite performance in the *PH* and Demodocus' three songs in *Od.* 8.[27]

Demodocus' song about Ares and Aphrodite is also relevant here, as it offers an important model for a mortal's narrative of a divine scene in front of an audience within the epic. In the introduction to Demodocus' song, it is clear that he is singing (*Od.* 8.266, φορμίζων ἀνεβάλλετο καλὸν ἀείδειν, 'play-ing his lyre, he began to sing beautifully'), while references to his musical instrument (φόρμιγγα: 8.67, 105, 254, 261) and the verb ἀείδειν (8.83, 266, 367, 514, 516, 521) repeatedly occur throughout the episode. Different verbs of speaking and singing introduce each of the three sections within Nestor's performance, although there are no references to musical instruments: he first sings in praise of Thetis (*PH* 4.129, ὕμνεεν) and then tells (4.131, ἔνισπε) of Peleus' wedding and does so accurately (4.144–5, καὶ τὰ μὲν ἂρ Νηλῆος ἐὺς πάις Ἀργείοισι / πάντα μάλ᾽ ἱεμένοις κατελέξατο). When Nestor reaches the section about Achilles' achievements, μέλπω is used at the beginning (4.147) and at the end of this section of the performance (4.163), thus indicating that he is singing this part of his performance. Quintus' choice of the verb μέλπω here could be taken as a departure from the Homeric ἀείδω, which is used of Achilles and Demodocus singing about κλέα ἀνδρῶν (in *Il.* 9.189 and *Od.* 8.73 respectively) and within Demodocus' third song (*Od.* 8.514, 516, 521), and as a variation of the use of μέλπομαι in Homer for bards entertaining guests at a feast in *Od.* 4.17–18 (in Sparta) and *Od.* 13.27 (in Phaeacia): μετὰ δέ σφιν ἐμέλπετο θεῖος ἀοιδός ('and the divine bard was singing among them').[28]

---

[27] As Eustathius (1.313) puts it when commenting on Demodocus' third song, καταστατικὴ δὲ ἔννοια τὸ ἔνθεν ἑλών, ᾗ χρῶνται καὶ οἱ μεθ᾽ Ὅμηρον ὁπηνίκα λόγου ἀφηγηματικοῦ κατάρχονται ('the "taking up [the story] from there" is a notion intended to appease, which those [coming] after Homer also use when they begin their narrative'). The collocation ἔνθεν ἑλών is also used by prose authors in the imperial period: e.g. [Longin.] *De subl.* 34.4; Chariton, *Callirh.* 8.7.9; D.Chr. 33.4; [Luc.] *Asinus* 6.1; Philostr. *VS* 1.529.

[28] In the *PH* the verb ἀείδω is used of bards singing about exploits from the (now completed) Trojan War (14.125, 142), while μέλπω describes the Greeks collectively singing of Victory (14.86, μέλποντες Νίκης ἐρικυδέος ὄβριμον ἀλκήν) and of the gods and the (deified) Achilles (14.330, μέλποντες μακάρων ἱερὸν γένος ἠδ᾽ Ἀχιλῆα; cf. *Il.* 1.472–4, οἳ δὲ πανημέριοι μολπῇ θεὸν ἱλάσκοντο / καλὸν ἀείδοντες παιήονα κοῦροι Ἀχαιῶν / μέλποντες Ἑκάεργον. See Leaf (²1902: 47) on the meaning of μολπή in the Homeric epics.

An important difference between Nestor's performance in *PH* 4 and his Homeric model relates to his source of inspiration. Demodocus' gift in singing is divine (*Od.* 8.43–5)[29] and he is inspired by the Muse (8.62–4, 8.73).[30] When Odysseus asks him to sing a third song, which he specifically asks to be about the Trojan Horse, he praises Demodocus and adds that he must have been taught by the Muse or Apollo, for he previously sang about the fate of the Achaeans λίην . . . κατὰ κόσμον ('very much in order', 8.489) as if he was present himself or heard it from elsewhere (8.487–91).[31] Quintus' Nestor, who has not received a special gift from the gods, can, of course, sing of Achilles' achievements and qualities as a first-hand witness, and it could be argued that the divine scene he describes at length is anyway visually present on the human plane within this epic: the wedding of Peleus and Thetis is depicted on Achilles' shield in *PH.* 5.73–9, with the Nereids leading the bride out of the sea and the gods feasting on Pelion's high peak in idyllic surroundings.

Nestor's detailed description of Peleus' wedding, however, seems extraordinary. Nestor himself has already been described earlier in the epic as someone familiar with 'old stories': when Zeus covered Troy in clouds and lightning and thunder resounded from the sky after Ganymede's request to be spared the sight of his city's destruction, Nestor recognised the god's intervention and recalled his past anger and fight against the Titans (8.461–9).[32] The Greeks then immediately heeded to Nestor's advice, for he knew stories of the past (8.480, ἀνέρι γὰρ πεπίθοντο παλαιῶν ἵστορι μύθων). Although Nestor does not have Demodocus' divine insight, he is presented as a figure of authority and a consummate performer, who is able to expand even on details of familiar divine scenes. The response of his internal listeners to the contents of his song is revealing, as they yearn to hear from him all about Peleus' wedding (4.145, μάλ' ἱεμένοις), whereas they already know the part of Nestor's song relating to Achilles' achievements (4.162, ἐπισταμένοισι καὶ αὐτοῖς).

[29] *Od.* 8.43–5, καλέσασθε δὲ θεῖον ἀοιδόν, / Δημόδοκον· τῷ γάρ ῥα θεὸς περὶ δῶκεν ἀοιδὴν / τέρπειν, ὅππῃ θυμὸς ἐποτρύνῃσιν ἀείδειν ('call the divine bard Demodocus; for the god has granted to him above all to delight with his song as his heart stirs him to sing').

[30] *Od.* 8.62–4, κῆρυξ δ' ἐγγύθεν ἦλθεν ἄγων ἐρίηρον ἀοιδόν, / τὸν περὶ Μοῦσ' ἐφίλησε, δίδου δ' ἀγαθόν τε κακόν τε· / ὀφθαλμῶν μὲν ἄμερσε, δίδου δ' ἡδεῖαν ἀοιδήν ('a herald approached leading the loyal bard, whom the Muse cherished above all and gave him both a blessing and an evil'); *Od.* 8.73, Μοῦσ' ἄρ' ἀοιδὸν ἀνῆκεν ἀειδέμεναι κλέα ἀνδρῶν ('the Muse stirred the bard to sing about glorious deeds of men').

[31] Hunter (2012: 98–9) tentatively suggests that Odysseus' comment may not necessarily include Demodocus' song of Ares and Aphrodite, since he cannot establish the accuracy of that song; yet, as Hunter (2012: 99) also mentions, Demodocus' gift to give delight ὅππῃ θυμὸς ἐποτρύνῃσιν to sing is acknowledged in Alcinous' words from the outset (8.45). For the parallel between Demodocus and Homer and the bard's 'objective and impartial' account, see Graziosi and Haubold (2005: 83).

[32] Nestor's description of Zeus's anger against the Titans in *PH* 8.465–9 recalls Hesiod's Titanomachy; cf. Hes. *Th.* 687–99 (esp. 693–8).

This brings us to two further important differences between Nestor and his Homeric models, which relate to the context and audience of each narrative: firstly, when Demodocus sings of Odysseus and his deeds in the presence of Odysseus himself, there is no indication in the text that the bard is aware of Odysseus' identity and that he has geared his narrative accordingly;[33] Nestor, by contrast, tells of Peleus and Thetis' wedding in the presence of Thetis herself, and of Achilles' achievements in the presence of the Greeks, who have witnessed these same achievements. Secondly, as the application of the language of battle and competition to the verbal arena indicates, there is emphasis on the competitive context of this performance (4.123–4, ἐριδμαίνεσκεν . . . / κείνῳ; 4.124, ἐπέων πέρι δῆρις ἐτύχθη; 4.126, εἰν ἀγορῇ ὑπόεικε).

THE WEDDING OF PELEUS AND THETIS (PH 4.128–43)

Let us now look closer at the narrative of Peleus' wedding and Achilles' achievements within Nestor's song to examine how he selects among available versions in the literary tradition and successfully gains the approval of the audience, including Thetis herself. Nestor has already praised her superiority among the sea goddesses in soundness of mind and in beauty (4.129–30, cited above) and now turns to Peleus' wedding feast (4.131, ἱμερόεντα γάμον Πηλῆος), which the immortal gods helped to devise (4.132, συνετεκτήναντο) around the mountaintops of Pelion. Nestor relates how they partook of an immortal feast (4.133–4, ἄμβροτον ὡς ἐπάσαντο / δαῖτα παρ' εἰλαπίνῃσιν) and underlines throughout the divine presence and opulence (4.133–4, ἄμβροτον . . . / δαῖτα; 4.134, εἴδατα θεῖα; 4.135, χερσὶν ὑπ' ἀμβροσίῃσι; 4.136, χρυσείοις κανέοισι; 4.137, ἀργυρέας . . . τραπέζας; 4.139, ἀμβροσίην . . . ἐνὶ χρυσέοισ<ι> κυπέλλοις), as well as the joyful atmosphere at the banquet (4.141–3, ἐπετέρπετο δ' οὔρεα πάντα / καὶ ποταμοὶ καὶ θῆρες, ἰαίνετο δ' ἄφθιτος αἰθὴρ / ἄντρά τε Χείρωνος περικαλλέα καὶ θεοὶ αὐτοί, 'all the mountains rejoiced, and the rivers and beasts, and the divine sky and the beautiful cave of Cheiron and the gods themselves took delight').

Such a positive description of the wedding of Peleus and Thetis from a mortal point of view is familiar from the earlier literary tradition, and the Chorus in Euripides' Iphigeneia at Aulis (Eur. IA 1036–79) offers a close parallel for this narrative before turning to Iphigeneia's imminent fate (IA 1080ff.). In the Homeric epics, however, although gifts made by the gods to Peleus are referred to in the Iliad (17.195–6, 18.84–5), his wedding with Thetis is mentioned only

---

[33] This seems also to be the case with Phemius in Odyssey 1 singing of the Greeks' returns, which Telemachus and Penelope can indeed hear. It has been noted that in his summary to Penelope, Odysseus omits Nausicaa and makes no mention of his extended stay with Circe (de Jong 2001: 563), but both women are absent.

in the final book of the epic, when Hera recalls the wedding feast following the comment by Apollo on Achilles' mistreatment of Hector's body (*Il.* 24.55–63).[34] Hera argues that, whereas Hector is a mortal (24.58, θνητός) nursed by a mortal woman, Achilles is the offspring of a goddess (24.59, θεᾶς γόνος), whom Hera brought up and gave away in marriage to the mortal Peleus (24.60–1, ἀνδρὶ πόρον παράκοιτιν / Πηλέϊ). She further adds that all gods went to the wedding and that Apollo too had feasted among them and held his lyre (24.62–3).

Two points within this speech are important for our purposes: first, that Hera gave Thetis to Peleus, and, secondly, that Apollo played the lyre among the feasting gods. Apollo's presence at the feast has caused difficulties in the literary tradition, as he is – directly or indirectly – responsible for killing the offspring of the union that is being celebrated:[35] a fragment by Aeschylus, for example, contains Thetis' direct accusation against Apollo for having sung at the feast for a long and happy life for Achilles (Aesch. fr. 350 Radt).[36]

These two points (namely, that Hera was responsible for arranging Thetis' wedding and that Apollo actively participated in the celebration) are important in Quintus' handling of the wedding of Peleus and Thetis.[37] Apart from Nestor's song and Achilles' shield, this union is discussed on four more occasions in the *PH*, which are all concentrated in Books 3–5 of the epic and will be examined below. Two passages – Hera's reproaches to Apollo (3.98–127) and to Zeus (4.49–55) – describe the gods' role in arranging the wedding and their participation in the feast, and two further passages – Thetis' lament (3.611–26) and the Nereids' departure into the sea (5.338–40) – describe the events leading to the marriage and cast light on Thetis' reluctance.

Let us start from Hera's reproaches in the *PH*, first to Apollo and then to Zeus, which elaborate the point that the goddess had made to Apollo in *Iliad* 24, namely that the gods' presence at the wedding feast implied a special bond between themselves and the couple. First, Hera accuses Apollo for having forgotten (3.99, λησάμενος, cf. 106 ἐξελάθου) that wedding which

---

[34] For early references to the wedding of Peleus and Thetis (esp. in the *Cypria*), see West (2013: 69–73).

[35] See Hadjicosti (2006) for an overview of the problem with reference to the *Iliad*, the relevant Aeschylean fragment, Catullus and Quintus.

[36] See Burgess (2004b) for convincing arguments against the suggestion that 'the *Iliad* 24 passage reflects a traditional story about a misleading prophecy of Apollo at the wedding of Peleus and Thetis'.

[37] That Hera brought up Thetis is also mentioned by Apollonius (A.R. 4.790–8) and Apollodorus (3.13.5), and had probably also featured in the *Cypria* (fr. 2), where Thetis refuses to marry Zeus as a favour to Hera; but the responsibility for arranging the marriage is also attributed to Zeus himself, either of his own accord or because he has heeded Prometheus or Themis, as is mentioned, for example, in the summary of Apollodorus. Apollo's presence in the post-Homeric tradition is often mentioned alongside that of the Muses (Pi. *N.* 5.22–5, Eur. *IA* 1040–8; Luc. *DMar.* 7: see *LIMC* s.v. 'Peleus').

the gods devised and where Apollo sat among the diners and sang of Peleus leading Thetis from the sea as his bride, while he joined the gods in making libations and praying for the birth of a child from that union (3.98–109).[38] In that same speech, Hera further predicts the arrival of Achilles' son from Scyros, and concludes by asking how Apollo will face Thetis when she visits Zeus's halls (3.125–7). Then, in *PH* 4, Hera accuses Zeus of having forgotten (4.50, λελασμένος, cf. 55, ἐξελάθου) Thetis, whom he formerly gave away in marriage to the godlike Peleus (4.50–1, ἥν ῥα πάροιθεν / ἀντιθέῳ Πηλῆι πόρες θυμήρε' ἄκοιτιν, cf. *Il.* 24.60–1, ἀνδρὶ πόρον παράκοιτιν / Πηλέϊ). She claims that Zeus himself arranged the immortal wedding, while all the gods feasted on that day and brought presents (4.52–4). Therefore, the responsibility for that marriage varies within Hera's three speeches in the *Iliad* and the *PH*: whereas Hera in the *Iliad* had said that *she* gave Thetis to the mortal Peleus (*Il.* 24.59–60, cited earlier), in her first reproach to Apollo she mentioned that *the gods* arranged the wedding (*PH* 3.99–100, τὸν ἀθάνατοι γάμον αὐτοὶ / ἀντιθέῳ Πηλῆι συνήρσαμεν), and later tells Zeus that *he* did so (4.51, ἀντιθέῳ Πηλῆι πόρες θυμήρε' ἄκοιτιν; 4.52, γάμον δέ οἱ αὐτὸς ἔτευξας).

The two remaining references to Peleus and Thetis bring to the foreground the bride's reluctance to marry the mortal groom. When lamenting over Achilles, Thetis recalls the numerous transformations she underwent to escape Peleus' bed until Zeus granted that she would bear a great son, who was, nevertheless, short-lived (3.611–26). Finally, the last reference to her marriage with Peleus in the *PH* is when the Nereids depart into the sea after the judgement over Achilles' arms: they are angered at Prometheus, as they recall (μνώμεναι) that it was at his prophecy that Zeus gave unwilling Thetis to Peleus (5.338–40).

With this background in mind, let us return to Nestor's own version of Peleus' wedding in his song. This version shares two notable features with the one adopted by Hera in her reproach to Apollo: both Nestor and Hera underline the collectivity in the gods' devising of the wedding (4.131–3, ὃ δ' ἱμερόεντα γάμον Πηλῆος ἔνισπε, / τόν ῥά οἱ ἀθάνατοι μάκαρες συνετεκτήναντο / Πηλίου ἀμφὶ κάρηνα, 'he told of her beautiful wedding with Peleus, which the blessed immortals helped devise at the peaks of Pelion'; cf. 3.99–100, τὸν ἀθάνατοι γάμον αὐτοὶ / ἀντιθέῳ Πηλῆι συνήρσαμεν, 'this wedding

---

[38] The marked contrast that the Iliadic Hera had made between mortality (Hector) and immortality (Achilles) is here brought to the foreground through the Posthomeric Hera's juxtaposition of the treatment that Apollo suffered at the hands of the mortal Laomedon (3.111–12, ὃ δ' ἀθάνατόν περ ἐόντα / θνητὸς ἐὼν ἀκάχιζε, 'and although [you were] immortal, he, a mortal, caused [you] grief') with Achilles' divine origin (3.116–17, ἢ γὰρ Ἀχιλλεὺς / ἤπιος ἄμμι τέτυκτο καὶ ἐξ ἡμέων γένος ἦεν, 'for Achilles was indeed kind to us and he was from our race').

we ourselves, immortals, helped arrange for god-like Peleus'),[39] and they both refer to the music at the feast.[40] Hera described Apollo singing about Thetis leaving the sea to become Peleus' bride (3.100–2), and the creatures and elements in the landscape coming together when he played the lyre (3.103–5),[41] while Nestor, too, describes the mountains, rivers and wild animals rejoicing (4.141, ἐπετέρπετο), and the air, Cheiron's cave and the gods themselves all taking delight (ἰαίνετο) (4.142–3) – but this is when the *Muses* (not Apollo) turn to song (4.141, Μοῦσαι δ' ἐς μολπήν). The presence of the Muses is a traditional element in the literary (and artistic, with the François Vase as a famous example) representation of the wedding of Peleus and Thetis; yet Nestor's departure from the version followed by Hera and his choice to focus on the Muses alone and make no mention of Apollo points to his consideration towards the audience of his performance. What is on display here is Nestor's eloquence and skill with words, as he takes care not to bring grief to Thetis, who is part of his audience. Nestor's focus on the opulence and divine presence at the famous wedding, together with the attention drawn from the outset to *Peleus'* ἱμερόεντα γάμον (with no mention of Thetis), attribute divinity, as it were, to a mortal who notoriously lacks it, as Thetis herself had complained a few lines earlier (*PH* 3.613–15, 621–4).[42]

ACHILLES' ACHIEVEMENTS (*PH* 4.144–61)

This attention on Nestor's part to his choice of material is also important in the next (section of his) song when he relates Achilles' achievements and takes further care to please the audience. Already from the start of this section, the audience responds enthusiastically to the choice of subject (4.146–8). Nestor chooses a starting point to glorify the hero with well-fitted words (4.148–9,

---

[39] Contrast Hera's reproach to Zeus in 4.52–4, where she attributes responsibility for the marriage to him alone: γάμον δέ οἱ αὐτὸς ἔτευξας / ἄμβροτον, οἳ δέ νυ πάντες ἐδαινύμεθ' ἤματι κείνῳ / ἀθάνατοι ('but you yourself arranged the divine wedding, and we all immortals feasted on that day'). Also, the versions adopted by Thetis and her sisters imply that – either because Prometheus told him or for no known reason – Zeus was responsible for this marriage.

[40] Like Apollo, Nestor, too, stands amidst the Greeks: 4.118, πρῶτος δ' ἐν μέσσοισιν ἀνίστατο Νηλέος υἱός ('the son of Neleus first stood up in the midst'); 4.128–9, τοὔνεκ' ἐν<ὶ> μέσσοισιν εὔφρονα Νηρηίνην / ὕμνεεν ('for this reason in their midst he sang for the wise daughter of Nereus'), cf. 3.100–1, εὖ δ' ἐνὶ μέσσοις / δαινυμένοις ἤειδες ('you sang well in their midst as they feasted').

[41] Cf. the effect of Orpheus' μολπῇσιν, according to his mother Calliope, in *PH* 3.638–41, as Vian (1963: 100, n1) points out.

[42] If we read Nestor's songs as individual parts of an encomium to Achilles (see below, pp. 53–4), then this would be a subtle beginning to the encomium with emphasis on Achilles' divine origin on *both* sides.

ὃ δ' ἄρ' ἔνθεν ἑλὼν ἐρικυδέα φῶτα / ἐκπάγλως κύδαινεν ἀρηρεμένοις ἐπέεσσι). The emphasis on these well-fitted words (4.149, ἀρηρεμένοις ἐπέεσσι) draws attention to the context of Nestor's performance and to the fact that he is keen to appeal to the audience. He is performing in a competition (cf. the repetition of ἀγών) and, unlike Odysseus before the Phaeacians (see p. 43, with note 26, above), Nestor relates events he has witnessed in the presence of other witnesses, so he takes care to choose the right material and relate it with the most appropriate words.[43]

A comparison with a parallel passage at the end of the *PH*, where the Greeks are celebrating their victory with songs about the Trojan War after the sack of the city, is telling (14.121–42). Arranged in linear sequence, the songs there offer an overarching account of the Trojan War from Aulis to the present moment: they start with the assembly of the Greek forces and largely concentrate on Achilles' achievements, from his sacking of twelve cities by sea and eleven cities by land and his defeat of Telephus, Eetion and Cycnus, to his victory over Hector and the dragging of the corpse around Troy, as well as his defeats over Penthesileia and Memnon. The songs move to the triumphs of other Greek heroes and conclude with those who entered the horse, with the sack of Troy and the victory feast itself. Through their comprehensive nature and position, these songs give a closural effect to the *PH*.[44]

Given that this section of Nestor's song focuses specifically on the deeds of Achilles, in whose honour the games take place, it is not surprising that Nestor omits events relating to Achilles' μῆνις. Nestor lists ten victims, whose deaths span the *Cypria*, the *Iliad* and the *PH*. This list does not follow strict chronology but, as we shall see below, is rather dictated by notions of symmetry and an attempt not to arouse memories of Achilles' raging behaviour that has not escaped criticism.

---

[43] Eustathius (1.303) attributes the pleasure derived from listening to Demodocus' second song, on the adultery of Ares and Aphrodite, to rhythm and harmony: τὴν μοιχείαν τῆς Ἀφροδίτης ἀκούων ἐτέρπετο ἐν φρεσὶ καθὰ καὶ οἱ ἄλλοι Φαίακες. εἰ δὲ μὴ ἐχρῆν ἐπὶ οὕτω φαυλοτάτῳ ἀκούσματι τὸν φιλόσοφον διαχέεσθαι, ἀλλ' ἔστιν εἰπεῖν ὡς οὐ τοῖς λεγομένοις ἁπλῶς χαίρει ἀλλὰ τῷ ῥυθμῷ καὶ τῇ ἐμμελείᾳ τοῦ σοφοῦ ἀοιδοῦ. ἴσως δὲ καὶ ταῖς τοῦ μύθου ἀλληγορίαις ἐμβαθύνων φιλοσοφώτερον, καὶ οὐ κατὰ τοὺς Φαίακας ἀκροώμενος καὶ αὐτός, οἳ ἄλλως τέρπονται ἀκούοντες διὰ τὸ φύσει δηλαδὴ τὰς ἐρωτικὰς ἐννοίας γλυκείας εἶναι ('listening to Aphrodite's adultery he (*sc.* Odysseus) rejoiced within just as the other Phaeacians. If the philosopher ought not to relax upon hearing such base things, one could argue that he delights not simply in what is being said but in the rhythm and harmony of the skilled bard. Perhaps also going deeper into the allegories of the story in a more philosophical manner, he himself does not listen in the manner of the Phaeacians, who take pleasure in listening in a different way because erotic stories are sweet by nature'). See Hunter (2012: 106).

[44] Other summaries of earlier episodes from the Trojan War in the *PH* are found at the opening (1.9–14) and the middle (7.379–81) of the epic. Achilles' exploits are the focus of these earlier summaries, and the choice of episodes included therein is determined by the immediate narrative context; this is further discussed in Carvounis (2019: 75–8).

Telephus and Eetion are mentioned together as objects of the verb ἐδάιξε (4.151). In older accounts (such as the *Cypria*), the Greeks land on Mysia and meet Telephus before they even reach Troy, so the mention of Telephus after Achilles' sacking of the surrounding cities upsets the traditional chronology of the latter's achievements. Achilles' treatment of both Telephus and Eetion testifies to his clemency: that Achilles healed Telephus' wound with the same weapon with which he had wounded him is referred to at the end of Nestor's song (4.172–7: see below), while Andromache herself had already testified in the *Iliad* to the respect that Achilles had shown to her father, Eetion (*Il.* 6.414–20).

Cycnus and Polydorus form the next pair of Achilles' victims (objects of the verb ἔκτανε), and Troilus and Asteropaeus follow suit. Cycnus and Polydorus are linked by their god-like characteristics: Cycnus is a god's son (*PH* 4.154, υἷα Ποσειδάωνος), while Polydorus, the youngest and dearest of Priam's sons (*Il.* 20.407–10), is described as ἀντίθεο[ς], both here and in his first appearance in *Iliad* 20, where his death had forced Hector to confront Achilles on the battlefield for the first time (*Il.* 20.419–54). Achilles' final achievements are his victories over Hector and Penthesileia (4.160), and Memnon (4.161), which take place in *Iliad* 22, *PH* 1 and *PH* 2 respectively. Nestor elevates Achilles' victims to elevate Achilles himself: Memnon here is described as υἱ<έ>α δῖον ἐυθρόνου Ἠριγενείης ('noble son of the early-born (Dawn) with the beautiful throne', 4.161) rather than as son of Tithonus, which is the case in *PH* 14 (14.135, υἱέα Τιθωνοῖο), and Cycnus is referred to here as a god's son (4.154, cited above), whereas in *PH* 14 he will be designated as Κύκνον . . . ὑπέρβιον (14.131).

For the episodes featuring Xanthus and Lycaon (4.156–8 and 4.158–9 respectively) Nestor mentions the reddening of Xanthus' streams and the bodies choking his flow, but not Achilles' confrontation with the river-god, while he omits Lycaon's plea and Achilles' merciless rejection, as well as Lycaon's subsequent death and Achilles' hurling of the body into the river (cf. *Il.* 21.118–20), and the boastful speech that provoked Xanthus' anger (21.136–8). Nestor mentions instead that Achilles killed Lycaon close to the river (ποταμοῦ σχεδὸν ἠχήεντος, *PH* 4.159) without exposing Achilles' raging and merciless side. Achilles' treatment of Lycaon's body has been described as an 'unnecessary and contemptuous action', which is followed by an 'insulting speech' that angers the river-god.[45] This view was also shared by ancient readers of the *Iliad*, and the παραποτάμιος μάχη features in Plato's *Republic* in his criticism of Homer and the poets: καὶ ὡς πρὸς τὸν ποταμόν, θεὸν ὄντα, ἀπειθῶς εἶχε καὶ μάχεσθαι ἕτοιμος ἦν ('and towards the river, who was a god, he was disobedient and ready to fight with him', *Resp.* 391b). The bT scholia on *Il.* 21.120 state that the fact that Achilles hurls into the

---

[45] Richardson (1993: 64) on *Il.* 21.120–38.

streams even those who died on the ground offers a possible cause for the river to plot against Achilles, and that he then speaks irreverently. Without omitting this famous incident from the *Iliad*, which is also recalled by the Trojans themselves at the very beginning of the *PH* (1.9–10), Nestor subtly avoids the more objectionable details of the incident.

The reference to Troilus seems to interrupt the sequence of Achilles' victims in *Iliad* 20 and 21, for after Polydorus, Achilles' next victim was Lycaon (21.34–135) and then Asteropaeus (21.140–210), whose death had prompted Xanthus' confrontation with Achilles (21.211–382). If Quintus' summary here were to reflect the sequence of duels related in the *Iliad*, we might have expected Lycaon to be mentioned instead of Troilus and before Asteropaeus. Troilus was mentioned by Priam at the end of the *Iliad*, where the old king lamented the excellent sons he lost in the war, among whom were 'godlike Mestor and Troilus who fights from a chariot (ἱππιοχάρμην)' (*Il.* 24.257), before focusing on the most recent loss of Hector (*Il.* 24.255–9). Neither Mestor nor Troilus is mentioned again in the Homeric epics; but whereas Mestor remains a minor figure in the literary tradition,[46] Troilus' death at the hands of Achilles was 'a popular story',[47] often represented in art from the archaic period onwards.[48]

Proclus' summary of the *Cypria* mentions Troilus' killing by Achilles without providing further detail. According to one version of Troilus' death (which may well have been that in the *Cypria*; cf. [Apollod.] *Epit.* 3.32; schol. ATV on *Il.* 24.257), Troilus was killed by Achilles in Apollo Thymbraeus' temple[49] and his death is associated in some versions with that of his sister Polyxena. Nestor here refers to Troilus with the adjective θηητόν (4.155)[50] and the narrator will later on underline Troilus' youth and beauty (4.418–35),[51] although it is implied that in this epic (and in *Aen.* 1.474–8) Troilus dies on the battlefield at the hands of Achilles (4.433–5). As with the wedding of Peleus, here too we witness Nestor opting for a version that befits Achilles.

This discussion of Nestor's presentation of the wedding of Peleus and Thetis and of Achilles' achievements has thus aimed to show that it is a presentation carefully handled to appeal to his audience; after all, Nestor is singing in the

---

[46] Richardson (1993: 299) on *Il.* 24.257: 'Oddly enough, neither Mestor nor Troilus is mentioned elsewhere in Homer. Apollodorus (*Epit.* 3.32) mentions Mestor in connexion with Akhilleus' raid on Aineias' cattle, and he crops up in some other late versions of the Trojan War (D.Chr. 11.77, Dictys 6.9).'

[47] Richardson (ibid.).

[48] For references, see West (2013: 121–2).

[49] See West (2013: 121); Vian (1963: 152, n2). In another version, Troilus is decapitated by Achilles: see Lyc. 313 (καρατομηθείς).

[50] The epithet θηητός does not occur in the Homeric epics, but it is found in Hes. *Th.* 31 for the staff that the Muses gave to Hesiod (*Th.* 31). The epithet is used by Tyrtaeus to describe a man's beauty (fr. 10.29 West) and this use is adopted in Hellenistic and later hexameter poetry.

[51] See Hornblower (2015: 187) on Troilus' eroticisation.

presence of Thetis herself and of the Greeks who fought alongside Achilles.[52] After every section of Nestor's song we witness the audience's reaction (4.130–1, ἣ δ' ἀίουσα / τέρπεθ'; 4.145–6, τοὶ δ' ἀίοντες / τέρπονθ'), and after the end of his performance, both the Greeks and Thetis herself applaud the performance as a whole (4.171–2, Ἀργεῖοι δ' ἄρα πᾶσιν ἐπευφήμησαν ἔπεσσιν / αὐτή τ' ἀργυρόπεζα Θέτις).[53] Thetis rewards Nestor with the horses that Telephus had given as a gift to Achilles after the latter healed his wound; Nestor thus receives a tangible token of Achilles' generosity and clemency.[54] In glorifying Achilles with well-chosen words (4.148–9, ἐρικυδέα φῶτα / ἐκπάγλως κύδαινεν ἀρηρεμένοις ἐπέεσσι), Nestor meets with unanimous approval and receives glory himself (4.179–80, οἳ δ' ἐς νῆας ἄγον μέγα κυδαίνοντες / ἀντίθεον βασιλῆα).

ENCOMIUM TO ACHILLES

If Nestor's song is read as a whole, it becomes apparent that the different parts of his song follow the structure of an encomium for Achilles. A basic pattern (with variations) for praise is recommended in theoretical treatments and *progymnasmata*, that is, elementary treatises in Greek and Latin from the imperial period.[55] 'Hermogenes' mentions as topics for the encomium race and city, family, events at birth, upbringing, education, physical and mental qualities; accomplishments, actions, length of life, manner of death, posthumous fame and descendants (15.18–17.1 Rabe).[56] Aphthonius in the late fourth/early fifth century suggests placing origin (γένος) first, divided into nation, city, ancestors and parents; then upbringing, divided into accomplishments, skill, laws; next actions, divided into mind, body and fortune; comparison; epilogue, with features appropriate to a prayer (22 Rabe).[57] Finally, Nicolaus of Myra in the fifth century, who, as Russell and Wilson note, has preserved a scheme that can be paralleled precisely to that of Menander Rhetor,[58] divides the encomium

---

[52] The competitive context of this performance is made explicit from the outset through the language of competition in the verbal arena (4.123–4, ἐριδμαίνεσκεν . . . / κείνῳ, 'contended with him'; 4.124, ἐπέων πέρι δῆρις ἐτύχθη, 'there was a fight with words'; 4.126, εἰν ἀγορῇ ὑπόειξε, 'yielded in the assembly'). For a narrative of the union between Peleus and Thetis and for Achilles' exploits from the *Iliad* and the Epic Cycle, see also, in the Greek side of the tradition, Pi. *I.* 8.49–58.

[53] If Nestor is relating more detail for Achilles' achievements than what the narrator gives us, then the people's praise cannot be directed at the narrator's artful summary, but rather at Nestor's tactful selection of subject matter (and, presumably, his artful choice of words, although Quintus' narratees cannot judge that).

[54] In this case, the epithet ἐυμμελίης (applied to Achilles in 4.173) is pointed.

[55] Russell and Wilson (1981: XVIII–XXXIV).

[56] Russell and Wilson (1981: XXVII).

[57] Russell and Wilson (1981: XXVIII).

[58] Cf. Agosti (2002) for a close comparison between an encomium to Diocletian that has been preserved on a papyrus fragment (*POxy* 4352, fr. 5.II.18–39) and Menander's treatise about the στεφανωτικὸς λόγος (422.16–20, p. 178 Russell and Wilson).

into proemium, origin, birth, education, accomplishments and actions, these last divided according to virtues, and not narrated chronologically.[59]

The structure of Nestor's performance points to an encomium for Achilles after similar rules.[60] He begins with Achilles' parents and divine origins, for he extols Thetis and sings of the wedding of Thetis and Peleus, where, as we saw, he underlines the divine presence, joy and opulence of the event, thus elevating Achilles' mortal father. Nestor then moves to the famous deeds of Achilles himself, from the cities he sacked by land and sea to the individuals he defeated in different phases of the war. Nestor subsequently praises Achilles' physical qualities before concluding with a prayer to see the latter's son Neoptolemus arrive from Scyros. That this praise is met with success is obvious from the reaction of the audience (see pp. 49–50, 53, above), who appreciate both the well-chosen words (4.149, ἀρηρεμένοις ἐπέεσσι)[61] and the content of Nestor's performance as a whole.[62]

Both the content and the competitive context of this performance show a distancing from the Homeric models and suggest a reflection in Quintus' epic of later practices. Competitions of all sorts have been part of Greek culture from the archaic period onwards, but from Hellenistic times and especially in the Roman Empire they are formally categorised and supported by the ruling authorities.[63] In the imperial period events in competitions seem to have proliferated from the first to the second century: it has been noted that whereas at around 20 CE there are seven events at games, among which are listed ἐπῶν ποιητής and ἐγκωμιογράφοι (which implies different competitions for epic poetry and poetic encomia),[64] at around 150–60 CE, there are twenty events, including the title of ἐγκωμιογράφος for the emperor, praise for the Muses, poet for the emperor and poem for the Muses.[65]

---

[59] Russell and Wilson (1981: xxviii).

[60] It is worth comparing Libanius' (prose) encomium of Achilles in Foerster vol. VIII.235–43, which includes, however, a more extensive account of individual aspects (such as, for example, Cheiron's contribution to Achilles' upbringing). There are some points shared with Nestor's performance, but Libanius is largely preoccupied with offering a positive narrative of Achilles' actions taken (mostly) from the *Iliad*.

[61] Cf. Nonn. *D.* 19.111, ἁρμονίην εὔρυθμον, which the audience applauds following Oeagrus' performance; see also note 43 above, on Odysseus' enjoyment of Demodocus' diction and style, as well as the subject matter of the second song in *Odyssey* 8.

[62] Other instances in the *PH* that attest to the interaction between rhetorical education and the literary tradition include the debate between Ajax and Odysseus in *PH* 5 for the arms of Achilles (see, for example, Maciver 2012b) and Calliope's speech of consolation to Thetis in *PH* 3.633–54 (see Carvounis 2019: xxvii–xxx).

[63] Remijsen (2014: 190–206). For the Hellenistic period, see Pallone (1984).

[64] Hardie (1983: 89).

[65] Gangloff (2010: 68). See now Bowie (2019) on specific examples of such poetic (and prose) performances.

More epigraphic evidence comes from the second and the early third centuries CE, and there is a decline across the empire in the latter half of the third century. There are also more competitions in the East than in continental Greece;[66] Aphrodisias in particular has provided substantial evidence for contests consisting of athletic and/or performing arts competitions that seem to be characteristic of this type of cultural activity taking place across the eastern part of the Roman Empire.[67] Epigraphic examples from Aphrodisias in the late second century CE offer a glimpse of this activity: in a schedule of prizes for a musical contest in Aphrodisias,[68] reference is made to prizes for (*inter alia*) a 'writer of encomia' (ἐνκωμιογράφῳ) who is mentioned in close proximity to a 'Cyclic flutist' (κυκλίῳ αὐλητῇ) (Roueché 52 I).[69] Another fragment refers to an 'adult harp-singer' (ἀνδρὶ κιθαρῳδῷ) in close proximity to a 'Latin poet' (ποιητῇ Ῥωμαικῷ) and to 'awnings and equipment for the theatre' (βήλων καὶ τῶν/ διὰ θεάτρου) (Roueché 52 II).[70]

Archaeological excavations have yielded material evidence that attests to a performative culture for later Greek literature;[71] the Kom el-Dikka auditorium in Alexandria and the Theatre of Aphrodisias are two important findings for declamation and festivals for the performing arts respectively.[72] More evidence has also helped cast light on the *Paneia* games in Panopolis, which offer a context for this agonistic performative culture in an area known as the place of origin for numerous Greek poets, where the games listed involve sports, theatrical and musical contests.[73]

Papyrus fragments attest to games featuring poetic contests,[74] as well as to poets' intentions to participate in such contests. An open reference to this agonistic culture for poetry is famously provided by the introduction to Claudian's Greek *Gigantomachia* at the end of the fourth century, where the poet mentions his hopes for praise by his audience upon hearing his verses.[75] Other fragments too can potentially yield further interesting readings: in an ethopoea assigned to the third century CE (*POxy* 3537r), Hesiod purports to be speaking

---

[66] Gangloff (2010: 59).

[67] Roueché (1993: 2–3).

[68] Roueché (1993).

[69] Before 'the athletic contest of the citizen boys' (εἰς δὲ τὸν γυμνικὸν τῶν πολειτῶν παί- / δων ἀγῶνα): Roueché (1993: 168–9).

[70] Roueché (1993: 173). In yet another schedule of prizes for a musical contest, reference is made again to the denarii ascribed to an 'encomium writer' (ἐνκωμιογράφῳ) before those ascribed to a 'poet' (ποιητῇ) (Roueché 53): Roueché (1993: 174).

[71] See Agosti (2006: 40).

[72] See Agosti (2012: 377–8).

[73] Miguélez-Cavero (2008: 258–60); van Minnen (2016: 59–60); Remijsen (2015: 115).

[74] See Rea (1996: 2) for references in the papyri to poetic competition.

[75] Later in the mid-fourth century CE, Libanius mentions ἐπίδειξις ἐπῶν (*Or*. 54, 37) and στίχων ἄμιλλαι (*Progymn*. VIII.540.18 Foerster): see Agosti (2006: 46 with n56).

after his meeting with the Muses.[76] This composition has attracted attention for its acrostic, consisting of a formulaic line familiar from the Homeric epics but absent from the Hesiodic tradition,[77] and for the fact that it shows 'Hesiod' transformed from bucolic to epic poet.[78] Another point of interest here is 'Hesiod's' determination to go to a place linked to 'a circle of contests' (κ]ύκλον ἀγώνων),[79] which could indicate a place for display of (poetic) prowess, and the readers may thus be encouraged to see here yet another such reference to contemporary poetic competitions.[80]

As has been attractively suggested, Nestor is here 'the equivalent of an epic singer' and Quintus thus provides 'a metapoetical commentary on his own role as a belated epic poet who has to shape a well-known tradition for a learned audience'.[81] This chapter has aimed to examine in further detail Nestor's attempts to appeal to his audience through his careful choice of events from the Trojan War and words with which to narrate these events. It has also been suggested here that Nestor's performance in *PH 4* can plausibly be considered to be a rare reflection of the agonistic culture in poetic performance that was widespread in the first centuries of the empire.[82]

---

[76] The title of this ethopoea seems to be the following: τίνας ἂν λόγου[ς Ἡσίοδος εἴπο]ι ὑπὸ τῶν Μουσῶν ε [μ]ενος. All the participles that have been suggested to fill the gap relate to Hesiod's sudden inspiration, e.g. ἐκ[διδασκόμ]ενος, ἐμ[πεπνευμ]ένος, ἔν[θεος γενόμ]ενος: see Parsons (1983: 62). On this fragment, see Miguélez-Cavero (2008: 316–40, with further bibliography).

[77] Agosti (1997), τὸν δ᾽ ἀπαμειβόμενος προσέφη.

[78] In 17–21 'Hesiod' expresses his aversion to the small (18, παύρην) song of weak farmers (17–18, ἀφαυροί / ... ἀγρο]ιῶται).

[79] Cf., e.g., Hes. *Th.* 91–2: ἐρχόμενον δ᾽ ἀν᾽ ἀγῶνα, θεὸν ὡς ἱλάσκονται / αἰδοῖ μειλιχίῃ, μετὰ δὲ πρέπει ἀγρομένοισι ('when he goes to an assembly, they greet him as a god with gentle reverence, and he is distinguished among those gathered'); cf. also *Il.* 24.1, λῦτο δ᾽ ἀγών. For the phrase κύκλον ἀγώνων, cf. (in the singular, κ. ἀγῶνος) A.R. 4.1602–10, where Triton leads the Argo forward to the sea like a man leading a horse into the 'circle of a racecourse' and running alongside it.

[80] There are more such hints in the papyri; for example, in *POxy* 63.4352 (c. 285) there is a reference to Capitoline Zeus (fr. ii.18, Ζεὺς ... Καπιτώλιος) and Rea (1996: 1–2) offers 'the theory that these verses were composed to be recited in a poetic competition at Capitoline games in Egypt'.

[81] Schmitz (2007b: 83).

[82] See note 15 above, for the suggestion put forward in Appel (1993: 70–1) that Quintus may here be drawing on personal experiences of such competitions. Further research on poetic performance will help cast light on the function of poetry and the performance of the *PH*: see Appel (1994b); cf. also Agosti (2012: 377–8) for the performance of Nonnus' poetry. 1 Earlier drafts of parts of this chapter were first presented in conferences on 'Greek Imperial Epic and Cultural History' (Cambridge, 3–5 July 2013) and 'The Poetry and Aesthetics of Late Antiquity' (Edinburgh, 3–4 September 2015). I would like to thank Emily Kneebone and Calum Maciver respectively for inviting me to these occasions, and those who participated in the discussions with comments, questions and feedback. I would also like to thank the editors of this volume, Silvio Bär, Emma Greensmith, Leyla Ozbek, for inviting me to contribute here and for their patience.

CHAPTER 4

A-Sexual Epic? Consummation and Closure in the *Posthomerica*[1]

Emma Greensmith

The world of imperial Greek epic is an intensely erotic space. The lustful adventures of Dionysus and his entourage, the *harpagē* that started the Trojan War, secret liaisons and encounters by lamplight – desire, sex and sexuality shape and permeate so many of the works from this period.[2] It is perhaps no surprise, therefore, that much of the recent critical output on this corpus has focused on sexual themes. In the growing scholarly attention in this era of poetry, eroticism has emerged as a central talking point: a means of communicating the value, interest and vitality of works once considered to lie outside the bounds of mainstream classical interest.

In this chapter, I consider the place of the *Posthomerica* in this discourse. Although Quintus' poem has itself received ample critical attention in recent years,[3] it seems not to share in the erotic obsessions of its imperial Greek siblings. Scenes of an obviously sexual inheritance are narrated without sexual details; nakedness and intercourse are minimalised; and romantic relationships remain surface-level, their lusty potential unfulfilled. If the reader comes to the epic looking for passion, they will be left bizarrely cold.

---

[1] The text of Quintus throughout is that of Vian (1963, -66, -69); of the *Iliad* that of Murray (²1999); of the *Odyssey* that of Murray (²1999). Translations of Quintus are adapted from James (2004), of Homer from Murray. The ideas in pp. 66–70 of this chapter have now been expanded in Greensmith (2020): especially 313–17.

[2] The period under question for the purposes of this chapter will be understood to range from the second to sixth century CE. On periodisation and imperial Greek epic, see e.g. the introduction of Hunter and Carvounis (2008). Relevant comments for the *Posthomerica* in Maciver (2012a: 15–26).

[3] See the Introduction to this volume for discussion and references.

I shall focus on this erotic absence in the *Posthomerica*, and argue that far from being a detriment of the poem, it offers a window into the specific identity poetics of the text. Quintus' pointedly passionless epic presents a profound meditation on closure, its literal and literary implications. By avoiding sexual forms of *telos*, the *Posthomerica* establishes its position as a text which refuses and frustrates any sense of completion. Continuing the *Iliad*, but never bringing it to a close, Quintus' 'asexual poetics' works to expound a Homeric text which defiantly ceases to end.

EROTICS AND EPIC

It would be far from controversial to chart the prevalence of erotic themes in Greco-Roman epic from its earliest manifestations. To take briefly the boldest, most familiar examples,[4] in the *Iliad*, *erōs* is repressed and refracted, set in contrast with the martial obsession embodied by *kleos* – with Briseis, sex object and spoil, providing a focal point for these two competing types of desire. More latent hints of sexual attraction – most famously between Achilles and Patroclus – have sparked generations of postscripts and speculation.[5] Equally evident are the different modalities of desire in the wandering narrative of the *Odyssey*, where the hero's entanglement with Calypso, Circe, Nausicaa (again repressed and counterfactual) and Penelope mould the course of the *nostos*.[6] Intense too is the ambiguous, dangerous attraction between Jason and Medea as it is shaped and reshaped by Apollonius.[7] And Dido, burning and frenzied, along with the cradle-snatching Amata, offers the potential, passionate alternative – or violent erotic derailment – of the *Aeneid*'s focused agenda.[8] Ovid's *Metamorphoses* give such themes an especially prominent place, as the sexual as much as bodily transformations of the characters tie together the poem's threads.[9]

For modern scholars focused on the epic genre, expounding its sexualised content can help to articulate the perennial excitement of the epic text. In a world increasingly sceptical about the desirousness of studying ancient literature

---

[4] Bibliography on the topic of *erōs/amor* in epic is vast. For a recent and broad survey (in epic and other genres), see Masterson, Rabinowitz and Robson (2015) with extensive bibliography; and, for cultural considerations, Skinner (2005). Further references for studies in individual epics given where relevant below.

[5] On this topic, see particularly Fantuzzi (2012).

[6] Especially: Felson-Rubin (1994); Cohen (1995).

[7] Book-length study in Beye (1982). Discussion also in Hunter (1993); Byre (2002); Papanghelis and Rengakos ([2]2008); Harder and Cuypers (2005).

[8] Cf. e.g. Gillis (1983); Farron (1993); Desmond (1994); Reed (2007); Cairns and Fulkerson (2015), especially chapters 8–9; and on Amata, Fantham (1998) is excellent.

[9] Seminally: Richlin (1992). See also Curran (1978); Robinson (1999); Bretzigheimer (1994); Anderson (1995).

at all, the well-known story content of mythological epic renders it a particularly useful vehicle to counter such dismissals. And these works' erotic themes can function as clear communicants of their passion and 'relevance'. Recent popular adaptations also testify to these effects. Madeline Miller's bestselling novel *The Song of Achilles* brings to the fore the hints of a homosexual relationship between the Iliadic Achilles and Patroclus; and the recent BBC series on the Trojan War was advertised as promising all of the 'sex and drama' of *Game of Thrones*.[10]

Imperial Greek epic seems to present a particularly good fit for this model. Many of the surviving Greek hexameter works from the Roman era make use of erotics extensively, explicitly and self-consciously. To consider some contrasting examples, Nonnus' *Dionysiaca* guides its hero through as many sexual adventures as military ones and begins and ends its encyclopaedic romp through mythology with violent and disturbing divine–mortal rapes. Colluthus' account of the rape – or abduction, or seduction[11] – of Helen tells the story of the *erōs* which caused the most canonical conflict of all, but often teasingly transfers the erotic locus away from the story's central couple and on to more twisted, wayward relationships. Musaeus' *Hero and Leander* reads like an epyllionic Greek novel, programmatically intent upon exploring ideas of seduction, desire and consent, with the opening subject of the lamp functioning as a reflexive motif for the poem's erotic agenda.

The marked presence of sexual themes in these imperial works can prompt a specifically late antique mode of cultural reflection, operating in texts written on the cusp of a rapidly changing world. How, we can ask, does eroticised epic combine or clash with the precepts of Christianity? How does it operate within changing political and cultural centres? Who read this sex-stuffed hexameter and why? Recent scholarship has tackled precisely such questions. Helen Morales has explored the sexual politics of Colluthus, considering, for example, the unexpected focus on the intense relationship between Helen and her distraught, abandoned daughter Hermione.[12] Simon Goldhill has considered the equally perverse 'erotics of death' in the *Dionysiaca*, as displayed in a scene of necrophilia to which I shall return.[13] Fotini Hadjittofi has looked at the rape scenes in the *Dionysiaca*, reading them in the light of Christian discourse around sex and violence.[14] A 2017 conference on imperial epic at the University of Cambridge focused directly on erotic ideology and cultural history, and explored the possible links between them.[15] Eroticism, it is clear, has played an

---

[10] See, for instance, the article about this series in *The Times*, 24 September 2016, which begins with the tricolon 'sex, scandals and sword-fights'.

[11] On the definition(s) of *harpagē* in this context, see e.g. Morales (2016: 61) with further references.

[12] Morales (2016).

[13] Goldhill (2015).

[14] Hadjittofi (2008).

[15] 'The Age of 'Hero's': Eroticism and Cultural History in Imperial Greek Epic', University of Cambridge, 3–4 July 2017.

important role in ushering in these texts from the canonical wilderness which they once inhabited.

If, however, desire makes epic, and makes these imperial epics, more critically desirable, a question is raised about the interpretative consequences when these themes are missing. The *Posthomerica* raises this question sharply. Unlike the later poems of Nonnus and Colluthus and Musaeus, the *Posthomerica* is not an erotic epic. It deals frequently with events of a sexual nature, but it does not fulfil their erotic potential. The poem contains no prolonged scenes of lovemaking, no homoerotics, no lingering depictions of nakedness. There is ample hyperbolised violence on the battlefield, a common way to visualise erotics in war, but this detail is gooey and gory – Philoctetes' gangrene (9.355–91), a twitching severed hand attached to a horse (11.191–200) – not beautiful or aestheticised. And the most famous rape in this segment of the saga, the assault of Cassandra by Locrian Ajax, is not directly narrated at all: it is refracted instead through the reaction of a goddess, happening, from the reader's perspective, 'off page' (4.416–29).

The usual explanations given for this sexual reticence are Quintus 'moralising' and his 'Homerising'. Given that, for all of the embedded hints discussed above, Homeric epic itself does not parade its sexual dynamics with proto-Nonnian flamboyance, it has been argued that through his even more muted sexual style Quintus is simply showing himself to be a good Homeric imitator.[16] This style has furthermore been viewed as an example of the poet's 'correction' of Homeric epic in the light of later moral and philosophical criticism: where, for example, critics like Xenophanes criticised the licentious portrayal of the Homeric gods, Quintus reflects this pattern of thought by reining in his own portrayals even more.[17] However, this corrective argument often ultimately becomes another way of saying that Quintus 'flattens' Homer;[18] it simply arrives at that conclusion by a different route. And it does not, at any rate, account for why Quintus chooses to centre his epic on episodes where eroticism is traditionally the central and most prevailing concern. Story content, of course, is always a choice – 'a poet does not need an excuse to write a poem'[19] – so it is a relevant question to ask why Quintus would cover this segment of the Cyclic story at all, only to forfeit the tone which fits the theme. Whilst the poet of the *Posthomerica* certainly read his Homer and his Homeric criticism closely, in order to account for the 'a-sexuality' of this epic, we must attempt a different route of explanation.

---

[16] See e.g. the introduction to James (2004), which strongly pursues this corrective reading. Further examples in the passages analysed below.

[17] See Wenglinsky (1999) and (2002).

[18] To use a term common in nineteenth-century pejorative assessments. Cf. e.g. Köchly (1850) with discussion in Vian (1959a: 145–6).

[19] Maciver (2012a: 8–9).

It is precisely this link between eroticism and style in the *Posthomerica* that the central part of this chapter will pursue. I shall look at three places in the epic where we would most expect to find erotic intensity: Achilles' encounter with the dead Penthesilea; Helen's re-seduction of Menelaus; and their eventual reunion in bed. I shall not read these scenes by trying to tease out passion where it seems to be missing. Rather, I shall suggest that eroticism is pointedly and powerfully removed from these expected places. The desire for desire is *set up*, and then always thwarted before the final climax. To characterise the effects of such a process, I want to term this a poetics of frustration. Many modern readers have in the past found Quintus' reticent, un-exuberant verse to be frus*trating*.[20] But 'frustration' instead suggests a more constitutive link between sexual gratification (and its denial) and poetic style, which lies at the heart of Quintus' agenda in his poem.

The theoretical language which can best capture this link comes from the deconstructionist concept of supplementarity. Understood in its broadest sense, supplementarity describes the process whereby 'a signifier [in this case, a source text] is so charged with an excess of energy that it generates further fictions, which serve to answer unanswered questions, fill "gaps", explain perceived contradictions, provide sequels and allow for appropriations in view of new circumstances'.[21] As the work of Charles Martindale,[22] Stephen Hinds,[23] Don Fowler[24] and others has finely shown, these ideas can account for the intertextual dynamics of many classical texts: the continuous re-reading and re-definition that characterises later poets' relationship to their earlier literary models, a process based on the constant striving for, but refusal of, textual closure. This interpretative system, though not necessarily explicitly sexual (although the frequent recourse in such scholarship to the Bloomian Oedipal complex shows how neatly the metaphorical lines can be drawn)[25] is directly mappable with discourses of desire: it focuses on questions of what to do with excess energy, and the longing created by the deferral of closure. It therefore offers a lens through which the age-old literary game of revision and re-reading can be understood as an erotically analogous process: another form of tension resistance and release.

---

[20] Cf. Lloyd-Jones' infamous condemnation (1969: 1) that Quintus served up 'an anaemic pastiche of Homer utterly devoid of life'. Further comments on this frustrating aspect of the epic in Middleton's chapter in this volume.

[21] Martindale (1993: 37) drawing on the biblical hermeneutics of, particularly, Kermode (1979) and (1983) is to my mind one of the clearest definitions of the concept, as defined for these purposes. For further on this formulation, see Steiner (1989) with relevant comments on closure at 82.

[22] Martindale (1993).

[23] Hinds (1998).

[24] Fowler (1997).

[25] Bloom (1973). For Bloom's use in discussions of classical literature, see particularly Martindale (1993: 36–8) and Chaudhuri (2014: 2–4).

Supplementarity will provide the framework for this discussion of the *Posthomerica* – a text which proves to be obsessed with problematising, in quite distinctive ways, the notion of Homeric closure. Through its position in the Homeric middle, and its claims to be speaking in Homer's voice, this is a poem which inserts itself within fixed literary boundaries, forcing open the space between Homer's two poems, a canonical duo which was by this era completed and closed.[26] The space created by the missing *erōs* in the poem, the sense of frustration created by making sexual scenes devoid of sexual fulfilment,[27] provides a prism for the poet to articulate the complexities of this inter-Homeric position: to display the effects of an epic defined by waiting, stasis and mediation. Quintus elides and combines ideas about sexual and narrative consummation, pointedly analogising the epic and the erotic *telos*, to focus attention on the challenges inherent to his task. *Almost* filling Homer's gap, the *Posthomerica* edges towards the closure of a new, expanded Homeric canon, but ultimately leaves it gaping open.

ACHILLES AND PENTHESILEA: NEUTRALISED NECROPHILIA . . .?

Within such a framework, let us first consider a passage which occurs in the first book of the poem and provides a dramatic and instructive example of Quintus' poetics of frustration. It is a scene steeped in a mythic tradition of violent, grotesque erotics, which, in this treatment, is denied and then diverted.

When Achilles kills the Amazon queen Penthesilea, in a scenario reminiscent of the aftermath of Hector's death in the *Iliad* (*Il.* 22.367–75), he and his fellow Greek soldiers gather around the fallen queen. Achilles removes her helmet, and they all stare at her face. They are struck by her beauty, which is enhanced in death by Aphrodite. Gazing upon the sight, Achilles feels remorse:

ἀμφὶ δέ οἱ κρατὸς κόρυν εἵλετο μαρμαίρουσαν
ἠελίου ἀκτῖσιν ἀλίγκιον ἢ Διὸς· αἴγλη·
τῆς δὲ καὶ ἐν κονίῃσι καὶ αἵματι πεπτηυίης
ἐξεφάνη ἐρατῇσιν ὑπ᾽ ὀφρύσι καλὰ πρόσωπα   660
καί περ ἀποκταμένης. οἳ δ᾽, ὡς ἴδον, ἀμφιέποντες
Ἀργεῖοι θάμβησαν, ἐπεὶ μακάρεσσιν ἐῴκει.
κεῖτο γὰρ ἐν τεύχεσσι κατὰ χθονὸς ἠΰτ᾽ ἀτειρὴς

---

[26] This is now a dominant reading of Quintus' poetics. I have discussed it in detail elsewhere (Greensmith 2020). See also Maciver (2012a: chapter 1), with further references.

[27] This lack of fulfilment will be considered often from the characters' and always from the reader's perspective.

Ἄρτεμις ὑπνώουσα, Διὸς τέκος, εὖτε κάμῃσι
γυῖα κατ᾽ οὔρεα μακρὰ θοοὺς βάλλουσα λέοντας·   665
αὐτὴ γάρ μιν ἔτευξε καὶ ἐν φθιμένοισιν ἀγητὴν
Κύπρις ἐυστέφανος κρατεροῦ παράκοιτις Ἄρηος,
ὄφρα τι καὶ Πηλῆος ἀμύμονος υἷ᾽ ἀκαχήσῃ.
πολλοὶ δ᾽ εὐχετόωντο κατ᾽ οἰκία νοστήσαντες
τοίης ἧς ἀλόχοιο παρὰ λεχέεσσιν ἰαῦσαι.   670
καὶ δ᾽ Ἀχιλεὺς ἀλίαστον ἑῷ ἐνὶ τείρετο θυμῷ,
οὕνεκά μιν κατέπεφνε καὶ οὐκ ἄγε δῖαν ἄκοιτιν
Φθίην εἰς εὔπωλον, ἐπεὶ μέγεθός τε καὶ εἶδος
ἔπλετ᾽ ἀμώμητός τε καὶ ἀθανάτῃσιν ὁμοίη.   (1.657–74)

From her head he removed the helmet, the brilliance of which equalled
the rays of the sun or the lightning of Zeus. Even in the dust and blood
where she had fallen, beneath her brows the beauty of her face could be
seen still undimmed by death. The Argives gathering round marvelled
to see how like the blessed immortals she was. She lay on the ground
in her armour, just like Artemis, Zeus's hardy daughter, sleeping when
her limbs are weary from hunting swift lions in the mountains. This
beauty even among the dead was the personal work of the fair-crowned
Cyprian goddess, the mighty war god's spouse, to inflict some suffering
on noble Peleus' son. Many there were who prayed that when they
returned to their homes, they might share the bed of a wife as lovely as
her. Even Achilles' heart felt unremitting remorse for killing her instead
of bringing her as his bride to Phthia the land of horses, because in
height and beauty she was as flawless as an immortal goddess.

Thersites then mocks Achilles for his weak, unwarlike sentimentality (1.716–40)
and Achilles kills him in angry retaliation (755–61). This story was well known
in the ancient tradition. The *Aethiopis*, according to Proclus' summary, narrated
how after killing Thersites Achilles sought purification on the island of Lesbos.
Propertius' brief mention of the encounter (3.115–16) singles out Penthesilea's
beauty, revealed in the removal of her helmet, which suggests that this was
a traditional feature of the tale. Lycophron gives a very violent version (*Al.*
999–1001), where Thersites gouges out one of Penthesilea's eyes and is killed
by Achilles because of this desecration of her body. The episode also fleet-
ingly occurs in another imperial Greek epic. Triphiodorus, with characteristic
brevity,[28] sweeps over it in just one line: describing how Achilles 'killed [the
queen] and despoiled her and gave her a funeral' (καὶ κτάνε καὶ σύλησε καὶ
ἐκτερέιξεν Ἀχιλλεύς, Triph. 39), he gives, as Miguélez-Cavero notes, a 'purely

---

[28] On Triphiodorus' poetics of speed, see Tomasso (2012) and Maciver (2020).

masculine' account of the relationship.[29] There are also versions which preserve a grimmer detail. According to some accounts, such as those preserved by Eustathius in his commentary on *Iliad* 2.220, Achilles engaged in necrophilia: he was so enraptured by Penthesilea's beauty, that he had sex with her corpse. Nonnus seizes upon this point. In a vignette during the Indian War (*Dion.* 35.21–36) he tells of an unnamed soldier's lust for a girl that he has killed; how he stares at her, touches her, 'and wants to have sex with her' (35.35). He proceeds to strip the corpse naked and fondle her breasts and limbs (35.31–4). This desire is explicitly modelled on the 'later' tale of Achilles and Penthesilea:[30]

> Καὶ νύ κε νεκρὸν ἔχων πόθον ἄπνοον, ὥς περ Ἀχιλλεύς
> ἄλλην Πενθεσίλειαν ὑπὲρ δαπέδοιο δοκεύων
> ψυχρὰ κονιομένης προσπτύξατο χείλεα νύμφης,
> εἰ μὴ Δηριαδῆος ἐδείδιεν ὄγκον ἀπειλῆς.   (*Dion.* 35.27–8)

He would have had a longing for a breathless corpse, like Achilles seeing another Penthesilea on the ground; he would have kissed the cold lips of the dust-covered girl, if he had not feared the weight of the threat of Deriades.

On the one hand, the *Posthomerica* preserves some standard features of the story. We find tropes of beauty, and the aesthetic revelation in the removal of the helmet (1.660, ἐξεφάνη ἐρατῇσιν ὑπ' ὀφρύσι καλὰ πρόσωπα; 673–4, ἐπεὶ μέγεθός τε καὶ εἶδος / ἔπλετ' ἀμώμητός τε καὶ ἀθανάτῃσιν ὁμοίη). However, Quintus completely omits any of the sexual reactions triggered by this sighting. Achilles does not touch Penthesilea at all. No one does in this scene, in comparison both to Nonnus and to Lycophron. Instead, he and all of the Greeks wish to marry her (1.669–74). Such intentions are in one sense evocative of the Odyssean suitors, who, when enraptured by Penelope's own divinely enhanced beauty (*Od.* 18.158–303), are further spurred on in their desire to win her as a bride (*Od.* 18.250–80). The urge for marriage to Penthesilea is equally multiplicitous (πολλοί, 669), unrequited and unfulfilled. However, unlike the Odyssean admirers, who are also overcome by a more overtly sexual desire – they wish to 'lie beside [Penelope] in bed' (. . . ἔρῳ δ' ἄρα θυμὸν ἔθελχθεν, / πάντες δ' ἠρήσαντο παραὶ λεχέεσσι κλιθῆναι, *Od.* 18.212–13) –

---

[29] Miguélez-Cavero (2013: 147). In this de-sexualised allusion to the story, Triphiodorus could arguably also qualify for the same line of argumentation that I am here pursuing for Quintus. However, the lack of narrative space dedicated to the episode in the *Sack of Troy* means that the tensional dynamics of *erōs* suggested vs *erōs* denied are not centralised to the same extent in Triphiodorus' treatment.

[30] It is later in the mythological tradition, as the Indian War precedes the Trojan one. On this scene, see especially Goldhill (2015).

there is here no explicit erotic impulse to accompany these nuptial designs. Achilles is then grieved at the loss of Penthesilea's 'beautiful strength' (ἐρατὸν σθένος, 719). As in Triphiodorus, this is a more masculine, martial quality which is admired, very different from the physicality of Nonnus, where the soldier is obsessed with the fleshy details of his victim's thigh. This grief is then compared to Achilles' former feelings for Patroclus (ἑτάροιο . . . Πατρόκλοιο, 721): a relationship which has the potential for amorous connotations, but this narrative pointedly falls short of fulfilling them.[31]

James' description of the passage reflects the usual line of explanation for its restrained tone: 'the socially respectable terms in which the attraction felt for Penthesilea is described reflects the overall moral tone of the poem, and they are equally in keeping with that of the Homeric epics.'[32] This is not, however, a straightforward removal of Achilles' more perverse form of attraction. The erotic version is still present in this scene. It is suppressed, deflected, and transferred into the unlikely voice-piece of Thersites.

Thersites' derisive speech first provides the missing language of erōs. Although he too talks of marriage (1.727), he also accumulates terms for lust and metonymies for sex: λιλαίετο, 1.725; γυναιμανέουσι, 735; ἐς λέχος ἱεμένης, 736; εὔαδεν εὐνή, 740. Achilles' reaction (755–61), complete with iambic moves of violence – tumbling teeth, falling face first, blood gushing out from the mouth – then provides an alternative physical release to the missing necrophilia. In the aftermath to the death of Hector, which the structure of the present scene closely resembles, after the Greeks marvel at Hector's beauty and form, they proceed repeatedly to stab his corpse (οἳ καὶ θηήσαντο φυὴν καὶ εἶδος ἀγητὸν / Ἕκτορος· οὐδ' ἄρα οἵ τις ἀνουτητί γε παρέστη, Il. 22.370–1). The killing of Thersites echoes this violent move: the penetration of Achilles' strike becomes, in a highly Homeric way, the deflected, distorted version of his other possible lusis in this story.

Quintus thus rewrites the episode so that it is characterised not by sex but by tension: erōs is repressed, un-released and then redirected. This tension is accompanied by symbols of delay, suppression and rerouted action of different types. The emphasis on Penthesilea's 'continued' beauty offers a suspension of the telos of death, akin, once again, to the preservation of Hector's corpse by the gods in the Iliad (Il. 23.184–91). The simile at 1.663 likens this beauty to Artemis 'sleeping' (ὑπνώουσα), offering another means of death-suspension via the comparison to a more temporary form of stillness. A further type of end point is deflected at 669–70, as Quintus describes how the Greeks wished that they had someone as lovely as Penthesilea 'when they returned to their homes'

---

[31] This detail thus serves as an example of how Quintus differs from Triphiodorus in that in his more extended treatment he gestures towards and then pulls back from the erotic potential of this scene.

[32] James (2004: 274).

(κατ' οἰκία νοστήσαντες). Mobilising the *nostos* verb most often used in Homer to indicate a happy escape,[33] the line offers a contrastive proleptic hint to the real *nostoi* of the Greeks – which, the reader knows, will not be quickly or happily achieved.[34] Through these markers, Quintus encourages the reader to align sexual and narrative consummation. Achilles' necrophilia becomes a form of *telos* that is *not* achieved, and its deflection crystallises the many different forms of delayed ending that the poem is intent upon exploring.

HELEN AND MENELAUS: THE DISROBING OF DESIRE

Achilles' 'asexual' response to Penthesilea provides a way to consider the tensional temporality of the poem as established from its earliest scenes. As the narrative continues, the dislocation of *erōs* becomes more intense, as the epic in the middle is forced to confront directly the issues associated with its own closure.

During the sack of Troy, after killing Deiphobus Menelaus discovers Helen in hiding, terrified that she is next to face his sword. Her fears are almost realised: Menelaus in a fit of jealousy moves to kill her, but his violence is checked by the intervention of Aphrodite:

ὀψὲ δὲ δὴ Μενέλαος ἐνὶ μυχάτοισι δόμοιο
εὗρεν ἑὴν παράκοιτιν ὑποτρομέουσαν ὁμοκλὴν
ἀνδρὸς κουριδίοιο θρασύφρονος, ὅς μιν ἀθρήσας
ὥρμαινε κτανέειν ζηλημοσύνῃσι νόοιο,
εἰ μή οἱ κατέρυξε βίην ἐρόεσσ' Ἀφροδίτη,
ἥ ῥά οἱ ἐκ χειρῶν ἔβαλε ξίφος, ἔσχε δ' ἐρωήν·   390
τοῦ γὰρ ζῆλον ἐρεμνὸν ἀπώσατο, καί οἱ ἔνερθεν
ἡδὺν ἐφ' ἵμερον ὦρσε κατὰ φρενὸς ἠδὲ καὶ ὄσσων.
τῷ δ' ἄρα θάμβος ἄελπτον ἐπήλυθεν· οὐδ' ἄρ' ἔτ' ἔτλη
κάλλος ἰδὼν ἀρίδηλον ἐπὶ ξίφος αὐχένι κῦρσαι,
ἀλλ' ὥς τε ξύλον αὖον ἐν οὔρεϊ ὑλήεντι   395
εἱστήκει, τό περ οὔτε θοαὶ βορέαο θύελλαι
ἐσσύμεναι κλονέουσι δι' ἠέρος οὔτε νότοιο·
ὣς ὃ ταφὼν μένε δηρόν· ὑπεκλάσθη δέ οἱ ἀλκὴ
δερκομένου παράκοιτιν· ἄφαρ δ' ὅ γε λήσατο πάντων,
ὅσσά οἱ ἐν λεχέεσσιν ἐνήλιτε κουριδίοισι·   400
πάντα γὰρ ἡμάλδυνε θεὴ Κύπρις, ἥ περ ἁπάντων
ἀθανάτων δάμνῃσι νόον θνητῶν τ' ἀνθρώπων.   (13.385–402)

---

[33] Cf. e.g. *Il*. 10.247, *Il*. 17.239.

[34] This prolepsis towards the chaos of the *nostoi* reaches its peak intensity in the final book of the poem (cf. e.g. 14.628–31). Further discussion below, p. 73.

At last, in the innermost part of the palace, Menelaus discovered his wife trembling in fear of the danger from her bold-hearted wedded husband. When he saw her, in his jealous state of mind he desired to kill her, and he would have done if the lovely Aphrodite had not restrained his anger, who made his sword fall from his hand and stopped his onrush. She dispelled his black jealousy and deep inside his heart and eyes she stirred up sweet desire. Unexpected amazement came over him, and seeing her brilliant beauty he could no longer put his sword to her throat. He stood there like a trunk of dead wood in a mountain forest, which neither the swift blasts of the north wind or south wind can shake when they hurtle through the air. Just so, astonished, did he stay a long time, his strength broken as he looked upon his wife. Suddenly gone from his mind were all the wrongs that she had done against their marriage bed, every one of them had been wiped away by the Cyprian goddess, who conquers the reason of gods as well as mortal men.

Once again, this sequence of events jars with traditional versions of the same story. In Aristophanes' *Lysistrata*, we hear how Helen bore her breasts in order to defend herself from Menelaus' anger:

ὁ γῶν Μενέλαος τᾶς Ἑλένας τὰ μᾶλά πα
γυμνᾶς παραυιδὼν ἐξέβαλ', οἰῶ, τὸ ξίφος. (Ar. *Lys.* 155–6)

When Menelaus saw the apples of the naked Helen, he dropped, I believe, his sword.

A scholium on this passage reveals that the same version occurred both in the *Little Iliad* and in Ibycus.[35] The encounter is also mentioned in Euripides' *Andromache*, where Peleus rebukes Menelaus for being seduced after seeing Helen's breast (627–31). It also appears several times in visual art in the sixth and fifth centuries BCE, where Helen is often depicted as removing her veil, the revelation of her face functioning as an alternative act of seduction.[36] In a scene from Stesichorus' *Sack of Troy*, Helen appears instead in front of the whole Greek army, and it is the force of this appearance which prevents them from stoning her:

ἆρα εἰς τὸ τῆς Ἑλένης κάλλος βλέψαντες οὐκ ἐχρήσαντο τοῖς ξίφεσιν; οἷόν τι καὶ Στησίχορος ὑπογράφει περὶ τῶν καταλεύειν αὐτὴν μελλόντων. φησὶ γὰρ ἅμα τῶι τὴν ὄψιν αὐτῆς ἰδεῖν αὐτοὺς ἀφεῖναι τοὺς λίθους ἐπὶ τὴν γῆν. (Σ Eur. *Or.* 1287 = fr. 106 F)

---

[35] Σ Ar. *Lys.* 155a = p. 12 Hangard; *Il. Parv.* fr. 28 *GEF*; Ibyc. fr. 296 *PMGF.*
[36] See Davies and Finglass (2014: 437), with examples.

Was it because they saw Helen's beauty that they did not use their swords? Stesichorus too describes something like this concerning the people who were intending to stone her. For he says that as soon as they saw her appearance, they let the stones fall to the ground.

In all of these accounts, whether full-scale disrobing or the coyer gestures found in the artwork, the message is to some extent the same: Helen has agency, and becomes, to varying degrees, the dominant force in her own survival scene, manipulating the male gaze of which she might otherwise be thought to be the victim. There is, however, no mention of the event in the *Odyssey*, in its description of Helen and Menelaus reunited in Sparta and the couple's retrospective account of her behaviour during the sack (*Od.* 4.1–289). Such an absence is, according to Griffin, unsurprising, since 'such a lurid episode is un-Homeric in atmosphere'.[37]

It is in this context that we must consider how Quintus shapes his version of the tale. The *Posthomerica* holds the conventional line regarding Helen's beauty, but it removes any direct agency from Helen, and bestows all power on to Aphrodite. Despite the goddess' potentially allegorical connotations – in other words, she could function in this scene as an outward manifestation of Menelaus' desire – there are no reinforcing details of the strength of this desire as Menelaus experiences it. Instead, with the generalising *gnōmē* (401–2) Quintus asserts the universal inescapability of the goddess' power: Menelaus' personal feelings are diffused into the wider collective of all mortals and immortals. Even once enraptured, Menelaus gazes not specifically at Helen's breasts, but at her κάλλος (394): like Achilles' remorse for Penthesilea's ἐρατὸν σθένος (1.719), an abstract concept takes the place of more explicit anatomical attraction.

In presenting this version, where Helen keeps her clothes on, Quintus could once again simply be read as being 'even more Homer than Homer': paying homage to his model, who had no place for such a lurid scene. What happens next, however, suggests a more complex relationship between *erōs* and Homeric poetics in this sequence:

ἀλλὰ καὶ ὣς θοὸν ἄορ ἀπὸ χθονὸς αὖτις ἀείρας
κουριδίῃ ἐπόρουσε· νόος δέ οἱ ἄλλ᾽ ἐνὶ θυμῷ
ὡρμᾶτ᾽ ἐσσυμένοιο· δόλῳ δ᾽ ἄρα ἄρ᾽ ἔθελγεν Ἀχαιούς.   405
καὶ τότε μιν κατέρυξεν ἀδελφεὸς ἱέμενόν περ
μειλιχίοις μάλα πολλὰ παραυδήσας ἐπέεσσι·
δείδιε γὰρ μὴ δή σφιν ἐτώσια πάντα γένηται·
'ἴσχεο νῦν, Μενέλαε, χολούμενος· οὐ γὰρ ἔοικε
κουριδίην παράκοιτιν ἐναιρέμεν, ἧς πέρι πολλὰ   410

---

[37] Griffin (2011: 336).

ἄλγε᾽ ἀνέτλημεν Πριάμῳ κακὰ μητιόωντες·
οὐ γάρ τοι Ἑλένη πέλει αἰτίη, ὡς σύ γ᾽ ἔολπας,
ἀλλὰ Πάρις ξενίοιο Διὸς καὶ σεῖο τραπέζης
λησάμενος· τῷ καί μιν ἐν ἄλγεσι τίσατο δαίμων.'
ὣς φάθ᾽· ὃ δ᾽ αἶψ᾽ ἐπίθησε. . . .   (13. 403–15)

Even so he picked up his sharp sword from the ground and made a
rush at his wife, but acted now with a different intention in his mind: it
was a trick to beguile the Achaeans. This time his brother Agamemnon
checked his zeal, who used many soothing words to change his mind,
for fear that all their efforts should have been for nothing: 'Come now,
Menelaus, control your anger. It is not fitting that you put to death your
wedded wife, for whose sake we have suffered so much, contriving
the ruin of Priam. Helen is not the one to blame, as you suppose, but
Paris for ignoring your table and Zeus the protector of host and guest.
So heaven has punished him painfully.' Thus he spoke, and Menelaus
quickly obeyed him.

Menelaus' rage towards Helen has by now been completely calmed by Aphrodite. However, he pretends otherwise, drawing his sword and running at
his wife again 'in order to beguile the Achaeans'. This is a strange turn of
events. What exactly is Menelaus trying to do here, and why? The insertion
of this moment, without narrative requirement or build up, suggests that its
importance may lie in its literary currency – its familiarity and recognisability.
The scenario of a son of Aretus deceiving the Greeks at a pivotal point in the
war may echo, subtly and implicitly, Agamemnon's famous test of the army
in *Iliad* 2.[38] There are hints to support this connection. The very presence of
Agamemnon, as the obstructer of Menelaus' plan, could remind us of his role
as the instigator of that original test. And the note that Agamemnon checked
Menelaus 'with words' (ἐπέεσσι, 407) echoes the king's Iliadic plan to test the
Greeks, and for the elders to restrain them, in the same way (πρῶτα δ᾽ ἐγὼν
ἔπεσιν πειρήσομαι, . . . / ὑμεῖς δ᾽ ἄλλοθεν ἄλλος ἐρητύειν ἐπέεσσιν, *Il.* 2.72–5).
This detail may seem inconsequential in isolation (it is, to be sure, a common

---

[38] This connection is more conceptual than strictly linguistic. The verb θέλγω is not found in
the Iliadic scene: it may thus be countered that, should Quintus have wished to evoke this
moment, he would surely gesture towards it more directly. However, as has been much discussed – e.g. in Maciver (2012c); Greensmith (2018) – Quintus' allusive strategies towards
Homer and his other models span the full spectrum, from direct quotation to, in Hinds' terms,
'more embedded ways of charting [his] inheritance' (Hinds 1998: chapter 1). It is thus my suggestion that the hints discussed above work to establish nodes of interaction with the Iliadic
scene, enabling but not compelling an interpretation based on its engagement.

enough dative plural, particularly in Homeric speech introduction formulae), but in aggregate, such connections are suggestive.[39]

If the lines do echo the trick from the *Iliad*, then we are faced once again with a moment in the *Posthomerica* which, in terms of the trajectory of the Trojan story, both propels us forwards and pulls us back. At this point in the narrative, the abduction of Helen is over; she and Menelaus are moving closer towards reunion. The way is paved for the 'future' of *Odyssey* 4, and the Helens who awaits us in tragedy. And yet this progression is stalled by the reperformance of rage, the reiteration of an episode from the Iliadic past, and one which emphasises how 'hoped for' endings are *not* always fulfilled. The deceitful dream which prompted Agamemnon's test made him a 'fool' (νήπιος, *Il.* 2.38) for believing that he would take the city of Priam on that day, 'when really Zeus was to bring many more woes before that' (*Il.* 2.35–40). In the present tense of Quintus' story, Troy *has* been sacked, and that deferred Iliadic end point has been reached. However, although the sack marks the end of Troy, it does not mark the end of the poem: there is another book to come – a continuation of this continuation. The unerotic nature of Helen's seductiveness and the precarious, insecure nature of her husband's desire thus helps to convey the elliptical shape of the epic at this point of the story, as we, like Menelaus, must wait for our ending still.

FINAL CONSUMMATIONS

Menelaus becomes a figure through which the reader can experience the *Posthomerica*'s deferment of its own conclusion. Despite the fiery finality of the sack and the removal of Helen's alternative bed partner, his sexual resolution is then further delayed, and comes only in the final book of the epic (Q.S. 14.149–79). His eventual sexual reunion with Helen takes the form of a bedroom scene, in which the couple converses, makes amends and finally makes love. The whole sequence is clearly reminiscent of the reunion of Odysseus and Penelope after the slaughter of the suitors (*Od.* 23.295–309):[40] the episode which comes immediately after the line regarded by Aristophanes and Aristarchus as the real end of Homer's poem.[41]

In this final reunion scene, Quintus again dilutes any active expressions of lust. It is, once more, Aphrodite (the goddess and/or the concept) who is responsible for Menelaus and Helen coming together: she is not only present,

---

[39] It also perhaps has resonances of Odysseus' charge at Circe in *Od.* 10.322, where he rushes '*as though* desiring to kill her' (ὥς τε κτάμεναι μενεαίνων).

[40] The initial order of conversation and copulation is reversed in the Quintan scene.

[41] Σ. *Od.* 23.296.

but 'hovering over their hearts' (πεπότητο περὶ φρένας, 152). The lovemaking itself is refracted into the world of simile:

ὡς δ᾽ ὅτε που κισσός τε καὶ ἡμερὶς ἀμφιβάλωνται
ἀλλήλους περὶ πρέμνα, τὰ δ᾽ οὔποτε ἲς ἀνέμοιο
σφῶν ἄπο νόσφι βαλέσθαι ἐπισθένει· ὣς ἄρα τώ γε
ἀλλήλοις συνέχοντο λιλαιόμενοι φιλότητος.   (14.175–9)

Just as ivy and a grapevine intertwine their stems so closely together that no wind is ever strong enough to separate them, thus those two clung closely in the passionate embrace of love.

The unusual choice of comparison, the ivy and the vine, may also echo a very similar image in Euripides' *Hecuba*, where Hecuba laments how she will cling to Polyxena even in her death:

ὁποῖα κισσὸς δρυός, ὅπως τῆσδ᾽ ἕξομαι.   (Eur. *Hec.* 398)

I will cling to her like ivy to an oak.

Quintus thus refers to a highly unerotic context – a distraught mother despairing for her child – and foreshadows the horrific sacrifice to which own his narrative will shortly turn (14.257–370), to embellish perversely this scene of sexual consummation.

The *erōs* is further and most firmly extinguished in this encounter by another narrative vehicle: that of memory. Aphrodite first makes the couple 'remember their former bed' (παλαιοῦ/λέκτρου ἐπιμνήσωνται, 152–3), with παλαιός providing a signpost for the act of looking backwards in literary and mythic time. Helen then begs Menelaus to 'forget' her former transgressions (163), and he agrees that it is wrong to keep 'recalling' evil deeds (165). As the scene ends, the memories become more positive, as the couple's 'hearts recalled how they were joined in marriage' (174). The act of recollection is repeated like a mantra: they remembered, they stopped remembering, they remember.

In studies of poetic allusion, memory has emerged as a key device for articulating *literary* recapitulations: characters' recollections of events from their past can reveal the textual 'memories' of the previous works which inform them.[42] Quintus here takes up this trope, but harnesses it as an anti-erotic,

---

[42] Studies of memory and allusion are copious and wide-ranging. Most relevant for my purposes are the readings of allusive memory in the Latin tradition, best epitomised by Conte's famous account of Ovid's Ariadne in the *Fasti* (1986). Later and related important analyses in Miller (1993); Barchiesi (1993); Hinds (1998). Further extended discussion in Greensmith (2020: chapter 5).

stalling move. Rather than revelling in the present act, narrator and characters alike in this scene are focused on re-enacting versions of their former selves. The whole action of the passage, the reunion necessary to continue to the next stage of the story, is driven by the memory of what came before: this is a progression – both sexual and narrative – *based on* repetition.

Now, the *Odyssey* 23 scene, which this reunion in its broadest shape 'recalls', is itself elliptical and implicit. There is no overt description of Odysseus and Penelope's lovemaking. Homer leaves them to it, and resumes his narration once 'the two had had their fill of the joy of love'. However, implicitness in this particular Homeric encounter can also serve a deeper interpretative purpose. It takes place after Odysseus has recalled to Penelope his own retrojecting narrative; selectively remembering his past, he famously omits the more exotic details of his sexual adventures as revealed in the *Apologoi*.[43] Earlier in the same speech, Odysseus also makes clear that this story is incomplete: the present-tense lovemaking with his wife is not the true consummation of his *nostos*. He will, in the future, go a-roving again:

> ὦ γύναι, οὐ γάρ πω πάντων ἐπὶ πείρατ᾽ ἀέθλων
> ἤλθομεν, ἀλλ᾽ ἔτ᾽ ὄπισθεν ἀμέτρητος πόνος ἔσται,
> πολλὸς καὶ χαλεπός, τὸν ἐμὲ χρὴ πάντα τελέσσαι.
> ὣς γάρ μοι ψυχὴ μαντεύσατο Τειρεσίαο
> ἤματι τῷ ὅτε δὴ κατέβην δόμον Ἄϊδος εἴσω,
> νόστον ἑταίροισιν διζήμενος ἠδ᾽ ἐμοὶ αὐτῷ.   (*Od.* 23.248–53)

> Wife, we have not yet come to the end of all our trials, but still hereafter there is to be measureless toil, long and hard, which I must fulfil to the end; for so did the spirit of Teiresias foretell to me on the day when I went down into the house of Hades to enquire concerning the return of my comrades and myself.

The Odyssean pillow talk provides a focal point for that epic's own problematic teleology:[44] it both contains its supposed 'ending' and expounds its profound lack of ending. In their desire to stop the *Odyssey* in Book 23, the scholia would place the marriage bed at the centre of the house as the end point of the poem. They therefore try to enforce a teleology that the *Odyssey*

---

[43] *Od.* 23.310–44. Odysseus does not mention Nausicaa at all, speaks only of Circe's 'wiles', and boasts of his endurance of Calypso's propositions and refusal of her promises, omitting the longevity of his stay with the nymph, during which he complied, begrudgingly or otherwise, to her lusts (cf. e.g. *Od.* 5.152–3, κατείβετο δὲ γλυκὺς αἰὼν / νόστον ὀδυρομένῳ, ἐπεὶ οὐκέτι ἥνδανε νύμφη).

[44] On Odyssean forms of closure (and the lack of it), see e.g. Quint (1993); Lowe (2000); Purves (2010).

simply does not have: because for Odysseus, of course, sex is always transitional not climatic, and his homecoming lovemaking with his wife will ultimately prove to be no exception. In his own euphemistic scene, Quintus plays on these anti-closural dynamics to bring his own sense of temporal unsettledness to bear on Menelaus' narrative – and, by extension, the narrative of his whole poem. As with Odysseus and Penelope in the *Odyssey*, sexual reunion is not the end of the story for Menelaus and Helen: they still need to return to Sparta and live their experiences in *Odyssey* 4. Nor is it the end of Quintus' poem: the narrative marches on, with almost five hundred more verses and another twist – the storm, the shipwrecks – to come. Quintus thus thwarts the neat marriage-bed conclusion on which Aristarchus' *Odyssey* – and, we may note, the Greek novel, a contemporary genre with the *Posthomerica* – relies. In place of sexual climax, Quintus instead ends his poem with an image of transition and suspension. Storms in epic are most often used to turn the narrative, or mark a point of changed direction: Odysseus, Aeneas, Jason, even Paris are all blown on to new heroic courses by them.[45] In the closing storm of the *Posthomerica*, however, we do not get to this new course: the storm just rages on, and we continue to wait for the *nostoi*, and indeed for the *Odyssey*, to emerge into the narrative present. In Menelaus' muted climax, we feel the force of this ellipsis.

CONCLUSIONS: EPIC WITHOUT END

By forging connections between sexual and narrative endings, Quintus is able to use the deferral of one to suggest the deferral of the other. His frustrated poetics aims to reveal, rather than to resolve, the problems of Homeric closure, and to expose the difficulties derived from working within closed canons with open endings.

To conclude my own exploration of this 'a-sexual' epic, I wish to focus briefly on the 'open endings' which remain here. What, for instance, is the role of scenes in the *Posthomerica* which, in contrast to those analysed here, do contain physical contact and the language of intimacy: those features which are so glaringly absent from the more conventional erotic moments? Particularly interesting in this respect is the figure of Neoptolemus, who is kissed a number of times throughout the epic,[46] and during a dream is kissed on the eyes and the neck by the ghost of his father Achilles (14.183). Why is tactility transferred from sexual encounters on to familial ones? What is the significance of intimacy in a dream, moments which in epic are usually bereft of physical

---

[45] For Paris as a storm-tossed voyager, cf. Colluthus 206–10.
[46] See Boyten (2010: 187–8).

contact? And how, to take another strand of enquiry, can we reconcile this poetics of frustration with other cultural-historical currents perceptible in the text: its so-called 'Stoic' ethos of restraint and *apatheia*,[47] or the 'aesthetic of excess' often said to characterise the gory battle scenes?[48]

In these and other respects, the chapter has sought to raise as many questions as it has answered. Therefore, without closing the topic, I end with a final word on the fundamental link with which I began, between erotic epic and critical response. Erotic themes have indeed contributed to new scholarly re-appreciation of other imperial Greek epics; but to sexualise the *Posthomerica* to try to make it fit this paradigm is to wilfully misread it. If we keep trying to turn Quintus into Nonnus, he will continue to seem impotent, because he will be deemed to fail at a poetic game that he does not try to play. It has been well and often said that in a corpus as diverse as that of imperial Greek epic, respecting differences remains a crucial task.[49] Quintus' *anti*-erotic poetics demonstrates how the epic must be approached on its own terms regarding its sexual dynamics too. If so, then the thrill of this imperial poem comes not from its *erōs*, but rather from the unsettling reading process that it requires, as the epic that abstains from sex forces its readers to confront their own frustrated longings and presumptuous desires – above all, that ever-present, but ever-evasive lust for critical closure.

---

[47] Maciver (2012a) is essential reading on this large and important topic.
[48] Cf. e.g. Ozbek (2007).
[49] Hunter and Carvounis (2008) are very cogent on this point.

CHAPTER 5

Images of Life and Death: Visualising the Heroic Body in Quintus Smyrnaeus' *Posthomerica*

A. Sophie Schoess

In his *Posthomerica*, Quintus famously presents his reader with a number of heroes and heroines whose stories continue on from the *Iliad*, as well as others who are newly introduced into the Trojan War narrative at this stage.[1] The new heroes and heroines are treated in great narrative detail and their genealogies and histories are incorporated into the storyline of the *Posthomerica*. Quintus draws the reader's attention to the novelty of his heroes' physical appearances by emphasising other characters' responses to them: Trojans and Greeks alike are described as they marvel at each figure foregrounded in the final stages of the war. The heroic bodies are literally put on display, both through physical descriptions and through the use of similes highlighting their fierceness and beauty. Quintus' focus on the visibility and visuality of his heroic characters allows him to draw on and connect literary and visual traditions surrounding the Trojan War and, in so doing, craft a highly visual epic.

This chapter examines Quintus' visualisations of heroic bodies in life and in death, and discusses their literary and visual influences. It focuses on three key heroic figures who fight and die in the *Posthomerica* and whose narratives are closely intertwined: Penthesileia, Memnon and Achilles.[2] The lives of these

---

[1] On the *Posthomerica*'s relationship with the *Aethiopis* and the Epic Cycle more generally, see Gärtner (2005: 28–9) with bibliography; Bär (2009: 78–84); Scafoglio's chapter in this volume. Cf. Scheijnen (2018: 89–90, esp. n1123).
The edition of the Greek text used throughout this chapter is Vian (1963); the translation is adapted from Hopkinson (2018).

[2] See Scheijnen (2016a: *passim* and 2018: 45–95). Other characters entering the war at this stage, such as Eurypylus on the Trojan or Neoptolemus on the Greek side, are also afforded detailed narratives, but their visual presentation is not nearly as extensive as that of Penthesileia, Memnon and Achilles. The Trojans, especially Helen, marvel at Eurypylus upon his arrival (Q.S. 6.125–32, 156–8; cf. 6.295–6), but the Greeks do not. Similarly, Odysseus and Diomedes initially marvel at Neoptolemus, but they do so because of his similarities with Achilles (Q.S. 7.176–7; cf. 7.461–3, 604–5).

three figures are linked not only through their roles in the Trojan War and their interactions with one another, but also through their divine parentage and patronage. Quintus draws attention not only to Achilles' role as the slayer of both Penthesileia and Memnon, but also to the roles played by Penthesileia and Memnon in the concluding narrative moments of the Cyclical, and especially the Homeric, *Achilleid*.[3] The crescendo of deadly encounters between divine offspring in the first two books of the *Posthomerica* (Q.S. 1.538–656 and 2.395–548) finds its epic climax in Apollo's intervention in Achilles' final battle (Q.S. 3.26–89).[4]

The connections between Penthesileia, Memnon and Achilles extend beyond the narrative and literary: Penthesileia and Achilles are connected, yet differentiated, through the Trojans' and Greeks' treatment of their bodies in life and death, while Memnon and Achilles are linked in life through divine interest in their physical strength and in death through divine displays of mourning. To appreciate the visual treatment of these three heroes, this chapter argues, Quintus' readers must draw not only on their familiarity with epic traditions,[5] but also on their knowledge of narrative visual art and its depiction of scenes from the Trojan War.[6] Yet Quintus blurs the distinction between literary and visual as he links evocations of visual artistic traditions with Homeric uses of visual language and *ekphrasis* to create a vivid narrative.[7] In this, Quintus follows in the footsteps of earlier imperial writers and in particular of representatives of the Second Sophistic movement,[8] who frequently foreground and explore the visuality of the Homeric poems.[9]

The visuality of Quintus' heroic narrative in the first three books marks out the bodies of Penthesileia, Memnon and Achilles as objects of the internal and, by extension, the external audience's gaze. While they are treated differently based on gender, allegiance and relative importance, all three elicit awed responses to their physical forms from friend and foe alike, responses that are described through distinctly visual language. This chapter examines Quintus' visual treatment of these three heroic characters and discusses how their bodies are presented as dynamic and fearsome in life, and yet awesome, still, in death. It addresses the varying degrees of divine investment in their lives, battles and deaths, and draws attention to their mortal and immortal audiences. In

---

[3] See, e.g., Scheijnen (2018: 93–5).
[4] E.g., Scheijnen (2016a; 2018: 45–93).
[5] On Quintus' engagement with Homer, see, e.g., Maciver (2012a: 7–13).
[6] See *LIMC* s.v. 'Achilles', 'Memnon' and 'Penthesileia.' Cf. Snodgrass (1998).
[7] Cf. Baumbach (2007); Maciver (2012a: 39–86).
[8] E.g., Bär (2010); cf. Schubert (2007); Maciver (2012a: 17–18).
[9] See, e.g., Squire (2011) and Squire and Elsner (2016). The authors of the surviving *Progymnasmata* consistently draw attention to Homer's poetic visuality, especially in relation to *ekphrasis* (see, e.g., duBois 1982: 9–27; Webb 2009: 42–59), a literary and rhetorical device that develops into an independent literary form in this period (Elsner 2002; cf. Maciver 2018: 83, n60).

so doing, this chapter highlights the narrative importance of visual language and description, and argues that Quintus uses the interplay between visual and literary to reflect on his heroes' visual and epic afterlives.

PENTHESILEIA

Quintus' Penthesileia enters the narrative at a moment of great fear and frustration for the Trojans. Following the death of Hector, so Quintus tells us in the opening of the *Posthomerica*, the Trojans are unable to shake the violent memory of Achilles' treatment of the Trojan prince and of his slaughter of many unnamed Trojans and their allies (Q.S. 1.1–17).[10] By emphasising the vividness of the Trojans' memories and their effect,[11] Quintus both invites the reader to revisit the epic events of the *Iliad*, and uses his own Homeric similes to set up the emotional and visual landscape into which Penthesileia is introduced.[12] The Amazon is immediately presented as a beacon of hope (Q.S. 1.62–83) and her divine beauty, θεῶν ἐπιειμένη εἶδος (Q.S. 1.19), is foregrounded, as is the Trojans' response to it.

Quintus' Penthesileia is introduced to two audiences simultaneously: to the reader she is presented as a strong and beautiful figure, eager for battle as a means of leaving behind the memory of accidentally killing her sister, Hippolyta, and the Erinyes, who haunt her because of it (Q.S. 1.20–32);[13] to the Trojans, unaware of her inner turmoil, she represents a vision of brightness and hope. The reader immediately recognises Penthesileia as a conflicted character, one whose past inevitably influences, even dictates, her present actions; the Trojans, on the other hand, see only her imposing beauty, bellicose character and physical strength, and are entirely taken with this external, visual narrative about the Amazon. Quintus invites his reader to create an image of Penthesileia informed by the Trojans' view of her, while also supplying narrative detail that animates the beautiful figure.

Penthesileia is compared to her companions through similes that make her seem a physical manifestation of beauty, light and hope:[14] she shines like Selene (Q.S. 1.37–40) and Eos (Q.S. 1.48–51) in the evening and morning

---

[10] Cf. Schmitz (2007b: 74–5).

[11] The narrative is framed by signposting verbs of remembering: μνησάμενοι (1.9) and ἔμιμνον (1.15). See Maciver (2012a: 130–2); Goldhill's chapter in this volume.

[12] See Bär (2009: 138–44); cf. Myers (2019: 33–40) on the anticipation of visuality and *enargeia* in the *Iliad*'s proem.

[13] It is worth noting that Quintus adds ἄφραστοι (1.31) to characterise the Furies. While ἄφραστος can mean 'unutterable' or 'marvellous', it is more likely used here to mean 'unseen', 'not perceived' (cf. Bär 2009: 194), highlighting again that the reader knows what Quintus' characters do not.

[14] See Bär (2009: 195–208); Maciver (2012a: 132–9). Cf. James (1978: 175–83).

skies. The effect of this radiance is explored through Trojan responses to the Amazon's arrival (Q.S. 1.53–83), as the Trojans are seen to throng around her and drink in her divine beauty (Q.S. 1.53–62). The scene is filled with visual language (ἐσίδοντο, 1.54; εἰδομένην, 1.56; εἶδος, 1.57; μάρμαιρον, 1.59) and the Trojans' reaction, ἐθάμβεον (Q.S. 1.54), in particular is linked with the language of *ekphrasis* and of viewing works of art.[15] Penthesileia's demure beauty, χάρις (Q.S. 1.61), is matched by her strength, ἀλκή (Q.S. 1.61), her threatening appearance, σμερδαλέον εἶδος (Q.S. 1.57), by her radiance, ἀγλαόν (Q.S. 1.57). The warrior queen is recognised as both frightening foe and demure maiden, characterised by her fine and beautiful face as much as by her physical strength (Q.S. 1.56–61),[16] and Quintus presents her as moving the Trojans to their first expression of happiness, ἀμφεγάνυντο (Q.S. 1.62), since the death of Hector. While the reader is witness to the internal conflict of the heroine and can therefore recognise the (self-)destructive potential of Penthesileia's eagerness for war, the Trojans, aware only of her outward appearance, are filled with a confidence that allows them to consign their fears and sadness to the past (Q.S. 1.62). Penthesileia is thus presented as a beautiful image on to which the internal audience projects its hopes.

Priam's response to Penthesileia's arrival is more nuanced than that of the other Trojans (Q.S. 1.74–85). Likened to a blind man who has regained his sight, Priam rejoices in Penthesileia's presence (Q.S. 1.84), but does not immediately forget his sorrows (Q.S. 1.84–5).[17] His prayer for her victory and the safety of the Trojans expresses both his hope and his grief (Q.S. 1.186–97), and it is answered with an omen that allows Priam to see what the other Trojans cannot, that Penthesileia is doomed to fail (Q.S. 1.198–204). Despite the subtlety and measuredness of Priam's response to Penthesileia, however, in its visual focus it still resembles that of the other Trojans. Quintus foregrounds the blind man's regained ability to see light as well as dark, drawing a direct link between Penthesileia and the divine light of day, ἱερὸν φάος (Q.S. 1.77) and φάος ἠριγενείης (Q.S. 1.79), as Priam looks at her for the first time, ἐσέδρακε (Q.S. 1.83). Again, the emphatic brightness of the Amazon's appearance highlights at once her feminine beauty and her physical strength, adding visual detail to the image in the reader's mind. Similarly, the omen observed by Priam depicting Penthesileia as a helpless dove in the talons of an eagle (Q.S. 1.198–200), and his response to it, draw attention to Penthesileia's

---

[15] On the association of *thauma* and *thambos* with the act of viewing works of art, see, e.g., Maciver (2012a: 54); Agosti (2014: 154); cf. Newby (2009: 326–7); Goldhill (2012).

[16] Cf. Vian (1954: 32–3).

[17] This theme of joy and grief mingled in Priam's heart frames the blindness simile: it is introduced in similar terms with στενάχοντος / καὶ μέγ' ἀκηχεμένοιο on the one hand, and ἰάνθη on the other (Q.S. 1.74–5). Compare Phoenix's response to Neoptolemus (Q.S. 7.630–9). Cf. Maciver (2012a: 139).

physical and visual presence: Priam recognises the beauty and vulnerability of her feminine strength, and understands that he will not see her return (Q.S. 1.201–2). By introducing Penthesileia from the Trojans' perspective, Quintus invites his reader to focus on her appearance rather than her narrative, and to imagine her radiant figure.[18]

This focus on Penthesileia's appearance and the response it elicits from various male audiences is partly mirrored in the Trojan women's reaction.[19] Though they view her from a distance, ἀπάνευθεν (Q.S. 1.403, 1.476), the women are similarly described as marvelling, θαύμαζον (Q.S. 1.404), and finally simply as watching, ἐσέδρακον (Q.S. 1.476). Their reaction to seeing Penthesileia outperform her male foes (Q.S. 1.420–1) is at once visual and literary: they are excited by Penthesileia's prowess, the image of the fearless and feared woman (Q.S. 1.404–24), and are simultaneously threatened by the epic and tragic realities awaiting women in war, the risk of capture and enslavement (Q.S. 1.425–35).[20] Their eagerness to enter war alongside their husbands and the Amazons is famously compared to that of bees in a hive (Q.S. 1.440–3),[21] while their act of abandoning their weaving indicates to the reader a disruption of the traditional, the epic, social order (Q.S. 1.444–6). Unlike Andromache, who, in the *Iliad*, follows Hector's instructions to return to her weaving and leave battle to men (*Il.* 6.490–3),[22] the Trojan women are here prepared to upset the order in an attempt to preserve it. It is Theano's call to reason that keeps the women from being killed in battle (Q.S. 1.447–50) and returns them to their traditional roles, spectators at a distance (Q.S. 1.475–6).

As in the case of Penthesileia's male audience, one figure stands out among the women in her response to the Amazon: Andromache feels no delight at her arrival and recognises the hopelessness of Penthesileia's situation from the start. Mingling grief over her lost husband and resentment over his being replaced as Troy's hero, Andromache anticipates Penthesileia's death even before Priam's omen (Q.S. 1.103–4). Andromache's direct comparison between Hector and Penthesileia[23] is revisited by other characters and the narrator to emphasise the similarity of the two warriors' roles, the hope and protector of Troy, and their shared fate as victims of Achilles (Q.S. 1.575–91, 2.10–25). Hector looms over Penthesileia as an epic male shadow, preserved through the memory of the Trojans and the song of Homer.

---

[18] See Webb (2009: 87–130) on the role played by the reader's imagination in *ekphrasis*.
[19] For a detailed discussion of the Trojan women's role in defining Penthesileia, see Schmiel (1986).
[20] Compare *Il.* 6.440–65, 22.59–65 and 24.725–45.
[21] See Maciver (2012c); cf. Lovatt (2013: 247–9).
[22] Compare also *Il.* 3.125–8 and 22.440–1; on weaving in Homer, see, e.g., Pantelia (1993).
[23] See Scheijnen (2016a: 85).

Much like the Trojans, the Greeks immediately respond to Penthesileia's physical presence with awe (Q.S. 1.205–10). Their reaction, however, is directly preceded by Priam's omen, which reframed the fierce warrior queen, for the external audience at least, as an innocent and vulnerable dove (Q.S. 1.198–204). Again, the reader is offered a picture that emphasises at once Penthesileia's strength and her weakness, while the internal audience responds only to her immediate and powerfully visual presentation (Q.S. 1.205–10). Where the reader's image of Penthesileia was initially characterised by her brightness, it now shifts to her fierceness, reminding the reader of depictions of Amazonomachies and of Penthesileia's encounter with Achilles in the visual arts.[24] The Greek response to the charge is divided between marvelling, ἐθάμβεον (Q.S. 1.205), at the mass of the Trojan army on the one hand and at the single figure of the Amazon on the other. While the Trojans are compared to a pack of wild animals (Q.S. 1.207), Penthesileia is likened to a force of nature (Q.S. 1.209). Penthesileia stands out, not only physically, but also in the kind of force she represents in this simile. It is this force on which the Greeks explicitly comment: καί νύ τις ἐν μέσσοισιν ἐποτρύνει πονέεσθαι· / φαίης κεν θεὸν ἔμμεν, ἐπεὶ μέγα μήδεται ἔργον (Q.S. 1.215–16).[25] Penthesileia is not identified in this speech, but rather has become an ominous and anonymous figure, τις, who drives on the Trojans like a god.[26] It is the tangible effect her presence has on both the Trojans – their readiness for battle (Q.S. 1.163–5) and renewed strength and unity on the battlefield (Q.S. 1.212–16) – and the Greeks – their initial desire for battle (Q.S. 1.220–5) and their subsequent flight (Q.S. 1.476–93) – that marks her as a divine force.

Quintus' description of Penthesileia's fighting, her success in driving back the Greeks and in killing her foes follows along typical epic lines, listing slain enemies (Q.S. 1.227–9)[27] and using similes to illustrate her ferocious strength (e.g., Q.S. 1.314–24).[28] The comparatively short description of the battle between Trojans, Amazons and Greeks does not stand out literarily, as Homeric tropes are employed throughout and the visuality of war is brought forward through descriptions of fallen warriors (e.g., Q.S. 1.345–9, 1.383–93) and corpses crowding the battlefield (e.g., Q.S. 1.350–3, 533–7). Quintus uses this visual language and description to enable his reader to visualise and animate the battle scene.

At the same time, Quintus' reader's point of reference for this Amazonomachy will not have been Homeric visuality – no such scene appears in

---

[24] See *LIMC* s.v. 'Amazons' and 'Penthesileia'; cf., e.g., von Bothmer (1957); Ridgway (1974); duBois (1991: 49–77).

[25] 'There is someone in their midst urging them to the task – you would think it was a god, so great is the exploit he has in mind.'

[26] Compare Q.S. 1.358–72. Cf. Scheijnen (2018: 62–70).

[27] Compare Q.S. 1.336–52 and 1.476–93. Cf. Kauffman (2018: 641–2).

[28] See Scheijnen (2018: 54–9, esp. n23) on the epic limitations of Penthesileia's *aristeia*.

the *Iliad* or *Odyssey* – but representations of mythical battles between Greeks, Trojans and Amazons in the visual arts, from wall paintings and painted pottery to marble reliefs and statue groups.[29] The larger battle scene is generic in its visuality and does not per se foreground individual narratives, though individual figures are represented in distinct moments of the battle: just as visual representations of Amazonomachies often depict figures on both sides as winning and losing their individual clashes,[30] so Quintus' narrative includes moments of success for both sides (Q.S. 1.225–308). A reader familiar with the visual type of the Amazonomachy is able to imagine the scene based on existing visual representations, and to connect the generic with the specific and the literary with the visual.

Alongside the visual focus on Penthesileia from the very beginning of Quintus' narrative, the generic visuality of the battle scene between Amazons and Greeks prepares the reader for the central visual tableau of this literary treatment: Penthesileia's confrontation with Achilles. While a few representations of other moments of Penthesileia's time in Troy do survive,[31] the majority of identifiable visual treatments of the Amazon's myth focus on her encounter with Achilles on the battlefield: their *monomachia*,[32] her pleading for her life,[33] and finally her death.[34] It is this famous and highly visual moment of confrontation between Penthesileia and Achilles for which the reader has been prepared by Quintus' visual treatment of the Amazon from the moment of her arrival in Troy. While initially both Achilles and Ajax rush at Penthesileia to end the slaughter of the Greeks, Quintus' Ajax removes himself from the scene almost immediately, allowing the visual focus to narrow on to the battle of the children of Thetis and Ares. Drawing on both visual and literary traditions within a single scene, Quintus links the meeting between Achilles and Penthesileia with Priam's omen (Q.S. 1.198–200) through the assertion that Ajax knew ὡς Ἀχιλῆϊ καὶ ἰφθίμη περ ἐοῦσα / ῥηΐδιος πόνος ἔσσεθ' ὅπως ἴρηκι πέλεια (Q.S. 1.571–2).[35] Priam's vision is here realised through an epic simile which clearly attributes the

---

[29] See, e.g., Stewart (1995); Martini (2013). See Madigan (1992: 70–3) on the similarities between the Trojan Amazonomachy depicted on the Ionian frieze of the Temple of Apollo at Bassai and that related in the *Posthomerica*.

[30] See, e.g., the Amazonomachies on the Ionian frieze of the Temple of Apollo at Bassai (Madigan 1992: 70–8); *LIMC* s.v. 'Penthesileia' 36.

[31] Penthesileia's arrival at Troy, for instance, is depicted on a few Hellenistic and Roman objects, including the *Tabulae Iliacae* (*LIMC* s.v. 'Penthesileia' 3a–7; for discussion, see Squire 2011: 186–7, esp. n128 with bibliography).

[32] E.g., *LIMC* s.v. 'Penthesileia' 21, 23, 32, 44, 55.

[33] E.g., *LIMC* s.v. 'Penthesileia' 11, 27, 30, 34, 39, 56.

[34] E.g., *LIMC* s.v. 'Penthesileia' 20, 37, 38, 40, 52–4.

[35] 'That for all her strength she would be an easy task for Achilles, just as a dove is for a hawk'. See Scheijnen (2016a: 89).

roles of defenceless victim and of violent killer to Penthesileia and Achilles respectively. The vividness of the simile further heightens the visuality of the scene itself, a scene which Quintus' readers would have encountered more frequently in the visual arts than in the epic tradition.[36] Yet, Achilles' speech anchors the moment in the epic tradition as well, as he draws an explicit comparison between Penthesileia and Hector.[37] The Trojan prince, too, was compared to a trembling dove in his final confrontation with Achilles (*Il.* 22.139–44), but where Penthesileia seeks out the confrontation with Achilles, Hector initially ran from it – a detail that at once illustrates the Amazon's warlike determination and her inexperience in this particular war. Unlike Hector and the Trojans, Penthesileia has not seen Achilles in battle and is therefore unprepared and ill-equipped to fight him. Once wounded, Penthesileia's thoughts resemble those of Hector before his fight with Achilles (Q.S. 1.601–9 and *Il.* 22.98–130): she ponders possible means of escape, though her fate has long since been decided. The swiftness of her wounding and of her death (Q.S. 1.594–629) demonstrates that the moment of epic confrontation here is in the service of bringing about the highly visual death of Penthesileia and Achilles' subsequent regret.

As has been noted elsewhere, Achilles, much like Ajax, does not respond to Penthesileia's battle prowess; he only sees in her a woman too feeble to warrant his attention as a warrior.[38] In many ways, Achilles' attitude towards Penthesileia reduces her status from the very moment they first meet in battle. That his perspective on Penthesileia should culminate in his thinking of her as a potential, now lost, bride (Q.S. 1.669–74, 1.718–21) does not come as a surprise to the reader. Indeed, familiarity with the poignant scene of Achilles' falling in love with Penthesileia in the visual arts combined with Quintus' description of Achilles' response to his female enemy prepare the reader for a shift in the Amazon's overall presentation.[39]

It is the Greeks' final response to Penthesileia's body that confirms this visual and narrative shift in the *Posthomerica*. Where Achilles has, from the outset, treated Penthesileia as primarily a woman, the other warriors have not; they saw in her a valiant ally and a formidable foe. Yet once Penthesileia has, with her death, relinquished her role as active combatant, her body is feminised and becomes the object of the penetrating male gaze. On her deathbed, she is transformed from a fearsome warrior into a vulnerable young woman

---

[36] On Penthesileia's literary history, see Fratantuono (2016: 208–12, esp. 210–12) on the literary treatment of her depictions in the visual arts.

[37] Compare Q.S. 1.105–9 and 2.10–25.

[38] E.g., Scheijnen (2016a: 89–90); Scheijnen (2018: 62–70).

[39] Cf. Schmiel (1986).

whose body is beautified by Aphrodite herself so as to prepare her specifically for Achilles' gaze (Q.S. 1.659–68):

τῆς δὲ καὶ ἐν κονίῃσι καὶ αἵματι πεπτηυίης
ἐξεφάνη ἐρατῆισιν ὑπ' ὀφρύσι καλὰ πρόσωπα   660
καί περ ἀποκταμένης. Οἳ δ', ὡς ἴδον, ἀμφιέποντες
Ἀργεῖοι θάμβησαν, ἐπεὶ μακάρεσσιν ἐῴκει.
Κεῖτο γὰρ ἐν τεύχεσσι κατὰ χθονὸς ἠΰτ' ἀτειρὴς
Ἄρτεμις ὑπνώουσα Διὸς τέκος, εὖτε κάμῃσι
γυῖα κατ' οὔρεα μακρὰ θοοὺς βάλλουσα λέοντας·   665
αὐτὴ γάρ μιν ἔτευξε καὶ ἐν φθιμένοισιν ἀγητὴν
Κύπρις ἐυστέφανος κρατεροῦ παράκοιτις Ἄρηος,
ὄφρά τι καὶ Πηλῆος ἀμύμονος υἷ' ἀκαχήσῃ.

Then the beauty of the face beneath her lovely brows could be seen, fallen though she was in the blood and dust. The Argives around them gazed at her and marvelled, since she resembled the immortals. Lying there on the ground in her armour she resembled Artemis, the unyielding daughter of Zeus, when she sleeps following a long and exhausting hunt after swift mountain lions; for Cypris of the fair garland herself, bedfellow of mighty Ares, had made her beautiful even in death so that even noble Peleus' son should feel remorse.

In death, Penthesileia's body becomes an object to be gazed at, an object whose sole purpose is to affect its male audience.[40] The Argive men again marvel at her figure but, unlike before, it is her beauty and her divine appearance, not her strength, that elicit this response.[41] Where, in battle, Penthesileia was compared to Athena, Enyo, Eris and illustrious Artemis (Q.S. 1.363–6), here she is reframed as the beautiful, peaceful and unprotected Artemis, not the fierce huntress characterised by her weapons in both literature and the visual arts.[42] Though her armour still protects her body, Penthesileia is defenceless to the male gaze, as is epitomised in the removal of her helmet (Q.S. 1.657–8) and the response this elicits from the assembled warriors.[43]

Through the removal of her helmet and the intervention of Aphrodite, Penthesileia has undergone a visual transformation from the armed warrior

---

[40] Cf. Homer, *Odysssey* 18.187–99.

[41] Compare Q.S. 1.625–9, where Penthesileia is likened to an ἄγαλμα, a literal object to behold; see Maciver (2012a: 142–3) for discussion.

[42] Cf. Maciver (2012a: 143–8). See Schoess (forthcoming) on the objectifying effect of the stripping of attributes.

[43] Cf. Madigan (1992: 74) on the symbolism of the fallen helmet in the visual arts.

princess to a generic, beautiful maiden: her beauty, essential to her description from the beginning of the *Posthomerica*, has here become her defining feature. Though hints of a sexualised viewing of her body could be detected immediately,[44] Penthesileia's armour protected her from it and reminded viewer and reader of her status as Amazon queen and warrior maiden. Her disarming and the exposition of her beautiful face here stand in strong contrast to her earlier arming scene (Q.S. 1.138–56), where to her delicate silver-white legs, κνήμῃσιν ἐπ' ἀργυφέῃσιν (Q.S. 1.142), she attached golden greaves, κνημῖδας χρυσέας (Q.S. 1.143).[45] The splendour of her divinely-wrought arms made her appear fierce and fearsome, likened by Quintus to one of Zeus's lightning bolts (Q.S. 1.153), a symbol of divine power. With the removal of her helmet, however, Penthesileia no longer commands her audience, but is shaped by it. Indeed, where visual depictions of Penthesileia often show her looking back at Achilles as she is dying,[46] Quintus presents his reader with an entirely passive figure at the mercy of her viewer.[47]

Penthesileia's death thus marks her literary and visual removal from the battlefield and therefore from the world of epic. Only in her burial at Troy, away from the Greeks' objectifying gaze, does Penthesileia regain her status as warrior (Q.S. 1.782–810). Unlike Hector, however, she does not receive an extended scene of public lament marking her short-lived inclusion in the epic narrative of the Trojan War. Still, she is mourned as a daughter of Troy and elevated through her burial beside the city's founder (Q.S. 1.800–3). Her story is forever linked with that of Troy, both in terms of narrative and in terms of the visual reminder of it: she now shares in Laomedon's μέγα σῆμα (Q.S. 1.788), an epic as well as topographical landmark.

MEMNON

Unlike Penthesileia, Memnon is not introduced as a vision, but rather as a promise, of hope. Indeed, his arrival is delayed narratively and rhetorically, allowing Quintus' Trojans to reflect on the loss of Hector, the Trojans' strength and protection (Q.S. 2.12–13). Thymoetes reminds the internal and external audience of Achilles' power and his ability and willingness to fight even the gods (Q.S. 2.14–15). While this particular detail foreshadows, for the reader, both his clash with Memnon and his death at the hands of Apollo, it is for the internal audience explicitly connected with Penthesileia's narrative: Achilles could fight and overpower her who put the other Greeks to flight

---

[44] See Lovatt (2013: 267) and Greensmith's chapter in this volume.
[45] Compare the potential for sensual viewing in Athena's arming scene (*Il.* 5.733–47).
[46] E.g., *LIMC* s.v. 'Penthesileia' 14, 17, 32, 34, 58g.
[47] Cf. Lovatt (2013: 306–8).

(Q.S. 2.16–17) and who seemed first like a goddess to her Trojan onlookers (Q.S. 2.19).[48] Indeed, the suggestion that Troy be abandoned as a direct consequence of these superior warriors' deaths is met by Priam's announcement that Memnon's arrival and aid are expected.

When Memnon finally enters the scene, the Trojans are jubilant, γηθόσυνοί μιν ἴδοντο (Q.S. 2.103), but he is not hailed as a vision as Penthesileia was. The simile describing the Trojans' response to seeing Memnon – comparing them to sailors relieved after a great storm (Q.S. 2.102–7) – uses the same imagery as that describing the Trojans' response to Penthesileia's death (Q.S. 1.630–42).[49] For the reader, this similarity adumbrates further suffering for the city.[50] In keeping with Memnon's less visual exposition, his reception by the Trojans is more subdued than Penthesileia's. It is worth noting, however, that where Priam's response to Penthesileia's arrival was more restrained than that of the other Trojans, his response to Memnon's arrival is more joyful than theirs (Q.S. 2.106). Focus is placed on Memnon's parents, Eos and Tithonus, their immortal story and Memnon's adventurous journey to Troy, biographical details that are here shared with the internal, the Trojan, audience, where Penthesileia's past and filiation were recounted only to the external audience. Priam's delight in Memnon finally leads to the first comparison between the hero and the gods, inspired by both his narrative and his appearance (Q.S. 2.131–2). That he rejects the Trojans' celebration of his battle prowess in favour of first proving himself (Q.S. 2.146–55) marks him again as different from Penthesileia, whose boasts and promises had proved unfulfillable (Q.S. 1.93–7). Indeed, Priam's immediate response, his admiration for Memnon's humility (Q.S. 2.156), stands in stark contrast to Andromache's rejection of Penthesileia's *hybris* (Q.S. 1.98–117), boosted by the narrator's calling the Amazon a fool, νηπίη (Q.S. 1.96–7).[51] Memnon's measured approach, the promise of his divine parentage, and his previous successes in battle thus appear to place him, at least for the internal audience, in a stronger position than the rash and exuberant Penthesileia.[52]

Quintus' subsequent introduction of a divine audience and his foregrounding of its perspective is characteristic of the overall presentation of Memnon's fight and death in the *Posthomerica*, as well as of the visuality employed in this episode.[53] At an Olympian banquet, held in parallel to the Trojan one in honour of Memnon, Zeus instructs the gods not to interfere in battle, at once reminding them of Iliadic losses (e.g., *Il.* 16.431–61) and anticipating the conflict between

---

[48] Compare, e.g., Q.S. 1.19, 56, 216 and 358–72.

[49] Compare Q.S. 1.353–6; see Vian (1954: 40–1).

[50] Compare Q.S. 2.43–8.

[51] Cf. Scheijnen (2016a: 85–7).

[52] See Scheijnen (2016a: 94–6).

[53] Cf. Myers (2019: 67–71).

Memnon and Achilles (Q.S. 2.164–82). That Zeus's order is brought forward at this point in the narrative emphasises Memnon's importance for both the internal audience and the reader, and simultaneously reinforces his difference from Penthesileia.[54] While Ares in his anger at his daughter's death had been stopped from interfering by Zeus's thunderbolt (Q.S. 1.675–715), here all the gods are addressed, implying a divine investment in Memnon and Achilles surpassing that of the Penthesileia episode.

Unlike the Amazon, who led the vanguard of the Trojan army into battle and was visually distinguished from her followers (Q.S. 1.138–81), Memnon enters the battlefield as part of the larger army (Q.S. 2.183–201), again indicating his more measured approach. The difference between Memnon and Penthesileia is most pronounced in the similes used to describe their attacks and the Greek responses to them.[55] Quintus initially includes Memnon in the picture of a unified and threatening Trojan army,[56] but immediately draws attention to the unique position of Achilles within the Greek host (Q.S. 2.193–214). The Trojans' might is emphasised as they move as one, like dark clouds (Q.S. 2.194) or like a swarm of wheat-eating locusts (Q.S. 2.197–8). It is this threatening image of strength and unity to which the Argives respond with marvel, ἐθάμβεον, but from a distance, ἀπάνευθεν (Q.S. 2.202) – not unlike the Trojan women in the Penthesileia episode. Though arming themselves as a group, the Greeks explicitly place their trust in Achilles' strength, κάρτεϊ Πηλείδαο πεποιθότες (Q.S. 2.204). Here, it is Achilles whose body is put on display through the vividness and brightness of the comparisons between his armour and Zeus's lightning bolts (Q.S. 2.207),[57] and between the hero and the sun god, Helius (Q.S. 2.208–11).[58] As with Penthesileia, Quintus' description of Achilles invites the reader to imagine a radiant warrior who at once combines beauty and fierceness. It is only once Achilles has been foregrounded on the Greek side that Memnon is finally positioned apart from the Trojan mass and presented as a fierce leader equal to Achilles (Q.S. 2.212). Where Ares' daughter was compared to Athena and Eris (Q.S. 1.179–81), Memnon is described as resembling the god of war himself (Q.S. 1.213),[59] a detail the reader is invited to incorporate into their visualisation of the scene.

---

[54] Compare divine discussions about the relative importance of mortal and semi-divine heroes in the *Iliad*, e.g., *Il.* 24.31–76.

[55] See above, p. 80.

[56] Cf. Goţia (2007: 89–90).

[57] Compare Q.S. 1.153; cf. Q.S. 2.378–87. For discussion, see Goţia (2007: 89–90) and Scheijnen (2016a: 96–7).

[58] Compare *Il.* 22.25–32, 317–21; cf. Lovatt (2013: 262–4). Note the similarities with Penthesileia's comparison with the goddesses Selene (Q.S. 1.37–41) and Eos (Q.S. 1.48–53), and more abstract forms of light, e.g., the light of morn (Q.S. 1.79).

[59] See Scheijnen (2018: 86, 61).

From the mortal audience's perspective, Memnon's presence on the battlefield thus initially appears less conspicuous than Penthesileia's. Yet Memnon commands the attention of a divine audience – attention Penthesileia was not afforded. More importantly, where Achilles and Ajax initially felt able to hold back from the melee when Penthesileia led the Trojans, they do not delay meeting Memnon's army.[60] Indeed, Achilles engages with Memnon on equal footing, in both verbal and physical contest, where he did not deem Penthesileia worthy of his attention.[61] To highlight how well matched the two heroes are, Quintus includes an indicative detail: Zeus, kindly disposed to both (Q.S. 2.458),[62] makes them untiring and greater, τεῦξε δ' ἄρ' ἀκαμάτους καὶ μείζονας (Q.S. 2.459), like to the gods, not mortals, οὐδὲν ὁμοίους / ἀνδράσιν, ἀλλὰ θεοῖσιν (Q.S. 2.459–60) – a delightful sight for Eris (Q.S. 2.460). Their *monomachia* is remarkable not only for its visual detail, but also for its striking sound: their immortal armour rings (Q.S. 2.466–7),[63] while the battle cry of their armies and the dust whirled up by their fighting reach the realm of the gods (Q.S. 2.467–70). The dust, clouding the skies and therefore the immortal view of the battle, is dispelled by one of the gods (Q.S. 2.481–2), and the devastation on the battlefield described in vivid detail (Q.S. 2.482–9).

The narrative focus of the clash is thus initially deflected, drawn away from Achilles and Memnon themselves to the gods watching from afar, ἀπάνευθεν Ὀλύμπιοι εἰσορόωντες (Q.S. 2.490–4).[64] The domains of the gods, sky and sea, alongside the earth reverberate with the sound of battle (Q.S. 2.495–7), again highlighting the striking sensory effect of the fight between the sons of Thetis and Eos. The reader witnesses this vivid scene alongside the divine audience, invested as much in the heroes' battle as in the divine response to it. In focusing the scene through the divine perspective, Quintus invites his reader to visualise the spectacle, drawing on their knowledge of visual representations of divine partisanship and intervention in battle,[65] as well as on their familiarity with Homeric narrative and visual language.

Quintus describes the responses of individual divinities to these sights and draws the reader into their emotional narratives: the Nereids tremble and fear for Achilles (Q.S. 2.497–9), while Eos fears for Memnon (Q.S. 2.500) and the daughters of Helius marvel, ἐθάμβεον (Q.S. 2.502), at the sight of the two heroes meeting in battle. The fierce investment of the gods in these two

---

[60] See Scheijnen (2016a: 99–100).

[61] Where Penthesileia's claim to divine parentage and success on the battlefield was derided by Achilles (Q.S. 1.553–91), he engages with Memnon's claim of having the superior immortal mother (Q.S. 2.412–51); see Scheijnen (2018: 88–92).

[62] Cf. *Il.* 22.167–87; see Myers (2019: 69–70) for discussion.

[63] Compare Q.S. 2.345–54.

[64] Cf. Q.S. 1.403 and 1.476.

[65] E.g., *LIMC* s.v. 'Memnon' 28, 30, 33, 34–7, 39, 40, 91.

heroes, nearly precipitating a divine battle, finally causes Zeus to direct the Fates, Κῆρες,[66] to the battlefield to decree the outcome (Q.S. 2.507–11), a popular scene in the visual arts.[67] Again, the gods' response is foregrounded (Q.S. 2.511–13), while the heroes continue their fight unaware (Q.S. 2.514–16). Their powerful bodies, standing out from the general fray,[68] are compared to those of Giants and Titans (Q.S. 2.518–19), and their performance is so compelling that Enyo preserves the balance of their fight (Q.S. 2.520–6) despite Zeus's earlier release of the Fates. The reader does not actually witness much of the fighting and, though Achilles and Memnon are the focus of the spectacle for the divine audience,[69] for the external audience the internal spectating becomes part of the spectacle. It is through the focus on the divine audience and their responses to the spectacular fight between the heroes that Quintus guides the reader's eye through the scene and enables them to visualise it. Just as Quintus compressed the battle between Penthesileia and Achilles, driving the narrative to its crucial visual moment, he here keeps short the description of the battle itself. Nevertheless, Quintus' conceit of divine interest in protracting the match allows him to highlight both its visual intensity and its epic importance. Unlike Penthesileia, who commanded the mortal audience's attention, Memnon and Achilles are the objects of the divine gaze, symbols of the epic traditions surrounding them, yet vividly animated.

Quintus devotes only a few lines to Memnon's death, moving swiftly from the evenly matched combat of the two heroes to the weighing of their fates and finally to the deadly blow and the stripping of Memnon's armour (Q.S. 2.538–48). It is again the divine responses to Memnon's death that are foregrounded, a number of which are familiar to the reader from the visual arts: Eos' mourning is described in great detail (Q.S. 2.549–50, 2.593–627, 2.635–41),[70] punctuated by descriptions of the Winds' carrying off Memnon's corpse (Q.S. 2.550–69),[71] the Ethiopians' divinely granted following the Winds (Q.S. 2.570–82), and the Trojans' and Greeks' mourning their fallen heroes (Q.S. 2.628–33). Memnon's death thus gives way to a different kind of spectacle, scenes of mortal and immortal mourning. Unlike Penthesileia, whose death prompted Aphrodite to remove her from the literary to the visual sphere and to recast her as an object of male desire, Memnon is elevated through his death and through the divine acts that ensure his eternal memory. Through the gods' intervention, drops of Memnon's blood falling to earth as he is borne away

---

[66] On Quintus' use of the Κῆρες, see Gärtner (2007: 227–40).

[67] E.g., *LIMC* s.v. 'Memnon' 14–25; see Burgess (2004a: 34–6) for discussion. On the interplay of light and darkness in this scene, see Goţia (2007: 97–8).

[68] Cf. *LIMC* s.v. 'Memnon' 28–60.

[69] E.g., Q.S. 2.467–89, 2.517, 2.527–37.

[70] Cf. *LIMC* s.v. 'Memnon' 91.

[71] Cf. *LIMC* s.v. 'Memnon' 62–89.

by the Winds become his *sēma* among mortals (Q.S. 2.557–8).[72] Though the removal of Memnon's body from the battlefield is itself spectacular, it is the divinely inspired removal of the entire Ethiopian army that leaves both Greeks and Trojans marvelling and speechless, θάμβησαν . . . ἀπειρεσίῃ δ' ἀνὰ θυμὸν / ἀμφασίῃ βεβόληντο (Q.S. 2.582–5). Quintus here draws on the Homeric trope of a hero's extrication from the battlefield by a divine benefactor shrouded from mortal sight (e.g., *Il.* 3.380–2 and 5.311–46) and extends it to include an entire army, adding to the divine spectacle.

Once the Winds have carried Memnon to the banks of Aesepus, Eos' final lament for her son commences (Q.S. 2.593–4). She echoes Memnon's and Achilles' earlier debate over the relative powers of Eos and Thetis (Q.S. 2.412–51), concluding that her role as bringer of light is not sufficiently respected by the gods (Q.S. 2.616–22). Her resolution to abandon her divine duties is emphasised by her mother's, Nyx's, darkening the night sky in support of Eos (Q.S. 2.625–7). The narrative of Eos' loss and grief, shrouded as it is in darkness, is visually foregrounded through Quintus' description.[73] When Zeus puts an end to Eos' mournful rebellion, the Ethiopians' burial of Memnon's body is put into narrative focus (Q.S. 2.640–3), though just like his death, it is afforded only a few lines. It is again a divine intervention that draws the reader's attention, this time a spectacle not hidden from sight: the Ethiopians are transformed into birds, forever tending Memnon's *sēma* and performing their rites in memory of their fearsome leader (Q.S. 2.643–50).[74] Quintus includes a curious detail here, that whether in Hades or in the Elysian plain (Q.S. 2.650–1)[75] Memnon would delight in the sight (Q.S. 2.652). In suggesting uncertainty about the afterlife of Memnon, Quintus goes against the narrative of the *Aethopis*, as summarised by Proclus, that Eos granted her son immortality, honoured as she was by Zeus.[76] Quintus' Memnon is given a different kind of immortality: his blood in the river Paphlagoneus will forever remind mortals of his wounds, his *sēma* is tended to with perpetual martial ritual and his divinely witnessed battle with Achilles is remembered in works of art and in Quintus' poem.

ACHILLES

Achilles' character and body – prominent and highly visible from the beginning of the Trojan War, in the *Iliad* and in the visual arts[77] – are already foregrounded

---

[72] Cf. Myers (2019: 30–1 and 145) on *Il.* 11.52–5.

[73] Cf. Goţia (2007: 99–100).

[74] For literary and visual treatments of the scene, see *LIMC* s.v. 'Memnonides'.

[75] Cf. Schmitz (2007b: 80–1).

[76] Compare Q.S. 3.766–83.

[77] The *LIMC* catalogue of visual treatments of Achilles' myth alone contains 922 items, ranging in theme from his childhood to his death.

in the first two books of the *Posthomerica*. Precisely because the reader is already familiar with them, they require less immediate narrative focus than had Penthesileia's or Memnon's. Indeed, the very first lines of the *Posthomerica* set out to bring to the reader's mind and inner eye the events of the *Iliad* and Achilles' role in them (Q.S. 1.1–17). Much like his Hector, Quintus' Achilles is characterised by his Iliadic past, highlighted through Homeric similes (e.g., Q.S. 1.571–2, 2.207) and comparisons with immortal beings (e.g., Q.S. 2.208–11, 2.518–19). In many ways, the first two books of the *Posthomerica* serve as a reminder of the final battle of the *Iliad*, drawing links between Hector and his Posthomeric heirs. The Trojan heroes perform an important narrative function in Achilles' story, emphasising his unmatched strength and highlighting that no mortal, not even the child of a god, can defeat him.[78] Equally, Penthesileia and Memnon both prepare the reader for Achilles' inevitable death, providing visual models for the impact of a semi-divine hero's fall,[79] even as they defer this death foretold so many times in the *Iliad*.

The first scenes of Achilles' raging and slaughtering Trojans in a quest to avenge Antilochus are reminiscent of his response to Patroclus' death in the *Iliad*, but are here interrupted by Apollo's intervention and the hero's death, a familiar scene in the visual arts.[80] As in the Memnon episode, attention is drawn to the divine audience and its response, though here the emphasis is more epic than visual, as references to the Epic Cycle and the *Iliad* in particular are foregrounded.[81] Even wounded, Achilles frightens the Trojans, who warily avoid him as they would a hurt, but angered animal (Q.S. 3.141–8).[82] The sound of his voice in his dying threat instills fear in them, leading them to believe him unharmed (Q.S. 3.167–75). Achilles' body, falling to the ground, has a similar effect, as it causes the earth to resound under his weight, and his armour to ring (Q.S. 3.178).[83] Having thus described in vivid detail the sounds surrounding Achilles' death, Quintus finally draws attention to the visual effect of his corpse, again framing it through the audience's response: the onlooking Trojans, εἰσορόωντες, tremble with fear, τρομέεσκον (Q.S. 3.180). Quintus emphasises each of these responses through an epic simile, and in so doing heightens the vividness of the scene, enabling his readers to visualise it.

From the moment of his death, Achilles' body is viewed from mortal and immortal perspectives, and lamented by humans and gods alike. On seeing

---

[78] Compare Q.S. 3.72–5. Note Quintus' choice not to include Paris in the scene. Contrast, e.g., *Il.* 22.358–60; Proclus' summary of the *Aethiopis* in his *Chrestomathy*; Apollodorus, *Epitome* 5.3–4.

[79] Cf. *Il.* 16.477–683.

[80] E.g., LIMC s.v. 'Achilles' 848–58; see Burgess (1995) for discussion.

[81] E.g., Q.S. 3.96–127, esp. 116–17 and *Il.* 24.32–63, esp. 59–63; for discussion, see Burgess (2004b). See also Q.S. 3.80–2 and *Il.* 22.359–60.

[82] See Jahn (2009: 100).

[83] Cf. Scheijnen (2017: 12–13).

Achilles' corpse, Paris is the first Trojan to respond, proposing to take it hostage and imagining the Trojans' reactions. The envisioned scene is reminiscent of Hector's treatment at the hands of the Greeks (Q.S. 3.196–9, 210–11 and *Il.* 22.367–404)[84] and foreshadows the Greek women's mourning Achilles (Q.S. 3.200–7 and 3.544–81). Through Paris' imagined scene, Quintus reminds his reader of the vivid description of Hector's death in the *Iliad* and invites them to linger on the image depicted so frequently in the visual arts.[85] Combining Homeric narrative and its visual reception, the moment is at once epic and visual.

The Trojan women's lament in the *Iliad* is paralleled here in their imagined joy at the death of Achilles. In a similar reversal, the captured women in the Greek camp lament the death of Achilles (Q.S. 3.544–81); they mourn him the way the Trojan women mourned Hector, and they do so sincerely, because he had shown them respect (Q.S. 3.549–50).[86] Briseis' lament in particular strikes a Homeric tone (Q.S. 3.560–73)[87] as it evokes Andromache's address to Hector in which she reminds him of her previous losses and of his unique role in her life (*Il.* 6.410–30). To Briseis and the other captive women, Achilles is no longer the man who killed their protectors and caused their lamentations;[88] he has become their guardian and it is his death, not the deaths he caused, they bewail.

The Greek warriors, too, respond to Achilles' death with lamentations (Q.S. 3.401–513), similarly evoking Homeric scenes.[89] Phoenix's speech in particular is reminiscent of his Iliadic address to Achilles: he tells again of his exile and welcome in the house of Peleus (Q.S. 3.465–9 and *Il.* 9.447–84) and of Achilles' childhood attachment to his foster father (Q.S. 3.470–9 and *Il.* 9.432–9, 485–95).[90] It is in his description of the preparation and presentation of Achilles' body that Quintus focuses most explicitly on its visual effect (Q.S. 3.533–43):

> Τὸν δ' ἐσιδοῦσ' ἐλέησε περίφρων Τριτογένεια·
> στάξε δ' ἄρ' ἀμβροσίην κατὰ κρ<ά>ατος, ἥν ῥά τέ φασι
> δηρὸν ἐρυκακέειν νεαρὸν χρόα κηρὶ δαμέντων·
> θῆκε δ' ἄρ' ἐρσήεντα καὶ εἴκελον ἀμπνείοντι·   535
> σμερδαλέον δ' ἄρα τεῦξεν ἐπισκύνιον περὶ νεκρῷ,
> οἷόν τ' ἀμφ' ἑτάροιο δαϊκταμένου Πατρόκλοιο

---

[84] Contrast the Greeks' respectful treatment of Penthesileia's body (Q.S. 1.782–8).

[85] E.g., *LIMC* s.v. 'Hector' 68–82.

[86] Compare Helen's lament for Hector (*Il.* 24.761–75).

[87] For a detailed discussion, especially of the visuality of Briseis' mourning, see Tsomis (2007: 187–94); cf.Vian (1954: 39–40).

[88] Compare Briseis' lament for Patroclus (*Il.* 19.282–300).

[89] Cf. Lovatt (2013: 372–3).

[90] Compare Q.S. 7.630–9;Vian (1954: 38).

χωομένῳ ἐπέκειτο κατὰ βλοσυροῖο προσώπου·
βριθύτερον δ' ἄρα θῆκε δέμας καὶ ἄρειον ἰδέσθαι.   540
Ἀργείους δ' ἕλε θάμβος ὁμιλαδὸν ἀθρήσαντας
Πηλείδην ζώοντι πανείκελον, ὅς ῥ' ἐπὶ λέκτροις
ἐκχύμενος μάλα πουλὺς ἄδην εὕδοντι ἐῴκει.

Wise Tritogeneia was struck with pity at the sight, and she let fall on
his head drops of ambrosia, known to prolong the freshness of dead
men's flesh. She made him seem fresh and as he was in life, and gave
the corpse just such a fierce expression as was on his grim face when
he was full of wrath at the death in battle of his comrade Patroclus; and
she made him more impressive and stronger in appearance. The Argive
troops were astonished to see Pelides stretched out so imposingly on the
bier, seemingly alive, as if he were only sleeping.

The scene reminds the reader of Aphrodite's beautifying Penthesileia's body
to ensnare Achilles. Unlike Penthesileia, however, Achilles is not made to
look less warlike and fearsome, but rather more so.[91] The facial expression of
the dead Achilles here serves as a visual reminder of the ferociousness of his
rage at the death of Patroclus, so vividly described in the *Iliad*. As with Penthesileia, the Greek army marvels, Ἀργείους δ' ἕλε θάμβος, at the divine effect
on the fallen warrior,[92] though this time it is not due to a shift in presentation,
but rather because Athena has emphasised his living features in death. Quintus returns again to the motif of Achilles' imposing size at the funeral, when
the Greeks easily gather his bones, conspicuous like those of Giants (Q.S.
3.723–5).[93] Achilles' body is thus visually impressive in death as in life, and his
imposing figure is emphasised by Athena's intervention, marking his body as a
visual reminder of his epic feats.[94]

As in the Memnon episode, Quintus draws attention to the divine mourn-
ers of Achilles' death, Thetis and her Nereid sisters (Q.S. 3.582–631). While
their lamentation for Achilles is a central theme in epic,[95] in the visual arts
Nereids are associated with death and burial more generally.[96] Quintus invites
his reader to connect the familiar image of the Nereids' mourning from the
Homeric epics with that from the visual arts, imbuing the simple scene with
intensity and vividness. In addition to echoes of Thetis' mourning Achilles'
fate in the *Iliad* and in the visual arts, there are a number of Posthomeric

[91] Cf. *Od.* 23.156–63.
[92] Compare *Il.* 22.369–71.
[93] See Lovatt (2013: 368–70) on Homer's treatment of the scene in the *Odyssey*.
[94] See Lovatt (2013: 371–2).
[95] See Tsagalis (2004).
[96] See Barringer (1995, esp. 59–66).

echoes of Eos' lament for Memnon, linking the heroes with one another, as well as the Cyclical tradition with Quintus' work. Here, too, parts of nature reverberate with the mother's lament, amplified by her parent (Q.S. 3.668–70; cf. 2.625–7). The rivalry between Eos and Thetis is continued as Thetis imagines Eos' rejoicing at her loss (Q.S. 3.608–10; cf. 2.616–22). Indeed, where the mourning Eos initially refused to bring light to the world, she is now seen exulting and bringing particularly bright light, λαμπρότατον φάος, to the Trojans and Priam (Q.S. 3.665–6; cf. 2.634–9). Thetis' final lament for Achilles, anticipated throughout the *Iliad* and widely featured in the visual arts, is here a faint echo of those earlier representations and instead is described as a familiar scene from mortal life (Q.S. 3.648).

Quintus' presentation of the end of Achilles' life reveals the hero's dependence on the epic tradition, and allows Quintus to highlight that, despite his popularity in the visual arts, Achilles remains defined by his Homeric treatment. This is made explicit in Calliope's address to Thetis, where the Muse foretells Achilles' immortal afterlife in epic song, eternally protected and renewed by the Muses themselves (Q.S. 3.633–48).[97] Calliope reminds Thetis that other divinities, too, have lost their semi-divine offspring (Q.S. 3.635–41), situating Achilles in a long line of heroes whose fates are remembered in oral and literary traditions. She moreover highlights that different standards apply to immortal parents (Q.S. 3.642–3), echoing Zeus's appeal to the gods before Memnon's encounter with Achilles (Q.S. 2.167–72) discussed above. In the most striking part of Calliope's address, she foretells Achilles' future in poetry, inspired by the Muses, οἱ κλέος αἰὲν ἐπιχθονίοισιν ἀοιδοὶ / καὶ μένος ἀείσουσιν ἐμῇ ἰότητι καὶ ἄλλων / Πιερίδων (Q.S. 3.645–7).[98] Through Calliope's words Quintus thus reflects on Achilles' poetic afterlife and *kleos*, and claims his own place in the epic tradition.

CONCLUSION

Throughout the *Posthomerica*, Quintus creates highly visual moments to foreground his epic heroes. The three heroes discussed Δ99 here stand out in their visual and, indeed, narrative treatment, reflecting their divine parentage and their prominence in the literary and artistic traditions surrounding the Trojan War. Quintus draws on these different traditions to enable his reader to visualise the scenes by drawing on visual representations, and to animate them with narrative detail. Though each character is treated differently, Quintus' visual focus – his use of visual language and physical description, and his evocation

---

[97] Compare *Od.* 24.60–1.
[98] Compare Helen's foretelling the Trojans' and her own future in song (*Il.* 6.354–8).

of visual representations familiar to reader and poet alike – is essential to the development of his characters and their narratives.

Quintus builds up to Penthesileia's most visual moment, her death at the hands of Achilles, with the use of epic similes and comparisons, but he allows the moment itself to evoke visual representations. In so doing, he connects the epic treatment of Penthesileia's battle at Troy with that in the visual arts, inviting his reader to draw on their shared knowledge not only of oral and literary traditions surrounding the Amazon, but also of visual traditions depicting her fight with Achilles, the hero's falling in love with the Amazon, and finally her death. Similarly, Quintus foregrounds Achilles' body through similes, divine comparisons and vivid descriptions of his fighting. This is not done to evoke specific types of images popular in the visual arts, but rather to emphasise the literary quality of Quintus' hero. Quintus draws on highly visual moments from Homer's *Iliad* to focus the reader's mind and inner eye and to create a vivid image that is at once visual and epic. Ultimately, however, Quintus uses the epic Muse, Calliope, to foreground the epic, not the visual, traditions surrounding Achilles. Memnon's body is less prominently displayed than Penthesileia's and Achilles', though it, too, is described by means of divine comparison and epic simile. From his battle with Achilles to the transformation of his companions, Quintus presents Memnon's brief time at Troy as a series of spectacles. He does so by framing the scene from a divine audience's point of view and by focusing the reader's viewing of the spectacle through this perspective. The various divine interventions in the episode create a vivid scene that reflects the gods' investment in Memnon and enhances the visibility of his body. In drawing on Iliadic models for his divine audience and its interventions, Quintus further highlights Memnon's epic nature. Quintus' epic heroes are thus reflections of their past representations in works of art and in literature. They are viewed through the eyes of their mortal and divine audiences who shape the reader's experience and understanding of the heroes' pasts, visual and literary, and their place in Quintus' epic world.

PART II

Religion, Gods and Destiny

A Non-Homeric Fate in Quintus of Smyrna's *Posthomerica*? Representation, Function, Problems

Calum A. Maciver

INTRODUCTION

In the *Posthomerica* (*PH*), all things are, at first glance, Homeric. It should present no surprise that the differences from the picture of fate given in the *Iliad* should be so manufactured as almost to escape the notice of the reader. Many of the expressions deployed to characterise the operations of *Aisa*, *Moira(i)* and the *Kēres* are Homeric formulations; the same is true for the actions of Zeus in determining the *telos* of the Trojan War. It would be very apposite if Quintus' representation of fate did in fact follow the lack of clarity on fate found in the *Iliad*, given the author's profoundly careful imitation of every facet of the Homeric poems. There are, nevertheless, differences which have far-reaching consequences for understanding the conceptual rework-ing of Homer's theology by Quintus. This *reworking* is really more a *reading* of Homer, an anachronistic positing of functions for fate and Zeus which Quintus is more drawing out of Homer rather than, with it, iconoclastically disfiguring Homer. Quintus' poetological game with the reader is that his poem is still the *Iliad*, given the smooth run-on from the *Iliad* with which the proem-less Book 1 of the *PH* begins.[1] The primacy of fate over Zeus, for

I express my gratitude to the organisers of the 2016 workshop and the editors of this volume. I received useful written feedback from Simon Goldhill and Emma Greensmith – my thanks to them both. The Greek text is from Vian (1963, -66, -69). All translations are my own.

[1] This has become more or less the established reading of Quintus' poetics – my own discussion (Maciver 2012a: 7–38) builds on a number of studies which argued a similar position – as far back at least as Köchly (1850). The lack of a proem, the in-proem in Book 12 and the shield of Achilles in Book 5 are all poetic sites which bring the nature of the *PH*'s 'Homeric' identity to the fore, given that they show subtle, key differences from Homer. For the overview of the evolution of scholarship on Q.S., see Bär (2009: 29–33).

example, should, therefore, be understood as Quintus' enlarging upon what is already largely apparent, but not fully worked out, in Homer.[2] Inevitably, too, given the temporal distance between compositions, later philosophical developments influence Quintus' portrait of the workings of the *kosmos*, as he articulates his own imperial reading of archaic Homer.[3]

In 2014, Ursula Gärtner published the latest contribution on the question of the function of fate in Quintus' *PH*. Her useful discussion and findings prove that the questions of the nature and function of Quintus' representations of fate and heroism are still just that – questions. In this chapter I will revisit the question of fate's identity and function in the *PH*,[4] to (re-)establish that Quintus does provide his poem with what is a non-Homeric apparatus both for fate and an idealised heroism in the *PH*, albeit one which is so carefully constructed that it exhibits its differences only subtly within the overwhelming Homeric tenor of the poem. I shall discuss Gärtner's objections to current and long-standing trends on fate and heroism in Quintus, above all her argument that the only markedly non-Homeric expressions on fate and 'Stoic' endurance are found in the speeches or reported speeches of characters, as opposed to the text of the primary narration. This is demonstrably not correct, as I shall show. I shall analyse the passages she raises, and will compare them with key passages spoken by the primary narrator, to illustrate that these characters are in fact vouching for, and verifying, the philosophy of the main fabric of the poem. I shall conclude with a discussion of the unified representation of fate in the *PH*, and shall touch upon some of the consequences of this difference.

QUESTIONS

I begin by summarising some of the points raised in Gärtner's 2014 article. Although she acknowledges that later philosophical presences can be detected throughout Quintus' poem, especially in the sententious, moralising statements which so mark the speeches of the characters,[5] she argues against reading a non-Homeric presence of later philosophical concepts in the main narrative of the *PH*, and in particular against Stoic formulations by the primary narrator, which would sit uncomfortably with the largely Homeric apparatus of

---

[2] The bibliography on the subject of fate in the *Iliad* is large (a discussion of the *status questionis* can be found in Wong 2002). Janko (1992: 5) gives the best summary of the lack of clarity on fate in the poem: 'The tangled relation between fate, human freedom and the gods was left for later writers to unravel.'

[3] See now Greensmith (2020) for the most recent and nuanced study of this imperial *articulation*.

[4] I shall be enlarging upon, but not varying the overall conclusions of, Maciver (2012a: 114–23).

[5] Gärtner (2014: 104–5), following the discussion of Köchly (1850: xcv–cvi); Vian (1966: 204); Maciver (2007: 268–70).

the poem. I shall return to the idea of Stoicism in the course of this chapter,[6] but shall address Gärtner's objections in two sections: first, on the idea of the necessity of endurance and the causality of fate in the speeches of several characters as differing from the pronouncements of the primary narrator; and second, on the overall function of fate in the *PH* compared with its function in the *Iliad*.

The key thrust of Gärtner's argument is that scholars have not taken into account sufficiently the context in which many of these moralising, seemingly Stoic, statements are made. She claims, first, that these apparently non-Homeric ideas are found only in the speeches of characters, not in the primary narration, that the characters formulate their own, varied statements on fate in order to excuse their own actions, and that very often these speeches recall similar speeches in Homer, but with this difference, that they apply popular morality to back up their arguments. Second, Quintus could easily have ironed out the irregularities found in the *Iliad*, but instead, according to Gärtner, does not contradict the contradiction in Homer that Zeus is both above fate and under fate. On the first issue, she raises, in particular, the speeches of Odysseus to the dead Ajax on the necessity for endurance (*PH* 5), and the interactions between Philoctetes and the Greek embassy in Book 9 of Diomedes, Odysseus and, later, Agamemnon, all of whom bring up the same theme of endurance, and more importantly, excuse their actions by referencing the primacy of fate. She expertly shows (for the first time in scholarship on the *PH*) that the principle of double determinism is just as evident in Quintus as it is in Homer. Philoctetes, for example, is coerced by Athena to relent in his anger towards his Greek comrades, but it is the means by which this is achieved, namely his renewed joy at seeing faces once so familiar to him, which underscores the Homeric double determinism at work behind his new-found friendliness.[7]

PRIMARY AND SECONDARY NARRATORS

Zu beachten ist, dass der Erzähler selbst nur an einer Stelle davon spricht, dass Aisa den Menschen bei ihrer Geburt unentrinnbar die Fäden zuspinnt, hierbei aber gerade nicht die Eigenverantwortung thematisiert. Alle anderen Stellen, auf die oft wegen ihres 'stoischen

---

[6] In using Stoicism, I do not imply that what I term as Stoic or Stoicism is either definitively a tenet of any stage of that school of philosophy or merely reflective of and similar to that school, for reasons which will become apparent. For more precise studies of Stoic cosmology up to Seneca's time, see the recent collection edited by Salles (2009).

[7] Gärtner (2014: 120); her discussion of double determinism is on 109–12, with reference in particular to Penthesileia in Book 1 and her reasons for going to Troy, and her death at the hands of Achilles.

Schicksalsgedankens' verwiesen wird, stammen aus dem Mund von
Personen, die die Eigenverantwortung für ihre vorherige Entscheidung
zumindest einschränken und sich selbst entschuldigen möchten, und
zwar in einer deutlichen Steigerung zu vergleichbaren Homerpassagen.
(Gärtner 2014: 125)

According to Gärtner (summarised in her conclusion, above), the primary narrator only in one place in Q.S. (11.274–7) states that *Aisa* spun the unbreak-
able threads of men's lives, at their birth, and that the narrator never dwells
upon human responsibility in relation to fate; all occurrences are found in the
mouths of characters, who seek to excuse their own actions publicly by allud-
ing to the causality of fate. We cannot, therefore, assign to the poet a unified
vision of a cosmos underwritten only by fate, but rather in the mouth of the
narrator we find much the same role for Zeus and fate as is found in the *Iliad*.
All of this is worth a second look.

A key sentiment in Q.S., discussed at length by Gärtner (2014: 117–23), is
the necessity for humans to bear all hardship that comes their way in life.[8] The
idea is closely bound up, in each occurrence, with the primacy of fate in causing the awful consequences certain characters, for example Ajax, Podaleirius
and Philoctetes, experience. It occurs in the extended speech of Odysseus to
the dead Ajax at the end of the *Hoplōn Krisis*, forming his gnomic conclusion
on why he was not responsible for Ajax's death, and why Ajax in fact was to
blame for his own death, urged on as he was by fate. Odysseus begins by placing the blame on some *Aisa* (5.579–82):

νίκην ἀμφεβάλοντ᾽ ἐρικυδέα, τῆς πέρι θυμὸν
ἀχνύμενος πάις ἐσθλὸς ἐυσθενέος Τελαμῶνος   580
ὤλετο χερσὶν <ἑ>ῇσι. Χόλου δέ οἱ οὔ τι ἔγωγε
α̲ἴ̲τ̲ι̲ο̲ς̲, ἀ̲λ̲λ̲ά̲ τ̲ι̲ς̲ Α̲ἶ̲σ̲α̲ πολύστονος ἥ μιν ἐδάμνα.

It was in anger at the victory that the
Noble son of valiant Telamon
Perished at my hands. But I was in no way responsible for
His anger, but some Fate, bringer of great grief, brought him low.

Gärtner, following earlier commentators,[9] rightly sees in this statement an
allusion to *Odyssey* 11.558–60, where, in a very similar formulation, Odysseus tells the shade of Ajax that no one else was responsible other than Zeus
himself for his death (οὐδέ τις ἄλλος / α̲ἴ̲τ̲ι̲ο̲ς̲, ἀ̲λ̲λ̲ά̲ Ζ̲ε̲ύ̲ς̲). In Q.S., Zeus has

---

[8] Thematised lists of *gnōmai* can be found in Maciver (2012a: 92, n28).

[9] Cf. Vian (1966: 41, n3) *ad loc.*

been replaced by fate (*Aisa*): given the close metrical parallels in the key lines (underlined), this is a highlighted change by Quintus – it is not Zeus who was responsible, but fate, and a clear shift away from the Homeric position of the agency of Zeus. Odysseus goes on to state that the quarrel for the arms of Achilles was a matter of excellence (or virtue, *Aretē*), the sort of contest that is always a source of delight for right-thinking men.[10] The emphasis on *aretē* as the topic of the quarrel (*neikos*) taps into the recurrent ethic of the poem,[11] emblematised on the very arms of Achilles for which they were both arguing. The central motif of the ecphrasis in Book 5 is the mountain of *Aretē* (5.49–56). Odysseus, with clear irony, is pointing to his rightful inheritance of the shield, over his defeated opponent, whose death proves that he was not characterised by the necessary *aretē*.[12] This is the first key reference Odysseus makes to the philosophy of the poem (and by extension, *kosmos*) in which he exists, awareness of which proves that Odysseus, almost poet-like,[13] is reinforcing the poem's ideals rather than, as Gärtner argues, coming up with his own popular morality in contrast to that found in the main narrative.[14] The key passage for Gärtner's discussion occurs at the end of Odysseus' speech, where the character concludes with a *gnōmē* on the necessity for endurance (Q.S. 5.594–7):

κεῖνος δ' ἐσθλὸς ἐὼν στυγερῇ ὑπὸ Δαίμονος Αἴσῃ
ἤλιτεν. Οὐ γὰρ ἔοικε μέγ' ἀσχαλάαν ἐνὶ θυμῷ·   595
<u>ἀνδρὸς γὰρ πινυτοῖο καὶ ἄλγεα πόλλ' ἐπιόντα</u>
<u>τλῆναι ὑπὸ κραδίῃ στερεῇ φρενὶ μηδ' ἀκάχησθαι.</u>

But he was a noble man who was led astray by an awful Fate
Of some god. It's not right either to give vent to anger too much.
For it belongs to a prudent man to endure with strength of mind
All ills which come his way and not to give way to grief.

A prudent man (Stoic sage?) is not overcome by grief but tolerates it with an unbending mind. This *gnōmē* comes just after Odysseus' restatement of the

---

[10] 5.592–3: ἀλλά μοι ἀμφ' ἀρετῆς νεῖκος πέλεν, ἧς πέρι δῆρις / τερπνὴ γίνεται αἰὲν ἐύφροσιν ἀνθρώποισι. In lines 590–1 Odysseus lists other subjects of quarrels (women, cities and wealth) – the type of causes of *neikos* found in the *Iliad*, not here in Q.S.

[11] For references and bibliography, see Maciver (2007: 259, n2).

[12] Discussion of the meaning and function of *Aretē* in Q.S. can be found in Maciver (2007) and Maciver (2012a: 66–86), with bibliography.

[13] Cf. Baumbach (2007: 122) on Odysseus' understanding of the shield's emblems as he tells Neoptolemus of his father's armour which will be his should he come to Troy. Odysseus as an ideal reader of the shield was its worthy recipient.

[14] Gärtner (2014: 118) is surely correct in asserting that Odysseus is derogatory to Ajax in that he emphasises his lack of cleverness here.

role of Fate (*Aisa*) in the downfall of Ajax (594–5): although (surely the force of ἐών here) Ajax was a noble man, he was led astray through the agency of a harsh fate brought upon him by a divine spirit. Thus he ends his concluding thoughts on the function of fate as the primary influence in his downfall. Then, according to Gärtner (2014: 119) Ajax speaks a 'popularstoisch[e]' *gnōmē*, one often found in Q.S., which pushes fate further into the background as Odysseus emphasises Ajax's incompetence as the ground of his madness and downfall. She argues that this is described only through the point of view of one of the characters, and is a further remove away from the type of sentiments found in Homer.

This is incorrect on two grounds. First, the connection of the *gnōmē* with its context must be taken into account. As Lardinois has clearly shown for *gnōmai* in Homer, it is the context which provides the impetus for a wisdom saying; the *gnōmē* is often a supporting, generalised reason why something is the case.[15] This case is no different here, exacerbated by the two instances of γάρ. Ajax was indeed a noble man, and so it must have been *Aisa* who led him to do what he did, because it is not right for someone to nurture grief in their heart; because, moreover, it is of the nature of a wise man to put up with all the ills that come his way and not to be overcome by grief. That is the only way to understand why Ajax did what he did, for he had been a man who was ἐσθλός. This popular-Stoic statement is used to explain the necessity of fate's involvement, as Ajax, so idealised throughout the epic,[16] would not have behaved in this way otherwise. Fate's role is brought to the forefront in the final words of his speech.

Second, Odysseus is tapping into the philosophy of both the primary and secondary narrative. Nestor speaks very similar words in his consolation of Podaleirius in Book 7, but in so doing echoes the very description of him made by the primary narrator in Q.S. Book 3, something missed by Gärtner. According to the *primary narrator*, Nestor was not overcome by grief in his heart at the death of his son Antilochus (3.7–9):

(. . .) ὅ δ' οὐ μέγα δάμνατο θυμῷ·
ἀνδρὸς γὰρ πινυτοῖο περὶ φρεσὶ τλήμεναι ἄλγος
θαρσαλέως καὶ μή τι κατηφιόωντ' ἀκάχησθαι.

(. . .) But he was not cut to the heart,
For it belongs to a man of wisdom to suffer pain bravely
In his mind and not to give in to torment in any way.

---

[15] See Lardinois (1997: 218), with my discussion in Maciver (2012a: 89).

[16] See Vian (1963: 132) on the idealisation of Ajax in Q.S. For the *gnōmai* which emphasise necessity of endurance in the face of pain or trouble, see Maciver (2012a: 92, n28).

The verbal parallels are immediately apparent. Nestor's behaviour and heroism has been validated by the projected voice of the poet,[17] a voice which strains throughout the *PH* to be identified as the same narrator responsible for the Homeric poems.[18] Here, however, grief is to be internalised – an enlargement of Achilles' advice to Priam in *Iliad* 24 (24.524) that there was no advantage in excessive grief, but also an improvement on Achilles: whereas Achilles poured out his grief in the *Iliad*, grief in this 'Homeric' poem is not to be exhibited in any way. This notion of *apatheia* is prevalent in Q.S.,[19] and is used by Odysseus to underline the inexorable power of fate: a prudent man such as Ajax did not show *apatheia*. Nestor, so often a *mise-en-abîme* of the poet's authorial voice,[20] given the full approval by the primary narrator, goes on, in Book 7, to give extended advice to Podaleirius on why it is not appropriate to grieve, mimicking the very language used in Book 3 of himself (7.44–55).[21]

Odysseus, then, evokes the philosophy of the *PH* as he speaks his words of grief to the departed Ajax. It becomes all the more likely that his sentiments on the function of fate are valid, and reflective of the philosophy of the poem at large, given that he is made to voice one of the key (stoical) ethics found repeatedly, in varied forms, throughout the poem. The appearance of the poem's philosophical fabric within his speech hints, further, at a more subtle characterisation of Odysseus as he makes his wise pronouncements over Ajax. Odysseus claims that he wishes he had never won the arms of Achilles (5.577–81) given the tragic consequences, yet his words elevate him to a superior state of wisdom, and emphasise that he, and not Ajax, is in tune with the *PH*'s prevalent wisdom on what it is to endure. It could even be argued that Odysseus is, like the poet himself, aware of what it is to be a hero in *this* poem. Odysseus shows awareness of the primary narrative of *Odyssey* 6 when he echoes the assimilation of Nausicaa to Artemis in his speech to her (6.149–52, picking up on the simile at 6.102–9).[22] His poetic identity as both character and *aoidos*, so emphasised in the *Odyssey*,[23] could be at play again in the *PH*,

---

[17] The same is true of the primary narrator's approbation of the conduct of Sinon at 12.387–8, formulated in very similar language (388): ἀνδρὸς γὰρ κρατεροῖο κακὴν ὑποτλῆναι ἀνάγκην.

[18] Useful discussion can be found in Bär (2009: 73–5).

[19] See James (2004: 82) and my own discussion at Maciver (2012a: 82) for further references. A particularly noteworthy parallel is found in the speech of the deified Achilles to his son Neoptolemus: a true hero neither gives in to pain nor overly rejoices in favourable events (14.201–3).

[20] Cf. Dällenbach (1989: 52) on the status of old people as 'organs of truth' and therefore embodiments of the poet, discussed at Maciver (2017: 271, n54).

[21] Further discussion at Maciver (2012a: 103–8). Nestor resembles, in characterisation, Cato, the Stoic sage of Lucan's *Pharsalia* (see, e.g., Lucan 2.380–95).

[22] Goldhill (1991: 67).

[23] See the excellent discussion of Goldhill (1991: 56–68).

where he adeptly taps into the philosophy of the *PH* to which he seems to have access, but to which Ajax did not. It serves to be poetically aware.

It is worthwhile to end this section on Odysseus with the prolepsis of Ajax's death earlier in the primary narrative of Book 5. When Ajax is defeated in the battle of words, he immediately experiences the physiological symptoms of madness, brought on by *Atē*.[24] At 331–2 we read:

> (. . .) ὅ δ' ὑστατίην ποσὶν οἶμον
> Ἤιεν οὐκ ἐθέλων. σχεδόθεν δέ οἱ ἕσπετο Μοῖρα.

> (. . .) That path, to be his last, he trod
> With unwilling feet. For at his side followed Fate.

'Er geht, doch Moira folgt ihm – wohl nicht mehr als eine Chiffre dafür, dass er zum Tod bestimmt ist, was sich an einer Reaktion erkennen lässt' (Gärtner 2014: 113).[25] But why would his final path be emphasised as one he embarks upon unwillingly, if *Moira* was merely a symbol for the certainty of his death? Just as Odysseus stated that prudent men do not give in to grief, and that therefore it was fate behind the downfall of Ajax, so here we have that very idea put into action. A similar picture is given of Penthesileia's final moments (discussed too by Gärtner 2014: 110–11) – the baleful fates of death (*Kēres*) spur her on to enter her one and only battle (πρώτην τε καὶ ὑστατίην δῆριν, 1.172).[26] The final moments of Ajax's life validate the philosophising spoken to him, in his death, by Odysseus.

PHILOCTETES

The most surprising moment in Quintus' relation of the embassy's meeting with Philoctetes in Book 9 is the ease and rapidity with which Philoctetes

---

[24] See the exhaustive study on *atē* by Cairns (2012), and especially p. 7 on the *atē* of Patroclus – the physical *atē* results from Patroclus' earlier misjudgements, just as Ajax here was unable to follow the ethical concepts of the *PH*.

[25] Translation: 'He leaves, but Moira follows him – really nothing more than a token for the fact that his death is determined, a fact which can be determined from his reaction.'

[26] Gärtner (2014: 110–12) has amply shown the notion of double determinism in the decisions of Penthesileia, but that notion does not undercut the vital place such personifications have in Q.S. They are found throughout the poem, and often have a direct influence on battle – e.g. at 1.273, where they direct arrows away from their targets. One of the strongest examples is in the speech of dying Paris to Oenone in Book 10, where he explains that he left her unwillingly, and that the *Kēres* led him to Helen (10.284–7) – it is of course in the interests of Paris to blame such figures rather than himself.

relents and ceases from his famous wrath.[27] Gärtner (2014: 119–23) discusses
the meeting and speeches between Philoctetes and the Greek embassy and
highlights that the characters in each case allude to fate to excuse their own
actions but proves, expertly, that double determinism is operative in the decision of Philoctetes to relent from anger: Athena is behind his acceptance of the
Greeks, but he too, on seeing his former friends, forgets his anger. The Greeks
do indeed excuse their behaviour and put the blame entirely on fate, but it
is important to emphasise that Philoctetes both heeds their words and speaks
the very same type of philosophy himself. Philoctetes exhibits all the signs of
sage-ness which Ajax lacked, and exemplifies the very type of hero Nestor
promotes in his consolation of Podaleirius in Book 7.

Diomedes and Odysseus approach Philoctetes on Lemnos and tell him that
no Achaean was to blame for his ills, but rather the *Moirai* (9.414–25):

(. . .) κακῶν δέ οἱ οὔ τιν' Ἀχαιῶν
αἴτιον ἔμμεν ἔφαντο κατὰ στρατόν, ἀλλ' ἀλεγεινὰς   415
Μοίρας, ὧν ἑκὰς οὔ τις ἀνὴρ ἐπινίσεται αἶαν,
ἀλλ' αἰεὶ μογεροῖσιν ἐπ' ἀνδράσιν ἀπροτίοπτοι
στρωφῶντ' ἤματα πάντα, βροτῶν μένος ἄλλοτε μέν που
βλάπτουσαι κατὰ θυμὸν ἀμείλιχον, ἄλλοτε δ' αὖτε
ἔκποθε κυδαίνουσαι, ἐπεὶ μάλα πάντα βροτοῖσι   420
κεῖναι καὶ στονόεντα καὶ ἤπια μηχανόωνται,
αὐταὶ ὅπως ἐθέλουσιν. Ὁ δ' εἰσαΐων Ὀδυσῆος
ἠδὲ καὶ ἀντιθέου Διομήδεος αὐτίκα θυμὸν
ῥηϊδίως κατέπαυσεν ἀνιηροῖο χόλοιο,
ἔκπαγλον τὸ πάροιθε χολούμενος, ὅσσ' ἐπεπόνθει.   425

No one from the Achaean army was to blame
For the evil he suffered, they said, except the grief-giving
Fates, who are not far from any man who walks the earth
But who roam about day on day, ever unseen,
Shadowing wretched mankind, sometimes, obeying their pitiless desires,
Breaking the might of mortals, at other times, without warning,
Giving them glory: they devise all things
For men, both grievous and gratifying,
As they will. He, then, listened to Odysseus
And godlike Diomedes and immediately stopped,
Effortlessly it seemed, the bitter anger in his heart,
Anger which had been so intense before, given all he'd suffered.

---

[27] For the most recent assessment of Philoctetes in Q.S., see chapter 7 in Greensmith (2020).

Odysseus and Diomedes explain the workings of the *kosmos* according to the philosophy of the *PH* and *easily* and *immediately* Philoctetes stops being angry,[28] despite how strong his wrath had been for all he had suffered. Against all previous representations of Philoctetes, tragic, epic (including the Epic Cycle) and prose (mythological handbooks),[29] Quintus reduces the tradition to an immediate acceptance by Philoctetes *because of* the exposition on the role of the *Moirai*.[30] According to Gärtner, as this speech is in the mouth of characters, it cannot be identified as representing the philosophy of the main narrative, but is used rather as a means of excusing actions. Yet Philoctetes' reaction, and the way in which he himself repeats the very ideas of endurance and right conduct so prevalent in Q.S., proves the value of the philosophy spoken by Odysseus and Diomedes: Philoctetes behaves just as Nestor had done when faced with extreme grief, as was highlighted by the primary narrator as a paradigm of steadfastness (in Book 3, discussed above). It belongs to a man who is noble so to behave, as Philoctetes himself states (9.518–24):

> ὦ φίλος, οὐ σοὶ ἐγὼν ἔτι χώομαι, οὐδὲ μὲν ἄλλῳ
> Ἀργείων, εἰ <καί> τις ἔτ' ἥλιτεν εἵνεκ' ἐμεῖο·
> οἶδα γὰρ ὡς <σ>τρεπτὸς νόος ἀνδράσι γίνεται ἐσθλοῖς,   520
> οὐδ' αἰεὶ χαλεπὸν θέμις ἔμμεναι οὐδ' ἀσύφηλον,
> ἀλλ' ὀτὲ μὲν σμερδνὸν τελέθειν, ὀτὲ δ' ἤπιον εἶναι.
> νῦν δ' ἴομεν ποτὶ κοῖτον, ἐπεὶ χατέοντι μάχεσθαι
> βέλτερον ὑπνώειν ἢ ἐπὶ πλέον εἰλαπινάζειν.

> Friend, I am not angry any more at you nor at any other of
> The Argives, if in fact anyone else wronged me.
> For I know that in good men the mind is amenable,
> Nor is it right always to be angry or headstrong
> But sometimes to be angry and sometimes to be gentle.
> But now let's retire to bed, since for one eager to fight
> It is better to sleep than to feast for too long.

That Philoctetes' behaviour is idealised is beyond doubt. He echoes the gnomic wisdom of Odysseus to the dead Ajax and Nestor to Podaleirius on the need

---

[28] The description of the Fates haunting wretched men every day (417–18) very closely matches the words of the primary narrator about the Furies at the beginning of Book 1 (31–2): ἄφραστοι· κεῖναι γὰρ ἀεὶ περὶ ποσσὶν ἀλιτρῶν / στρωφῶντ', οὐδέ τι ἔστι θεὰς ἀλιτόνθ' ὑπαλύξαι.

[29] It is likely that Q.S. did have access to the Epic Cycle: see the brief discussion in Baumbach and Bär (2007b: 1) and Bär and Baumbach (2015).

[30] There are a number of similarities between this exposition and that by Nestor on fate in Book 7 – for references, see Maciver (2012a: 120).

to control anger (521), and foreshadows the advice given by the apparition of
Achilles when he appears to Neoptolemus in Book 14 in his statement that one
should sometimes be angry, and sometimes gentle (522 – with which compare
14.201–6). The parallel is all the more important in that Achilles enlarges on the
figure of *Aretē* found on the shield of Achilles in Book 5. Gärtner's insistence
on separating the information found in the primary narrative from the words of
secondary narrators overlooks the vital connections and elaborations of symbols
and gnomic wisdom in the primary narrative recurrent in key speeches by key
figures in the secondary narration. The wisdom of the primary narrative should
not be kept apart – the poem itself, through these many overlapping phrases,
encourages the two types of narration to be held together.[31]

Gärtner (2014: 120) shows that in speaking to Nestor, Agamemnon speaks
only of his own folly (*atē* – 9.115–20, in contrast to his public shirking of
responsibility at *Iliad* 19.86–7, where he puts the blame on Zeus, *Moira* and
Erinys), but in speaking to Philoctetes publicly, Agamemnon blames the gods
and fate (9.491–511):

ὦ φίλ', ἐπειδή πέρ σε <u>θεῶν ἰότητι</u> πάροιθε
Λήμνῳ ἐν ἀμφιάλῳ λίπομεν βλαφθέντε νόημα,
μὴ δ' ἡμῖν χόλον αἰνὸν ἐνὶ φρεσὶ σῇσι βαλέσθαι·
οὐ γὰρ ἄνευ μακάρων τάδ' ἐρέξαμεν, ἀλλά που αὐτοὶ
ἤθελον ἀθάνατοι νῶιν κακὰ πολλὰ βαλέσθαι   495
σεῦ ἀπὸ νόσφιν ἐόντος, ἐπεὶ περίοιδας ὀιστοῖς
δυσμενέας δάμνασθαι, ὅτ' ἀντία σεῖο μάχωνται.

. . . .

πᾶσαν ἀν' ἤπειρον πέλαγός τ' ἀνὰ μακρὸν ἄιστοι
<u>Μοιράων ἰότητι</u> πολυσχιδέες τε πέλονται   500
πυκναί τε σκολιαί τε, τετραμμέναι ἄλλυδις ἄλλη·
τῶν δὲ δι' αἰζηοὶ φορέονθ' <u>ὑπὸ Δαίμονος Αἴσῃ</u>
εἰδόμενοι φύλλοισιν ὑπὸ πνοιῆς ἀνέμοιο
σευομένοις· ἀγαθὸς δὲ κακῇ ἐνέκυρσε κελεύθῳ
πολλάκις, οὐκ ἐσθλὸς δ' ἀγαθῇ· τὰς δ' οὔτ' ἀλέασθαι   505
οὔτ' ἄρ' ἑκών τις ἑλέσθαι ἐπιχθόνιος δύνατ' ἀνήρ·

---

[31] The ancients identified the voice of the narrator in the speeches of characters – see Lardinois (1997: 233). Most of the moral statements in the *PH* occur in *gnōmai* in the speeches of secondary narrators. Of the 132 *gnōmai* in the poem, 99 are spoken by characters, leaving 33 in the voice of the primary narrator. This contrasts with 3 out of 154 *gnōmai* in the *Iliad* in the primary narration (for the statistics, see Maciver 2012a: 91–3). Most of the philosophising statements are indeed in the mouth of characters in Q.S., but a markedly high proportion of overlap with the morality of the primary narrative exists compared with Homeric practice.

χρὴ δὲ σαόφρονα φῶτα, καὶ ἦν φορέηθ' ὑπ' ἀέλλαις
οἴμην ἀργαλέην, στερεῇ φρενὶ τλῆναι ὀιζύν.
Ἀλλ' ἐπεὶ ἀασάμεσθα καὶ ἠλίτομεν τόδε ἔργον,
ἐξαῦτις δώροισιν ἀρεσσόμεθ' ἀπλήτοισι,   510
Τρώων ἥν ποθ' ἔλωμεν ἐυκτίμενον πτολίεθρον.

Friend, I grant that before – by the will of the gods –
We left you behind on sea-girt Lemnos – deluded as we were;
All the same, don't put bitter anger in your mind,
For not without the gods did we do these things, but I guess the gods
Themselves wished to bring many evils on us
In your absence, given how expert you are at slaying
The enemy with arrows, whenever they face you in the fight.

. . . .

Across the whole land and wide sea, unseen
And branched are the [paths of life], by the Fates' will,
Crowded and twisted, turning in all different directions.
Men are carried across them by Divine Fate
Like leaves whirling in the wind's
Breeze. A good man often lights upon an evil
Path, and an evil man upon a good path. A man cannot escape
Them nor can a man on earth, of his own will, choose them.
A man must be prudent and if he is carried by the winds
On a path of pain, he must endure misery with an unbending mind.
But since we have been deluded and have erred in this deed,
We will bestow countless gifts on you right away,
If ever we sack the well-built city of the Trojans.

The principle of double determinism is very clearly present here: they acted by the will of the gods/Fates, but they still committed folly, and for that reparation is due. Gärtner (2014: 122) is correct to state that the idea of endurance is once again found in this passage, but it cannot be separated from the other information in his speech. She rightly points out that the speech is very similar to Nestor's exposition of Fate in Book 7 (discussed below), but there was no need for Nestor to give that information to excuse *his* behaviour as she (rightly) claims Agamemnon is doing here. It is undoubted that reference to a third party allows Agamemnon to lessen the severity of his actions (as he does in the *Iliad*), but that does not mean that the information on fate is merely used for that purpose alone, or that it is in essence, according to the fabric of the poem as a whole, *not* valid. Once again, Philoctetes' fulfilment of the idealised philosophy of endurance and *apatheia*, raised again here (507–8, in close resemblance to previous statements on endurance), shows not only that in the actions of mortals in this poem this philosophy can be realised (and suddenly, in the case of Philoctetes), but that Agamemnon's advice is merely a restating of what is found throughout the poem.

The near-effortlessness with which Philoctetes accepts the excuses of the embassy to Lemnos is what sets Quintus' version against tradition above all, and it could be argued that Quintus highlights this difference with tradition in his use of 'before' in reference to the hero's anger: ἔκπαγλον τὸ πάροιθε χολούμενος (9.425, quoted above). Philoctetes on hearing the words of Odysseus and Diomedes ceases to be angry despite how much he had raged before both in the real sense, on the island, abandoned, but metapoetically too, in previous poetic versions which portrayed his unabated anger, especially in the famous example of Sophocles' eponymous play.[32] The contrast with the tragic representation of Philoctetes' unceasing rage is all the more remarkable given the lingering advertisement of Philoctetes' suffering,[33] and in particular the noxiousness of his wound (9.355–97). Quintus gives pointed scrutiny to his character's tragic past only to sweep it away, to draw attention to how different his account is: his type of philosophy evident in his idealised, Stoicised, heroes, brings successful outcomes where more archaic versions failed.

FATE

I have tried to establish that a markedly non-Homeric philosophy can be detected within the *PH*. In each case, however, the non-Homeric notions are often camouflaged within very obvious Homeric constructions.[34] The differences between Homer and Q.S. are most clearly seen in the presentation of fate. In this final section I will analyse the key passages where fate is described, beginning with Nestor's re-presentation of the 'jars of Zeus' paradigm from *Iliad* 24. The standard scholarly position is that Quintus combined a traditional Homeric point of view of fate and Zeus's operations in the *kosmos* with influence of Stoic ideas.[35] Gärtner (2014: 126) states in her conclusion that Quintus

---

[32] I owe this latter interpretation on the metapoetics of 'before' to Simon Goldhill.

[33] As astutely pointed out to me by Emma Greensmith.

[34] Heinze (1993: 202–3) claims something similar for Virgil's *Aeneid*.

[35] Köchly (1850) and Vian (1963, -66, -69). James and Lee (2000: 12–13) list previous scholarship on Stoicism in Q.S., something they themselves acknowledge as present in particular in the omnipotence of fate and in the description of the destination of souls after death. On the latter, Quintus presents a not entirely coherent mix of neo-Pythagorean/Orphic ideas within a traditional Homeric picture. I discuss this in Maciver (2017).

in fact, similar to Lucan,[36] wants to make no profound Stoic statements himself, but taps into the readers' knowledge of Stoicism by inserting certain Stoic ideas into the poetic code of the poem, in order to bring these very ideas into a space for discussion.[37] She sensibly concludes: 'Die *PH* sind sicher nicht anti-stoisch, aber auch nicht paradigmatisch stoisch.'[38] Q.S. was writing a Homeric poem, and therefore an oversimplified, non-Homeric system of thought would ruin the poetic ideology the poem represents.

In the representation of fate, however, Quintus has pointedly ironed out the differences in Homeric representations – in Q.S., fate is omnipotent, and above Zeus himself.[39] In Book 7, Nestor explains to Podaleirius why it is that grief comes the way of mortals (7.71–84):

ἐσθλά τε καὶ τὰ χέρεια θεῶν ἐν γούνασι κεῖται,
Μοίρης εἰς ἓν ἅπαντα μεμιγμένα. καὶ τὰ μὲν οὔ τις
δέρκεται ἀθανάτων, ἀλλ' ἀπροτίοπτα τέτυκται
ἀχλύι θεσπεσίῃ κεκαλυμμένα· τοῖς <δ'> ἐπὶ χεῖρας
οἴη Μοῖρα τίθησι καὶ οὐχ ὁρόωσ' ἀπ' Ὀλύμπου   75
ἐς γαῖαν προΐησι· τὰ δ' ἄλλυδις ἄλλα φέρονται
πνοιῇ<ς> ὣς ἀνέμοιο· καὶ ἀνέρι πολλάκις ἐσθλῷ
ἀμφεχύθη μέγα πῆμα, λυγρῷ δ' ἐπικάππεσεν ὄλβος
οὔ τι ἑκών. ἀλαὸς δὲ πέλει βίος ἀνθρώποισι·
τοὔνεκ' ἄρ' ἀσφαλέως οὐ νίσεται, ἀλλὰ πόδεσσι   80
πυκνὰ ποτιπταίει· τρέπεται δέ οἱ αἰόλον εἶδος
ἄλλοτε μὲν ποτὶ πῆμα πολύστονον, ἄλλοτε δ' αὖτε
εἰς ἀγαθόν. Μερόπων δὲ πανόλβιος οὔ τις ἐτύχθη
ἐς τέλος ἐξ ἀρχῆς· ἑτέρῳ δ' ἕτερ' ἀντιόωσι.

Good and evil fortunes lie on the knees of the gods above,
All mixed together into one by the Fates. And none of the
Gods sees those fortunes which have been made invisible,
Wrapped in a divine mist. Fate alone gets her

---

[36] Not all scholars would agree with this representation of Stoic ideas in Lucan: see the discussion of Colish (1985: 265–75) for the prevalence of Stoicism in the *Pharsalia*.

[37] Silius Italicus is a useful *comparandum* for a picture of Stoic endurance in characters to an extent much closer to the internalisation of grief of characters such as Nestor and Sinon in the *PH*. See, e.g., *Punica* 15.819–20 (Hannibal suppresses his tears) and 1.179–81 (King Tagus endures torture, but his mind remains untouched). See Colish (1985: 284–5).

[38] Translation: 'The *PH* is definitely not anti-Stoic, but it is not paradigmatically Stoic either.'

[39] For a recent study of Stoic fate, see Meyer (2009). One branch of early Stoicism saw Zeus and fate as synonymous (see Meyer 2009: 80). This is not quite the case in Q.S.: sometimes there is overlap, and sometimes fate is definitively characterised as superior to Zeus – Zeus as represented as an anthropomorphic, Homeric-like god.

Hands on them and hurtles them towards earth from Olympus,
But blindly. And they, one after another, are borne
As though by gusts of wind. Often a good man
Is overwhelmed by great trouble, but, unwillingly, wealth falls to a
Pernicious man. Blind is life for mankind.
Therefore, not unerringly do men go, but with their feet they
Often stumble. Appearances are prone to change and turn
Sometimes into grief-bringing trouble, and sometimes, in turn,
Into fortune. No mortal lives a completely happy life
From beginning to end: different people meet with a different fate.

In *Iliad* 24, Achilles states that it is Zeus who mixes these outcomes, and knowingly bestows them on mortals (24.527–33):

δοιοὶ γάρ τε πίθοι κατακείαται ἐν Διὸς οὔδει
δώρων οἷα δίδωσι κακῶν, ἕτερος δὲ ἑάων·
ᾧ μέν κ' ἀμμίξας δώῃ Ζεὺς τερπικέραυνος,
ἄλλοτε μέν τε κακῷ ὅ γε κύρεται, ἄλλοτε δ' ἐσθλῷ·   530
ᾧ δέ κε τῶν λυγρῶν δώῃ, λωβητὸν ἔθηκε,
καί ἑ κακὴ βούβρωστις ἐπὶ χθόνα δῖαν ἐλαύνει,
φοιτᾷ δ' οὔτε θεοῖσι τετιμένος οὔτε βροτοῖσιν.

For there are two urns that stand in the threshold of Zeus, and they give varying gifts – the one urn evil, the other good. When Zeus who delights in thunder mixes these and bestows them on someone, sometimes that person meets with ill, and sometimes good. But when Zeus bestows on someone a portion from the urn of ills, he makes the man a failure, and grinding poverty drives him over the shining earth, and he walks honoured neither by gods nor mortals.

This passage functions as a very suitable model: Nestor is trying to persuade someone to stop grieving, just as Achilles was with Priam. This Iliadic passage is also one of the most famous on the arbitrariness of good and bad fortunes which life brings. That aspect has been strengthened in Q.S. by the fact that the *Moira* does not look where she sends the good and bad outcomes to the ground. Zeus, however, has been replaced, in terms of agency, by the *Moirai*. In Q.S. he neither mixes the good and bad outcomes, nor dispatches them. He does not even get to see them, wrapped as they are in a mist. All things, however, seem to originate from the gods – they lie on the lap of the gods (itself a Homeric formulation – *Iliad* 17.514 and 20.435), and in a sense are god-breathed in origin. That is as far as their role goes – the actual good and bad fortunes originate from them. Quintus thus provides scope for the Homeric notion of divine origins, but the agency is entirely changed (ostentatiously so).[40] Fate's primacy is clear, indubitably presented by Nestor, who, when it comes to a description of souls after death, prefaces his remarks with *phatis* (7.87) (an expression not used in Homer) to emphasise that he is reporting popular, contemporary belief, *not* the authorised Homeric version. For fate, he is rewriting Homer, or adjusting focus from Zeus on to *Moira*, drawing the reader, as it were, to go back to the *Iliad* for a second look and replace Zeus with *Moira*, or to read Zeus qua *Moira*.

For Gärtner,[41] the picture is unclear: Zeus is more powerful than fate in places, and subordinate in others – an apparent ploy by Quintus to be as inexact as Homer, and thus faithfully Homeric. In the passages which she lists as exemplary of the all-powerfulness of Zeus, however, Zeus is not all-powerful – Quintus nowhere contradicts the strongest statements of the subordination of Zeus to fate given at 2.172, 11.272–3, and especially 13.558:

2.172 (the words of Zeus, where he states that there is no point in any god supplicating him, given his subservience to fate):

(. . .) Κῆρες γὰρ ἀμείλιχοί εἰσι καὶ ἡμῖν.[42]

(. . .) For the deathly fates are unfeeling even of us.

11.272–3:

<Αἶσα> ἅζετο δ᾽ οὔτε Ζῆνα πελώριον οὔτέ τιν᾽ ἄλλον
ἀθανάτων. (. . .)

For she is a respecter of neither mighty Zeus nor any other
Of the gods. (. . .)

13.558–60 (Troy fell):

(. . .) οὐδέ οἱ αὐτὸς
Ζεὺς ὕπατος χραίσμησεν ἀπ᾽ αἰθέρος, οὕνεκα Μοίραις
εἴκει καὶ μεγάλοιο Διὸς μένος. (. . .)

---

[40] James (2004: 307) *ad loc.* rightly compares Plato's myth of Er (*Resp.* 617D–E) for the role of fate in the allotment of fortunes – there are no clear verbal parallels, unfortunately. It is plausible to suppose that Quintus is applying the figure from a later rewriting of the Platonic version.

[41] *Contra* almost all scholars of Q.S. of the twentieth century – listed in her footnote 11 (Gärtner 2014: 100).

[42] According to Wenglinsky (2002: 177), there is no clearer statement in Q.S. on the relationship between the gods and Fate.

(. . .) Which Zeus himself
On high did not stop from heaven, because to the Fates
Even the power of mighty Zeus yields. (. . .)

The last example seems to allude to the situations in the *Iliad* (Books 16 and 22, the deaths of Sarpedon and Hector respectively) where Zeus seemed capable of overturning fate to save his favourites. Quintus could not be any clearer or bolder in putting fate first. It would therefore be very strange for Quintus to undermine these *very bold statements* (the like of which cannot be found in Homer) by stating the very opposite. These are the passages Gärtner cites to support her claim:

2.507–13:

Καί νύ κε δὴ μακάρεσσιν ἀμείλιχος ἔμπεσε δῆρις,
εἰ μὴ ὑπ' ἐννεσίῃσι Διὸς μεγαλοβρεμέταο
δοιαὶ ἄρ' ἀμφοτέροισι θοῶς ἑκάτερθε παρέσταν
Κῆρες· ἐρεμναίη μὲν ἔβη ποτὶ Μέμνονος ἦτορ,   510
φαιδρὴ δ' ἀμφ' Ἀχιλῆα δαΐφρονα· τοὶ δ' ἐσιδόντες
ἀθάνατοι μέγ' ἄυσαν, ἄφαρ δ' ἕλε τοὺς μὲν ἀνίη
λευγαλέη, τοὺς δ' ἠὺ καὶ ἀγλαὸν ἔλλαβε χάρμα.

And now cruel strife would have broken out among the gods
Had not the two Fates of death, by the command of
Loud-thundering Zeus, come to the sides of both camps,
Swiftly. A dark Fate entered the heart of Memnon,
A light one to warlike Achilles. On seeing this
The immortals let out a huge shout: ruinous pain gripped
Some, but the others were taken by glorious and triumphant joy.

The *Kēres* may come to stand on either side by the commands of Zeus, but he has no determination or knowledge of the outcomes; similarly, in the picture Nestor paints to Podaleirius, the good and bad fortunes lie on the knees of the gods, but they know neither their nature or eventual application. There is no contradiction here.

2.593–8:

δύσετο δ' ἠελίοιο φάος· κατὰ δ' ἤλυθεν Ἠὼς
οὐρανόθεν κλαίουσα φίλον τέκος, ἀμφὶ δ' ἄρ' αὐτῇ
κοῦραι εὐπλόκαμοι δυο<καί>δεκα, τῇσι μέμηλεν   595
αἰὲν ἑλισσομένου Ὑπερίονος αἰπὰ κέλευθα
νύξ τε καὶ ἠριγένεια καὶ ἐκ Διὸς ὁππόσα βουλῆς
γίνεται. (. . .)

The sun set. Dawn came down from
Heaven weeping for her beloved son, and around her
Came her twelve fair-haired maidens, whose task
Is always the high paths of revolving Hyperion,
Both night and dawn and as many things as Zeus
Decrees. (. . .)

The inclusion of this passage as illustrative of Zeus' omnipotence over fate is
puzzling. Zeus can decree (especially in his function of god of the heavens and
celestial functions) Dawn's domain and duties, without contradicting, undermining or interfering with fate's primacy. All things originate from Zeus but
are allocated by fate.

2.661–4:

δείδιε γὰρ <δὴ> Ζηνὸς ἄδην ἄλληκτον ἐνιπήν,
ἐξ οὗ πάντα πέλονται ὅσ' Ὠκεανοῖο ῥέεθρα
ἐντὸς ἔχει καὶ γαῖα καὶ αἰθομένων ἔδος ἄστρων.

But [Dawn] didn't forget her path,
For she was afraid of Zeus's firm and irreversible command,
From whom stem all things, as much as is contained within
The streams of Ocean, the earth itself and the seat of the shining stars.

Zeus as origin of all things in the world once again matches Nestor's 'fortunes
on the lap of the gods' idea, but the primacy and supremacy of Fate is not
undone by this passage – these are two very different things (compare Q.S.
14.100, below).

4.56–61:

ὣς ἄρ' ἔφη· τὴν δ' οὔ τι προσέννεπεν ἀκάματος Ζεύς.
Ἧστο γὰρ ἀχνύμενος κραδίην καὶ πολλὰ μενοινῶν,
οὕνεκεν ἤμελλον Πριάμου πόλιν ἐξαλαπάξειν
Ἀργεῖοι, τοῖς αἰνὸν ἐμήδετο λοιγὸν ὀπάσσαι
ἐν πολέμῳ στονόεντι καὶ ἐν βαρυηχέι πόντῳ·   60
καὶ τὰ μὲν ὣς ὥρμαινε τὰ δὴ μετόπισθε τέλεσσεν.

So she spoke but invincible Zeus didn't respond to her.
For he sat downcast in heart, lost in his thoughts.
Soon enough the Argives would destroy the city of
Priam, but he planned for them terrible ruin

In grievous war and in the loud-roaring sea.
The matters he so devised then he later brought about.

Zeus will indeed accomplish all of this, all of which has been fated – he is not
by any necessity undoing what Fate has already established, but is a character
fulfilling what has been fated.[43] As stated elsewhere in the primary narrative
in Q.S., by fate all things fade and all things grow – the means by which that
happens, in this case Zeus, are predicated upon fate.

8.458–60 (words of Nestor in battle):

Τοῖσι μὲν <ἄρ> τεράεσσι πιθώμεθα· τῷ γὰρ ἔοικε
πάντας <ἀεὶ> πεπιθέσθαι, ἐπεὶ μάλα φέρτατός ἐστιν
ἰφθίμων τε θεῶν ὀλιγοσθενέων τ' ἀνθρώπων.   460

We must obey these portents, as we all
Ought to obey such things, always, since he is by far the strongest
Of all mighty gods and short-lived men.

Again, there is no contradiction here. A dichotomy is made between gods and
men, but it is quite clear that fate is not included in the bracket 'gods', and
'all' refers to those traditional Olympians and mortals on earth. There is no
explicit statement here on Zeus's primacy over fate. Nestor goes on to speak
of the Titans and what happened to them when they challenged Zeus. None
of this refers to fate.

10.329–31:

(. . .) ἦ γὰρ ἔμελλον
κείνου ἀποφθιμένοιο καὶ αὐτῇ Κῆρες ἕπεσθαι   330
ἐσσυμένως· ὡς γάρ οἱ ἐπέκλωσε<ν> Διὸς Αἶσα.

(. . .) For the deathly Fates
Were about to meet her quickly after his
Death. For the fate of Zeus had so spun it for her.

Gärtner (2014: 99–100) states that this Iliadic formulation Διὸς Αἶσα illustrates
the *Gleichsetzung* (equal setting) between Zeus's will and that of fate. Rather,
I would argue, we have a repetition of what was found in Nestor's recasting
of the Iliadic jars of Zeus, once again. Things originate from Zeus (almost as

---

[43] Cf. Jupiter's pronouncement in Virgil, *Aeneid* 1.262: *volvens fatorum arcana movebo.*

though this is a genitive of origin, rather than a possessive genitive). In a discrete, non-oral text, the reader must qualify statements against clearer stipulations of the same theme. In this case, the reader already knows that the gods do not see nor dispense fortunes to men – only fate does, and throughout Q.S. it is *fate* which spins mortals' destinies. That is how we are to reread this formulation Διὸς Αἶσα in Homer, according to Quintus. There is no sense, again, that Fate is subordinate to Zeus.

Finally, 14.97–100:

> ἀλλ' οὐ μὰν ὑπὲρ Αἶσαν ἐελδόμενοί περ ἀμύνειν
> ἔσθενον· οὐδὲ γὰρ αὐτὸς ὑπὲρ μόρον οὐδὲ Κρονίων
> ῥηιδίως δύνατ' Αἶσαν ἀπωσέμεν, ὃς περὶ πάντων
> ἀθανάτων μένος ἐστί, Διὸς δ' ἐκ πάντα πέλονται.   100

But not beyond Fate were they strong enough to defend the city,
Despite their desire to do so. For even the son of Kronos himself cannot,
Beyond destiny, thrust Fate away lightly, Zeus who is the strongest
Of all the gods, and from whom are all things.

According to Gärtner (2014: 99), we find this contradiction already in Homer. There is indeed a lack of clarity in Homer, but it is not present in Quintus, even in this passage. I discuss these lines at length in my 2012 study (2012a: 117–18), and rehearse my findings briefly here: the Trojans cannot override fate, just as Zeus could not (as emphasised at the end of Book 13). ῥηιδίως (line 99) can be read as referring to what seemed possible in the *Iliad* – namely, that Zeus could easily ignore fate and follow his own course of action (in the cases, for example, of Sarpedon and Hector). Taken together with all of the passages on fate discussed above, what is *not* being emphasised here is that Zeus could still, even in the *PH*, thrust Fate away at all, easily *or* with difficulty. What seemed light for Zeus to accomplish in the *Iliad* was in fact impossible, even though Zeus is the strongest of the gods, and from whom all things originate that exist (Διὸς δ' ἐκ πάντα πέλονται). All things may come from him, but he has no control over outcomes, that is, whatever fate has in store.

CONCLUSION

Quintus presents a unified conception of fate in the *PH*: the references to fate and to the function of Zeus are not contradictory, but are couched in Homeric phrasing and settings which seem, in some places, to present a picture that is purely Homeric. Quintus had a difficult task to keep as closely as possible to the ideologies presented in the Homeric texts but to adapt the theology and cosmology into a uniform pattern, one clearly influenced by later philosophical systems.

In previous publications, I have followed Francis Vian and Alan James, among others, in seeing Stoic values in the *PH*, from the mountain of *Aretē* to the many stoical *gnōmai* throughout the poem. Gärtner raises the point, at the end of her article, that a true Stoic would not *blame* fate for their actions. In mainstream Stoic thinking this is correct. Is this a case of Quintus marrying Homeric and non-Homeric ideas, leaving the seams for all to see, or is there a more complex reason? It is undoubted that much of the non-Homeric philosophy in the *PH* is at least influenced by Stoicism or later developments of Stoicism. An obvious *desideratum* is the classification of the philosophies in Q.S. – can they be mapped on to extant Stoic treatises, of any of the three periods of Stoicism? It is simply not sufficient to state that something is not Stoic either because it is written after the flourishing of mainstream Stoicism, or because there are *some* statements which do not cohere with Stoicism. The opportunity remains open for categorisation to a more accurate and plausible degree of the non-Homeric philosophy of Q.S.

Ursula Gärtner's article, the impetus for this chapter, has moved scholarship forward in analysis of the motivation, whether personal or divine, of the poem's characters and their actions. She has proved beyond doubt the presence of double determinism in Q.S., yet another aspect in the poetics of the *PH* wherein Quintus carefully follows Homer. The representation of fate, like much of the poem's moral fabric, has Homeric semblances, but betrays later philosophical influences whereby Quintus reads Homer through a lens coloured by Stoicism, already centuries after the earliest Stoic readings of Homer. As much as Quintus exerts a Homeric identity, his belatedness is to the fore in his presentation of fate and the divine in the *PH*.

CHAPTER 7

Disempowering the Gods

Katia Barbaresco

W hen it comes to the divine in the *Posthomerica* (*PH*), anyone who reads this poem will mostly find the same gods as in Homer and Hesiod and will notice that they seem to behave very similarly to Homeric gods: they attend a divine council (*PH* 2.164–82), they intervene in mortal affairs (e.g. 3.26–92, Apollo kills Achilles; 5.360–4, Athena turns Ajax mad; 12.395–415, Athena blinds Laokoon and in 12.447–80 kills his children; 13.326–32, Aphrodite helps Aeneas escape), they interact and speak with mortals (e.g. Thetis in 4.95–7, 110–17), they even answer a prayer, sending Eurypylos to aid the Trojans (6.117–20), and they fight among themselves (12.160–216). All things considered, it doesn't surprise us if both Tychsen (1807) and Köchly (1850) thought that this poem should be dated to the pagan revival, approximately under the reign of Julian II (331–63 CE).[1] Although, as we have briefly hinted, the gods of the traditional pantheon appear and sometimes take action in the *PH*, they do so much less frequently and, above all, much less effectively.[2] In

I would like to thank the editors and also Prof. Alberto Camerotto, Prof. Filippomaria Pontani, Prof. Michael Trapp and Dr Pavlos Avlamis for their helpful suggestions and questions, all of which significantly improved this chapter. Of course, any mistakes that may remain are my own.

[1] Köchly (1850: IV–V). On a possible solution on the dating of the *PH*, see Baumbach and Bär (2007b: 1–8).

[2] According to Wenglinsky's (2002) analysis, the Olympians are mentioned 410 times in the *PH*, but 1,352 times in the *Iliad*: an Olympian gets mentioned once every 21 lines in the *PH*, once every 12 lines in the *Iliad*. She states (p. 44) that fewer mentions indicate minor importance 'in propelling the action of the *Posthomerica*'. See also Bär (2016: 218). On the gods' brief and perfunctory intervention in the *PH*, see James and Lee (2000: 11): 'One simply quantitative measure of this is the proportion of speeches spoken by deities, which is about 10 per cent in the *PH*. as a whole, compared with 27 per cent in the *Iliad*.' See Allan (2006) for a study on the long-stated difference between divine intervention and double motivation in the *Iliad*, the *Odyssey* and the wider corpus of early Greek hexameter poetry.

fact, Köchly had to state that Quintus' gods 'are only pale shadows patterned after the Homeric images, doing almost the same things, but lacking all blood and vigor, so that one could easily believe that the poet himself no longer had any faith in their vitality and power'.[3]

Scholarship on Quintus has come a long way since these first remarks, analysing various aspects of the divine in the *PH*. One of the characteristics that has often attracted scholarly attention is the relationship between the gods and the personifications of Fate:[4] as early as Köchly's edition, the abundance of passages where the Keres, Moirai and Aisa are said to have supreme control over both mortals and immortals was highlighted,[5] and more recent scholarship[6] has pointed out that, as the traditional divinities and their actions become less effective on mortal affairs, the personifications of Fate and minor gods often take on their role and narrative relevance.[7] In the last two decades much attention has been given to understanding why Quintus gives such great importance to Fate: it has been argued to reflect Stoic doctrine,[8] the popular philosophical trends of his time or a mixture of these elements.[9] Although some interpretative ideas will be proposed, the goal of this chapter is not to try and explain why traditional divinities are often superseded by the Keres, Moirai or Aisa in the *PH*. This study stems from the idea that Quintus does not merely replace the Homeric *Götterapparat* with the figures of Fate, but instead that the

---

[3] Translation by Paschal (1904: 40). Köchly (1850: v): *Dii quidem apud Quintum nil sunt nisi tenuissimae umbrae per imitationem pietatis fide fervoreque carentem ex splendidis Homeri imaginibus descriptae; agentes quidem eadem fere introducuntur, sed omni sanguine et vigore carent, ut facile videas poëtam ipsum de eorum vita et potestate nihil amplius credidisse.* Hedén (1912: 97) thinks that Quintus was a Christian.

[4] For a definition of 'personification', see Gärtner (2007: 213).

[5] Köchly (1850: v–vii).

[6] See Paschal (1904: 16, 40–3); Hedén (1912: 112–13, 187–8); Duckworth (1936: 64); Kakridis (1962: 164–78); Vian (1963: xv–xvi); Ferrari (1963: 13–16); García Romero (1985; 1986); Wenglinsky (2002: 76–83); James (2004: xxvii–xxix); Carvounis (2007); Gärtner (2007; 2014); Maciver (2012a: 108–13, 116–18); Bär (2016: 226–7); Ferreccio (2018: xxi–xxiv).

[7] Even though Apollonius of Rhodes also makes room for other divinities like Hekate and Rhea, the plot of the *Argonautica* is still determined, like the Homeric poems, by the gods of the traditional pantheon: most of the fourth *logos* talks about the *nostos* of the Argonauts, which is long and arduous because of Zeus' decision (4.557–61) to make the Argonauts suffer terribly all the way home. See Hunter (1993: 78, 88–9). The problematic relationship between mortals and gods in the *Argonautica* is well presented in Glei (²2008: 13–15), with references to important scholarly contributions. See also Elderkin (1906: 29–32); Klein (1931); Lesky (1966: 734); George (1972: 47–52); Feeney (1991: 57–98).

[8] Maciver (2007: 265–7; 2012a: 70–1, 106–7); Campagnolo (2010/11: 27–37); Langella (2016). In his study on the conception of the afterlife in the *PH*, Maciver (2017) considers not only Stoicism but also Orphism and neo-Pythagoreanism. Remarks on Stoicism in the *PH* are previously found in Paschal (1904: 11, 41); Vian (1959a: 27; 1963: xvi–xvii); García Romero (1985; 1986; 1989a; 1989b; 1990). See also Maciver's contribution in this volume.

[9] Gärtner (2014: 105, 126), where she concludes that the *PH* is certainly not anti-Stoic, but neither paradigmatically Stoic. See also Kakridis (1962: 171–81); Bertone (2000: 69–71).

author's behaviour towards the gods is twofold: whenever tradition does not strictly require the gods' presence or intervention, he puts into action various techniques and uses certain expressions to deprive the traditional gods – and especially the Olympians – of their influence over mortals; on the other hand, when tradition requires it, and also in the descriptive parts, he retains their effective role. Understanding Quintus' twofold usage of the gods clarifies why at first sight we sense the presence of the traditional divinities in this poem, but at the same time we cannot shake off the feeling that they lack 'all blood and vigor'.[10] On the one hand this chapter considers the different sequences of the poem, showing both that the Olympians are somehow actively present in the descriptive parts of the poem as much as (or even more than) in the narrative ones, and that the descriptive parts are a means to unearth and resonate with some Homeric passages or peculiar mythical variants. On the other hand, it analyses some passages in which Quintus makes his lack of belief in the Olympian gods and in their intervention clear.[11]

WHEN AND WHY DO QUINTUS' OLYMPIANS NOT ACT?

We have already stated that Quintus' Olympians do not usually intervene in mortal matters: indeed, they themselves sometimes prevent other divinities from actively reacting to what happens in Troy.[12] More often than not it is Zeus who holds the other Olympians off: after the death of Penthesileia, her father Ares would have wanted to take revenge on Achilles and the Myrmidons (1.675–88), but he is stopped by Zeus's lightning and thunderbolts; during the only divine council of the *PH* (2.164–82)[13] Zeus deters the Olympians from going on the battlefield and pleading with him to save any of the fighting mortals, but no later than the next day, Eos deflects the sharp spears from her son Memnon (2.289–90), and later, while Achilles is duelling with Memnon, the gods would have

---

[10] See my note 3 above. Cf. Paschal (1904: 41): 'In his portrayal of the gods it cannot be doubted that Quintus has made an effort to preserve their Homeric character. Perhaps he never admitted to himself that he had lost faith in them. At any rate, it will be patent to any reader that his gods have nearly the same relations among themselves and to the Greeks and Trojans as in Homer. In fact, he seems to take pains that this shall be so.' See also Elderkin (1906: 29): 'Even in the stronghold of epic Zeus and Athena have lost power. In noticeable fashion they and Hera recede from immediate participation in the events of the *Posthomerica*.'

[11] Some of the arguments here expressed have lately benefited from the thorough analysis of the gods in the *PH* in Wenglinsky's (2002) unpublished doctoral dissertation.

[12] About gods preventing other gods from interfering with mortals, see Bär (2016: 219), who considers this an inner-fictional fact that transforms Homeric double motivation into 'what one might call Posthomeric "double motivation *ex negativo*"'.

[13] On the singularity of this theme in the *PH*, in contrast with Quintus' much more often over-Homerisation, see Bär (2016: 220–2).

burst into fighting (2.507–13) had not Zeus intervened sending the Keres to the heroes' side, thus sealing the outcome of the duel. It is instead Athena who prevents Ares from facing Neoptolemos in a duel (8.340–3), and Zeus steps in with thunder[14] only after, to prevent the two gods from fighting among themselves. When Apollo leaps down from Olympos to strike Neoptolemos down (just like he did with his father Achilles in 3.26–62), the god is at first restrained by birds of omen and other signs (9.308–9), but eventually decides to act anyway and is stopped by the intervention of Poseidon (9.309–23), who tells him to go back to the sky, lest Troy be swallowed into the ground.

Although they do not succeed in their attempts, we must notice that the gods do try several times to interfere with mundane issues, as if they did not remember having agreed with Zeus not to meddle with mortals in the second *logos* (2.164–82). Why do they behave like this? Quintus must surely know that the Homeric gods also tried – and sometimes managed – to take part in Trojan and Achaean affairs even after Zeus's prohibition on doing so (*Il.* 8.10–40).[15] If we should not expect the Homeric poems to be utterly consistent, since their discrepancies probably 'arise from the oral technique of composition by themes and formulas',[16] should we postulate a similar reason to interpret the numerous attempts of Quintus' gods to meddle with mortals? Or is Quintus only trying to emulate Homer also in this respect? As Włodzimierz Appel (1994b) and Mario Cantilena (2001) convincingly stated, it is probable that the fourteen *logoi* were composed in writing one at a time to be recited in public at competitive festivals, and were put together only later by the author, thus creating the *PH* as we now know it.[17] This kind of composition would explain not only the gods' attempts

---

[14] On Zeus's use of thunder in the *PH*, see Carvounis (2008: 66–71).

[15] Cf. *Il.* 5.755–67, where Zeus sends Athena to stop Ares on the Trojan plain. See how many times the Olympians try to intervene even in the books following Zeus's prohibition: *Il.* 8.198–212 (Hera refrained by Poseidon), 311 (Apollo diverts an arrow from Hektor), 350–484 (Hera and Athena are stopped by Iris, sent by Zeus), 10.515–25 (Athena and Apollo go among the ranks), 11.163–4 (Zeus saves Hektor), 11.402–3 (Zeus saves Sarpedon), 13.1–80 and 206–39 (Poseidon goes among the ranks), 351–60 (both Poseidon and Zeus go among the ranks), 434–44 (Poseidon makes Idomeneus kill Alkathoos). On the divine *stasis* in *Iliad* 8, see Kelly (2007: 44–7, 422–5); on its aftermath, see Carvounis (2008: 64–5). On the initial lack of response of the gods to Zeus's prohibition, see Person (1995); Foley (1995); Porter (2011).

[16] Lord (1938: 440). For the oral theory, which explains such discrepancies as an inevitable byproduct of oral composition in performance, unconcerned about self-contradiction, see also Notopoulos (1964: 48). For the analytic theory, that considers these inconsistencies as proof of the *Iliad*'s origins in multiple sources, see Kullmann (1960; 1981; 1991); Burgess (2015). For a different approach that construes 'the contradictions as evidence for the view that while Homer has asked for one story, the Muse has given him another slightly different story', see Satterfield (2011: 1–20). Cf. *Od.* 8.492–502, when Odysseus asks Demodokos for a story, but Demodokos starts his tale from another point of the *oimē*. See Camerotto (2009: 33–4).

[17] Appel (1994b: 4–5) understands the title τὰ μεθ' Ὅμηρον as τὰ μεθ' Ὅμηρον ἔπη. Agosti (2006: 40–9) suggests that some parts of Nonnus' *Dionysiaca* might also have been recited in public.

to interfere in the *logoi* following the second one – which strikes us as strange, since Quintus' gods usually respect Zeus's orders[18] – but also major discrepancies: in *logoi* 6–9 the Achaean wall suddenly appears but is never mentioned in any of the other preceding or following *logoi*; in 10.343–60 Hera and the Seasons speak about the imminent wedding of Helen to Deiphobos, Helenos' resentment and capture by the Achaeans, the killing of Alkathoos and the taking of the Palladion, but none of these events, albeit included in the *Little Iliad*, will eventually be narrated extensively in the *PH*.[19] If considering the various *logoi* almost as independent would account for most of the gods' attempts from the third *logos* onwards, it would still not justify the instances in the second *logos*, namely Eos' effective intervention to shield her son (2.289–90) and the Olympians' shot at fighting among themselves (2.507–13).

Therefore, I would like to suggest another explanation: Quintus does not seem to like the Olympians having overt influence over mortals, but at the same time he cannot totally suppress the divine and mythological presence, since it is, as Eustathius would later say, 'the soul of poetry'.[20] When compared to the gods' great importance in propelling the action in archaic epic, sometimes Quintus' divinities give us the impression of being defunctionalised characters. As we will see in this chapter, Quintus uses various techniques to disempower his gods while keeping them in his poem. Making gods hinder one another is one of them: it is a means to involve the Olympians in his narrative without making them have a real influence over mortals' life. In these aborted attempts to intervene on the battlefield Quintus displays a peculiar usage of *if not*-situations.[21] By saying that Ares 'would have made that day a day of grief for the Myrmidons had not Zeus himself on Olympus scared him'[22]

---

[18] For the prominent role of Zeus among the other gods in the *PH*, see Vian (1963: XVI); Wenglinsky (2002: 45–9, 166–76). Cf. *PH* 12.206–16.

[19] On this prophecy, see Mondino (1957: 134–6, 139); cf. Tychsen (1807: XLIII); Köchly (1850: XXXI–XXXII).

[20] Eust. *in Il.* B 450–2 (van der Valk 252.27–8): ψυχὴ γάρ τις οἷον ὁ μῦθος τῷ τῆς ποιήσεως σώματι δι' ὅλου παρενεσπαρμένος αὐτοῦ: 'for myth is a soul, as it were, to the body of poetry, being strewn throughout it' (translation by van den Berg 2017). Van den Berg (2017: 130): 'Myths are thus essential to poetry (. . .) and can be invented completely at the poet's own discretion. Eustathios especially considers tales involving the gods to be mythical.' Cf. Eustathius, *in Il.* A 1 (van der Valk 11.8–9).

[21] For a definition of *if not*-situation, see de Jong (²2004a: 68): 'In the *Iliad* we find 38 passages of the type: "and now x would have happened, if somebody had not done y". I call these passages *if not*-situations and consider them a special type of counterfactuals.' For Homer's usage of *if not*-situations, see also van den Berg (2017: 143–4). Quintus' *if not*-situations ('Beinahe-Episoden') have been studied in Nesselrath (1992: 53–66; 2019: 579–82), with a special focus on their structure and wording. On Quintus' usage of *if not*-situations to envision events that are impossible for cultural reasons, see Barbaresco (2021).

[22] This and all the other translations of the *PH*, unless otherwise stated, are taken from Hopkinson (2018). All translations of the *Iliad* and the *Odyssey* are those of Murray and Wyatt (²1999) and Murray and Dimock (²1999), respectively.

(1.689–90), the intervention of Ares on the battlefield is only envisioned, but never actually comes to pass. If we look at the other divine attempts to interfere with mortals, we realise that this way of avoiding divine intervention becomes a pattern, for these *if not*-situations are used three out of four times: 'the gods would have fallen into a fierce fight among themselves had not Zeus' sent the Keres (2.507–11), and Ares would have 'openly fought against [Neoptolemos] himself' and would even have revealed his supernatural nature to the mortals,[23] had not Athena stepped in to stop him (8.341–3).[24] Thanks to this narrative strategy, the poet creates a sense of suspense by describing an alternative situation to his audience: he gives a glimpse of what a deity could do, thus increasing expectations and catalysing the attention of the public,[25] and then he immediately brings the plot back to its course, thus excluding any real divine interference in the life of mortals. Since the listeners and readers already know how the story ends, the poet's artistry lies in his ability to create prospects that differ from the traditional plot and in his constant threats to do what cannot be done, viz. violate the traditional plot. If in the Homeric poems *if not*-situations usually imply the intervention of a god (or a great hero) to save a mortal[26] or to prevent the defeat of Achaeans or Trojans,[27] in these three instances Quintus uses this narrative technique for a different purpose: the gods no longer intervene to solve otherwise unsolvable situations, but it is their very involvement that seems unutterable, almost beyond belief, just like

---

[23] On the visibility of the gods on the battlefield in the *PH* and *Iliad*, see Barbaresco (forthcoming).

[24] Nesselrath (1992: 58), after having compared this episode with Hes. *Scut.* 443–56, states that in this case Quintus shifted from a confrontation between god and man (Ares vs Neoptolemos) to a purely divine level (Ares vs Athena and then Zeus). He demonstrates that, when it comes to the 'Beinahe-Episoden', later Greek epic poets like Quintus seem to follow Homer's (and especially the *Iliad*'s) steps rather than Apollonius of Rhodes' ones (Nesselrath 1992: 48). As Vian (1988: 290) notices, conflicts among the Olympians cease only after the theomachy in *PH* 12.

[25] Cf. *schol.* bT Hom. *Il.* Θ 217a (Erbse): καί νύ κ' ἐνέπρησεν: εἰς ἄκρον τοὺς κινδύνους εἴωθεν ἐξάγειν ἀεί, καὶ ἐναγώνιον ποιήσας τὸν ἀκροατὴν τῇ προσδοκίᾳ εὐθὺς τὴν ἴασιν ἐπιφέρει. 'He (sc. Homer) is wont always to maximise the danger, and having put the reader in a state of agony by means of the expectation, he at once adduces the remedy' (translation in Nünlist 2009). On ἐναγώνιος and *if not*-situations, see Nünlist (2009: 142–3).

[26] Divine intervention in narrator text: *Il.* 3.373–5, 5.22–4, 311–13, 15.459–64, 20.288–91, 21.211–13, 22.202–4; hero's intervention: *Il.* 5.679–80, 7.104–8, 8.90–1, 17.613–14. Divine intervention in character text: *Il.* 11.750–2, 18.454–6. Gods saving other gods in character text: *Il.* 5.388–90 (Hermes saves Ares), 14.258–9 (Night saves Hypnos), 18.397–9 (Eurynome and Thetis help Hephaistos).

[27] *Il.* 2.155–6, 8.130–2, 217–18, 12.290–3, 16.698–701, 17.319–25, 21.544–6. The Trojan retreat is avoided thanks to the seer Helenos in 6.73–6, to Polydamas' advice in 13.723–5; the Achaeans' retreat happens thanks to Paris' killing of Machaon in 11.504–7. All these passages are commented in de Jong (²2004a: 70–81).

the death of a great hero or the premature victory of a party, and therefore can only be envisaged.[28]

As for Eos' diversion of the Achaean spears that would have otherwise hit her son Memnon (2.289–90), I think that, just like the Homeric narrator, not even Quintus is primarily focused on avoiding self-contradiction: the motif of a god deflecting a weapon from his or her protégé was so widely used in epic (e.g. *Il.* 4.127–39, 8.309–12, 13.554–5, 15.458–65, 521–3, Hes. *Scut.* 455–6)[29] that – as Alessia Ferreccio suggests – it would have hardly bothered any reader[30] – or, I would add, any listener: in this case the topos overpowers the need for consistency. At any rate, Eos' intervention is not totally effective, since it does not stop Memnon from dying.

WAS IT REALLY GOD'S WORK?

Quintus seems to be at pains to involve gods in narrative and yet he tries to do it as unobtrusively as possible. Sometimes he does so by hinting at an alleged intervention of the gods in mortal matters, other times by inserting the adverb που, 'maybe, supposedly'. Homer uses this adverb only in the speeches of characters, who often employ it when speaking of the gods, their doings and belongings,[31] whereas three times in Apollonius' *Argonautica* it is the author himself who voices overt uncertainty over divine doings (1.996–7, 1.1140, 4.557–8):[32] if Homeric characters use που because they are not all-knowing,[33]

---

[28] In Homer there is only one *if not*-situation that describes a god intervening to prevent another god from meddling with humans: in *Il.* 15.121–42 Zeus would have burst out with anger at the other gods, had Athena not kept Ares from killing Deiphobos to avenge his son Askalaphos. Yet here the focus is not, as in the *PH*, on the aftermath for humans, but rather on the wrath of Zeus towards the other Olympians. See de Jong (²2004a: 76–7); Nesselrath (1992: 27; 2019: 573, 580). Similarly – although they are not formally *if not*-situations – the two episodes when Zeus considers sparing Sarpedon (*Il.* 16.431–8) and Hektor (*Il.* 22.167–76) 'raise the possibility that Zeus could bring about a radically different outcome', as Allan (2006: 8) states, and thus create tension, which is dissolved only after Hera's and Athena's words. Cf. Call. *Hymn. Del.* 133–52, where the river-god Peneios offers to let Leto give birth by his streams, but then Ares arrives and, being enraged, is about to destroy the river: this does not happen only because Leto gives in, thanks Peneios and moves on to another island.

[29] See Fenik (1968: 67, 104, 142). Quintus modifies this scheme in 7.595 (divine armour stops the weapons), 11.479–80 (both Aphrodite and the shield stop the blows), 13.187 (see p. 129, below), 13.326–32 (Aphrodite clears the road to let her son and his family pass).

[30] Ferreccio (2014: 164). See also Vian (1963: 66, n7).

[31] Bolling (1929: 100) cites *Il.* 1.178, 2.116, 3.308, 9.23, 10.70, 13.225, 14.69, 120, 16.514, 21.83, *Od.* 4.74, 4.181, 6.173, 190, 9.262, 11.139, 14.119, 227, 17.424, 19.80. See also Ebeling (1880, -85) s.v. που.

[32] On Homer's and Apollonius' usage of που, see Hunter (1993: 108–9); Cuypers (2005: 41–5).

[33] Sicking (1993: 59): 'With που a speaker presents his statement as a surmise whose accuracy he does not vouch for.'

in these instances Apollonius too seems to deduce the facts of his story, rather than knowing them.[34] This can recall Herodotus, who also uses κου in narrator-text (e.g. 5.1.3, 7.214.2) to speak about divine signs, like the earthquake in 6.98.1 and a divine dream in 7.12.1.[35] Although in *PH* 1.360–1 and 13.234–5 που is found in the speeches of an anonymous Trojan and of Priam, who speak about the will of Zeus and the decision of the Keres,[36] Quintus generally seems to follow Herodotus' and Apollonius' lead, using it many times, also for Eos' intervention (2.290).[37] The narrator is uncertain about Memnon's habitation after his death: he might be in the House of Hades or among the blessed ones in the Elysian plain: *PH* 2.650–2, εἰν Ἀίδαο δόμοισιν / ἠέ που ἐν μακάρεσσι κατ' Ἠλύσιον πέδον αἴης.[38] When Apollo and the Winds take Glaukos' body to Lykia and the nymphs create an ever-flowing river, the author says that this was supposedly made by the immortals to honour Glaukos (4.11–12, ἀλλὰ τὰ μέν που / ἀθάνατοι τεύξαντο γέρας Λυκίων βασιλῆι, 'such were the honours paid by the immortal gods to the king of the Lycians'). During the running race at Achilles' funeral, when the runners are about to reach the finish, Teukros trips: perhaps it was the immortals who stopped his limbs, for 'some god or evil spirit made him trip over the annoying branch of a deep-rooted tamarisk bush' (4.200–2, δὴ τότε που Τεύκροιο μένος καὶ γυῖα πέδησαν / ἀθάνατοι· τὸν γάρ ῥα θεὸς βάλεν ἠέ τις ἄτη / ὅζον ἐς ἀλγινόεντα βαθυρρίζοιο μυρίκης).[39] Antiphos does not die at the hands of Eurypylos, because he is supposed to be killed by the Kyklops, since this appears to please Moira (8.127, ὡς γάρ που στυγερῇ ἐπιήνδανε Μοίρῃ, 'such was the pleasure of hateful Fate'). The warrior Kleodoros is shot to death by Paris' arrows, and this may have been decided by a *daimōn*: 10.220–1, ὡς γάρ νύ που ἤθελε δαίμων / θήσειν αἰνὸν ὄλεθρον, 'no doubt in accordance with the will of some god who wished to

---

[34] See Cuypers (2005: 40, 44).

[35] On these passages, see Sicking (1993: 57–8).

[36] Cf. *PH* 7.195–7: Οὐ γὰρ ἔοικε / θνητῶν τεύχεσι κεῖνα, θεοῦ δέ που Ἄρεος ὅπλοις / ἶσα πέλει, where Odysseus tells Neoptolemos that his father's arms are not like the arms of mortals, but can be considered as good as those of Ares. See Tsomis (2018a: 146).

[37] In his unpublished doctoral dissertation Boyten (2010: 254–60) offers a table of interactional particles, and links Quintus' usage of που to that of Herodotus.

[38] As noted by Maciver (2017: 135), the whole *PH* is incoherent in its presentation of the Netherworld.

[39] Cf. *Il.* 23.773–6, where it is Athena that makes Ajax slip on excrement (ἀλλ' ὅτε δὴ τάχ' ἔμελλον ἐπαΐξασθαι ἄεθλον, / ἔνθ' Αἴας μὲν ὄλισθε θέων, βλάψεν γὰρ Ἀθήνη, / τῇ ῥα βοῶν κέχυτ' ὄνθος ἀποκταμένων ἐριμύκων, / οὓς ἐπὶ Πατρόκλῳ πέφνεν πόδας ὠκὺς Ἀχιλλεύς), and Verg. *Aen.* 5.327–30, where there is no divine involvement in Nisus' slipping on blood (*iamque fere spatio extremo fessique sub ipsam / finem adventabant, levi cum sanguine Nisus / labitur infelix, caesis ut forte iuvencis / fusus humum viridisque super madefecerat herbas*). Quintus, whose divinities intervene only here in the *athla*, appears not to choose any of these versions, but instead he lets his audience choose what happens. On the meaning of *atē* in the *PH*, see Ozbek (2007: 173, n23).

bring death'. The authorial voice states that 'the gods must have made (. . .) for mortals to admire' (11.97–8, ἀλλὰ τὸ μέν που / ἀθάνατοι τεύξαντο καὶ ἐσσομένοισιν ἰδέσθαι) the rock of Korykos – the birthplace of the slain warrior Archelochos – inside which there is a perpetual fire that burns the roots of the palm trees that grow around it, and yet they bear abundant fruit. Athena is explicitly said to determine the death of Laokoon's sons (12.447–8), whilst the setting of the cave where the two mighty serpents, 'surviving spawn of dread Typhon', lived at that time (12.451, ναίεσκον ἔτ') is described as mythical: by stating that it is only said to be beneath a rugged rock (12.449, δὴ γάρ που πέλεν ἄντρον ὑπὸ στυφελώδεϊ πέτρῃ) and by calling it dark and inaccessible to mortals (12.450, ἠερόεν, θνητοῖσιν ἀνέμβατον), the author seems to be detached from the supernatural framework of this killing.

In none of these instances but the last is an Olympian mentioned as the one responsible for the happenings: in *PH* 4.12, 401, 11.98 it is the immortals, in 8.127 Moira and in 10.220 it is a *daimōn*. The same thing occurs in 13.544–51, where Laodike is said to have 'stretched her arms to the sky and prayed to the blessed, unwearying gods that the earth should swallow her up before she sullied her hands by working as a slave'. Not only do we find here the impersonal form 'they say' (13.545, ἐνέπουσιν) and the unspecified 'blessed ones' (13.546, εὐχομένην μακάρεσσιν ἀτειρέσιν), but not even afterwards do we discover which of the gods takes action: it is just 'one of the gods' (13.548, θεῶν τις; 549 ἐννεσίῃσι θεοῖο) that hears and answers Laodike's prayer.[40] Right after Laodike is swallowed by the earth, Quintus tells of the faintness of Elektra, one of the stars of the Pleiades, who is again said (13.551, φασι) to conceal 'her body in mist and cloud' (13.552–3, ἑὸν δέμας ἀμφικαλύψαι / ἀχλύι καὶ νεφέεσσιν), becoming 'hidden and unseen' out of grief for the destruction of her son's city (13.556–7, ἣ δ' ἄρα μούνη / κεύθεται αἰὲν ἄιστος).[41] Quintus' scepticism is expressed not only by the generic and impersonal verbal forms, but best of all by the statement that follows these two episodes, 'perhaps the immortal gods' good sense brought these things to pass, and perhaps not' (13.560–1, ἀλλὰ τὸ μέν που / ἀθανάτων τάχ' ἔρεξεν ἐὺς νόος ἠὲ καὶ οὐκί), where not only do we find the που, but also τάχα, 'maybe, probably': almost like an historian, Quintus does not say if this was the gods' doing or not, but

---

[40] Laodike's prayer is taken into account in Wenglinsky (2002: 317), whereas Schubert (2007: 350–2), after Vian (1969: 119, 123–4), explains why this alleged episode takes place right after Aethra's one. Other versions of Laodike's myth (Lyc. *Alex.* 314–22, 494–503, schol. Lyc. *Alex.* 319a Leone, Euph. fr. 58 Powell, Parth. *Narr. am.* 16, Apoll. *Epit.* 5.25, Plut. *Cim.* 4.6, Paus. 10.26.7, Triph. 660–3) are examined by Ciampa (2009).

[41] This myth too is found only in post-classical authors such as Ov. *Fast.* 4.177–8 and Hyg. *Fab.* 192 (cf. schol. A Hom. *Il.* Σ 486 Erbse, schol. MDΔVUA Arat. *Phaen.* 259 Martin) and commentaries (Serv. *in Georg.* 1.138, Eust. in *Il.* Σ 485 van der Valk 1155.56–7). On Elektra's story, see Gärtner (1999) and Vian (1969: 151, nn6–7).

reports the events as alleged by some (13.545, ἐνέπουσιν; 13.551, φασι).[42] The author chooses to place this assertion at a programmatic point, almost at the closure of this *logos*, thus declaring his lack of belief in these myths, just before going back to the mortals' doings in Troy, where the Argives are ravaging the city, and Eris, 'Strife incarnate', holds the battle's issues.[43] The adverb που is found again right at the end of the *PH*, after the storm that makes most of the Achaeans shipwreck: although Quintus does say that it is Poseidon that causes the earthquake that destroys the Achaean wall (14.646–54), the author seems to be more focused on the naturalistic than on the divine side of the phenomenon, as noticed by Vian,[44] and then he comments: 'Such it seems (ἀλλὰ τὰ μέν που) was the result of the immortal gods' resentment' (*PH* 14.654–5).[45] As it happens, Quintus' account of the Trojan War ends with the surviving Achaeans being guided in their voyages not by a named deity, but by an anonymous god (14.657, θεός).

There is still one more turn of phrase that causes us to believe that Quintus 'no longer had any faith in [the Olympians'] vitality and power':[46] the expression 'one of the gods' that we have just found in Laodike's episode (13.548). Just like the που, this too is meaningful because it is the authorial voice that uses it and not only the characters. In Homer the idea that it is 'one of the gods' that intervenes in mortal matters is found only in character-speech, for the narrator usually states which one of the gods actually takes action,[47]

---

[42] On Herodotus' *Zurückhaltung* on divine matters and habit of not naming the god who intervenes, see Roettig (2010: 88–97). On divine (and thus?) contested (ἀμφήριστον) myths, see Call. *Hymn. Jov.* 4–8, where the poet says that he is in doubt (ἐν δοιῇ μάλα θυμός) because some say (φασι) that Zeus was born in the Idaean mountains, some others in Arkadia. About this hymn, see, among others, Fuhrer and Hunter (2002), and Hopkinson (1984: 144): 'whether or not Callimachus believes in the Zeus he here represents, and, if he did, whether he believed these particular myths of his birth and portion to be the true ones – these questions are as irrelevant as they are unanswerable.'

[43] Way's (1913) translation of *PH* 13.563. This verse is omitted by the Hydruntinus branch of the tradition. Vian notes that οὐκί (13.561) is suspected by many, but puts it in his edition, along with other editors like Köchly, who however proposes ἠέ τις Αἶσα (cf. Apoll. Rhod. 3.328, Ζηνὸς νόος ἠέ τις αἶσα) or ἠδὲ καὶ ἀλκή in his apparatus. Zimmermann conjectures ἠέ καὶ αὐταί (13.559, Μοίραις). Cf. ἠὲ καὶ οὐκί in *Il.* 2.238, 300, 10.445, *Od.* 1.268 (about a divine decision), 4.80, 632, 11.493. Some of my comments on Elektra's episode are drawn from Vian (1969: 151, n8). On Zeus and the Moirai in 13.558–60, see Gärtner (2007: 226, 239).

[44] Vian (1969: 203, n3). See also Carvounis (2019: 281–2).

[45] Ἀλλὰ τὸ/τὰ μέν που is used in *Od.* 4.181 of a god's jealousy, and later by Quintus only and only for divine actions: 3.624 (Zeus), 4.11 (the immortals), 10.342 (Zeus), 11.97 (the immortals), 13.234 (the Keres), 13.560 (the immortals), 14.167 (Oblivion), 14.654 (the immortals).

[46] Köchly; see my note 3 above.

[47] Character-speech: *Il.* 5.191, θεός νύ τις, but also τις (. . .) θεῶν, θεῶν (. . .) τις, or οὔ τις (. . .) θεῶν (*Il.* 13.55, Poseidon takes Kalchas' likeness; 68, Ajax does not recognise Poseidon; 15.290, Thoas does not recognise Apollo; 17.338, Aeneas recognises Apollo but tells his comrades that 'one of the gods' spoke to him). *Il.* 17.469, τίς τοί νυ θεῶν; 20.453, 24.374, 564, *Od.* 5.221, 10.157,

and the same can be said of Apollonius' *Argonautica*, although it is rare for not even the author to name the god that has intervened.[48] Although Quintus does place expressions like θεός (12.254), δαίμων (1.723, 5.181, 12.255), κακὸς δε τις (. . .) δαίμων (5.422), θεὸς ἤ δαίμων τις (9.229), θεῶν (. . .) τις (9.262), ἀθανάτων τις (3.42), οὐδὲ θεῶν τις (13.472) in dialogical sequences, he also employs them in narrative ones.[49] In 1.380 it is one of the blessed (μακάρων τις) that holds Achilles and Ajax away from the fray, and also that clears the battlefield of the dust in 2.481, whereas either a god or a *daimōn* is said to save some of the shipwrecked mortals in 14.627–8.[50] It is known that Homeric characters do not name the divinities they interact with because they are disguised or impossible to identify, whereas the authorial voice, being all-knowing, does name them. Rather than thinking that the *PH*'s author (or the *Argonautica*'s) – who often does not name the gods that interact with mortals – is not all-knowing, I think that this type of expression intentionally displays Quintus' distance from the Homeric *Götterapparat*.

One of the most significant cases that shows Quintus' detachment is in 9.80–2, where the intervention of any god at all is doubted: Deiphobos is 'either emboldened and made fearless by some god or self-prompted to war' (καὶ τότ' ἄρ' ἢὲ θεῶν τις ὑπὸ φρένας ἔμβαλε θάρσος / Δηιφόβῳ καὶ θῆκε μάλ' ἄτρομον, ἢὲ καὶ αὐτόν / θυμὸς ἐποτρύνεσκε ποτὶ κλόνον). Although a situation in which divine intervention is questioned can already be found in

---

18.407; 22.429, τις θεός; 24.182, 373. *Od.* 14.178; 23.63, τις ἀθανάτων; 15.46, ἀθανάτων ὅς τις. In *Od.* 4.364–5 Odysseus, who is both a narrator and a character here at the same time, after the usual τις (. . .) θεῶν mentions the name of Eidoteia. In *Il.* 6.108 the authorial voice says that the Achaeans fear that a god (τιν' ἀθανάτων) has descended from the sky to help their enemies, but this is clearly the perspective of the mortals, not that of Homer. A *daimōn* is said to be the one responsible for the happenings in *Od.* 6.172, 10.64, 17.445. On these expressions in the Homeric poems that usually entail that the mortal has not recognised the god that has intervened, see Chantraine (1952: 50–6).

[48] Apoll. Rhod. 1.820, τις θεός; 871, τις (. . .) θεός; 2.316, τι θεῶν χατέωσι νόοιο; 3.323, θεὸς δέ τις; 691, τις θεός; 776, θεὸς ἤ τις Ἐρινύς. Apoll. Rhod. 1.681; 4.1591, μακάρων τις. On θεός, δαίμων and που in the *Odyssey* and in Apoll. Rhod., see Feeney (1991: 85–9). On the *Argonautica*'s narrator, who does not have full knowledge of events, see Knight (1995: 286–9).

[49] The frequency of some of these expressions is listed in one of Wenglinsky's (2002: 38) useful tables, although she comes to a conclusion with which I disagree (42): 'the very fact that the poet attributes actions to unidentifiable divine entities indicates that he conceives of a unified divine power, of which individual deities represent, as it were, various aspects, united in purpose.' Kakridis (1962: 164–7) thinks, after Hedén (1912), that these expressions are due to Quintus' ἀμηχανία to choose a particular deity: this inability is caused by his great distance from the Homeric gods.

[50] Vian (1969: 201, n8) briefly compares this passage with Aesch. *Ag.* 661–3, but in the tragedy the messenger says that it was not a mortal but a god that saved them from the shipwreck: ἡμᾶς γε μὲν δὴ ναῦν τ' ἀκήρατον σκάφος / ἤτοι τις ἐξέκλεψεν ἤ 'ξῃτήσατο / θεός τις, οὐκ ἄνθρωπος, οἴακος θιγών.

Il. 6.438–9, ἤ πού τίς σφιν ἔνισπε θεοπροπίων εὖ εἰδώς, / ἤ νυ καὶ αὐτῶν θυμὸς
ἐποτρύνει καὶ ἀνώγει ('either someone well skilled in soothsaying told them,
or perhaps their own heart urges and commands them to it'), and in *Od.*
16.356–7, ἤ τίς σφιν τόδ' ἔειπε θεῶν, ἠ' εἴσιδον αὐτοί / νῆα παρερχομένην
('either some god told them of this, or they themselves caught sight of the
ship of Telemachus as she sailed by'), it must be noticed that both of these
are character-speeches, whereas in the *PH* the statement is made by the narrator.[51] Similarly, in the *Argonautica*'s προέκδοσις Hypsipyle does not know
the reason for the madness of her people: 'it might have been either from
a god or from their own folly' (*schol.* L Apoll. Rhod. 1.801–3b Wendel, ἐν
δὲ τῇ προεκδόσει· (. . .) καὶ τότ' ἔπειτ' ἀνὰ δῆμον ἄατος ἔμπεσε λύσσα, οὐκ
οἶδ' ἤ θεόθεν ἤ αὐτῶν ἀφροσύνῃσι). The final edition of the *Argonautica* tells
us instead that the cause of the disaster was the anger of Aphrodite. Things
are different in the *PH*: in 13.187 the old Ilioneus begs Diomedes to spare
him, and the hero is said to be restrained for a moment either by a god
or by a momentary forgetfulness of his anger (ἤ χόλου ἀμβολίη ἤ καὶ θεοῦ
ὀτρύνοντος), but eventually decides to kill his enemy, as is the norm in epic.
Therefore, if the two Homeric instances can be explained as peculiar types of
'listing (. . .) possible alternative motives (cf. e.g. *Il.* 5.811f.)',[52] the *PH* cases
reveal a different motive: since the alternatives are uttered by the authorial
voice, it appears that it is the author himself that does not believe in any
divine intervention in the business of battle.

WHEN AND WHY DO QUINTUS' OLYMPIANS ACT?

Although on the aforementioned occasions Quintus uses *if not*-situations to
avoid actual divine intervention, makes anonymous deities intervene or even
questions their very intervention, sometimes the Olympians do intervene
in the *PH*, both in descriptive sequences and occasionally also in narrative
ones, thus causing major progress in the plot. In considering Quintus' handling of the gods we need to reflect on what we deem as divine action, for
it can be nuanced: it could take not only the form of divine councils, where
decisions about mortal matters are made, or of verbal or physical interactions

[51] Aristarchus athetised *Il.* 5.433–9 as inappropriate for Andromache. Cf. Apoll. Rhod. 3.327–8,
καί σφ' ἀπέρυκεν / ἡμέας οἰκτείρων Ζηνὸς νόος ἠέ τις αἶσα, again in character-speech, and Verg.
Aen. 12.320–2, *incertum qua pulsa manu, quo turbine adacta, / (. . .) casusne deusne, / attulerit; pressa
est insignis gloria facti*, where the authorial voice asks whether it was chance or a god (Iuturna?)
that hit Aeneas.

[52] Kirk (1990: 219). For double motivation in the *PH*, see Gärtner's (2014) study, which is more
focused on the statements found in character-speech – where characters try to justify themselves by blaming the gods or the Keres – than on the authorial voice.

between gods and humans, but could also entail gods interacting with each other without mortals even realising it or the recollection of the great deeds of the Olympians in descriptive sequences, namely similes and excursuses.

As for the interaction of one or more gods with one another, we can mention the grand scene of the *theomachia* in *PH* 12.160–216, where, even though the divinities hurl entire peaks of Mount Ida at each other (12.185–9), the mortals are 'not put in fear – it was the gods' will that men should remain ignorant of that divine conflict' (12.184–5).[53] Just in between Ajax's madness and his slaying of sheep, Quintus inserts the arrival of Eos and a mythological digression (*PH* 5.395–403):[54] if the gods do not usually speak or have any kind of interaction in the *PH*, here the author makes Hera both come back from a visit payed to Tethys, the wife of the Ocean, and meet and kiss Hypnos. This digression allows Quintus not only to add the meeting of Hera with two gods, but also to recall the *Dios apatē* (*Il.* 14.231–360), by stating that Hera considered Hypnos to be her son-in-law from the time he helped her to put Zeus to sleep.[55] In sneaking this scene in at the break of a new day, the author manages to add a divine episode to his poem without making any god have any interaction with mortals, who are not even aware of this encounter.

Many of the other excursuses are biographical, stemming from the death of a hero on the battlefield. In these digressions there is 'little if any pathos (. . .), and the slain man does not remain in the narrative spotlight for very long; he seems rather wholly forgotten, and the narrative never returns to him'.[56] Some of these descriptive scenes are in fact more focused on myth than on dying warriors. When Podaleirios finds out that his brother Machaon has been killed, he goes on a killing spree and slaughters two warriors: Kleitos, son of a nymph (*PH* 6.455–67), and Lassos, son of another nymph, Pronoe, who had given birth to him near the river Nymphaios, close to a cave that 'is said to be sacred' (*PH* 6.471–2, τὸ δὴ φάτις ἔμμεναι αὐτῶν / ἱρὸν Νυμφάων) to the Paphlagonian and Herakleian nymphs. This cave is immense to behold, suitable for deities, with mixing-bowls crafted in stone, Pans and many nymphs, looms and distaffs marvellous to look at for mortals, who can

---

[53] On the *theomachia* of the *PH*, see Carvounis (2008) and Campbell (1981: 56–60), who not only compares it with the *Iliad*'s one, but also to divine strife in Vergil, Plato's *Republic*, Silius Italicus and Nonnus' *Dionysiaca*.

[54] On epic digressions, see Austin (1966) and Gaisser (1969).

[55] On the specific verbal echoes between this passage and the *Dios apatē*, see James and Lee (2000: 199–200). On this alleged kinship between Hera and Hypnos, see Wenglinsky (2002: 284), who concludes: 'Quintus presents obligations of kinship, rather than greed or lust, as the motivation for Sleep's action.'

[56] Kauffman (2018: 638). For the biographies of minor warriors in Q.S., see Kauffman (2018: 639): 'Death scenes, in his treatment, often become the starting point for a kind of tourism, in which the reader is expected to envision the strange and dazzling sights that the poet presents for him.'

access it only from the north, for the south way can only be used by the gods
(*PH* 6.477–82). Such a long digression is both reminiscent of the *Argonautica*
(2.727–45), from which the cave in *PH* 6 derives the location of the cave and
its being an entrance to Hades, and of the *Odyssey* (13.102–12), where a cave
very similar to the one in *PH* 6 is described: it is sacred to the nymphs and
said to be on Ithaka, is full of bowls and amphoras filled with honey, water
streams and looms used by the nymphs themselves.[57] The deaths of other warriors are a means to unearth peculiar mythical variants: Zelys' killing brings
out a digression on his homeland (*PH* 10.125–37), Phrygia, where he lived
near another cave sacred to the nymphs, where Selene once fell for Endymion
and lay beneath some oak trees, where 'even to this day traces of where they
slept can be seen' (*PH* 10.131–2). Cow milk was spilled near those oaks, and
even now there is a spring marvellous to look at, for it is an optical illusion: it
looks like a lake of white milk from a distance, but is instead limpid water that
soon solidifies.[58] Leto's labour near the river Xanthos in Lykia (*contra Hymn.
hom. Ap.* 115–18) is recalled in the excursus on the birthland of Laodamas, a
warrior killed by Neoptolemos (11.20–6), whereas further ahead the slaying of
Archelochos brings up Hephaistos' otherwise unknown ever-burning rock of
Korykos, in Cilicia (11.91–8).

Of these sites, three out of four are said to be a marvel to mortals: *PH*
6.471, ἄντρου θηητοῖο, 'a cave of marvels'; 482–3, τὰ καὶ περὶ θαῦμα βροτοῖσιν
εἴδεται, 'an astonishing sight' for the mortals who see it; 10.133–4, οἱ δέ νυ
φῶτες / θηεῦντ' εἰσέτι κεῖνο, 'still visible today'; 11.93, ἥ τε βροτοῖσι /
θαῦμα πέλει, 'an extraordinary sight for mortals to see', just as Niobe's rock is a great
wonder to the 'passing travellers': 1.299, ἣ δὲ πέλει μέγα θαῦμα παρεσσυμένοισι
βροτοῖσιν. This last marvellous location is introduced at the point of death of
a warrior as well (Dresaios, 1.291–306) and, like the cave in *PH* 6, strongly
reminds us of Homer (*Il.* 24.614–17, cf. Eust. *in Il.* Ω 615–18 van der Valk
1367.55–1368.28, Paus. 1.21.3). Rather than using all these excursuses to
describe the birthplaces and lives of the slain warriors, as is Homer's custom,
or exploiting them to offer 'fleeting side-glimpses into various recesses of
history, learning or life', as Apollonius does,[59] Quintus seems to employ them

---

[57] For a comment on the similarities between these three passages, see James (2004: 305). Vian
(1966: 86) seems to deem Quintus' Pans and nymphs to be statues, whereas in the *Odyssey* they
are real. Πᾶνες is Rhodoman's emendation of πάντες, attested by all the manuscripts. Bertone
(2000: 84–90) gives an eschatological explanation of this passage, comparing it with Homer,
Apollonius and Porphyry's *De antro nympharum*.

[58] A petrified stream is found also in Strabo 5.4.13, Ov. *Met.* 15.312–14, Plin. 2.226. For other
literary reference to the amour of Endymion and Selene, see Tsomis (2018b: 105–17). On the
whereabouts of this cave (Phrygia or Caria), see Vian (1959a: 133–4).

[59] Fränkel (1952: 154). For the numerous and various excursuses, typical of Hellenistic poetry,
found in Apollonius' *Argonautica*, see Fränkel's article. On Homer's catalogues of slain warriors and biographical excursuses, see Beye (1964). Wenglinsky (2002: 102–5) examines other

as convenient ways to insert divine scenes in his poem: on the one hand the author shows – especially lesser – gods and nymphs acting, but on the other hand all these divinities belong to and act in a mythical past and none of them comes into contact with either the Trojan or Achaean heroes.

Quintus manages to recall the Olympians and their great deeds by hinting at them in similes, in a way that strongly reminds us of Apollonius' *Argonautica*.[60] Aphrodite's adultery is evoked in *PH* 14.47–57, where Helen's shame, patent among the Achaeans when she walks by Menelaos' side, is compared to Aphrodite's: after having slept with Ares the goddess was caught in Hephaistos' trap in plain view of all the Olympians. The link with *Odyssey* 8.266–366 is more than clear, although Quintus does not introduce this tale as a *divertissement*, but instead highlights its moralising aspects.[61] After Oinone has flung herself on Paris' pyre, the other nymphs are amazed and reproach Paris' behaviour towards his first wife (*PH* 10.464–78), while the herdsmen stand 'no less shocked than the assembled Argives had been at the sight of Evadne stretched out upon and embracing the body of her husband Capaneus, victim of Zeus' devastating thunderbolt' (10.479–82). Even more than in *PH* 14.47–57, in this passage an Olympian is seen actively intervening in mortal life, punishing a mortal: Kapaneus' death by Zeus's thunderbolt is told in Aeschylus' *Seven Against Thebes* (ll. 423–56) and the fate of Euadne, who threw herself on her husband's pyre, is narrated at length in Euripides' *Suppliants* (ll. 985–1072), and later recalled by others (e.g. Ov. *Ars am.* 3.21–2, *Trist.* 5.14.38, *Pont.* 3.1.111, Stat. *Th.* 12.777–809). If these two similes refer to the doings of Aphrodite, her divine audience and of Zeus, there are others that involve the Gigantomachy instead: for example in *PH* 1.179–81 Quintus compares the way Penthesileia fights to the way Athena fought the Giants, in 11.415–19 Aeneas fights like Zeus against the Giants, making the entire earth shake, and in 14.582–7 Ajax's prolonged death scene becomes a means to evoke Athena's thrusting the island of Sicily over the giant Enkelados.[62] Since in the imperial period 'Gigantomachies were very much in vogue',[63] we can see that Quintus does engage with this trend, but far from describing them at length in narrative sequences, he prefers to hint

digressions, like that of the petrification of Hekabe, and compares them with some of Apollonius' ones. On Quintus' digressions that strongly recall some passages of Apollonius' *Argonautica*, see Ozbek (2011). On the Hellenistic tradition of mentioning surviving landmarks, followed in the *PH*, see Carvounis (2014: 191–208).

[60] For a brief overview of Apollonius' insertion of the Olympians in aetiological stories and in myth, see Hunter (1993: 78–9), where he also states that 'the diminution in the prominence of the divine was an Apollonian experiment with significant consequences for the subsequent epic tradition'.

[61] On this simile, see Maciver (2012a: 168–71) and Tomasso (2010: 168–9). Cf. Luc. *D. Deor.* 17, 21.

[62] On Quintus' numerous similes regarding the Gigantomachy or the Titanomachy, see Carvounis (2008: 70) and Wenglinsky (2002: 111–15).

[63] Campbell (1981: 57).

at them briefly in his similes, thus granting a sense of divine participation in human affairs, but at the same time confining the gods to mythological backgrounds on many occasions.[64]

As for the intervention of the gods in narrative sequences, it has previously been stated that the gods intervene because they are some sort of servants of Fate, which pulls the strings of the *PH* plot,[65] but I think that the divide that determines whether the gods do or do not intervene in the *PH* is tradition. For the oral, archaic phase of epic the *oimē* is the way a poet 'uses the legendary matters and their articulation, both of which are traditional'.[66] By the time Quintus writes his epic poem in the imperial period, almost a thousand years have passed since the composition of the Trojan Epic Cycle, during which a wide range of versions of each episode had been given. It is patent that Quintus has done his readings and is thus fully aware of the accumulated range of possibilities from which he now has to choose. It is especially because of this learnedness, together with the religious and cultural milieu of the first centuries CE (see pp. 136–7, below), that he skilfully manipulates the mythical material. Whenever the consensual version of an episode strictly implies the intervention or the apparition of a god, Quintus sticks to it, but when there is no well-established tradition that implies it, then Quintus avoids divine intervention or at least makes it as unobtrusive as possible. Quintus' compliance with tradition can be perceived by comparing the way he engages with tradition in three passages of the third *logos*, all of which concern the relationship between deities and mortals.

The first of these excerpts regards Achilles' killers. The *Iliad* states three times that a deity is involved in his killing: in 19.416–17 (ἀλλὰ σοὶ αὐτῷ / μόρσιμόν ἐστι θεῷ τε καὶ ἀνέρι ἶφι δαμῆναι, 'but for you yourself it is fated to be vanquished in fight by a god and a mortal') the horse Xanthos tells Achilles that both a god and a man will kill him, whereas Hektor is more precise and mentions Paris and Apollo (22.359–60, ὅτε κέν σε Πάρις καὶ Φοῖβος Ἀπόλλων / ἐσθλὸν ἐόντ᾽ ὀλέσωσιν ἐνὶ Σκαιῇσι πύλῃσιν, 'when Paris and Phoebus Apollo slay you, valorous though you are, at the Scaean gates'),

---

[64] Wenglinsky (2002: 5) states that in the *PH* divine 'unseemly' features are devaluated and – therefore – 'confined to the 'mythological background' of the poem or to the speech of mortal characters'. The Homeric poems too treat some mythological episodes, especially those involving really serious violence among the Olympians, as belonging to a superseded past, e.g. *Il.* 1.590–4, 8.12–16, 478–81, 15.18–24, 18.394–9.

[65] According to Vian (1963: xvi) all gods, Zeus included, are nothing but docile executors of Fate's will. See also Vian (1959a: 27). Cf. *PH* 7.70–6, *Il.* 17.514–15. On these passages, see Gärtner (2007: 222–4). See also García Romero (1986); Duckworth (1936: 64); Paschal (1904: 42). Gärtner (2014: 100) doubts the almightiness of Fate in the *PH*.

[66] My translation of Camerotto (2009: 21): 'Le forme stesse di ripresa dei materiali della leggenda, ovvero gli argomenti e la loro articolazione narrativa, sono tradizionali e sono rappresentate dalle oἶμαι.'

and Achilles himself says that his mother foretold that he would be killed by Apollo's arrows (21.277–8, ἥ μ' ἔφατο Τρώων ὑπὸ τείχεϊ θωρηκτάων / λαιψηροῖς ὀλέεσθαι Ἀπόλλωνος βελέεσσιν, 'saying that beneath the wall of the mail-clad Trojans I should perish by the swift missiles of Apollo'). The *Aethiopis* – followed by Eur. *Andr.* 655, *Hec.* 387–8, Verg. *Aen.* 6.57–8 and Ov. *Met.* 12.580–609, 13.501 – deemed both Apollo and Paris accountable for Achilles' death, although in many extant sources from Pindar onwards Apollo appears to be the only one responsible for the killing (Pi. *Pae.* 6.79–82, *Pyth.* 3.101, Aesch. fr. 350 Radt, Soph. *Ph.* 334–6, Eur. *Andr.* 52–3, Hyg. *Fab.* 107, 113, Hor. *Carm.* 4.6.3–12).[67] Therefore, if one of the two branches of tradition does not consider Paris implicated in this matter, both the branches acknowledge Apollo's involvement. This means that anyone who listened or read about the death of Achilles would have expected Apollo to intervene. As it happens, Quintus does not suppress the god's intervention, but instead he chooses the variant in which Apollo acts alone (*PH* 3.26–90), without any involvement of Paris. As Silvio Bär notices, choosing this branch of tradition 'may serve to emphasize the lack of interaction (. . .) between humans and gods'.[68]

Towards the end of the third *logos* we can find the other two passages where I believe Quintus comes up with two solutions to two different situations. The first circumstance is very similar to the one we have just analysed and is thus solved in a very similar way. The Nereids, having heard the lamentation of the mortals for Achilles' death, make their way to the Achaean camp to mourn the son of Thetis (*PH* 3.582–94), and are joined at once by the Muses (3.594–6). All of this coincides with what we know of the *Aethiopis*[69] and read in the *deuteronekyia* of the *Odyssey*,[70] where the ghost of Agamemnon tells Achilles that Thetis arose from the sea with the Nereids (*Od.* 24.47–9) to grieve for her son, and that shortly after the nine Muses raised his dirge (24.60–2, cf. Pi. *Isth.* 8.56a–60, Lyc. *Alex.* 273–4). Quintus considerably expands the Odyssean account, but does not seem to further this divine meeting with mortals at any rate. His only divergence from the – known – tradition is in fact that the *Odyssey* says that Nestor calms down the Achaeans, who, scared at the sight of the

---

[67] For the *Aethiopis*, see *Aeth. arg.* 69.15–16 (Bernabé), Τρεψάμενος δ' Ἀχιλλεὺς τοὺς Τρῶας καὶ εἰς τὴν πόλιν συνεισπεσὼν ὑπὸ Πάριδος ἀναιρεῖται καὶ Ἀπόλλωνος. Cf. Apoll. *Epit.* 5.3, διώξας δὲ καὶ τοὺς Τρῶας πρὸς ταῖς Σκαιαῖς πύλαις τοξεύεται ὑπὸ Ἀλεξάνδρου καὶ Ἀπόλλωνος εἰς τὸ σφυρόν. On the mythical variants of Achilles' death, see Sodano (1947); Vian (1959a: 31–2; 1963: 91–3); Burgess (2009: 38–9).

[68] Bär (2016: 223). On Achilles' death by Apollo in the *PH*, see also Wenglinsky (1999, esp. 80–3).

[69] For the *Aethiopis*, see *Aeth. arg.* 69.19–21 (Bernabé), ἔπειτα Ἀντίλοχόν τε θάπτουσι καὶ τὸν νεκρὸν τοῦ Ἀχιλλέως προτίθενται. Καὶ Θέτις ἀφικομένη σὺν Μούσαις καὶ ταῖς ἀδελφαῖς θρηνεῖ τὸν παῖδα. See West (2013: 153–4).

[70] On Aristarchus' rejection of *Od.* 24.1–204 and on the probable pre-Iliadic features of these verses, see Russo, Fernández-Galiano and Heubeck (1992: 356–7, 365–7), with reference to important scholarly contributions.

Nereids, would have otherwise escaped and boarded the ships (*Od.* 24.50–7, cf. Tzetz. *Posth.* 435–6, 452–8), whereas in the *PH* it is Zeus himself who 'endowed the Argives with great and fearless courage so that they would not be terrified at the sight of that noble band of goddesses going openly through their midst' (*PH* 3.595–7). It is not uncommon for gods to encourage men in the *PH*; indeed, this is one of the few divine actions that occurs almost as often as in the *Iliad*.[71] We must notice that this type of intervention allows the poet to insert divine influence without making any god appear or have visible, tangible contact with mortals. So once again the audience would expect the Nereids and the Muses to participate at the funeral of Achilles and would also anticipate the mortals being afraid of the goddesses' arrival, and so Quintus fulfils these expectations, but he does so giving this scene a twist: just as Apollo does not act together with Paris, neither can a mortal, viz. Nestor, now mediate between the gods and humans.[72] Zeus himself has to intervene, and Quintus makes him do it in a very subtle way, thus keeping the mortal world detached from that of the immortals.

He does so also right at the end of this *logos*, when he inserts the arrival of Poseidon at the Trojan shore: in *PH* 3.766–83 the sea god promises Thetis Achilles' apotheosis and divine honours on the Isle of Leuke.[73] Neither Homer nor any other extant text mentions Poseidon's presence and promise at Achilles' funeral, so we either have to consider that it comes from a now lost, maybe local mythographic account,[74] or we are led to believe that this is original to Quintus. In the latter option, the author does not have to cope with a long-standing tradition that wanted Poseidon to have contact with mortals, so he can make Poseidon step upon the shore unseen by men (*PH* 3.767–8, ἤλυθεν Ἐννοσίγαιος ἐπ' ἠόνας· οὐδέ μιν ἄνδρες / ἔδρακον, 'then the Earthshaker (. . .) came to the shore. No man could see him'), stand unnoticed by the Nereids and speak to Thetis alone: just as in *PH* 8.341–3 Athena prevents Ares from revealing himself to Neoptolemos, in this case too Poseidon does not show himself to the mortals, for there is no well-established tradition with which Quintus must cope. But why does Quintus add Poseidon to this scene? Quintus might be taking Poseidon's intervention either from this now lost mythographic account, or from the only other extant text that mentions the sea god with respect to Achilles' afterlife, which

---

[71] Wenglinsky (2002: 288, n298) lists 23 examples in the *PH* and 53 in the – much longer – *Iliad*.

[72] Cf.Vian (1959a: 33), who thinks that Q.S. makes Zeus (and not Nestor) reassure the Greeks out of concern for plausibility. On Quintus' usage of the verses athetised by Aristarchus, see Vian (1959a: 33–4).

[73] On the Odyssean and post-Homeric traditions of Achilles' afterlife, see Maciver (2017), but also Vian (1963: 125, n5, n7);Vian (1969: 159–63, 185 n2).

[74] Cf.Vian (1963: 93), according to whom only the meeting of Poseidon and Thetis is ascribable to a mythographic account on Achilles' death.

is Philostratus' *Heroikos*,[75] which could owe Poseidon's involvement to this lost account too. The *Heroikos* is a dialogue almost contemporary to the *PH*, where Achilles is said to be killed by Paris at Thymbraios, the sanctuary of Apollo. According to this dialogue his funeral was attended neither by the Muses nor by the Nereids (51.7), but after his death a great wave dashed against the Achaean camp and during the night the loud lamentation of Thetis was heard (51.8–11, cf. *Od.* 24.48–9). After the funeral, in which only mortals took part, Thetis beseeched Poseidon to send up from the sea an island[76] where Achilles and Helen – for according to Philostratus they were in love – could dwell (54.5–6).

TOWARDS A CONCLUSION

The *Heroikos'* version of Achilles' death, funeral and afterlife shows an even clearer divide between gods and mortals than the one we find in the *PH*, and an even greater revision of the Homeric poems. However this hypothetical lost account of Achilles' funeral might have described Poseidon's involvement, we must note that neither Quintus nor Philostratus makes the sea god interact with mortals. It goes without saying that the nature of Philostratus' dialogue is very different from that of Quintus' epic poem, but – by comparing these two works – we cannot help but notice the underlying tendency of the writers of the imperial era to correct, refute or emend Homeric matters. This is achieved in various ways and to varying degrees, from the complete rewriting of the Trojan War in Dio Chrysostom's *Trojan* oration, that exposes Homer's alleged lies, to minor revision focused on criticism of the Homeric representation of the gods.[77] Just think of Lucian's *Dialogues of the Gods*, where the divinities are shown in their everyday life, full of uncertainties and mistakes, or the *Zeus Catechised*, that highlights the inconsistencies of divine omnipotence struggling with the power of fate. Philostratus' *Heroikos* fits well into this scenario, rejecting extraordinary events such as Achilles'

---

[75] Vian (1963: 125, n7). Grossardt (2006: 740) believes that Q.S. takes Poseidon's intervention from the *Heroikos*, but he admits that both Q.S.'s and Philostratus' versions could go back to a common source. On the dating and relationship between the *Heroikos* and the *PH*, see Grossardt (2006: 134–7), who thinks that many details of Achilles' funeral in the *PH* derive from the *Heroikos*. See also Bär (2010: 287–8).

[76] According to Arr. *Peripl. M. Eux.* 21.1 it is Thetis that creates the island: ταύτην λέγεται Θέτις ἀνεῖναι τῷ παιδί. See Belfiore (2009: 229–30).

[77] On epic correction of the traditional material aimed at reconciling it with criticism of poetry (like the *scholia*, Plutarch and Eustathius), see Feeney (1991) and, specifically on the *PH*, Wenglinsky (1999; 2002), Barbaresco (forthcoming).

divinely wrought armour, the fight against the river Scamander and the talk-ing horses (47, 48.11–13, 50.1–3).[78]

Quintus' PH also dovetails with this framework, seeing as he modifies the Homeric Götterapparat. Quintus' peculiar usage of *if not*-situations allows him to let his audience sometimes envision the intervention of the Olympians with-out making it really happen. The assiduous use of που in episodes that entail divine intervention in mortal matters, the numerous unnamed and unspecified deities (θεός, δαίμων, θεῶν τις etc.) interacting with humans, and the usage of impersonal verbal forms (PH 13.445, ἐνέπουσι; 13.551, φασί) make us question his real beliefs, just like, to an even greater degree, the author's clearly stated doubt regarding Laodike and Elektra's myths (13.560–1). Scepticism is made apparent when the authorial voice lists possible and, more importantly, non-divine alternatives for the deeds of his warriors. Since he cannot totally sup-press the divine apparatus, Quintus seems to find an alternative dimension to speak about the gods and make them act by inserting divine episodes in similes and digressions. He tends to avoid the intervention of the gods as often as he can, or at least seeks to make it less overt, as in PH 3.767–8. Notwithstanding all of this, when we compare Quintus' poem to other works composed in the context of the Second Sophistic, like the ones briefly mentioned above, but also the Latin prose accounts of the Trojan War by Dictys Cretensis (*Ephemeris belli Troiani*) and Dares Phrygius (*De excidio Troiae Historia*),[79] where the gods are utterly absent, we have to admit that the PH still 'gives us a generally tra-ditional impression',[80] even when it comes to the divine.

---

[78] For an overview of the conception of Homer in the Second Sophistic, see Kim (2010a), with chapter 4 on Dio Chrysostom's *Trojan*, chapter 5 on Lucian's *True Stories* and chapter 6 on Philostratus' *Heroikos*. On the *Heroikos'* refutation of Homer, see, among others, Mestre (2004: 127–42) and Berenson Maclean and Bradshaw Aitken (2001: LX–XCII); on its religious and philosophical content, see Mantero (1966: 19–142). For some remarks on the relationship between this dialogue, Homer, Dio and Lucian, see Bär (2010: 289–94) and Mantero (1966: 145–224). On Lucian's parody of Homer and the Homeric Götterapparat, see Camerotto (1998: 175–91); Berdozzo (2011); Gassino (2012/13).

[79] For a study of these Latin accounts of the Trojan War, see the recent volume edited by Brescia *et al.* (2018). For a survey of their links to the Second Sophistic and revisionism of Homer, see, in the same volume, Bär (2018b), but also Usener (2007). Some remarks on the relationship between myth and history in Herodotus, Thucydides, Lucian, Philostratus, Dictys and Dares are found in Prosperi (2013: 1–18).

[80] Bär (2010: 308). Feeney (1991: 262): 'Epic narrative (. . .) achieves its characteristic effects prin-cipally through stunning and extraordinary displays of power, to which the gods above all contribute. Epic stripped of all this becomes sub-epic, as the epic cycle becomes in the bald and godless prose of Dictys and Dares.'

CHAPTER 8

Animal and Human Sacrifice in Quintus of Smyrna

Jan N. Bremmer

Animal sacrifice continues to fascinate us.[1] In the last decade alone, we have had several collections, one monograph and a sizable number of articles on the topic of Greek sacrifice.[2] Most of these studies, though, have concentrated on the classical and Hellenistic periods. Much less attention has been paid to the Roman period. The only major study of animal sacrifice in that period concentrates on important authors such as Strabo, Plutarch and Pausanias, but does not pay any attention, for example, to the Greek novel,[3] which I have studied elsewhere, as it is an important source for sacrifice in the earlier Roman period.[4] However, Quintus of Smyrna does not appear to have received any attention in this respect.[5] He is even absent from Fred Naiden's study of Greek sacrifice, although the title promises an analysis of the subject in the Roman period too. Unfortunately, we cannot be certain about Quintus' time and place of origin. He is now generally located at about 200–300 CE,[6] and the plausible influence of Philostratus' *Life of Apollonius* and *Heroikos* on Quintus suggests the earlier decades of that century.[7] Similarly uncertain is his place of origin. He is especially familiar with the Troad,[8] but his knowledge of Lycia may well

---

[1] For a recent historiography, see Graf (2012); less satisfactory, Jacquemin (2014).

[2] Most recently, Pirenne-Delforge and Prescendi (2011); Ekroth and Wallensten (2013); Naiden (2013); Bielawski (2017); Hitch and Rutherford (2017); Bielawski (2019).

[3] Petropoulou (2008). See also Pernot (2005), who concentrates on Aelius Aristides and Lucian; Ullucci (2012).

[4] Bremmer (2018), which I freely use in this contribution.

[5] I mainly use the Budé edition of Vian (1963, -66, -69) and the translation by James (2004), although sometimes somewhat adapted.

[6] For a recent, sceptical survey of the various suggestions, see Bär (2009: 12–23).

[7] *Life of Apollonius*: Greensmith (2020: 268–9). *Heroikos*: Grossardt (2006: vol. 1, 134–5).

[8] Paschal (1904: 12–13).

suggest an origin from that region,[9] as northern Lycia was a centre of literary productivity in the second century with various novels probably being written there.[10] Whatever the answers to these questions may be, Quintus may certainly represent an interesting example of what people thought about sacrifice in the earlier third century, even within the constraints of his poetic tradition. At the same time, Quintus also provides several descriptions of human sacrifice, in which he mostly varies early epic sources, but with his own emphases, as we will see below.

In this contribution I will begin by looking at the descriptions of animal sacrifice. Admittedly, these are not numerous, but they may still be able to help us to fill in some gaps in our knowledge of sacrificial practices and traditions in the third century. I will then turn to the poem's cases of human sacrifice and conclude by asking which people sacrifice, when, where, how, why, what and to whom in Quintus. But before we come to those questions, let us now turn to the relevant passages of animal sacrifice, of which I will first look at normal sacrifices, then at 'non-standard' ones, and conclude with a case of a rejected sacrifice.

ANIMAL SACRIFICE

Let us start with a simple mention of sacrifices as typical for the relations with the gods. After Achilles' death, Poseidon appears to Thetis, although not to the Greeks, and exhorts her to stop lamenting because (3.771–80):

Οὐ γὰρ ὅ γε φθιμένοισι μετέσσεται, ἀλλὰ θεοῖσιν,
ὡς ἠὺς Διόνυσος ἰδὲ σθένος Ἡρακλῆος·
οὐ γάρ μιν μόρος αἰνὸς ὑπὸ ζόφον αἰὲν ἐρύξει
οὐδ' Ἀΐδης, ἀλλ' αἶψα καὶ ἐς Διὸς ἵξεται αὐγάς·
καί οἱ δῶρον ἔγωγε θεουδέα νῆσον ὀπάσσω   775
Εὔξεινον κατὰ πόντον, ὅπη θεὸς ἔσσεται αἰεὶ
σὸς πάις· ἀμφὶ δὲ φῦλα περικτιόνων μέγα λαῶν
κεῖνον κυδαίνοντα θυηπολίης ἐρατεινῆς
ἶσον ἐμοὶ τίσουσι. Σὺ δ' ἴσχεο κωκύουσα
ἐσσυμένως καὶ μή τι χαλέπτεο πένθεϊ θυμόν.   780

He (Achilles) won't be dwelling with the dead but with the gods,
like noble Dionysos and mighty Herakles,
he won't be kept in darkness forever either by fearful Fate

---

[9] Schürr (sine anno).
[10] Cf. Bremmer (1998: 167–70).

or by Hades, but soon he shall come to Zeus's light.[11]
And I will present him with a god-fearing island,
in the Euxine Sea, where your son shall be a god forever.
The tribes that live around shall greatly glorify him
and with lovely sacrifices honour him
no less than me. So stop your wailing
immediately and do not hurt your heart with grief.

Poseidon clearly wants to comfort Thetis with the assurance of a special fate for her son. That is why he compares Achilles with Dionysos and Herakles, both of whom were also sons of a mortal parent (Diod. Sic. 4.15.1). The combination of Dionysos and Herakles is old and occurs already in the *Iliad* (14.323–4). Equally old must be the idea that they arrived late in heaven, as both Hecataeus (*FGrH* 1 F 300) and Herodotus (2.145) call them, together with Pan, the youngest of the Greek gods. Achilles, then, will not be going to the underworld but he will be given an island in the Black Sea where they will worship him as a god. Part of this idea was traditional, as in the *Aethiopis* (Arg. 4b West) Achilles is translated to Leuke, and Alcaeus (fr. 354 Voigt) already mentions him as ruling over Scythia. Leuke has been identified with the island of Ostrov Zmeinyy, and Achilles' cult on the island and its neighbouring regions is well attested through lapidary graffiti, statues and inscriptions.[12] The concept of the island as gift of Poseidon also occurs in Philostratus' *Heroikos*, and may well be derived from there by Quintus.[13]

What is striking, though, in this passage, is the fact that Quintus stresses that Achilles will be a god and that the surrounding peoples will honour him with lovely sacrifices.[14] In Homer and long afterwards, Achilles is a hero, and his ontological status is never spoken of as being a god. It seems to be only in the Roman period that we first hear him explicitly being called 'a god' (Dio Chr. 36.14). Like other great Greek heroes, such as Ajax, Diomedes and Herakles, his status apparently moved between the categories of divinity and hero.[15] As I have argued elsewhere, the category of cultic hero is a relative latecomer in Greek religion and should not be projected back into the Bronze Age, as it is not attested before the sixth century BCE.[16] In any case, the status of Achilles

---

[11] Q.S. 3.774, ἀλλ' αἶψα καὶ ἐς Διὸς ἵξεται αὐγάς ~ *Il.*13.837, ἠχὴ δ' ἀμφοτέρων ἵκετ' αἰθέρα καὶ Διὸς αὐγάς.

[12] Shaw (2001); very important, Hupe (2006).

[13] Cf. Grossardt (2006: vol. 2, 740) on Philostr. *Her.* 54.5.

[14] The expression does not mean 'with incense and sacrifices', *contra* Burgess (2009: 129).

[15] Parker (2011: 110).

[16] Bremmer (2019a: 85–93) (first published in 2006). My argument has been accepted by Gordon (2013), with an excellent *Forschungsgeschichte*, but unpersuasively contested by Parker (2011: 287–92).

does not seem to have been a point of issue for the inhabitants of the Pontic region, who never called him either a god or a hero.

What is markedly unusual, though, is the qualification of the sacrifices to Achilles as 'lovely'. Outside Quintus (note also 14.332, ἐρατὴ δὲ θυηπολίη), the qualification is unique in Greek literature. So why would he have used this adjective? One reason might be the differences between heroic and divine sacrifices. Recent discussions have shown that the old binary opposition 'Olympian' versus 'Chthonian' sacrifice is a modern construction, although inspired by various passages from late antiquity.[17] Instead, there is now the tendency no longer to differentiate between Olympian and Chthonic divinities, but rather between heroic and divine sacrifices, even though there are no clear-cut dividing lines between these two.[18] However, in the time of Quintus, we can find a more clear demarcation between divine and heroic sacrifices in Philostratus and, albeit somewhat later, Porphyry.[19] It may well be that this division is in the background of our passage. In any case, by calling the sacrifices 'lovely' Quintus makes sure that we have here normal sacrifices to the gods, not heroic sacrifices which might have contained black victims, holocausts, distinctions regarding the consumption of food, prescriptions to consume the meat on the spot or other features of sacrifices to heroes.

Although this particular sacrifice is not described in any detail, we are better served in Quintus' last book, where we can find a more substantial description of a 'standard' sacrifice after the victory of the Greeks (14.101–10):

Ἀργεῖοι δ' ἄρα πολλὰ βοῶν ἐπὶ μηρία θέντες
καῖον ὁμῶς σχίζῃσι, καὶ ἐσσύμενοι περὶ βωμοὺς
λείβεσκον μέθυ λαρὸν ἐπ' αἰθομένῃσι θυηλῇς
ἦρα θεοῖσι φέροντες, ἐπεὶ μέγα ἤνυσαν ἔργον.
Πολλὰ δ' ἐν εἰλαπίνῃ θυμηδέι κυδαίνεσκον   105
πάντας ὅσους ὑπέδεκτο σὺν ἔντεσι δούριος ἵππος.
Θαύμαζον <δὲ> Σίνωνα περικλυτόν, οὕνεχ' ὑπέτλη
λώβην δυσμενέων πολυκηδέα· καί ῥά ἑ πάντες
μολπῇ καὶ γεράεσσιν ἀπειρεσίοισι τίεσκον
αἰέν. (. . .)   110

The Argives laid out many ox thigh bones (μηρία)
with kindling wood and burned them together. Then, moving around
     the altars,
they poured sweet wine upon the blazing sacrifices
to thank the gods because they had made that great accomplishment.

[17] Cf. Parker (2011: 80–4, 283–6); Henrichs (2019: 129–48) (first published in 2005).
[18] Cf. Parker (2005).
[19] Philostratus, *Her.* 53.8, 11–13 with Grossardt (2006: vol. 2, 719–20, 726–8) *ad loc.*

During their merry feast they loudly celebrated
all those who with their weapons had entered the Wooden Horse.
They admired the famous Sinon for having endured
the grievous torture of the enemy. And all of them
kept honouring him with song and with an endless flood of gifts.

The description clearly does not go into great detail, as it passes over the selection of the animals, the procession to the altar and the kill. It gets straight to the point, so to speak, by concentrating on the actual sacrificing of the bulls. But what does the Greek mean when it says that they put μηρία on the logs of wood? Vian, James and Carvounis all translate with 'thighs',[20] but that is not correct. As various scholars have recently shown, the term – whether it is μηρία or its synonym μῆρα, which Quintus uses more often – means thigh bones, not whole thighs,[21] which indeed burn very well with the right doses of fat.[22] The logs of wood are sometimes represented on fifth-century Athenian vase paintings with remarkable precision and clearly have to suggest the piety of the sacrificers, as will be the case here.[23]

On the burning wood and thigh bones, the Greeks poured μέθυ λαρόν, 'sweet wine' (103). Vian translates the expression with 'vin pur', but that is clearly wrong. The Greeks normally made libations with their usual drinking wine, that is, wine mixed with water. It is only in 'non-standard' libations that they used either unmixed wine or just water.[24] Wine libations are well attested both in texts and on vase paintings. Athenian vases often portray the sacrificer pouring a libation from a cup in his right hand, while he extends his left hand in a gesture of prayer. The custom was clearly traditional, since in the *Odyssey* (3.359–60) Nestor also performs a libation on the burning sacrifice.[25]

As a reason for their sacrifice, Quintus gives that they performed it ἦρα φέροντες, a Homeric expression (*Il.* 14.132; *Od.* 3.164), of which Quintus is rather fond.[26] Here, it probably means 'thanking, returning a favour'. Indeed, gratitude was one of the main reasons for sacrifice in ancient Greece. As Theophrastus (F 584A Fortenbaugh) noted, 'there are three reasons one ought to sacrifice to the gods: either on account of honour or on account of gratitude or on account of a want of things.' The sacrifice having been performed, the meat will have been used for the meal as was normal. In literature, the division

---

[20] Carvounis (2019: 71).

[21] Dieu (2016); Ekroth (2018: 93–5); Nussbaum (2018a; 2018b).

[22] As is experimentally shown by Morton (2015).

[23] For the wood in sacrifices, see van Straten (1995: 167–8); Gebauer (2002: 442–3).

[24] As was shown by Graf (1980).

[25] Cf. Rudhardt (²1992: 240–5) (texts); van Straten (1995: 134–6) (vases); Gaifman (2018: 17–43).

[26] Q.S. 1.803, 2.605, 5.163, 10.462, 14.445. Note that the expression is not explained in any of the commentaries on Quintus.

and distribution of meat is regularly described in detail, but its consumption is hardly ever mentioned. Similarly, vase paintings never show anyone eating, although the various phases of sacrifice are often represented.[27] And indeed, in this passage, too, it is not so much the food that receives attention but the 'glories of men',[28] in particular those of Sinon, whose mutilations are mentioned but not detailed,[29] as that would have spoilt the happy atmosphere of the feast.

A final joyful sacrifice takes also place after the killing of Polyxena (14.331–5; below, pp. 151–5):

> Αἶψα δὲ δαῖτ' ἐπάσαντο βοῶν ἀπὸ μῆρα ταμόντες
> ἀθανάτοις· ἐρατὴ δὲ θυηπολίη πέλε πάντη·
> οἳ δέ που ἀργυρέοισι καὶ ἐν χρυσέοισ<ι> κυπέλλοις
> πῖνον ἀφυσσάμενοι λαρὸν μέθυ· γήθεε δέ σφι
> θυμὸς ἐελδομένων σφετέρην ἐπὶ γαῖαν ἱκέσθαι.   335

> Immediately they feasted, after cutting the ox thigh bones
> for the immortals, a lovely sacrifice (θυηπολίη) it was in every way.
> Now from goblets of both silver and gold, no doubt,
> they drank the sweet wine which they'd drawn off, their spirits high
> in expectation of reaching their native countries.

The description does not add new details to what we have seen already. It is noteworthy, though, that the cutting out of the thigh bones is the only detail mentioned from the whole of the sacrificial ritual, and we will have to come back to this (below, pp. 156–7). Tine Scheijnen notes that θυηπολίη occurs only twice in Quintus, with the only other time being used after Poseidon's foreshadowing of Achilles' deification. According to her, 'the recurrence of the word enhances the obvious connection between Poseidon's prophecy and its current completion: in Book 14, Achilles' deification is realised. He has shown his new power, and the Achaeans have experienced and acknowledged it.'[30] However, this interpretation is hardly persuasive. Admittedly, the only other time the term θυηπολίη occurs in Quintus is in the passage in Book 3 which we have discussed above, but, as we see in this section, there are not that many sacrifices in Quintus, and the term can also be found several times in one of Quintus' epic models, Apollonius Rhodius.[31] More importantly, though, the sacrifice is not intended for Achilles in particular, but it is explicitly said to be 'for the immortals' (14.332). Not every repetition of a term is necessarily significant.

[27] As is noted by Schmitt-Pantel (1985: 150).Vases: Gebauer (2002: 448–70).
[28] For the expression, see Watkins (1995: 173–8); Massetti (2019: 113–18).
[29] They are described in Q.S. 12.367–73.
[30] Scheijnen (2018: 343).
[31] Apoll. Rhod. 1.967, 1.1124, 4.772, 4.995; cf.Vian (²2008).

Having seen three joyful sacrifices, let us now turn to a somewhat less happy occasion. Right at the beginning of his epic, Quintus introduces Penthesileia, the queen of the Amazons, who had come to Troy to assist the Trojans against the Greeks.[32] According to Hellanicus (*FGrH* 4 F 149 = F 149 Fowler) and others, she had come in order to kill some warriors, as otherwise she would not be allowed to get married. This motif, which apparently is not yet found in the *Aethiopis*,[33] is later varied by the idea that the queen had killed a fellow Amazon by accident,[34] and Quintus is the first to turn this Amazon into her sister.[35] Yet it remains somewhat obscure why participating in the war would have helped Penthesileia in connection with her pollution of murder. And that is precisely the motif that receives the most attention from Quintus, who gives as an additional reason for Penthesileia to come that (1.28–32)

ὄφρα καθηραμένη πέρι λύματα λυγρὰ φόνοιο
σμερδαλέας θυέεσσιν Ἐρινύας ἱλάσσηται,
αἵ οἱ ἀδελφειῆς κεχολωμέναι αὐτίχ' ἕποντο   30
ἄφραστοι· κεῖναι γὰρ ἀεὶ περὶ ποσσὶν ἀλιτρῶν
στρωφῶντ', οὐδέ νυ[36] ἔστι θεᾶς ἀλιτόνθ' ὑπαλύξαι.

She might purify herself of the baneful stains of bloodshed,
appeasing with sacrifices of cakes the dreaded Erinyes,
who in instant wrath for her sister were following her,
unseen. For constantly on the heels of offenders (ἀλιτρῶν)
they move, and no sinner (ἀλιτόνθ') can escape those goddesses.

Quintus applies here a well-known literary topos, namely, that of the Erinyes pursuing murderers of kin.[37] It is rather doubtful that the Erinyes still belonged to lived religion in his time, as we do not hear about them any more after the fourth century.[38] Even if it is the case that this absence of evidence may be caused by the absence in our sources of cases of homicide, which provide the best examples of these vengeful spirits,[39] it is a fact that Erinyes had not been spoken of in a long time, and a literary elaboration seems more than probable in this case. This is all the more likely given that at the end of the fifth century, witness Euripides' *Orestes* (38), they had started to become identified with the

---

[32] West (2013: 130–41); add Pilz (2011).

[33] Cf. Fowler (2013: 541).

[34] Diod. Sic. 2.46.5; Apollod. *Ep.* 5.1; Servius on Verg. *Aen.* 1.491.

[35] Cf. Bär (2009: 183–7), on Q.S. 1.23–4.

[36] Bär (2009: 194) persuasively keeps the manuscripts' νυ instead of Vian's τι.

[37] See also the commentary by Bär (2009: 189–90) on Q.S. 1.27–32.

[38] Mikalson (1983: 50–2); Parker (1983: 124–8).

[39] Thus Jameson (1993: 118).

Eumenides, a process we can also observe in the more or less contemporary Derveni Papyrus.[40]

Originally, the Erinyes belonged exclusively to the world of myth, not, like the Eumenides, of cult. They were the female avenging spirits in cases of family murders,[41] but usually only of the parents and the eldest sons.[42] The idea that the Erinyes would go after Penthesileia because of the murder of her sister is clearly a later innovation by Quintus. On the other hand, his use of the term ἀλιτρός for offending and the corresponding verb ἀλιταίνω shows that he knew the right vocabulary, as ἀλιτρός 'often figures in texts about crime and its punishment by the gods', although this observation by Annette Harder (on Call. *Aet.* fr. 75.68–9)[43] perhaps insufficiently notes the serious character of the crime; the related ἀλιτηρός is 'one of the strongest terms denoting a religious offender'.[44]

But what about the θυέεσσιν with which Penthesileia hoped to appease the Erinyes and to purify herself? As the Erinyes were figures of mythology, not of cult, we do not have any ancient mention of sacrifices to the Erinyes. It is different of course in the case of the related Eumenides and Semnai Theai, with whom they became largely identified in tragedy and who did receive sacrifices.[45] However, for us it is important to note that the combination 'purificatory sacrifice' is relatively late in Greek and starts to be found only in the Roman period.[46] If we assume, though, that Quintus had real sacrifices in mind, which ones would he have thought of? Unfortunately, the sense of θυέεσσιν is not immediately clear, although it already occurs in Homer (*Il.* 6.270). Vian and James translate it with 'sacrifices' and Silvio Bär with 'Rauchopfer'. In a detailed discussion, Casabona, in what is still the best account of sacrificial terminology, has persuasively argued that the term can mean either 'sacrifice in general' or 'cake'.[47] The latter may well have been what Quintus had in mind, as we know from the Derveni Papyrus that the Eumenides received a combination of wineless libations and cakes as offerings (§ 17 Kotwick = VI.7 Kouremenos).[48] On the other hand, Quintus may have just followed Homer without any specific thoughts about the sacrifices. We simply do not know.

---

[40] Bremmer (2019b: 204).

[41] Hall (2018).

[42] Parker (1983: 196).

[43] Harder (2012: vol. 2, 650).

[44] Parker (1983: 270). For the vocabulary, see Hatch (1908); Latte (1920/21: 257).

[45] Cf. Henrichs (1991: 169–79); Zerhoch (2016: 308–9); for the complicated relationships between Eumenides, Erinyes and Semnai Theai, see also Sommerstein (1989: 6–12); Johnston (1999: 279–87); Schlatter (2018: 165–9).

[46] Cf. Georgoudi (2017: 108–9).

[47] Casabona (1966: 109–17), overlooked by Graziosi and Haubold (2010: 155) on *Il.* 6.270.

[48] For the combination of wineless libations and sacrificial cakes, see Henrichs (2019: 71–4). For cakes in Greek sacrifices, see Kearns (2011); García Soler (2014); Meirano (2017).

Having looked at standard and 'non-standard' sacrifices, let us conclude this section with a rejected sacrifice. Following the punishment of Laokoon and his sons (12.500–9),

Τρῶες δ᾽ ἀθανάτοισιν ἐπεντύνοντο θυηλὰς   500
λείβοντες μέθυ λαρόν, ἐπεί σφισιν ἦτορ ἐώλπει
λευγαλέου πολέμοιο βαρὺ σθένος ἐξυπαλύξειν.
Ἱερὰ δ᾽ οὐ καίοντο, πυρὸς δ᾽ ἐσβέννυτ᾽ αὐτμή,
ὄμβρου ὅπως καθύπερθε δυσηχέος ἐσσυμένοιο·
καπνὸς δ᾽ αἱματόεις ἀνεκήκιε· μῆρα δὲ πάντα   505
πῖπτε χαμαὶ τρομέοντα· κατηρείποντο δὲ βωμοί·
σπονδαὶ δ᾽ αἷμα γένοντο· θεῶν δ᾽ ἐξέρρεε δάκρυ,
καὶ νηοὶ δεύοντο λύθρῳ· στοναχαὶ δ᾽ ἐφέροντο
ἔκποθεν ἀπροφάτοιο. (. . .)

The Trojans prepared sacrifices to the immortals
with libations of sweet wine, hoping in their hearts
to be relieved of the heavy weight of woeful war.
Their victims, though, refused to burn and the fires went out,
as if a heavy shower of rain had fallen.
The smoke that rose was bloodstained, all thigh bones
fell quivering to the ground and the altars collapsed.
Libations turned to blood, the gods shed tears,
and temples were wet with gore. The sound of groans came out
from unexpected places. (. . .)

The list with portents continues for a while, but the message is crystal clear: the gods do not accept this sacrifice. Rejection of sacrifice by the gods is not unusual in Greek literature. Fred Naiden has collected twenty-nine examples, from Homer to Sopater,[49] but as with the successful sacrifices in Quintus, he has overlooked this passage, which certainly is one of the most dramatic examples of such a rejection. Naiden was drawn to the subject by noting the neglect of the place of the gods in sacrifice in the studies by Burkert and Vernant. This is a justified observation, as the gods clearly come short in the best studies of sacrifice in the second half of the twentieth century,[50] whereas our passage is one more example of the important place of the gods in the sacrificial ritual.

---

[49] Naiden (2006).

[50] This is also one of the main points in his well-researched, but not always persuasively argued *Smoke Signals for the Gods* (Naiden 2013). Both in that book and in his article on rejected sacrifices, he has overlooked that I made the same point in Bremmer (²1999: 43); see also Bremmer (2019a: 335).

In archaic poetry, such a series of omens is unusual, as Stanford (ad *Od.* 12.395–6) already noted.[51] Normally, the gods reject a sacrifice or dreadful human behaviour with a single gesture. When Athena refused the robe of the Trojan women, she (that is, her statue) 'tossed back her head in refusal'.[52] When Cleomenes offered a sacrifice to Hera to receive further success, a flame shot out from the breast of her statue, which Cleomenes, surely rightly, interpreted as a negative reaction of the goddess,[53] and Artemis showed her disgust at the offering of unclean human victims by letting her statue turn away from its base on its own and closing its eyes (Eur. *IT* 1165–7). In Quintus' case, though, we have a whole series of portents, which are rather unique, but the best parallel is probably the passage in Vergil's *Aeneid* regarding the Palladion. After the Greeks had stolen it (2.171–5, trans. Horsfall 2008),

> *Nec dubiis ea signa dedit Tritonia monstris.*
> *Vix positum castris simulacrum: arsere coruscae*
> *luminibus flammae arrectis, salsusque per artus*
> *sudor iit, terque ipsa solo (mirabile dictu)*
> *emicuit parmamque ferens hastamque trementem.*   175

Tritonia gave signs of this by no uncertain portents.
The statue had just been set down in camp. Dancing flames
blazed from her upwards-turned eyes and salt sweat passed over her limbs.
Three times she actually leaped from the ground (a wonder to relate),
carrying her round shield and quivering spear.

Although earlier scholars were strongly divided regarding the idea of Quintus actually having read the *Aeneid*, in recent years scholars have become more receptive to the idea.[54] If it was indeed the case that he had read Vergil's poem, we cannot be sure if he did so in Latin or in translation, as Greek translations of Vergil did exist.[55] In any case, our passage might well be one of those where Vergilian influence should not be excluded.[56]

HUMAN SACRIFICE

Having taken a first look at animal sacrifice, let us now turn to the cases of human sacrifice. I will start with a non-realised human sacrifice. When Odysseus

---

[51] Stanford (²1971: vol. 1, 417).
[52] *Il.* 6.311, with Graziosi and Haubold (2010: 165–6) *ad loc.*
[53] Hdt. 6.82.2, with Hornblower and Pelling (2017: 198) *ad loc.*
[54] Gärtner (2005); James (2007); Fratantuono (2016); Ozbek (2018).
[55] Fisher (1982: 176); Tomasso (2010: 140–6); Maciver (2011).
[56] Similarly, James (2004: 332–3), but note the scepticism of Campbell (1981: 170) *ad loc.*

proposes the trick of the Trojan Horse to the Greeks, he also suggests that as part of the scheme (12.32–8),

> (. . .) Ἀλλά τις ἀνὴρ
> θαρσαλέος, τόν τ᾽ οὔ τις ἐπίσταται ἐν Τρώεσσι,
> μιμνέτω ἔκτοθ<εν> ἵππου ἀρήιον ἐνθέμενος κῆρ,
> ὅς τις ὑποκρίναιτο βίην ὑπέροπλον Ἀχαιῶν   35
> ῥέξαι ὑπὲρ νόστοιο λιλαιομένων ὑπαλύξαι,
> ἵππῳ ὑποπτήξας εὐεργέϊ τόν ῥ᾽ ἐκάμοντο
> Παλλάδι χωομένη Τρώων ὑπὲρ αἰχμητάων.

> (. . .) But one man
> of courage, unknown to anybody of the Trojans,
> must stay here next to the horse and steel his warrior heart.
> He must pretend the Achaeans wanted to sacrifice him for their return,
> but that he escaped their brutal violence by cowering under the splendid
>   horse
> that they had made to appease the anger that Pallas felt for the spearmen
>   of Troy.

We have here a suggestion of human sacrifice to enable a return for the Greeks from Troy. In fact, our sources never mention human sacrifices in order to make a return or a departure possible except for the sacrifice of Iphigeneia as described in the *Cypria*.[57] It seems likely that her sacrifice is here in the background of the suggestion. Such an echo is all the more probable, since Quintus, as we will see below, also explains the sacrifice of Polyxena as a means to prevent storms penning up the Greek fleet.

We hear more about this sacrifice later in the same book when Sinon details the supposed plans of the Greeks (12.379–84):

> (. . .) Ἀμφὶ δὲ νόστου
> ἐννεσίη<ς> Ὀδυσῆος ἐμοὶ μενέαινον ὄλεθρον,   380
> ὄφρά με δηώσωσι δυσηχέος ἄγχι θαλάσσης
> δαίμοσιν εἰναλίοις. Ἐμὲ δ᾽ οὐ λάθον, ἀλλ᾽ ἀλεγεινὰς
> σπονδάς τ᾽ οὐλοχύτας τε μάλ᾽ ἐσσυμένως ὑπαλύξας
> ἀθανάτων βουλῇσι παραὶ ποσὶ κάππεσον ἵππου·

> (. . .) To ensure
> their return they planned to kill me on the advice of Odysseus,
> sacrificing me beside the sounding sea

---

57 For this much-discussed case, see, with extensive bibliography, Bremmer (2019a: 373–402).

to the gods of the deep. But seeing this I made a dash
away from their grievous libations and barley grains,
and by the immortals' will I fell at the feet of the horse.

Once again, we hear of a sacrifice to ensure safe return,[58] but this time Sinon
provides more detail. It is noteworthy that, both here and in the earlier passage, the human sacrifice should take place to guarantee a safe return. Unfortunately, we have no other detailed source about Sinon's ploy. Although he
did appear in the *Iliou Persis* (Arg. 10 Bernabé = Arg. 2a West) and the *Little
Iliad* (F 12 West), none of our earlier sources mention a possible human sacrifice except Vergil, where the Delphic oracle gives the following advice to the
Greeks, according to Sinon (*Aen.* 2.116–19, trans. Horsfall 2008):

> *Sanguine placastis ventos et virgine caesa,*
> *cum primum Iliacas, Danai, venistis ad oras;*
> *sanguine quaerendi reditus animaque litandum*
> *Argolica.* (. . .)

> With the blood of a slaughtered virgin you appeased the winds,
> Greeks, when you first came to the shores of Ilium.
> With blood you must seek your return, and the offering must be made
> of an Argive's life. (. . .)

We are surely encouraged to see a Vergilian influence (see above, p. 147)
here in the motif of the appeasement of the gods with a human sacrifice for
a safe return. On the other hand, the sacrifice itself is described with typically
Greek, not Roman, details. But first we have to note that Quintus ascribes the
purported sacrifice to δαίμοσιν εἰναλίοις, the only time that he uses the plural
of δαίμων, a word of which he is rather fond. He could have used the word
θεοῖσιν, which he regularly uses elsewhere, but δαίμοσιν probably reflected
better the negative meaning of the supernatural beings to whom Sinon was
supposed to be sacrificed. In Homer, δαίμων was still used whenever the presence of the divine remained vague enough not to be pinned upon one of
the major deities or when it was felt that a god intervened for a short period
directly and concretely in their life, but with Empedocles we can observe the
beginning of a negative development of the word, which became normal in
later antiquity.[59] In any case, in Greek religion, such human sacrifices did not
take place and its mention here is a case of 'invention of tradition'.

---

[58] On the passage, see also Bär (forthcoming a).
[59] De Jong (²2004a: 158, 239–40); Bremmer (2019c). Major deities: note the exceptions of *Il.*
3.420 and *Od.* 3.166.

As regards the particulars of the sacrifice, we have already discussed the libations, but here we also hear of the barley groats, which were an indispensable part of the classic sacrifice. In the description of a sacrifice in the *Odyssey*, Nestor pronounced a prayer, after which the other participants in the sacrifice 'threw the barley groats forward' (3.447), but in classical times they were, now perhaps mixed with salt, thrown on the altar and the victim during and/or after the prayer.[60] In fact, the barley groats had become so prominent that Herodotus (1.132) noted their conspicuous absence in Persian sacrifices. However, in later literary descriptions of sacrifice, the barley groats seem to disappear, and in inscriptions we do not hear of them any more after the end of the third century BCE.

We leave the area of deceit and trickery with another sacrifice, that of the Trojan prisoners for Achilles. Evidently, one can debate whether this is a proper sacrifice or just ritual slaughter. It would carry us too far to discuss this problem here in detail. Let it suffice to observe that the killing of the Trojans is not a proper sacrifice, but that its combination with the usual sacrificial victims will at least have evoked sacrifices for the average reader. I think that this is as far as we can go.

After the Greeks had collected an enormous amount of wood for Achilles' pyre (3.678–82),

> Ἀμφὶ δὲ τεύχεα πολλὰ πυρῇ περινηήσαντο
> αἰζηῶν κταμένων, πολλοὺς δ' ἐφύπερθε βάλοντο
> Τρώων δῃώσαντες ὁμῶς περικαλλέας υἷας   680
> ἵππους τε χρεμέθοντας εὐσθενέας θ' ἅμα ταύρους,
> σὺν δ' ὀίάς τε σύας τ' ἔβαλον βρίθοντας ἀλοιφῇ·

Round the pyre they piled a quantity of armour
from men killed in battle. There too they slaughtered many
of the fairest sons of Troy and threw them on the pyre,
together with neighing horses and powerful bulls
and, thrown there also, sheep and fine fat pigs.

As has often been observed, the main inspiration for this scene is the funeral of Patroclus in the *Iliad* (23.166–83), which is partially reflected in Achilles' report of his own funeral in the *Odyssey* (24.65–70). From the former, Quintus took the horses,[61] bulls, the sheep and the slaughtered Trojans (680, δῃώσαντες ~ *Il.* 23.176, δηϊόων), who are notably absent from the *Odyssey* passage. Interestingly, Quintus does not mention the dogs, which might not have looked

---

[60] Bednarek (2017); Paul (2018); Bednarek (2019).
[61] For horse sacrifices, see Georgoudi (2005a).

heroic enough in his eyes, but he adds pigs. The combination of bulls, sheep and pigs conforms to a well-known sacrificial triad in Greece, the *trittoia*, which is already mentioned in the *Odyssey* (11.130), and probably goes back much earlier.[62] Perhaps, we may note that these three male victims also occur in Vergil's description of the funeral of Pallas (*Aen.* 11.197–9), although they should perhaps not be seen as an instance of the Roman *suovetaurilia* sacrifice.[63] Once again, Vergil may well be in the background of this Quintan passage.

Our final example of a human sacrifice is one that was well known in antiquity: the sacrifice of Polyxena, who, with Iphigeneia, perhaps is the most famous human sacrificial victim in antiquity.[64] We turn to the last book of Quintus' epic, which describes the departure of the Greeks. After they had celebrated their victory and finally gone to bed, Achilles appeared to his son Neoptolemos, whom he asked to sacrifice Polyxena because he was terribly angry with the Greeks, and Agamemnon in particular. If they did not do it, he would send storm after storm to prevent their departure. But he would not object to Polyxena being properly buried away from his grave (14.209–22). Quintus follows here a familiar strand of the tradition, although the oldest evidence did not yet speak of Polyxena's sacrifice. According to the *Cypria* (F 34 Bernabé = 27 Davies), Odysseus and Diomedes fatally wounded her during the capture of Troy.[65] However, virtually at the same time, a more gruesome variant arose. According to Proclus' summary of the *Iliou Persis* (p. 89 Bernabé = Arg 4c West), Stesichorus (S 135–6 Davies = F 118 Finglass), Ibycus (F 258)[66] and Simonides (F 557), Polyxena was sacrificed to the ghost of Achilles and slaughtered by his son Neoptolemos. The dramatic detail that it was the ghost of Achilles himself who requested the sacrifice was probably first introduced by Sophocles (F 522–8 Radt), but became the standard version in later poets.[67]

The reason for Achilles' continuing anger remains obscure in our text, as does the choice of Polyxena. In Euripides (*Hec.* 94–5), just one of the Trojan women is requested without any name, but the passage is likely to be a later interpolation,[68] and we simply do not have enough early evidence to recover the reason for Polyxena's selection. Martin West's suggestion that, as a daughter

---

[62] Cf. Stengel (1910: 195–6); add *CGRN* 25.A. fr. 12.5, 8, 11 (Athens), 32.41 (Thorikos); van Straten (1995: 14–18) (vases); Watkins (1995: 197); Santos (2008).

[63] Horsfall (2003: 152).

[64] For the literary and iconographical evidence, see Touchefeu-Meynier (1994); add *SEG* 45.2150; Tuna-Norling (2001); Linant de Bellefonds (2009); with detailed bibliography, Bremmer (2019a: 352–7), which I freely use here. For modern representations, see Posner (1991).

[65] For a slightly different interpretation of the passage, see Hedreen (2001: 136–7); West (2013: 55, n1) ascribes the notice to a prose history of Cyprus, which is possible, but not compelling.

[66] Robertson (1970).

[67] Cf. Eur. *Hec.* 37–44; *Anth. Pal.* 9.117; Ov. *Met.* 13.441–8; Sen. *Tro.* 168–202; Triph. 686–7.

[68] West (2013: 242); Battezzato (2018: 86).

of the defeated enemy king, she might have been chosen to give Achilles a consort in the underworld, is wholly speculative and lacks any convincing parallels. However, the threat of penning up the Greek fleet with storms is clearly taken from the myth of Iphigeneia and is also found in Aeschylus;[69] a variant of this motif is the lack of wind, which we frequently find in Euripides' *Iphigeneia in Aulis* (10, 88, 352, 1596).

The Greeks did not hesitate and immediately performed the sacrifice (14.257–62, 267–9):[70]

> Ὡς φάμενοι ποτὶ τύμβον Ἀχιλλέος ἀπονέοντο.
> Τὴν δ' ἄγον, ἠΰτε πόρτιν ἐς <ἀ>θανάτοιο θυηλὰς
> μητρὸς ἀπειρύσσαντες ἐνὶ ξυλόχοισι βοτῆρες,
> ἣ δ' ἄρα μακρὰ βοῶσα κινύρεται ἀχνυμένη κῆρ·   260
> ὣς τῆμος Πριάμοιο πάις περικωκύεσκε
> δυσμενέων ἐν χερσίν. Ἄδην δέ οἱ ἔκχυτο δάκρυ
> (. . .)
> ὣς ἄρα καὶ Πριάμοιο πολυτλήτοιο θυγατρὸς
> ἑλκομένης ποτὶ τύμβον ἀμειλίκτου Ἀχιλῆος
> αἰνὸν ὁμῶς στοναχῇσι κατὰ βλεφάρων ῥέε δάκρυ·

That said, they left for the tomb of Achilles
leading Polyxena like a heifer for sacrifice to a god,
torn by herdsmen from its mother in the woods,
and she, in its heart's distress, calls loudly and pitifully.
Such then was the lamentation of Priam's daughter,
in the hands of her enemies shedding copious tears.
(. . .)
So now, as the daughter of much-enduring Priam
was dragged toward the tomb of merciless Achilles,
cruel tears flowed from her eyes accompanied by her groaning.

The scene evokes the procession of a sacrifice, but not in the traditional manner of the animal or, for that matter, of the human sacrifice. The scene starts with the 'leading' (ἄγον) of Polyxena, a verb that is normally used for leading animals by hand.[71] As such it would be perfectly fitting, as we can see animal victims being led in that manner on representations of sacrificial processions

---

[69] Aesch. *Ag.* 148–9, 214–15. For lack of wind, note also Eur. *IT* 15–16; Soph. *El.* 564; Ov. *Met.* 13.183–4; cf. Diggle (2007: 147–50).

[70] Given the subject of my contribution, I concentrate exclusively on the sacrifice itself, as a full commentary on the whole of Quintus' passage would far exceed my space and competence.

[71] Cf. Chantraine (1956: 32–3).

on vase paintings.[72] Traditionally, most processions were led by a well-dressed girl, the *kanēphoros*,[73] but here the only girl is Polyxena, who, poignantly, twice has been called εὔπεπλον, 'well dressed'. (14.214, 241). She is compared to a heifer, as was not unusual in ancient Greece, where young girls were often compared to unruly young animals, such as heifers, fillies or even fawns.[74] However, Quintus' allusions here will also no doubt include the moments in Euripides where both Polyxena and Iphigeneia are also compared to a heifer,[75] in this case even a very young one.[76]

It belonged to the ideology of Greek sacrifice that an animal voluntarily went to the altar, and sometimes could almost hardly wait to be sacrificed.[77] However, the reality was more stubborn, and ideology and practice did not always concur: vases sometimes show us ephebes struggling with the victim or the ropes tied to its head or legs in order to restrain it. Euripides liked to put voluntary human victims on the stage.[78] Aeschylus (*Ag.* 236–7), however, was more 'realistic': his Agamemnon ordered the sacrificial servants to gag Iphigeneia and wrap her in clothes. An Attic red-figure oinochoe of about 430–420 BCE even shows Iphigeneia clearly being dragged to her death.[79] This is also the case with Quintus' Polyxena, who has to be 'dragged' (14.268, ἑλκομένης) to Achilles' grave.

There is a brief delay in the action with Hekabe remembering a frightening dream and lamenting her and Polyxena's fate (14.272–303), but then the pace quickens again. When they arrived at the tomb of deified Achilles (14.305–17),

δὴ τότε οἱ φίλος υἱὸς ἐρυσσάμενος θοὸν ἄορ   305
σκαιῇ μὲν κούρην κατερήτυε, δεξιτερῇ δὲ
τύμβῳ ἐπιψαύων τοῖον ποτὶ μῦθον ἔειπε·
'Κλῦθι, πάτερ, σέο παιδὸς ἐπευχομένοιο καὶ ἄλλων
Ἀργείων μηδ' ἥμιν ἔτ' ἀργαλέως χαλέπαινε·

---

[72] For the sacrificial procession, see, most recently, van Straten (1995: 14–30); Bonnechère (1997: 63–89); Gebauer (2002: 17–212).

[73] Van Straten (1995: 14–24); Roccos (1995).

[74] Heifer: *Hymn to Demeter* 174. Fillies: Nisbet and Rudd (2004: 154–5) on Hor. *Carm.* 3.11.9.

[75] Eur. *Hec.* 206, 525–6 (Polyxena), *IT* 359–60, *IA* 1081–3 (Iphigeneia); see also Spinoula (2000: 159–60).

[76] Is there an allusion to Homer here? Cf. Q.S. 14.258–9, τὴν δ' ἄγον, ἠύτε **πόρτιν** ἐς <ἀ>θανάτοιο θυηλὰς / μητρὸς ἀπειρύσσαντες ἐνὶ ξυλόχοισι βοτῆρες ∼ *Il.* 5.161–2, ὡς δὲ λέων ἐν βουσὶ θορὼν ἐξ αὐχένα ἄξῃ / **πόρτιος** ἠὲ βοὸς ξύλοχον κάτα βοσκομενάων.

[77] Meuli (1946: 226, 254–5, 266–7) (= Meuli 1975: 950, 982, 995–6); see also van Straten (1995: 100–2); Himmelmann (1997: 38–40); Gebauer (2002: 181, 203). This is unpersuasively contested by Naiden (2013: 83–90); see also Georgoudi (2008: 139–53); Parker (2011: 129–30).

[78] From the huge bibliography, see, most recently, Oikonomopoulou (2004); Roselli (2007); Bremmer (2019d).

[79] Kahil and Linant de Bellefonds (1990: 708–9), no. 1; cf. Mylonopoulos (2013: 69–70).

ἤδη γάρ τοι πάντα τελέσσομεν ὅσσα μενοινᾷς   310
σῇσιν ἐνὶ πραπίδεσσι· σὺ δ' ἵλαος ἄμμι γένοιο
τεύξας εὐχομένοισι θοῶς θυμηδέα νόστον.'
Ὣς εἰπὼν κούρης διὰ λοίγιον ἤλασεν ἄορ
λαυκανίης· τὴν δ' αἶψα λίπεν πολυήρατος αἰὼν
οἰκτρὸν ἀνοιμώξασαν ἐφ' ὑστατίῃ βιότοιο   315
Καί ῥ' ἣ μὲν πρηνὴς χαμάδις πέσε· τῆς δ' ὑπὸ δειρὴ
φοινίχθη περὶ πάντα. (. . .)

Then his beloved son first drew his swift sword.
With his left hand he held the maiden back, while with his right
touching the tomb, he spoke the following words:
'Father, hear the prayer of your son and of the other
Argives and be no longer harsh and angry with us.
Soon we shall have carried out everything
that you have set your heart on. So be propitious to us
and quickly grant the sweet return for which we pray.'
With that he plunged his lethal sword into the throat
of the maiden. Quickly the life that she loved left her,
as she uttered a pitiful wail on the threshold of death.
She fell to the ground face downward and her neck
all the way round was reddened. (. . .)

It is striking that we do not hear any details which would normally be part
of a sacrifice, such as mention of the sacrificial basket, libations or the groats.
Instead, Neoptolemos holds Polyxena back, surely in order to prevent any
struggling or resistance; similarly, at Polyxena's sacrifice in Euripides' *Hekabe*,
there were 'selected youths' present to check 'any leap your calf' should make,
as Thaltybios tells Hekabe (525–6). In Euripides' *Hekabe*, Polyxena is standing
(524),[80] like Iphigeneia on several vase paintings,[81] and it is clear that in Quintus,
too, she is represented standing, as later she falls on to the ground. Although
representations of Polyxena's sacrifice are rare,[82] at the beginning of the sixth
century an archaic Attic vase painter and in its last decades an Ionian sculptor
pictured Polyxena being lifted up like an animal,[83] and Aeschylus describes the

---

[80] Battezzato (2018: 145), *ad* 524, is somewhat confusing at this point, as he compares representations of Iphigeneia, but the latter is lifted up above the altar.

[81] Attic oenochoe: see my note 79 above. Apulian volute krater: Kahil and Linant de Bellefonds (1990: 710), no. 4; Taplin (2007: 159–60). Selinuntine lekythos: Marconi (1994); Mylonopoulos (2013: 68–9).

[82] For Etruscan representations, see Steuernagel (1998: 42–4), reviewed by Bonnechère (2000).

[83] Schwarz (2001); Reinsberg (2003; 2004); Linant de Bellefonds (2009: 431), *add.* 5*; Mylonopoulos (2013: 76–8); Corfù (2016); Draycott (2018).

sacrificing of Iphigeneia in his *Agamemnon* in the same manner.[84] Apparently, there was no fixed tradition about the way Polyxena was sacrificed.

It was always common, though, to pronounce a prayer just before the actual kill, as is already the case in the *Odyssey*.[85] In essence, Neoptolemos' prayer is not unlike his prayer in the *Hekabe* (534–41), although much shorter and with no attention to the blood. And as in the case of the *Hekabe*, the prayer will not be fulfilled for many of the Greeks. In hindsight, as the readers know of course, the sacrifice will prove to be futile.[86]

No other details of a normal animal sacrifice are mentioned, but the text immediately proceeds with the actual killing, which is performed by Neoptolemos. He pierces Polyxena's throat with his sword, just as he does in the *Hekabe* (567); similarly, in the case of Iphigeneia, Achilles wishes Artemis to receive the 'pure blood from the throat of the beautiful virgin' as the sacrifice from the Greek army and Agamemnon (Eur. *IA* 1574). It is noteworthy that the use of a sword was not the right way of sacrificing. In the standard animal sacrifice, the sacrificer used a special knife, the *machaira*, which was brought in the sacrificial basket and taken out only at the very last moment.[87] However, the sword and the prominence of blood points instead to the *sphagia*, the sacrifice before a battle.[88] Quintus clearly continues a tradition already found in Aeschylus' *Agamemnon*, whose comparison of Iphigeneia to a she-goat (232, *chimaira*) alludes to such a *sphagia*.[89] In the battle-line sacrifice, a sacrificial victim – on vase paintings usually a ram – is killed by the piercing of its neck or throat. In reality, the piercing must have resulted in a heavy spurt of blood, but we are never shown it on the vase paintings, although our text is very clear in this respect.[90] But why is it noted that Polyxena fell 'face downward'? The expression is Homeric and typical for warriors dying.[91] Yet, can it perhaps also be that this is an allusion to her gesture in the *Hekabe* where she falls 'concealing for male eyes what had to be concealed' (568–70)? The scene was very well known in antiquity and repeatedly imitated, mentioned or alluded to by Roman authors, for example Ovid (*Met.* 13.479–80; *Fasti* 2.833–4) and Pliny (*Ep.* 4.11.9), Greek poets (*Anth. Pal.* 16.150) and even Christian writers, such as Clement of Alexandria (*Strom.* 2.144.1) and the editor of the *Passio Perpetuae et Felicitatis* (20.4), who lets Perpetua rearrange her clothes

---

[84] Aesch. *Ag.* 231–8, to be read with the observations by Maas (1951) and Radt (1973: 121).

[85] *Od.* 3.445–6; Eur. *El.* 803; Isaeus 8.16; Agatharchides *FGrH* 86 F 5; Apoll. Rhod. 1.425.

[86] As noted by Battezzato (2018: 147).

[87] Plato F 98 Kassel/Austin; Ar. *Pax* 948 with schol.; Eur. *El.* 810, *IA* 1565; Philostr. *VA* 1.1; Suda κ 318; cf. Durand (1986: 103–15); Bonnechère (1999); Georgoudi (2005b).

[88] Jouan (1990/91); Gebauer (2002: 280–5); Dillery (2005: 200–9); Parker (2009); Jameson (2014: 98–144).

[89] For the importance of blood in the *sphagia*, see Jameson (2014: 104–8).

[90] Cf. Ekroth (2005: 13–14).

[91] Graziosi and Haubold (2010: 87, 165) on *Il.* 6.42–3, 307; Carvounis (2019: 155) on Q.S. 14.316.

after being tossed by a cow in the arena.[92] Given his readers' deep familiarity
with the scene, Quintus may have felt it necessary to at least allude to Polyxena's
fall with decency.

CONCLUSION

With the sacrifice of Polyxena, we have come to the end of our discussion. To
what extent can we answer the questions posed in our introduction? I would
like to note the following points:

1. Let us start by observing that the animal sacrifices are hardly described in
    any detail. We do not hear of specifics about the age, colour, gender or
    place to consume the meat – details which are so prominent in the *leges
    sacrae*. This absence can also be observed in the Greek novels, and these
    detailed prescriptions may well have been typical of the various sanctuaries
    and played a much smaller role in sacrifices in everyday life outside the
    sanctuaries. On the other hand, it is also typical of Quintus' epic that he
    minimises references to religious ritual,[93] and this tendency may also have
    played a role in his descriptions of sacrifice.
2. The reasons for sacrifice vary. As we have seen, it can be a way of show-
    ing the divinity of the worshipped supernatural being (3.771–8), an act of
    gratitude (14.101–10), a way of having a nice banquet (14.331–5), a means
    of appeasing the Erinyes (1.28–32), and an attempt at gaining the favour of
    the gods (12.500–9). None of these are out of the ordinary, and Quintus
    clearly moves within the sacrificial tradition of his poetic predecessors.
3. Yet it is rather striking that when he zooms in on a sacrifice, Quintus sin-
    gles out elements that were probably no longer practised in his own time.
    The thigh bones are not mentioned any more in the *leges sacrae* after the
    third century BCE, and in the 'sacred laws' we last hear of the barley groats
    in the second century BCE. In this respect, it also looks significant that the
    term οὐλοχύται already becomes explained in Homeric and lexicographi-
    cal scholarship of the early Roman period.[94] Apparently, the sacrificial
    ritual had become simplified over the course of the centuries, perhaps
    under Roman influence. This makes it all the more interesting to observe
    that Quintus selects precisely those elements of the sacrifice to emphasise.
    There seems to be an antiquarian interest in Quintus, or a wish to focus on

---

[92] Braun (1983); Friesen (2016).
[93] Cf. Wenglinsky (2002: 328): 'Quintus' limited description of sacrifice'; Wenglinsky (2002: 347).
[94] Aristonicus on *Od.* 3.445 Carnuth; Apion fr. 96 Neitzel; Apollonius Soph. p. 124 Bekker;
      Pollux 1.33.

specifically Greek elements of sacrifice in the Roman world, which would deserve further investigation.

4. There is not much attention to the specific gods to whom the Greeks sacrifice. The singling out of Achilles is noticeable, but in the other cases we only hear of sacrifices 'to the gods' or 'to the immortals', except in the case of the Erinyes. This is even the case in the rejected sacrifice, whereas often in Greek tradition such rejections are ascribed to one god.[95] This minimising of the role of individual gods fits a general pattern of Quintus' *Posthomerica*, in which the gods are clearly less important than in Homer's epics and are largely depersonalised.[96] Moreover, the status of the figure of Zeus has been heightened in comparison to that of the other gods.[97] It may well be that the growing autocracy of the emperor also exerted a certain influence on Quintus' pantheon. The deification of Achilles might suggest a rejection of the belief in heroes, which is attested for the Epicureans.[98] The latter also rejected the interference of the gods in human life,[99] which is a clear characteristic of Quintus' epic.[100] In this connection, we might perhaps also note the prominent Epicurean inscription of Diogenes in Lycian (see above, pp. 138–9) Oenoanda and the popularity of Epicureanism, atheism lite, among the Greek elites in Asia Minor.[101]

5. As regards human sacrifice, Quintus clearly imagines it as happening like animal sacrifice, witness his mention of 'libations and barley groats' in the case of Sinon (12.383). This is perhaps not surprising, as there was no fixed tradition regarding a ritual of human sacrifice. The poets therefore took details from their knowledge of practised sacrifices, that is, from animal sacrifices. But Quintus is reticent in his particulars, and it is perhaps note-worthy that in this case he mentions 'innocent' parts of the ritual with no description of the knife or the killing. It is different with Polyxena, but in her case, too, Quintus is sparing with details. This restraint fits the general tenor of his work, which in general avoids the more excessively graphic details.[102] It is clear that Homer's description of Patroclus' funeral and the Epic Cycle's account of Iphigeneia were enormously influential, given

---

[95] Naiden (2006: 196).

[96] For the gods in Quintus, see Wenglinsky (2002); Bär (2016).

[97] Wenglinsky (2002: 347); Bär (2016: 222–3).

[98] Plut. *Mor.* 420cd; Ps. Plut. *Mor.* 882b (= Epicurus fr. 393 Usener).

[99] O'Keefe (2010: 155–6).

[100] Bär (2016: 219). See also Barbaresco's contribution in this volume.

[101] Scholz (2017: 170–3) (popularity); for the inscription, see, most recently, Hammerstaedt, Morel and Güremen (2017).

[102] Wenglinsky (2002: *passim*). But for exceptions, see Kauffman (2018), with an interesting dis-cussion of Quintus' reference to an arena spectacle (6.531–7), the pervasiveness of which is also illustrated by its occurrence in dreams; cf. Quintus' slightly younger contemporary Artemidorus 2.54; Barbaresco (2019).

the regular connection between human sacrifice and the enabling of the Greek fleet to set sail (12.35, 379–80; 14.216–17). Yet we have also seen that Quintus did not follow his examples slavishly but felt free to invent, for example, a human sacrifice to the gods of the deep (12.382) or the *trittoia* of Achilles' funeral (3.681–2).

In the end, sacrifice plays only a minor role in Quintus' epic. Yet even in this minor part we can observe typical characteristics of his epic: the avoidance of more excessive graphic details, the non-intervention of the gods and the attention to typically Greek, not Roman, elements of sacrifice. In this way, sacrifice is still an important prism for acquiring a better insight into the mental and religious world of this obscure and underestimated poet.[103]

[103] I am most grateful to Raphael Brendel and, especially, Silvio Bär for information and comments and to Emma Greensmith for her kind and skilful correction of my English.

PART III

Between Narratology and Lexicology

A Narratological Study of the Role of the Fates in the *Posthomerica*

Eirini Argyrouli

Fate is a typical element in epic poetry from the Homeric poems onwards. Its main personifications are Κήρ/Κῆρες, Μοῖρα/Μοῖραι, and Αἶσα. In this chapter I will examine the role of Fate in Quintus Smyrnaeus' *Posthomerica* (*PH*) in order to understand how the narratological devices used help the poet to create a specific representation of Fate in his work. Having as a basis Irene de Jong's narratological study of the *Iliad*,[1] I will look at Quintus' text and study three narratological aspects in connection to the Fates: focalisation, space and time. Specifically, I will address the following three questions: first, how does the presence of the Fates affect time in the *PH*? Secondly, what is the special placement of the Fates in the space where the action unfolds? And, thirdly, how does focalisation function in instances where the Fates are involved in the action, and how do they influence the narration in these episodes?[2]

Quintus' *PH* is a sequel to the *Iliad*. It follows the *Iliad* in terms of language and form, and it also shares its narrative techniques, plot sequences and imagery.[3] One of the major Homeric concepts that Quintus adopts and reforms is that of

---

[1] De Jong (²2004a).

[2] Prior to addressing these questions, it would be helpful to introduce some basic narratological terms, starting with the narrator, the narratee and focalisation: the 'voice' that tells the story is the narrator. In the *PH* there is an external narrator, which means that he is not a character in the story but tells the events as an omniscient storyteller. He is also 'primary', which means that he is the main voice that narrates and we learn the events through his point of view. In de Jong's (2014: 47) words, 'The viewing of the events of the fabula is called focalization: there is the seeing or recalling of events, their emotional filtering and temporal ordering, and the fleshing out of space into scenery and persons into characters.' The primary, external narrator focalises and tells a story to us; we are his audience and we are the external (because we are not characters of the story) narratees (de Jong 2004b).

[3] Maciver (2018: 71–89) gives an analytical account of the *PH* as a sequel of the *Iliad*.

Fate. In the *Iliad* it is presented as a power that determines human life. Scholars of Homer have tried to interpret different aspects of Fate and to examine the balance between its power and the power of the gods.[4]

The following three passages of the *Iliad* give a clear idea of what the 'Homeric' Fate is. The first is that of the golden scales. In Book 22 of the *Iliad* the narrator describes the battle between Achilles and Hektor. During their fight, Zeus presents the golden scales. He places on them δύο κῆρε and he weighs the fateful portions of each hero. The scale is heavier on Hektor's side and this determines that his αἴσιμον ἦμαρ ('the fatal day of death') has arrived. Indeed, he is killed by Achilles in this same episode (22.209–13):

> 1. καὶ τότε δὴ χρύσεια πατὴρ ἐτίταινε τάλαντα,
> ἐν δ' ἐτίθει δύο κῆρε τανηλεγέος θανάτοιο,   210
> τὴν μὲν Ἀχιλλῆος, τὴν δ' Ἕκτορος ἱπποδάμοιο,
> εἷλκε δὲ μέσσα λαβών· ῥέπε δ' Ἕκτορος αἴσιμον ἦμαρ.
> ᾤχετο δ' εἰς Ἀΐδαο, λίπεν δέ ἑ Φοῖβος Ἀπόλλων.

> Then the Father balanced his golden scales, and in them
> he set two fateful portions of death, which lays men prostrate,
> one for Achilleus, and one for Hektor, breaker of horses,
> and balanced it by the middle; and Hektor's death-day was heavier
> and dragged downward toward death, and Phoibos Apollo forsook him.[5]

The Fates in this episode do not act; they are placed on the scales by Zeus. Neither gods nor humans challenge the result of the scales because there is a common acceptance that fate is inevitable.[6] Their presence is decisive for the disclosure of the outcome of the battle, but they are not presented as personified active deities and they do not intervene in the action. The weighing of the scales is an incident that is included also in Book 3 (540–1) of the *PH*. In these passages, Fate is not an acting, personified deity; rather, it functions as a power, a representation of the idea that human life and death is predetermined.[7]

---

[4] Scholarly works in the latest decades regarding the Fates in the *Iliad* include: Morrison (1997: 273–96), who sees in the *Iliad* a tendency of Homer to discretely undermine and question the fated predestination by projecting alternative outcomes to the story; outcomes, however, that never are fulfilled. Sarischoulis (2016: 81–105) argues that fate in the *Iliad* predetermines a mortal's death but not one's choices during one's life, and that therefore there is space for free will and not everything is controlled by the Fates. See also Ehnmark (1999: 359–68) and Pirenne-Delforge and Pironti (2011: 93–114).

[5] All translations of the *Iliad* are taken from Lattimore (1951).

[6] Morrison (1997: 274).

[7] Schein (1984: 47) observes that Moira in the *Iliad* never brings gifts or blessings. The positive things are given to humans by the gods. Quintus follows Homer in this respect, presenting the Fates as bearers of death. On this aspect, see Gärtner (2007: 238).

The gods of the *Iliad* seem to know beforehand the way a mortal is to die, but they do not cause, provoke or cancel the fated events.[8] For example, in Book 16, Zeus seems upset that Sarpedon is destined to die. He knows that 'it is destined that the dearest of men, Sarpedon, must go down under the hands of Menoitios' son Patroklos' (*Il.* 16.433–4) and he reveals to Hera that he considers two options: one is to save Sarpedon by removing him from the battle; the other is to accept that his end has arrived (16.431–8):

2. τοὺς δὲ ἰδὼν ἐλέησε Κρόνου πάϊς ἀγκυλομήτεω,
Ἥρην δὲ προσέειπε, κασιγνήτην ἄλοχόν τε·
'ὤι μοι ἐγών, ὅ τέ μοι Σαρπηδόνα φίλτατον ἀνδρῶν
μοῖρ' ὑπὸ Πατρόκλοιο Μενοιτιάδαο δαμῆναι.
διχθὰ δέ μοι κραδίη μέμονε φρεσὶν ὁρμαίνοντι,   435
ἤ μιν ζωὸν ἐόντα μάχης ἄπο δακρυοέσσης
θείω ἀναρπάξας Λυκίης ἐν πίονι δήμωι,
ἢ ἤδη ὑπὸ χερσὶ Μενοιτιάδαο δαμάσσω.'

And watching them the son of devious-devising Kronos
was pitiful, and spoke to Hera, his wife and his sister:
'Ah me, that it is destined that the dearest of men, Sarpedon,
must go down under the hands of Menoitios' son Patroklos.
The heart in my breast is balanced between two ways as I ponder,
whether I should snatch him out of the sorrowful battle
and set him down still alive in the rich country of Lykia,
or beat him under at the hands of the son of Menoitios.'

Hera seems quite surprised that Zeus wants to change the ancient destiny that hangs above Sarpedon. She then challenges him to actually do it (ἔρδ'), but prepares him that the rest of the gods will react (16.439–49):

3. τὸν δ' ἠμείβετ' ἔπειτα βοῶπις πότνια Ἥρη·
'αἰνότατε Κρονίδη, ποῖον τὸν μῦθον ἔειπες;   440
ἄνδρα θνητὸν ἐόντα, πάλαι πεπρωμένον αἴσηι,
ἂψ ἐθέλεις θανάτοιο δυσηχέος ἐξαναλῦσαι;
ἔρδ'· ἀτὰρ οὔ τοι πάντες ἐπαινέομεν θεοὶ ἄλλοι.
ἄλλο δέ τοι ἐρέω, σὺ δ' ἐνὶ φρεσὶ βάλλεο σῆισιν·
αἴ κε ζὼν πέμψηις Σαρπηδόνα ὅνδε δόμονδε,   445
φράζεο, μή τις ἔπειτα θεῶν ἐθέλησι καὶ ἄλλος
πέμπειν ὃν φίλον υἱὸν ἀπὸ κρατερῆς ὑσμίνης.
πολλοὶ γὰρ περὶ ἄστυ μέγα Πριάμοιο μάχονται
υἱέες ἀθανάτων. (. . .)'

---

[8] Richardson (1990: 138–9).

In turn the lady Hera of the ox eyes answered him:
'Majesty, son of Kronos, what sort of thing have you spoken?
Do you wish to bring back a man who is mortal, one long since
doomed by his destiny, from ill-sounding death and release him?
Do it then; but not all the rest of us gods shall approve you.
And put away in your thoughts this other thing I tell you;
if you bring Sarpedon back to his home, still living,
think how then some other one of the gods might also
wish to carry his own son out of the strong encounter;
since around the great city of Priam are fighting many
sons of the immortals. (. . .)'

Hera warns Zeus that the rest of the gods might feel resentment towards him
if he intervenes, and they too might as well try to save their own favourite
mortals from fated death. Hera's words make Zeus realise that he must not
save Sarpedon. The infringement of destiny seems to be a rather complex
matter, so eventually, he does not dare to provoke it.[9] Once again Fate in this
passage is not presented as a personified divinity, but, as a power that controls
the life of Sarpedon.

Quintus follows Homer in retaining in his poem the role of Fate as a
controller of human life, but he gives new traits to it and reshapes its traditional
representation[10] and increases the presence and importance of the Fates in his
epic. In the *PH* there are 87 references to the Fates.[11] Scholars have already discussed the role of the Fates in the *PH*. Francis Vian, Francisco Antonio García
Romero and Calum A. Maciver see traces of the Stoic idea of determinism
in the strong role of Fate in the epic. Maria Wenglinsky analyses the different
ways the gods are represented in the *PH* as compared to Homer's *Iliad* and
Odyssey, Apollonius' *Argonautica*, Virgil's *Aeneid* etc. – among other deities, she
also studies the case of the Fates. Ursula Gärtner dedicated a full chapter to Fate
in its different personifications in Quintus' epic.[12] In the next three sections

---

[9] Schein (1984: 63–5) and Richardson (1990: 194–5) observe that the fated events are never
challenged and the possibility of Zeus overpowering fate is never put to the test in this passage.

[10] Bär (2016: 227); Wenglinsky (2002: 79). See also García Romero (1985: 105); James and Lee
(2000: 11–13); Gärtner (2007: 238; 2014: 100–1).

[11] *PH*: Book 1: 173, 193, 204, 307, 310, 390, 493, 591, 651, 680; Book 2: 13, 172, 236, 266, 361, 483,
510, 515; Book 3: 14, 41, 44, 331, 615, 650, 757; Book 4: 433; Book 5: 34, 332, 536, 582, 594, 601,
611; Book 6: 13, 392, 561; Book 7: 10, 75, 247, 289, 613, 669; Book 8: 11, 109, 127, 152, 173, 319,
323, 474; Book 9: 145, 416, 500; Book 10: 97, 107, 109, 286, 304, 330, 344, 377, 405, 428; Book 11:
39, 105, 140, 151, 185, 272, 296; Book 12: 171, 523, 527, 548, 564; Book 13: 126, 154, 177, 235, 280,
494, 559; Book 14: 97, 293, 365, 563.

[12] Vian (1963: XVI); García Romero (1985: 101–6); Wenglinsky (2002); Gärtner (2007: 211–40);
Maciver (2012a: 101–23); Bär (2016: 215–30). See also Gärtner (2014: 97–219) and the chapter
of Maciver in this volume, which discuss the relation of Quintus with the Stoic ideology.

I will look into passages from the *PH* where the Fates play a determining role, and I will analyse their narratological ramifications.

TIME

The first question on which I will focus is how the presence of the Fates influences the flow of time in the story. Often, the narrator places the Fates in passages where he alludes to a future development, that is, in a prolepsis. A prolepsis is used in order to prepare the narratees 'for later developments by announcing them beforehand, either implicitly or explicitly'.[13] The effect of this device 'depends to a large degree on the fact that their information reaches the narratees, but not the characters'.[14] In the *PH*, we often see that when the Fates approach a hero or intervene in the action, it is connected to an early announcement of the character's death.

An example of prolepsis is found early in *PH* 11, where Aineias and Eurymachos spread panic among the Greeks who flee, trying to save their lives. At this moment, one of the Argives finds the courage to turn against the two heroes (11.184–92):

4. Ἔνθα τις Ἀργείων, ἢ κάρτεϊ πάγχυ πεποιθώς,
ἢ Μοίρης ἰότητι, λιλαιομένης μιν ὀλέσσαι,   185
φεύγοντ᾽ ἐκ πολέμοιο δυσηχέος ἵππον ἔρυκε
γνάμψαι ἐπειγόμενος ποτὶ φύλοπιν, ὄφρα μάχηται
ἀντία δυσμενέων. Τὸν δ᾽ ὀβριμόθυμος Ἀγήνωρ
παρφθάμενος μυῶνα κατ᾽ ἀλγινόεντα δάιξεν
ἀμφιτόμῳ βουπλῆγι· βίη δ᾽ ὑπόειξε σιδήρου   190
ὀστέον οὐταμένοιο βραχίονος· ἀμφὶ δὲ νεῦρα
ῥηιδίως ἤμησε· φλέβες δ᾽ ὑπερέβλυσαν αἷμα.

Now one of the Argives, either too confident in his strength
Or else because his death had been determined by Fate,
Stopped his horse's attempt to flee the din of battle,
Eager to turn it back to the fray, that he might face
And fight the foe. Stouthearted Agenor was, however,
Too quick for him and slashed his sensitive upper arm
With a two-edged battle-ax. The bone of his smitten arm
Yielded to the force of steel, the sinews were severed
Easily and blood came spurting from the veins.[15]

---

[13] Schmitz (2007b: 70).

[14] De Jong (2007: 25). See also de Jong (²2004a: 86).

[15] The textual edition of the *PH* used in this chapter is that by Vian (1963, -66, -69). All translations are taken from James (2004).

The anonymous Greek hero does the opposite to the rest of the Argives. While they run away from the Trojans, he turns and fights against them. Here the narrator intrudes and explains what drove him to do this: 'either too confident in his strength / Or else because his death had been determined by Fate'. The narratees are being informed of the fact that the hero is going to be killed very soon.[16] This glimpse into the future increases the tension and strengthens the role of the primary narrator as a storyteller who knows not only the present and the past, but also the future.

Another asset of prolepsis is that it creates dramatic irony because the characters are oblivious to the fact that their moment of death is close.[17] This is observed in the next passage from Book 3 (11–17):

5. (. . .) τοὶ δὲ καὶ αὐτοὶ
καί περ ὑποτρομέοντες ἐυμμελίην Ἀχιλῆα
τείχεος ἐξεχέοντο μεμαότες, οὕνεκ' ἄρα σφι
Κῆρες ἐνὶ στέρνοισι θράσος βάλον· ἦ γὰρ ἔμελλον
πολλοὶ ἀνοστήτοιο κατελθέμεν Ἀϊδονῆος   15
χερσὶν ὑπ' Αἰακίδαο δαΐφρονος, ὅς ῥα καὶ αὐτὸς
φθεῖσθαι ὁμῶς ἤμελλε παρὰ Πριάμοιο πόληι.

(. . .) But they,
In spite of their fear of Achilles of the ashwood spear,
Poured out eagerly from their gates, because their breasts
Were filled with courage by the Fates. For many of them
Would soon descend to Hades' house of no return
At the hands of Aiakos' valiant grandson, who himself
Was soon to perish likewise close to Priam's city.

The Trojans march in the battlefield 'in spite of their fear of Achilles', because the Κῆρες have filled them with courage. There are two prolepses in this passage. First the narrator foreshadows the deaths of many of the Trojans and then the death of Achilles. In both cases the Fates lead the characters to destruction. However, the most tension comes from the information that Achilles will soon die, because he is one of the central heroes of the poem.

Examples (4) and (5) demonstrate the function of prolepsis in the *PH*. In both cases the Fates have decided the future of a character, and the omniscient narrator brings the knowledge about the future to the narratees through a

---

[16] Schmitz (2007b: 67) explains that in passages such as this one we have 'short-range prolepses' because the information given to us will be fulfilled a few lines later.
[17] De Jong (²2004a: 86–7).

prolepsis. This foreshadowing of an event that is predefined by the Fates is something that we notice a further eight times in the poem.[18]

SPACE

In the *PH* the place of the mortals is on the battlefield and the space of the gods (most of the time) is somewhere far above (typically on Mount Olympos), where they observe everything from a distance. Occasionally the gods might come down to Troy in order to defend or to avenge a character.[19] Quintus chooses to personify Fate, and as a physical presence, Fate needs physical space, and that space is the battlefield.[20] Silvio Bär observes that the gods seem consciously to choose to stay out of human affairs, unlike the Fates, who are always found around the mortals,[21] and their presence on the battlefield is connected to death. Their proximity to characters is expressed with words such as ἀμφί, ἐγγύθεν, σχεδόθεν and ἄγχι. When they come close to a mortal, they either bring or foreshadow someone's death. Such an instance is found in Book 8 (5–12):

6. Τοὺς μὲν <γαρ> πάις ἐσθλὸς Ἀχιλλέος ὀτρύνεσκεν   5
ἀντιάαν Τρώεσσιν ἀταρβέα θυμὸν ἔχοντας,
τοὺς δ' ἄρα Τηλεφίδαο μέγα σθένος· ἦ γὰρ ἐώλπει
τεῖχος μὲν χαμάδις βαλέειν νῆάς τ' ἀμαθῦνειν
ἐν πυρὶ λευγαλέῳ, λαοὺς δ' ὑπὸ χερσὶ δαΐξαι.
ἀλλά οἱ ἐλπωρὴ μὲν ἔην ἐναλίγκιος αὔρη   10
μαψιδίη· **Κῆρες δὲ μάλα σχεδὸν ἑστηυῖαι**
πολλὸν καγχαλάασκον ἐτώσια μητιόωντι.

One side was encouraged by the worthy son of Achilles
To go and face the Trojans with intrepid spirits,
The other by Telephos' powerful son, who expected
To dash the wall to the ground, destroy the ships
With dreadful fire, and lay his murderous hands on the men.
But all his hope was built upon the air,
Empty. **The Fates were standing very close to him,**
Laughing in utter scorn of his futile designs.

---

[18] Instances of prolepsis related to the Fates in the *PH*: 1.390–3, 3.43–4, 5.331–2, 7.611–13, 8.127–9, 10.329–31 etc.

[19] Wenglinsky (2002: 259) observes that, in contrast to the gods in the *Iliad*, the gods in the *PH* often effect the action from afar, without descending onto the battlefield in order to perform their actions.

[20] Passages from the *PH* where the position of the Fates is mentioned include: 1.309–11, 1.390–2, 2.361–2, 2.514–16, 3.43–4, 5.34–6, 5.331–2, 9.145–7, 12.564–6, 13.493–5.

[21] Bär (2016: 219).

Eurypylos was hoping to break the Greek wall, burn the ships and kill many men. None of his plans will come to fruition, and this is understood by the ironic laugh of the Κῆρες. The narrator mentions that they 'were standing very close to him'. It is typical to see the Fates coming very close to a character whose moment of death is approaching. We never read that they approach a hero who does not subsequently die. Thus, judging from their laughter and the proximity to Eurypylos, we understand what will happen next. The spatial position of the Fates as such can work as a prolepsis itself; realising that the Fates are coming very close to a character leads us to the conclusion that she/he will die.

There are many instances in the *PH* where the presence of the Fates is the lever that brings together the space and time of the narration and moves the story forward. However, this is not always the case. In the next example we can see that the Κῆρες are standing next to the Trojans who are already dying at the hands of the Greeks (13.124–32):

7. Ἄλλοι δ᾽ ἀμφ᾽ ἄλλοισιν ἀπέπνεον· οἳ δ᾽ ἐκέχυντο
πότμον ὁμῶς ὁρόωντες ὀνείρασιν· **ἀμφὶ δὲ λυγραὶ**   125
Κῆρες ὀιζυρῶς ἐπεγήθεον ὀλλυμένοισιν.
Οἳ δ᾽ ὥς τ᾽ ἀφνειοῖο σύες κατὰ δώματ᾽ ἄνακτος
εἰλαπίνην λαοῖσιν ἀπείριτον ἐντύνοντος
μυρίοι ἐκτείνοντο· λυγρῷ δ᾽ ἀνεμίσγετο λύθρῳ
οἶνος ἔτ᾽ ἐν κρητῆρσι λελειμμένος. Οὐδέ τις ἦεν,   130
ὅς κεν ἄνευθε φόνοιο φέρε στονόεντα σίδηρον,
οὐδ᾽ εἴ τις μαλ᾽ ἄναλκις ἔην. (. . .)

Crowded together they breathed their last, some lying sprawled
Who'd only seen their death in their dreams. **Surrounding them**
The dismal Fates delighted in their miserable deaths.
Just like pigs in the palace of a wealthy prince
When he prepares an abundant banquet for his people,
They were killed in thousands and with their grisly gore was mingled
The wine that was left in the mixing bowls. No one at all
Could then have carried his steel unstained by bloodshed,
However feeble a fighter. (. . .)

During the great slaughter of the Trojans by the Greeks, the Fates surround them, laughing. They stand ἀμφί, so very close around the ones who die. Again, they seem to engage with what is happening around. They do not intervene, but they are present and observe. They are delighted to see what is happening – probably because it is the fulfilment of their plans.

In the *Iliad*, it can be observed that there is no instance in the whole poem where the Fates as personified deities are present in the battle; rather, the Olympians come down to intervene in the action, and other deities such as Deimos, Enyo, Eris and Phobos stir up the fights.[22] The only possible exception is in Book 18 (533–7) where Eris, Kydoimos and Ker are depicted on the shield of Achilles as being present in a battle – but even then, they are not included in the storyline.[23] In the rest of the epic, heroes very often refer to Fate, even the narrator tells that certain events happen according to Fate, but it is a lifeless Fate that does not come down to the battlefield mingling with mortals.

Contrary to this Iliadic practice, the Fates in the *PH* act like persons. They wander between mortals and they intervene in actions. Quintus stimulates a new approach to the traditional imagery of epic poetry but he still keeps a close eye on his model poem. Thus we observe delicate differences in the representation of different elements which are never destructive of the original. In the next section I will explain how the interventions of the Fates influence the narration and the role of the narrator.

FOCALISATION

In this part I will analyse the use of focalisation and embedded focalisation in the *PH*. We speak of embedded focalisation when the primary narrator-focaliser 'hands over focalization (but not narration) to one of the characters, who functions as F2 (focalizer 2) and, thereby, takes a share in the presentation of the story'.[24] This, in turn, helps us, the narratees, to better understand the perception of the characters.

The key indication of embedded focalisation is usually a verb of perceiving, thinking, feeling or speaking – or the use of emotional language.[25] There are many verbs which Quintus uses for this purpose, like for example νοέω, θαυμάζω and φαίνομαι. These verbs function as signs that a character is perceiving an event and thinks, feels or speaks in a certain way about it and, for a limited time, functions as internal, secondary narrator-focaliser and takes the reins of the narration.

In the *PH*, the primary and the secondary narrators take their turns in focalising very often. A traditional case of embedded focalisation is, for example,

---

[22] See for example *Il.* 4.40, 5.333, 13.299–300, 15.119, 20.48–50.
[23] See Coray (2016: 231–2).
[24] De Jong ([2]2004a: 101–2).
[25] De Jong (2004b: 18–22).

a passage from Book 8 where Neoptolemos manages to kill Eurypylos after a cruel battle between the Greeks and the Trojans (8.217–20).

8. ἦ ῥα καὶ ἐκ νέκυος περιμήκετον εἴρυσεν αἰχμὴν
ἐσσυμένως· Τρῶες δὲ μέγ' ἔτρεσαν εἰσορόωντες
ἀνέρα καρτερόθυμον· ὁ δ' αὐτίκα τεύχε ἀπούρας
δῶκε θοοῖς ἐτάροισι φέρειν ποτὶ νῆας Ἀχαιῶν.   220

With that he tore his great long spear from the corpse
in a flash. The Trojans were filled with terror at the sight
of that brave hero, who quickly stripped his victim's armour
for his nimble comrades to take to the Achaean ships.

The scene is focalised through the Trojans, who function as secondary narrator-focalisers. The markers of embedded focalisation are a feeling (μέγ' ἔτρεσαν) and a visual experience (εἰσορόωντες). The Trojans feel fear for what they see: Neoptolemos. To their eyes, Neoptolemos is 'strong-hearted'. They see him taking the armour of the dead Eurypylos and giving it to his comrades to take it to the ships. They observe the fast movement of their foes as the scene unwraps. The phrase νῆας Ἀχαιῶν points out that they take the armour to the Greek side of the battlefield, that is, far from the Trojans.

This is a typical example of embedded focalisation in the *PH*, and as I mentioned earlier, it is a narratological device that is very often used in this epic. What is striking, however, is that there is never embedded focalisation in scenes where the Fates are involved in the action. Let us take, for example, a passage from Book 12 (519–24):

9. (. . .) Μάλα μυρία δ' ἄλλ' ἐφαάνθη
σήματα Δαρδανίδῃσι καὶ ἄστεϊ πῆμα φέροντα·   520
ἀλλ' οὐ δεῖμ' ἀλεγεινὸν ἐπὶ Τρώων φρένας ἷξε
δερκομένων ἀλεγεινὰ τεράατα πάντα κατ' ἄστυ·
Κῆρες γὰρ πάντων νόον ἔκβαλον, ὄφρ' ἐπὶ δαιτὶ
πότμον ἀναπλήσωσιν ὑπ' Ἀργείοισι δαμέντες.

(. . .) Unnumbered other portents appeared,
Presaging ruin for Dardanos' people and city.
No daunting fear, however, impinged on the Trojans' minds,
Despite the sight of all these daunting marvels among them
The Fates had robbed them all of sense, so that after the banquet
They might meet their doom of death at the hands of the Argives.

When the Trojans drew the Wooden Horse into their city, 'unnumbered other portents appeared' that were revealing the upcoming destruction of

Troy. The whole of nature was thrown into confusion. Nevertheless, the Trojans were unable to understand what was really going on because 'the Fates had robbed them all of sense', they were out of their minds and they were behaving in a way that was not 'logical' or 'correct'. This mental blindness or delusion of the characters results as a misconception of reality. Consequently, the characters' actions lead them straight to their destruction.

Narratologically speaking, the blindness – or, at least, the false perception of reality – is expressed by the absolute lack of embedded focalisation: people who have lost their ability to perceive reality would not be able to focalise anyway. There is no verb of feeling, seeing or perceiving in this passage, which would indicate embedded focalisation. On the contrary, there is a clear statement that the Fates affected the logical thinking of characters. In a way, the physical inability of the Trojans is also expressed narratologically: the primary narrator takes the reins of storytelling and describes by himself all the events that followed the introduction of the Wooden Horse in Troy. The narratees who read the story and already know from the epic tradition that the city is going to fall feel sympathy with the Trojans because they understand that they are absolute victims of Fate, being unable to escape their doom.

This blindness, or wrong perception of reality, however, does not only apply in the case of a collective delusion. It can also happen to individual characters whom the Fates approach with destructive intentions. For example, in Book 10, the narrator dedicates a passage to the death of Eurymenes, a comrade of Aineias. He is a minor character who had no role earlier in the poem and who only becomes known to us a few moments before his death. Fate encouraged him to attack the Greeks bravely. The incident is described as follows (10.97–109):

10. **Καὶ τότε Μοῖρ' ἀίδηλος ἐπέχραεν Ἀργείοισιν**
Εὐρυμένην, ἕταρον κρατερόφρονος Αἰνείαο.
ὦρσε δέ οἱ μέγα θάρσος ὑπὸ φρένας, ὄφρα δαμάσσας
πολλοὺς αἴσιμον ἦμαρ ἀναπλήσῃ ὑπ' ὀλέθρῳ.   100
Δάμνατο δ' ἄλλοθεν ἄλλον ἀνηλέι Κηρὶ ἐοικώς·
οἱ δέ μιν αἶψ' ὑπόεικον ἐφ' ὑστατίῃ βιότοιο
αἰνὸν μαιμώωντα καὶ **οὐκ ἀλέγοντι μόροιο.**
Καί νύ κεν ἔργον ἔρεξεν ἀπείριτον ἐν δαῒ κεῖνος,
εἰ μή οἱ χεῖρές τ' ἔκαμον καὶ δούρατος αἰχμὴ   105
πολλὸν ἀνεγνάμφθη· ξίφ<ε>ος δέ οἱ οὐκέτι κώη
ἔσθενεν· **ἀλλά μιν Αἶσα διέκλασε·** <τὸν δ'> ὑπ' ἄκοντι
τύψε κατὰ στομάχοιο Μέγης· ἀνὰ δ' ἔβλυσεν αἷμα
ἐκ στόματος· τῷ δ' **αἶψα σὺν ἄλγεϊ Μοῖρα παρέστη.**

Then **it was that destructive Fate set onto the Argives Eurymenes**, companion of stouthearted Aineias,

> **Filling his heart with ample courage for him to lay low**
> **Many before he fulfilled his fate with his own death**.
> He killed in all directions like a pitiless Doom.
> Men shrank before him at once, as at the end of his life
> He raged so **fiercely with no thought of his fate.**
> That man would have wreaked immeasurable havoc in battle,
> Had not his arms grown weary and the head of his spear
> Been bent a long way back. The hilt of his sword had lost
> Its strength and snapped **as it was fated**. Then he was struck
> In the gullet by the spear of Meges. Blood spurted out
> From his mouth and pain and **Fate were at his side in a flash**.

In this passage, there is reference to two personifications of fate, Μοῖρα and Αἶσα, and they use Eurymenes for a double purpose: the death of many Argives and eventually the death of the hero himself. Eurymenes is inspired to fight with great courage, moments before he is killed.[26] There is no indicator of embedded focalisation: Eurymenes does not think, or see, or realise that his fate-driven courage leads him to death. On the contrary, there is a clear mention of his inability to focalise: he was not thinking of his Fate – and not thinking means not focalising. The destiny is in the hands of the Fates in the same way that the narration is in the hands of the primary narrator. The character is a mere puppet danced towards destruction.

In all the instances in the *PH* where the Fates cause wrong perception of reality, there are some standard characteristics. First, the Fates decide that a character should die. Second, they mentally manipulate the character.[27] This results in one acting out of context and without logic. This behaviour brings death to the character, so fate's plan is fulfilled. Finally, in all these instances the characters never focalise, the primary narrator describes the entire scene and the narratees do not receive any information about the feelings of the characters. This lack of embedded focalisation in scenes where the Fates intervene and 'blind' the characters is a common motif in the *PH*.[28]

No similar manipulation of the narration occurs in the *Iliad*. Fate is described as a power which ensnares humans and leads them to death – but

---

[26] Wenglinsky (2002: 267) observes that in the *Iliad* such scenes of manipulation of weapons are usually implemented by the Olympians, whereas in the *PH* the Fates can do the same. For example, in this passage Aisa manipulates Eurymenes' sword.

[27] Gärtner (2007: 236) reminds us of the passage from Book 7 where Nestor tells that human life is blind. Indeed, according to the text the mortals are blind not because they cannot see the world around them, but because they cannot see the ways Fate knits their lives. This word play with vision and the Fates is something that we very often notice in the *PH*; the narrator often employs an exchange between the seen and the unseen, blindness and visuality.

[28] The same blocking of embedded focalisation is observed in the following passages of the *PH*: 1.170–3, 1.388–402, 2.357–67, 2.507–16, 11.272–82, 12.562–75, 14.360–5.

this is mostly a poetic expression rather than an actual delusion or blindness caused by it. A characteristic example is found in Book 5, where the death of Amphios is described (5.610–14):

11. τὼ δὲ πεσόντ᾽ ἐλέησε μέγας Τελαμώνιος Αἴας·   610
στῆ δὲ μάλ᾽ ἐγγὺς ἰών, καὶ ἀκόντισε δουρὶ φαεινῷ,
καὶ βάλεν Ἄμφιον Σελάγου υἱόν, ὅς ῥ᾽ ἐνὶ Παισῷ
ναῖε πολυκτήμων πολυλήϊος· ἀλλά ἑ μοῖρα
ἦγ᾽ ἐπικουρήσοντα μετὰ Πρίαμόν τε καὶ υἷας.

As these fell great Telamonian Aias pitied them
and stood close in and made a cast with the shining javelin,
and struck Amphios, Selagos' son, who rich in possessions
and rich in cornland had lived in Paisos, but his own destiny
brought him companion in arms to Priam and the children of Priam.

In this passage, the role of Fate is marked differently as compared to that in the *PH*. It is mostly a literary reference and it equates the Fates with death. Nowhere in the *Iliad* is there a scene in which they, as personified divinities, 'blind' a character.

CONCLUSION

Quintus reshapes the portrayal of Fate while maintaining the traditional characteristics that Homer transfused to them. The main idea is that Fate predetermines human life and that it has power to control the moment and the way a mortal should die. Both gods and humans admit its power and they do not challenge it. However, in the *PH*, more often than in the *Iliad*, Fate is presented as a personified divinity. The Fates are placed on the battlefield and have an impact on the development of the story. On a narratological level, their presence interacts with the concepts of time and space and strengthens the role of the primary narrator.

The narratees are often informed about an incident before it happens in the form of a prolepsis. A typical execution of this narratological device is to have the narrator tell an event that has been decided by the Fates prior to its actualisation. More often prolepsis has to do with the death of a character; this pushes the story forward because every death in the epic fulfils a part of the story and leads to the eventual sack of Troy.

In the *PH* the battlefield seems to be the natural space of the Fates, as this is the place where human destiny is determined. Their physical presence establishes them as acting, personified entities in the poem. Additionally, their appearance in the same space as humans enables them to intervene in the action. On the other hand, in the *Iliad*, the Fates never appear as acting characters on the battlefield. This constitutes a difference in the representation of fate between the two poems.

The Fates tend to step into the action and 'blind' characters. When this happens, the mortals do not have a clear understanding of reality and thus do not act as logical beings, but in a way that leads them to destruction. In such moments the Fates take control over human life and in the same way that the story is driven by Fate, the narration is led by the primary narrator. As I explained earlier in this chapter, there is never embedded focalisation when a character is blinded. I argued that there is no space for the focalisation of a character who is unable to see reality clearly. The role of the primary narrator gets stronger as he is the only real 'observer' of the events that take place in such scenes of 'blindness'.

Quintus' *PH* offers insightful material for narratological observations, but very little scholarly work has so far been undertaken on this aspect of the epic. This chapter has examined only the small part of the poem that is connected to the Fates. However, it would be rewarding to expand narratological studies which focus on the *PH* per se or in comparison to other works of its genre.[29]

---

[29] I would like to thank my professors from the National and Kapodistrian University of Athens, Sophia Papaioannou and Katerina Carvounis, who kindly offered their feedback on the subject of this chapter.

CHAPTER 10

Wielding Words: Neoptolemus as a Speaker of Words in Quintus' *Posthomerica*

Tine Scheijnen

'Néoptolème est le moins loquace de tous les personnages de la Suite d'Homère (. . .) C'est qu'il est avant tout un homme d'action, soucieux "non de paraître un héros, mais de l'être".'[1]

Speech has served as marker for heroic characterisation since Homer, as earlier studies have shown.[2] Vian understands Neoptolemus' – indeed limited – speech use in Quintus as such an indication of heroism: he is a doer of deeds, rather than a speaker of words. This observation is more than correct: the actions of Neoptolemus are lifesaving and praiseworthy on more than one occasion. Still, he also has a remarkable way of wielding his words. Both in length and in contents, his brief interventions stand out and add to his characterisation. Vian continues:

Il ne se laisse pas griser par les éloges qu'on lui décerne de tout côté, il évite la jactance, se refuse à faire des promesses; avec la tranquille assurance de l'homme conscient tout à la fois de sa valeur et de la fragilité des choses humaines, il ne prend la parole que pour s'en remettre au bon vouloir des Dieux.[3]

This chapter was written under the European Union's Seventh Framework Programme (FP/2007–2013) with the support of the European Research Council Starting Grant Novel Saints (Grant Agreement n. 337344) at Ghent University. Many thanks to Berenice Verhelst, Elena Langella and the editors of this volume for their valuable comments.

[1] Vian (1966: 104). 'Neoptolemus is the least talkative character of the *Posthomerica* (. . .). He is primarily a man of action, eager "not to show oneself as a hero, but to be one".'

[2] Martin's *The Language of Heroes* (1989) is, of course, a prime example.

[3] Vian (1966: 104). 'He does not lose his head over the eulogies he is showered with, he avoids bragging, refuses to make any promises; with the calm assurance of a man aware both of his valour and the delicacy of human things, he only takes the floor to commend himself to the will of the gods.'

This has led to the observation that Neoptolemus is an efficient speaker,[4] possibly a Stoic figure[5] or an ideal hero.[6] While meritorious in their own right, such conclusions do not fully explore the plot developments in which this new hero appears, nor the function of his words in that narrative context. Neoptolemus stands in relation to other heroes, old and new, whose behaviour can put that of Neoptolemus in perspective. Such dynamics will be studied here. This contribution compares Neoptolemus' heroic discourse to that of his Aeacid family and to that of the other new heroes in the *Posthomerica* (*PH*). I argue that Neoptolemus not only develops his own way of speaking in reaction to the old Aeacid habits and the more 'modern' fashion of new champions, but that Achilles' son also undergoes a personal development of his heroic identity, of which his speaking behaviour forms an important marker. I will trace both hypotheses, not from a rhetorical point of view,[7] but primarily in the light of the heroic customs and beliefs that are expressed in Neoptolemus' speeches – and those of his peers. The conclusion will reflect on the possible implications of these observations for Quintus' literary contextualisation.

SPEAKERS OF WORDS IN HOMER AND QUINTUS

Phoenix was once charged with instructing Achilles 'to be both a speaker of words and a doer of deeds' (μύθων τε ῥητῆρ' ἔμεναι πρηκτῆρά τε ἔργων, *Il.* 9.443). Indeed, a hero needs both skills to successfully defend his heroic position. While triumph in battle obviously brings glory, a hero uses speech in various situations to defend or establish his status:[8] he gives counsel in the assembly (ἀγορά);[9] on the battlefield he exhorts his peers, challenges and scorns his foes.[10] Such speech use remains important in Quintus' epic.[11] It comes as

---

[4] Boyten (2007; 2010); Langella (2018). Boyten further investigates if Neoptolemus could be deemed a better hero than his father in Quintus.

[5] Calero Secall (1998b); Langella (2016).

[6] Toledano Vargas (2002).

[7] This topic has been explored elsewhere: on Quintus in his imperial rhetorical context (Second Sophistic and/or broader), see Baumbach and Bär (2007a); Bär (2010); Maciver (2012b); Avlamis (2019); on rhetorical influence in Book 5, see Bär (2010: 296–7); James and Lee (2000: 16), following Elderkin (1906); on Quintus' use of direct speech, see Verhelst (2017), in comparison to Homer, Apollonius and especially Nonnus; on Neoptolemus' speech already Boyten (2007; 2010: 185–7); Langella (2017/18: 114–19, 134–8; 2018). Quintus will also be included in the fifth volume of the Brill *Studies of Ancient Greek Narrative* (Bär forthcoming b).

[8] Martin (1989: 96–7).

[9] On εὐβουλία and honour in the *Iliad*, see Schofield (1986) and Horn (2014: 60–2).

[10] On 'Leistung und Agonalität' in Homer, see Horn (2014: 46–64).

[11] On flyte in Quintus, see Maciver (2012b: 611–12), referring to Martin (1989: 67–77); on flyte in Homer, see more recently also Horn (2014: 100–3).

no surprise, then, that the most prominent heroes are also prominent speakers, both in the *Iliad* and the *PH*.[12]

Table 10.1 measures a character's speech use according to two parameters: the number of speeches and the total length of his/her speeches in lines. Both methods reveal the same nine (in the case of the *Iliad*) or six (in the case of the *PH*) names as the most prominent speakers. On top of the *Iliad* list feature Achilles and his two antagonists, followed by two important divinities, two Achaeans renowned for their speaking skills (Nestor and Odysseus) and, finally, Priam and Diomedes. Quintus' top speakers are all Achaeans, four of them the same as in the *Iliad*. In addition, Ajax Major and Neoptolemus enter the lists.

Table 10.1

	Iliad		*Posthomerica*	
	Speeches	**Lines**	**Speeches**	**Lines**
RANKING	*(average 7.7)*	*(average 81)*	*(average 2.5)*	*(average 29.6)*
1	Achilles	Achilles	Neoptolemus	Nestor
	87	983	19	198
2	Hector	Agamemnon	Nestor	Odysseus
	49	589	14	188
3	Agamemnon	Nestor	Odysseus[13]	Ajax Major
	47	532	8	152
4	Zeus	Hector	Ajax Major	Achilles
	39	522	8	120
5	Nestor	Zeus	Achilles	Neoptolemus
	33	378	8	117
6	Hera	Odysseus	Agamemnon	Agamemnon
	31	348	8	75
7	Odysseus	Hera		
	31	257		
8	Diomedes	Diomedes		
	26	226		
9	Priam	Priam		
	25	213		

[12] Statistical information and the data for some of my own calculations are derived from the online database 'Direct Speech in Greek Epic Poetry', a digital appendix to Verhelst's (2017) monograph. On the speech ratio of Quintus compared to Homer, see James and Lee (2000: 16), relying on Elderkin (1906) and Verhelst (2017: 24–32).

[13] The four heroes with an equal number of speeches are ranked according to their number of speech lines in the epic.

Ajax is not a minor speaker in the *Iliad*,[14] but given his important role in the debate of *PH* 5, his increased speech use in Quintus is no surprise. Neoptolemus, of course, is a new character. His appearance at once marks his prominence in the epic and draws attention to the brevity of his interventions, briefly mentioned above.[15] Indeed, he is by far the most frequent speaker of the epic, but uses considerably fewer lines to do so than, for example, his father. Achilles has eight speeches, which are on average fifteen lines long. The general average in the *PH* is 11.8 lines per speech,[16] but Neoptolemus' only 6.2 lines. In total, even Achilles has more speech lines than Neoptolemus, although the former is a speaking character in only four books. Despite being constantly compared to his father on other levels,[17] Neoptolemus seems to steer away from his father's practice as regards speech use: in length as well in content, there are considerable differences. This will be discussed in more detail below. A final observation, which should first be brought into relation with Neoptolemus, is the marked decrease of Diomedes' direct speech in the *PH*.[18]

Diomedes, in general, receives only limited attention in Quintus.[19] He mostly yields his place to two other characters: Ajax Major as a hero of strength and Neoptolemus as an impetuous youngster.[20] Four out of his five speeches occur in a context where he tries to exhort the army to battle, but only one is successful.[21] In addition, he challenges Achilles after the murder of Thersites (Q.S. 1.767–81; no speech) and kills an imploring old man during the sack (Q.S. 13.181–207). Similar actions in the *Iliad* were coloured by his youth: he was a promising young hero in full heroic development.[22] In Quintus, a less experienced hero takes his place and even follows Diomedes' lead on two occasions. The only successful battle exhortation by Diomedes, in Book 7.422–30, sends Neoptolemus into his first fight. Diomedes' last feat, slaying the old man,

---

[14] He holds the twelfth place for numbers (nineteen speeches) and the thirteenth place for length (137 lines).

[15] Verhelst (2017: 30, n85).

[16] Vian (1966: 104, n1).

[17] For an overview of this feature in this epic and existing research on the topic, see Scheijnen (2015) and especially chapter 4 in Scheijnen (2018).

[18] Quintus' Diomedes ends in the eleventh place for numbers (five speeches, like Menelaus and Priam, but with fewer speech lines) and in the fifteenth place for length (only thirty-nine lines).

[19] Mansur (1940: 16–19).

[20] Mansur (1940: 18); Combellack (1968: 12); Calero Secall (1998a: 78, n1), following van der Valk (1952) and Tsomis (2018a).

[21] Besides two speeches in Book 4, he speaks in the assembly of Q.S. 6.41–67, where he is overruled by Calchas. In Book 7, he exhorts Neoptolemus, this time with success.

[22] While still learning his rhetorical skills (Martin 1989: 124–30), Diomedes is often named as an exemplary hero in both battle and council. For his character in Homer, see also Andersen (1978) and Horn (2014: 62, n264).

serves as a double for Neoptolemus' killing of Priam.[23] As a result, it could be argued that Diomedes' speeches mainly occur in contexts that either characterise him as a hero by Neoptolemus' side, or in situations where he actually seconds the young hero's actions. Diomedes has become a hero of reference.

As a young, sometimes impetuous warrior, Neoptolemus is perhaps not unlike Diomedes. The youth of Achilles' son forms an important pillar of his characterisation in the *PH*, as I argue elsewhere.[24] This also resounds in Neoptolemus' way of speaking. As a speaker, Neoptolemus is one of kind, as becomes clear when comparing his speech use to that of his peers.

FAVOURITE *TOPOI* IN HEROIC SPEECH IN QUINTUS

During the first battle in the *PH* and in her own first speech, the Amazon queen Penthesilea shouts out (Q.S. 1.331–4):

πῇ νῦν Τυδεΐδαο βίη, πῇ δ' Αἰακίδαο,
ποῦ δὲ καὶ Αἴαντος; **τοὺς γὰρ φάτις ἔμμεν ἀρίστους·**
ἀλλ' ἐμοὶ οὐ τλήσονται ἐναντία δηριάασθαι,
μή σφιν ἀπὸ μελέων ψυχὰς φθιμένοισι πελάσσω.

Where now is the might of Tydeus' son, where that of Achilles
Or of Ajax? **They are famed as your best**,
Yet they will not dare to face me in combat,
For fear I take souls from bodies and send them to the dead.[25]

This marks the beginning of a battle for superiority between her and Achilles. Earlier, Andromache had already murmured: 'you (Penthesilea) haven't the strength to fight the fearless son of Peleus. (. . .) Hector was your better by far (σέο πολλὸν ὑπέρτερος) with the spear, but for all his strength he was killed and grieved by the Trojans' (Q.S. 1.100–6). While facing the Amazon, Achilles likewise scorns her twice: 'we (Ajax and Achilles) are far the greatest warriors in the world (μέγα φέρτατοί εἰμεν ἐπιχθονίων ἡρώων)' (Q.S. 1.577) and 'for we are far the greatest warriors (μέγα φέρτατοί εἰμεν ἡρώων), great light of Danaans, but the bane of Trojans' (Q.S. 1.649–50).[26] This urge to be the best,

---

[23] For this scene, see Boyten (2007: 320–6) and Scheijnen (2018: 290–302).

[24] Scheijnen (2015; 2018: 209–19). Similar observations have been made about Triphiodorus (Miguélez-Cavero 2013: 214–15).

[25] Quintus of Smyrna: translations by James (2004), text edition by Vian (1963, -66, -69). Homer's *Iliad*: text and translation by Murray and Wyatt (²1999). Homer's *Odyssey*: text and translation by Murray and Dimock (²1999).

[26] See also Scheijnen (2016b).

to claim such a title for oneself, is well known from Homer (Horn 2014: 46–50): one may think of Peleus' instructions to Achilles 'always to be bravest (αἰὲν ἀριστεύειν) and preeminent above all (ὑπείροχον ἔμμεναι ἄλλων)' (Nestor: *Il.* 11.783–4).[27] In the *Iliad*, the words ἄριστος Ἀχαιῶν are doubtlessly the most famous phrase to draw attention to this continuous heroic contest, and it mostly relates to Achilles.[28] His speeches on the battlefield in *PH* 1 indicate that such superlative discourse is still important for Achilles in Quintus. The strife for heroic superiority continues, and it is a matter of words as much as of deeds. This is confirmed by a sample count of adjectives expressing 'excellence' which are used in a comparative way in heroic discourse (direct speech).

The graph in Figure 10.1 represents the occurrence in character speech of the following superlative and comparative forms that are used in a discourse of heroic supremacy, and which imply that the excellence of a hero is considered on a larger heroic scale:[29] the superlative forms ἄριστος, ὑπέρτατος, φέριστος, φέρτατος, προφερέστατος, κρατερώτατος, the Posthomeric (and Homeric) *hapax* βασιλεύτατος and the adjective ἔξοχος, which in itself has superlative

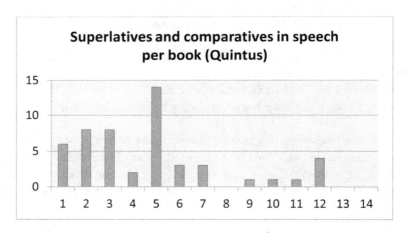

Figure 10.1

<hr />

[27] Similarly Glaucus in *Il.* 6.206–10.
[28] For example *Il.* 1.88–91, 243–4 and 407–12. See also Nagy (1979: 26–41) and Edwards (1984). Variants of ἄριστος Ἀχαιῶν also occur, but this would lead us too far for the present discussion. See e.g. Horn (2014: 155–7).
[29] I only focus on adjectives with a positive meaning (e.g. 'better than' or 'best'), not on those implying one's inferiority (e.g. 'worst' or 'worse than'). These graphs only include the occurrences of these adjectives in the specific narrative context of heroic qualification. Occurrences of the same adjectives elsewhere (e.g. in general phrases such as 'it would be best to …') are left out.

meaning;[30] the comparative forms ἀμείνων, ἀγαυότερος, ὑπέρτερος, φέρτερος, ἀρείων, once ἀτιμότερος and once πινυτώτερος. These cases include vocatives, challenges ('you think you are . . .'), negations ('. . . you are not'), explicit claims and comparisons that are expressed by the hero himself or by one of his friends, foes or peers. I have counted fifty-one such instances. Thirty-eight are found in first five books of the *PH*, fourteen in Book 5 alone. With two exceptions, they always relate to a specific hero or heroes. A few characters frequently form the subject of such comparisons, or frequently use such expressions themselves.

The graph in Figure 10.2 is based on the same data as the first, but only shows the results for a selection of heroes in the *PH*. Most of these comparatives and superlatives either refer to the speaker's own superiority (e.g. 'I'm better than you in birth as well as in bodily strength', Achilles to Memnon: Q.S. 2.433) or are used to undermine the superiority of someone else (e.g. 'Palamedes was your better in strength as well as intelligence', Ajax Major to Odysseus: Q.S. 5.198–9). In fact, five out of Ajax's eight cases and all of the cases in which Achilles is the speaker are self-referential. In contrast, Diomedes and Neoptolemus never use comparatives or superlatives for self-reference.

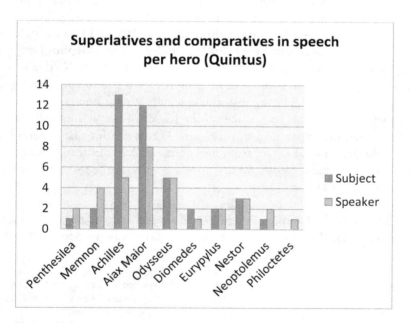

Figure 10.2

---

[30] Other adjectives in the positive form, such as ἀμύμων, are, despite a possible connotation of excellence (for ἀμύμων, see Campbell 1981: 29), not taken into account. An apparent comparative context is often lacking in these cases.

The three new Trojan champions only receive such 'compliments' because they give them to themselves: all superlatives marking superiority for Penthesilea, Memnon and Eurypylus are found in their own speeches. The superiority of Achilles and Ajax Major is most often recognised by others: Achilles' by seven other speakers and Ajax's by six.[31]

There is a clear concentration of the use of comparatives and superlatives in heroic speech, and by extension of the use of heroic (self-)characterisation, in the first five books of the *PH*. This speech motif is particularly related to Achilles and Ajax Major, who are by far its most frequent subjects *and* speakers. Achilles and Ajax are the characters most often praised as 'better than' or 'best of': thirteen and twelve times throughout the epic, respectively. This is reminiscent of Homer's interest in the ἄριστος Ἀχαιῶν and connects the characterisation of both Aeacids in the *PH* to their counterparts in the *Iliad* (where Ajax was often named the second best, after Achilles).[32] Odysseus firmly takes the third place in the Posthomeric list. His dispute with Ajax in Book 5 is essentially a debate about the nature of heroic excellence and a defence of their own supreme position therein.[33] The third Aeacid, however, keeps a remarkably low profile in these graphs. Neoptolemus once scorns Deiphobus by denying the latter's assumed superiority (Q.S. 9.250) and once respectfully addresses Nestor as a very wise man (Q.S. 12.275). The young hero is only once the subject of such a comparison himself. When Phoenix states that Neoptolemus is superior to Eurypylus as Achilles was to Telephus (ὑπέρτερος, Q.S. 7.665), Neoptolemus quickly intervenes with the words: 'Old fellow, the judges of my prowess in battle will be almighty Fate and the powerful god of war' (Q.S. 7.668–9).[34] Throughout the epic, the young hero seems less concerned with defining his own place on the ladder of heroic hierarchy and less flattered when others do him this honour. This is a habit that Neoptolemus remarkably does not take over from his father and Ajax. Instead, a list of other *topoi* repeatedly mark Neoptolemus' speeches (the numbers of the speeches refer to Table 10.2):[35]

a)   'This is in the hands of the gods/fate': speeches **2**, **3**, **4**, **5**, **16** (twice, he refers to god(s) preventing a specific situation from happening: **8** and **11**).

---

[31] Some of these instances are in fact challenges: 'it is said you are the best' or 'you believe yourself to be the best'. Still, these cases recognise the fact that the addressee makes an important claim or already takes a prominent position on the ladder of heroic hierarchy.

[32] For example *Il.* 17.279–80 = *Od.* 11.550–1, *Il.* 2.768–9, *Il.* 7.226–8 and *Od.* 11.469–70 = *Od.* 24.17–18. On Ajax and Achilles in the *PH*, see Scheijnen (2016a) and chapter 3 in Scheijnen (2018).

[33] See Maciver (2012b); Scheijnen (2016a; 2018: 132–45).

[34] See also Boyten (2010: 186); Tsomis (2018a: 371); Langella (2017/18: 549).

[35] What follows are paraphrases reflecting the general idea of each *topos*, not translations.

Table 10.2

SPEECHES BY NEOPTOLEMUS IN THE *POSTHOMERICA*					
Number	Book	from	to	length	addressee
1	7	179	181	3	Odysseus and Diomedes
2	7	220	225	6	Odysseus and Diomedes
3	7	288	291	4	Deidamia
4	7	668	669	2	Phoenix
5	7	701	704	4	Agamemnon
6	8	15	22	8	Myrmidons
7	8	147	161	15	Eurypylus
8	8	210	216	7	Eurypylus
9	9	50	60	11	Achilles
10	9	248	252	5	Deiphobus
11	9	261	263	3	Deiphobus
12	9	275	283	9	Greeks
13	11	217	220	4	Greeks
14	12	67	72	6	Calchas
15	12	275	280	6	Nestor
16	12	298	302	5	Nestor
17	13	238	240	3	Priam
18	14	235	245	11	Greeks
19	14	308	312	5	Achilles

b) References to his father: **3**, **5**, **6**, **7**, **8**, **9** (in **18**, he recalls his father's dream, and in **19**, he addresses him as a god).

c) Sometimes including the specific wish not to shame Achilles or to honour his heroic reputation: speeches **3**, **5**, **9**.

d) Exhortations to be brave/scorning cowardice: speeches **6**, **11**, **12**, **13**, **14**, **15**, **16** (speech **10** is the only one spoken by Neoptolemus referring to a heroic position of superiority: 'you think you are πολλὸν ἄριστος, but now face me').

e) Some of the cases in 'b' or 'd' include a resolution 'not to die before', or rather 'to die than not to meet his goal': speeches **3**, **12**, **13** and **16**.

Together with the brevity of Neoptolemus' speeches, recurring motifs such as (a) have led Vian and other scholars after him to describe Neoptolemus in terms of modesty and idealism, as referred to in the introduction to this chapter. A clear tendency towards this kind of behaviour is tangible in certain characters of the epic. It is often related to Stoic influences and/or the development of a new kind of heroism in the epic.[36] With regard to expressions of modesty, in particular, Neoptolemus is not alone. Eurypylus' reply to Paris in Book 6 sounds fairly similar: 'It rests upon the knees of the immortals as to who will die and who will survive the violent fray. For my part, as duty bids and my fighting powers permit, I'll stand in defense of the city and also swear an oath not to return before either killing or being killed' (Q.S. 6.309–14).[37] Both this speech and, for example, Neoptolemus' reaction to Agamemnon (quoted at the end of the previous section) are situated at the welcome of the champion into the army's ranks. They both counter the high expectations of their host. Memnon was also careful with promises: 'A feast is not a place to make enormous boasts, nor yet to commit oneself to a promise, but quietly to dine in the hall and make appropriate plans; whether or not I am brave and strong you soon shall learn in battle; that is where the strength of a man is seen' (Q.S. 2.148–55). This, in turn, seems to be an implicit reaction to – and better practice than – Penthesilea's boasts one book earlier (Q.S. 1.93–7).[38] Her attempt to engage in the battle for heroic hierarchy with Achilles and Ajax had a disastrous outcome. Ever since, newly arriving champions tend to keep a low profile on their intentions. Rather than an individual trait, this tendency to be 'modest' is introduced as a new (good) practice early in the PH. Although this behaviour does not completely erase traces of individual ambition and, occasionally, boasting,[39] it still forms a distinguishable trait of new heroes that arrive in Troy during the PH. As this attitude in speech becomes more frequent, the use of superlatives in the discourse of individual heroic excellence, a typical marker of the heroic mode of Achilles and Ajax, decreases after the first books. Neoptolemus' speeches are clearly influenced by and form a marked example of this new fashion.

While crafting his own 'modern' speech use by sharing the verbal caution of his newly arrived peers, Neoptolemus also, and prominently, voices a few other recurring interests in his speeches: references to his father are omnipresent (topoi (b) and (c) in the list) and his speeches are full of heroic gnōmai about bravery (topos (d), sometimes strengthened by (e)).[40] Both of these tendencies serve the

---

[36] On Stoic influences, see e.g. Ferrari (1963: 52); Vian (1963, -66, -69); Hadjittofi (2007); James (2007); Maciver (2007); Gärtner (2009); Maciver (2012a); Langella (2016); Maciver (2017), Langella (2017/18); Maciver's contribution in this volume. See Langella (2016: 557, n16) for more complete references on this topic. On other types of idealism and heroism, see e.g. Toledano Vargas (2002); Kneebone (2007); Langella (2018: 302).

[37] Tsomis (2018a: 357–8).

[38] Vian (1963: 48); Calero Secall (1995); Ferreccio (2014: 72); Scheijnen (2016b: 95).

[39] For example Eurypylus boasts about his own invincibility in his flyte to Neoptolemus (Q.S. 8.138–45). Memnon engages in a discourse about individual superiority – and that of his mother – with Achilles (Q.S. 2.412–29).

[40] On gnōmai in Quintus, see chapter 3 in Maciver (2012a). It should be noted, both here and below, that Neoptolemus is not the only one in the PH prone to the use of gnōmai, or even this

same goal: that of a son trying to find his place in the lingering shadow of his renowned father.[41] Throughout the epic, Neoptolemus is frequently recognised as his son (e.g. Q.S. 7.689–91) or even mistaken for him (e.g. Q.S. 7.537–8). The comparison is made explicit on various occasions, in both character speech (e.g. Q.S. 7.185–6) and narrator text (e.g. Q.S. 7.433–4). Neoptolemus also cultivates this likeness by wearing his father's weapons (Q.S. 7.445–51) and, not unimportantly, by repeatedly expressing his desire to be like his father. For example, the heroic *gnōmai* of *topos* (d) hail bravery and scorn cowardice; they explicitly voice the same heroic code of Achilles and Ajax. Both elder Aeacids on the battlefield often scorned specific cases of cowardice (e.g. against the arrow that killed Achilles, in Q.S. 3.68–82 and 3.435–58) and Ajax was a severe advocate of the same belief in Book 5 (181–236 and 292–305). Neoptolemus goes further. He makes these heroic values explicit in his speeches in more general wordings, resulting in gnomic claims about prowess and bravery. This way, he shows himself a clear student of his father's beliefs. He feels the specific need to express his position as an heir following in their footsteps. Obviously, the countless references to his father (*topos* (b)) and – most notably – his desire not to shame him (*topos* (c)) complement the same intention. His looks, the armour he wears and his battle successes may stage Neoptolemus as an exact copy of his father, but his speeches prove otherwise: in many ways, they reveal the insecurity of a young man from a new generation, facing a mighty legacy to which he wants to do honour. At the end of Book 7, Quintus illustrates this with a fitting simile: Neoptolemus is not the lion, but his cub, suddenly finding himself alone in his father's world (Q.S. 7.715–22).[42]

THE COURSE OF NEOPTOLEMUS' WORDS: HEROIC DEVELOPMENT?

Neoptolemus' speeches mark his growth as a hero.[43] The contexts in which Neoptolemus speaks evolve in a telling way – and so do the *topoi* he uses. Book 7, the book in which he is introduced, gives him five speeches.[44] In

---

kind of heroic *gnōmai*. He does use them more often than others in heroic contexts, however. More than on the *gnōmai* as such, this chapter focuses on the position and function of such expressions in the progressive characterisation of Neoptolemus as a young hero.

[41] A much-debated topic: see e.g. Boyten (2007; 2010); Maciver (2012a); Scheijnen (2015; 2018); Langella (2016; 2017/18; 2018).

[42] My interpretation of and more bibliography on Neoptolemus' characterisation can be found in Scheijnen (2015) and in chapter 4 of Scheijnen (2018); similarly on the lion cub simile Scheijnen (2018: 191); also recently Tsomis (2018a: 378).

[43] Other views on Neoptolemus' transition from adolescence to heroic maturity, compared to Telemachus and/or Jason, are provided by Boyten (2010: 206–13) and Tsomis (2018a: 244–6).

[44] For a complete overview, see also Langella (2018: 289–91).

the very first one, he welcomes Odysseus and Diomedes to Scyros, but also betrays his ignorance of his visitors' heroic world: he does not recognise them (speech 1 in Table 10.2). The second speech, in which he accepts to sail to Troy, and the third one to his mother voice his intention to join that heroic world and to do something 'worthy of the Aeacids' (speech 3).[45] He arrives and joins his first battle without further direct speech, until he is welcomed in the Achaean camp that evening. Then follow two (very) brief interventions in which he first rebukes Phoenix not to voice any high expectations ('the judges of my prowess in battle will be almighty Fate and the powerful god of war', Q.S. 7.668–9, speech 4) and then underlines to Agamemnon that he would have loved to meet his father alive, to prove he will not shame him (speech 5). These first speeches of Neoptolemus have a remarkable focus: four of them include *topos* (a), a modesty claim about any high expectations that are imposed on him; two, moreover, express the hope to be worthy of his father. Book 7 introduces Neoptolemus to the story and, despite his first success on the battlefield, the young hero's personal main concern is clearly the large pressure to prove himself in this new context.

His first battlefield speech occurs soon after, at the beginning of Book 8. He exhorts the Myrmidons to be brave and leads them into the fight (speech 6). This is the warrior speaking for the first time. His two other speeches in the same book are addressed to Eurypylus, before and after the latter's defeat. Neoptolemus uses these occasions to shape his own heroic identity and the perception he wishes to create on the battlefield. He does this in a peculiar way: first, he points out to Eurypylus the different battle accessories that should have helped him recognise 'the son of Achilles' (speech 7). After dealing him the fatal blow, Neoptolemus again boasts that Achilles' mighty spear, specifically, has done its job (speech 8). As I argue elsewhere, Neoptolemus proves his heroic worth by slaying the enemy he was summoned for. At the same time, however, he grants his father every glory for this achievement.[46] It seems as if the young hero is not quite self-confident enough yet to assume his own position on the heroic scale; he defines himself in terms of Achilles' large shadow.

A decisive turning point is Neoptolemus' visit to his father's grave at the beginning of Book 9. The tomb is visible from the sea, but Odysseus had wisely spared Neoptolemus the sight during their arrival (Q.S. 7.403–6). Two books later, Neoptolemus makes his own decision to visit the tomb. In an emotional speech, he regrets never having met his father, but assures him that his legacy is being carried out: 'your spear and your son in the fray are filling the foe with terror' (9.58, speech 9). This is a logical vow given Neoptolemus' earlier

---

[45] More on this speech by Tsomis (2018a: 180–1).
[46] Scheijnen (2018: 199–205).

self-representation on the battlefield.[47] Still, something changes after this visit. Later in the same book, Neoptolemus rejoins battle with no less than three speeches. He challenges Deiphobus (speech 10), scorns him when he escapes (speech 11) and exhorts the Achaeans (speech 12). In none of these speeches does he refer to his father. A recurring *topos*, however, is (d): the scolding of cowardice (speech 11) and the praise of bravery (speech 12). Neoptolemus still hails these ideals, but now clearly and repeatedly on his own behalf. In Book 9, he does not (any longer?) need his father's reputation to shine on the battlefield. The young hero appears to have undergone an evolution: in Books 7 and 8, he had dealt with the burden of his father's legacy, and he now feels confident enough to proceed on his own behalf. This does not imply that he distances himself from his father; quite on the contrary, he still hails the same heroic code of bravery, which he expresses in strong *gnōmai* such as 'I would rather die than be called unfit for war (ἀπτόλεμος)' (Q.S. 9.283, speech 12). This tendency neatly continues in his next speech, during the battle of Book 11. He has only one speech there, which he uses to rebuke his men for a cowardly flight: 'It is far better to perish in battle than to opt for feeble flight' (Q.S. 11.219–20, speech 13). He converts his initial aim 'If I am to perish (. . .), let me first do something worthy of Aiakos' bloodline' (speech 3) to a more general battle cry, of which he himself becomes the interpreter – thus inspiring others to follow him.[48] Neoptolemus seems to have constructed his own heroic identity, strongly inspired by his father's legacy, but now he is mature enough to carry it out on his own behalf. In the last battles around Troy, the young hero has developed leadership skills.

This identity, this newly shaped self-confidence is put to the test in Book 12, when Neoptolemus faces a new speaking context for the first time: assembly. In the first of two meetings in this book, Calchas insists on a new strategy, which Odysseus delivers: the ruse of the Trojan Horse. Neoptolemus is quick to react. His intervention is brief and gnomic, as we would expect of him: 'Let us not, then, look for a trick or any kind of stratagem. Work with the spear is the one true test of champions. Brave men always prevail in battle' (Q.S. 12.70–2, speech 14). These words are perfectly in line with the heroic code and identity the boy has chosen for himself. Only, their message is not accepted in this new context, as Odysseus points out that 'the dauntless valour of your invincible father was [not] sufficient to sack the wealthy city of Priam' (Q.S. 12.77–8). Neoptolemus' suggestion is declined. The young hero's reaction is inappropriate for an assembly: together with Philoctetes, he plans a violent revolt against the new plans. They are only

---

[47] Scheijnen (2018: 205).

[48] On the expression 'better to die than to fail' in battle exhortations, see Verhelst (2017: 86, n14). For this case, see also Tsomis (2018a: 369–70).

stopped by Zeus's lightning bolt (Q.S. 12.84–103). Reluctantly, they yield
to divine power. Such a reaction is reminiscent of Achilles' intention to slay
Agamemnon in *Iliad* 1 and Athena's timely intervention (*Il.* 1.198–222).[49]
There are differences, though, the most important being that Achilles' anger
is acknowledged as rightful by the goddess. Athena only urges him to express
it by words (1.211) rather than by weapons. Neoptolemus must learn the same
lesson in *PH* 12; in the assembly, words are the way to disagree, not violence.
In Book 12, moreover, Neoptolemus must truly yield to the assembly's decision. Instead of being secretly supported by the gods, as Achilles was, his son
must now learn to follow the others' advice. The second assembly serves to
realign views: although the ruse must be carried out, Nestor finds a wise way
to appeal to Neoptolemus' heroic pride.[50] He mentions the κλέος that can
be won in such a ruse and suggests that he himself, as an old man, might
take up arms for that reason (Q.S. 12.264–73). Triggered by both statements, Neoptolemus speaks again, twice. The abundant mention in the second assembly of concepts such as θάρσος, ἀριστεύς and κλέος, all of which
are central to Neoptolemus' beliefs, make it possible for the young hero to
respond in the gnomic wordings he is used to: 'we, the young men, hungry
for battle, will enter [the horse] eager to do your bidding' (Q.S. 12.279–80,
speech 15) and 'I would rather be the war god's glorious victim than escape
from Troy with a burden of disgrace' (Q.S. 12.301–2, speech 16). Helped
by Nestor in this subtle way, Neoptolemus leaves his second assembly with
unhurt pride, leading the other heroes into the horse. However, his final
intervention is also marked by the modesty he so often displayed in Book 7:
'If the gods choose otherwise, so be it also' (speech 16). Neoptolemus has
toned down, as if he accepts Nestor's lesson and his (still inexperienced) position in this assembly. At the same time, he is grateful for the opportunity
to express his heroic beliefs once more. He will gladly carry them out during
the sack, as he bellows at Priam in the hubbub of the next book: 'As you are
my foe I shall not leave you among the living' (speech 17).

   One final and decisive step in Neoptolemus' heroic development is taken
in the last book of the *PH*, Book 14. The young hero will speak twice more,
but not before he has received a long dream vision of his father: his first and
only encounter with Achilles. This speech, which I discuss at greater length
elsewhere, is of central importance for our evaluation of Neoptolemus' growth
as a hero, for two reasons: it helps us to identify the 'checklist' of heroic features that Achilles would have wanted his son to follow; and it sends Neoptolemus on his final mission in the *PH*, a mission that marks the conclusion of

---

[49] Vian (1969: 92, n4) and James (2004: 329) rather see the parallel with Nestor and Diomedes in
   Iliad 8.
[50] Schenk (1997) and Scheijnen (2018: 244–55).

his development.[51] The 'checklist' can be found in the first part of Achilles' speech (Q.S. 14.187–91 in particular, here paraphrased):[52]

- Stop mourning me (for I am with the gods now).
- Put my strength into your heart.
- Always be the Ἀργείων πρόμος in battle and yield to no one.
- In the assembly, obey your elders.
- And all will call you εὔφρων.

Each of these pieces of advice Neoptolemus has learned (by himself) to implement in his heroic behaviour through the course of his actions. Arriving in Troy as the mourning son (cf. e.g. his speech 5 to Agamemnon and 9 to Achilles), Neoptolemus has quickly learned to incorporate his father's force in his own battle successes (explicitly so in both of his speeches to Eurypylus in Book 8, and again in speech 9, to his father). As from Book 9, the boy has developed his leadership skills to encourage and exhort the other Achaeans on the battlefield. He therefore could easily be called a πρόμος ('foremost fighter', 'champion', 'one fighting in front').[53] Finally, he had his first experiences in the assembly in Book 12. Although he seemed ill-disposed to listen to anyone, by the end of the second meeting he is convinced by and has expressed his respect for Nestor, who has taught him an important lesson. It then appears that Neoptolemus has checked all of Achilles' 'boxes' to be regarded as εὔφρων. Moreover, an intertextual level is added to this heroic checklist by the word πρόμος: Carvounis has shown that the word occurs only this once in the PH and establishes a firm link with Odysseus' description of Neoptolemus to Achilles in the underworld scene of Odyssey 11. Achilles had first asked: 'But come, tell me tidings of my son, that lordly youth, whether or not he followed to the war to be a leader (πρόμος)' (Od. 11.493–4).[54] Odysseus' ensuing report to Achilles can to a major extent be compared to Neoptolemus' actual progress in the PH (Od. 11.504–37, again paraphrased):[55]

- Odysseus brought Neoptolemus to Troy from Scyros.
- In council, Neoptolemus was always the first to speak and never erred; only Nestor and Odysseus surpassed him.

---

[51] Achilles' dream appearance has received ample attention in earlier research, especially by Maciver (2012a) and Carvounis (2019: 98–122); see also Boyten (2010). For my own interpretation and more detailed references, see Scheijnen (2018: 322–37).

[52] Carvounis (2019: 109).

[53] LfgrE s.v. πρόμος.

[54] Carvounis (2019: 109–10). See also Scheijnen (2018: 335), drawing on the 2005 dissertation version of Carvounis' book.

[55] See also Langella (2018).

- In battle, he was always foremost, yielding to no one in his prowess.
- He slew many; most notably Eurypylus, who was second only to Memnon.
- When Odysseus led everyone into the horse, he was the only one without fear, eager to start battle.
- After the sack, he left for home, completely unharmed.

Odysseus indeed took part in the expedition to fetch Neoptolemus in *PH* 7. The young hero's battle prowess as a πρόμος is undeniable. The specific example to prove this is the defeat of Eurypylus, indeed the main opponent of Neoptolemus *and* the first champion to arrive after Memnon, who was (in turn) the most honourable adversary of Achilles in the *PH*. Less is known about what happens inside the horse, but Neoptolemus led the way in, and eagerly.[56] In the entire epic, Neoptolemus remains unharmed.[57] So far as we can see, then, Quintus has painted a picture of Neoptolemus that fits perfectly into the description of Odysseus which, in the chronological order of the myth, will of course only take place *after* the *PH*. It therefore suffices that the picture is complete at the end of Book 14. Interestingly, one detail mentioned by Odysseus does not yet entirely fit the state of Neoptolemus at the time of his father's appearance: his behaviour in council. So far, Odysseus and Nestor have indeed surpassed him.[58] In Book 12, the young hero yielded to Odysseus by accepting the plan and to Nestor in realising how the ruse could benefit him. However, at the beginning of Book 14 Neoptolemus has not quite yet reached the state of rhetorical supremacy referred to in the underworld. As Langella notes, a considerable part of Neoptolemus' speeches in the *PH* consists of replies to someone else.[59] In the assemblies, particularly, he has not been the first to speak and he has occasionally been found to be struggling in such a context. This changes drastically when Neoptolemus awakens from his encounter with Achilles – which brings us to the second reason why the dream appearance was important. Achilles' order in the final part of that speech is the immediate instigator of Neoptolemus' last action (and last words) in the *PH*. This action and these words allow the young hero to fulfil the final criterion of Odysseus' description in *Odyssey* 11.[60]

Achilles, who has recently become a god, wants Neoptolemus to give him his share of loot from the sack: Polyxena, in the form of a human sacrifice. This is at once a way for Achilles to bring the news of his deification to the Achaeans (who may, until now, have been unaware of this)[61] and to bring

---

[56] That Neoptolemus is the first one to enter the horse does not necessarily imply that he is the leader: in *PH* 13, Odysseus appears to be in command (Q.S. 13.34–50).

[57] Boyten (2010: 233).

[58] Carvounis (2019: 109).

[59] Langella (2018: 291).

[60] See also Carvounis (2019: 109).

[61] Vian (1969: 186, n1).

Achilles' own heroic glory to its climax in the *PH*: Polyxena is the new Briseis, she must serve as his γέρας. The term γέρας is not mentioned by Achilles. We find it in Neoptolemus' first of two speeches in Book 14: speech 18, in which he addresses the assembled Achaeans. This meeting in the agora is called by the young hero himself and he is the first and only one to speak, summarising only the relevant parts of Achilles' long speech to Neoptolemus.[62] Some parts were private between father and son (especially the list of heroic advice), but the sacrifice is to be carried out publicly, to honour Achilles. Neoptolemus correctly interprets this request as a claim of the γέρας that is Achilles' rightful due. He explains this to the Achaeans, in addition to the (breaking?) news that his father now is a god and will punish them, should they not meet his demands. As soon as the Achaeans, in response to Neoptolemus' announcement, implore Achilles as a god, a raging storm begins (14.246–52). The army acknowledges Achilles' new powers (Q.S. 14.254–6) and prepares the sacrifice. This entire chain of events is triggered by Neoptolemus' speech, which sets in motion the final part of Achilles' deification: a god he may already be, but in order for him to be worshipped, this knowledge must be spread. Neoptolemus devotedly takes up the role of intermediary, thus also displaying a new kind of leadership, now in the assembly. He personally slays Polyxena on the altar and invokes his father in what are Neoptolemus' last words in the epic (Q.S. 14.308–12):

κλῦθι, πάτερ, σέο παιδὸς ἐπευχομένοιο καὶ ἄλλων
Ἀργείων, μηδ' ἧμιν ἔτ' ἀργαλέως χαλέπαινε:
ἤδη γάρ τοι πάντα τελέσσομεν, ὅσσα μενοινᾷς   310
σῆσιν ἐνὶ πραπίδεσσι· σὺ δ' ἵλαος ἄμμι γένοιο
τεύξας εὐχομένοισι θοῶς θυμηδέα νόστον.

Father, hear the prayer of your son and of the other
Argives and be no longer harsh and angry with us.
Soon we shall have carried out everything
That you have set your heart on. So be gracious to us
And quickly grant the sweet return for which we pray.

The speech begins with words typical for prayer (κλῦθι, πάτερ, line 308).[63] They end with the word νόστος, which forms an important motif throughout Book 14.[64] As the storm ceases, the real importance of Neoptolemus' final speech crystallises: not only has the son, by taking the lead in this ritual, ensured his father's worship as a god on earth, he has also provided the Achaeans

---

[62] For intertextual links, see Carvounis (2019: 122).

[63] In Quintus, these exact words have been used for Zeus once before (Q.S. 1.186). See Carvounis (2019: 153–4) and Scheijnen (2018: 342).

[64] Scheijnen (2018: 343–5).

with the means to leave Troy and start for home: a quiet sea.[65] In the process, Neoptolemus has checked the last box on his heroic 'to do' list: to be a foremost speaker. He now also masters the art of the assembly. Neoptolemus has completed his development, fulfilled the heroic advice his father gave him and is ready to be described to him as a valiant, successful youth in the underworld, 'later' in the *Odyssey*.

CONCLUSION

The growth of Neoptolemus as a young hero aims indeed to arrive at the point where his character is completely 'up to date' with the picture Odysseus is about to paint of him in the *Odyssey*. What is a chronologically logical concern (the *PH* takes place before the *Odyssey*) is in fact a literary choice: Homer predates Quintus and Quintus' poetics are resolved to engage with the expectations of a Homeric readership. Still, Quintus is not a slave of Homer: regarding the figure of Achilles, for example, Book 14 presents a paradox. Achilles is deified by Quintus, where *Odyssey* 11 portrays him as a repenting ghost. Other traditions about Achilles' afterlife have been more influential here than Homer.[66] Quintus' dealing with Neoptolemus appears to be more straightforward: his character is progressively constructed towards 'who he must be in the *Odyssey*' (cf. the 'checklist').

Still, the comparison of his speech use to that of other heroes reveals that, in the process of his growth, the youth seems to take steps away from his old (Homeric?) inheritance and, in many ways, is also a hero of 'a new generation'. Why does young Neoptolemus not favour the beloved superlative discourse of his forefathers – despite its continuity with the *Iliad*? What does it mean that many of the newly arrived champions (particularly starting with Memnon) share a discourse of modesty instead – even on the battlefield? Neoptolemus and his peers adhere to a new fashion that perhaps could be deemed 'modern' (compared to Homer) in the cultural context of Quintus.[67] The debate about Stoic (or similar) influences has been referred to above. In addition, Tsomis has argued that such discourse has been ongoing long before the Stoa and that Quintus may well have been influenced for this by contemporary popular beliefs.[68] Such influences could indeed convey an impact on the ideological motivations behind certain heroic behaviour in the *PH*.

---

[65] Boyten (2007: 328; 2010: 199–202).

[66] Full interpretation and more references in Scheijnen (2018: 322–37); also Carvounis (2019: 98–102).

[67] On Quintus' speech use compared to other epic authors until Nonnus, see Verhelst (2017).

[68] Tsomis (2018a: 83–105).

As pointed out in the introduction to this chapter, modesty has had a strong impact on the perception of Neoptolemus' heroic characterisation as a whole; this becomes increasingly clear when the character of Neoptolemus is considered on a larger intertextual scale. Langella, for example, compares how Neoptolemus is portrayed as an orator by Quintus, Dictys and Dares: she identifies clear differences but also a possible dialogue between these works.[69] Indeed, Quintus takes his position as an at first view Homer-abiding poet in an era of thorough Homeric revisionism. The more extreme strands of this tendency[70] show no mercy for Homeric characters in their rigorous rewritings. In order to take a position *against* such rewritings, Quintus not only looks back to Homer; he also seems to take things one step further. Could his emphasis on modesty serve as a counterpart for the more cruel, unnuanced portrayals of Neoptolemus in other works?[71] Such a hypothesis would imply that, in order to portray Neoptolemus as a reasonable, Homer-worthy character, he paradoxically could (should?) be portrayed as more modest than Homer might have done (or did, with his father Achilles).

On a text-internal level, it should be observed that Neoptolemus' modesty is embedded in specific contexts: the vast majority of speeches in which he is careful occur in Book 7, before or just after his arrival in Troy; one more is found in Book 12, after he has expressed his respect for Nestor in the assembly. It has been the goal of this contribution to illustrate how, through the course of the narrative, this specific trait has a clear role, alongside other *topoi*, to paint a multi-faceted image of the young hero: modest and careful at first, but fierce and – judging from his speeches – more and more confident as a leader of the Achaeans. That his final performance focuses on the worship of his father and the finalisation of his own characterisation to join with the *Odyssey*, brings us back to the beginning of this conclusion: if anything, Neoptolemus is a character of paradoxical influences, both traditional and 'modern'. It shows us once more how Quintus' epic carefully navigates between those two poles.

---

[69] Langella (2018).
[70] So identified by Avlamis (2019).
[71] For example Boyten (2007; 2010).

CHAPTER 11

Stepping out of Place: σχέτλιος in Quintus of Smyrna's *Posthomerica*

Jordan Maly-Preuss

Epic storylines are founded on a bedrock of resistance: the focal characters resist adversaries, inclement circumstances and ordinary limitations on behaviour. An epic hero would hardly fulfil his role without anyone to oppose, nor would Helen or Penelope garner such attention if they did not defy others' expectations for their conduct, whether by abandoning a marriage or preserving it long after it has been popularly deemed void. Among the many possible means of highlighting a character's resistance within epic is to describe them with the epithet σχέτλιος. Both characters and extradiegetic narrators employ this evaluative epithet to designate those who depart from an expected path, whether these expectations derive properly from the speaker's individual judgement or from broader social mores. This practice persists in Quintus of Smyrna's *Posthomerica*, where persons termed σχέτλιος (hereafter, 'schetliasts')[1] can be seen specifically to resist what the speakers deem to be the schetliasts' proper social roles. In the following I analyse Quintus' usage of σχέτλιος against the background of previous poetic (primarily epic) usage and find that the valence he develops is distinctly 'Posthomeric'.[2]

The epithet σχέτλιος, which I argue should be understood as possessing a basic sense of 'resistant', is most studied and perhaps best remembered for its appearances in Homer,[3] though it enjoyed a robust existence throughout all periods of literature from archaic epic to Nonnos and in every major

---

[1] I coin the term 'schetliast' on analogy with 'scholiast'; the form σχετλιαστής is attested in *Suda*, ed. Adler, B 43.

[2] I employ 'Posthomeric' throughout to mean only 'pertaining to the *Posthomerica*'.

[3] The most substantial treatments (all re Homer) are Brunius-Nilsson (1955: 42–4); Hohendahl-Zoetelief (1980: 53–62); Vanséveren (1998); Kelly (2007: 309–10); Stocking (2011); Wilson (1971: 293–4) re tragedy; Dickey (1996: 164) re prose.

genre except New Comedy and invective, with about 400 extant occurrences before Quintus.[4] Both general and etymological lexica illustrate the difficulty of characterising the word in all its guises,[5] as even in archaic epic it occurs in widely varying social contexts and with substantially differing emotional content, manifesting not only criticism and challenge but also teasing and praise.[6] I have elsewhere conducted a thorough study of σχέτλιος in archaic epic,[7] finding that across forty instances the word exhibited a stable underlying valence, resistance to order. I further found that the particular instantiation of order that characters resisted was consistent within each poem but variable between poems, as poets aligned the epithet with the conceptual programmes of their works. Thus, for instance, Hesiod's *Erga* employs σχέτλιος to label those who resist Zeus's justice,[8] while in the *Homeric Hymns* the epithet emphasises well-controlled divine reproduction as important for maintaining order.[9] Indeed, even later semantic developments cohere with a basic sense of 'resistant'. Whereas archaic epic σχέτλιος can be characterised as 'active', labelling concerted resistance on the part of the targets, in tragedy and later poetry (notably Apollonios of Rhodes' *Argonautica*) the word acquires a further 'passive' sense, in which targets are not agents but patients, and speakers employ the term to indicate that targets' circumstances resist order.[10] In oratory and prose, meanwhile, the connotations are simplified: here it is overwhelmingly moral order that is resisted,[11] whereas epic and tragic schetliasts can surpass ordinary limits without earning disapproval.[12]

Silvio Bär and Anastasia Maravela have recently issued a call for increased application of diachronic narratology to epic;[13] I concur that such an approach is crucial for establishing a thorough understanding of post-archaic epic poetics, and this chapter demonstrates what can be achieved using this lens. My study employs the varied perspectives of lexicography, narratology, narrative intertextuality and analysis of social and conversational dynamics;[14] I devote

---

[4] Assessed through *TLG* search, 20 January 2020.

[5] Cf. Chantraine (1968); Frisk (1970); *LSJ* ([10]1996); Beekes (2010); Montanari (2015).

[6] E.g., criticism/challenge: *Il.* 17.150; teasing: 10.164; praise: *Od.* 12.21.

[7] Oxford MPhil dissertation (2018).

[8] *Erga* 15, [124], 187, 238, 254.

[9] *h.Ap.* 322, *h.Aph.* 254.

[10] E.g., Eur. *Andr.* 31, *Hec.* 783, *El.* 120. Cf. Wilson (1971), Peradotto (1990) on active/passive senses of the (perceived) τλα- epithet family (σχ., τάλας/τλήμων, 'miserable/daring').

[11] E.g., *Hdt.* 6.138.23, Dion. Hal. *Ant. Rom.* 11.1.3.13, Dio Cass. 45.23.2.2.

[12] *Il.* 10.164; *Od.* 11.474, 12.21, 13.293; Eur. *Alc.* 741. Cf. Richardson (1993: 115); de Jong (2001: 297, 329); Parker (2007: 199); Bowie (2013: 146).

[13] Bär and Maravela (2019).

[14] For my models in analysis of social and conversational dynamics, see Beck (2005; 2012); Scodel (2008).

roughly equal attention to speakers and targets, individual σχέτλιος-speeches[15] and superstructural phenomena (such as patterning of related scenes). My treatment of *comparanda* for Posthomeric σχέτλιος-instances, however, is necessarily weighted towards specific works. Quintus' primary intertexts for σχέτλιος were evidently the *Iliad* and *Odyssey*, as his usage most closely resembles Homeric patterns; I therefore privilege comparison with Homer, and by extension archaic epic. Next in priority are the *Argonautica* and tragedy, as these incorporate the epithet into characters' conversations (Quintus places nine of his ten σχέτλιος-instances in character-speech); then archaic lyric and epigram and other post-archaic epic, in all of which narrator-uttered σχέτλιος predominates (whereas Quintus has only one such occurrence). Throughout the chapter I focus upon inheritance and innovation within epic social and structural dynamics for σχέτλιος.

Across extant epic, character-speakers nearly always explain what it is about the schetliasts' behaviour that merits the description; narrator-uttered σχέτλιος also frequently receives justification.[16] These explanations inform both the intra- and extradiegetic audiences of the speakers' intentions and also, when considered in the aggregate, reveal the characteristic valence that σχέτλιος exhibits in each poem. Quintus' particular valence for σχέτλιος shows the greatest affinity with those seen in three archaic epics: the *Iliad*, the *Odyssey* and the pseudo-Hesiodic *Aspis*. Iliadic characters' explanations for σχέτλιος reveal that the schetliasts in that poem resist order-directed change: speakers allege that schetliasts are neglecting their social duties and urge them to enact more cooperative behaviour. Odyssean σχέτλιος-speakers more typically voice comment upon past actions that have irrevocably breached ordinary limits; *themis*, the system of principles that governs interactions and sets limits, is the primary form of order resisted.[17] In the *Aspis* the explanations for σχέτλιος instead reveal an understanding of order as reason, which the schetliasts resist by losing their self-possession or causing others to do so. Posthomeric σχέτλιος is typified by a blending of these aspects, with an infusion of a 'cognitive' emphasis upon schetliasts' mental states.[18] Posthomeric σχέτλιος-speakers claim that schetliasts' inaccurate self-perceptions have prompted the current conflicts; they base their explanations upon proper social limits while attempting

---

[15] I term 'σχέτλιος-speeches' all speeches containing σχ.; for *PH* this includes a single narrator-uttered 'σχέτλιος-speech', which is complicated by narrating a character's thoughts. I denote these speeches as 'speaker→target' when speakers directly address targets and as 'speaker to hearer re target' when speakers address remarks about targets to third parties.

[16] Homeric explanations for σχ.: Brunius-Nilsson (1955: 42–3); Hohendahl-Zoetelief (1980: 62); Vanséveren (1998: 255); *LfgrE* s.v.; Kelly (2007: 309–10).

[17] See Burkert (1977) on *themis*; Yamagata (1994: 72–8) for *themis* in Homer; Austin (1975: 130–78) for the importance of order in *Od*.

[18] Maravela (2019) finds that Quintus' νήπιος also has cognitive emphasis.

to position themselves as authorities over schetliasts. The change they desire is that the schetliasts realise their (allegedly) proper social roles as the speakers' inferiors. These features are conveniently exemplified in the first σχέτλιος-speech in the poem, to which we now turn.[19]

PH 1.447–74:[20] THEANO PREVENTS THE TROJAN WOMEN FROM RUSHING ON TO THE BATTLEFIELD

Theano's speech is a notable outlier among σχέτλιος-speeches in the *Posthomerica*, in the gender pairing of speaker and target and in the mildness of the speaker's attitude.[21] At the same time it evinces the depth of Quintus' interaction with his antecedents, as the temporal patterning surrounding the epithet exhibits the same paradigm that is characteristic of Iliadic σχέτλιος-speeches. Serving as an exemplar and a point of contrast, then, Theano's address to the Trojan women provides a lens for discerning the characteristic aspects of Posthomeric σχέτλιος usage and engagement with earlier trends.

Let us first consider gender dynamics. Only here in the poem does a woman address a female schetliast, a phenomenon rare across epic, limited to Aphrodite targeting Helen (*Il.* 3.414), Penelope addressing her handmaids (*Od.* 4.729)[22] and Kirke criticising Medea (*Arg.* 4.739), and exceptionally rare elsewhere (the only other such occurrence in all of extant Greek literature is Soph. *Ant.* 47, where Ismene targets Antigone). When women in epic call other women σχετλίη/σχέτλιαι, certain situational factors obtain, equally in Apollonios and Quintus as in Homer. Named female speakers only call other women σχετλίη in direct address,[23] only apply σχετλίη to women over whom they have authority,[24] and reliably elicit a compliant or conciliatory response

---

[19] Greek texts employed (punctuation occasionally altered): *Il.*, West (1998, 2000); *Od.*, West (2017); *Arg.*, Vian (1974, -80, -81); *PH*, Vian (1963, -66, -69). All translations are my own.

[20] Speech introductory lines are crucial for interpreting emotional and interpersonal functioning of speeches (cf. Beck 2005: 13–15, 32–45 and speech introductory lemmata in Kelly 2007); I therefore regularly include such lines in citations.

[21] Discussions of this speech: Bär (2009: 116–17); Boyten (2010: 62–3); Scheijnen (2018: 59–61); Carvounis (2020: 145–53). Theano's resonance as a character: Carvounis (2019: 156–7).

[22] The only other woman→women instance in extant Greek literature. The specific word form σχέτλιαι is extremely rare: elsewhere only Call. *Hec.* fr. 318 Pfeiffer, σχέτλιαι ἀνθρώπων ἀφραστύες.

[23] At *Od.* 23.150 (Ithakan passersby re Penelope), the speaker group may include low-rank women, but this is anonymous τις-speech: the prohibition against named speakers holds. Indeed, no named character of either sex censures an absent woman with σχ., though a woman may thus censure an absent man, e.g. *Il.* 8.361 (Athene re Zeus to Hera), *Arg.* 1.807 (Hypsipyle re Lemnian men to Jason).

[24] Viz., Aphrodite is Helen's tutelary deity, Penelope owns her handmaids and Kirke receives Medea as a supplicant.

from the female schetliasts they address.[25] As we shall see, Theano's speech manifests all these qualities. Desiring to prevent the Trojan women from rushing on to the battlefield, Theano speaks to them immediately and directly. As a Trojan woman herself, she is entitled to criticise their misguided notions; as the women's elder, she speaks from a superior position and convinces them to remain within Troy (PH 1.475–6). Theano's success at influencing her targets is shared by female σχέτλιος-speakers elsewhere in the poem: when Hera castigates Apollo for shooting Achilles, she wins a contrite response (speech: 3.96–127; response: 129–33); when Oinone excoriates Paris for requesting her aid, he turns away from her dwelling (speech: 10.307–27; response: 328, 332–3). The last female-uttered σχέτλιος-speech in the Posthomerica is Kassandra's rebuke of the rejoicing Trojans (12.539–51), which far from prompting faith in her warnings provokes scorn and threats (552–61). But this is poor Kassandra's lot; her failure set against the other women's success highlights her impotence, not least because she comes last, so that an alert audience is in a position to notice the contrast. Kassandra, the final explicitly named σχέτλιος-speaker in the poem, is the inverse of Theano, the first speaker: Theano, who believes that the Trojans may still prevail (1.470–2), is heeded and averts disaster from Troy for a time; Kassandra, who knows that Troy is doomed to fall, is ignored and cannot prevent the inevitable. The poem's first twelve books, which narrate the events before the fall of Troy, are thus bookended by these two σχέτλιος-speeches, coming as they do at the beginning and end of what we could call the 'pre-lapsarian' section.

Along with its female-only context, the second major distinction between Theano's speech and all other σχέτλιος-speeches in the poem is its speaker's benevolent intention towards her addressees.[26] Whenever a woman is called σχετλίη by another character elsewhere in epic this entails criticism of her behaviour,[27] never mere observation that she has exceeded ordinary limits, but in Theano's case the criticism is merely pragmatic, with no concomitant moral disapproval or personal enmity. In this, Quintus departs from his antecedents. In all three of the other female-to-female speeches listed above, the speaker's

---

[25] Helen does go to Paris' bed (Il. 3.418–20), Eurykleia mollifies Penelope (Od. 4.742–58) and Medea accepts Kirke's rebuff without opposition (Arg. 4.749–52).

[26] Though Kassandra utters warnings, these are not unmixed with frustration and despair (PH 12.544–9). Her tone recalls not only tragic σχ. but narrator-uttered σχ. in Arg., which usually expresses the target's suffering (1.1302, 2.1028, 3.1133, 4.916, 4.1524; but 4.376 conspicuously employs the critical tone of Arg. character-speech).

[27] Besides the instances discussed, characters criticise women as schetliasts at Il. 24.33 (mixed group); Od. 23.15; Erga 15, 187 (mixed); Aspis 149; Nonn. Dion. 25.340 (mixed). Cf. Arg. 3.1133: the narrator expresses not criticism but pity, showing influence from tragedy, where σχ. more frequently indicates speakers' recognition of targets' sufferings than their faults, e.g. PV 644; Eur. Hec. 783, IA 932. Narrators do criticise women in mixed-gender groups, e.g. Call. Hymn 3.124.

emotional state is overtly described in the speech introductory line(s), and the content of the speech further elucidates the speaker's attitude towards her target: Aphrodite is angry (χολωσαμένη, *Il.* 3.413) and threatens Helen (414–17), Penelope laments loudly (ἀδινὸν γόωσα, *Od.* 4.721) and blames her handmaids for Telemakhos' successful departure (727–4),[28] and Kirke pities the weeping Medea (μυρομένην ἐλέαιρεν, *Arg.* 4.738) but refuses to condone her actions (745–8).[29] For Theano, the narrator describes not her experiential state at the time of speaking, but instead a fixed characteristic, her shrewdness (πύκα φρονέουσα Θεανώ, 'level-headed Theano', *PH* 1.449).[30] We must look at Theano's speech and the reaction it elicits to discern her sympathetic attitude towards her addressees. She intervenes to save their lives, as is implied both in the narrator's framing (447–50) and in her warning to the Trojan women that they are no match for the Greek warriors (454–5), and besides σχέτλιαι she employs no term of criticism harsher than νήιδες ('naïve', 453). Theano does not deride the women for attempting to enter a decidedly masculine sphere, but instead presents reasoned argument against entering battle founded upon the pragmatic point that they are unskilled (451–69), rather than raising any moral point about the inherent wrongness of female participation in combat.[31] She ends by encouraging her fellow Trojan women to take greater confidence in their own safety (470–4).[32] All these elements point to a desire to do the women good, and to a correspondingly gentle valence for σχέτλιαι: Theano deploys the epithet to seize the women's attention, not to deride them.[33]

Theano differs in her attitude from all other σχέτλιος-speakers in the *Posthomerica*; she is the only one who seeks to avert an action before it is taken, and so though her criticism is urgent it need not be scathing, as the women have

---

[28] Penelope engages in prospective lament: Kelly (2012).

[29] Hunter (2015) *ad Arg.* 4.745–52 sees Kirke's dismissal of Medea as 'modelled on' Aiolos' dismissal of Odysseus (*Od.* 10.72–6). The presence of σχέτλιος in both exchanges strengthens the connection: Odysseus to Aiolos and family (*Od.* 10.69, a failed supplication) and Kirke→Medea (*Arg.* 4.739, refusing further assistance).

[30] Picking up πύκα from *Il.* 5.70, ὅς ῥα νόθος μὲν ἔην, πύκα δ' ἔτρεφε δῖα Θεανώ, 'Who (Meges), though he was a bastard, exalted Theano raised carefully'.

[31] Indeed, Theano's gnomic statement (*PH* 464–6) seems to frame male/female division of labour as contingent rather than necessary, though she recommends compliance; cf. Scheijnen (2018: 60–1). Bär (2009: 102, 117) notes the narrator's ambiguous framing; Boyten (2010: 63) believes the narrator rejects epic gender norms. Intriguingly, after Ismene calls Antigone σχετλία (*Ant.* 47), she also argues against resisting the male/female distinction (*Ant.* 61–2, 67–8). We need not conjecture that Q. intended correspondence between the scenes; nevertheless, Ismene is also the only other extant female→female speaker who means her target well when calling her σχετλία.

[32] Theano seems to insinuate that the women *would* need to fight if calamity truly arrived; some later do (*PH* 13.118–22). Cf. Scheijnen (2018: 60 n34).

[33] *Contra* Boyten (2010: 62), who states that Theano employs σχέτλιαι 'dismissively'.

as yet committed no misdeed.[34] Theano's concern for avoiding disaster in the present is reflected in her explanation for calling the Trojan women σχέτλιαι. Theano employs the same rhetorical patterning present in Iliad σχέτλιος-speeches: a past–present–future/alternative frame, in which speakers justify σχέτλιος by naming schetliasts' current behaviour, support their claims with reference to past events that have created the present circumstance, and envision either a future scenario that will result if schetliasts do not change or an alternative scenario that would improve upon the present.[35] A straightforward example of this pattern is Il. 9.628–33, where Ajax speaks to Odysseus about Achilles: Ajax uses past tense to describe the origin of Achilles' resistance (Ἀχιλλεύς / ἄγριον ἐν στήθεσσι θέτο μεγαλήτορα θυμόν, 'Achilles has hardened his proud heart', 628–9) and justifies his choice to call Achilles σχέτλιος by naming Achilles' current behaviour with the present tense (οὐδὲ μετατρέπεται, 'he is not swayed', 630). He then contrasts this with a generalising statement about the better alternative that a less obstinate person would adopt (καὶ μὲν τίς τε κασιγνήτοιο φόνοιο / ποινὴν ἢ οὗ παιδὸς ἐδέξατο τεθνηῶτος, 'another man would instead even accept the bloodprice if his brother or son were killed', 632–3). The rhetorical patterning outlined admirably suits attempted persuasion, the prevailing Iliadic σχέτλιος-speech type.[36]

Theano's speech displays this same Iliadic patterning.[37] Her initial challenge to the women not only questions their behaviour but serves to explain her choice to call them σχέτλιαι (PH 1.451–5). For illustrative purposes I have annotated this passage: justifications for σχέτλιος are in **bold**, support in *italics*, and real or intended consequences are <u>underlined</u>. Mentions of experience, or lack thereof, are indicated with {braces}.

> **Τίπτε ποτὶ κλόνον** αἰνόν, ἐελδόμεναι πονέεσθαι,
> **σχέτλιαι**, {*οὔ τι πάροιθε πονησάμεναι περὶ χάρμης*},
> ἀλλ' ἄρα {*νήιδες*} ἔργον ἐπ' {*ἄτλητον*} μεμαυῖαι,
> **ὄρνυσθ'** {ἀφραδέως}; <u>Οὐ γὰρ σθένος ἔσσεται ἶσον</u>
> <u>ὑμῖν καὶ Δαναοῖσιν {ἐπισταμένοισι} μάχεσθαι.</u>   455

---

[34] Kassandra desires to prevent disaster (PH 12.539–551), but does not expect success (546); she reacts, moreover, to a pre-existing situation – the Trojans are already ignoring the portents when Kassandra speaks. Theano, by contrast, responds to Hippodameia's previous speech urging the women to fight (PH 1.406–35), and dissuades them from ever entering the battlefield.

[35] These elements need not occur in chronological order.

[36] Speakers attempt to persuade hearers (who are not themselves necessarily the targets of σχ.) in all Il. σχέτλιος-speeches except 10.162–7, 16.198–209 and 18.5–14 (10/13x).

[37] Elsewhere in PH Thersites' (1.731–7) and Kassandra's (12.544–6) explanations for σχ. engage most closely with the Iliadic paradigm, as they urge their targets to change present behaviour.

Why are you rushing into dread battle eager for the struggle,
Wayward ones, never before partakers in combat,
Yet naïvely zealous for unfamiliar action?
Your strength will not be equal to your foes'
Since the Greeks have been well trained for war.

Theano's argument runs thus: '**Why** are you rushing into battle (justification), *since* you have no experience (support), <u>and indeed</u> your strength will not suffice to contend with the Greeks (negative alternative: consequences of action)?' At first glance the clause directly following σχέτλιαι would seem to offer the justification, with its negative opening. But the logic of Theano's speech and its kinship with Iliadic framing of σχέτλιος weigh against such an interpretation here. If we accept σχέτλιαι as appositive with the 'you' of ὄρνυσθε ('you are rushing'), then it belongs to the main clause in Theano's extended question and accords with the overall logic of her speech – the women resist their proper social role precisely by meaning to enter battle, not by having never before experienced combat. Theano's justification for σχέτλιαι, then, is the overarching question 'Why are you rushing into battle?' (extended over 451–4), which employs a present-tense verb like the Iliadic justifications discussed above. Her supporting material, the women's inexperience (452–3), references their past behaviour; she then envisions a negative future, their inevitable failure (454–5), that will result if they continue on their present course. In predicting a stark future for her target, she resembles Aphrodite threatening Helen, as both speeches are successful dissuasions.[38] Aphrodite also foretells destruction for Helen if she chooses to fight against her patron goddess' will (μέσσῳ δ' ἀμφοτέρων μητίσομαι ἔχθεα λυγρά, / Τρώων καὶ Δαναῶν, σὺ δέ κεν κακὸν οἶτον ὄληαι, 'And I will devise excruciating enmity [towards you] on both sides, from the Trojans and the Greeks, and you would perish under your miserable fate', *Il.* 3.416–17).

Aphrodite's speech is an outlier among σχέτλιος-speeches in the *Iliad*, as Theano's is in the *Posthomerica*. Iliadic σχέτλιος-speakers do not usually employ the epithet in direct attacks on their targets;[39] σχέτλιος-speakers in the *Posthomerica* usually do.[40] The difference lies in what the speakers desire from

---

[38] Successful dissuasions through σχέτλιος-speech are rare, occurring elsewhere only at *Od.* 12.115–26 and Soph. *Phil.* 927–62. Medea claims disingenuously to have dissuaded herself with a σχέτλιος-speech (Eur. *Med.* 869–93).

[39] In addition to *Il.* 3.414, only 17.150 (Glaukos threatens Hektor with withdrawal of Lykian troops) and 24.33 (Apollo challenges Athene, Hera and Poseidon in the gods' council) = 3/13x (23.1%).

[40] *PH* 1.733, 2.414, 3.114, 5.211, 6.388, 10.318 = 6/10x. I take 13.380 as embedded focalisation, but Menelaus' thoughts occur while he physically attacks the Trojans, producing an effect similar to that of verbal attack in direct address.

their targets: the paradigm of the competitive–cooperative dichotomy will aid in elucidation.[41] In their essence, Iliadic σχέτλιος-speeches urge reintegration of cooperative motives into schetliasts' behaviour;[42] the speakers' envisioned outcomes, if achieved, would in most cases benefit the schetliasts as well as the speakers and their broader communities. This is why Iliadic σχέτλιος is not inherently denunciatory,[43] though it can certainly convey bitterness (*Il.* 8.361) or even fury (22.41). Fundamentally, however, speakers wish for their relationships with schetliasts (or the schetliasts' integration into their own communities) to experience not further damage but amelioration.[44] Speakers in the *Posthomerica*, by contrast, employ σχέτλιος competitively, desiring their targets to acknowledge the speaker's superiority. Restoration of the breach in relational order would not mean increased cooperation between persons of closely coordinated status but increased stratification. Quintus' speakers believe that, through a failure of perception, their targets have developed inaccurate views of themselves that conflict with their proper roles. These views have led the targets to attempt to occupy new roles, resulting in social dislocation. This dislocation, in turn, can in most cases be corrected – but only through the targets' acknowledgement of the speakers' superiority.

Despite her benevolent attitude towards the other Trojan women, Theano does exhibit the mindset just described. She underscores the women's inexperience four times in three lines (*PH* 1.452–4) before contrasting it with the Greek warriors' skill in combat (see the annotated passage above). From listening to Hippodameia's argument that they could fight effectively against men (406–35), the Trojan women have naïvely lost sight of their own naïveté and are attempting to become warriors – but as Theano reminds them, they are neither Amazons nor men, and so lack the training necessary to succeed (454–60). They should instead attend decently to their looms (467–8), thus resuming their proper role in relation to others. Theano does not demand that the other women submit to her, but merely to her argument; her claim to superiority here rests merely in her greater prudence – a marked contrast with the poem's other σχέτλιος-speakers, who explicitly crave to be acknowledged as authorities

---

[41] The classic statement of competitive–cooperative dichotomy in Homeric values is Adkins (1960), esp. 30–60. Adkins's views on Homeric ethics have been justly criticised as reductionist (e.g. Long 1970; Finkelberg 1998 with fuller bibliography), but his familiar paradigm serves here as a useful explanatory model without necessitating acceptance of his interpretation of Homer.

[42] Thus Hainsworth (1993) *ad Il.* 9.630: 'by honouring Akhilleus the Achaeans have a claim in turn to his co-operation.'

[43] *Contra* Van Hook (1916); Hohendahl-Zoetelief (1980); Vanséveren (1998); Stocking (2011).

[44] *Il.* 22.41–2 has a sardonic version: Priam says of Achilles, σχέτλιος, αἴθε θεοῖσι φίλος τοσσόνδε γένοιτο / ὅσσον ἐμοί· τάχα κέν ἑ κύνες καὶ γῦπες ἔδοιεν, 'Obdurate man, if only he were to become as beloved to the gods as he is to me! – Then dogs and vultures would swiftly devour him.' Priam opines that his relationship to Achilles would be greatly ameliorated by this desirable outcome.

set above their targets. As we shall see, it is this quality in Thersites' σχέτλιος-speech, the next in the *Posthomerica*, that leads to his demise.

Our discussion of Theano's address to the Trojan women has allowed us to establish the basic connotative parameters for Quintus' σχέτλιος: namely, that it treats a crucial lack of awareness in its targets, informs them that they are violating their proper social roles and emanates from a position of superiority. It has also provided a point of comparison against which we can now define the prevailing social trends in Posthomeric usage. Though the *Posthomerica* has four female σχέτλιος-speakers (Theano, Hera, Oinone, Kassandra), it has only one female target, the Trojan women; all its other targets are either male or mixed groups.[45] In having more female speakers than targets, and more male schetliasts than female, Quintus adheres to persistent epic etiquette for the term.[46] He likewise maintains the apparent epic prohibitions against an individual male character addressing an individual female character as σχετλίη or any character directly referring to themselves as σχέτλιος.[47] Although Quintus' speakers have competitive aims, these do not supersede the most basic standards of social decorum surrounding σχέτλιος in epic. Indeed, Quintus in one point increases the apparent decorum of the term. Whereas in archaic epic mortals may employ the epithet of gods and gods of mortals,[48] in the *Posthomerica* speakers confine allegations of schetliast status to those on their own ontological plane. Quintus' speakers evidently perceive that hierarchical reinforcement of social positions is best undertaken within one's own sphere, god to god, woman to woman, warrior to warrior.[49]

Out of these patterns emerges the typical Posthomeric schetliast, a mortal male who receives criticism from another mortal character for his behaviour as a warrior.[50] Whereas Iliadic σχέτλιος has been mistakenly characterised as

---

[45] Male: Achilles (*PH* 1.733, 2.414), Apollo (3.114), Odysseus (5.211), Nireus (6.388), Paris (10.318), Greek expeditionary force (13.16); mixed groups: Trojans (12.544, 13.380).

[46] Female σχέτλιος-speakers: archaic epic, 13/40 speakers (32.5%); *Arg.*, 4/10 (40%); all other literary hexameter through Nonnos, 1/11 (9.1%). Female schetliasts: archaic, 7/40 (17.5%); *Arg.*, 2/10 (20%); all other, 3/11 (27.3%, in mixed groups only). Male schetliasts: archaic, 29/40 (72.5%); *Arg.*, 8/10 (80%); all other, 9/11 (81.8%).

[47] Neither of these prohibitions holds for tragedy: male→female (expressing sympathy, not challenge), Eur. *Hec.* 783, *IA* 932; self-reference, *PV* 644. Epic characters call themselves σχ. only when reporting others' speech (e.g., *Il.* 16.203, *Od.* 12.279).

[48] Mortals re gods (all with absent schetliast): *Il.* 2.112, 9.19; *Od.* 3.161, 10.69. Gods re mortals: *Il.* 5.403 (absent schetliast); *Od.* 12.21, 12.116, 13.293, 20.45 (all direct address). Apollonios already restricts cross-boundary σχ. to god→mortal (*Arg.* 4.739).

[49] Separation between mortals and gods: Wenglinsky (2002: 288–306, 338–49).

[50] Achilles (1.733, 2.414), Odysseus (5.211), Nireus (6.388), Greek expeditionary force (13.16) = 50%; cf. *Il.* 53.8% (Achilles (9.630, 16.203, 22.41), Nestor (10.164), Hektor (17.150, 22.86), Patroklos (18.13)); *Od.* 11.1% (Odysseus (9.494, 12.279)); *Arg.* 30% (Lemnian men (1.807), Jason (4.376), Argonauts (4.1047)).

a term that highlights schetliasts' martial prowess,[51] for Posthomeric σχέτλιος this interpretation comes nearer the truth, though with a crucial difference: it is the speakers, not the targets, in the *Posthomerica* whose prowess is proclaimed with the epithet. I will now consider in greater detail the social functioning of these power claims. The final section, then, will discuss the tendency of consecutive σχέτλιος-speeches to form thematically meaningful clusters.

CLAIMS TO POWER

Though the consistently negative valence of Quintus' σχέτλιος coheres with poetic practice for many centuries prior,[52] Quintus creates a distillation of tradition that is uniquely his own. Most Posthomeric σχέτλιος-speakers pronounce harsh judgements from a position of assumed authority that in other poems had been reserved to the narrator.[53] As noted in our discussion of Theano's speech, Theano presents a major and Kassandra a partial exception to this trend; they are the only speakers who do not desire to enact either social or physical violence upon their targets. Oinone, on the other hand, declares in the most savage of all σχέτλιος-speeches in the poem (10.307–27) that she would like to repay Paris by rending him with her teeth and lapping up the blood like an animal (315–17). Her speech is also the one in which the speaker–target pair could have been expected out of all those in the *Posthomerica* to have had the most cooperative relationship (as a nymph married to a prince), until the events that brought them into conflict and instead rendered their interactions competitive. When σχέτλιος-speakers express dissatisfaction with family members in earlier epic, by contrast, they explicitly wish the schetliast to appreciate and include them more (whether or not this is still possible at the time of the speech).[54]

---

[51] Horowitz (1975); Oguibénine (1998);Vanséveren (1996; 1998) correctly refutes their claims.

[52] After classical tragedy, all poetic occurrences are negative.Though character-speakers and narrators may use σχ. to identify suffering rather than transgression (e.g. Eur. *Andr.* 1179, Call. *Hymn* 5.78, *Arg.* 4.1524, Dion. Per. *Orbis descriptio* 668), this entails negative attendant circumstances; the prior neutral sense did not.

[53] Narrator-uttered σχ. regularly displays definitive negative (often explicitly moral) judgements: e.g., *Od.* 21.28, *Th.* 488, *Erga* 238,Theogn. 733, Call. *Hymn* 3.124, *Arg.* 4.445, Sibylline Oracles 14.61, Opp. *Hal.* 4.11, ps-Opp. *Cyn.* 1.244.These narrators' judgements resemble prose usage; see note 11.

[54] See especially *Il.* 8.373 (Athene to Hera re Zeus), ἔσται μὰν ὅτ' ἄν αὖτε φίλην γλαυκώπιδα εἴπῃ, 'But wait and see; he will call me his light-eyed darling again' and *Arg.* 1.807–8 (Hypsipyle to Jason re Lemnian men), δηρὸν ἐτέτλαμεν, εἴ κέ ποτ' αὖτις / ὀψὲ μεταστρέψωσι νόον, 'We held out for a long while, in case they should at last turn their minds back [towards us]'; cf. *Il.* 8.361–3 (Athene to Hera re Zeus), 22.59–76 (Priam→Hektor), 22.81–99 (Hekabe→Hektor); *h.Ap.* 322–5 (Hera→Zeus); *Arg.* 1.807–9 (Hypsipyle to Jason re Lemnian men), 4.368–71 (Medea→Jason).

Oinone expresses no such longing, but instead mockingly upends the family dynamics of earlier σχέτλιος-speeches: she fortifies the breach between herself and Paris, bidding him seek the help of his new wife and family (*PH* 10.313–14, 319–20, 324–7).

The harsh tone of Posthomeric σχέτλιος also entails an assertion of social dominance over its targets. This stands in contrast to archaic usage, where the reactions of characters called σχέτλιος in direct address indicate that σχέτλιος-speeches are not necessarily interpreted by their targets as an affront.[55] When Diomedes calls Nestor σχέτλιος in the *Doloneia*, characterising him as over-active for his age (*Il.* 10.163–7), Nestor good-humouredly agrees with him (169–71). Odysseus utters a σχέτλιος-speech to Polyphemos while captive in his cave (*Od.* 9.345–52), and far from objecting to Odysseus' characterisation of himself, the Cyclops appreciates the proferred wine and offers his captive a gift (355–6).[56] Nor are these the only occurrences in earlier epic where the speaker carries their point without causing evident offence, though they are at an interpersonal disadvantage to their target (as Diomedes is with respect to age and Odysseus with respect to brawn).[57] Quintus' σχέτλιος-speakers, meanwhile, do tend to provoke resentment, as they claim not only that they know better than their targets, but that their superior knowledge gives them authority over the schetliasts in question. As the only σχέτλιος-speech in the poem uttered by a speaker who is unambiguously socially inferior to his target,[58] Thersites' disparagement of Achilles provides an object lesson in these power claims, as well as a counterpart to the Homeric examples just discussed. Achilles' homi-cidal response to Thersites' censure (1.741–7) evinces the challenge to the tar-get's social position that Posthomeric characters issue in speeches where they employ the epithet.[59] Achilles cannot countenance a person who is manifestly inferior claiming to have authority over him, as he states clearly in his rebuttal to the now dead Thersites (1.750–4).[60] The Trojans likewise reject Kassandra's assertion of authoritative knowledge, though this reaction underscores their

---

[55] See Hohendahl-Zoetelief (1980: 57–62).

[56] Cf. Hohendahl-Zoetelief (1980: 57) on Polyphemos' mild reaction.

[57] Cf. *Il.* 16.202–9 (Achilles quotes Myrmidons targeting him; he permits resumption of battle), *Od.* 12.278–302 (Eurylokhos reproaches Odysseus and gains consent to land on Thrinakia), *Arg.* 4.1030–57 (Medea beseeches Argonauts for protection and wins their support).

[58] In every other case the speaker either has equivalent social standing to the target (Memnon→Achilles, 2.414; Aias→Odysseus, 5.211; Eurypylos→Nireus, 6.388; Oinone→Paris, 10.318; Trojans re Greeks, 13.16) or is socially superior (Theano→Trojan women, 1.452; Hera→Apollo, 3.114; Kassandra→Trojans, 12.544; Narrator/Menelaus re Trojans, 13.380).

[59] Scheijnen (2018: 76) recognises that the affront extends beyond Thersites' axioms: 'Thersites need not be wrong in the meaning of his words; his insolence lies elsewhere.' A substantial portion of that insolence is employing σχ.

[60] Maciver (2012a: 76, n144) observes that Thersites is positioned as an authority over Achilles through intertexts with *Il.*

own poor discernment: they aggressively scorn her, predicting for her 'a fate worse than Laokoön's' (ἀργαλεώτερον ἄλγος / . . . Λαοκόωντος, 12.559–60).

The audacity of the position taken by Posthomeric σχέτλιος-speakers is further illustrated by Eurypylos' vaunting over the vanquished Nireus (6.384–9).[61] This is the only time in extant epic that a warrior calls his defeated foe σχέτλιος in battlefield vaunting:[62] a stark indicator that Posthomeric σχέτλιος substantially departs from previous epic paradigms. Nowhere else in any genre of surviving poetry prior to Quintus had the term been employed by character-speakers as a means of asserting individual social dominance, as it is consistently in the *Posthomerica*.[63] In archaic epic, by contrast, the term highlights situational power imbalances from below. Though speakers may outrank their targets, by employing σχέτλιος they acknowledge an inability to compel or restrict the schetliasts in the present circumstances.[64] Even when an archaic σχέτλιος-speaker has social authority over their target, for example in Aphrodite's threat to Helen (*Il.* 3.413–17) or Penelope's reproach of her handmaids (*Od.* 4.721–34), the target's recalcitrance constitutes a temporary imbalance in the regular power relationship.[65] Quintus inverts this power dynamic; his characters, rather than identifying irregularities to which they object, instead actively promote disparity at their targets' expense – a change in the interpersonal significance of σχέτλιος that represents Quintus' most pronounced break with prior tradition in the usage of the epithet.

One further example will encapsulate the differences I have identified between Homer's and Quintus' σχέτλιος-speeches. In addition to Eurypylos' vaunting σχέτλιος-speech, the *Posthomerica* also contains the only battlefield flyting speech[66] that incorporates σχέτλιος (Memnon targeting Achilles,

---

[61] No warrior calls another individual σχ. in *PH* after this; the last individual targeted is Paris (Oinone speaks, 10.318). Scheijnen (2018: 256–7) finds that explicit comparisons between warriors cluster in the first five books, with Eurypylos uttering the last such claims (*PH* 6.388, 415). Neoptolemos and Philoktetes, who never boast of their superiority (257), are likewise never associated with σχ.

[62] Though Odysseus vaunts over Polyphemos with a σχέτλιος-speech (*Od.* 9.474–9), this is not standard battlefield vaunting but quasi-comic adaptation of tropes familiar from *Il.*: Odysseus shouts from aboard ship at a living foe, who hurls a boulder that misses; Walsh (2005: 153–6) analyses this within a 'mounting rage' sequence. See Parks (1990); Kyriakou (2001); Beck (2005: 165–90) for Homeric vaunting generally; Kelly (2007: 294–5) for stones in Iliadic combat.

[63] Despite the triumphant tone in *Od.* 9.474–9, Odysseus explains σχ. by citing Polyphemos' androphagy (478–9), not his own victory.

[64] This is one of several major arguments posed in my MPhil dissertation.

[65] Walsh (2005: 142) notes that Helen's prior insult (*Il.* 3.403–12) 'damages Aphrodite's honor'; S. West in Heubeck, West and Hainsworth (1988: 239) renders Penelope's explanation for σχ., 'not even you (from whom I might have expected some loyalty)', cf. Hohendahl-Zoetelief (1980: 56–7).

[66] Flyting speeches are taunts issued by opponents before combat, whereas vaunting speeches are delivered by victors over their vanquished foes.

2.411–29).[67] The word is absent from archaic flyting speeches for good reason: no warrior would taunt another by admitting that his target had for the time being gained the upper hand. The only instance of a Homeric warrior calling another σχέτλιος on the battlefield is *Il.* 17.140–68, where Glaukos rebukes Hektor, his ally, for failing to retrieve Sarpedon's body – an interaction wholly different from a flyting speech, despite its antagonistic tone.[68] Where Glaukos argues from the ethical standard of community bonds, Memnon stresses individual prowess and accurate self-image as the desirable standards. Glaukos severely criticises Hektor's performance in combat (142–3, 166–8), but does not contrast this with claims of his own superior prowess; Memnon, meanwhile, both derides Achilles' alleged self-assessment as the greatest of warriors, descended from the most powerful mother (*PH* 2.414–16), and declares that he, Memnon, is superior both in martial potential (412–13) and maternal descent (416–29).[69] Both speakers justify their use of σχέτλιος by questioning the schetliast's future efficacy in battle: yet whereas Glaukos claims that Hektor has violated the regular social obligations between warriors (πῶς κε σὺ χείρονα φῶτα σαώσειας μεθ' ὅμιλον / . . . ἐπεὶ Σαρπηδόν' . . . / κάλλιπες, 'How will you be able to rescue a lesser man from the fray . . . when you have left Sarpedon behind?', *Il.* 17.149–51), Memnon asserts that Achilles has developed an inaccurate sense of superiority (τίπτε σὺ Τρῶας ἀνηλεγέως ὀλέεσκες, / πάντων εὐχόμενος πολὺ φέρτατος ἔμμεναι, 'Why did you keep cruelly slaughtering the Trojans, thinking that you were far mightier than everyone [else]?', *PH* 2.414–15). Glaukos expressly desires for Hektor to reform his behaviour,[70] while Memnon suggests that Achilles should reform his attitude about himself, and by so doing acknowledge Memnon as the greater warrior. The same motivation appears in Aias' first speech to Odysseus during the contest for the arms of Achilles (*PH* 5.180–236),[71] where the explanation for σχέτλιος closely echoes Memnon's (τίπτε βίῃ πολὺ φέρτατος ἔμμεναι ἄλλων / εὐχόμενος μέσσοισιν ἔχες νέας, 'Why, given your boasts that you were by far the mightiest of all, did you maintain your ships in the middle of the line?', 211–12). Aias calls Odysseus σχέτλιος as a reinforcement of his overall argument that Odysseus is attempting

---

[67] On this speech, Campagnolo (2010/11: 280); Ferreccio (2014: 217–18); Scheijnen (2018: 88–90). Homeric flyting: Martin (1989: 68–77); Parks (1990); Beck (2005: 165–90); Walsh (2005). Posthomeric flyting: Maciver (2012b).

[68] Long (1970: 124), Scodel (2008: 51–2) discuss Hektor's cooperative response, an improbable reaction to flyting. Glaukos' speech is properly a hostile exhortation: Beck (2005: 152–64) on hortatory speeches.

[69] Campagnolo (2010/11: 281): 'Memnone vuole contestare l'avversario sottolineando che la sua superiorità è solo presunta' ('Memnon desires to challenge his opponent, stressing that [Achilles'] superiority is merely reputed').

[70] Hence Glaukos' threat to withdraw the Lykian troops if his demands are not met (*Il.* 17.146–8, 154–5).

[71] On this speech, Maciver (2012c); Scheijnen (2018: 138–41).

to fill a social role he has not merited, that is, rightful heir to Achilles as 'best of the Achaians' (ἄριστος Ἀχαιῶν, 5.125).[72]

CLUSTERING OF σχέτλιος-SPEECHES

I will now turn from discussing Posthomeric σχέτλιος-speeches in the aggregate to examining how sequential σχέτλιος-speeches can illuminate one another's pragmatic function in the narrative by forming thematic clusters around one character or plot movement.[73] Theano's speech forms a linked pair with the next σχέτλιος-speech in the poem, Thersites' abuse of Achilles (PH 1.722–40).[74] In both cases Penthesileia serves as the motivating focal figure. As a beautiful female warrior, Penthesileia inspires those who see her with desires both martial and sexual.[75] Yet not all onlookers are equally affected by the longings the Amazon queen inspires: Theano, as we have seen, dissuades her companions from yielding to the Amazon's charms; now Thersites rebukes Achilles for falling under Penthesileia's sway. Recurrent forms of the word ἔρως, 'passionate desire', underscore the thematic link between the two reactions to Penthesileia that occasion these speeches. While she still lives, the sight of the Amazon's prowess rouses desire for battle in Hippodameia (πολέμοιο . . . ἔρως, PH 1.404), which same emulative desire Hippodameia then raises in the other Trojan women (speech: 406–35; women's response: πάσῃσι δ' ἔρως στυγεροῖο μόθοιο / ἔμπεσεν, 'and lust for dread battle filled them all', 436–7). Once Achilles has slain Penthesileia and gazes upon her lying dead before him, he too is moved to desire her, not as a role model but as a partner (657–74, 718–21), when he sees the beauty of her form (she has 'lovely brows', ἐρατῇσιν . . . ὀφρύσι, 660 and 'lovely vigour', ἐρατὸν σθένος, 719).[76] Theano and Thersites, who seek to quell the impulses Penthesileia stimulates in others, also parallel one another: both attempt to regulate their own sphere, targeting members of their social group (Theano the other Trojan women, Thersites another Greek warrior),

---

[72] Scheijnen (2018: 257): 'Odysseus and Ajax make ample use of comparative adjectives to support their cases'; in this context, σχ. can be understood as equivalent to a comparative adjective.

[73] Maravela (2019) finds similar clustering in PH instances of νήπιος ('naïve').

[74] Thersites' speech: Maciver (2012a: 75–9); Scheijnen (2018: 74–7). Connections between Thersites and Penthesileia: Schubert (1996).

[75] Penthesileia as object of desire: Bär (2009: 195–8 and passim); Boyten (2010: 49–52); Maciver (2012a: 144–8); the chapters by Greensmith and Schoess in this volume.

[76] Penthesileia also 'smiles alluringly', μειδίαεν . . . ἐρατεινόν (PH 1.58); see Bär (2009: 243–5). She inspires five of six ἔρως-derived terms in Book 1. The exception is the epic idiomatic phrase 'desirable feast', δαιτός . . . ἐρατεινῆς (1.120; see Bär 2009: 375–6). Even here, however, the word ἐρατεινῆς stands at the transition of narrative focus to Penthesileia's experiences (PH 1.121–81): the reader is primed to consider the Amazon's desirability as well as that of the feast.

and both only appear in the narrative for the scene in which they deliver their σχέτλιος-speeches and experience their targets' reactions.

This type of σχέτλιος-speech cluster occurs in more elaborated form elsewhere in the *Posthomerica*. Thersites' speech participates not only in a Penthesileia-themed doublet, but also in a sequence of three successive σχέτλιος-speeches that have Achilles as their focal figure. First Thersites derides Achilles for regretting Penthesileia's death (1.722–40), then Memnon attacks him with battlefield flyting (2.410–29) and, finally, Hera upbraids Apollo for killing him (3.96–127). The final three σχέτλιος-speeches in the poem also form a chain, this time to address the fall of Troy: Kassandra decries the Trojans' disregard of the portents that spell their doom (12.539–51), after which the Trojans mock the Greeks for their supposed retreat (13.14–18) and Menelaus correspondingly mentally abominates the Trojans while slaughtering the city's inhabitants (13.374–84, of which I take 378–84 to be embedded focalisation).[77]

In his patterning of these sequences, Quintus imitates epic precedent;[78] his apparent model is a similar cluster of three σχέτλιος-speeches in the *Iliad*, the final three in that poem. Like Quintus' sequence in the same position, this Iliadic chain focuses upon a defeat of Troy, in its case by clustering around Hektor:[79] Priam beseeches Hektor to seek refuge within Troy's walls (*Il.* 22.37–76), Hekabe adds her voice to the supplication (22.81–9) and after the outcome of Hektor's refusal, Apollo brings a formal suit against Athene, Hera and Poseidon for opposing the restitution of Hektor's body (24.32–54).[80] Quintus sensitively identifies the conceptual patterns in the Iliadic three-speech sequence and employs them in his own Destruction of Troy sequence to good effect, demonstrating an interest in imitating Homeric syntactic framing for σχέτλιος not only on the sentence level, but also in the scene-by-scene outworking of what I call

---

[77] Wenglinksy (2002: 346) concurs; Scheijnen (2018: 308–9) acknowledges the possibility but inclines against. *Pace* Scheijnen, Menelaus' thoughts are highlighted and explicitly validated (Τρωσὶ κακὰ φρονέεσκε τὰ δὴ θεὸς ἐξετέλεσσε / πρέσβα Δίκη, 'he contemplated evil toward the Trojans, and these very things the venerable goddess Justice accomplished', *PH* 13.377–8). The following explanatory γάρ (378) marks the transition to enumerating the thoughts Justice fulfils; cf. de Jong (²2004a: 110–12) re φρονέω and γάρ with embedded focalisation in *Il.* Furthermore, when the narrator restates Menelaus' name (385), this need not entail prior departure from his experiences, but could indicate shift of focus from thoughts to deeds.

[78] There is also one certain doublet from drama, the two σχέτλιος-occurrences in Soph. *Phil.*: Neoptolemos tells Philoktetes what he said to the Atreidai when they deprived him of Achilles' arms (368–70), then Philoktetes calls Neoptolemos σχ. when deprived of his bow (929–30).

[79] The downfall of Hektor in *Il.* emblemises the coming (extradiegetic) downfall of Troy.

[80] I disagree with Scodel (2008: 151, n34) that Apollo targets all the Olympian gods; cf. Macleod (1982: 90–1).

'event syntax'.[81] In each case, impending death approaches and then overtakes the focal figure;[82] in each case as well, the first two speeches fail in their objective while the third succeeds. Priam and Hekabe both fail to convince Hektor to seek his own safety (*Il.* 22.78, 91), but Apollo wins Zeus's approval for the ransom of Hektor's body (24.64–76); the Trojan revellers scorn Kassandra and her warnings (*PH* 12.552–61) and then mistakenly believe themselves safe from the Greeks (13.19–20), but Menelaus' tirade against the Trojans in embedded focalisation occurs while he is successfully slaughtering them (13.374). Furthermore, both of these sequences encompass the movement of their focal object into Troy. In the Iliadic sequence, Hektor as a schetliast resists entering the city, but will be brought back post mortem once he is a victim of others' behaviour as schetliasts. In the Posthomeric cluster, Ὄλεθρος (Destruction) is explicitly described as coming ever closer (ἐν ποσὶ κεῖμεθ' Ὀλέθρου, 'we lie at the feet of Destruction', 12.543; οὐδ' ἄρ' ἐφράσσατ' ἐπὶ προθύροισιν Ὄλεθρον, 'they did not consider that Destruction was on the doorstep', 13.20),[83] until it rampages within the walls of Troy itself (δηίοισιν ἀνηλέα τεῦχεν ὄλεθρον, '[Menelaus] dealt pitiless destruction upon his enemies', 13.374). Destruction is thus construed almost as a character in its own right,[84] standing just outside the city and then being conveyed inside only after it has 'perished' in the eyes of the Trojans (insofar as they believe, once the Greeks have 'departed', that the possibility of

---

[81] Our Iliadic σχέτλιος-sequence is not the only such in epic, though Quintus' sequences seem most closely modelled upon it; several more occur in *Il.*, *Od.* and *Arg.*, of which three exhibit the pattern I have identified (two speeches treating the same focal figure and basic concept, the second intensified, then a speech related to the death of the focal figure). These are *Od.* 9.345–52 (Odysseus→Polyphemos in cave), 473–9 (Odysseus→Polyphemos from ship) and 492–9 (companions→Odysseus, fearing Polyphemos will kill them); *Od.* 11.472–6 (Achilles' shade→Odysseus in underworld), 12.20–7 (Kirke→Odysseus and companions returned from underworld) and 115–41 (Kirke→Odysseus, warning him not to risk Kharybdis); and *Arg.* 4.354–90 (Medea→Jason, fearing he will surrender her to Apsyrtos), 4.445–9 (Narrator→Eros, decrying the god's destructiveness) and 4.738–48 (Kirke→Medea, condemning her deeds after Apsyrtos' death). Though the *Od.* sequences end with potential rather than actual death for Odysseus, and the focal figure in the *Arg.* sequence is neither target nor addressee but an absent party, the essential pattern holds.

[82] Homeric sequences of three elements building towards the focal figure's death occur elsewhere, e.g.: the suitors thrice throw missiles at Odysseus (*Od.* 17.462–66, 18.394–8, 20.299–302) and the third time Theoklymenos foretells their downfall (20.350–7), cf. Fenik (1974: 180–8); Kelly (2008: 188); Steiner (2010: 137); the suitors are thrice listed in a specific order (17.336–506, 21.141–268, 22.8–329), the third time while being massacred; see Reece (1995). See de Jong (2001: xix) for further bibliography on triadic structures and typical numbers in Homer.

[83] Vian (1969: 129, n1); Ferreccio (2018: 213); Scheijnen (2018: 275) also note a connection between these lines.

[84] Cf. Vian (1959a: 210; 1969: 129, n1); Vian and Battegay (1984) s.v. ὄλεθρος; Gärtner (2007: 213, n19); Ferreccio (2018: 213); *contra* Wenglinksy (2002: 78, n75).

Troy's fall has likewise vanished: ἦ ῥ' ἅλιον Δαναοὶ στρατὸν ἐνθάδε πουλὺν ἄγειραν, 'See, the Greeks mustered their huge army here in vain!', 13.15).[85]

The same patterns just demonstrated occur in Quintus' earlier, Achilles-focused sequence, displaying even tighter correspondences with Iliadic precedent. The parallelism between the Iliadic Hektor sequence and the Posthomeric Achilles sequence is closer with respect to the focal figures (Achilles forms a more obvious counterpart to Hektor than does semi-personified Destruction) and also to the relational dynamics of the speeches within their respective sequences. Where the speaker, addressee and perspective on the war's outcome all differed from the first to the second speeches in the Destruction of Troy sequence, in the Hektor- and Achilles-focused chains the participants and the points of view are more stable. In both these chains the addressee of the first and second speeches is the same (Hektor in the *Iliad*, Achilles in the *Posthomerica*) and the first two speakers occupy the same essential position in relation to this addressee (Priam and Hekabe as Hektor's parents, Thersites and Memnon as Achilles' adversaries). The speakers also express the same basic concept to the focal figure, with repetition producing an intensifying effect: Hektor's parents each implore him to avoid single combat with Achilles, Hekabe with an especially emotive plea;[86] Achilles' verbal attackers each denigrate his prowess in relation to their own standards, Thersites as Achilles' inferior but Memnon as his potential equal.[87] The correspondence between the third speeches in these sequences is also tighter, as in both cases one of the slain focal figure's major divine advocates (Apollo for Hektor, Hera for Achilles) accuses the hero's major divine opponent(s) (Athene, Hera and Poseidon against Hektor; Apollo against Achilles) of misconduct in effecting his current state (bodily state post mortem or actual demise).[88] Finally, and most intriguingly, Hera's accusation of Apollo in Quintus' sequence continues and expands upon her response to Apollo's σχέτλιος-speech at the end of the Iliadic sequence.[89] Homer's Hera reminds Apollo of his participation at the wedding of Peleus and Thetis (*Il.* 24.55–63), drawing the moral that he ought to show favour to Achilles as their offspring (59–63). Quintus reverses Hera's and Apollo's roles, so that Hera is the one who calls Apollo σχέτλιος, but her argumentation is the same as in the *Iliad*: by playing the lyre and taking part in the libation at the wedding, Apollo incurred an obligation to Thetis' progeny

---

[85] The Greeks and Trojans become thematically assimilated to one another during the Sack (Avlamis 2019: 171–4), adding another connection between *PH* 13.16 and 13.380.

[86] Hekabe entreats Hektor for compassion, baring her breast (*Il.* 22.80); Martin (2015) finds that breast-baring supplications in Homer and Attic tragedy consistently fail.

[87] Memnon potentially equal to Achilles: Vian (1963: 49); Boyten (2010: 115–19); Scheijnen (2018: 88–90).

[88] On Hera→Apollo: Wenglinsky (2002: 231–40); Ferreccio (2018: 32) with respect to σχ.

[89] See Wenglinksy (2002: 237–8) on correspondences between these speeches; she notes σχ. in both. Hadjicosti (2006) discusses both scenes but omits this link.

(*PH* 3.99–109). Whereas Apollo wins his suit in the gods' assembly at the end of the *Iliad*, now that he has killed Achilles in the *Posthomerica*, Hera retaliates by accusing Apollo before the other gods and emerges victorious: Apollo silently acknowledges her castigating σχέτλιος-speech and cedes place (3.129–33). Quintus' Achilles sequence is thus capped by an *oppositio in imitando* of the concluding episode in the *Iliad*'s Hektor sequence.[90]

Here we return to the authority claims that Posthomeric speakers make over their targets. Though the Iliadic Hektor sequence and the Posthomeric Achilles sequence show strong structural correlation with one another, they differ widely in their speakers' intentions towards the focal figures. The speakers in the Iliadic cluster seek to preserve both Hektor's person and his social ties, displaying the general cooperative orientation of Iliadic σχέτλιος-speakers. Priam, Hekabe and Apollo all urge their addressees not to neglect their social obligations (Hektor's to his parents and city, the pro-Greek divine faction's to Hektor as a pious worshipper), but they do not pose as if they were offering instruction in the very nature of parent–child or divine–mortal ties. Rather, they argue from a basis of values that are presumed to be shared by the addressee. Quintus' speakers, by contrast, do affect to educate their targets in the elementary aspects of their social relationships: Thersites offers sententious guidance on the dangers of sexual infatuation and the duty of a warrior to avoid such motivations and devote himself instead to martial pursuits (*PH* 1.736–40),[91] Memnon informs Achilles that his descent from Thetis is nothing to boast about (2.426–9) and Hera undertakes to instruct Apollo in the ethical parameters by which he ought to have judged Achilles to be his friend and the Trojans his foes (3.96–127). These speakers adopt a patronising tone, true to Posthomeric form, communicating that their targets are not competent to discern and act within their proper social roles.

CONCLUSION

As discussed in the introduction to this chapter, the poets of archaic epic used the epithet σχέτλιος to signify resistance against forms of order specific to the conceptual programmes of their particular poems. Though I have shown that Quintus' σχέτλιος usage most closely resembles that in the *Iliad*, the changes to schetliasts' behaviour demanded by Posthomeric σχέτλιος-speakers are unique

---

[90] Bär (2016) discusses Quintus' practice of making 'singularit[ies]' from 'conventional motif[s]' involving gods in Homer (229). Hera's σχέτλιος-speech accords with this, as the only one in *PH* with a divine speaker, addressee or target: gods frequently participate in σχέτλιος-speeches in archaic epic (speakers 11/40x, addressees 6/40x, targets 11/40x).

[91] Scheijnen (2018: 76): 'This entire speech could be read as a maxim about proper behaviour in a heroic society, and a warning about possible reprimand.'

within extant epic, and indeed within ancient Greek poetry generally. Only Quintus shifts rhetorical focus from schetliasts' actions to their self-perceptions and from cooperative aims to competitive, hierarchical ones. While it is possible that Quintus interpreted the *Iliad*'s σχέτλιος-speeches in a cognitive and competitive light and sought merely to imitate this, I consider it more probable, given the evidence presented in this chapter, that he preferred to craft a different significance for σχέτλιος specific to the *Posthomerica*. Yet this raises the question of why Posthomeric σχέτλιος-speakers emphasise (allegedly) correct social roles as the pertinent form of order. Previous scholarship on the mortal and immortal spheres, heroism and excellence, and characterisation in the poem contributes to understanding the main thematic concerns in the *Posthomerica*,[92] yet the apparent importance of adhering to social roles merits further investigation. It seems especially suggestive that σχέτλιος is never straightforwardly uttered by the Posthomeric narrator, who occasionally explicitly opposes σχέτλιος-speakers' views.[93] Further work on Posthomeric conversation and its narratorial framing could illuminate the place of social roles in the poem's thematic system.

My analysis of Posthomeric σχέτλιος also indicates the fruitfulness of a specifically lexical approach to narratology. Anastasia Maravela has recently applied diachronic narratology to the epithet νήπιος ('naïve'),[94] finding that it forms significant clusters not unlike those I have described for σχέτλιος. Our work is in fact intimately aligned, as these terms do not merely form their own clusters, but repeatedly create combined clusters.[95] This intriguing phenomenon deserves attention for its own sake, but also for its broader implications. The event syntax exhibited in σχέτλιος-sequences and the meta-clustering of σχέτλιος and νήπιος suggest that other prominent words and formular idioms may display similar patterns, both in the *Posthomerica* and in epic generally. Were these to be uncovered, we would gain greater diachronic insight into epic narrative structuring on the scene level, which would in turn contribute another perspective to the increasing body of evidence on Quintus' innovation with respect to his predecessors.

---

[92] Among which are Wenglinsky (2002); Boyten (2010); Maciver (2012a); Bär (2016); Scheijnen (2018).

[93] E.g., *PH* 12.562–4, 13.19–20.

[94] Maravela (2019).

[95] Penthesileia cluster: *PH* 1.96, 134, 374 (νήπιος), 452, 733 (σχέτλιος); Hera→Apollo: 3.114 (σχέτλιος), 125 (νήπιος); Oinone and Paris: 10.318 (σχέτλιος), 329, 474 (νήπιος); misguided Trojans: 13.16 (σχέτλιος), 20 (νήπιος).

CHAPTER 12

Renewing Homer with Homer: The Use of Epithets in Quintus of Smyrna's *Posthomerica*

Alessia Ferreccio

Focusing attention on the epithets used in the *Posthomerica*, especially for gods and heroes, is a good method for accessing the poetic universe of Quintus, his style and his relationship with tradition; it also confirms the results obtained by more recent studies that have swept away the unflattering assessments of Q.S.'s epic and have restored it to its full literary dignity.

Incomprehension can arise when an unwatchful reader mistakes its strong and pervasive adherence to the Homeric model for monotony and lack of inventiveness. Therefore, the aim of this paper is to investigate Q.S.'s relationship with Homer precisely in terms of the feature that appears to be the most Homeric of all, namely lexis, focusing particularly on the epithets reserved for gods and heroes. While at first sight the lexis may appear to be an example of imitation in the pejorative sense of the term, what we in fact find is evidence of interesting originality and active imitation that competes with its model in a kind of long-distance ἀγών.

We can thus imagine the poet as a skilful weaver who uses Homeric threads, or epithets, for the weft of his poem, which he weaves in a non-Homeric manner, deploying *iuncturae* that have no equivalent in Homer, while for the warp he interlaces the non-Homeric threads in a Homeric manner, creating an iridescent fabric that proves to be both old and new at the same time.

HOMERIC EPITHETS

The basic assumption from which to start is that Q.S. is faithful to Homer, so much so that the lexis of the *Posthomerica* can rightly be termed 'hyper-Homeric':[1]

---

[1] In the words of Costantino Lascaris, Q.S. is ὁμηρικώτατος and μέγιστος ζηλωτὴς τοῦ Ὁμήρου; cf. Köchly (1850: CXI–CXII).

80 per cent of the vocabulary used by Q.S. is taken from Homer, including both some *hapax* as well as epithets and *iuncturae* that are almost completely missing from the rest of epic and literary production.[2]

Within this adherence to the model, Q.S.'s Homeric lexis is often used in a way we could call 'non-Homeric', producing in the attentive reader an effect of departure from the norm and novelty. This result is achieved both by creating unusual and unexpected combinations and by the semantic extension of some terms.

Renewing *Iuncturae*

A characteristic feature of Q.S.'s poetics lies in the way he assembles elements of Homer's mode of expression in an innovative fashion, using a technique that enables him to differentiate himself from Homer precisely at the moments when he refers to him and quotes him: a prime example is the *iunctura* φόνον στονόεντα (Q.S. 1.208, a total of 13 times), which sounds Homeric – because the terms are Homeric – but which does not exist in that collocation in Homer's epics.

Regarding only the collocations of epithet + theonym, there are 226 original combinations.[3] Let us look at some examples in which the constituent elements are all Homeric but are combined in a way that is not to be found in Homer:

Il. 5.672 *et al.*, ἐρίγδουπος Ζεύς	Q.S. 2.177, ἐρίγδουπος Κρονίδης
	Q.S. 1.578, ἐρίγδουπος Κρονίων
	Q.S. 1.694, ἐρίγδουπος πατήρ
Il. 10.553, κούρη αἰγιόχοιο Διός	Q.S. 14.421, κούρη ἐριγδούποιο Διός
	Q.S. 12.386, κούρη μεγάλοιο Διός
Il. 1.206 *et al.*, θεὰ γλαυκῶπις Ἀθήνη	Q.S. 12.447, θεὰ μεγάθυμος Ἀθήνη
	Q.S. 12.154, θεὰ πολύμητις Ἀθήνη

The syntagma πολύμητις Ἀθήνη (Q.S. 12.154) sounds truly surprising, because the adjective πολύμητις, 'very cunning', is applied to Athena, whereas in Homer's epics it is typically associated with Odysseus, almost as if Q.S. were

---

[2] Out of a total number of adjectives used by Q.S., 720 are Homeric and 220 non-Homeric; see Vian (1959a: 146–62, 182–92; 1963: XL–LII). With regard to the epithets used to qualify the gods, 190 out of 232 are Homeric; cf. Ferreccio (2018: XXVII). On *hapax legomena* in the *Posthomerica*, cf. Appel (1994a).

[3] Cf. Ferreccio (2018: XXXV).

extending the prime characteristic of the pupil, shrewdness, also to the god that protects him.[4]

Q.S. 2.138–9, περίφρων Ἀμφιγυήεις / Ἥφαιστος κλυτὸν ἔργον

is modelled on

Il. 1.607–8, περικλυτός Ἀμφιγυήεις / Ἥφαιστος

Q.S. replaces the Homeric περικλυτός, 'illustrious', with περίφρων, a term that is isometric and phonically similar, and at the same time he also evokes it in the next line in the expression κλυτὸν ἔργον. The new epithet applied to Hephaestus, περίφρων, 'very wise', is surprising, because in the Homeric poems it is an appellative used only for female figures: Aegialeia (Il. 5.412), Arete (Od. 11.345), Eurycleia (Od. 19.357, 491; 20.134; 21.381) and especially Penelope (Od. 1.329 et al.: a total of 55 occurrences).

Another example of a small 'aprosdokēton effect' is the hexametric close κλυτὰ μητιόωσα (Q.S. 2.437, a unicum in the preserved literature), which calls to mind κακὰ μητιόωσα (Il. 15.27), turning a negative value into a positive: the two iuncturae are isometric, come at the close of the hexameter and are almost homophonous, but have two opposite meanings: in the Iliad Hera is accused by Zeus of scheming against Heracles, while in the Posthomerica Thetis is praised for her noble thoughts.

A similar game of mirrors is set up between the line endings:

Il. 22.15, θεῶν ὀλοώτατε πάντων   Q.S. 2.87, πάντων ὀλοώτατε φωτῶν

In the passage from the Iliad Achilles accuses Apollo – guilty of having duped the hero by taking on the appearance of the Trojan Agenor – of being 'the most ruinous of all the gods'; shortly before the god mocks him because the Pelides does not understand who he has before him and tries in vain to kill an immortal. Q.S. cites the vocative ὀλοώτατε in the same position in the line – the sole example in the entire epic production – likewise as the incipit to a speech reacting to a provocation, this time uttered by Polydamas, who, accused of cowardice by Paris, rebukes the Trojan prince for being 'the most ruinous among all men'. Thus Q.S., through the shrewd use of quotation,

---

[4] In Homer's epic poems there are 87 occurrences of πολύμητις, 86 of which are loci in which it is an epithet of Odysseus (18 in the Iliad: 1.311, 440; 3.200, 216, 268; 4.329, 349; 10.148, 382, 400, 423, 488, 554; 14.82; 19.154, 215; 23.709, 755 and 68 in the Odyssey: 2.173 et al.) and one passage in which it is the appellative of Hephaestus (Il. 21.355). It is a hapax in the Posthomerica.

suggests a subtle and allusive parallel between Apollo and Paris, the objects of the reproach, both archers – one divine, the other human – and both defenders of the Trojans.

Renewing the *iuncturae* also means applying Homeric epithets to other divinities and other heroes than those in the Homeric epics. The most significant cases in point are βοῶπις, 'that has large eyes', an epithet specific to Hera in Homer and Eos in the *Posthomerica* (2.643), and γαιήοχος, 'that holds the earth', an appellative exclusive to Poseidon in the Homeric epics and referring to Oceanus in Q.S. 2.208.[5] It so happens that the exchange of epithets is not only an index of stylistic *variatio* but also conceals possible intertextual allusions, as in the dialogue at a distance between *Il.* 24.32–54 and Q.S. 3.98–127. In the passage in Homer, Apollo condemns the gods, including Hera, who takes the floor immediately afterwards, at line 55, for being σχέτλιοι, 'cruel', because they have allowed the dead body of Hector to be profaned by Achilles without intervening. In the *Posthomerica*, Hera in a long reprimand harshly accuses Apollo of being σχέτλιος, because he was responsible for killing Achilles, son of Thetis, at whose marriage to Peleus the god had played the lyre, happy as he was at the union. Q.S. thus recalls the Iliadic situation by means of the reference to σχέτλιος, but turns it on its head: Apollo passes from accuser to accused; Hera moves from the role of the one who must defend herself to the one who attacks; the dead body in question is not Hector, but his killer and archenemy, Achilles[6].

Also regarding the titles given to the heroes, Q.S. plays with epithets, often casting aside Homeric combinations in favour of others hitherto unexplored:

- Nestor: never the patronymic Νηληιάδης (13 times in Homer) or the periphrase Γερήνιος ἱππότα (36 times in the Homeric poems), but Νηλέος υἱός (2.243), not found in Homer;
- Thrasymedes: none of the epithets he has in the Homeric epics, but ἀγακλεής, 'very famous' (2.268), εὐμμελίης, 'armed with a strong pole' (2.342) and ἰσόθεος, 'equal to the gods' (6.540; 12.319);
- Antilochus: not διοτρεφής, 'divine' (*Il.* 17.685; 23.581), but the near-synonym θεοειδής (2.244), never applied to him in the Homeric epics; not πεπνυμένος, 'wise' (*Il.* 23.570, 586), but the synonym εὔφρων (3.517);
- Achilles: not δῖος, 'divine' (δῖος Ἀχιλλεύς counts 57 occurrences in the *Iliad*), replaced by the synonyms ἀντίθεος (4.385), θεοειδής (11.234) and ἰσόθεος (14.180);
- Hector: never κορυθαίολος, 'shaking the crest' (38 times in the *Iliad*).

---

[5] Cf. Ferreccio (2018: 136–7, 210–11).

[6] On σχέτλιος cf. in this volume Jordan Maly-Preuss, Chapter 11, pp. 194–213.

Another strategy deployed by Q.S. to renew the apparatus of epithets within the tradition is to apply to the Achaeans epithets that in the Homeric epics are predominantly applied to the Trojans, and vice versa:

- ἀντιθέα: 'god-like': in the Homeric epics this epithet (in its feminine form) is only used for Penelope (*Od.* 11.117; 13.378), while in the *Posthomerica* it designates Trojan heroines: Hecuba (13.503), and women who sided with the Trojans: the Amazon Clonia (1.235), and Helen (2.97; 6.152; 13.525). The fact that an epithet exclusive to Penelope, a model of the faithful woman, is used to refer to Helen, the paradigm of marital infidelity, sounds antiphrastic;
- εὐμμελίης: 'armed with a strong pole': this epithet is used exclusively for Trojans in the *Iliad* (*Il.* 4.47 *et al.*), while in the *Posthomerica* it comes to indicate primarily Greek warriors (Q.S. 2.342 *et al.*);
- θρασύς: 'bold': in the *Iliad* this is always an attribute of Trojans and in particular of Hector (*Il.* 12.60 *et al.*); in Q.S. it qualifies his greatest adversary and killer, Achilles (Q.S. 2.430 *et al.*);
- παιδοφόνος: 'one who kills children': Priam contemptuously calls Achilles, who was guilty of the murder of his son Hector, παιδοφόνος (*Il.* 24.506, *hapax Homericum*), whereas Q.S. transforms it into the allotrope παιδοφονεύς (Q.S. 2.322, *hapax* in the *Posthomerica*)[7] with which Nestor apostrophises Memnon, killer of his son Antilochus;
- ὑπείροχος: 'eminent': the epithet used of Achilles in *Il.* 11.784 characterises his victims Penthesileia and Memnon in Q.S. 1.250 and 2.298;
- χολωθείς: 'angered': in *Il.* 16.320 the Trojan Maris, angered by the death of his brother Atymnius (κασιγνήτοιο χολωθείς), speared to death by Antilochus, attacks Antilochus, but is killed by Thrasymedes, Antilochus' brother; in Q.S. 2.294 Thrasymedes, enraged by the death of his brother Antilochus (ἀδελφειοῖο χολωθείς), kills the Trojan Laomedon. The weave of intertextual references is particularly dense at this point: the same pair of brothers, Thrasymedes and Antilochus, are the protagonists of the two passages, but while in the *Iliad* they are victorious and slaughter their enemies, in the *Posthomerica* they find themselves in extreme difficulty, to the point that Antilochus ends up being killed. Reinforcing the connection is the position in both passages in the close of the *iunctura* κασιγνήτοιο χολωθείς, which however Q.S. changes into ἀδελφειοῖο χολωθείς.

The mode of 'passing into the enemy camp' also involves the proper name Μέγης. In the *Iliad* he is a Greek hero who carries out acts of war together with

---

[7] On παιδοφονεύς, cf. Ferreccio (2011).

Nestor, Thrasymedes and Antilochus (*Il.* 10.102–76; 16.313–25; 19.238–9), while in the *Posthomerica* it is also the name of a Trojan, father to the warrior Polymnius, killed during Thrasymedes' attempt to protect Nestor from Memnon's attacks (2.292).

Renewing Epithets

As mentioned above, the *imitatio cum variatione* of Homer can also involve the lexical sphere. In this vein Q.S. uses a Homeric term with a semantic nuance different from the model. Let us take a look at some examples.[8]

In the *Odyssey* – there are in fact no occurrences in the *Iliad* – θεουδής has the meaning of 'pious', 'godfearing' and is often inserted into the formulaic expression ἦε φιλόξεινοι καί σφιν νόος ἐστὶ θεουδής, uttered by Odysseus (*Od.* 6.121; 9.176; 13.202), or in one case by Alcinous (*Od.* 8.576), to signal an encounter with an unknown people whose customs are unfamiliar and whose respect or lack of respect for the gods one wishes to determine. θεουδής is furthermore the irreproachable king who, devoted to the gods, is faithful to justice (*Od.* 19.109–11, ὥς τέ τευ ἦ βασιλῆος ἀμύμονος, ὅς τε θεουδής / [ἀνδράσιν ἐν πολλοῖσι καὶ ἰφθίμοισιν ἀνάσσων] / εὐδικίας ἀνέχῃσι, 'as [the fame] of a perfect king, who godfearing / is lord over many fierce men and holds up justice') and, in the words of Eurycleia, the soul of Odysseus, hated and persecuted by Zeus despite having a pious heart devoted to the gods (*Od.* 19.363–4, ἦ σε περὶ Ζεὺς / ἀνθρώπων ἤχθηρε θεουδέα θυμὸν ἔχοντα, 'Surely Zeus / hated you among men, though you had a godfearing heart'). Apollonius Rhodius uses the adjective in its Homeric meaning, as is clearly evident in 2.1179–80, Ζεὺς ἐτεὸν τὰ ἕκαστ' ἐπιδέρκεται, οὐδέ μιν ἄνδρες / λήθομεν ἔμπεδον οἵ τε θεουδέες †οὐδὲ† δίκαιοι, 'Zeus truly sees everything and we humans who fear the gods and the just cannot escape him.'[9] In the *Posthomerica*, θεουδής is used both with a different meaning – not 'godfearing' but more generally 'divine' – and to indicate phenomena or things, and no longer persons as in the *Odyssey* or in the *Argonautica*: the divine rain, longed for by the peasants who rejoice at the sight of a rainbow appearing over the sea, in the same way as the Trojans express their delight at the arrival of Penthesileia (1.63–5, ὡς δ' ὁπότ' ἀθρήσαντες ἀπ' οὔρεος ἀγροιῶται / Ἶριν ἀνεγρομένην ἐξ εὐρυπόροιο θαλάσσης, / ὄμβρου ὅτ' ἰσχανόωσι θεουδέος, 'as when the rustics, observing from a mountain / Iris the rainbow rising up from the immense sea, when they yearn for the divine rain'); the island in the Euxine Sea, where Achilles will live on after death and will receive divine honours (3.775–6, καί οἱ δῶρον ἔγωγε θεουδέα νῆσον ὀπάσσω / Εὔξεινον κατὰ πόντον, ὅπη θεὸς ἔσσεται αἰεί, 'and I will give as gift to

---

[8] On the extension of the meaning of a term in the *Posthomerica*, see Ferreccio (2014: XXIII; 2018: XXXI).

[9] Cf. also A.R. 2.849 and 4.1123, referring to the hero Idmon and to Alcinous, respectively.

him a divine island / within the Euxine Sea, where he will be a god forever')
and the armour of Achilles, divine in that it has been forged by a god, Hephaestus (5.587, θεουδέα τεύχε').

It is possible that Q.S. interpreted the passage from *Od.* 19.109–11 taking
θεουδής to mean 'godlike', 'divine',[10] and that he therefore adopted it with this
broader and more generalised meaning.[11] However, it may also reflect a debate
about the meaning of the adjective, traces of which can be found in the scholia
and in ancient lexica. According to the sch. *Od.* 6.121a–d Pontani, θεουδής can
mean both θεοῖς ὅμοιος, 'divine', 'godlike', and ὁ θεοῖς ἀρέσκων, 'agreeable to
the gods', and δεισιδαίμων, 'afraid of the gods', 'religious'. The fact that ancient
commentators raised questions about the meaning of θεουδής in the *Odyssey*
suggests that several interpretations may have been held possible and that Q.S.,
as an expert on Homer and a refined *poeta doctus*, consciously chose to use the
epithet in the acceptation he considered to be correct.[12]

A similar procedure to that carried out on θεουδής – broadening of meaning
and elevation of referent – involves the term εὔφρων, which in the Homeric
epics is an epithet for wine (*Il.* 3.246, οἶνον ἐύφρονα), a participant at a symposium (*Il.* 15.99, τις ἔτι νῦν δαίνυται εὔφρων) and of θυμός (*Od.* 17.531, θυμὸς
εὔφρων), and has the meaning of 'cheerful', 'joyful' (*Il.* 15.99; *Od.* 17.531) or 'giving comfort' (*Il.* 3.246). In the *Posthomerica*, εὔφρων is never used in its Homeric
acceptations, but rather with the meaning of (1) 'favourable', 'generous', referring to heroes who die to save their companions (Achilles 3.549 and 787) or
their father (Antilochus in 3.517) or, in most occurrences, of (2) 'wise', 'able',
'expert': the Trojans (5.157), Testor (6.68), Polydamas (6.505), Deidamia (7.184),
Odysseus (8.113), Lernus (10.221), Anchises (13.315), Neoptolemus (14.191),
the gods Athena (10.353 and 13. 420), Hephaestus (2.440 and 3.738) and Thetis
(4.128 and 9.29). The meaning of 'able' is particularly appropriate in the passages
where εὔφρων is the epithet of Hephaestus, the blacksmith who made Achilles'
armour and the amphora in which the bones of the deceased hero were placed.
The 'Homeric' choice of using a word to be found in Homer, therefore, conceals within it a 'non-Homeric' intent, because it is used in acceptations that can
be found in post-Homeric works, for example, in Apollonius Rhodius, where
εὔφρων is the epithet used for the goddess Concord (2.718) and the Hesperides

---

[10] Cf. Bär (2009: 257–8).

[11] One can note a process of generalisation of meaning also in the case of the verb ὀαρίζω, which
in Homer specifically expresses the idea of married couples or lovers spending time together
intimately or conversing confidentially (cf. the conversation between Hector and Andromache in *Il.* 6.516; the amorous encounter between two lovers in *Il.* 22.127–8), while in the
Posthomerica, over and above the Homeric meaning (cf. Paris confabulating with the nymphs
in 10.366; Helen and Menelaus in the tent in 14.150), it has the more generic sense of 'conversing': cf. 2.113; 6.150; 10.343, 361; 14.253.

[12] For other lexical and mythological choices that presumably reflect erudite discussions, cf.
Ferreccio (2018: XLII–XLIV).

(4.1411) and means 'benevolent', and in the tragedians, where it means 'wise' (cf. Aesch. *Ch.* 88 and *Supp.* 378).[13]

The broadening of the semantic field of εὔφρων involves – again in the same direction of 'cheerful' > 'wise' – also its nominal derivative, εὐφροσύνη, which, if in Q.S. 2.112; 5.69 and 14.124 it means 'cheerfulness', 'joy' as in the Homeric *loci* (*Od.* 6.156; 9.6; 10.465; 20.8; 23.52),[14] in other passages in the *Posthomerica* it is used to indicate one of the qualities that makes Thetis stand out among the Nereids, 'wisdom' (4.129–30, ὡς πάσῃσι μετέπρεπεν εἰναλίῃσιν / εἵνεκ' ἐυφροσύνης καὶ εἴδεος, 'how she surpassed all the sea goddesses / with her wisdom and beauty'), and the 'wisdom' which, if mixed with the words of men, gives them great strength, unlike the vigour without πινυτὴ μῆτις, the 'wise prudence' that leads nowhere (5.262–5, μέγα γὰρ κράτος ἀνδράσι μῦθος / γίνετ' ἐυφροσύνῃ μεμελημένος· ἠνορέη δὲ / ἄπρηκτος τελέθει μέγεθός τ' εἰς οὐδὲν ἀέξει / ἀνέρος, εἰ μή οἱ πινυτὴ ἐπὶ μῆτις ἕπηται, 'Speech becomes mighty power for men / when it is mixed with wisdom; vigour / is impotent instead, and the big size of a man comes to nothing, / if wise prudence doesn't help').[15]

ἄτλητος and πολύτλητος, epithets that in fact share the same etymological root, move along a similar path, from a passive meaning in Homer to a sense that is (also) active in the *Posthomerica*. In the Homeric epics ἄτλητος refers to pain that cannot be borne, thus 'unbearable', 'intolerable' (*Il.* 9.3, πένθος; 19.367, ἄχος);[16] in the *Posthomerica* it retains the Homeric meaning in 1.453 and 9.457, but in 6.14 it is used to characterise Thanatos as the divinity 'that cannot bear', and is hence 'implacable'.

Similarly, the *hapax homericum* πολύτλητος connotes the γέροντες, elderly people 'that have suffered much' (*Od.* 11.38), and has a passive value that the term retains in Q.S. 1.135, 182; 5.45, 361; 8.411; 10.369; 13.544; 14.267, 557; in other *loci*, however, it is converted into the active acceptation, 'that causes suffering', and thus 'grievous', 'painful', and refers to old age (Q.S. 2.341 and 13.319, γήραϊ . . . πολυτλήτῳ), labour pains (Q.S. 11.25, ὠδίνεσσι πολυτλήτοισιν) and life (Q.S. 13.477, πολυτλήτου βιότοιο). Particularly worthy of note is the association of πολύτλητος with old age, γήρας, because it is at one and the same time an evident allusion to the passage cited above in the *Odyssey*, the only occurrence of the adjective in Homer, and a differentiation from it, since the meaning of the adjective changes.

The *hapax homericum* ἀνούτατος describes the warrior who roams around the battlefield as yet uninjured, 'unwounded', 'unharmed' (*Il.* 4.540), a value

[13] On the meanings of εὔφρων, cf. Fraenkel (1950: 365–7).

[14] εὐφροσύνη means 'joy' also in A.R. 2.1149; 4.69, 1037, 1167.

[15] In Q.S. 4.275 the most appropriate meaning of εὐφροσύνη as a characteristic of Achilles' female slaves is restraint, reserve (cf. Vian 1963 *ad loc.*, 'retenue'), which can be understood as a variant of wisdom and prudence in women who have been made slaves.

[16] Cf. also A.R. 2.858; 3.578 *et al.*

that the term has in the sole occurrence in Apollonius Rhodius (2.75) and in two *loci* in the *Posthomerica*: 2.530 and 13.143. There is a different context for 3.175, where the Trojans think that Achilles is ἀνούτατος, because, although he has been mortally injured, he continues to hit out at the Trojans (3.149–63); also when Achilles collapses and holds himself up with his lance, his enemies take flight, terrorised by his rage (3.169–75). In my view, seeing the Trojans as fearing Achilles because they believed he had not been hit is an unsatisfactory reading, since in the previous lines it is repeated several times that the Pelides had been injured: Apollo shoots an arrow and hits the hero in the heel (3.61–2), he falls heavily to the ground and complains that he has been the target of the arrow (3.62–82), he extracts it from the wound and throws it far away (3.83–5). The Trojans do not come close to him even though he is βλήμενος, hit (3.140–1), just as peasants do not approach the lion wounded by the hunter, who though pierced does not back away, εὖτε λέοντος / ἀγρόται ἐν ξυλόχοισι τεθηπότες, ὅν τε βάλησι / θηρητήρ, ὃ δ' ἄρ' οὔ τι πεπαρμένος ἦτορ ἄκοντι / λήθεται ἠνορέης, 'as in the forest the rustics are frightened by a lion, whom a hunter wounded, and though the javelin stands in his heart, the lion doesn't forget his courage' (3.142–5). Apollo's arrow does not lay him low, and in fact the injury arouses his wrath and fervour: ὣς ἄρα Πηλείδαο χόλος καὶ λοίγιον ἕλκος / θυμὸν ἄδην ὀρόθυνε. θεοῦ δέ μιν ἰὸς ἐδάμνα, 'so wrath and his deadly wound incited / Peleides' soul entirely. But the god's dart tamed him' (3.147–8). Bearing in mind the repetition and the underlining of the motive for injuring Achilles as an exceptional event, it would seem more appropriate to understand that the Trojans, when they observe the strength and rage that still grip the hero, think that he is 'inviolable', and thus 'invulnerable' to any aggression;[17] this meaning of ἀνούτατος expands the Homeric value of the term and would later be picked up again by Nonnus.[18]

In the epic lexicon, μητιόων retains its verbal sense ('excogitating') and is constructed using the object that is being excogitated; and this is how it is used in various passages in the *Posthomerica*.[19] But the occurrences of μητιόων in Book 5

---

[17] Cf. Trypanis (1970: 51); Appel (1994a: 17); *contra* Way (1913) and Vian (1963), who translate ἀνούτατος as 'woundless' and 'unharmed', respectively.

[18] Cf. e.g. *D.* 10.17; 16.157, 382; 25.352; 26.82; 30.292; 39.92; 40.49; 47.670.

[19] Cf. *Il.* 15.27, πέμψας ἐπ' ἀτρύγετον πόντον κακὰ μητιόωσα; 18.312, Ἕκτορι μὲν γὰρ ἐπήνησαν κακὰ μητιόωντι; 20.153, ὥς οἳ μέν ῥ' ἑκάτερθε καθήατο μητιόωντες; *Od.* 1.234, νῦν δ' ἑτέρως ἐβόλοντο θεοὶ κακὰ μητιόωντες; 6.14, νόστον Ὀδυσσῆϊ μεγαλήτορι μητιόωσα; 8.9, νόστον Ὀδυσσῆϊ μεγαλήτορι μητιόωσα; otherwise in *Il.* 7.45, ἤ ῥα θεοῖσιν ἐφήνδανε μητιόωσι it has a verbal sense, but is constructed without the object; A.R. 3.24, τοῖον μητιόωσα παροιτέρη ἔκφατο μῦθον; 210, τοῖσι δὲ νισσομένοις Ἥρη φίλα μητιόωσα; Q.S. 2.437, πασάων δὲ μάλιστα Θέτιν κλυτὰ μητιόωσαν; 3.94, οἳ δ' ἄρα καὶ Δαναοῖς, δι<ὰ δ'> ἄνδιχα μητιόωντες; 655, ὣς φάτο Καλλιόπη πινυτὰ φρεσὶ μητιόωσα; 8.12, πολλὸν καγχαλάασκον ἐτώσια μητιόωντι; 9.11, τρέψον ἀφ' ἡμετέρης ὀλοὰ φρεσὶ μητιόωντα; 13.411, ἄλγε' ἀνέτλημεν Πριάμῳ κακὰ μητιόωντες; 14.423, δὴ τότε μητιόωσα βαρὺν καὶ ἀνηλέα πότμον.

reveal a different use of the term, deployed as an epithet of Agamemnon (5.135), Prometheus (5.338) and Odysseus (5.429, 571). The context in which μητιόων is an attribute of Agamemnon argues rather for the acceptation of 'wise': the Atreides is called upon, together with Idomeneus and Nestor, to judge who among the Greek heroes is worthy of receiving the armour of Achilles (5.134–5, ἦτεε δ' Ἰδομενῆα κλυτὸν καὶ Νηλέος υἷα / ἠδ' ἄρα μητιόωντ' Ἀγαμέμνονα, 'He asked glorious Idomeneus and Neleus' son / and wise Agamemnon'). When it is the appellative of Odysseus, the adjective would appear better rendered as 'perspicacious', 'astute', in line with the Homeric characterisation of the hero. Following his approach of innovation within the tradition, Q.S. uses, very close together, μητιόων, 'astute', in its 'new' guise as adjective and the verb from which it derives, μητιόω, 'excogitate', which recalls the Homeric use of μητιόων. Menelaus must not become angry with the shrewd Odysseus, but rather with the gods, who are plotting the downfall of the Achaeans (5.428–9a, μὴ νῦν, ὦ Μενέλαε, μέγ' ἀχνύμενος περὶ θυμῷ / σκύζεο <u>μητιόωντι</u> Κεφαλλήνων βασιλῆι, / ἀλλὰ θεοῖς οἳ νῶιν ὀλέθρια <u>μητιόωνται</u>, 'Now, Menelaus, albeit grieved at heart, / don't become angry with the shrewd king of Cephallenians, / but with the gods who plot our ruin'). More ambiguous is the shade of meaning of μητιόων – whether 'wise' or 'astute' – in reference to Prometheus, who in the myth stands out for the astuteness he puts in play when stealing fire from the gods and in the deception he uses in dividing up meat for the sacrifices, also orchestrated at the expense of the Olympians, and for the knowledge, in the meaning both of knowledge of the future and as accumulated knowledge to be passed on to humans who need to be taught all the *technai*.[20] In the passage in the *Posthomerica*, Prometheus is mentioned as the figure ultimately answerable for Thetis' suffering due to the death of Achilles, because he was responsible for revealing to Zeus the prophecy about the son of the goddess, who would be greater than the father. Precisely because of this prediction, the gods forced the Nereid to marry a man, Peleus, whose offspring would by definition be mortal (5.338–40, αἳ δὲ μέγα σκύζοντο Προμηθέι μητιόωντι / μνώμεναι ὡς κείνοιο θεοπροπίῃσι Κρονίων / δῶκε Θέτιν Πηλῆι καὶ οὐκ ἐθέλουσαν ἄγεσθαι, '[The Sea nymphs] were very angry against the wise (*or* watchful) Prometheus, / remembering that Zeus, moved by his prophecy, married Thetis to Peleus, though she was not willing').[21] The mention of the prophecy would tend to support the meaning

[20] On the deception of the fire and the sacrifice to Zeus, cf. Hes. *Th.* 535–57, 565–7; *Op.* 49–52; Aesch. *Pr.* 109–11, 252–3; Apollod. 1.7.1; on the prophecy of Prometheus to Io: Aesch. *Pr.* 700–41; 786–818; 823–76 and to Zeus: Aesch. *Pr.* 168–76; 755–70; 908–27; 947–51; Q.S. 5.338–40; Apollod. 3.13.5; on the teaching of *technai* to men, Aesch. *Pr.* 441–71; 476–506.

[21] The lines continue with Cymothoe, one of the Nereids, who rejoices at the fact that Prometheus has been chained to the rocks of the Caucasus and suffers the torment of the eagle that devours his liver because he has revealed the ancient oracle about Thetis' son ousting his father (5.341–5). This version of the myth appears to have no other attestations and is perhaps the fruit of the poet's inventiveness; cf. Vian (1966: 31–2, n5); James and Lee (2000: 109–10).

of 'wise', 'knowing', but the negative context of censure and condemnation in which Prometheus is mentioned, together with the epic apparatus of the epithets that mark him out and that allude to his machinations (e.g. Hes. *Th.* 546 and *Op.* 48, ἀγκυλομήτης, 'of crooked counsels'; *Th.* 511, ποικίλος αἰολομήτις, 'versatile and astute'; *Th.* 521, ποικιλόβουλος, 'of varied counsels'; Opp. *H.* 5.6, πολυμῆτα, 'very cunning', 'very watchful'), suggests that the sense of 'watchful', 'astute' is equally valid.

Also the occurrences of μητιόων that are in line with Homeric use reveal the stylistic peculiarity of Q.S., namely his *innovatio in imitando*. μητιόωσα is used to refer to Athena both in the Homeric epics and in the *Posthomerica*, but whereas in the *Odyssey* Athena 'contrives the return' of Odysseus (*Od.* 6.13–14, θεὰ γλαυκῶπις Ἀθήνη, / <u>νόστον</u> Ὀδυσσῆϊ μεγαλήτορι <u>μητιόωσα</u>, 'the goddess, Athena with gleaming eyes, / contriving the return of greathearted Odysseus'; 9.7–9, Παλλὰς Ἀθήνη / . . . / <u>νόστον</u> Ὀδυσσῆϊ μεγαλήτορι <u>μητιόωσα</u>, 'Pallas Athena /. . . / contriving the return of greathearted Odysseus'), in Q.S. 14.419–42 the goddess, furious with the Greeks because of the rape of Cassandra by Ajax Oileus in her temple, ponders a grim and merciless destiny (14.423, <u>μητιόωσα</u> βαρὺν καὶ ἀνηλέα <u>πότμον</u>, 'pondering a stark and unmerciful destiny') and unleashes a terrible storm at sea in an attempt to prevent the heroes from returning to their homeland. This reversal comes as a surprise to the attentive reader, as the mention of Athena μητιόωσα immediately recalls the image of the goddess who was the principal architect of Odysseus' return to Ithaca.

Again regarding the use of a Homeric term also with a meaning not to be found in Homer, it is worth pointing out κρυερός, which in the Homeric epics refers to fear and lament (*Il.* 13.48, φόβος; *Il.* 24.524; *Od.* 4.103; 11.212, γόος) and always has the figurative/metaphorical value of 'chilling', 'dreadful', while in the *Posthomerica*, besides being used in the Homeric sense in connection with battle (1.487, χάρμη) and terror (5.366; 7.543, φόβος), it also qualifies water (3.527; 10.420), hail (7.134), the Boreas wind (1.625; 8.205) and winter (2.601; 9.72), and thus takes on the concrete meaning of 'icy'. Q.S.'s *usus* proves to be even more significant when one observes that Hesiod and Apollonius Rhodius also used κρυερός in the abstract Homeric acceptation, as an epithet for a curse, ἀρά (*Th.* 657), Hades (*Op.* 153) and commands from the king (A.R. 2.210; 3.390).

The opposite procedure – that is, Q.S.'s use of a term that has a concrete meaning in Homer and to which he gives an abstract value – is reflected in the occurrences of ζέω, which in Homer indicates the boiling of water in preparation for a bath (*Il.* 18.349; *Od.* 10.360) and the seething waters of the river Xanthus – likened to the simmering of a cauldron – generated by the prodigious red-hot wave of heat that is the work of Hephaestus (*Il.* 21.362–5), but which in the *Posthomerica* is used only once to describe Ocean's actual boiling caused by the wave of heat that Zeus, furious at the Titans (8.464), hurled at the earth and the sea, in a situation similar to the battle Hephaestus fought against Scamander in the *Iliad* (21.362–5). In its other occurrences ζέω takes on a figurative meaning and describes turbulent feelings in the soul, such as the fervour of war (2.256; 3.140, 163; 8.173–4) and anger (5.324, 379, 385; 6.461).

There are some examples where Q.S. explores the full semantic spectrum of a term, exploiting both its Homeric and its post-Homeric values: a case in point is πορφύρω, which describes (1) being unquiet, the agitation of the heart in the chest (13.24–5, ἀμφὶ δέ οἱ κῆρ / ἄσπετα πορφύρεσκε κατὰ φρένα, 'his heart / was agitated tremendously in his chest'; 14.41–2, ἐν δέ οἱ ἦτωρ / ἄσπετα πορφύρεσκε κατὰ φρένα, 'her heart / was agitated tremendously in her chest'), as in Homer (οἱ κραδίη πόρφυρε, 'his heart was unquiet': *Il.* 21.551; *Od.* 4.427, 572; 10.309); (2) 'meditating and pondering' (1.706; 2.85; 5.355; 6.33; 9.246), according to the *usus* of Apollonius Rhodius (1.461; 2.546; 3.23, 397, 456, 1161, 1406); (3) 'turning red' (14.47), referring to the cheeks of Helen, which blush from αἰδώς, and 'being red', in reference to blood (14.319).[22]

NON-HOMERIC EPITHETS

Thus far we have examined some examples of how Q.S. renewed the Homeric material through the use of unexpected formulas or semantic expansions; let us now turn to a review of the ways in which Q.S. introduces a non-Homeric epithet into a clearly Homeric fabric.[23]

The first strategy deployed by Q.S. entails the use of terms that are reminiscent of Homeric terms. Let us look at some examples.

The collocation ἐϋσθενέων Ἀργείων (1.716 *et al.*),[24] used as a replacement for Ἀχαιῶν χαλκοχιτώνων (*Il.* 1.371 *et al.*),[25] to which it is isometric, constitutes a perfect 'Homerising' formula; despite sounding Homeric, the adjective ἐϋσθενής is not attested in the Homeric epics.

---

[22] Starting from the Alexandrine age, πορφύρω becomes confused with πορφύρα and inherits its value, meaning 'becoming red' or 'being red' (Theoc. 5.125; Bion 2.19; Maec. in *AP* 9.249.3; Agath. in *AP* 10.14.1; Nonn. *D.* 45.308) and 'turning purple' (Nonn. *D.* 44.106); cf. Chantraine (1968–80) s.v.

[23] The apparatus of divine epithets in the *Posthomerica* comprises 42 non-Homeric terms; cf. Ferreccio (2018: XLVI).

[24] Cf. also Q.S. 2.390; 3.435; 4.76, 293; 6.85; 7.3; 9.3, 289; 11.332; 14.633.

[25] Cf. also *Il.* 2.47, 163, 187, 437; 3.127, 131, 251; 4.199; 6.454; 7.275, 444; 8.71; 10.136, 286, 367; 12.352; 13.272; 15.56; 17.414; 18.105; 23.575; 24.225; *Od.* 1.286; 4.496; cf. *Il.* 10.287, χαλκοχίτωνας Ἀχαιούς.

Instead of the Homeric νεφεληγερέτα,²⁶ 'gatherer of rainclouds', the customary epithet of Zeus, in the *Posthomerica* we find attested the albeit highly rare allotrope νεφεληγερής (4.80): a further confusing element is the association of this attribute with Zephyrus and not Zeus, as one would expect on the basis of the Homeric text. But also on this occasion the novelty of the combination is kept in check by the initial assonance of the names of the two divinities, an open allusion to and citation from the Homeric model.

Similarly, the peculiar feature of possessing whirlwind-swift feet is indicated not by the word ἀελλόπους, used in Homer exclusively as an epithet of Iris (*Il.* 8.409; 24.77, 159), but rather the allotrope ἀελλοπόδης (Q.S. 10.189). Also it is not used to characterise the goddess but Hermes, her masculine counterpart in the role of celestial messenger.

The epithet of Eos, φαέσφορος, 'bringer of light' (2.186 and 656), not to be found in the Homeric epics, calls to mind the action of the goddess as described in the *Iliad*: φόως φέροι (*Il.* 11.1–2, Ἠὼς δ' ἐκ λεχέων παρ' ἀγαυοῦ Τιθωνοῖο / ὄρνυθ', ἵν' ἀθανάτοισι φόως φέροι ἠδὲ βροτοῖσι, 'Dawn arose from her couch from beside noble Tithonus, / to bring light to immortals and to mortal men'; 19.1–2, Ἠὼς μὲν κροκόπεπλος ἀπ' Ὠκεανοῖο ῥοάων / ὄρνυθ', ἵν' ἀθανάτοισι φόως φέροι ἠδὲ βροτοῖσιν, 'Dawn with saffron-coloured veil arose from the streams of Oceanus, / to bring light to immortals and to mortal men').

Q.S.'s expertise in the art of allusion is particularly significant in two epithets applied to Hephaestus, both of which are non-Homeric: πυκινόφρων, 'skilful' (5.98) and the extremely rare χαλκεοτέχνης, 'smith' (2.440).²⁷ Both describe a well-known quality that is often mentioned by Homer, the technical skill of the god in the art of metallurgy, but without drawing on the Homeric terminology of equal significance, πολύφρων (*Il.* 21.367; *Od.* 8.297, 327) and κλυτοτέχνης (*Il.* 1.571; 18.143, 391; *Od.* 8.286). These are not to be found in the *Posthomerica* but are alluded to via their replacements: πυκινόφρων, which is a compound using -φρων like the Homeric πολύφρων, and χαλκεοτέχνης, which plays a game of deconstructing and reconstructing the Homeric terms κλυτοτέχνης and χαλκεύς (in reference to Hephaestus: *Il.* 15.310).

The second strategy deployed by Q.S. is the *ex novo* coining of terms that nonetheless contain 'echoes of Homer'.

On the face of it, the *hapax totius Graecitatis* ῥοδόπεπλος, 'that has a rosy veil', 'that has a rosy garment', an epithet of Eos (Q.S. 3.608), appears to be genuinely Homeric, so well is it constructed; however, in fact it is a term

---

²⁶ *Il.* 1.511, 517, 560; 4.30; 5.631, 736, 764, 888; 7.280, 454; 8.38, 387, 469; 10.552; 11.318; 14.293, 312, 341; 15.154, 220; 16.660; 17.198; 20.10, 19, 215; 21.499; 22.182; 24.64; *Od.* 1.63; 5.21; 9.67; 12.313, 384; 13.139, 153; 24.477.

²⁷ The other attestation of χαλκεοτέχνης occurs in a funereal epigram (*Epigr. sepulc.* 2.341.1 Cougny).

that is not attested outside the *Posthomerica*. The Homeric nature of the new formation is ensured by the two terms that comprise it, recurrent in many Homeric epithets: -πέπλος is present, among others, in κροκόπεπλος – which, to reaffirm the allusiveness of the new coinage ῥοδόπεπλος, is a qualifying adjective precisely for Eos in the *Iliad* (*Il.* 8.1; 19.1; 23.277; 24.696) – and in τανύπεπλος (*Il.* 3.228; 4.305; 18.385, 424; *Od.* 12.375; 15.171, 363). Undoubtedly the prefix ῥοδο- calls to mind the most famous of the epithets of Aurora, ῥοδοδάκτυλος, 'rosy-fingered' (*Il.* 1.477 *et al.*), yet significantly enough Q.S. banished it from the *Posthomerica*, as he did κροκόπεπλος.

A similar genesis is involved in another Homeric-style neologism, which was also probably created by Q.S.,[28] and likewise used to qualify Eos: ῥοδόσφυρος, 'rosy-ankled' (1.138), which this time combines the usual ῥοδο- with -σφυρος, on the model of the Homeric καλλίσφυρος, 'with beautiful ankles' (*Il.* 9.557, 560; 14.319; *Od.* 5.333; 11.603).

A Homeric overtone also accompanies another compound using -πέπλος: ἀγλαόπεπλος, 'with a beautiful veil', an epithet of Thetis in Q.S. 11.240, the only literary attestation of the term,[29] inspired not only by the above-mentioned κροκόπεπλος, 'with saffron-colored veil', and τανύπεπλος, 'that wears a long peplos, long-robed', but also by εὔπεπλος, 'having a lovely peplos' (*Il.* 5.424; 6.372, 378, 383; 24.769; *Od.* 6.49; 21.160).

κυανοκρήδεμνος, 'with dark veil', is also an epithet attested only in the *Posthomerica* (for Thetis: 4.115, 381; 5.121) and fashioned from Homeric material: κυανο-, the basis of Homeric compounds – such as κυανοχαίτης, κυανῶπις, κυανόπεζα, κυανοπρῴρειος, κυανόπρωρος[30] – and κρήδεμνον, thus similar to the Homeric καλλικρήδεμνος, 'with beautiful veil' (*Od.* 4.623) and λιπαροκρήδεμνος, 'bright-veiled' (*Il.* 18.382), the latter two being terms that are avoided in the *Posthomerica*.

μεγαλοβρεμέτης, 'loud-thundering', is a new coinage by Q.S., who revamps the apparatus of divine epithets by introducing the appellative *hapax totius Graecitatis* for the probably more traditional and icastic prerogative of Zeus, his role as master of thunder and lightning (2.508). Instead of 'copying' Homer by using the well-known ὑψιβρεμέτης, 'high-thundering' (*Il.* 1.353; 12.68; 14.54; 26.121, *Od.* 5.4; 23.331), Q.S. eschews the unoriginal reference – ὑψιβρεμέτης has no right to be in the *Posthomerica* – and recreates the Homeric model by taking its pieces apart and putting them together again.

---

[28] Cf. Ferreccio (2018: 140, n361).

[29] Apart from in the *locus* in the *Posthomerica*, ἀγλαόπεπλος is testified only by an epigraph found in Termessos, in Pisidia (modern-day Turkey), and dated from the third century CE (TAM III 1 590.1).

[30] κυανοχαίτης: *Il.* 13.563 *et al.*; *Od.* 3.6 *et al.*; κυανῶπις: *Od.* 12.60; κυανόπεζα: *Il.* 11.629; κυανοπρῴρειος: *Od.* 3.299; κυανόπρωρος: *Il.* 15.693 *et al.*; *Od.* 9.482 *et al.*

CONCLUSIONS

If taken singularly, the *variationes* from Homer may appear of little significance, even imperceptible or, worse still, an index of scant ability or a lack of acquaintance with the model. Taken together, however, they suggest an express design, attributable to Q.S.'s profile as a *poeta doctus* who makes allusiveness one of the strategies of his poetics. Q.S. does not adopt the principle of authority, according to which composing an epic means imitating Homer, wearily repeating him, but rather he follows the principle of imitation according to the criterion of ζῆλος, competitive emulation. The challenge he faces is also to reproduce in a different epoch the expressive context that generated the Homeric epics, recreating, *cum variatione*, the Homeric formularity and the stylemes of the oral tradition[31] – and to become an *alter Homerus*.

Q.S. is not only in competition with Homer; at the same time he also sets his audience the challenge of tracking down and decoding the allusions scattered throughout his epic poem.

---

[31] Thus Cantilena (2001: esp. 63 and 69), who calls Q.S. a 'transitional' poet.

CHAPTER 13

Polychronic Intertextuality in Quintus of Smyrna's *Posthomerica*

Vincent Tomasso

The 2012 film *Django Unchained* informs the audience that its narrative takes place in '1858' 'somewhere in Texas'. This chronological and spatial specificity generates expectations that are by turns reinforced and disrupted by the film's soundtrack. There is instrumental music that a typical audience member might associate with the late nineteenth century. For instance, Giuseppi Verdi's version of 'Dies Irae' (1874) plays over a Ku Klux Klan attack,[1] and in another scene a musician at Calvin Candie's plantation strums Beethoven's 'Für Elise' (published in 1867) on a harp. Tarantino also employs tracks from Italian spaghetti western films, such as 'His Name Was King' (composed for *Le Chiamavano King* (Romitelli 1971)) and the film's theme, 'Django', which appeared in *Django Unchained*'s namesake, *Django* (Corbucci 1966). This source is particularly appropriate, given that spaghetti westerns are *Django Unchained*'s primary reference point. The soundtrack also consists of popular songs from a variety of eras, such as Jim Croce's 1973 song 'I Got a Name', and the 2012 'Unchained', a remix of James Brown's 1973 song 'The Payback' and Tupac Shakur's 2006 song 'Untouchable'.[2] The soundtrack that results from this mixture interrupts the audience's experience of the film's late nineteenth-century narrative, causing them to reflect on how their present informs the past, and vice versa.

The soundtrack of Tarantino's *Django Unchained* parallels the diction of Quintus of Smyrna's third-century CE epic *Posthomerica* (henceforward *PH*). Like Tarantino's film, the *PH* draws its audience's attention to that epic's

---

[1] Robbins (2015: 281) contends that 'Dies Irae' is anachronistic for *Django Unchained*, but it is nevertheless effective in its evocation (for the audience) of 'nineteenth-century-ness'.

[2] Robbins (2015) argues for the thematic coherence of *Django Unchained*'s soundtrack.

imbrication in the past and in the present. On the one hand, the past predominates in the *PH*: according to Constantine Lascaris, a fifteenth-century CE Greek scholar, Quintus is Ὁμηρικώτατος, 'most Homeric'.[3] This is confirmed by the fact that a majority of Quintus' lexicon is taken from the Homeric poems, estimated by one scholar to be 3,000 words, or 80 per cent.[4] The other 20 per cent derives from sources outside the Homeric corpus. While the *PH*'s predominant references are the two Homeric epics, Quintus also includes a wide sweep of Greek literature in an attempt to articulate and channel the power of the Greek past. Such relationships between texts are called 'intertextuality', which many studies of Quintus have interrogated – in fact, this could be said to be the object of every investigation of the *PH*. Intertextuality is concerned with elucidating the relationships one text has with other texts, and because there are so many kinds of relationships, there are many different ways analyses can be focused. Studies of the *PH*'s intertextuality often focus on genre and/or theme, such as Stoicism.[5]

This chapter's analysis will be focused on a different type of intertextuality in the *PH*: Quintus' use of words that do not appear in the Homeric lexicon but which do appear in other Greek texts. I call this type of intertextuality 'polychronic', in the sense of the two Greek words that form that compound: 'many' 'times'. That is, such intertexts draw the audience's attention to the variety of time periods from which the embedded texts derive. This term neatly parallels the term 'polyphonism' that has been applied to Homer by Richard Martin and to Quintus by Emma Greensmith. According to Martin, 'polyphonism' refers to how epic is an 'ambitious supergenre' through its 'inclusion of every other form of song-making', such as praise/blame poetry, proverbs and lyric songs.[6] Greensmith applies this to the *PH*, specifically to Quintus' engagement with Homer, Hesiod and Callimachus.[7] Polyphonic intertextuality is therefore an integral mode of Quintus' poem, along with polychronic intertextuality. The latter is not meant to exclude the former, or other types of intertextuality, such as use of Homeric *hapax legomena* or relationships with other imperial epic poets.[8] Indeed, it complements them; if we do not take a variety of angles, our understanding of how Quintus interacted with other texts will not be nuanced enough.

---

[3] Greek text: Köchly (1850: CXI).

[4] Paschal (1904: 22). I have reservations about Paschal's data, considered in more detail below, but the figure just cited gives a solid general impression. See also Vian (1959a: 182; 1963: XL–XLIII); James and Lee (2000: 21–2).

[5] On Stoicism in the *PH*, see Maciver (2012a).

[6] Martin (1997: 166; 2009: 17).

[7] Greensmith (2018: 274).

[8] On Quintus' use of Homeric *hapax legomena*, see Appel (1994a), and on his engagements with other imperial epic poets, see Maciver (2016).

The foundation of this chapter's analysis is the 13 lists of words in Paschal's 1904 study of the *PH*.[9] He finds 800 words that Quintus employs that do not appear in either the *Iliad* or the *Odyssey* but do appear in other Greek texts. This is important groundwork for understanding Quintus' polychronic intertextuality, but there are a few issues with the words listed there. First, new editions of the texts in question mean that some words appear in earlier texts. An instance of this is the adjective λαοφόνος, -ov, 'people-killing' (*PH* 1. 593), which appears in Paschal's 'Alexandrine Poets Except for Apollonius Rhodius and Nicander' category. Indeed, this adjective is in line 53 of *Idyll* 17 by the third-century BCE poet Theocritus, but it also appears three hundred years earlier in line 87 of Bacchylides' *Ode* 17. Another issue is stems. For instance, the adverb ἀργαλέως, 'difficultly', appears first in Theognis, but it is misleading to call it an 'un-Homeric word', because the stem ἀργαλέ- appears 60 times in the *Iliad* and *Odyssey*. Third, it is not immediately apparent whether an ancient audience would have associated the words in Paschal's lists with the text that each appears in. To be fair, this was not a concern of Paschal's, and he should not be faulted for it, but it is an important characteristic for my purposes. The adjective ὀβριμόθυμος, -ov, 'brave', is an example. That adjective appears 27 times in the *PH*, and Paschal indicates that that word appears first in the *Homeric Hymns*. ὀβριμόθυμος, -ov is a *hapax legomenon* in the *Homeric Hymns*, appearing in the masculine vocative singular in the Homeric Hymn to Ares line 2. However, it is not confined to that text; it also appears in line 140 of Hesiod's *Theogony*. On the one hand, this data point is revealing for Quintus' poetic practice, since the *Theogony* is an epic, and Hesiod is one of Quintus' primary hypotexts. Additionally, ὀβριμόθυμος is applied only to the god Ares in both the *Homeric Hymn* and the *Theogony*. On the other hand, Quintus' use of ὀβριμόθυμος does not tell us much about the relationship between the *PH* and the *Homeric Hymns*. Lastly, Paschal includes words that are inflected identically in both the *PH* and one other text, but those words can appear in other forms in other texts. An example is the noun ζήλοιο (*PH* 6.37, 9.344, 10.298 and 10.489), 'jealousy, zeal', which Paschal lists in his 'Apollonius Rhodius' category; indeed, that word appears at *Argonautica* 1.616 in the epic dialect genitive singular. However, the lemma ζῆλος, -ου, ὁ is used much earlier, in the Hesiodic *Works and Days* (line 195), and appears 766 times prior to the *PH*.

This chapter presents some of the results I obtained by sifting Paschal's data. To arrive at the words that I felt best represent Quintus' polychronic intertextuality, I kept in mind the following criteria: (1) the word <u>must not</u> appear in the Homeric poems, (2) the word <u>must</u> appear first in the text under consideration and (3) the word <u>must not</u> appear in Greek literature before the *PH*. My process was to cross-reference the words in Paschal's lists, which were derived from

---

[9] Paschal (1904: 22–7).

Zimmerman's 1891 text and other emendations made through 1901, with Vian's text of the *PH*, published from 1963 through 1969. Once I verified that Paschal's reading was the same as Vian's, I ran a *Thesaurus Linguae Graecae* search on that word. If that search revealed that the word did not appear in the Homeric epics and only appeared in one other author, I then investigated Homeric parallels in the word's entry in the Liddell–Scott–Jones *Greek–English Lexicon*, as well as in Cunliffe's *A Lexicon of the Homeric Dialect*. The resulting data consists of words that often are not highly relevant to the texts in which they first appear – in other words, they do not have marked meta-significance to the text or to genre. The emphasis in this polychronic intertextuality is the temporal position of the text making intertextual references above all other considerations.

The dating of many of the texts is being reconsidered constantly, and in discussing them I defer to the current dating consensus; in no way am I arguing chronology in this chapter. In any case, Quintus' audience probably felt that broad century numbers were sufficient indications of texts' temporality. For instance, while the modern scholarly community is concerned with the date of the *Homeric Hymn to Hermes*, its placement in a collection indicates that ancient Greeks felt that it was 'archaic'. For the purposes of this chapter, I concur with the typical dating of Quintus to the second half of the third century CE.[10]

Polychronic intertextuality impels us to reflect on the composition of the *PH*'s audience. The poem consists of a predominating texture of Homericism, including both words that appear frequently in the Homeric lexicon and *hapax legomena*,[11] studded here and there with references to other texts. This requires an audience that is both attentive to and aware of, or at the very least willing to investigate, changes in the Homeric texture. We can parallel this situation to Apollonius of Rhodes' third-century BCE epic *Argonautica*. Arguments made about Apollonius' use of Homeric *hapax legomena* typically depend on an elite audience.[12] Apollonius' audience would need to be able both to guess that a given word was a *hapax legomenon* and then consult copies of the Homeric poems in order to confirm this, which would probably mean that the *Argonautica*'s ideal audience was composed of 'scholar-poets' – individuals who lived and worked in the Library of Alexandria.

This, I argue, was true of Quintus' audience to a greater or lesser extent. In the first place, imperial Greek culture was, similar to Hellenistic Alexandria, a 'world not just of the book, but of the very big book' – an intertextual culture, as demonstrated by the many quotations of the Homeric poems in the third-century Athenaeus' *Deipnosophistae*.[13] The deliverers of

---

[10] Summary: Baumbach and Bär (2007b: 2–8).

[11] See Appel (1994a).

[12] Maciver (2016: 531, n14) points out that including Homeric *hapax legomena* was a common practice in Greek imperial poetry.

[13] Goldhill (2009b: 96–7).

these quotations were products of the highest levels of education, and the setting for Athenaeus' dialogue, a dinner party, is elite as well. Education at every stage made use of the Homeric poems: beginning students were assigned passages to practice the alphabet, read aloud and memorise,[14] and advanced students composed *progymnasmata* ('preliminary exercises') in the style of, and/or in response to the *Iliad* and *Odyssey*.[15] Those who were able to avail themselves of this system were called the *pepaideumenoi*, the educated elite, who were both author and audience of the *PH*.[16] Whether Quintus was actually a sophist, like Dio and other Homeric revisionists such as Philostratus and Lucian, is a matter of debate,[17] but immaterial for this chapter. But since the focus of this chapter is intertextuality – and intertextuality of a very specific kind, that would probably require a high level of education to be aware of – Quintus' audience would probably have attained a high level of education that enabled them to apprehend the sophisticated intertextuality of the sort analysed in this chapter.

Quintus' sustained relationship with the Homeric epics is well documented: almost every word of the *PH* is derived from the *Iliad* and/or *Odyssey*. His use of *hapax legomena* from the Homeric epics, however, indicates an even closer relationship. Apollonius of Rhodes' use of Homeric *hapax legomena* has been investigated thoroughly,[18] and it is notable that in some cases Quintus uses Homeric hapaxes that do not appear in the *Argonautica*. Take the verb παππάζω, 'to call someone "papa"', which Dione uses in her declaration to Aphrodite at *Iliad* 5.408: οὐδέ τί μιν παῖδες ποτὶ γούνασι <u>παππάζουσιν</u>, 'and children do not at all <u>call him "papa"</u> at his knees'.[19] Quintus' Phoenix employs the same verb in his lament over Achilles' body: πολλάκι <u>παππάζεσκες</u>, 'you often used to <u>call me "papa"</u>' (*PH* 3.474). That this word was typically associated with Homer is confirmed by Apollonius' first–second century CE *Homeric Lexicon*, in which he defines this verb, with a quotation from the Odyssean Nausicaa, as ὠνοματοπεποίηται παρὰ τὸ τὰ παιδία τοῖς πατράσι λέγειν προσφωνοῦντα πάππα· 'πάππα φίλ', οὐκ ἂν δή μοι ἐφοπλίσειας ἀπήνην' (*Od.* 6.57), 'coined by children addressing their fathers

---

[14] Examples discussed at Morgan (1998: 39–44) (handwriting) and Cribiore (2001: 134) (memorisation); cf. Kennedy (2003: XI) (memorisation).

[15] For an overview of the stages of education at this time, see Webb (2017). On the Homeric epics' primacy in Greek education, see Cribiore (2001: 194–7). On *progymnasmata* generally, see Kennedy (2003). For *progymnasmata* that engage the Homeric epics, see Miguélez-Cavero (2008).

[16] Cf. Maciver (2012a: 18).

[17] See Maciver (2012a: 17–18), who discusses the debate, with further bibliography.

[18] See Kyriakou (1995).

[19] I have made use of the list of Homeric *hapax legomena* that appear in the *PH* in Appel (1994a: 101–16).

with the word "papa": "Dear papa, would you not get a wagon ready for me.'"[20] The adjective φυγοπτόλεμος, -ον, 'cowardly', appears only in Odysseus' Cretan lie to his swineherd Eumaeus: ἐπεὶ οὐκ ἀποφώλιος ἦα / οὐδὲ φυγοπτόλεμος, 'since I was neither idle nor cowardly' (Od. 14.212–13). This adjective is an insult that the Posthomeric Thersites utters against Achilles at PH 1.740, and Paris employs it in the same way in his insult of Polydamas at PH 2.68. As with παππάζω, the only appearances of this word before Quintus are discussions in grammatical treatises. In the second century, Aelius Herodian discusses φυγοπτόλεμος three times in his works, including On the Iliad's Prosody and On the Odyssey's Prosody.[21] By incorporating Homeric hapax legomena such as these, Quintus draws attention to his close relationship with Homer, unmediated by other texts.

Quintus' audience probably understood Hesiod's Theogony to be from the same stratum of 'hallowed antiquity' as, if not slightly later than, Homer. Unlike the Iliad and Odyssey, the Theogony is not a heroic epic, but all three works are composed in dactylic hexameters and overlap in narrative material at various points. These two elements cause the Theogony to be the focus of Quintus' intertextuality at several points.[22] Hesiodic intertexts add to Quintus' polychronism in that Hesiodic poetry is distinguishable from Homeric poetry through lexicon. Although much diction is shared between them, perhaps suggesting a common tradition, some is not, and I focus on two particular examples here. The first is the verb περιάχω, 'to echo around, resound', which appears unaugmented in the third-person singular of the imperfect at Theogony line 678 in a description of the sea mirroring the sounds of the Olympians and Titans fighting: δεινὸν δὲ περίαχε πόντος ἀπείρων, 'the endless sea was resounding fearfully'. Quintus is fond of this verb, as is demonstrated by the six times that he uses it in the PH. Although an aorist form of this verb, περιήχησεν, does appear at Iliad 7.267, Quintus gives his intertexts a Hesiodic bent by using only the imperfect, and, in several cases, the exact form of Theogony 678. This is the case at PH 2.605 (a description of the mountains echoing the noise of Achilles and Memnon fighting), 11.382 (the noise created by the advance of an Achaean contingent), 14.416 (the noise of the ocean dashing against departing Achaean ships), 14.483 (the noise of the Winds in a cave) and 14.534 (the noise on land when Athena kills little Ajax).

---

[20] Appel (1994a: 23) argues that Quintus' use of παππάζω is an interpretation of Homer.

[21] Appel (1994a: 47–8) investigates the one instance of φυγοπτόλεμος in the Homeric epics and their two reappearances in the PH, concluding that Quintus has changed the metrical position in the second appearance (the first is identical); the meaning is the same in all three cases.

[22] Nearly every analysis of the PH has dealt with the Book 12 proem and its engagement with the Theogony. See especially Maciver (2012a: 34–8), and Greensmith (2018).

The adverb συνωχαδόν, 'continually', appears at *Theogony* line 690 in the narrator's description of the comportment of Zeus at the outset of the Olympians' war with the Titans: ἀστράπτων ἔστειχε <u>συνωχαδόν</u>, 'he was hurling lightning bolts <u>continuously</u>'. συνωχαδόν is glossed by a scholiast on Hesiod,[23] which demonstrates that this adverb was infrequent enough that those who encountered it required assistance to make sense of it. The scholiast obliges by equating the meaning of συνωχαδόν with the much more common adverb συνεχῶς, which is employed 1,754 times in Greek literature, from the eighth through the second centuries. In fact, the uncontracted form, συνεχέως, appears in line 636 of the *Theogony*, which suggests that Quintus' audience would have associated συνωχαδόν with Hesiod. Aside from a brief discussion of συνωχαδόν in the second-century CE grammarian Apollonius Dyscolus' treatise *On Adverbs*, it surfaces next at *PH* 14.517 in the narrator's description of the Achaeans' ships in a storm: αἳ γάρ ῥα <u>συνωχαδὸν</u> ἀλλήλῃσιν / αἰὲν <ἐν>ερρήγνυντο, 'they kept smashing into one another <u>continuously</u>'.[24]

The next polychronic intertext comes from Paschal's list of 'early lyric poets', from the seventh century to the fifth century. The substantive ἀμφιπερικτίονες, 'dwellers all around', appears at *PH* 6.224 and twice in archaic lyric poetry. In *PH* 6 it describes how the Ceryneian Hind was uprooting the neighbours' plots in the ecphrasis of the armour of Heracles' grandson Eurypylus: Κεμμὰς δ' εὖ ἤσκητο θοὴ πόδας, ἥ τ' ἀλεγεινῶν / ἀμφιπερικτιόνων[25] μέγ' ἐσίνετο πᾶσαν ἀλωήν, 'A swift-footed hind had been well fashioned, and she was greatly destroying the neighbours' vineyard.' This substantive appears once in the poetry of the seventh-century BCE Callinus and once in the poetry of the sixth-century BCE Theognis.[26] The closest Homeric dialect word is the adjective περικτίονες, 'living nearby',[27] which is close to ἀμφιπερικτίονες, but the form that Quintus employs in this instance triggers memories of archaic lyric through a Homeric prism. This is particularly so given that ἀμφιπερικτίονες does not appear in any other authors besides Callinus and Theognis.[28]

The *PH*'s connection to Attic drama of the sixth to fourth century BCE on the level of narrative content has been explored before,[29] and the fragments of an imperial tragedy *Ptocheia* that survive demonstrate the vitality of Greek

---

[23] The scholiast on the BMM² manuscript in Flach (1876).

[24] Vian (1969: 117, n3) notes that this adverb has a different, though related, meaning in the *Theogony* and the *PH*, and he compares, without comment, the related adverb συνοχηδόν, 'in confinement', in a *Palatine Anthology* epigram.

[25] Vian (1966: 76) notes several manuscript readings for this word.

[26] Martin (1997: 156–9) compares the language of Homeric similes to that of Theognis' poetry.

[27] Several of the *PH* manuscripts read περικτιόν or περίκτιον here (Vian 1966: 76). The adjective περικτι- appears four times in the *Iliad* and twice in the *Odyssey*.

[28] Campbell (1981: 190) discusses four phrasings that are common to Theognis' poetry and *PH* 12.

[29] The standard study is Paley (²1879).

drama in Quintus' and his audience's world.[30] In his mid-fifth-century tragedy *Agamemnon*, Aeschylus has Cassandra use the noun ἄλυξις, -εως, ἡ, 'escape', in her prophetic certainty that she cannot escape her own impending death: οὐκ ἔστ' ἄλυξις, 'escape is impossible' (1299). ἄλυξις next appears in the *PH*, on two occasions: at 1.478, the narrator describes the Achaeans' terror at not being able to escape death at the hands of the Amazon Penthesilea (οὐδέ σφιν θανάτοιο πέλε στονόεντος ἄλυξις), and at 12.212, Zeus uses the word to indicate what will happen if the Olympians do not stop fighting (οὐδ' ἔσσεται ὕμμιν ἄλυξις). In the Homeric poems, the idea of 'escape' is conveyed by words deriving from the ἀλε- and ἀλυ- roots: the verbs ἀλεείνω, ἀλέομαι and ἀλύσκω, and the noun ἀλέη. The chorus applies the adjective εὔπρωρος, -ον, 'with a good prow', to ships in the Greek armada in Euripides' late fifth-century tragedy *Iphigenia at Aulis* (line 765). In the *PH*, the word appears four times (1.824, 4.29, 4.283 and 5.330), also as an epithet of ships. A similar idea is conveyed in the Homeric epics through the adjective εὔπρυμνος, -ον, 'with a good stern/poop deck', at *Iliad* 4.248 in Agamemnon's description of the Achaeans' ships. The adjective μονάμπυξ, -υκος is applied to horses four times in the extant plays of Euripides. In different passages, it refers to the piece of armour that covers a horse's nose, as well as an indication of a horse working alone. It appears at *Alcestis* line 428, *Suppliants* lines 586 and 680, and *Helen* line 1567, in addition to *PH* 4.545, where the narrator employs it to describe the horses in one of the competitions of Achilles' funeral games. Homer uses the related adjective ἄμπυξ, -υκος at *Il.* 22.469, though not with respect to horses, but rather in a description of how Andromache throws off her veil in her grief at Hector's death and disfigurement.

The fact that Hesychius defines the noun ῥοῖβδος, 'a rushing noise or motion', indicates that it was an unfamiliar word to his readers in the fifth and sixth centuries CE, and it was probably the same for Quintus' audience a few hundred years earlier. ῥοῖβδος is associated with classical drama, appearing before Quintus only in the fifth-century tragedian Sophocles and the late fifth/early fourth-century comedian Aristophanes. In Sophocles' *Antigone* line 1004, the Theban prophet Tiresias declares that a bird omen he has witnessed is not without meaning (πτερῶν γὰρ ῥοῖβδος οὐκ ἄσημος ἦν), and in Aristophanes' *Clouds* line 407, Socrates declares how lightning is created when gusts of wind ὑπὸ τοῦ ῥοίβδου, 'with a rushing noise', run into clouds. ῥοῖβδος appears twice in the *PH*: in a description of the noise that Zeus makes in response to Ares going to Ida (1.699), and in a simile comparing the noise made by the fighting Achaeans and Trojans to the ἀκαμάτῳ . . . ῥοίβδῳ, 'limitless rushing' of a hurricane (10.70). The first instance in particular presents a stark difference with Quintus' intertexts, since a version of this episode also

---

[30] Parca (1991).

appears in Book 15 of the *Iliad*. There, Athena stops her brother from leaving Mount Olympus, since she and the other gods fear Zeus' χόλος καὶ μῆνις (15.122); Quintus repeats the essential details of the episode (*Iliad* 15: Ares wants to take revenge for his son Ascalaphus' death; *PH* 1: Ares wants to take revenge for his daughter Penthesilea's death), but his use of a non-Homeric, non-epic noun from non-Trojan War narratives highlights his text's polychronicity.

From Herodotus' *Histories* of the fifth century BCE come two words that Quintus reuses. The verb, ἐπάγω, 'to bring to', appears at *Odyssey* 14.392 and *Odyssey* 19.445, and so Quintus adds to the Homeric texture of his poem by using this verb at *PH* 9.107 in Deiphobus' speech to his fellow Trojans about how there is sun after a storm: Ζεὺς ἐπάγει μερόπεσσι δι' ἠέρος εὔδιον ἦμαρ. Quintus also uses an Ionic form of that verb, ἐπαγινέω, which never appears in the *Iliad* or the *Odyssey*, but is used by Herodotus, whom Longinus described as one of the most Homeric (Ὁμηρικώτατος) of authors.[31] The historian uses the verb in his reporting of the Egyptian king Psammetichus' attempt to find out whether his people were the oldest. Psammetichus has two Egyptian children taken from their parents and raised in isolation: ἐντειλάμενος . . . τὴν ὥρην ἐπαγινέειν σφι αἶγας, 'he commanded [a shepherd] to bring goats to them from time to time' (*Histories* 2.2.9–11). The same verb form appears at *PH* 6.234–55 in the ecphrasis of Eurypylus' shield: τῷ δ' ἄρα θεσπεσίοιο βαθὺν ῥόον Ἀλφειοῖο / ὄβριμος Ἡρακλέης ἐπαγίνεεν, 'And to it (king Augeas' stables) strong Heracles was bringing the deep current of the marvellous Alpheus.' Quintus is pointedly drawing the audience's attention to Herodotus by using this verb, since his Herodotean hypotext also uses ἐπάγω (18 times); ἐπαγινέω is a *hapax legomenon* in the *Histories*. At *PH* 12.404, the narrator employs the verb περιστρωφῶντο in his description of the Trojan priest Laocoön's punishment: περιστρωφῶντο δ' ὀπωπαὶ, 'and his eyeballs were rolling around'. A participial form, περιστρωφώμενον, describes the movement of an individual named Mys to oracular shrines at *Histories* 8.135. The separate elements of this compound, περί and στρωφάω, appear frequently in both Homeric epics, and Cunliffe includes several περι- verb compounds, but never together.

Ozbek has analysed the *PH*'s treatment of medical issues in the Homeric epics and in post-Homeric medical texts, concluding that Quintus sometimes allows Homer, at other times post-Homeric texts to guide his medical discourse.[32] The text *On Fractures* has been connected to the mid-fifth-century/ early fourth-century BCE physician Hippocrates, but there are doubts about whether it was actually authored by him or someone else in his tradition. In any case, this text is likely to derive from the classical period, and the verb

---

[31] Longinus, *De subl.* 13.3.
[32] Ozbek (2007). See also James (2005: 371) and Bär (2009: 273–5).

ἀμφιθνήσκω appears here and in the *PH*.[33] In *On Fractures*, it appears in the context of the author's description of what happens when a fracture causes necrosis: ἀμφιθνήσκουσιν αἱ σάρκες, 'the flesh withers' (section 33 line 3). The Posthomeric Teucer employs this verb in his exhortation to his fellow warriors: κείνοις ἀμφιθάνωμεν, 'or we die around them' (6.44–50). The simplex form of this verb, θνήσκω, appears frequently in the Homeric epics (138 times), in addition to compound forms like ἀποθνήσκω (4 times), but the context of the *PH* of Teucer's encouraging of the Achaeans after the death of the physician Machaon is especially poignant in its counterpoint.

Quintus makes use of some of the diction of a poet of the late fourth to mid-third century BCE, Callimachus. Callimachus' influence (or lack thereof) on the *PH*'s poetics has been a point of investigation for years, primarily in terms of Quintus' proem in Book 12.[34] In his *Hymn to Artemis*, Callimachus uses the adjective τετραβόειος, ον, 'of four bull-hides', in a description of Cyclopes' φάεα μουνόγληνα σάκει ἴσα τετραβοείῳ, 'eyes equal [in size to] a shield made of four bulls' hides' (*In Dianam* line 53). This adjective does not appear again until *PH* 6.547, where it describes a shield that protects Aeneas from Teucer's onslaught in battle: ἤρκεσε γάρ οἱ πῆμα σάκος μέγα τετραβόειον, 'his shield of four bulls' hides defended him from pain'. This adjective was an obscure word, as noted by a scholiast on Callimachus' hymn, who defines the adjective as τετραπτύχῳ, 'fourfold'.[35]

From a bit later in the third century BCE comes Apollonius of Rhodes' *Argonautica*. The shared genre and intertextual practices of Apollonius and Quintus result in a large number of lexical correspondences, narrative references and adapted phrasings,[36] but my focus here is on the smaller subset of words shared by the *Argonautica* and the *PH*. My first example derives from the verb παραθερίζω, which means 'to graze in passing' and is used very infrequently in extant Greek literature. It appears first in the *Argonautica* (*Arg.* 2.601) and next in the *Posthomerica* (*PH* 10.238). In the *Argonautica* it takes the form of the third-person plural aorist παρέθρισαν that describes how the Clashing

---

[33] ἀμφιθνήσκω also appears in the second-century CE physician Galen's *Commentary on Hippocrates' On Fractures* 3, but the relevant passage is a quote from *On Fractures*.

[34] Quintus' relationship with Callimachus was a focus of scholarship as early as the mid-eighteenth-century Teubner edition of the *PH* (Köchly 1850: III) and continues to be debated. See further Vian (1963: XL); Maciver (2012a: 34–8); Bär (2007: 45–51); Greensmith (2018).

[35] Pfeiffer (1953).

[36] Vian (2001) is a study on the influence of the *Argonautica* on the *PH* that cites many places in Vian's earlier studies of the *PH* in which he discusses Quintus' engagement with Apollonius. Vian focuses on thematic and narrative resonances between the two epics and explicitly says that he will avoid lexical topics 'which would have been inevitably incomplete' (2001: 285). On adapted phrasings, see Campbell (1981: 198) ('Apollonius Rhodius' in the index). On a simile that appears in both Apollonius and in Quintus, see Maciver (2012c).

Rocks take off a piece of the Argo as the ship passes between them: ἔμπης δ᾽ ἀφλάστοιο παρέθρισαν ἄκρα κόρυμβα, 'nevertheless they grazed the high stern of the ship's poop deck'. In the *PH* it takes the form of the third-person singular aorist παρέθρισε when the narrator describes how Philoctetes' arrow strikes Paris: ἀλλὰ παρέθρισε χειρὸς ἐπιγράβδην χρόα καλόν (*PH* 10.238), 'but it grazed the beautiful skin of his hand'. These are the only two appearances of this verb between Homer and Quintus. Nothing from that stem appears in Homeric poetry (in other words, a word with the θεραιζ- root, though the verb θερίζω appears as early as Aeschylus' *Suppliants* 636). My second example derives from the verb παραλιταίνω, 'to do wrong', which appears twice in the *Argonautica* (παρήλιτες at 2.246 and παρήλιτον at 3.891) and twice in the *PH* (παρήλιτον at 10.305 and 12.417).[37] *Arg.* 2.246 is part of Zetes' question to Phineus: ἦ ῥα θεοὺς ὀλοῇσι παρήλιτες ἀφραδίῃσιν, 'Did you do the gods wrong in your destructive foolishness?' At *Arg.* 3.891 Medea speaks: ἦ μέγα δή τι παρήλιτον, 'I did a great wrong.' At *PH* 10.305, Paris speaks to his ex-wife Oenone: εἰ καί τι παρήλιτον ἀφραδίῃσιν, 'even if I did some wrong in my foolishness'. At *PH* 12.417 the narrator is describing the Trojans' fear that they have done something that might offend Athena: μὴ δή τι παρήλιτον ἀφραδίῃσι, 'lest they did some wrong in their foolishness'.[38] There is no item in the Homeric lexicon formed from the same stem.[39]

In his *Idyll* 24 of the second century BCE, Theocritus depicts the infancy and early life of Heracles. Early in that poem, the hero's mortal stepfather Amphitryon orders his slaves to οἴσετε πῦρ ὅτι θᾶσσον ἀπ᾽ ἐσχαρεῶνος ἑλόντες, 'Take fire from the hearth and bring it quick as you can' (line 48). The noun ἐσχαρεών, -ῶνος, ὁ also appears four times in Quintus' epic: (1) *PH* 5.504, (2) *PH* 12.569, (3) *PH* 13.147 and (4) *PH* 14.26. The second instance is particularly notable in this context, which is a description of the frantic Cassandra's attempt to burn the Wooden Horse: αἰθομένης ἔτι δαλὸν ἀπ᾽ ἐσχαρεῶνος ἑλοῦσα, 'having seized a still-burning piece of wood from the hearth'. Quintus draws his audience's attention to the fact that he is borrowing from Theocritus by using a participle of the verb αἱρέω as the following word.

In the following century, Moschus uses the adjective βαρύδουπος, -ον, 'loud-roaring', to describe Poseidon: καὶ δ᾽ αὐτὸς βαρύδουπος ὑπεὶρ ἅλα Ἐννοσίγαιος / κῦμα κατιθύνων, 'Above the sea the loud-roaring Earthshaker himself straightened the waves' (*Europa* lines 120–1). The components of this compound adjective, the adjective βαρύς and the noun δοῦπος ('loud noise'), appear frequently in the *Iliad* and the *Odyssey* (36 times and 13 times,

---

[37] On this sharing, see, with little comment ('Quintus takes up Apollonian expressions'), Vian (2001: 293).

[38] Discussion of textual readings of this passage at Vian (1969: 219).

[39] Vian (1969: 28, n4) argues that Paris' speech in these lines echoes Parthenius 4.

respectively), but βαρύδουπος appears only in Moschus and Quintus before the fourth century CE. In the *PH* this adjective is applied to Lemnos' beaches when Odysseus and Diomedes persuade Philoctetes to join the Achaeans: Οἳ δέ μιν αἶψ' ἐπὶ νῆα καὶ ἠϊόνας βαρυδούπους / καγχαλόωντες ἔνεικαν, 'Rejoicing, they quickly carried him to his ship and the loud-roaring shores' (*PH* 9.426–7).

The adjective ἀνδροβόρος, -ον appears in the Sibylline Oracles in a description of Mark Antony (Book 11 line 291). Lines 161–89 of this same book prophesise the outcome of the Trojan War, and so we might expect ἀνδροβόρος to occur in that context. But it does not; instead, it appears several hundred lines later in a comparison of Mark Antony to a lion: συνοικήσεις δὲ λέοντι ἀνδροβόρῳ, 'you (Cleopatra) will marry and live with a man-devouring lion' (11.290–1). The *PH* applies this same adjective to the flesh-eating horses of the Thracian king Diomedes in an ecphrasis on Eurypylus' shield: Διομήδεος ἵπποι / ἀνδροβόροι (6.246–7).

From the late first-century BCE/early first-century CE Strabo's *Geography* comes the adjective βαθύστομος, -ον, which the writer applies to caves in a Middle Eastern country: σπήλαια βαθύστομα, 'deep caves'. Quintus' narrator applies this same adjective to the Amazon Penthesilea's axe, describing it as βουπλῆγι βαθυστόμῳ (*PH* 1.133). Cunliffe lists eight words that are compounds of the adjective βαθύς, -εῖα, -ύ, 'deep' (38 times in Homer); βαθύστομος, -ον, that adjective combined with the noun στόμα, -ματος, τό, 'mouth' (28 times in Homer), does not appear in either the *Iliad* or the *Odyssey*.

Around the time of Marcus Aurelius' co-emperorship with his son Commodus in 177–80, Oppian wrote a didactic epic about aquatic life and the practices of fishermen titled *Halieutica*. The *Halieutica* has proved important in studies of the *PH*, since Quintus interfaces with Oppian's epic on three occasions (at *PH* 7.569–75, 9.172–7 and 11.62–5), which has led to the common assertion that the *Halieutica* provides a *terminus post quem* for the *PH*.[40] A study by Emily Kneebone extended that idea into Quintus' poetic practice.[41] Given the *Halieutica*'s Homericising tone, overlap with the *PH* is inevitable,[42] but it is striking when Oppian's and Quintus' diction overlap in words that do not appear in the Homeric corpus, nor, indeed, anywhere else in extant Greek literature. For instance, the participle περιπλήθουσα, 'being very full', appears at *PH* 14.290 in Hecuba's lament as her city falls: τί δ' ὕστατον ἀχνυμένη κῆρ / κωκύσω

---

[40] See, e.g., James and Lee (2000: 6); Baumbach and Bär (2007b: 3); Bär (2009: 15–16); Maciver (2012a: 3). For a commentary on Quintus' adaptations, see James (2004: 310) on lines 569–75, 316 on lines 167–79, and 323 on lines 60–6.

[41] Kneebone (2007).

[42] On Homericising in Oppian, see, e.g., Bartley (2003).

πολέεσσι <u>περιπλήθουσα</u> κακοῖσιν, 'Grieving at heart and <u>very full</u> of many evils, what am I to lament last?' This form, the feminine nominative singular participle, also appears at *Halieutica* 2.348, 4.397 and 4.500. This is a compound of the verb πλήθω, 'to be full of', which appears with some regularity in Homeric poetry; the adjective περιπληθής, 'very full of people' is a *hapax* at *Odyssey* 15.405.[43] A scholiast's gloss of this word with the participle μεστουμένη, 'being full of', which is found 46 times in authors through the third century CE, suggests that audiences had difficulty understanding this word's meaning – perhaps because that the word was confined to Oppian's work.[44]

The adjective θρασύφρων, 'with a bold mind', is particularly notable as a shared word because of its frequency in those two texts: it appears once in the *Halieutica* (θρασύφρονες at 1.112) and a striking 15 times in the *PH*.[45] In their commentary on Book 5 of the *PH*, James and Lee remark on the phrase θρασύφρονος Αἰακίδαο at 5.5 that the adjective 'was possibly coined by Oppian' and is used as alternative for the Homeric adjectives δαΐφρων and κρατερόφρων.[46] To these two adjectives, I add the metrically equivalent πολύφρων (10 times) and ταλασίφρων (13 times). The line that contains this adjective refers to sea bass: λάβρακές τ' ἀμίαι τε <u>θρασύφρονες</u> ἠδὲ χρέμητες, '<u>bold-minded</u> bass, tunny and sea crows' (1.112). A scholiast on Oppian's gloss of θρασύφρονες goes on for several lines, describing how this word refers to these fish's daring to attack larger marine life (τολμηροὶ ἐν τῷ δάκνειν δελφῖνας). As with περιπλήθουσα, this indicates that readers in the scholiast's time were confused by θρασύφρων.

The shared features of the *Halieutica* and the *PH* mean that the latter's intertexts with the former are more numerous, but Quintus also engaged prose texts of the same time period.[47] Whereas the texts considered previously either came from the distant past or were poetry, diction of more contemporary prose texts would have been much more jarring. Sometime in the mid-first/early second centuries, Plutarch uses the verb ἐνομόργνυμι in the middle voice, meaning 'to impress', twice in the *Moralia* (*Cicero* 32.7.2 and *Against the Stoics on Common Conceptions* 1081B.4). The narrator applies this same verb to the snake that bit Philoctetes: στυφελοῖσι τόν οἱ <u>ἐνομόρξατ'</u> ὀδοῦσι, '[a wound] that it <u>caused</u> with its cruel fangs' (*PH* 9.385). This verb appears in both Homeric poems without the -μο- infix

---

[43] Verb and participle forms of πλήθω appear 11 times, the adjective οἰνοπληθής once, the noun πλῆθος three times and the noun πληθύς 17 times.

[44] Scholia 348 in a hypothesis to Book 2 in Bussemaker (1849).

[45] We perhaps should also include the two instances in the epic *Cynegetica* (at 3.51 and 3.296) if we think that the author of that poem conceived of his work as a supplement to the *Halieutica*.

[46] James and Lee (2000: 39).

[47] James and Lee (2000: 22) note that Quintus tends to avoid words typical of prose texts.

and without a gamma; in the middle voice, it is associated with the gods' laughter (*Il.* 1.599 and *Od.* 8.326).[48]

The adverb δράγδην, 'by hand', is employed at *PH* 13. 90–1 in a description of victims during the sack of Troy: οἳ δ' ἄρα χερσὶ / δράγδην ἔγκατ' ἔχοντες ὀιζυρῶς ἀλάληντο, 'Others held entrails in their hands as they wandered around miserably.' δράγδην appears for the first time in the late first-century/early second-century CE Plutarch in his essay *On the Failure of Oracles* in a description of the numerous problems with philosopher Empedocles' poetry: δράγδην λαμβάνοντας ἐκ τῶν ἐπῶν τῶν Ἐμπεδοκλέους ἁμαρτίας καὶ ἄτας καὶ πλάνας θεηλάτους (418E5), 'failures, errors and mistakes caused by the gods from Empedocles' poetry by the handful'. In the next century, Lucian uses the same adverb in his dialogue *Lexiphanes*, a satire of the much-discussed Second Sophistic phenomenon of correcting spoken Greek, in the context of activities in a gymnasium undertaken by one of the interlocutors: ὁ δὲ μολυβδαίνας χερμαδίους δράγδην ἔχων ἐχειροβόλει (section 5 line 6), 'the other threw the large lead weights that he held in his hands'. For an audience enmeshed in the Homeric poems, this instance recalls the scenes in which Iliadic heroes throw rocks at one another on the battlefield. In particular, Diomedes' attack on Aeneas parallels *Lexiphanes* in terms of diction and theme: ὁ δὲ χερμάδιον λάβε χειρί, 'and he picked up a rock with his hand' (*Il.* 5.302).[49] Although δράγδην's usage statistics depart from the normal characteristics of the data in this chapter, since two authors post-Homer and pre-Quintus use it, Plutarch and Lucian are both prose authors of the imperial period, and so they can be considered together for the purposes of polychronic intertextuality. Quintus combines the archaic and the imperial, as he uses both χερσὶ and δράγδην. It is especially significant that Quintus chose to use a word from *Lexiphanes*, which pokes fun at the cultural phenomenon of Atticising.[50] Quintus highlights his diction in this instance by also employing χερσὶ, 'with their hands', in the previous line, which echoes the Iliadic χειρί. The Homeric epics never use δράγδην, but the related noun δράγμα appears twice (*Il.* 11.69 and 18.552) and the participle δραγμεύων once (*Il.* 18.555). Even though the basic sense of the word, 'that which can be held in the hand', is inherent to all of these words, in the Homeric epic the noun refers to corn, whereas the adverb is never so used. The adjective βαθυσκόπελος, -ον, 'with high cliffs', appears first in the third-century *Philosophy from Oracles* by the philosopher Porphyry. He prefaces one such oracle with a description of a location: βαθυσκοπέλους ἀνὰ πρῶνας θῆρας ὀρειονόμους ἐλάαν Λητωίδι κούρῃ, 'to drive mountain-ranging animals for Leto's daughter

---

[48] James and Lee (2000: 22) note that Quintus also has the tendency of Atticising texts of the imperial period to use the middle voice.

[49] = *Il.* 8.321 = *Il.* 20.235.

[50] On this phenomenon, see Kim (2010b). James and Lee (2000: 22) note the few Attic features of the *PH*'s language and style.

through promontories <u>with high cliffs</u>'. Especially striking in this instance is the Homeric flavour of Porphyry's words; in particular, the infinitive ἐλάαν is used seven times in the *Iliad* and ten times in the *Odyssey*. Quintus describes wooded areas with the adjective βαθυσκόπελος, -ον (βαθυσκοπέλου διὰ βήσσης, 1.316 and βαθυσκοπέλοιο . . . βήσσης, 5.372), and his Hera applies the adjective to crags that came to hear Apollo's song (βαθυσκόπελοί τε κολῶναι, 3.104). Cunliffe lists nine adjectives that compound βαθυ- with another noun, as well as the noun σκόπελος, but βαθυσκόπελος, -ον does not appear in either the *Iliad* or the *Odyssey*.

Near the end of the second century or possibly at beginning of Quintus' own century,[51] the sophist Lucius Flavius Philostratus, whose other work is prose, tried his hand at composing poetry. In one of his epigrams that survives in the *Greek Anthology*, he employs the verb περιπτώσσω, 'to fear greatly', in his ecphrasis of a picture of the hero Telephus: οὗ καὶ τειρομένοιο <u>περιπτώσσοντες</u> Ἀχαιοὶ / φύρδην Τευθρανίας νεῦνται ἀπ' ἠιόνος, 'Where the Achaeans, <u>greatly fearing</u> distressing [Telephus], have gone away headlong from the Teuthranian bank' (AP 16.110.7–8). Telephus is not a character in Quintus' epic, though he is mentioned as Eurypylus' father, and he had an important role in the Achaeans' mis-landing in Mysia, prior to the events of the *Iliad*. The uncompounded form, πτώσσω, 'to fear', appears nine times in the *Iliad* and *Odyssey* combined, as well as in a wide variety of genres and time periods thereafter, though still infrequently (37 times) before the *PH*. Quintus uses that uncompounded form on six occasions and the compounded form once, which the narrator uses to describe the Trojans' fear of Locrian Ajax in battle: οἳ δὲ <u>περιπτώσσοντες</u> ἀμύμονος ἀνέρος ἀλκήν, 'They <u>in great fear</u> of the might of the excellent man' (*PH* 11.445). This narrative overlap, in addition to its application to the Achaeans rather than the Trojans, explains Quintus' decision to use it as an intertext.

The final set of polychronic intertexts to be discussed in this analysis are words coined by Quintus himself.[52] When he uses words of his own making, Quintus draws his audience's attention to their present moment in the third century. An example is the adjective ἀνερκής, -ές, which the Posthomeric Nestor employs to describe the state of the Achaeans after Achilles' death: στρατὸν εὐρὺν <u>ἀνερκέα</u> θῆκας Ἀχαιῶν, 'you made the Achaeans' wide army <u>defenceless</u>' (*PH* 3.494). This adjective never appears in the Homeric epics, but its two components, the alpha privative and the noun ἕρκος, do. This adjective is a *hapax legomenon* in the *PH*, and it does not appear elsewhere

---

[51] If the *communis opinio* about the date of the *PH* in the second half of the third century is right (see above), Quintus probably post-dates Philostratus, whose dates are usually given as circa 170–247/250.

[52] Vian (1959a: 168–74) is an investigation of Quintus' neologisms, which he concludes are botched attempts at Homeric imitation ('D'une manière plus ou moins consciente . . .').

in Greek literature after Quintus' epic. Quintus underscores this particular neologism by including words derived from the ἔρκ- root 22 times in his epic. Another example is the adjective μεγαλοβρύχοιο, which appears once in the *PH* in a simile. In his speech before the Achaeans justifying why he should receive Achilles' armour, Ajax compares himself to a lion and his rival Odysseus to a dog: ὅσσον τίς τε κύων <u>μεγαλοβρύχοιο</u> λέοντος, 'as much as some dog is [weaker] than a <u>loud–roaring</u> lion' (5.188). The Homeric epics feature several adjectives formed from compounds with the adjective μέγας, μεγάλη, μέγα (Cunliffe lists four), and the other element of this Posthomeric adjective is related to the verb βρυχάομαι, 'to roar' (three times in the *Iliad*, twice in the *Odyssey*). In this respect, μεγαλοβρύχοιο does not differ from Quintus' formation of new words elsewhere in the *PH*; a scholiast's use of it to gloss ἐριβρύχεω, 'loud-bellowing', in Hesiod's *Theogony* (line 832) suggests that the word Quintus used was more familiar to the scholiast's audience in a later century. Quintus highlights his neologism by also using a variation on ἐριβρύχεω, ἐρίβρυχος, in the description of a lion (*PH* 3.171).

Near the midpoint of *Django Unchained*, protagonists Django and Dr King Schultz visit plantation owner Calvin Candie in the hopes that they can rescue Django's wife from Candie's ownership. In a parlour where Candie conducts gladiator-style fights to the death between slaves, Django encounters an Italian owner named Amerigo Vessepi, played by none other than Franco Nero, who, several decades earlier, played the title character in the Italian spaghetti western *Django* (Corbucci 1966). 'What's your name?' Amerigo inquires. 'Django,' Django replies. 'How do you spell it?' Amerigo asks. Django obliges, adding, 'The "D" is silent.' 'I know,' Amerigo responds, before finishing his shot of tequila and departing. This scene complements the soundtrack discussed in the introduction to this chapter, in that it compels the audience to confront the film's oscillation between the past of the narrative (historically, the late nineteenth century; generically, the western) and the present of the audience.

In a similar way, Quintus signposts the polychronic texture of the *PH* through his polychronic intertextuality. Paschal's estimation that 80 per cent of the *PH*'s lexicon is to be found in the Homeric poems sets the dominant tone of Quintus' epic through the *Iliad* and *Odyssey*, much as the setting, plot and characters of *Django Unchained* recall the heyday of western film production in the 1950s and 1960s. The remaining 20 per cent of the *PH*'s lexicon has been investigated in this chapter, in terms of how those words make the audience aware of the various chronological strata of Quintus' epic. In turn, those strata reveal the ambition of the *PH* to be an epic that is at once archaic, classical, Hellenistic and imperial. Through Quintus' polychronic intertextuality, Homer is both a possession of the Greek past and of the third-century present.[53]

[53] My thanks to this volume's editors for their energy and care, especially to Emma Greensmith for her perceptive comments on a draft of this piece that helped clarify my argument. Thanks also to the anonymous press reader.

PART IV

The Struggle with the Literary Past

The Dissolution of Troy: Homeric Narratology in the *Posthomerica*

Fran Middleton

Locating suspense in the *Posthomerica* is one of the poem's central challenges. Over the course of the twentieth century, scholars repeatedly criticised the poem for lacking any such driving force, with the result that one German handbook insisted Quintus' work lacked all 'tension and life' ('Spannung und Leben'), while a later commentator wrote in English that the poem is 'empty of inspiration' and its verses are little more than a 'leaden echo' of Homer.[1] The poem even seems to thematise its lack of inspiration, as its poet fails to appeal to the Muse in the work's opening lines and so fails to provide any frame of reference for the story he begins.[2] The reader is left on their own to make sense of *Posthomerica*'s parade of secondary characters and the deaths which close down one episode and then the next. As a sequel, the narrative's direction therefore appears to remain the *Iliad*'s, onwards ever towards the fall of Troy. In this chapter, however, I argue that Quintus does not adopt the narrative drives of Homeric epic so straightforwardly, but instead transmutes them.

Following his book-length discussion of 'foreshadowing' and 'suspense' in Homer, Virgil and Apollonius of Rhodes (1933), George Duckworth (1936) produced an article on the same matters in Quintus of Smyrna.[3] In the main, Duckworth defends the *Posthomerica*, arguing that the poet builds suspense in a manner similar to Virgil, primarily by leaving the outcome of events unknown

---

[1] Schmid and Stählin ([6]1924: 964); Knox (1985: 715). Cf. Duckworth (1936: 58); Schmidt (1999: 41); Maciver (2012a: 7–8).

[2] It is nonetheless possible to draw connections between the *Posthomerica*'s opening and other epic proems. See Bär (2007).

[3] Cf. Rengakos (1999) on 'Spannungsstrategien' in the Homeric epics, which responds to Duckworth's discussion to focus on the differences in technique between the *Iliad* and the *Odyssey*.

rather than making clear what will happen. There is, nonetheless, a certain lack of foreshadowing, which we expect to build the reader's anticipation (71): 'Where Quintus departs from Homer is in his failure to give in detail any fore-knowledge of the later part of his poem. The technique of Quintus . . . tends to lessen the unity of the *Posthomerica* as a whole.' This raises the question of what aspects of the poem's later parts we might expect to see foreshadowed, and so what is missing. More recent studies operate on the assumption that the poem works towards the expected end of the Trojan myth: the fall of Troy.[4] As I discuss in the first part of this chapter, the *Posthomerica* is undoubtedly concerned with the fall of Troy, which is framed as an act of λύσις: 'release' or 'dissolution'. This is a key term in the *Iliad* as the *Posthomerica* activates it, connecting the 'ransoms' of Chryseis and Hector – the two *termini* of the poem's ring composition – the fall of Troy and the loosening of Troy's κρήδεμνα ('veils'), which is to say its walls. However, throughout the *Posthomerica* more broadly, λύσις notably does not provide the poem with *urgency* as a τέλος. Instead, this idea frequently marks moments of pause and retardation in the narrative. If there is suspense in the *Posthomerica*, then it is produced by the fall of Troy as a source of delay, rather than as a thwarted goal.

What, then, may be understood as the *Posthomerica*'s narrative τέλος, if not the Trojan myth's conclusion? In the second part of this chapter, I argue that we should be willing to recognise the answer that arises from looking in the most obvious place. The poem closes with the gods bringing down a storm on the Achaeans and allusion to the dangers of their νόστοι. This of course connects the *Posthomerica* to the Trojan story's further continuation in the *Odyssey*.[5] The sea nonetheless provides a sense of urgency throughout the *Posthomerica*, as Odysseus and Diomedes cross that water to bring Neoptolemus and Philoctetes to the battlefield. These moments foreshadow the Achaeans' return to the sea, ironising the difficulties Odysseus is doomed to face. This foreshadowing provides the poem with momentum, which is set in tension with the ongoing difficulties faced by those characters who seek the fall of Troy so that they might return home. As the *Iliad*'s τέλος becomes the *Posthomerica*'s source of delay, the *Odyssey*'s source of delay becomes the *Posthomerica*'s τέλος.

---

[4] Schmitz (2007b), for example, takes this line in his study of the *Posthomerica*'s use of prolepsis and analepsis: 'the *Posthomerica* have a more "natural" τέλος in Troy's fall.' Bär (2007: 33) and Maciver (2012a: 21, n72; 132) also refer to 'the fall of Troy' as the poem's τέλος. See Greensmith's chapter in this volume for a different approach to this issue.

[5] Maciver (2012a: 23) follows consensus when he remarks that the *Posthomerica*'s 'purpose, at the absolute basic level, is to tell the story of the Trojan War where the *Iliad* leaves off up to the point at which the *Odyssey* begins'. However, the poem's relationship to the *Odyssey* is less extensively discussed than its relationship to the *Iliad* and the *Aeneid*, which Gärtner (2005) for example concentrates on.

λύσις AS A FORCE FOR DELAY

The association between λύσις and the resolution of a narrative goes back to Aristotle. In *Poetics* 18 (1455b24–1456a32), Aristotle defines λύσις as the denouement of a tragic plot: the resolution of those complications he describes as δέσις.[6] The term is further used throughout ancient scholarship on Homer, following Aristotle's use of the term in his *Homeric Problems*.[7] As René Nünlist describes (2009: 11–12), a typical format for scholia on the Homeric poems by the third century CE was for a question to be posed and an answer to be offered, generally with an explanation of what kind of answer is required in response to the problem. For example, a problem might be answered with a 'solution from diction', λύσις ἐκ τῆς λέξεως, a particular understanding of what a word means,[8] or with a 'solution from character', λύσις ἐκ τοῦ προσώπου, an understanding of how the narrative is focalised. In the *Posthomerica*, as I shall show, λύσις recognisably carries this idea of 'resolution' as it describes the fall of Troy, but it refers to the end of what we might recognise as the Trojan *fabula*, to use formalist terminology – the war's sequence of events – rather than the denouement of the *Posthomerica*'s *sjuzhet*, the shape of its plot. In this way, the poem distinguishes itself from the *Iliad* and distorts the recognised principles of the *Iliad*'s narrative.

As Antonios Rengakos notes, it is only relatively recently that scholars have appreciated that narrative tension might be a feature of Homeric epic,[9] and the idea remains contentious. Erich Auerbach's reading of Odysseus' scar (1953: 3–23) famously argues that Homer's digressions are not intended to cause the reader any concern for the narrative's progress: 'For the element of suspense is very slight in the Homeric poems; nothing in their entire style is calculated to keep the reader or hearer breathless. The digressions are not meant to keep the reader in suspense, but rather to relax the tension' (4). Many scholars continue to emphasise the so-called paratactic nature of the Homeric epics, suggesting that excursus develops rather than frustrates the narrative. Egbert Bakker (1999) in particular defends the relevance of Auerbach's remarks against what he calls the trend of increasingly 'literary' readings of Homer (11). We might compare the disputes raised with Auerbach by scholars such as Norman Austin (1966), Michael Lynn-George (1988: esp. 1–49) and Charles Segal (1994: 6–9), who consider the Homeric epics to be structured and suspenseful.

---

[6] See Goldhill (2009a) for discussion of the role played by λύσις in Sophocles' tragedies.

[7] See MacPhail (2011: 2–3). Cf. Combellack (1987: 202), who notes Porphyry's own recollection of the history surrounding Homeric problem-solving.

[8] See Combellack (1987) on this type of solution in particular.

[9] Rengakos (1999: 308): 'Daß die "Spannung" keine Kategorie des Epischen ist, gehörte bis vor wenigen Jahrzehnten zu den Dogmen der Homerforschung, und entsprechend gering war auch das Interesse, das die Interpreten der Ilias und der Odyssee diesem Thema entgegenbrachten.'

The *Posthomerica* takes a line on this Homeric problem, repeatedly high-lighting the idea of λύσις as the outcome of the Trojan War. This reminds the reader of those moments in the *Iliad* when Aristotelian λύσις appears to be written into the Homeric poem's events. The attitude is most apparent at the end of *Posthomerica* 11, when after the book's extended descriptions of battle the narrator remarks (499–501):

(. . .) οὐ γάρ τι κακοῦ παύοντο **μόθοιο**
οὐδέ σφιν μάλα δηρὸν ὑπ᾽ Ἄρεϊ τειρομένοισιν   500
ἔσκε **λύσις καμάτοιο**· πόνος δ᾽ ἄπρηκτος ὀρώρει.[10]

(. . .) In no way was there an end to the evil **clamour of battle**.
Not for those weakened by Ares for all too long
was there ever release from toil. The labour had become unending.

Again and again, ἔσκε (11.501) suggests, one might have hoped for the clamour of battle (μόθος, 499) to cease, but the resolution of suffering (λύσις καμάτοιο, 501) does not come. This comment appears to echo the Greek perspective, building on a speech given by Philoctetes two books earlier, as he encourages the Achaeans to fight until the Trojan walls have fallen (9.537–9):

'Εἰ δ᾽ ἄγε <δὴ> πολέμοιο μεδώμεθα· μηδέ τις ἡμέων
μιμνέτω ἐν νήεσσι, **πάρος κλυτὰ τείχεα λῦσαι**
Τροίης εὐπύργοιο καταπρῆσαί τε πόληα.'

'Come on then, let us plan for war. Let none of us
hang back in ships **until the famous walls** of Troy
have fallen, its beautiful towers – and the city has been burnt to dust.'

The phrase Philoctetes uses, πάρος κλυτὰ τείχεα λῦσαι, translates literally as 'until the famous walls are dissolved'. It is not a violent image, but it is evocative, recalling the way λύειν is used throughout both the *Posthomerica* and the *Iliad* to describe the body's collapse in death. The *Posthomerica* in particular associates λύειν with death: it is explicitly used in this context on sixteen out of twenty-nine instances of the verb.[11] The reader also recalls how the *Iliad*

---

[10] This text follows Vian (1963, -66, -69), as do all passages of the *Posthomerica* below.

[11] This is after my own count, including compounds. The verb explicitly describes death at 1.253, 312, 762; 2.252, 296, 544; 3.162, 307; 5.272, 296; 6.596, 7.582; 10.140, 236; 11.84, 489. A number of other moments refer to release from suffering, while 9.538 and 12.441 both refer to the fall of Troy. I will discuss below the important simile of 11.307–15, when the verb is used in a familiar way to describe the unfastening of various parts of a ship, only to tie the semantics of this to the moment of death and the unfastening of bodies on the battlefield, which should influence our reading of several other descriptive passages.

uses λύειν to describe the destruction of cities. In *Iliad* 2.117–18, for example, Agamemnon describes Zeus as the god ὃς δὴ πολλάων πολίων **κατέλυσε** κάρηνα / ἠδ' ἔτι καὶ **λύσει** ('who has **destroyed** the heights of many cities indeed, and will go on **destroying** them').

The *Iliad* and the *Odyssey* use the verb λύειν to describe the fall of Troy at two pivotal moments, connecting the verb to the city's destruction and referring (back) to this τέλος of the *Iliad*. In *Iliad* 16.97–100, Achilles prays to Zeus, Athena and Apollo after Patroclus has asked if he might borrow Achilles' armour. He requests that he and Patroclus alone might escape death and break through the walls (**loose the** holy **veils**) of Troy: νῶϊν δ' ἐκδῦμεν ὄλεθρον, / ὄφρ' οἶοι Τροίης ἱερὰ **κρήδεμνα λύωμεν** (16.99–100). The moment is overshadowed by the narrator's comments in 16.46–7, which frame Patroclus' request for Achilles' arms as an action that will lead to his demise. The scene marks the *Iliad*'s move into its final third and looks towards Achilles' fatal engagement in battle, ironising Achilles' prayer and foreshadowing Achilles' own fate. As Odysseus returns to Ithaca, he takes counsel with Athena and asks her to fill him with courage so that they might destroy the suitors (13.383–91), οἷον ὅτε Τροίης **λύομεν** λιπαρὰ **κρήδεμνα** ('just as when **we were loosing the** bright **veils** of Troy', 13.388). This moment looks to the *Odyssey*'s own end point, which is framed to mirror the projected τέλος of the *Iliad* and to reject the *Oresteia* paradigm, which Odysseus exclaims he might have fallen prey to without Athena's advice in 13.383–5. In both poems, the reference to Troy's fall comes at a crucial turning point, emphasising to the reader how characters' choices shape the Homeric narrative as they anticipate forthcoming events in the plot.

Activating λύσις as a structural key to the *Iliad*, the *Posthomerica* further recalls the role of 'ransom' – another translation of the λύσις – in the *Iliad*'s composition. As Keith Stanley (1993: 29–32) discusses, the *Iliad*'s ring composition has been recognised in modern scholarship at least as far back as the nineteenth century, and the term λύσις is used to describe the release of Chryseis' and Hector's body throughout *Iliad* 1 and 24. Hector's speech in *Iliad* 6.441–65 famously draws together his own fate and the fate of the city, and Hector's λύσις in Book 24 draws on the added significance that has been built into this term over the course of the poem, now recalling Achilles' comments in Book 16 and the increasing association between λύσις and death, emphasised not least as Hector is returned as a corpse. Achilles describes himself to Hector explicitly as 'the one who loosened your knees', ὅς τοι γούνατ' ἔλυσα, after stabbing him in *Iliad* 22.335, and Andromache reminds the audience of Hector's significance in her lament of 22.477–514: οἶος γάρ σφιν ἔρυσο πύλας καὶ τείχεα μακρά, she says ('you alone protected [the Trojans'] gates and high walls', 507). As Chryseis' λύσις instigates the plot and the *Iliad*'s Aristotelian δέσις, Hector's λύσις stands for not only the poem's solution but the greater collapse of Troy.

In the *Posthomerica*, the moment of Troy's loosing veils is described explicitly as a τέλος, but this does not mark the end of the poem, inviting the reader to recognise the transforming relationship between this poem's plot and the narrative drives of the *Iliad*. *Posthomerica* 12.436–43 sees λύειν used to describe the Trojans' self-defeating welcome of the Wooden Horse into the city, recalling the images of *Iliad* 16.100 and *Odyssey* 13.388. Rather than the *Iliad*'s projected dramatic climax, a mirror to the catharsis of Hector's funeral, this is a moment of pause, awe and anticipation:

> αὐτοὶ δ' ἐστέψαντο κάρη· μέγα δ' ἤπυε λαὸς
> ἀλλήλοις ἐπικεκλομένων. Ἐγέλασσε δ' Ἐνυὼ
> δερκομένη **πολέμοιο κακὸν τέλος**· ὑψόθι δ' Ἥρη
> **τέρπετ', Ἀθηναίη δ' ἐπεγήθεεν.** Οἳ δὲ μολόντες
> ἄστυ ποτὶ σφέτερον **μεγάλης κρήδεμνα πόληος** 440
> **λυσάμενοι** λυγρὸν ἵππον ἐσήγαγον· αἳ δ' ὀλόλυξαν
> Τρωιάδες, πᾶσαι δὲ περισταδὸν εἰσορόωσαι
> **θάμβεον ὄβριμον ἔργον** ὃ δή σφισιν ἔκρυφε **πῆμα**.

And they wreathed their heads. The people called out to each other
with raised voices, just as they were called on. **Enyo laughed**,
seeing the city's terrible fate – **and from high up, Hera
enjoyed the view, while Athena rejoiced.** Those coming
into their town loosened **the veils of their great city**
as they led the baneful horse inside. The women of Troy
cheered, all of them gathering to look upon **the creation,
which was amazing and formidable**, and was certainly hiding **a
disastrous end** for them.

Three goddesses stand watch over the horse's passage, and the divine conflict which has framed the Trojan War is momentarily set to one side. War herself watches and laughs (ἐγέλασσε, 12.437), while Hera on the side of the Trojans and Athena on the side of the Greeks both look on the moment with joy (τέρπετο, ἐπεγήθεεν, 438). Marked as the 'end point', the τέλος, of the war (438), the moment nonetheless seems to act like those references to Troy's veils in the *Iliad* and *Odyssey*: a turning point between the back-and-forth of those battles up until now, not least the exchanges in Book 11, and the one-sided conquest of the Trojans which is to follow. It is a phrase repeated ironically in 14.117, as the Greeks congratulate each other on their victory 'fearless at heart' (ἀταρβέα θυμόν, 14.115), before the events and their consequences which follow.[12]

---

[12] Cf. Campbell (1981: 151), who discusses the difficulties of this phrase in Book 12.

This frames the poem differently from the Homeric epics, as Troy's fall is openly displayed, rather than set as the vanishing point between the *Iliad* and the *Odyssey*'s prospective and retrospective modes of view. While the poet emphasises the misery to follow from this moment in the *Posthomerica*, the πῆμα (12.443) concealed by the horse, the audience is encouraged to share the awe felt by the Trojan women, who are astounded by the great work (θάμβεον ὄβριμον ἔργον, 12.443).

As a result, this scene distorts an Iliadic understanding of Troy's λύσις, which now becomes the τέλος of the Trojan War but not the resolution of the *Posthomerica*'s narrative. The description of the goddesses' reaction and that of the Trojan women becomes a moment of retardation and suspense, at odds with what one expects of references to Troy's λύσις in the *Iliad* and *Odyssey*. This reaction to the Homeric epics develops throughout the *Posthomerica*, and allows us to better understand the seemingly interminable nature of Book 11: the battles of the *Posthomerica*, we might say, are all excursions and sources of delay, rather than flawed attempts at building momentum. The death of Penthesileia produces a moment of reflection and awe, rather than a will for revenge (1.659–74): she lies 'in dust and blood' on the ground (ἐν κονίῃσι καὶ αἵματι, 659), just as those heroes who die in Book 11 will later, in 11.314, scattered like parts of a ship loosened after a storm (11.307–15). It is Ares who reacts violently to the Amazon's death, only to be held back by Zeus (1.675–715). Dawn is similarly the first to react when Achilles kills Memnon (2.549–69), before the grieving Aethiopians are veiled in mist (2.580–2) and both the Greeks and Trojans together pause to marvel at the sight (ἀμφὶ δὲ Τρῶες / καὶ Δαναοὶ θάμβησαν, 2.582–3). When Achilles is killed, the Trojans immediately react passively with fear (3.179–85), before Paris urges them to claim the body (3.186–211).

Indeed, death and λύσις repeatedly hold the poem back. As Book 11 suggests that 'release from toil' has not come (λύσις καμάτοιο, 11.500–1), the phrase plays on the uses of λύειν at 11.311 to describe the fallen bodies, and 11.84 and 11.489 to describe Abas and Toxaechmes' deaths. As it is not yet total, the λύσις of slain warriors is a frustrating force in the narrative, just like the protracted fall of Troy. There are two scenes prior to this in which the idea of λύσις καμάτοιο also frames narrative excursus. In the second half of Book 10, we learn the story of Oenone, Paris' first wife, who mourns for her former husband and ultimately kills herself by leaping on the hero's funeral pyre. It is night, 'which brings mortals release from toil' (μερόπεσσι λύσιν καμάτοιο φέρουσα, 10.437), that allows Oenone to escape the notice of her father and maidservants and make her way to Paris' pyre. This phrase echoes a comment from the narrator in 7.762, when Neoptolemus is held back from killing Eurypylus by night, 'which brings men release from toil' (ἥ τ' ἀνθρώποισι λύσιν καμάτοιο φέρουσα). Killing Eurypylus is the primary reason he has been brought to the battlefield; just as in the case of Oenone, night's release diverts the narrative from its path.

In the narrative of the *Iliad*, slaughter is the engine of the plot, lending momentum to the fall of Troy whether we understand that this is held in suspense or not. Diomedes' mastery of the battlefield invites Hector's retaliation, which invites Patroclus to kill Sarpedon, Hector to kill Patroclus and Achilles to kill Hector. The *Posthomerica* recounts the series of deaths which follow, allowing the story of Troy to reach its final conclusion, but this poem describes death in such a way that it is transformed into the end of momentum, the fall of Troy producing episodes more reminiscent of Auerbach's 'relaxing' digressions than the moments of foreshadowing offered by the *Iliad*. As Frederick Combellack (1968: 16) remarks, 'Quintus has a somewhat un-Homeric interest in depicting the sufferings which the war brings to people in general, combatants and non-combatants alike', and Pavlos Avlamis (2019) has more recently emphasised how the destruction of Troy in *Posthomerica* 13 takes on the tone of a spectacle treated in ecphrasis.

We may read this approach in the scene which precedes the long sequence of Paris' death and the final third of the *Posthomerica*. When Philoctetes encounters Paris on the battlefield, he is initially unable to kill him, catching Cleodorus of Rhodes instead. This leads to a moment of reflection, as the Greek hero calls on Paris before aiming for him again (10.223–38):

Τὸν δ' ὡς οὖν ἐδάμασσε Πάρις στονόεντι βελέμνῳ,
δὴ τότε δὴ Ποίαντος ἀμύμονος ὄβριμος υἱὸς
ἐμμεμαὼς θοὰ τόξα τιταίνετο καὶ μέγ' ἀΰτει· 225
    'Ὦ κύον, ὡς σοὶ ἔγωγε φόνον καὶ κῆρ' ἀίδηλον
δώσω, ἐπεί νύ μοι ἄντα λιλαίεαι ἰσοφαρίζειν·
καί κεν ἀναπνεύσουσιν ὅσοι σέθεν εἵνεκα λυγρῷ
τείροντ' ἐν πολέμῳ· **τάχα γὰρ λύσις ἔσσετ' ὀλέθρου**
ἐνθάδε σεῖο θανόντος, ἐπεί σφισι πῆμα τέτυξαι.' 230
    Ὣς εἰπὼν νευρὴν <μὲν> εὔστροφον ἀγχόθι μαζοῦ
εἴρυσε, κυκλώθη δὲ κέρας, καὶ ἀμείλιχος ἰὸς
ἰθύνθη, τόξον δὲ <λυγρὴ> ὑπερέσχεν ἀκωκὴ
τυτθὸν ὑπ' αἰζηοῖο βίῃ· μέγα δ' ἔβραχε νευρὴ
ἰοῦ ἀπεσσυμένοιο δυσηχέος. Οὐδ' ἀφάμαρτε 235
δῖος ἀνήρ· **τοῦ δ' οὔ τι λύθη κέαρ, ἀλλ' ἔτι θυμῷ**
ἔσθενεν· οὐ γάρ οἱ τότε καίριος ἔμπεσεν ἰός,
ἀλλὰ παρέθρισε χειρὸς ἐπιγράβδην χρόα καλόν.

So, then, Paris laid him low with a killing shot,
and right after this the great son of noble Poeas
eagerly drew his swift bow and raised his voice to shout,

    'You dog, I will bring you a dark end and bloody death,
since now you think you can match yourself against me –
and all of them will die, those who struggle on

in this baneful city because of you. **Soon there will be an end to suffering,**
at the moment when you are dead, since you have brought them this disaster.'

Saying this, he pulled the well-spun bowstring
back to his chest – the bow circled round – and the piercing arrow
was set true. But the poisoned tip of the arrow reached past the bow,
just a little, by the force of its strength. The string shuddered violently
once the keening arrow had been released. The godlike man
did not miss, **but Paris' heart was not yet stilled.** Instead, his spirit
still brought him strength. For now, the arrow did not bring mortal injury,
but did enough to kill him later by grazing the fine flesh of his hand.

Jeering at his opponent, Philoctetes claims that the end of the war will
come quickly once Paris is dead (10.229–30). The Trojans are instead due to
suffer πῆμα, 'misery', 'disaster' (230), the same word as that promised by the
narrator in his description of the Trojan Horse (12.443). Taking these comments in the spirit of an Iliadic boast, this speech could read as a moment of
foreshadowing, urging the poem on towards a τέλος of Troy's fall. However,
as this scene responds to the *Iliad*, we note how the λύσις ὀλέθρου Philoctetes
promises ('release from destruction', 229) is not imagined to follow simultaneously as a result of Paris' death, but τάχα: 'soon', 'forthwith', 'probably'. This
new requirement for Paris' death contradicts and tears open the association
with Hector and Troy, which allows Hector's death in the *Iliad* to stand for
Troy's fall in synecdoche. Rather, Troy's fall is an ever-protracted process,
with new requirements ever introduced.

This delay is a growing source of suspense throughout the *Posthomerica*, and
even here Paris is not killed cleanly, but struck with a poison arrow in a non-
fatal place (237). His heart does not fail – τοῦ δ' οὔ τι λύθη κέαρ (236) – and
this echoes the similar delay to Memnon's death in *Posthomerica* 2.252, when
he is attacked by Antilochus and his survival is described with the same phrase.
Against the poem's other uses of λύειν, these moments remind us that λύσις is
a slow, drawn-out process, rather than a discrete moment which here has been
deferred. The term does not provide urgency, even as it is activated in the *Iliad*
as a term which drives the Homeric plot to the fall of Troy.

NARRATIVE URGENCY IN THE *POSTHOMERICA*

The *Posthomerica* is a frustrating poem,[13] transforming the *Iliad*'s narrative logic
so that the forces which bring urgency to the *Iliad*'s plot – the fall of Troy
and reciprocal killing – become forces for delay. It is not surprising, therefore,

---

[13] See Greensmith's chapter in this volume.

that readers have insisted that the *Posthomerica* contains no tension at all, these moments of delay unmatched by any propelling force. However, the *Posthomerica*'s many moments of pause are challenged on at least two key occasions by episodes where events move remarkably quickly. These both depict Odysseus and Diomedes journeying over the sea to retrieve those warriors who will allow for Troy's fall.

At first, the swiftness with which these figures are retrieved might seem to contradict my argument in the first half of this chapter, that the fall of Troy is a force for delay in the poem. However, we may make sense of these episodes as we recognise the means by which Neoptolemus and Philoctetes are brought to Troy, namely over the sea, the poem's point of focus in its final lines. It is the sea to which the *Posthomerica* aims itself, driving towards the *Odyssey* and activating that poem's source of delay as its own source of urgency.

The first journey Odysseus makes with Diomedes is to Scyros, described in 6.96–113 and 7.169–75. The episode is interrupted, so we might say delayed, by description of Eurypylus' *aristeia*, which carries between the two books. The journey is nonetheless straightforward, only slowed by its narration. The first passage makes clear how different this journey is from any that might be expected for Odysseus in the *Odyssey*:

Καί ῥ᾽ ὅτε δὴ παύσαντο κορεσσάμενοι μέγ᾽ ἐδωδῆς,
δὴ τόθ᾽ ὁμῶς Ὀδυσῆι περίφρονι Τυδέος υἱὸς
νῆα θοὴν εἴρυσσεν ἀπειρεσίης ἁλὸς εἴσω·
καρπαλίμως δ᾽ ἤια καὶ ἄρμενα πάντα βαλόντες,
ἐν δὲ καὶ αὐτοὶ ἔβαν, μετὰ δέ σφισιν εἴκοσι φῶτες   100
ἴδμονες εἰρεσίης, ὁπότ᾽ ἀντιόωσιν ἄελλαι
ἠδ᾽ ὁπότ᾽ **εὐρέα πόντον** ὑποστορέῃσι γαλήνῃ.
Καί ῥ᾽ ὅτε δὴ κληῖσιν ἐπ᾽ εὐτύκτοισι κάθισσαν,
τύπτον ἁλὸς μέγα κῦμα· πολὺς δ᾽ ἀμφέζεεν ἀφρός.
Ὑγραὶ δ᾽ ἀμφ᾽ ἐλάτῃσι **διεπρήσσοντο κέλευθοι**   105
νηὸς ἐπεσσυμένης· τοὶ δ᾽ ἱδρώοντες ἔρεσσον.
Ὡς δ᾽ ὅθ᾽ ὑπὸ ζεύγλῃσι βόες μέγα κεκμηῶτες
δουρατέην ἐρύσωσι πρόσω μεμαῶτες ἀπήνην
ἄχθεϊ τετριγυῖαν ὑπ᾽ ἄξονι δινήεντι
τειρόμενοι, πουλὺς δὲ κατ᾽ αὐχένος ἠδὲ καὶ ὤμων   110
ἱδρὼς ἀμφοτέροισι κατέσσυται ἄχρις ἐπ᾽ οὔδας·
ὣς τῆμος μογέεσκον ἐπὶ στιβαρῆς ἐλάτῃσιν
αἰζηοί· **μάλα δ᾽ ὦκα** διήνυον εὐρέα πόντον.

And so, when they finished their meal, more than satisfied,
it was that moment when the son of Tydeus, with careful Odysseus,
nonetheless drew **a speedy ship** down into the boundless sea.

Quickly they threw together their provisions and all their equipment,
and off they went. Twenty men went with them,
**experienced oarsmen who knew what to do when the winds
     were against them
and when calm overtook the wide sea.**
And when they were sat in the well-made benches,
they beat the bay's high surf, and the sea foam frothed around them.
Watery ways were carved out by the oars
of the rushing ship. They rowed bathed in sweat.
**Just as when oxen toil hard beneath the yoke,
struggling to drag forward a wooden waggon,
which groans from its burden beneath the spinning axle;
they bear it, and great streams of sweat flow down both their
     necks
and their shoulders, towards the earth –**
so at that moment did the strong oarsmen struggle against the stiff oars
and with great haste they were making it through the wide sea.

The overriding impression provided for this journey is its speed. As we
might expect for any Homeric ship, that taken by Odysseus and Diomedes
is described as 'speedy' (θοός, 6.98). This idea is nonetheless developed as the
heroes are described acting 'quickly' as they crew the ship (καρπαλίμως, 99)
and as the vessel takes to the sea it is finally described to travel 'very swiftly'
(μάλα δ' ὦκα, 113). The way this urgency is framed further sets it at odds with
the *Odyssey* as the passage foreshadows the poem's closing lines.

In line 105, the ship is described making its way to Scyros: 'the watery
routes were cut through' (ὑγραὶ ... διεπρήσσοντο κέλευθοι). The use of
διαπράσσειν ('cut through', 'complete') with κέλευθοι ('routes') is uncommon
in Homer, though both words are familiar terms to describe movement over
a large area and sea routes respectively. As a result, the passage recalls the few
moments when they are used together: first, *Iliad* 1, when Agamemnon has
released Chryseis. Here the Greeks return from their sacrifices and we learn
that the ship 'made its way, cutting a route through the swell' (ἡ δ' ἔθεεν κατὰ
κῦμα διαπρήσσουσα κέλευθον, 1.483). The *Posthomerica* passage further recalls
Telemachus' journey away from Ithaca, when the same line is used at *Odyssey*
2.429 after Athena lends her aid to the journey (2.420–1). This fulfils Telemachus' request to the assembly of *Odyssey* 2, to give him a speedy ship and
twenty comrades to cut a path as he seeks news (νῆα θοὴν καὶ εἴκοσ' ἑταίρους,
/ οἵ κέ μοι ἔνθα καὶ ἔνθα διαπρήσσωσι κέλευθον, 2.212–13).

These moments in the *Iliad* and the *Odyssey* are scenes of progress and
urgency, set in contrast with the poems' central problems. The Greeks' journey in *Iliad* 1 resolves the danger of Apollo's plague, only to be contrasted

with Achilles' brooding anger, described immediately afterwards in 1.488–92. Telemachus' journey is a response to Odysseus' continuing absence and sets itself in contrast with Odysseus' immobile position on Ogygia, described in *Odyssey* 1.11–21. Further details link the *Posthomerica*'s journey to Pylos with Telemachus' travels in the *Odyssey*,[14] contrasting Odysseus in the *Posthomerica* with his son in the poem to come. The speedy ship taken by Odysseus and Diomedes (*Posthomerica* 6.98) corresponds to that asked for by Telemachus (*Odyssey* 2.212), as does the crew of twenty men (*Posthomerica* 6.100; *Odyssey* 2.212). Like Telemachus' journey in the *Odyssey*, Odysseus and Diomedes' journey to Scyros expands the geographical space discussed by the epic, connecting the poem's primary setting with new locations. The journey's outcome further evokes Telemachus' travels as Odysseus and Diomedes come to meet Neoptolemus and recognise him in 7.176–7 as 'similar to Achilles in his beautiful body' (Ἀχιλῆι δέμας περικαλλὲς ὁμοῖον, 177). Telemachus is recognised as taking on the form if not speech of his father by Athena as Mentes (*Odyssey* 1.206–9), by Nestor (3.123–5) and by Helen and Menelaus (4.141–50).

The description of the crewmen in *Posthomerica* 6.107–11 reinforces the difference between the role played by this Odyssean journey and those Odysseus ever fails to complete in the *Odyssey*. The crew are described as working like oxen or cattle (βόες, 6.107), labouring under the yoke. This is not necessarily a surprising image, but as we are minded to recall the *Odyssey* here, not least through Odysseus' character as well as the more detailed references, we remember the crucial obstacle to Odysseus' return home: his crew's death after eating the cattle of the Sun. This is the only event from the *apologoi* mentioned in the *Odyssey*'s proem, 1.8–9 (νήπιοι, οἳ κατὰ βοῦς Ὑπερίονος Ἡελίοιο / ἤσθιον). As Odysseus' crew work like βόες in the *Posthomerica*, they are transformed into figures whom we may contrast against Odysseus' crew in the later poem: at this moment they are loyal and provide no problem at all to the narrative's progression, leading it onwards rather than holding it back.

The crew are further described as skilled in rowing (ἴδμονες εἰρεσίης, 6.101), whether the winds set themselves against the ship (ὁπότ' ἀντιόωσιν ἄελλαι, 101) or whether the seas are smooth (101). In a subtle way, this foreshadows the problems which lie ahead for Odysseus, when he will have to travel through many stormy seas. This comment also foreshadows the threat which arises in the final lines of the *Posthomerica*. Rather than closing with Poseidon's earthquake and Troy's flooding, the poem remarks on the Greeks' journeys home, suggesting that 'each made it to another place, as a god guided each man, as many as escaped the miserable winds over the sea' (ἄλλη δ' ἄλλος ἵκανεν, ὅπῃ

---

[14] Cf. Vian (1966: 71), who notes further similarities between this passage and Telemachus' departure from Ithaca.

θεὸς ἦγεν ἕκαστον, / ὅσσοι ὑπὲρ πόντοιο λυγρὰς ὑπάλυξαν ἀέλλας, 14.657–8). As the sea journey to Scyros goes smoothly, it urges the poem onwards to an end when the seas change and Poseidon has become enraged. Francis Vian (1969: 156) suggests the poem's final passage 'is presented as a digression' ('est présenté comme une digression'), but we may recognise how it corresponds to the sea journeys of 6, 7 and 9, which Vian also notes the centrality of (1966: 47–9).[15]

The speed of the journey to Scyros is echoed by the journey back to Troy, described in 7.394–417: αἶψα δὲ δὴ μέγα λαῖτμα διήνυε ποντοπορεῦσα ('swiftly the sea-sailing ship cut across the great gulf', 397). This is matched by the journey to and from Lemnos in Book 9, as Odysseus and Diomedes journey to find Philoctetes.[16] Unlike the journey to Scyros, the outward journey (9.333–52) is not interrupted by any lengthy excursus, only a description of Lemnos' history in myth (338–52). The return journey (434–43) is similarly straightforward, and this time Athena even lends her aid to urge the ship onwards (436–7), recalling the goddess's aid to Telemachus in Odyssey 2.420–1. These sequences continue to foreshadow the difficulties Odysseus will face at sea, and the τέλος of the Posthomerica's plot in those troubles of the Odyssey. The journeys are beguilingly simple, and they make a mockery of the journeys Odysseus will take in his Homeric poem.

Throughout Odysseus and Diomedes' encounter with Philoctetes, the reader is struck by both the episode's urgency and the threat of the sea, and the poem's description of Odysseus' swift sea journeys yokes these ideas together, framing the episode on Lemnos as one pivotal to the Posthomerica's plot. This is not, however, a moment which turns the poem towards the fall of Troy, even as Philoctetes' return allows him to kill Paris and help push the Trojans back behind their walls. Instead, the poem looks towards the sea and the primary source of delay in the Odyssey. Against all expectations, Philoctetes is not upset to see Odysseus and Diomedes. His anger is described in 9.398–403, as he prepares to shoot at the two men with an arrow, but just as quickly Athena causes his anger to fade away (403–5). After Odysseus and Diomedes speak to Philoctetes in one short, reported speech of 410–22, we are reminded again that Philoctetes' anger has vanished and the three men take immediately (αἶψα, 426) to the ship. Philoctetes' wound is similarly healed in six lines, 9.461–6, with no delay to the narrative.

Rather than dwell on these key features in the myth of Philoctetes, his anger and his wound, the Posthomerica labours most to describe Philoctetes' state as he lies waiting in the cave. We are not concerned for him as a warrior, but as a mortal, threatened by the sea. On first arriving, Odysseus and Diomedes look

---

[15] Cf. Maciver (2012a: 21–4) on the thematic structure of the Posthomerica.
[16] See also Goldhill's chapter in this volume.

on him with awe (9.353–60), while the narrator first compares the hero to a
wild beast, then a cave, hollowed out by the sea (9.378–91):

οἳ δ' ὅτε δὴ Λήμνοιο <πέδον> κίον ἠδὲ καὶ **ἄντρον**
λαΐνεον τόθι κεῖτο πάϊς Ποίαντος ἀγαυοῦ,
δὴ τότ' ἄρά σφισι θάμβος ἐπήλυθεν, εὖτ' ἐσίδοντο   355
ἀνέρα λευγαλέῃσιν ἐπιστενάχοντ' ὀδύνῃσι
κεκλιμένον στυφελοῖο κατ' οὔδεος. ἀμφὶ δ' ἄρ' αὐτῷ
οἰωνῶν πτερὰ πολλὰ περὶ λεχέεσσι κέχυντο·
ἄλλα δέ οἱ συνέραπτο περὶ χροΐ, χείματος ἄλκαρ
λευγαλέου. (. . .)   360

. . .

Ὡς δ' ὅτ' ἐπὶ προβολῇσι πολυκλύστοιο θαλάσσης
πέτρην παιπαλόεσσαν ἀπειρεσίης ἁλὸς ἅλμη
δάμναθ' ὑποτμήγουσα μάλα στερεήν περ ἐοῦσαν,   380
τῆς δ' ἄρα θεινομένης ἀνέμῳ καὶ κύματι λάβρῳ
χηραμὰ κοιλαίνονται ὑποβρωθέντα θαλάσσῃ·
ὣς τοῦ ὑπίχνιον ἕλκος ἀέξετο πυθομένοιο
ἰοῦ ἄπο, στυφελοῖσι τόν οἱ ἐνομόρξατ' ὀδοῦσι
λυγρὸς ὕδρος, τόν φασιν ἀναλθέα τε στυγερόν τε   385
ἔμμεναι, ὁππότε μιν τέρσῃ περὶ χέρσον ἰόντα
ἠελίοιο μένος· τῷ καὶ μέγα φέρτατον ἄνδρα
τεῖρε δυσαλθήτοισιν ὑποδμηθέντ' ὀδύνῃσιν.
ἐκ δέ οἱ ἕλκεος αἰὲν ἐπὶ χθόνα λειβομένοιο
ἰχῶρος πεπάλακτο πέδον **πολυχανδέος ἄντρου,**   390
θαῦμα μέγ' ἀνθρώποισι καὶ ὕστερον ἐσσομένοισι.

Then they came to the land of Lemnos and the **rocky
cave** where the child of noble Poeas lay.
Right at that moment a feeling of awe struck them,
as they looked upon the man groaning over the pains that racked him,
lying on the rough ground. Beside him
many feathers of birds were piled up around the bed –
but they were also sewn together around his flesh, as a defence
against the bitter cold. (. . .)
. . .
**Just as when the wash of the boundless, ever-thrashing salt-sea
dashes against the crags, and cuts under their rugged stone
despite its great strength,
and the rock is struck by the wind, so that caves,
gnawed out by the sea, are hollowed by the furious surf –**
so the wound grew under his foot, because of the rotting poison

which the baneful water-snake infected him with
through its rough fangs, which they say is incurable
and deeply painful, when the **strength of the sun** weakens the creature,
moving over the sand; through this it even weakens the bravest man
by far, who is laid low by unshakeable pains.
Out of the seeping wound, ever more ichor fell to the earth
and stained the floor of the **wide-yawning cave**,
a great wonder for mortals and all who would be born later.

As at other moments of death or destruction in the *Posthomerica*, the sight of
Philoctetes brings a pause to the narrative. Diomedes and Odysseus are caught in
awe (θάμβος, 9.355), and the yawning cave, covered in the ichor of Philoctetes'
wound (389–90), becomes a great wonder, θαῦμα μέγα (391), for both the men
present and for those yet to come. In both instances, the cave itself may be read
as the object of wonder just as much as Philoctetes. Like those bodies which fall
to the ground and mingle with the blood and dust of the battlefield, Philoctetes
and the cave seem to be almost mingling together: the poet describes the great
many feathers (οἰωνῶν πτερὰ πολλὰ, 358) which not only surround the hero's
bed (358), but also (ἄλλα δέ, 359) cling to his skin (συνέραπτο περὶ χροΐ, 359).
The later simile makes it possible to directly assimilate Philoctetes and the cave
he is living in, and the sea buffets him to near disintegration just like Oenone
who melts like a forest in thaw (10.415–20).

There is a great deal of tension in the scene, as Philoctetes is caught
like an animal in a trap (9.364–6), and threatened by the raging sea. In the
simile of 377–82, the sea is not only πολυκλύστος ('many-surging', 'ever-
thrashing', 378), but boundless (ἀπειρεσίη, 379). It 'dashes against', 'breaks',
'tames' (δάμνατο, 380) the ragged rocks despite their great strength (μάλα
στερεήν περ ἐοῦσαν, 381), building on the image of Philoctetes as a beast
to mark the sea's power. These rocks are subdued and carved into hollows
(χηραμὰ, 382) by wind and a 'lashing wave' (κύματι λάβρῳ, 381), 'eaten up'
(ὑποβρωθέντα, 382) by this violent sea. In these lines we hear a clear fore-
echo of the storm which closes the poem, from 14.487–658, as Zeus accepts
Athena's supplication and Iris brings her message to the rocky, cave-ridden
island of Aeolia, home of the winds (14.474–7). This destroys the Achaeans'
ability to sail (497–504), leaving them at the mercy of the ἄελλαι (504) which
close the poem (658).[17]

Fore-echoes of the poem's end appear in similes throughout the *Posthomerica*'s opening books, framing the 'real' parts of each battle and the death
of the poem's heroes as steps towards the poem's end, even as they also provide moments of pause and reflection. This inverts the relationship we expect

[17] Carvounis (2007) discusses this episode in detail, though not as the poem's τέλος.

between simile – typically recognised as a moment of digression – and the narrative, but helps account for the narrator's extensive use of similes through-out the *Posthomerica*.[18] In Book 1, for example, Penthesileia's appearance is lik-ened to Zeus's lightning, in the moments before he brings the rain and winds (1.153–6), while the Greeks are described fleeing from her army of Amazons and falling like trees in a forest, battered by a storm (1.487–91). Memnon's army and the other Trojan allies rush from the gates like a swarm of locusts which nonetheless take on the form of swollen rainclouds (2.198–9), while his assault on the Greeks is described to be like a river driven to flood by storming rain (2.345–52). When Achilles is shot by Apollo, he falls like a tower struck by a whirlwind and an earthquake (3.63–5),[19] and the cries of the mourn-ing Achaeans flood the shores like great waves from the sea (3.508–11).[20] To honour Achilles, Zeus sends for Aeolus, who brings a storm to Troy in a clear fore-echo of events at the poem's end (3.694–718), and there is a faint echo again in Achilles' funeral games, as Epeius and Acamus fight like storm clouds in the wind (4.349–52). When the Trojans drag the Wooden Horse into their city, it creaks and complains like a ship dragged into the sea (12.427–32).

Throughout the *Posthomerica* the reader is caught in a tension between the fall of Troy, λύσις, the τέλος of the war, and the storm-driven seas, the τέλος of the poem. I discussed earlier how λύσις may come to stand for the forces of urgency in the *Iliad*, and the importance of the sea to the *Odyssey* scarcely needs rehearsing.[21] We should nonetheless remember how the sea not only thwarts Odysseus' return to Ithaca in the first half of the poem, but frames the *Odyssey*'s famously obscure τέλος. The prophecy of Teiresias, reported to the Phaeacians in 11.121–31 and then repeated to Penelope in 23.267–77, sug-gests that Odysseus will not be free from suffering until he finds the land of those men οἳ οὐκ ἴσασι θάλασσαν ('who know not of the sea', *Odyssey* 11.122; 23.269). Alex Purves (2010: 65–96) discusses this prophecy in detail as one which not only invites the Homeric audience to imagine Odysseus leaving

---

[18] Kneebone (2007) highlights the depth of meaning to be found in the *Posthomerica*'s similes, noting the long history of scholars' attention to these passages, and often their dismay (p. 285). Combellack (1968: 17), for example, remarks that 'Quintus was clearly impressed by the merits of the Homeric simile, since he sows them in his poem with a generosity that in places seems excessive.' Maciver (2012a: 125–92) discusses the issue of the *Posthomerica*'s similes at length.

[19] Vian (1963: 98, 169) notes how this develops the *Iliad*'s use of towers as similes for Echepolus, who dies like a crashing tower in *Iliad* 4.462, and Ajax's shield, which acts as a bastion in 11.485. In the *Posthomerica*, it is the description of the storm destroying the tower that Achilles is compared to which becomes significant.

[20] As Vian (1963: 115) suggests; cf. the description of *Iliad* 14.392–401, when the two armies come against each other. In the *Iliad*, however, the image of the sea is set against that of a forest fire and the wind through trees.

[21] Dougherty (2001), for example, discusses the power of the sea in the *Odyssey* and for the *Odyssey* at length. Cf. Purves (2010: 70–3).

the sea and his troubles behind, but the means of his κλέος and identity, the genre of epic itself. While the sea in the *Posthomerica* is drawn more closely to the problem of the *Odyssey*'s storms and Poseidon's wrath, rather than understood as a difficult space in itself, the poem's use of sea travel and the threat of storms makes use of the *Odyssey*'s structural tensions. The dangers of nature which Odysseus must leave behind become the bourne which the *Posthomerica*'s heroes cannot avoid, even as they are delayed by those forces which bring about Troy's fall.

CODA

We may understand the narratological forces of the *Posthomerica* as transmuted versions of those which structure the *Iliad* and *Odyssey*. These produce narrative tension in the poem and even provide for readerly pleasure. However, the question remains of what significance these transformations would have held for the poem's imperial readers. There is little space left for me to explore this issue in detail, but I would close by noting the continuities between the *Posthomerica*'s treatment of death and the sea – not least in the scene of Philoctetes' suffering – and more famous third-century interpretations of Homer. Porphyry's *On the Cave of the Nymphs* offers a commentary on *Odyssey* 13.102–12 which follows what was likely a more widespread understanding to read Odysseus' departure from the cave as an allegory for the soul's escape from the body.[22] This lends symbolic weight to the forces of the *Posthomerica*; the poem becomes increasingly evocative.

Two passages from Porphyry's dense discussion in particular colour our reading of Philoctetes as a mortal caught between life and death, between the desired pause of λύσις and the urgent threat of the sea. First, in section 9 of *On the Cave of the Nymphs*, Porphyry summarises his study of caves in general:

Ὅτι μὲν οὖν σύμβολον κόσμου τὰ ἄντρα καὶ τῶν ἐγκοσμίων δυνάμεων ἐτίθεντο οἱ θεολόγοι, διὰ τούτων δεδήλωται· ἤδη δὲ καὶ ὅτι τῆς νοητῆς οὐσίας εἴρηται, ἐκ διαφόρων μέντοι καὶ οὐ τῶν αὐτῶν ἐννοιῶν ὁρμώμενοι. **τοῦ μὲν γὰρ αἰσθητοῦ κόσμου διὰ τὸ σκοτεινὰ εἶναι τὰ ἄντρα καὶ πετρώδη καὶ δίυγρα, τοιοῦτον δ᾽ εἶναι τὸν κόσμον διὰ τὴν ὕλην ἐξ ἧς συνέστηκεν ὁ κόσμος, καὶ ἀντίτυπον καὶ ῥευστὸν ἐτίθεντο·** τοῦ δ᾽ αὖ νοητοῦ διὰ τὸ ἀφανὲς αἰσθήσει καὶ στερρὸν καὶ βέβαιον τῆς οὐσίας· οὕτωσὶ δὲ καὶ τῶν μερικῶν ἀφανῶν δυνάμεων, καὶ μᾶλλόν γε ἐπὶ τούτων τῶν

---

[22] On the history of this interpretation, see Lamberton (1986: 318–24). Cf. Lamberton's further discussion of the treatise (119–33); Pépin (1965). Johnson (2013: 265, 275–6) notes the continuities between *On the Cave of the Nymphs* and both Egyptian and Jewish theology.

ἐνύλων. κατὰ γὰρ τὸ αὐτοφυὲς τὸ τῶν ἄντρων καὶ νύχιον καὶ σκοτεινὸν καὶ πέτρινον ἐποιοῦντο τὰ σύμβολα.

So, the theologians suggested that caves are a symbol of the cosmos and the powers which structure it; this has been made clear by what I have said. But it has also already been observed that caves are a symbol of mental essence, though theologians are driven to this conclusion for other reasons and not the same ideas. **On the one hand, they suggested caves are a symbol of the cosmos as it may be perceived because they are dark, rocky and damp, and the cosmos is like this because of the matter which the cosmos is made out of, both solid and liquid.** But they are also symbols of thought as they resist observation, and as they are both unyielding and steadfast in essence. Thus they are symbols of both individual, invisible powers and, moreover, for these reasons, those with material form. For, in accordance with caves' self-creating nature, theologians used to derive symbols from their gloominess, their darkness, and their rockiness.

Caves are understood to be analogous with the cosmos, which on account of its material (ὕλη) is dark (σκοτεινά), damp (δίυγρα) and unstable (ῥευστόν). Later, in section 11, Porphyry explains that souls are attracted to such moisture on the mortal plane as one finds in caves, but eschew that moisture (and physicality, γένεσις) after death:

ἀνάγκη τοίνυν καὶ τὰς ψυχὰς ἤτοι σωματικὰς οὔσας ἢ ἀσωμάτους μέν, ἐφελκομένας δὲ σῶμα, καὶ μάλιστα τὰς μελλούσας καταδεῖσθαι εἴς τε αἷμα καὶ δίυγρα σώματα ῥέπειν πρὸς τὸ ὑγρὸν καὶ σωματοῦσθαι ὑγρανθείσας. διὸ καὶ χολῆς καὶ αἵματος ἐκχύσει προτρέπεσθαι τὰς τῶν τεθνηκότων, καὶ τάς γε φιλοσωμάτους ὑγρὸν τὸ πνεῦμα ἐφελκομένας παχύνειν τοῦτο ὡς νέφος· ὑγρὸν γὰρ ἐν ἀέρι παχυνθὲν νέφος συνίσταται· παχυνθέντος δ' ἐν αὐταῖς τοῦ πνεύματος ὑγροῦ πλεονασμῷ ὁρατὰς γίνεσθαι. καὶ ἐκ τῶν τοιούτων αἷ συναντῶσί τισι κατὰ φαντασίαν χρώζουσαι τὸ πνεῦμα εἰδώλων ἐμφάσεις, αἱ μέντοι καθαραὶ γενέσεως ἀπότροποι.

Therefore, it is also necessary for souls – whether they are embodied or disembodied, though nonetheless connected to a body, and especially those destined to be bound to blood and otherwise liquid bodies – to turn towards moisture and to be embodied as they are moistened. For this reason, by the release of bile and blood, the souls of the dead are forced out, and those souls eager for a body are fattened as they take on the moist air, just like a cloud. For a moist cloud clumps together once it has been fattened in the air, and souls become visible when the air within them is fattened by an excess of moisture. As a consequence of this process, the images of those spirits who appear before people, just as they imagine, clinging to the air, which are pure nonetheless as they turn away from physicality – they also become visible.

It is due to the moistening of souls by the body, so Porphyry suggests, that corpses release their liquid, in particular bile (χολή) and blood (αἷμα) as the soul leaves. In the cave on Lemnos, described as both rocky (λαῖνεον, *Posthomerica* 9.353) and cold if not damp enough for Philoctetes to require his covering of feathers (359–60), the reader is invited to observe how the environment interacts with both the moisture of Philoctetes' body and the threat of the sea. This is seen to be a marvellous phenomenon, as I have already noted (389–91), in the manner of other deaths throughout the *Posthomerica* and as one would expect from the moment of the soul's exodus. In particular, we might compare Oenone's death in Book 10, as she not only melts like a forest in a spring, as I noted above (10.415–22), but like wax melting in the heat of a candle (434) before the fire reduces her and Paris' corpse to one set of ashes (μιῇ δ' ὑποκάββαλε τέφρῃ, 484). The herdsmen who see this look on the phenomenon in awe (ἐθάμβεον, 479). Even the water-snake, the cause of Philoctetes' suffering, is described to bite more fiercely when it has been struck by the heat of the sun (9.385–7), a reminder of the conflict between heat, light and those forces of the wet, physical world.

Porphyry's discussion of souls underscores the wonder felt by those looking on Philoctetes after he is healed by Podaleirius in 9.460–88. Philoctetes is compared to an ἄρουρα, 'a cultivated field' (473), which has wilted on account of a heavy storm's flooding rain (ἥν τε πάρος φθινύθουσαν ἐπέκλυσε χείματος αἰνοῦ / ὄμβρος ἐπιβρίσας, 474–5) before it is revived by winds (ἀνέμοισι, 475). The Greeks cannot stop looking at him in awe, like a man who has risen from the dead (Ἀργεῖοι δ' ὁρόωντες ἅτ' ἐκ θανάτου ἀνιόντα / ἀνέρα θαυμάζεσκον, 480–1). This resurrection Philoctetes achieves recalls the experience of the soul after death, freed from the cave and its attendant moisture, and it is what allows him to call for Troy's own λύσις at the end of Book 9, insisting that no one should stay among the ships 'before we have dissolved the famous walls of well-fortified Troy' (πάρος κλυτὰ τείχεα λῦσαι / Τροίης εὐπύργοιο, 538–9), which I discussed above. It is his transformation over the course of Book 9 which draws the narrative back towards Troy's destruction, away (temporarily) from the destructive force of the sea.

Throughout *On the Cave of the Nymphs*, there is awareness of λύσις as the process of death, though Porphyry is typically more concerned with the material state of souls. Death (θάνατος) is described as λυσίπονος ('toil-relieving') in section 18, while section 25 describes the power of the warm South Wind to melt the soul away from the body, an action which is described twice through the verb διαλύειν. This draws on a Platonic meaning of λύσις, which dates back to the *Phaedo*. *Phaedo* 67d in particular sees Socrates ask, 'So is this what we call death, the release (λύσις) and separation (χωρισμός) of the soul from the body (ψυχῆς ἀπὸ σώματος)?' As Jonathan Zecher (2015: 70–2) discusses, this idea was echoed by philosophers well into the Common Era, and the definition was generally accepted even though its precise meaning remained less than clear. As moments of λύσις become moments of reflection in the *Posthomerica*, rather than moments of urgency, the poem appeals to a Neoplatonic reader who is concerned more by the threat of mortal suffering rather than the escape of souls after death. The death of heroes and the fall of Troy is an attractive, marvellous diversion from the slings and arrows of continuing mortal existence, which nonetheless remains a threat throughout the *Posthomerica* and overwhelms the poem at its close.

CHAPTER 15

'Why So Serious?' The Ambivalence of Joy and Laughter in the *Iliad*, *Odyssey* and *Posthomerica*

Arnold Bärtschi

CONTRASTING EFFECTS OF EPIC JOY AND LAUGHTER

Joy is one of the universal 'basic emotions' and plays a pivotal role in human interaction. The same holds true regarding its various types of physical manifestations like laughter and smile.[1] They can either bring pain or pleasure (λύπη καὶ ἡδονή) depending on the context and the target at which they are directed. For this reason, their intentional manipulation can have an extremely precarious impact on members of an ancient Greek society that is concerned with public shame to a high degree.[2] Therefore, joy and laughter have been an integral part of the characterisation of literary characters since the Homeric poems. One of the most famous depictions of the proverbial 'Homeric laughter' is the banquet scene at *Il.* 1.595–9 where a hobbling Hephaistos is ridiculed by his fellow gods. Since they openly laugh at the expense of another individual (ἄσβεστος (. . .) γέλως, 1.598), their ridicule has the devaluating effect of derision. This negative manifestation of joy, however, stands in stark contrast to the subtle and heartfelt smile of Hera (μείδησεν, 1.595; μειδήσασα, 1.596) recognising her son's well-meant attempt to dispense the tension in the wake of her dispute with Zeus.[3]

[1] On the universality of joy, cf. Konstan (2006: 3–40), who interprets the characteristics of χαρά in Arist. *EN* 2.1105b22 and *De an.* 403a18 and compares them to modern definitions of 'basic emotions'. On ancient emotions, cf. Desclos (2000); LaCourse Munteanu (2011); Sanders and Johncock (2016); the work of the research network 'Emotions through Time: From Antiquity to Byzantium (ETT)' based at the University of Edinburgh.

[2] Cf. Arist. *Rh.* 2.1.1378a19–22 (ed. Ross 1959). On the social function of joy and laughter, cf. Halliwell (1991: 279–80; 2004; 2008: 5–7).

[3] On the ridicule of Hephaistos, cf. e.g. Willcock (1978: 196) *ad* 599; Kirk (1985: 112–14) *ad loc.*; Collobert (2000: 134–8); Pulleyn (2000: 272) *ad* 595–6; Halliwell (2008: 58–63); Ratinaud-Lachkar (2010: 154–5).

This brief example perfectly illustrates the necessity of a context-sensitive interpretation of epic joy and laughter, especially since this aspect has not yet received scholarly attention in a systematic manner.[4] This particularly applies to a precise distinction between positive and negative forms of joy (joy vs *Schadenfreude*) and its physical manifestations (laughter or exultation vs derision and smile vs sneer).[5] This categorisation depends on whether they have a beneficial or disadvantageous effect on their target.[6] A systematic analysis of Homer's *Iliad*, *Odyssey* and Quintus of Smyrna's *Posthomerica* (*PH*) not only allows us to compare their use of vocabulary and emphasis on positive vs negative emotions, but also to examine the specific functionalisation of joy and laughter in each poem.[7]

Based on these preliminary considerations and a complete collection of reference material, this chapter has a threefold aim.[8] First, a brief comparative overview will present the lexical similarities and characteristics of the poems. Second, an exemplary contextualisation of selected expressions within their narrative frame of the poems will illuminate their varying functions in the narrative. Throughout this chapter, a special focus lies on the transforming process recognisable in the *PH*. Third, the examination of three selected Posthomeric passages will show their character as serious parodies of Homeric scenes whose comic effect is reversed into their opposite.[9] This kind of close but innovative

---

[4] On Homeric joy and laughter, cf. Latacz (1966); Halliwell (2008: 51–99). On their sinister effects, cf. Hewitt (1928); Pisanello (1999).

[5] To some extent, this analysis includes related terms denoting encouragement, applause, consent, boast or rebuke, but only if they have a joyous colouring. The same holds true for the terms εὐφροσύνη, εὔφρων, χαρίεις, χαρίζομαι, χάρις. On the risk of overlap between these lexical fields, cf. Latacz (1966: 172–3, 232–3). By following Latacz (1966: 126–7), I omit the terms χαροπός and χάρμη. However, in contrast to Latacz (1966: 160, 217–18, 231–2), this analysis includes the terms χαίρω, γαίων, τέρπομαι, ἰαίνομαι.

[6] This distinction is based on the classification of emotions according to Ortony, Clore and Collins (1988: 15–33). Cf. also Halliwell (1991; 2008: 19–38), who distinguishes between 'playful' and 'consequential' laughter. On the direction of emotions, cf. Pellizer (2000). Aspects regarding humour and comic effect, however, cannot be considered.

[7] Genette's concept of hypertextuality, which stresses the transformative process between hypotext and hypertext, forms the basis of this comparative examination; cf. Genette (1997: 5–10). Genette himself uses the *PH* as an example to illustrate the hypertextual subgenre 'serious imitation' but devaluates it as a work of epigonism; cf. Genette (1997: 242–4). On intertextuality in the *PH*, cf. Vian (1959a); Maciver (2012a); U. Gärtner (2017); Scheijnen (2018).

[8] Due to its quantity, the complete collection of material will be available on the following website as soon as the collective volume has been published: https://rub.academia.edu/ArnoldBärtschi. Because the collection of material heavily relies on the use of the *TLG*, the Greek texts follow the respective text editions of Allen (²1919) for the *Odyssey*; Allen (²1920) for the *Iliad*; Vian (1963, -66, -69) for the *PH*. Translations follow Rieu (2003) for the *Iliad*; James (2004) for the *PH*.

[9] The adjective 'Posthomeric' is used to denote affiliation with the poem *PH*. On literary parody, cf. Freund (1981: 14–15, 27–8), who distinguishes between purely comic 'trivial' and 'serious' parody, which he further subdivides into 'total' and 'instrumental' parody. While 'total'

reshaping of the Homeric tradition evokes a unique effect that permeates the *PH* and is firmly linked with the rather serious conception of its literary world, which is reflected by the citation in the title.[10]

EXPRESSING JOY AND ITS PHYSICAL MANIFESTATIONS WITH WORDS

Table 15.1 in the Appendix shows that all three poems make use of a wide array of verbs, nouns, adjectives and adverbs denoting joy. While the *Iliad* contains the smallest number of passages representing joy in a positive way (164x) and the *Odyssey* the largest number of passages (220x), the *PH* occupies the middle ground (190x). However, it shows the highest density of expressions due to its minor number of verses compared to the Homeric poems. The most common vocabulary to denote these emotions is basically shared by all three poems (e.g. γηθέω, εὐφραίνω, ἰαίνομαι, τέρπομαι, χαίρω). Preferences for active or medio-passive conjugation regarding this basic vocabulary are evident but do not create special meaning apart from clarifying the direction of the emotion. The *PH* overall shows a quantitative preference for these basic terms, while the Homeric poems make use of a greater range of exclusive expressions (ἀσπάσιος, ἄσμενος, γηθοσύνη, εὐφραίνω, εὔφρων, ἦδος, τερπικέραυνος, χαρίεις, χαρίζομαι). Finally, the *PH* features more compound verbs (ἀμφιγάνυμαι, ἐπιγηθέω, ἐπικαγχαλάω, ἐπιτέρπω) in contrast to the simplex forms predominant in the Homeric poems. This relatively homogeneous use of vocabulary with a positive effect regarding the targets contrasts with the amount of widely varying passages representing *Schadenfreude*, which is characterised by a disadvantageous effect on its targets. In contrast to the *Odyssey* (4x) and the *Iliad* (23x), the *PH* (51x) contains significantly more instances of this negative emotion. However, it is striking that no term is reserved for this specific form of joy exclusively, which underlines the need to carefully contextualise each occurrence.

Table 15.2 in the Appendix, which lists physical manifestations of joy with positive and negative effects, allows us to draw different conclusions. In contrast to Table 15.1, terms concerning smiles and laughter show a smaller range

---

parody' criticises its hypotext, 'instrumental parody' uses the parodic form only to convey an independent message. The examination of parodic transformation consists of the following steps: recognising the parodied hypotext, identifying the modification procedure as well as its scope and determining the resulting effect. On successful applications of Freund's parodic concept to ancient texts, cf. Ax (1984; 1991; 1993).

[10] The opening citation is taken from the movie *The Dark Knight*, TC 00:29:32–5 (Director: Christopher Nolan, GB/US 2008, Warner Bros. Pictures) and reflects the twisted and tragicomic world view of the villain Joker.

and are mostly limited to certain verbs (e.g. γελάω, μειδάω, ἐπίαχω). However, certain verbs also denoting joy (e.g. ἀγάλλομαι, καγχαλάω) reappear in this list. To pinpoint the exact meaning of other verbs is especially difficult because they can also refer to unspecific forms of inarticulate clamour (ἐπίαχω, καγχαλάω) and thus heavily rely on contextualisation.[11] Some terms, however, are exclusively used for derision (γέλοιος, γέλως, ἐπιμειδάω, ἐπιγελάω, ἐπικαγχαλάω, ἐπὶ μακρὸν αὖω, ἐφεψιάομαι, καθεψιάομαι, λωβεύω) and the verb κερτομέω with its derivations is of special importance (ἐπικερτομέω, κερτομία, κερτόμιος, φιλοκέρτομος).[12] While the *Odyssey* slightly favours positive laughter (*Iliad*: 5x; *Odyssey*: 8x; *PH*: 3x) and the *Iliad* positive smiles (18x; 8x; 6x), the *Iliad* as well as the *PH* contain notably more instances of positive exultation (12x; 4x; 18x).[13] Although sneers (2x; 0x; 1x) carry almost no weight, derision clearly overshadows its positive counterpart (45x; 35x; 23x). Since these differences stem from the varying narrative contexts of their respective poems, separate interpretations will subsequently illuminate the following aspects: first, the high number of smiles in the *Iliad* (18x, below, pp. 270–2). Second, the superior number of passages featuring derision in the *Iliad* (46x) and the *Odyssey* (35x) compared to the *PH* (23x, below, pp. 272–3). Third, the numerous manifestations of exultation in the *PH* (18x) in combination with the predominance of Posthomeric *Schadenfreude* (51x, below pp. 273–5).

DIVINE LAUGHTER IN DECLINE

In the *Iliad* and, to a smaller degree, in the *Odyssey*, positive smiles and laughter foremost characterise the blessed carefreeness of the gods.[14] This becomes apparent especially in the established epithets φιλομμειδής (Aphrodite), τερπικέραυνος (Zeus) and τερψίμβροτος (Helios).[15] 'Burlesque' scenes like the harmless and even playful theomachy (*Il.* 20.3–74; 21.385–513), the mockery of Hephaistos the cupbearer (*Il.* 1.595–9) as well as the ridicule of Ares and

---

[11] Cf. Halliwell (1991: 284).
[12] On the complex semantics of this word family, cf. Clarke (2001).
[13] On the nuances of these terms in general, cf. Lopez Eire (2000).
[14] Regarding laughter, cf. *Il.* 15.101; 19.362; 21.508. Regarding smiles, cf. *Il.* 1.595; 1.596; 5.426; 8.38; 14.222; 14.223; 15.047; *Od.* 5.180; 13.287. On divine blessedness, its limitations and relation to the mortal realm, cf. Burkert (1960: 139–41); Clarke (1969: 249); Levine (1982b); Macleod (1982: 3–4); Burkert (1983: 352–6); Garvie (1994: 293–5) *ad* 266–369; Collobert (2000: 140–1); Lopez Eire (2000: 32–3); Halliwell (2008: 58–69).
[15] Cf. φιλομμειδής at *Il.* 3.422; 4.10; 5.375; 14.211; 20.40; *Od.* 8.362. Cf. τερπικέραυνος at *Il.* 1.419; 2.478; 2.781; 8.2; 11.773; 12.252; 16.323; 24.529; *Od.* 7.164; 7.180; 14.268; 17.437; 19.365; 20.75; 24.24. Cf. τερψίμβροτος at *Od.* 12.269; 12.274.

Aphrodite (*Od.* 8.266–369) underline this depiction of the Homeric gods.[16] This jovial interaction between Homeric gods, however, is not at all lacking the negative effects of derision and *Schadenfreude*.[17] In the latter scene, for example, the inconsequential derision of the assembled gods is directed at the adulterers and, at the same time, the cheated Hephaistos himself (ἄσβεστος (. . .) γέλως, 8.326) and renewed by a joking Hermes (8.339–43). However, the passage also contains a counterpoint in Poseidon, who vehemently opposes this kind of behaviour and prepares the eventual reconciliation of the gods in conflict (8.344–5).[18]

Meanwhile, the *PH* draws a completely different picture of divine joy and laughter. Here, the Olympian gods are systematically marginalised and almost completely overshadowed by divine personifications of aspects of war and fate.[19] Consequently, they get almost no opportunity to smile and laugh in a positive and carefree manner and thus lose their characterisation as blessed and divine beings.[20] In fact, their joyous Homeric nature is downright stolen and transformed in a negative way by personifications of war, who enjoy derision and *Schadenfreude* throughout the poem.[21]

In contrast to the 'burlesque' ridicule among the Homeric gods themselves, mortal men are the primary target of divine *Schadenfreude* and derision in the *PH*. Moreover, the number of Posthomeric instances clearly outweighs the Homeric usage. Some of the Olympian gods behave in much the same manner as personifications of war, especially when the destruction of Troy is clearly impending.[22] Consequently, the Posthomeric gods adapt to the behaviour of lesser divine personifications and forfeit their blessed grandeur, which

---

[16] On the 'burlesque' divine, cf. Burkert (1960; 1983: 351–67); Muth (1992: 8–39); Ballabriga (2000); Halliwell (2008: 78–80).

[17] Regarding derision, cf. *Il.* 1.599 (Olympian gods); 4.6 (Zeus, two terms); 5.419 (Zeus); 21.389 (Zeus); 21.408 (Athene); 21.409 (Athene); 21.427 (Athene); 21.508 (Zeus); 21.519 (Olympian gods); *Od.* 8.326 (Olympian gods); 8.343 (Olympian gods); 8.344 (Poseidon). Regarding *Schadenfreude*, cf. *Il.* 5.760 (Apollon and Aphrodite); 7.61 (Apollon and Athene); 11.73 (Eris); 20.23 (Zeus); 21.390 (Zeus); 21.423 (Athene).

[18] On the ridicule of Ares and Aphrodite, cf. Burkert (1960); Heubeck, West and Hainsworth (1988: 369–70) *ad loc.*; Brown (1989); Muth (1992: 17–20); Garvie (1994: 293–308) *ad loc.*; Pisanello (1999: 97–100); Collobert (2000: 134–8); Halliwell (2008: 78–84).

[19] Cf. Paschal (1904: 40–2); Vian (1963: xiv–xvii); Wenglinsky (1999: 80–5; 2002); Gärtner (2007; 2014); Bär (2016). Cf. also the chapter of Maciver in this volume.

[20] Regarding laughter, cf. Q.S. 2.210 (Helios); 6.3 (Gaia and Aither). Regarding smiles, cf. 5.72 (Aphrodite); 5.88 (Poseidon).

[21] Regarding derision, cf. Q.S. 1.191 (Aisa); 11.152 (Ares); 12.437 (Enyo). Regarding *Schadenfreude*, cf. Q.S. 2.486 (Olethros); 8.12 (Keres); 8.191 (Eris); 8.324 (Keres and Moros); 8.425 (Enyo); 9.146 (Keres); 11.161 (Eris); 13.126 (Keres).

[22] Regarding divine *Schadenfreude* directed at mortal enemies, cf. Q.S. 2.513 (Olympian gods); 3.136 (pro-Trojan gods); 3.608 (Eos); 3.665 (Eos); 4.46 (pro-Trojan gods); 10.334 (Hera); 11.168 (Apollon); 11.178 (Apollon); 13.418 (Hera and Athene); 14.547 (Athene); 14.629 (Athene).

is why they seem to be transformed into malevolent gods of destruction.[23] This change of their behaviour reaches its climax when Athene destroys the Greek fleet at the end of the poem (Q.S. 14.419–631) and Poseidon, with the help of Zeus, washes away the wall of the abandoned military camp of the Greeks (Q.S. 14.632–55).[24] This drastic change in the depiction of the representatives of the divine realm hints at a shift concerning the overall atmosphere of the *PH* compared to the Homeric poems.

DERIDING OPPONENTS ON THE BATTLEFIELD

This Posthomeric transformation of divine joy and laughter also becomes apparent in the depiction of the mortal realm itself and the battlefield in particular. In the *Iliad* and *PH* alike, it forms the main setting as well as the dominant narrative context of derision. Trash talk, taunts and ridicule before and after martial encounters constitute an important aspect of heroic warfare and are as much part of the fight between two warriors as the duel itself.[25] But while Homeric warriors prefer open derision as an external expression of malevolence (45x) compared to the internal emotional process of *Schadenfreude* (23x), the opposite holds true for Posthomeric warriors, who give vent to *Schadenfreude* more often (51x) than to derision (23x).

This Posthomeric preference for the more 'decent' emotion *Schadenfreude* could either be based on the problematic nature of derision in Greek society in general or be explained by specific intertextual influence of the *Odyssey*.[26] There, derision is mainly related to the hubristic behaviour of the suitors and their allies, which leads to their inevitable doom and thus serves as an extremely negative foil.[27] Moreover, such ill conduct is explicitly rejected twice in the *Odyssey*: first, by Odysseus, who dissuades the nurse Eurykleia when she is about to rejoice at the sight of the dead suitors (*Od.* 22.409–12); second, by Penelopeia, who similarly warns Eurykleia against premature *Schadenfreude* (23.59). The almost exclusive restriction of positive forms of

---

[23] However, cf. Wenglinsky (1999: 80–5; 2002), who stresses the explicit problematisation of the destructive behaviour of the gods.

[24] James (2004: 632–55); Carvounis (2007); Scheijnen (2018: 345–58); Bärtschi (2019: 342–54); Carvounis (2019: 186–283).

[25] Cf. Hewitt (1928: 437–8); Parks (1990); Halliwell (2008: 25–30, 53–8).

[26] On the destructive effects of aischrology in Greek society, cf. Halliwell (1991: 285–9); Lowry (1991: 10–57); Halliwell (2004; 2008: 22–38).

[27] On the deriding behaviour of the suitors, cf. *Od.* 2.323; 16.087; 16.354; 18.34–5; 18.40; 18.100; 18.111; 18.350 (two terms); 19.370; 19.372; 20.177; 20.263; 20.346; 20.347; 20.358; 20.374; 20.390; 21.376. Cf. also Hewitt (1928: 441–3); Levine (1980; 1982a; 1982b: 97–100); Colakis (1986); Levine (1987); Guidorizzi (1997); Halliwell (2008: 86–98).

joy and laughter to Odysseus and his allies further stresses his rejection of negative emotions.[28]

Since derision is dismissed as the behaviour of hubristic people in such an explicit manner in the *Odyssey*, it seems to be ill-suited for characterising heroes in the *PH* as well, whose ideals are, above all, aimed at moderation and inner balance. Among others, Nestor is depicted several times as the ideal paradigm of such an even-tempered hero (Q.S. 3.1–9; 3.514–25; 5.599–612a; 7.16–95).[29] Despite the dissuasive foil of the suitors of the *Odyssey* and the Posthomeric ideal, the Posthomeric heroes are nevertheless extremely prone to *Schadenfreude*, which gives them negative traits of character. As a consequence, this discrepancy begs the question if the heroic ideals of moderation personified by Nestor are really of notable relevance to the literary world of the *PH*.

GREEK EXULTATION AND TROJAN SCHADENFREUDE

This issue is related to the numerous passages featuring exultation in the *PH*, which provides insight into the overall Posthomeric reworking of the Homeric representations of joy and its physical expressions. Most instances of exultation in the *PH* are manifestations of universal joy of the Greek army or single Greek heroes (11x). In particular, they appear in the context of the funeral games in honour of Achilles and the capture of Troy.[30] In contrast, the Trojan army and heroes only rarely exult (3x).[31] This significant imbalance is directly linked with victory and success among the two war parties and illustrates the devastating course of the war from a Trojan perspective. Although the Greeks lose their champions Achilles and Aias, they later gain Philoktetes and Neoptolemos as new allies. The Trojans, however, lose their newly arrived champions Penthesileia, Memnon and Eurypylos one after another without being able to permanently replace them.[32]

Considering this one-sided exultation reserved for the Greeks, it is surprising that the exact opposite is the case regarding the representation of *Schadenfreude*. The Trojans and single Trojan heroes display this negative emotion

---

[28] On positive instances of laughter in the *Odyssey*, cf. Stanford ([2]1971: 387–8) *ad loc.*; Levine (1982b: 97–100; 1983); Colakis (1986: 138–40); Russo, Fernández-Galiano and Heubeck (1992: 290–1, 318–19) *ad loc.*; Hoffer (1995); Lateiner (2005); Halliwell (2008: 86–97); Westra (2010: 146–7).

[29] On this Posthomeric ideal of heroism, cf. Mansur (1940: 37–9); Vian (1963: xxxv–xxxvii); García Romero (1989b; 1990); Maciver (2007); Boyten (2010); Maciver (2012a: 66–86; 103–19); Langella (2016); Scheijnen (2018).

[30] Cf. Q.S. 4.198 (Greeks); 4.460 (Aias); 4.585 (Agamemnon); 7.353 (Neoptolemos); 7.688 (Agamemnon); 8.39 (Greeks); 9.527 (Myrmidons); 11.386 (Agamemnon and Menelaos); 14.85 (Greeks); 14.232 (Greeks); 14.329 (Greeks).

[31] Cf. Q.S. 1.161 (Penthesileia); 1.166 (Penthesileia); 10.45 (Trojans).

[32] Cf. Jahn (2009: 91–3).

more often (16x)[33] than their Greek adversaries (8x).[34] Moreover, it is either focused on characters like Penthesileia and Memnon, who show this negative emotion shortly before they die, or reserved for the Trojan collective in the face of the death of Achilles. In the aftermath of his fall at Q.S. 3.174–9, Trojan *Schadenfreude* is underlined 11x in 750 lines, which is additionally emphasised by derision of Trojans and pro-Trojan gods.[35] In the light of the inevitable doom of Troy and its inhabitants, this cumulative display of negative feelings evokes an effect of tragic irony.

Furthermore, this emphasis on destructive emotions is underlined by frequent juxtapositions of the reactions of both war parties to the same event. While the death of Achilles, for example, delights the Trojans and their divine helpers, the shock and grief of the Greeks resulting from this loss is explicitly set against Trojan malevolence (Q.S. 3.399–400): τοῖος ἄρ᾽ Αἰακίδης δηΐων ἐπικάππεσε γαίῃ, / χάρμα φέρων Τρώεσσι, γόον δ᾽ ἀλίαστον Ἀχαιοῖς ('Such was Achilles when he fell in the land of his foes, / Bringing joy to Trojans but endless grief to Achaians').[36] This technique of immediate contrast between joy and grief is already present in the Homeric poems, especially at Il. 16.599a–601, where the Greek grief due to the death of Bathykles immediately contrasts the joy of the Trojans:[37] πυκινὸν δ᾽ ἄχος ἔλλαβ᾽ Ἀχαιούς, / ὡς ἔπεσ᾽ ἐσθλὸς ἀνήρ· μέγα δὲ Τρῶες κεχάροντο. / στὰν δ᾽ ἀμφ᾽ αὐτὸν ἰόντες ἀολλέες ('The loss of this brave man was a heavy blow to the Greeks; but the Trojans were delighted and massed in numbers round Glaucus'). However, this narrative technique, which illustrates just how close joy and grief are depending on the perspective, is used much more frequently in the *PH*.[38] This has an equalising effect

---

[33] Cf. Q.S. 1.395 (Penthesileia); 1.484 (Trojans); 2.357 (Memnon); 2.378 (Memnon's companions); 3.187 (Paris); 3.200 (Trojan women); 3.208 (Priamos and the Trojan elders); 3.400 (Trojans); 3.496 (Trojans); 3.609 (Axios and Priamos' family); 4.17 (Trojans); 4.21 (Trojans); 4.32 (many a Trojan); 4.47 (Trojans); 6.648 (Trojans); 11.336 (Trojans).

[34] Cf. Q.S. 1.747 (Greeks); 4.207 (Aias); 5.146 (winner of the ὅπλων κρίσις); 5.321 (Odysseus); 8.336 (Neoptolemos); 10.206 (Philoktetes); 13.83 (Greeks); 13.358 (Menelaos).

[35] Regarding *Schadenfreude*, cf. Q.S. 3.136 (pro-Trojan gods); 3.608 (Eos); 3.665 (Eos). Regarding derision, cf. Q.S. 3.136 (pro-Trojan gods); 3.398 (Leto); 4.46 (pro-Trojan gods). Cf. 4.19 (many a Trojan). Cf. also Bärtschi (2019: 307–8).

[36] Cf. similarly Q.S. 3.135–8; 3.493–7; 3.665–71; 4.13–19; 4.43–7.

[37] On contrasting reactions, cf. Il. 2.266a–270; 3.41–5; 6.484; 7.214–16 (two instances); 13.344; 15.101b–103a; 16.599a–601; 17.472b–473; 18.130–3; 18.230–4a; 18.834b–835a; 21.45–8; 23.342–3a; Od. 8.538; 15.400–1; 17.530–8 (two instances); 19.471a; 19.513; 20.82; 20.301a–302b; 21.57; 21.105 (two instances); 22.411–12 (two instances); 23.59–61 (two instances). Cf. also 2.268–70 (beating of Thersites); 7.214–15 (swaggering Aias); 17.471–2 (death of Patroklos). Cf. also Lavigne (2008: 121–3).

[38] Cf. Q.S. 1.62; 1.72–3; 1.84–5a; 1.373–5; 1.391–3a; 1.484b–485b; 1.739–40; 2.3–5a (two instances); 2.19–20; 2.377b–378; 2.493–4; 2.512b–513; 2.632–3 (two instances); 3.135–7a; 3.400–1; 3.476b–482a; 3.495–7; 3.665–8a; 4.13–19 (two instances); 4.43b–47; 5.145–8a; 5.321; 5.652b; 6.298–300a; 7.327; 7.461–2; 7.632–6 (four instances); 7.724–5a; 8.195–6a; 9.57–9;

on the perception of both war parties, which forestalls a one-sided reading of the *PH* as either pro-Greek or pro-Trojan.[39] On the one hand, this results in alternating sympathies towards Greeks and Trojans alike. On the other hand, this seemingly equal depiction does not reduce the problematic characterisation of the Posthomeric heroes displaying negative emotions and expressions more excessively than their Homeric counterparts.

This holds true even more because of the explicit propagation of heroic ideals embodied in Posthomeric champions like Nestor, who functions as a contrastive foil. For this reason, the heroes of the *PH* in general are characterised more like men driven by destructive emotions than moderate consideration. Also, this undermining depiction of the Posthomeric heroes prepares and supports Athene's complaints at the end of the poem when she asks Zeus for permission to destroy the Greek fleet because of the universal depravity of mankind (Q.S. 14.427–42). Intertextual allusions to Hesiod's succession of races underline the validity of her argument. Zeus sanctions this plan by agreeing verbally (Q.S. 14.443–8) and transferring his lightning, the symbol of his sovereignty, to his daughter (Q.S. 14.449–50). In retrospect, the unfavourable depiction of the Posthomeric heroes earlier in the poem prefigures their eventual doom at the hands of the gods that leads to the end of the heroic age.[40]

TREACHEROUS AND AMBIVALENT JOY

This inevitable fate of the Posthomeric heroes is prepared by three additional narrative techniques: first, the depiction of treacherous joy, second, the portrayal of ambivalent joy, and, third, the use of serious parodies of Homeric scenes featuring laughter and derision. In the light of the impending destruction of Troy, Trojan *Schadenfreude* has a distinctly tragic effect. However, the same holds true regarding the individual fates of specific heroes fighting on behalf of Troy, namely Penthesileia, Memnon and Eurypylos. Each of their arrivals at Troy are met with exuberant joy highlighted by several similes;[41]

9.183; 11.335b–336a; 12.356–7; 12.544–5; 12.552; 12.576–8a; 13.383–4; 14.181b–182; 14.397b–399; 14.407b–409a; 14.541; 14.616a; 14.628b–631. Cf. also Bärtschi (2019: 193–4, 208–9, 272–3, 299, 307).

[39] On an overall balanced portrayal of Greeks and Trojans, cf. Stoevesandt's (2004) examination of the *Iliad*; Jahn's (2009) analysis of the depiction of fear and flight in the battles of the *PH*.

[40] On Athene's intervention and the end of the *PH*, cf. Wenglinsky (2002: 183–4); Carvounis (2007); Bär (2016: 225–6); Scheijnen (2018: 346–55); Bärtschi (2019: 185–254, 351–2); Carvounis (2019: 186–283).

[41] On Penthesileia, cf. Q.S. 1.62; 1.69; 1.72; 1.75; 1.80; 1.84; 1.90. On Memnon, cf. Q.S. 2.103; 2.106; 2.125. On Eurypylos, cf. Q.S. 6.124; 6.127; 6.128; 6.129–30; 6.295; 6.298. On the similes, cf. Q.S. 1.63–72; 1.76–83; 2.103–6; 6.125–8. Cf. also Bärtschi (2019: 268–70).

however, the inclusion of intertextual and proleptic hints ensures that these emotions are marked as false hopes implicitly and explicitly.[42]

The entrance of Penthesileia right at the beginning of the poem is of particular importance because the hope she symbolises for the Trojans weighs all the heavier considering their desperate prospects after the death of Hektor that form the starting point of the poem (Q.S. 1.1–17).[43] Her fate thus becomes paradigmatic for all external allies of Troy who follow in her footsteps. Of course, the educated reader knows from the beginning that Penthesileia will die at the hands of Achilles, but her doom is stressed several times throughout Book 1, first by inclusion of a compassionate speech of Andromache during the welcome festivities (1.100–13) and later by a misleading dream promising victory (1.124–31). The attribute δολόεντος (1.125), a proleptic hint at its fatal consequences (1.126–7) and an explicit explanation of the narrator (1.134–7), who characterises the deceived Penthesileia as νηπίη (1.134), highlight the true nature of the dream.[44] The Amazon's intense joy (γήθεε ἐν φρεσὶ πάμπαν, 1.132) thus becomes undoubtedly treacherous and ironic.

In the ensuing battle, the treacherous joy felt by the Trojans hoping for victory reflects her unfounded self-confidence and leads to further judging (νήπιος, 1.374) and proleptic comments of the narrator (1.373–5): ὣς ἄρ' ἔφη Τρώων τις ἐνὶ φρεσὶ πάγχυ γεγηθώς, / νήπιος· οὐδ' ἄρ' ἐφράσσατ' ἐπεσσύμενον βαρὺ πῆμα / οἳ αὐτῷ καὶ Τρωσὶ καὶ αὐτῇ Πενθεσιλείῃ ('Such words were spoken in jubilation by some Trojan. The fool was not aware of grievous woes approaching. Woes for him, for Troy, and for Penthesileia herself'). Finally, the Trojans themselves recognise their error, but only after Penthesileia has fallen victim to Achilles' superiority (2.18–20): καὶ γὰρ ἔην ἔκπαγλος· ἔγωγέ μιν ὡς ἐνόησα, / ὠισάμην μακάρων τιν' ἀπ' οὐρανοῦ ἐνθάδ' ἱκέσθαι / ἡμῖν χάρμα φέρουσαν· ὃ δ' οὐκ ἄρ' ἐτήτυμον ἦεν ('Such terror she inspired that when I saw her / I thought that some immortal had come from heaven to earth / To bring us joy, which after all was not the case'). Although the elder Thymoites in his speech explicitly stresses the proximity of joy (χάρμα, 2.20) and grief as well

---

[42] Cf. Q.S. 1.132–7; 1.373–5; 2.20; 2.410b–11; 3.476b–82a; 6.17b–18; 6.298–300a; 12.356–7; 12.441b–3; 12.544–5; 12.552; 12.576–8a; 13.383–4. Cf. also the Homeric antecedents of this narrative device at Il. 9.74–7; 13.609b; 18.130–3; 21.45–8; 24.490–2. On the general importance of prolepses in the PH, cf. Duckworth (1936); Schmitz (2005: 122–6; 2007b). Cf. also the chapter of Middleton in this volume.

[43] On the starting point of the PH, cf. Bär (2009: 140) ad 1–17; Maciver (2012a: 130–2); Fratantuono (2016: 212); Scheijnen (2018: 35, n99); Bärtschi (2019: 197–8). Cf. also the chapter of Goldhill in this volume.

[44] On proleptic hints at Penthesileia's demise, cf. Duckworth (1936: 72–3); Sodano (1951: 60–3); Vian (1963: 5); James (2004: 239, 270) ad loc.; Bouvier (2005: 46–9); Bär (2009: 315–29, 362–6, 383–4) ad loc.; Maciver (2012a: 139); Fratantuono (2016: 217–18); Scheijnen (2018: 50–2); Bärtschi (2019: 276–7). On contrasts in the presentation of Penthesileia in general, cf. Schmiel (1986); Schubert (1996).

as the vanity of false Trojan hope (οὐκ (. . .) ἐτήτυμον, 2.20), the Trojans later fall into exactly the same trap when Memnon and Eurypylos arrive.[45]

In the case of the joyful welcome of Penthesileia, treacherous joy is combined with, and intensified by, the equally tragic use of ambivalent joy.[46] The most prominent example of this narrative device among Homeric passages is the tearful laughter of Andromache at *Il.* 6.484 (δακρυόεν γελάσασα).[47] As soon as the Trojans behold Penthesileia, their sorrow is replaced with joy (Q.S. 1.62): λαοὶ δ᾽ ἀμφεγάνυντο καὶ ἀχνύμενοι τὸ πάροιθεν ('All around her the grief of the people changed into joy'). Priamos' continuing grief resulting from the loss of Hektor, however, overshadows the Amazon's arrival and creates an ominous feeling that intensifies the prolepses hinting at Troy's doom from the perspective of a single non-combatant. This contrast is extensively illustrated by a rainbow simile focused on the aspect of joy (1.63–72a) and followed by a brief *gnōmē* about the alluring effect of hope (1.72b–73). Furthermore, Priamos' immense sorrow (μέγ᾽ ἀκηχεμένοιο, 1.75) contrasts only a small amount of joyous relief (τυτθὸν ἰάνθη, 1.75). A long simile featuring a suffering blind man slowly and partially regaining his eyesight (1.76–83) illustrates Priamos' inner conflict and stresses the ambivalent nature of this shimmer of hope. An explicit comment of the narrator complements this inner perspective (1.84–5a): παῦρον μὲν γήθησε, τὸ δὲ πλέον εἰσέτι παίδων / ἄχνυτ᾽ ἀποκταμένων ('He felt a little joy, though still outweighed by grief / For the death of his sons'). A disadvantageous bird omen later confirms his scepticism and leaves him heartbroken in the process once more (198–204). Throughout the portrayal of Priamos' inner struggle, intensifying adverbs (τυτθόν, 1.72; βαιόν, 1.80; παῦρον, 1.84) highlight the ambivalence of joy in this exceptional situation and thus greatly contribute to a nuanced characterisation.[48] Table 15.3 in the Appendix shows that the *PH* makes use of a wider array of intensifying terms to elaborate on a fine gradation of context-sensitive representations of joy compared to the Homeric poems. Particularly the high number of adverbs as well as the involvement of different seats of emotions, which generally play a major role in the emotional life of epic heroes from Homer onward, mark the Posthomeric usage.[49]

---

[45] Cf. Duckworth (1936: 73–4); Bär (2009: 251–3) *ad loc.*; Scheijnen (2018: 81–5).

[46] Cf. Q.S. 1.62; 1.72–3; 1.84–5a; 2.3–5a (two instances); 2.632–3 (two instances); 7.327; 7.632–6 (four instances); 9.183; 14.19b; 14.397b–399; 14.407b–409a; 14.541; 14.616a; 14.628b–631.

[47] Cf. also ambivalent joy at *Il.* 6.484; 7.212a; 13.344; 15.101b–103a; 18.230–4a; 23.10; 23.97b–98; *Od.* 2.301; 4.102a; 4.372; 8.538; 9.356; 11.212; 14.465; 15.400–1; 17.530–8 (two instances); 19.213; 19.251; 19.471a; 19.513; 20.82; 20.301a–302b; 21.57; 21.105 (two instances); 21.429. Cf. also Antin (1961); Pisanello (1999); Halliwell (2008: 53–5).

[48] On Priamos' nuanced characterisation, cf. Bär (2009: 251–87) *ad loc.*; Maciver (2012a: 134–9).

[49] On seats of emotions in the Homeric poems, cf. Jahn (1987).

Similarly, the return of Neoptolemos to the Greek camp after his first battle at Troy mirrors the contrast between the universal joy of an army and the ambivalent mingling of joy and grief of individual non-combatants' reactions (Q.S. 7.619–727). This scene proves that the portrayal of ambivalent joy is no narrative device exclusive to only one of the war parties. Here, the likeness of Neoptolemos to his deceased father brings back grievous memories to Phoinix (7.631–6) and Briseis (7.723–7).[50] Furthermore, the subsequent depiction of Trojan joy at the sight of Eurypylos (7.728; 7.729) immediately contrasts (Τρῶες δ' αὖτ' ἀπάνευθε, 7.728) this renewal of hopeful joy on the part of the Greeks (7.619–727). Thus, ambivalent joy contributes to the overall atmosphere of the *PH* in the same way as the rampant malignity of its heroes, Greek and Trojan alike. Not only do they favour negative emotions like *Schadenfreude* and are ignorant regarding their tragic presumptuousness, but moreover, they are also incapable of feeling untroubled joy. This lack of entirely positive joy and laughter as well as the systematic undermining of their seemingly relieving effect in key moments of the narrative has serious implications regarding the literary world of the *PH*, from which light-heartedness seems to be completely absent. An atmosphere of seriousness and an ominous apocalyptic mood are predominant and, throughout the poem, foreshadow the destruction of the Trojans and Greeks in Q.S. 13 and Q.S. 14, respectively.

Finally, certain passages that intertextually allude to Homeric scenes featuring laughter and derision present a climax of this ambivalent depiction of joy and its physical expressions. In the last part of this chapter, the theomachy of the Olympian gods, the beating of Thersites and the foot race during the funeral games in honour of Patroklos will be interpreted in contrast to their Posthomeric counterparts. However, whereas Homeric laughter contributes to a comic dissolution of tensions in these passages, their Posthomeric transformation evokes exactly the opposite effect and thus parodies the Homeric hypotexts in a serious way.[51]

TWO ENTIRELY ANTITHETICAL THEOMACHIES

The Posthomeric re-enactment of the Homeric theomachy (Q.S. 12.160–218a) excludes every form of carefree joy and laughter predominant in the Iliadic scenes (*Il.* 20.3–74; 21.385–513) and shows how closely to each other divine and mortal realms are elaborated in the *PH*. In the *Iliad*, Zeus enjoys the

---

[50] Cf. Greek joy at Q.S. 7.604; 7.639; 7.642; 7.646; 7.675 (twice); 7.686; 7.688; 7.692; 7.702. Regarding Phoinix's ambivalent joy, cf. Q.S. 7.632; 7.634; 7.635; 7.636. Regarding Thetis' ambivalent joy, cf. 7.724. On Neoptolemos as a second Achilles, cf. Scheijnen (2018: 192–7); Bärtschi (2019: 248–54). Cf. also the chapters of Greensmith and Scheijnen in this volume.

[51] On alternative modes of reception, cf. also the chapter of Renker in this volume.

spectacle of his fellow gods battling each other as an uninvolved spectator after personally inciting the conflict by lifting the ban on divine interference in the mortal war (*Il.* 20.20–30). Not only does he express *Schadenfreude* in the face of their burlesque banter (20.23; 21.390) but he also derides the wounded gods (21.389; 21.508). He thus re-enacts the battle in the mortal realm and evokes the same behaviour in his fellow gods.[52]

In comparison to this light-hearted conflict without severe consequences, Zeus does not approve of the Posthomeric theomachy, so that it quickly evolves into a serious divine conflict of cosmic proportions (Q.S. 12.162–89a). As soon as Zeus recognises what is going on behind his back, he appears in a thunderous epiphany and sends Themis to warn the disobedient gods about his destructive might (189b–218a). As Carvounis has shown, this Posthomeric reworking contains numerous verbal echoes to the Iliadic theomachy as well as to other scenes that showcase Zeus's anger and threats against his fellow gods.[53] The combination of these passages has a drastic effect because it stresses Zeus's fearsomeness, which is reflected in the fearful reaction of the gods. Since this characterisation is predominant throughout the poem, it does not leave any room for carefree divine joy and laughter, which is so characteristic in the Homeric hypotexts.[54]

Since the intertextual relation between the Homeric hypotext and the Posthomeric hypertext is clearly marked, the process of parodic reworking underlying the Posthomeric theomachy as well as its range, spanning several scenes of the *Iliad*, is easily discernible.[55] The transforming process includes a complete omission of joy and laughter, a substitution of these affects by fear as well as a conflation of different Homeric scenes. These changes erase the possibility of a comical reading in the *PH*. Consequently, this Posthomeric reworking reverses the effect of the scene and creates a parody with a serious

---

[52] Regarding *Schadenfreude*, cf. *Il.* 21.423 (Athene). Regarding derision, cf. *Il.* 21.408 (Athene); 21.409 (Athene); 21.427 (Athene); 21.519 (pro-Greek gods). Regarding sneering, cf. *Il.* 21.434 (Hera); 21.491 (Hera). On the Homeric theomachy, cf. Hewitt (1928: 446–7); Latacz (1966: 72–3, 154–5); Levine (1982b: 97–101); Burkert (1983: 352–6); Golden (1989: 9–11); Edwards (1991: 288–9) ad loc.; Richardson (1993: 85–7) ad loc.; Postlethwaite (2000: 263–5) ad loc.; Wenglinsky (2002: 195–9); James (2004: 329–30) ad 162–218; Carvounis (2008); Halliwell (2008: 64–9); Bärtschi (2019: 260–1).

[53] On the Posthomeric theomachy and its references to the *Iliad*, cf. Campbell (1981: 56–60) ad loc.; Vian (1988: 290); Wenglinsky (2002: 195–9); James (2004: 329–30) ad 162–218; Carvounis (2008); Bär (2016: 223–4); Bärtschi (2019: 257–61).

[54] Cf. Q.S. 12.200 (ὑπὸ φρένας ἔμπεσε δεῖμα); 12.201 (ἔτρεμε γυῖα); 12.202 (περιδδείσασα); 12.214 (τρομέοντες). For other instances, cf. Q.S. 2.209 (μάλα γάρ μιν ἀπειρέσιον τρομέεσκον). Cf. also Wenglinsky (2002: 166–7); Carvounis (2008: 67–70). Bärtschi (2019: 361–3) nevertheless acknowledges the possibility of a comic reading of the theomachy due to its hyperbolic elaboration.

[55] On marked intertextuality, cf. Broich (1985); Helbig (1996); Zogg (2014: 13–29).

meaning that is critically directed at the Iliadic hypotext.[56] At the same time, this serious parody substantially contributes to the serious atmosphere of the poem by reflecting on its innovative transformation.[57] Finally, the theomachy comes right after the construction of the Wooden Horse (Q.S. 12.1–159) and before its infiltration into Troy (218b–585). This position in the narrative marks the end of pro-Trojan divine intervention and explains this serious last effort of the gods in favour of their supported party.[58]

THE BEATING AND MURDER OF THERSITES

Several Posthomeric scenes in the mortal realm exhibit similar instances of serious reworking of Homeric passages, for instance the killing of Thersites by Achilles (Q.S. 1.722–66). In the Iliadic episode (*Il.* 2.211–77), Thersites functions as a mouthpiece of voices that criticise the power structures inside the Greek army. Furthermore, Thersites' subsequent beating by Odysseus and the ensuing universal derision dissolve some of the tension that remains in the aftermath of the suspense-packed confrontation between Achilles and Agamemnon, which is explicitly mentioned by a concessive clause (ἀχνύμενοί περ, *Il.* 2.270):[59] οἳ δὲ καὶ ἀχνύμενοί περ ἐπ' αὐτῷ ἡδὺ γέλασσαν ('The others, disgruntled though they were, had a good laugh at him'). The introduction of Thersites as a challenger of kings (ἐριζέμεναι βασιλεῦσιν, 2.214) aiming at amusing his fellow warriors (γελοΐϊον Ἀργείοισιν, 2.215) explicitly stresses this double function. Odysseus himself explicitly identifies this behaviour as derision of his superiors (2.256b, σὺ δὲ κερτομέων ἀγορεύεις, 'your speech was one long sneer') and punishes him according to the principle 'an eye for an eye' by making him the target of derision as well. The pitiful state of the beaten Thersites, however, strongly contrasts with the universal mockery of the Greeks and at least hints at the ambivalence of their derision at the expense of a defenceless individual (2.265–9):[60]

---

[56] Cf. Carvounis (2008: 63); Bär (2016: 223). On this special case of a parodic reworking of a comic hypotext, cf. Verweyen and Witting (1979: 126–8).

[57] Most (1993: 34–40) similarly interprets the parodic elaboration of the *Batrachomymachia* as elucidation of the poem's innovative reworking of the literary tradition. Cf. also Verweyen and Witting (1979: 62–9); Most (1993: 29–34); Schmitz (2007a: 24–5).

[58] Cf. Vian (1969: 72; 1988: 289–90); Wenglinsky (2002: 195); Carvounis (2008: 62).

[59] On the Homeric Thersites episode, cf. Ebert (1969); Willcock (1978: 200–1) *ad loc.*; Funke (1981); van Thiel (1982: 148–9); Kirk (1985: 138–42) *ad loc.*; McGlew (1989: 290–2); Lowry (1991); Schubert (1996: 115–16); Postlethwaite (2000: 52–3) *ad loc.*; Brügger, Stoevesandt and Visser (2003: 69–75) *ad loc.*; Halliwell (2008: 69–76); Rousseau (2013); Scheijnen (2018: 70–7).

[60] On the ridicule of Thersites, cf. Hewitt (1928: 438–9); Ebert (1969: 162–3); Funke (1981: 251–7); Kirk (1985: 143–4) *ad loc.*; Lowry (1991: 25–8); Brügger, Stoevesandt and Visser (2003: 74, 82) *ad* 221–2a and 256; Halliwell (2008: 48–52, 71–6).

ὡς ἄρ' ἔφη, σκήπτρῳ δὲ μετάφρενον ἠδὲ καὶ ὤμω   265
πλῆξεν· ὃ δ' ἰδνώθη, θαλερὸν δέ οἱ ἔκπεσε δάκρυ·
σμῶδιξ δ' αἱματόεσσα μεταφρένου ἐξυπανέστη
σκήπτρου ὕπο χρυσέου· ὃ δ' ἄρ' ἕζετο τάρβησέν τε,
ἀλγήσας δ' ἀχρεῖον ἰδὼν ἀπομόρξατο δάκρυ.

So he spoke, and struck him on the back and shoulders with the sceptre. Thersites cowered and burst into tears. A bloody bruise raised by the gold-studded sceptre swelled up on the man's back. He sat down, terrified and in pain, looked helplessly around and brushed away a tear.

Meanwhile, the appearance of Thersites in the *PH* ends on a much grimmer note. When Achilles pities the slain Penthesileia (Q.S. 1.718–21), he is mocked by the malicious Thersites (1.722–40) and kills him in the heat of the moment (1.741–7). The Greeks react in the same manner as they did in the *Iliad*, but in doing so, they immediately sanction this manslaughter of an ally by expressing *Schadenfreude* (1.746b–747): αἶψα δ' ἄναλκις ἀπὸ μελέων φύγε θυμὸς / ἀνέρος οὐτιδανοῖο. χάρη δ' ἄρα λαὸς Ἀχαιῶν ('Quickly the feeble spirit fled from the frame of that man / of no account, which pleased the whole Achaian army'). Later, the Greeks renew their universal approval of this crime (μέγα φρεσὶ κυδαίνοντες, 825) when they bury Thersites' corpse without proper funeral honours. Achilles' impulsive act almost leads to bloodshed with Diomedes, who is characterised as a distant relative of Thersites and his only defendant after his death (1.767–74). Only the persuasion of the Greek leaders keeps both heroes from fighting against each other (1.775–81).[61] In juxtaposition to the earlier mythical tradition, the killing of Thersites does not split the entire Greek army in the *PH*; the consequences, in fact, are tremendously played down and reduced to a personal quarrel between Achilles and Diomedes. According to testimonies on the *Aithiopis*, both the killing of Thersites and the consequent quarrel with serious disputes had been part of the literary tradition before the *PH*. However, due to the fragmentary transmission of the Epic Cycle and its uncertain status as hypotexts of the *PH*, there exists no possibility of verifying the intertextual relation between the poems.[62]

---

[61] On the Posthomeric Thersites episode and its implications for the heroic code of the poem, cf. Mansur (1940: 5–6, 18–19); Schubert (1996: 115); James (2004: 241) *ad* 716–81; Boyten (2010: 51–4); Fratantuono (2016: 229–30); Scheijnen (2018: 70–7).

[62] Cf. the testimonies Apollod. *Epit.* 5.1 (numbering of Wagner 1894); Procl. *Chr.* 172–84 (numbering of Severyns 1963). On the highly debated intertextual status of the Epic Cycle, cf. Severyns (1926); Mansur (1940: 47–55); Sodano (1951); Vian (1959a: 20–2, 87–94; 1963: XXIII–XXX, 6–10); Ebert (1969: 167–8); Lowry (1991: 27–8); Sánchez Barragán (2001: 90–1); James (2004: XVII–XXI); Bouvier (2005: 45–6); Gärtner (2005: 28–9); Bär (2009: 78–9); Tomasso (2010: 12–16); Fantuzzi (2012: 277–8); Bär and Baumbach (2015: 604–14). Cf. also the chapter of Scafoglio in this volume.

In contrast to the Epic Cycle, the *Iliad* undoubtedly serves as a hypotext of the Posthomeric scene, because structural and verbal parallels clearly mark intertextuality between the passages. The narrator introduces Thersites' appearance (*Il.* 2.211–23; Q.S. 1.748–9; 1.825–7), his mocking speech (*Il.* 2.224–44a; Q.S. 1.722–40) is followed by a reprimanding answer (*Il.* 2.244b–264; Q.S. 1.755b–766), a form of punishment (*Il.* 2.265–70; Q.S. 1.741–7a) and an approving speech of the Greeks (*Il.* 2.271–8a; Q.S. 1.750–5a). Achilles' mention of Thersites' earlier mocking speech at Q.S. 1.759–60 additionally marks the intertextual relation.[63] However, the differences become much clearer when weighed against these parallels. Both in the *Iliad* (*Il.* 2.212–23; 2.246–64; 2.271–7) and the *PH* (Q.S. 1.747b–754; 1.757–65), Thersites is explicitly characterised as a problematic and insignificant member of the Greek army. However, he is not equipped with pitiful character traits in the *PH*, which removes every possibility for the reader to sympathise with him. At the same time, he loses his function as a jester and stress reliever and even becomes the cause of dangerous discord within the army. Consequently, these modifications completely reverse the purpose of his character and lead to a serious parodic reworking. Furthermore, the devaluating speech of Achilles, which mirrors the speech of Odysseus, is set at the end of the passage (Q.S. 1.755b–766) and thus resembles derision of slain foes on the battlefield. Verbal parallels to Achilles' earlier derision of Penthesileia strengthen this functionalisation and intertextuality with *Il.* 16.776. Ultimately, these changes result in a mean and cold-hearted characterisation of Achilles and the Greek army as a whole, who not only follow their affects without reasoning, but also treat one of their own deceased in the same way they would mock a fallen foe.[64] This general conduct ultimately confirms Athene's complaints about the depravity of mankind at the end of the poem.

A MERRY FOOT RACE GONE AWRY

The context of the funeral games in honour of the deceased Achilles contains a last example regarding the seriousness of the Posthomeric heroes. While the funeral games in honour of Patroklos in the *Iliad* provide an opportunity for mostly innocuous competition between the Greek champions, things again escalate in the Posthomeric foot race. The intertextual relation between both foot races is once again marked by several verbal parallels and is furthermore strengthened by the portrayal of Aias, son of Oileus, as one of the main competitors. In contrast to the Iliadic race, which portrays Aias, son of Oileus,

---

[63] On intertextuality between the Homeric and Posthomeric episodes, cf. Schubert (1996: 111–16); James (2004: 274–5) *ad loc.*; Boyten (2010: 105); Maciver (2012a: 75); Scheijnen (2018: 71–2).

[64] On Achilles' ambivalent characterisation, cf. Mansur (1940: 5–7); Scheijnen (2018: 76–7).

slipping and falling headfirst into dung (*Il.* 23.773–84), Teukros seriously hurts his ankle by tripping over a tamarisk branch in the *PH* (Q.S. 4.199–214). This treacherous plant, in turn, intertextually refers to the branch causing the destruction of a chariot at *Il.* 6.38–41.[65] Although the circumstances of the incidents are elaborated quite differently, both instances portray the *Schaden-freude* and derision of the Greek spectators. The Iliadic reaction follows Aias' short speech in which he self-ironically comments on his mishap (23.780–4):

στῆ δὲ κέρας μετὰ χερσὶν ἔχων βοὸς ἀγραύλοιο   780
ὄνθον ἀποπτύων, μετὰ δ' Ἀργείοισιν ἔειπεν·
ὢ πόποι ἦ μ' ἔβλαψε θεὰ πόδας, ἣ τὸ πάρος περ
μήτηρ ὣς Ὀδυσῆϊ παρίσταται ἠδ' ἐπαρήγει.
Ὣς ἔφαθ', οἳ δ' ἄρα πάντες ἐπ' αὐτῷ ἡδὺ γέλασσαν.

He stood there with his hands on one of the animal's horns and, as he spat out dung, said to the Greeks: 'Damn it! It was the goddess tripped me up – the one who always dances attendance on Odysseus, like a mother.' So he spoke, and they all laughed delightedly at him.

Although the Greeks laugh at the expense of Aias, he takes part in the joke and bears the derision like a good sportsman.[66] In contrast to this amusing ending of the scene, the derision in the *PH* carries a much meaner undertone (Q.S. 4.205b–208):

(. . .) Οἳ δ' ἰάχησαν   205
Ἀργεῖοι κατ' ἀγῶνα. Παρήϊξε<ν> δέ μιν Αἴας
γηθόσυνος· λαοὶ δὲ συνέδραμον, οἵ οἱ ἕποντο,
Λοκροί, αἶψα δὲ χάρμα περὶ φρένας ἤλυθε πάντων·

(. . .) A shout went up
From the Argives at the contest as past him Ajax darted
Exultant, and his followers came running up,
The Lokrians, all of them possessed by sudden joy.

Although Teukros' injury is not the direct object of the joy of Aias (γηθόσυνος, Q.S. 4.207) and the Lokrians (χάρμα περὶ φρένας, 4.208), the victory directly depends on it, nonetheless. Consequently, this portrayal of joy leaves a bitter aftertaste of *Schadenfreude* at the expense of an injured contender. Finally, Aias'

---

[65] On the intertextual relation between the Homeric and Posthomeric episodes, cf. Vian (1963: 131–4); James (2004: 290–1) *ad* 200–5.

[66] On the Homeric depiction of ridicule directed at Aias, cf. Hewitt (1928: 439); Whitman (1958: 164–5); MacLeod (1970: 53–4); Levine (1982b: 97–9); Kirk (1985: 144) *ad* 270; Pisanello (1999: 97–8); Halliwell (2008: 98–9).

roles during both incidents additionally highlight this shift in tone and perfectly illustrate the deleterious development of characters from one poem to the next: while he himself is the object of mockery in the *Iliad*, he now practises the same sort of devaluation in the *PH*, which amounts to another reversal of effect due to a serious parodic reshaping of the hypotext.

CLOSING REMARKS

In conclusion, the representation of joy and its physical manifestations in the *PH* clearly evokes the Homeric tradition, but significantly transforms its use. As a result of the portrayal of Posthomeric gods and heroes as excessively prone to *Schadenfreude* and derision, the overall tone of the *PH* drastically changes compared to the Homeric poems. Due to the predominance of *Schadenfreude* and exultation, the use of ambivalent and treacherous joy as well as the parodic reworking of joyous Homeric scenes, a serious atmosphere pervades all parts of the poem. Eventually, carefree joy and laughter thus lose their Homeric function of relief and considerably contribute to an ambivalent characterisation of the Posthomeric heroes as representatives of a depraved humankind that deserve to be destroyed at the close of the poem.[67]

APPENDIX

Table 15.1 Joy and *Schadenfreude* in the *Iliad*, *Odyssey* and *Posthomerica*

Emotion	Term	*Il.*	*Od.*	Q.S.	Emotion	Term	*Il.*	*Od.*	Q.S.
Joy (+)	ἀγάλλομαι	2	1	2	Joy (+)	πολυγηθής	1		4
	ἀμφιγάνυμαι			1		πολυπαίγμων		1	
	ἀπονίναμαι	1	4	2		ποτιττέρπω	1		
	ἄσμενος	2	3			τερπικέραυνος	8	7	
	ἀσπάσιος	3	7			τερπνός			4
	ἀσπασίως	5	5	10		τέρπομαι	24	62	16
	ἀχάριστος		2			τέρπω	3	6	2
	γαίω	4				τερπωλή		1	3
	γάνυμαι	3	1	2		τερψίμβροτος		2	
	γηθέομαι			1		χαίρομαι	11	9	19
	γηθέω	18	17	32		χαίρω	26	50	9
	γηθοσύνη	1	1			χαρίεις	2	1	
	γηθόσυνος	4	2	4		χαρίζομαι	11	9	
	ἐπαγάλλομαι	1		1		χάρις	5	1	1
	ἐπήρατος	1		3		χάρμα	3	2	9

[67] I would like to thank the editors for including this chapter in the collective volume and, in particular, Silvio Bär, Alexandra Scharfenberger and Philipp Karkutt for their helpful remarks.

ἐπιγηθέω			3	Schaden-
ἐπιτέρπομαι		1	8	freude
εὐφραίνομαι		1		(–)
εὐφραίνω	5	2	1	
εὐφροσύνη		5	1	
ἔϋφρων	2	1		
ἐψιάομαι		2		
ἥδομαι		1		
ἦδος	3	2		
θυμαρής	1	3	6	
θυμηδής		1	9	
ἰαίνομαι	5	6	16	
ἰαίνω	4		8	
ἰυγμός	1			
καγχαλάω			5	
κυδαίνω		1	8	
μείλια	2			
ὀνίναμαι	1			

ἀγάλλομαι	2		
ἀσπασίως		1	
γάνυμαι			1
γηθέω	5		17
γηθοσύνη	1		
γηθόσυνος			1
ἐπιγηθέω			1
ἐπιτέρπομαι			5
θυμηδής			1
ἰαίνομαι			5
καγχαλάω			3
κυδαίνω			3
κυδιάω			2
τέρπομαι	4		1
χαίρομαι	5		3
χαίρω	2	3	
χάρις			1
χάρμα	4		7

Table 15.2 Physical Expressions of Joy in the *Iliad*, *Odyssey* and *Posthomerica*

Expression	Term	Il.	Od.	Q.S.	Expression	Term	Il.	Od.	Q.S.
Laughter (+)	γελαστά		1		Derision (–)	αὔω	4		1
	γελάω	3	6	2		γελάω	6	8	6
	γέλως		1			γέλοιος	1		
	ἐκγελάω	1				γέλως	1	6	
	καγχαλάω			1		ἐκγελάω		2	
Smile (+)	ἐπιμειδάω	3	1			ἐπεύχομαι	17	2	2
	μειδ(ι)άω	10	6	6		ἐπιγελάω			1
	φιλομμειδής	5	1			ἐπικαγχαλάω			5
Exultation (+)	ἀγάλλομαι			1		ἐπικερτομέω	2	1	
	ἐπαγάλλομαι	1				εὐχωλή	6		
	ἐπεύχομαι			1		ἐφεψιάομαι		2	
	ἐπίαχω	5		2		καγχαλάω	1		1
	ἐπικαγχαλάω			2		καθεψιάομαι		1	
	καγχαλάω	2	2	9		κερτομέω	2	6	4
	κυδαίνω	1				κερτομία	2	1	
	κυδιάω	3		2		κερτόμιος	3	3	
	ὀλολύζω		2	1		κυδιάω	1		2
Sneer (–)	μειδ(ι)άω	2		1		λωβεύω		2	
						παραβλήδην–	1		1
						φιλοκέρτομος		1	

Table 15.3 Itensifying terms in the *Iliad*, *Odyssey* and *Posthomerica*: total instances (negative emotions)

Term	*Il.*	*Od.*	Q.S.	Term	*Il.*	*Od.*	Q.S.
ἀάσχετον			1	θυμῷ	12 (2)	7	7 (4)
ἀγλαόν			1 (1)	ἱερὴ ἴς		1	
ἄδην			1	ἱερὸν μένος		2 (1)	
αἰνῶς		1		κατὰ θυμόν	1 (1)	1 (1)	2 (2)
ἀλεγεινά			1 (1)	κῆρ	2	2	1
ἀλίαστον			2 (1)	λυγρόν			1 (1)
ἄλληκτον			1	μακρά			1
ἄμοτον			1	μάλα	1 (1)	1	2
ἀνὰ θυμόν			3	μάλιστα			2 (1)
ἀνὰ φρένας			1 (1)	μέγα	7 (3)	2 (1)	30 (9)
ἀπειρέσιον			1	μέγας	1		
ἄσβεστος	1 (1)	2 (3)		μεγάλα			3 (3)
ἀτειρέσιον			1	νόον			1
ἀχρεῖον		1		νόος			4 (1)
βαιόν			1	πάγχυ			2 (1)
γναθμοῖσι ἀλλοτρίοισιν		1 (1)		πάμπαν			2
ἔνδοθι			1	περὶ θυμόν			1
ἔνδον		1	1	περὶ φρένας			1 (1)
ἐν(ὶ) θυμῷ	1	3 (1)	1	περὶ φρεσί			2
ἐνὶ στήθεσσι	3 (2)			πόλλα			1
ἐν(ὶ) φρεσί	1	2	9 (3)	πολλόν			1
ἐπὶ μακρά			1	τόσσον			1
ἐπὶ μακρόν	4 (4)		1 (1)	τυτθόν			1
ἐρατεινόν			2	ὑπὸ κραδίη			2
ἐτώσιον			1	ὑπὸ φρεσί			1
ἡδύ	4 (4)	5 (5)		φίλον ἦτορ	2	3	
ἦτορ	1		6 (5)	φίλον κῆρ		2 (1)	
θαρσαλέον κῆρ			1	φρένα	8 (1)	4	
θυμόν	3	3	11	φρένας		1	3
θυμός	1	5	6	φρεσί	2 (1)	1	6 (4)

CHAPTER 16

Reshaping the Nature of Heroes: Heracles, Philoctetes and the Bow in Quintus Smyrnaeus' *Posthomerica*

Leyla Ozbek

INTRODUCTION

In the second part of Book 9 of Quintus' *Posthomerica*, Odysseus and Diomedes must momentarily abandon the battlefield and travel to the island of Lemnos in order to bring Philoctetes to Troy. During the Achaean fleet's initial voyage towards Troy, the hero is famously abandoned on Lemnos after having been bitten by a snake. As the myth narrates, Philoctetes, an exceptional archer, is the rightful possessor of the bow of Heracles, which the hero donated to him while on his funeral pyre.[1] This bow – the famous *toxon* of Heracles, the mighty hero – is always described and treated as if it were more than a mere weapon. In this, Quintus makes no exception. Nevertheless, he addresses this extraordinary weapon in an original way.

The aim of this chapter is to examine the way in which Quintus deals with the famous myth regarding Heracles, Philoctetes and the siege of Troy. It contextualises it within the mythic tradition, highlighting where Quintus follows the predominant tradition as well as the moments where he chooses original or underexploited paths to describe this exceptional weapon. In his short description of the bow's story and construction, Quintus carefully chooses every

I wish to thank Silvio Bär, Nicola Barbagli, Emma Greensmith and Fabio Guidetti for their valuable suggestions and criticisms.

[1] The myth usually includes the need to bring both Philoctetes and his bow to Troy. This is, for instance, the version of Sophocles' *Philoctetes*. In this tragedy, one must also interpret in this sense ll. 1055–66, in which Odysseus pretends that only the bow is necessary and not Philoctetes (the lines have the dramatic purpose of highlighting the suspense at this point of the plot, a tension that culminates with the exit of Odysseus and Neoptolemus with the bow). See e.g. Budelmann (1999: 92–132); Finglass (2006); Schein (2013: 279–80). The 'fake ending' represented by the exit of the two characters is examined by Seale (1972 and 1982).

word and model, deciding which to follow and which to alter. By choosing and partially altering the literary models of the *Iliad* and the *Odyssey*, Quintus presents a bow with a similar technical structure to the weapons possessed by some important archers of the *Iliad* and, most of all, by Odysseus in the *Odyssey*. Quintus' elaboration of the previous epic models, together with his choice to describe the bow as a weapon constructed by Heracles himself, provides a new portrayal, both for the internal and the external audience, of Philoctetes: he is a mighty hero who possesses a mighty weapon and is a warrior and a leader in line with Heracles and the most important heroes of the Achaeans.

AT TROY: THE IMPORTANCE OF PHILOCTETES' ARRIVAL

In the second part of the *Posthomerica*, Neoptolemus, Achilles' son, starts to become the true protagonist and leader of the Achaean army. In Book 7, persuaded by Odysseus and Diomedes, he arrives from Scyros to take on his father's role. At Troy, he manages to stop the long *aristeia* of Eurypylus (Priam's nephew), finally confronting and killing him (8.133–220). However, following the death of the last hero summoned by Priam to protect the city after the death of Hector, the battle continues to rage, now involving even the gods. This balance, forcibly tipped by various divine interventions, prevents the Achaeans, now unstoppably commanded by Neoptolemus, from winning this important battle too quickly and savagely.

In Book 9, when the battle begins anew after a day of truce, the odds appear to be again tipped by the intervention of the gods. This foreshadows a stalemate similar to the battle of the prior two days. From a tactical point of view, this moment of stalling hits the Achaeans the hardest, since, following the arrival of Neoptolemus, they experienced a series of victories and a surge of hope for the end of their ten-year siege and the final conquest of Troy. While the Achaeans are still struggling to win the day, something occurs that will change the outcome of the war, urging them to temporarily abandon the battlefield: just as with Neoptolemus in Book 8, the prophet Calchas announces that the Achaeans cannot win the war and conquer Troy without Philoctetes in their ranks, whom they guiltily abandoned on Lemnos during the voyage of the fleet to Troy (9.326–9).

Following Calchas' advice,[2] the Achaeans send an embassy to Lemnos, led by Odysseus and Diomedes (as was also the case for Neoptolemus) in order to bring Philoctetes to Troy. The similarities between the embassy sent for

---

[2] Usually this advice is given by Helenus (see e.g. *Il. parv.* A.1.6–7 PEG = *Procli Iliadis parvae enarratio* 6–8 EpGF, Tz. *ad* Lyc. 911, Soph. *Ph.* 604–19 and 1341–2, Eur. *Ph.* test. iii a Kn., 9–11 and fr. 789b Kn.). Quintus, however, assigns it to Calchas (as in Apollod. *Epit.* 5.8–10, which nevertheless differs from the chronology of the *Posthomerica* in various points). At this point of the narrative, Helenus has not yet been captured by the Achaeans.

Neoptolemus and the one sent for Philoctetes include not only the protagonists (the two ambassadors and Calchas), but also the level of urgency with which the narrative conveys the necessity of the hero's presence at Troy. The Achaeans remove two of their mightiest warriors, Odysseus and Diomedes, from the battlefield in order to accomplish a mission that is considered fundamental to the outcome of the war.

The reasons that necessitate the arrival of Philoctetes and Neoptolemus, and the 'divine way' in which they are summoned, also link these two heroes in a different, somewhat elevated status in comparison to the other chiefs of the Achaeans. This is a focal point of their characterisation throughout the whole narrative. Their status is highlighted especially during the assembly regarding the Wooden Horse, when the two heroes – alone against all the other Achaeans – take a stance against this 'trick', which was suggested by Odysseus and approved by Calchas (12.84–6).[3] In this central point of the story, the narrator makes an important comment highlighting directly the fundamental feature that links Neoptolemus and Philoctetes from the beginning: both heroes have come to fight at Troy 'by the gods' will' (12.92, ἄμφω γὰρ βουλῇσι θεῶν ἐς δῆριν ἵκοντο).[4]

This contextual and narrative similarity is one of the techniques used by Quintus to highlight the importance of Philoctetes. The arrival of the hero at Troy and his subsequent actions are pivotal to Quintus' narrative. Philoctetes will become one of the new protagonists, along with Achilles' son, of the last part of the war. Once on the battlefield, Philoctetes immediately takes the stage and shows his importance (and his abilities as an archer) by killing Paris, the lead archer of the enemies, thus ending the line of Priam's direct male descendants who have fought in the war. The exceptionality of Philoctetes – as a war hero and leader, as well as an outstanding archer – is stressed in two ways. First, it is emphasised by the words of Calchas, who urges the Achaeans to retrieve from Lemnos the mighty hero (described here through the expression Φιλοκτήταο βίη, 9.328), the 'expert in war and its miseries' (9.329, πολέμοιο δαήμονα δακρυόεντος). Second

---

[3] τῷ (sc. Calchas) δ' ἄρα πάντες ἀριστῆες πεπίθοντο / νόσφι Νεοπτολέμοιο δαΐφρονος, οὐδὲ μὲν ἐσθλόν / πεῖθε Φιλοκτήταο νόον κρατερὰ φρονέοντος ('all the chiefs were persuaded except for warlike Neoptolemus and the noble mind of stout-hearted Philoctetes'). In this case, they stand together against a solution that they find unfair and 'unheroic', taking a stance especially against Odysseus (cf. in particular 12.66–72, with Hopkinson 2018: 583, n3): a stance that immediately reminds the audience of the plot of Sophocles' *Philoctetes* and of the Sophoclean characterisation of these three heroes.

[4] The Greek text of the *Posthomerica* is taken from Vian (1963, -66, -69). For Q.S. 9.333–546, I use my edition of the text, soon to appear in Ozbek (forthcoming). The English translation is taken from Hopkinson (2018), in prose. As regards the *Iliad* and the *Odyssey*, I follow West (1998, 2000; 2017); I follow these critical editions because they are the most up to date, especially regarding the ancient manuscripts and *testimonia* collated and quoted: obviously, the Homeric text read and employed by Quintus was the text of the late-antique *vulgata*, a text with phonetic and textual choices different from the text reconstructed by West. The translation of the *Iliad* comes from Verity (2011), while the translation of the *Odyssey* from Wilson (2018).

(and above all), his importance is expressed in Quintus' initial portrayal of the character, which is developed through the description of the weapons he carries.

AT LEMNOS: PHILOCTETES, THE CAVE AND (FINALLY) THE BOW

Quintus uses Odysseus and Diomedes as an internal audience to portray Philoctetes' character and his living conditions on Lemnos in an effective way. Through their eyes (and their feelings of awe, surprise and even disgust), Quintus is able incisively to describe the cave, in which Philoctetes lives a primitive and almost feral life, as well as his degraded physical status (9.353–75). In a crescendo of pathos, Quintus then focuses the eyes of the ambassadors on the hero's wound (9.375–91). Following a tradition which is already present in fifth-century tragedy, but emphasising it in a way even more elaborate and intense, Quintus gives a description of Philoctetes' general condition and of his wound, including medical details which often border on the gruesome.[5]

Regarding the wound, Quintus stresses its internal putrefaction and gangrenous colour (9.375–6), then focuses on its dripping humour that permanently stains the floor of the cave (9.389–90). The description is expanded by the presence of two similes used to convey the awe and disgust of the internal – as well as external – audience. Philoctetes is compared to a beast biting off its leg while caught in a trap (9.365–70); his foot, consumed by gangrene, is compared to a sea rock gradually worn away by the waves of salt water and the gusts of the wind (9.378–85).

Near Philoctetes' bed, always within reach, lies his most valuable possession: the quiver full of arrows imbued with the venom of the Hydra of Lerna, and near it the bow (9.392–7):

καί οἱ πὰρ κλισίην φαρέτρη παρεκέκλιτο μακρή
ἰῶν πεπληθυῖα· πέλοντο δ' ἄρ' οἳ μὲν ἐς ἄγρην,
οἳ δ' ἐς δυσμενέας, τοὺς ἄμπεχε λοίγιον ὕδρου
φάρμακον αἰνομόροιο· πάροιθε δέ οἱ μέγα τόξον   395
κεῖτο πέλας, γναμπτοῖσιν ἀρηράμενον κεράεσσι
χερσὶν ὑπ' ἀκαμάτοισι τετυγμένον Ἡρακλῆος.

Near where he lay was laid his huge quiver full of arrows tipped with deadly venom from the lethal Hydra, some to be used for hunting and others against his enemies. Nearby within reach was the great bow made by Heracles' tireless hands from bent horns.

---

[5] On Quintus' attention to medical details, see Ozbek (2007).

Quintus carefully studies every detail of this climactic and emotional description. He skilfully builds his narrative from a spatial point of view, in order to bring more suspense to the description. The hollow cave, partially shaded by the sun, is filled with objects and details that the two characters focus on only gradually. In this way, Quintus places Philoctetes' most famous possession at the very end of the overview, leaving the audience waiting in anticipation from the beginning of the description to hear about the very last item to be described: the bow of Heracles.

THE GIFT: FROM ONE HERO TO ANOTHER HERO

Quintus gives great importance to the *toxa* of Philoctetes, making them a symbol that embodies the character who possesses them. In doing so, he includes into the narrative also the former owner of the weapons, Heracles.[6] This helps him to skilfully manipulate the story to better fit his narrative intentions.

As noted, the bow appears in a place of honour at the very end of the first description of Philoctetes. In this way, Quintus focuses the audience's attention on two specific features regarding the object: its construction and its structure. Regarding the construction of the bow, the narrator stresses a detail which, among all the extant traditions, is present only in this passage. The last line of the description points out that the weapon was made by Heracles himself with his own hands (9.397). This goes against all the traditions concerning the bow, which is always said to be a creation of Apollo, who then gifted it to Heracles. This tradition is attested from very early times, found already in e.g. Hes. fr. 33a.29 M—W and continuing for centuries not only in literary works but also in the mythographic tradition (see e.g. Apollod. 2.4.11).[7] By turning Heracles into the maker of this outstanding bow, who at the beginning of his myth is just a hero, a leader and a mighty warrior – not a god – Quintus builds for the audience a subtle yet acute similarity between Heracles and Philoctetes.

The aim of this passage is to portray Philoctetes as a warrior who possesses extraordinary abilities. This is achieved by Quintus not only through the details regarding the construction of the weapon but also (and most of all) with a description of its structure. In his definition of the design and material of the bow, Quintus chooses not to break with the previous tradition as he did with its construction. Instead, he follows and elaborates on certain previous epic models regarding famous weapons – and most of all famous leaders – as

---

[6] On the importance of Heracles in the Greek epic tradition, see Bär (2018a), who quotes this passage of the *Posthomerica* on p. 103 and n12.

[7] On the literary and mythographic sources, see Napolitano (2002: 175, n220) and Boardman (1988: 729).

a way of inserting Philoctetes into the lineage of the most important warriors and archers of the epic tradition.

QUINTUS' HOMERIC MODELS (TWO COMPOSITE BOWS?)

The structure of Philoctetes' bow derives primarily from two Homeric bows which, compared to all the other weapons, possess certain outstanding features – and in the latter example, can be used only by an outstanding archer and leader: the bow of Pandarus, briefly described in the *Iliad*, and the bow of Odysseus, detailed throughout the *Odyssey*.

In the case of the bow of Pandarus, it is important that a testimony, albeit a very synthetic one, already exists in the *Iliad* of a bow that is not just the traditional weapon described within this narrative but a weapon technically defined as a 'composite bow', likely of Asian origin (it is worth noting that Pandarus, who fights for the Trojans, comes from Anatolia, in particular from the region along the river Aesepus, at the base of Mount Ida).[8] This kind of weapon (which will be analysed in detail below) possesses particular characteristics of range and power, achieved through a complex process of composition and the assemblage of different parts and materials.

In *Iliad* 4, Athena, disguised as Laodocus, looks for Pandarus in order to lure him into shooting an arrow towards Menelaus. Athena is specifically searching for Pandarus for this extremely difficult task because this hero is a mighty archer who possesses an exceptional bow. It is described immediately after, when Athena 'swayed the thoughts of a thoughtless man' (4.104) and subsequently Pandarus decided to take his bow and arm it for the shot.

The description of the weapon is brief, but it reveals precise and particular details (Hom. *Il.* 4.105–11):

αὐτίκ' ἐσύλα τόξον ἐΰξοον ἰξάλου αἰγός   105
ἀγρίου, ὅν ῥά ποτ' αὐτὸς ὑπὸ στέρνοιο τυχήσας
πέτρης ἐκβαίνοντα, δεδεγμένος ἐν προδοκῆσιν,
βεβλήκει πρὸς στῆθος, ὁ δ' ὕπτιος ἔμπεσε πέτρῃ.
τοῦ κέρα ἐκ κεφαλῆς ἐκκαιδεκάδωρα πεφύκει·

---

[8] Archaeological and historical surveys have proven that, from the post-Mycenaean era onwards, the structure of the bow used by the Greeks was not developed from the Mycenaean model but rather from a configuration coming from the Asiatic continent (probably through Anatolia and the Middle East). See (with different opinions) especially Borgna (1992), and also Miltner (1937); Lorimer (1950: 276–89); McLeod (1965); Snodgrass (1967: 39–40); Rausing (1967: 95–9), who gives a chronological and geographical list of the different types of bow, from the simple asymmetric to the Turkish composite (pp. 129–51); Luce (1975: 109); Napolitano (2002: 142).

καὶ τὰ μὲν ἀσκήσας κεραοξόος ἤραρε τέκτων,   110
πᾶν δ' εὖ λειήνας χρυσέην ἐπέθηκε κορώνην.

At once he took out his well-polished bow, made from the horns
of a full-grown wild goat that he himself had once shot in the chest
as it emerged from a rocky place while he waited in a hide,
and he hit it in the chest; and it fell backwards on to the rock.
On its head grew horns of sixteen palms' length, and
these a craftsman who worked in horn had fitted together,
smoothing the whole bow skilfully, and adding a tip of gold.

Quintus' description of the bow of Philoctetes contains many similarities with
this Homeric passage, which is probably one if its models. Pandarus' bow is
made with the horns of a wild goat (4.105–6, ἰξάλου αἰγός / ἀγρίου) killed
by Pandarus himself during a hunt. The majestic horns were then fixed one
against the other by the maker (who is a skilled artisan, a τέκτων, 4.111) to form
the inner core of the bow (4.111, τὰ (sc. κέρα) μὲν ἀσκήσας κεραοξόος ἤραρε
τέκτων). The procedure of Heracles in Quintus' description is more synthetic
than that of Homer, but it is strikingly similar in its focal points. The core of
the weapon is defined in the same way and with similar wording. Heracles, in
making his bow, uses 'bent horns' (9.396, γναμπτοῖσιν . . . κεράεσσι), meaning
that they probably derive from a goat, and places them one against the other
(9.396–7, γναμπτοῖσιν ἀρηράμενον κεράεσσι / . . . τετυγμένον (sc. τόξον)). It is
also noteworthy that the same verb is used in the two passages to describe the
technical detail of fixing the horns with their tips facing opposite sides (Il.
4.111, ἤραρε – Q.S. 9.396, ἀρηράμενον) and that the term used to define the
maker/making of this complex artisanal artefact has the same root (Il. 4.111,
τέκτων – Q.S. 9.397, τετυγμένον).

The bow described in Iliad 4 (and remodelled in Posthomerica 9) shares
fundamental characteristics with the weapon technically called a 'composite
bow'. Of course, when compared with archaeological artefacts or with their
description in technical treatises, the Homeric description of the structure
of this weapon is less precise and articulate (and sometimes slightly different in minor details). This is related to the fact that the Homeric description
must be contextualised within its framework and as a part of a literary poem,
which has its own narrative rules and aims. Furthermore, scholars agree that
during the period of composition/assemblage of the Homeric epics into the
two poems that we have come to know there was likely no precise evidence
or complete knowledge about this particular weapon.[9] This is why the Iliad

---

[9] For an analysis of the bows and arrows described in the Homeric epics, see Schaumberg
(1910: 68–92); Bulanda (1913); Lorimer (1950: 289–302). On the knowledge of the composite
bow in the Homeric epics, see Lorimer (1950: 289–300), who presents the disadvantage of

and the *Odyssey* (especially the *Iliad*) contain just scattered details and hints regarding this kind of bow.[10]

From a technical perspective, the structure of the composite bow results from the assemblage of different materials joined with glue of animal origin. The weapon is composed of pieces of wood joined together along their length, a core of horn (usually the long horns of the *Capra aegagrus*, widespread especially on Crete),[11] and layers of sinew. This composite structure gives the bow a good ratio of flexibility, resistance and overall stability, thus providing the shot with more precision, power, speed and range in comparison to what can be achieved with a simple wooden bow (which is usually also larger). Given its complexity, this bow requires a high degree of technical knowledge to be assembled, which is probably why, in the passage of the *Iliad*, the narrator highlights the skills of the craftsman who built Pandarus' bow.[12]

Along with its structure and the materials used, this weapon also differs in usage from the simple wooden bow, especially in the method of stringing (i.e. how the bowstring is attached to its tips). In order to arm it, the archer usually needs to block one end under his knee and place the other upon his opposite leg. The act of bending the weapon with his legs gives the archer's hands greater freedom to operate the ends of the bow, thus permitting him to attach the string to the limbs.[13]

seeking excessive precision and technical consistency in two literary texts; Rausing (1967: 97–8); Borgna (1992: 64–5 and 84). In the past, scholars were overconfident of the precise knowledge regarding composite bows in Homer. This has led to some misunderstandings involving various disciplines and different subjects. For instance, Bulanda (1913: 77–8), while commenting *Il.* 4.105–11, quotes the archaeological discovery, in a Theban tomb from the first dynasty, of a bow composed of just two horns. The scholar (criticised by Rausing 1967: 97–8) goes as far as identifying this bow with the weapon possessed by Pandarus, quoting as parallels some bows depicted on vases belonging to the geometric style and a particular model of a Scythian bow. However, this Theban bow is probably a unique piece that was not built to be used as a real weapon but only for religious and/or symbolic purposes; see especially Lorimer (1950: 288–9), and also Rausing (1967: 136).

[10] According to Borgna (1992: 89 and 91), the *Iliad* and the *Odyssey* represent two different case studies, given the overlapping of different periods of composition and the substantial amount of time elapsed between the (final) versions of the two works. Because of this, we find in the more recent *Odyssey* a new perception of the archer (probably deriving from Anatolian influence) and the insertion of new and more advanced details regarding his weapon. In the *Odyssey*, the role of the archer (and subsequently of his weapon) is not only perceived as being more valuable, but it also takes centre stage. The hero of the work is, this time, an archer, who will end the plot thanks to his outstanding bow (see also Lorimer 1950: 289).

[11] Schaumberg (1910: 76) and Borgna (1992: 64) identify that this particular species of goat was killed by Pandarus in *Il.* 4.105–6 (see also Lorimer 1950: 279 and Rausing 1967: 97–8).

[12] See, among others, Luce (1975: 110) and Borgna (1992: 65). On the importance of highly specialised artisans as bow craftsmen, see Borgna (1992: 74–6).

[13] See Bulanda (1913: 90–6); Lorimer (1950: 292); Rausing (1967: 28); Luce (1975: 110); Borgna (1992: 23).

These details (transposed into literary works, with all the methodological differences mentioned earlier) permit us to identify in the Homeric epics not only Pandarus' weapon in the *Iliad* as potentially a composite bow, but also the most famous weapon of the *Odyssey*: the bow of Odysseus. In this latter poem, the weapon of Odysseus is identified by a series of adjectives which appear to convey details of a composite bow, such as παλίντονον ('bent backward', 21.11, 21.59),[14] ἀγκύλα ('curved', 21.264, used also for Pandarus' bow in *Il.* 5.209),[15] and κάμπυλα ('bent', 'curved', 9.156, 21.359, 21.362, used also for Pandarus in *Il.* 5.97).[16]

Furthermore, when in Ithaca Odysseus takes his bow into his hands after about twenty years of disuse, his first concern is whether the parts made of horn are intact. Hence, he peruses the weapon inch by inch, to be certain that parasites have not gnawed and damaged the horn (*Od.* 21.393–5, ὃ δ᾽ ἤδη τόξον ἐνώμα / πάντῃ ἀναστρωφῶν, πειρώμενος ἔνθα καὶ ἔνθα, / μὴ κέρα ἶπες ἔδοιεν ἀποιχομένοιο ἄνακτος, 'the master was already handling / the bow and turning it this way and that, / to see if worms had eaten at the horn / while he was gone').[17]

The composite nature is also highlighted in the most famous part concerning the bow: the 'trick' of its stringing, a technique which only Odysseus knows and whose description is strikingly similar to the stringing of a composite bow. In *Odyssey* 21, when Telemachus and the suitors try to string the bow, they fail miserably. The narrator highlights how the suitors attempt to attach the string with all their strength but with no success, even when they light a fire and apply grease to warm the bow (21.178–85, 21.246).[18]

---

[14] In the *Iliad*, this adjective also identifies the bows of other outstanding archers, marking the exceptionality of the weapons (Teucer's bow: 8.266, 15.443; Dolon's bow, which ends in Odysseus' hands after the killing of the former: 10.459).

[15] As with παλίντονον, in the *Iliad* ἀγκύλα occurs only to describe the weapons of two exceptional archers: Pandarus (see above) and Paris (6.322).

[16] As with the first two cases, in the *Iliad* this adjective identifies the same group of outstanding archers/bows (apart from the already quoted Pandarus, Paris: 3.17; Dolon: 10.333; Teucer: 12.372), with the addition of Artemis, a deity known for her ability in using the bow (21.502). On these three adjectives, see especially Borgna (1992: 64–5), partly enhancing Schaumberg's opinion; Lorimer (1950: 291–2 and 298); Rausing (1967: 97–8).

[17] Moreover, even if the meaning of the rare term γωρυτός in 21.54 is debated, a great number of ancient and modern scholars of the *Odyssey* believe that the bow was also kept in a specific case in order to protect it, especially from parasites which might attack and ruin the parts made of horn (*Od.* 21.51–4, Penelope takes the bow of her husband from the bedchamber: ἣ δ᾽ ἄρ᾽ ἐφ᾽ ὑψηλῆς σανίδος βῆ· ἔνθα δὲ χηλοί / ἕστασαν, ἐν δ᾽ ἄρα τῇσι θυώδεα εἵματ᾽ ἔκειτο. / ἔνθεν ὀρεξαμένη ἀπὸ πασσάλου αἴνυτο τόξον / αὐτῷ γωρυτῷ, ὅς οἱ περίκειτο φαεινός, 'she stepped inside, / onto the pallet where the scented clothes / were stored in chests, and reached to lift the bow / down from its hook, still in its shining case').

[18] The action of slightly heating them is a technique sometimes used for composite bows to make them more flexible, since heat has an effect on the parts made of sinew or animal glue (for the sources testifying this technique, see Rausing 1967: 68).

Odysseus, however, has no problem stringing his bow. As Luce notes,[19] the narrator points out how the suitors and Telemachus always tried to string the bow while standing. In 21.124, Telemachus is standing (στῆ) while trying to bend it (στῆ δ' ἄρ' ἐπ' οὐδὸν ἰὼν καὶ τόξου πειρήτιζεν, 'he stood astride the threshold and began / to try the bow'); the same formulaic line is used for Leiodes, the first who tries to string it after Telemachus' attempt (21.149). Odysseus, meanwhile, who came into the hall and sat down during the suitors' attempts (21.243, ἕζετ'), is said to be in this same position (21.420, αὐτόθεν ἐκ δίφροιο καθήμενος) while swiftly notching and shooting the arrow through the axe heads (21.419–23):

τόν ῥ' ἐπὶ πήχει ἑλὼν ἕλκεν νευρὴν γλυφίδας τε,
αὐτόθεν ἐκ δίφροιο καθήμενος, ἧκε δ' ὀϊστὸν   420
ἄντα τιτυσκόμενος· πελέκεων δ' οὐκ ἤμβροτε πάντων
πρώτης στειλειῆς, διὰ δ' ἀμπερὲς ἦλθε θύραζε
ἰὸς χαλκοβαρής. (. . .)

He laid it (sc. the arrow) on the bridge,
then pulled the notch-end and the string together,
still sitting in his chair. With careful aim,
he shot. The weighted tip of bronze flew through
each axe head and then out the other side.

This leads to the hypothesis that he was also in this same position mere seconds before his shot, when he handles the bow and attaches the string to its tips with the same rapidity and smoothness (21.405–9):

αὐτίκ' ἐπεὶ μέγα τόξον ἐβάστασε (sc. Ὀδυσσεύς) καὶ ἴδε πάντη,   405
ὡς ὅτ' ἀνὴρ φόρμιγγος ἐπιστάμενος καὶ ἀοιδῆς
ῥηϊδίως ἐτάνυσσε νέην περὶ κόλλοπι χορδήν,
ἅψας ἀμφοτέρωθεν ἐϋστρεφὲς ἔντερον οἰός,
ὣς ἄρ' ἄτερ σπουδῆς τάνυσεν μέγα τόξον Ὀδυσσεύς.

After examining the mighty bow
carefully, inch by inch – as easily
as an experienced musician stretches
a sheep-gut string around a lyre's peg
and makes it fast – Odysseus, with ease,
strung the great bow.[20]

---

[19] Luce (1975: 110).

[20] The narrator twice highlights the smoothness of Odysseus' actions (21.407, within the simile, ῥηϊδίως; 21.409, ἄτερ σπουδῆς). This ease in handling the bow surprises even the suitors (21.396–403).

If one considers the characteristics of a composite bow, this is of course the most effective stringing position since, as previously noted, the archer is free to block the bow on his legs and string it with both hands.

All these details, whether analysed singularly or together, lead us to believe Odysseus' weapon had the form of a composite bow, similar to those described in the *Iliad* but with more elaborate characteristics. Quintus, then, while describing the weapon of Philoctetes, recalls these fundamental models, activating in the audience a resonance that is composite like the bow he is depicting. He is using and innovatively altering the models present in the *Iliad* and the *Odyssey*, while at the same time he is also showing how the details in these two poems were already the subject of elaboration, expansion and modification.

A WEAPON WORTHY OF AN OUTSTANDING HERO

In conclusion, Quintus follows the models of the *Iliad* and the *Odyssey* for his description of the bow of Philoctetes: it is a 'special' bow that needs a particular assemblage and is made from different materials. The assemblage of this exceptional *toxon* by Heracles is a fundamental feature for the characterisation of Philoctetes in this passage (and in the whole poem); through this seminal detail, Quintus highlights the connection between Philoctetes and the most famous hero of the previous generation. In describing his bow as an outstanding weapon, probably a composite that shares its characteristics with the bow of the greatest hero of the *Odyssey* (and partially with those of certain outstanding archers from the *Iliad*), Quintus situates Philoctetes – until now an outcast, not in any way valued – within the lineage of the most famous archers of the epic tradition. With three lines describing Philoctetes' weapon and its assemblage by Heracles, Quintus skilfully erases the contingent status of the hero at Lemnos for the audience. Philoctetes is no longer an invalid outcast living a savage life but comes to be – as he was before, and will be again – one of the leaders of the Achaean army and of the entire Trojan saga.

CHAPTER 17

Quintus and the Epic Cycle

Giampiero Scafoglio

STATUS QUAESTIONIS

The relationship between Quintus' *Posthomerica* and the Epic Cycle is a challenging and controversial subject that has fuelled the scholarly debate for almost two centuries, starting from the skeptical stance taken by Hermann Köchly in the middle of the nineteenth century.[1] The complexity of the issue finds confirmation in the opposite reactions of scholars, either definitely approving and supporting or firmly rejecting this stance: if Frederick Paley maintained the traditional view and did not even hesitate to consider Quintus' development of the matter and plot as a true reflection of the Epic Cycle,[2] Ferdinand Noack assumed on the contrary that the subject itself of the *Posthomerica* reveals the intention to fill a gap in mythical narrative between the *Iliad* and *Odyssey*, and thereby demonstrates the loss of the Epic Cycle by Quintus' time.[3] In the twentieth century, the most important scholar of the Epic Cycle, Albert Severyns, considered the Cyclic poems among the sources of the *Posthomerica* and proposed some convincing parallels, though he was not sure about direct imitation.[4] The most important scholar of Quintus' epics, Francis Vian, after a thorough examination of the analogies with and differences from the Epic Cycle (as far as it can be reconstructed on the basis of the surviving evidence), reached the conclusion that Quintus followed the Cyclic poems at several points, especially in the first part of the *Posthomerica*, but most likely with an indirect approach, by

I warmly thank Leyla Ozbek for her useful and kind help.

[1] Köchly (1850: VIII–XXXII).
[2] Paley (²1879: 2).
[3] Noack (1892: 770).
[4] Severyns (1925: 153–61, and elsewhere).

the means of intermediate sources.[5] Today scholars are still divided: if Jonathan Burgess adopts a more positive position, counting the Epic Cycle among the main sources of the *Posthomerica*, Alan James conversely takes for granted the loss of the Cyclic poems by Quintus' time, repeating almost exactly the old argument by Noack; Calum Maciver, in turn, is tentatively possibilist.[6]

Bär and Baumbach have recently made the point, laying down some methodological criteria concerning the potential engagement of later epics with the Epic Cycle in general.[7] They recall, in fact, three caveats that must not be ignored in tackling this issue: first, we do not know for sure when the Epic Cycle was lost;[8] accordingly, we cannot assume Quintus' direct knowledge of these poems. Second, the Epic Cycle was not a set of coherent poetic works, 'but rather a conglomeration of different (and differing) hexameter texts that were thematically arranged around the Homeric epics':[9] it is possible that Quintus knew some parts of the set, or some individual poems, but not others, so that each section or episode of the *Posthomerica* requires a specific assessment with respect to its supposed source(s). Third, most important, the methods and tools of traditional source criticism turn out to be inadequate to explore the relationship between a later and an earlier text, a relationship that is not limited to, and does not even necessarily require, a direct approach with the model(s). In other words, intertextuality is not only a textual matter, based on first-hand imitation, but a cultural phenomenon in the broader sense, potentially involving intermediate models, as well as overlaps and stratification of several sources. In my view, this third caveat is a further issue, but it is at the same time the keystone to overcome the first two problems: the gaps and weakness in our knowledge on the Epic Cycle (mainly on the date of its loss, but also on the profile of the individual poems) cannot prevent us from evaluating (at least in general terms) the importance and role played by the Epic Cycle in the content, structure and plot of the *Posthomerica*.

---

[5] Vian (1959a: 17–109, esp. 87–94).

[6] Burgess (2001: 45); James (2004: XIX); Maciver (2012a: 8–9). For a 'positive' view cf. also Zanusso (2013: XXIV–XXIX; 2014); and Tsomis (2018b: 21–2), who speaks of an *aemulatio*, consisting of 'Anpassung' and 'Neurung', carried out by Quintus at the same time towards Homer and the Epic Cycle.

[7] Bär and Baumbach (2015).

[8] Ioannes Philoponus, in his commentary on Aristotle's *Analytica posteriora* 77b32, testifies that the poems of the Epic Cycle fell into disuse after Peisander of Laranda composed his *Heroic Theogamies* (Wallies 1909: 156–7), in the first half of the third century CE, that is probably the time of Quintus Smyrnaeus or a few decades earlier (Baumbach and Bär 2007a: 1–8; Bär 2009: 14–23). It should be noted, though, that he does not speak of an immediate and complete loss, but of a gradual process that does not exclude the survival of some copies in the following centuries (Scafoglio 2004a).

[9] Bär and Baumbach (2015: 605). I fully agree with the idea of 'a conglomeration of different (and differing) hexameter texts' on mythical subjects, while their arrangement 'around the Homeric epics' seems to me a result of later (notably Alexandrine) criticism: Scafoglio (2016: 441–2).

Furthermore, when we think about the possible mediation between Quintus' poem and the Epic Cycle, we should not focus (as some scholars do) only or mainly on mythographic handbooks: we have to take account of the interferences by other poetic models (both from the classical period and Hellenism), as well as theoretical treatises, first of all Aristotle's *Poetics*, which have represented an important interpretative filter or grid for both the Homeric and Cyclic epics from antiquity up to today. There can be little doubt that Quintus approached the Epic Cycle, and compared it to the Homeric poems, in view of Aristotle's *Poetics* and/or of Alexandrian criticism, which follows in the footsteps of the philosopher of Stageira. Giovanni Cerri has recently investigated the Aristotelian (and Alexandrian) influence on Quintus' usage of the Epic Cycle, concluding that the *Posthomerica* were intended to replace the latter, eliminating its defects (in the light of Peripatetic criticism) and getting closer to the model of epic perfection, that is Homer.[10]

With these premises, I will try to outline an overview of Quintus' ideas and work on the Epic Cycle, assuming that he read (at least a part of) it – which seems to me objectively probable – but considering the straight knowledge and direct imitation of the Cyclic poems as neither a certainty nor even a *condicio sine qua non* for the intertextual relationship.

THE *POSTHOMERICA* AS A CYCLIC POEM

The *Posthomerica* are in many respects a Homeric poem: this is how they were intended by their author and perceived by their audience: Quintus would have appreciated, and many readers of his time would have shared, the appellative of Ὁμηρικώτατος that the Byzantine scholar Costantine Lascaris attributes to him.[11] The imitation of the *Iliad* can indeed be recognised in several episodes, in many aspects and at different levels of Quintus' text.[12] But the identification with Homer is even stated by the author of the *Posthomerica* (in an allusive way) in the invocation to the Muses that introduces the catalogue of the warriors entering the Wooden Horse (12.306–13): here the poet evokes the initiation that the goddesses gave him, when he was still a beardless boy who pastured his flocks 'in the fields of Smyrna'. By means of a metaliterary device that goes back to Hesiod, but passes through Alexandrian poetry too,[13] Quintus recalls his city of origin, which is at the same time one of the most accredited candidates among the cities that competed for the title of Homer's birthplace. Scholars have not failed to recognise the self-representation of Quintus as an *alter Homerus*, a

---

[10] Cerri (2015).

[11] *Sc.* in his preface to the manuscript *Matritensis gr.* 4686.

[12] Maciver (2012a); Zanusso (2013: XXII–XXIV, XL–XLIV).

[13] Cf. Hes. *Th.* 22–34; Call. Fr. 1.21–40 and 2 Pfeiffer.

self-representation that finds confirmation in (and gives a meaning to) the far-reaching imitation of the *Iliad* realised in the *Posthomerica*.[14]

Nevertheless, it is precisely the mix of literary references crowded into the invocation to the Muses that reveals Quintus' intention to present himself not only as a 'new Homer', but also as a 'Hesiodic' and Alexandrian poet: Quintus looks at Homer and tries to reproduce his kind of poetry through the prism of Hellenistic culture and mindset, which largely depends on Aristotle's *Poetics*, for aesthetics and Homeric criticism. Moreover, the primacy of the author of the *Iliad* as an epic model excludes the possibility of an imitation that is truly worthy of him; and the concept of an *alter Homerus* already implies the imitative and even epigonal character of the poet coming after Homer and pretending to 'double' Homer.[15] Now, who are, before Quintus, the poets coming after Homer and pretending to double Homer? According to the Aristotelian and Alexandrian view, they are the authors of the Epic Cycle. Each of them seems to be in fact an *alter Homerus*, from the standpoint taken by Aristotle and his followers, for several reasons: they continue and complete Homer's work, filling the gaps before, between and after the *Iliad* and *Odyssey*; they (try to) imitate Homeric epics in general matter, individual episodes and style; they borrow epithets, phrases and whole sentences from the Homeric texts (and even if this is, at least to some extent, a consequence of the formulaic technique due to oral tradition, the perception of Homeric imitation is unavoidable). According to Aristotle and his followers, however, they inevitably remain on a lower plane than Homer (we will see why, and with what consequences on Quintus' self-awareness). The appellative νεώτεροι and its variants, which scholiasts and other ancient scholars usually attribute to them,[16] express not only their chronological posteriority, but also (and perhaps above all) their inferiority in cultural stature and literary quality, with respect to Homer.

Indeed, the *Posthomerica* are similar to the Epic Cycle for their subject and specifically for their complementary role to Homeric epics. Actually, the Cyclic poems were composed to fix the mythical tales of the oral tradition down in writing, just like the *Iliad* and *Odyssey*; but later readers failed to recognise their original purpose and saw them as a big picture of the prequels, interlude and aftermath to the Homeric epics: it was Alexandrian scholars who asserted this point, based on Aristotle's criticism. The outcome of this process of subordination of the Epic Cycle to the Homeric epics is clearly recognisable in the general presentation and structure of the summaries included by Proclus in

---

[14] Cerri (2015: 145–7). *Homerus novus* (not slavish imitator of Homer): Baumbach and Bär (2007a: 37–40 and *passim*).

[15] When I speak of 'epigonal' character, I am not expressing my own view of course, but the inherent judgement of Quintus' self-representation, that fits with Aristotelian and Alexandrian criticism considering Homer as archetypal paradigm of epic poetry. Cf. the *excursus* (below).

[16] Severyns (1928: 31–92); Nagy (2009: 291–3).

his *Chrestomathy*, with the artificial construction of continuity and consistency between the matters of the individual poems, all neatly arranged (by appropriate work of cutting and sewing) around the *Iliad* and *Odyssey*.[17] The subject of the *Posthomerica*, with its evident intention of filling the gap between the two Homeric poems, fits perfectly with the (supposed) aim and outlook of the Epic Cycle, whether Quintus read the latter through the eyes of a later reader, or he knew it from a set of summaries forming a continuum and gravitating around the *Iliad* and *Odyssey*, just like what we find in Proclus' *Chrestomathy*.

Even the title *Posthomerica* reveals the purpose to complete Homer's narration (although referring generally to 'the events following the Homeric epics', while the poem includes only the matter coming after the *Iliad*). It is true that, precisely speaking, the manuscript tradition attributes two titles to Quintus' poem, notably παραλειπόμενα Ὁμήρου (in the codices of the family H) and Τὰ μεθ' Ὅμηρον (in those of the family Y):[18] the former is more appropriate, even though the latter has had better luck; but neither of them seems to be authentically dated back to the author (or even to the archetype Ω). Byzantine scholars and copyists must have added both titles to the poem, and some of them in fact quote the latter:[19] this says a lot about the perception of the poem by the audience over time. I think this is precisely the idea that Quintus wanted to give the readers about his work, i.e. the idea of continuity and complementarity with Homeric epics.

Now, the continuity between the matters of the individual poems of the Epic Cycle is emphasised in the set of summaries constructed by Proclus, and we have reason to believe that this is what usually happened in mythographic collections of the same kind. But the same continuity already existed, or sometimes was constructed on purpose, within the tradition of the original poetic texts. This is why we find an 'alternative ending' of the *Iliad*: a distich transmitted by the scholium T *ad Il.* 24.804a, that connected this poem with its ideal continuation, belonging to the Epic Cycle, that is the *Aethiopis*:

ὣς οἵ γ' ἀμφίεπον τάφον Ἕκτορος· ἦλθε δ' Ἀμαζών,
Ἄρηος θυγάτηρ μεγαλήτορος ἀνδροφόνοιο.

So they busied themselves with Hector's funeral. And an Amazon came,
a daughter of Ares the great-hearted, the slayer of men.[20]

This 'alternative ending' (which τινὲς γράφουσιν, as the scholium says, *sc.* in place of the last line of the *Iliad*) announces the arrival of the Amazons, which

---

[17] Cf. Scafoglio (2004a: 49–57; 2004b: 305–8).

[18] For these symbols and an overview of the manuscript tradition of the *Posthomerica*:Vian (1963: XLV–LI, LIV–LV).

[19] *Schol.* A D Gen. *Il.* 2.219; Eustath. *Prooem. in Il.* 5.

[20] Text and translation by West (2003).

was the starting point of the plot of the *Aethiopis*. What was then the origin of this distich? What was its role in the oral and/or in the written tradition of the *Iliad* and/or of the *Aethiopis*? It is possible that it dated back to the oral culture, in which the mythical episodes were initially all relatively autonomous (as individual songs or rhapsodies) and at the same time all potentially connected with each other, according to the choice and inspiration of the aeds, as well as to their practical needs (most of all, their allotted time) and to the circumstances they were in, including the requests and expectations of the audience. Thus, we can imagine the oral tradition as a large container or reservoir full of tales, or rather songs (with contents already fixed in a provisional form), that the aeds could choose and combine in different ways. Against this backdrop, it is easy to figure out the function and usefulness of 'alternative endings' (such as the quoted lines) that allowed the aeds to pass smoothly from one song to another.[21]

However, even if one were to believe that the distich at issue has been introduced at a later stage at the end of the *Iliad* and/or at the beginning of the *Aethiopis*, or better between the former and the latter, we cannot ignore its importance, as well as its specific function, which consisted in creating a continuity between the two poems. Quintus aims to create the same continuity with the *Iliad*, as he does not start his poem with the proem, which is a conventional, unmissable feature of epics from Homer onwards, almost a distinctive mark of the literary genre. Instead, he recalls the last events of the *Iliad* and thus creates a direct connection with its end (1.1–4):

Εὖθ' ὑπὸ Πηλείωνι δάμη θεοείκελος Ἕκτωρ
καί ἑ πυρὴ κατέδαψε καὶ ὀστέα γαῖα κεκεύθει,
δὴ τότε Τρῶες ἔμιμνον ἀνὰ Πριάμοιο πόληα
δειδιότες μένος ἠὺ θρασύφρονος Αἰακίδαο.

When godlike Hector had been vanquished by the son of Peleus
and the pyre had consumed him and the earth had covered his bones,
the Trojan forces stayed inside the city of Priam
terrified of the noble might of bold-hearted Achilles, grandson of Aeacus.[22]

Then, a little later, he announces the arrival of the Amazons with a sentence (1.18–19) that is strongly reminiscent of the distich quoted by the scholium T *ad Il.* 24.804a:

καὶ τότε Θερμώδοντος ἀπ' εὐρυπόροιο ῥεέθρων
ἤλυθε Πενθεσίλεια θεῶν ἐπιειμένη εἶδος.

---

[21] Scafoglio (2004b: 307–8). *Contra*, Davies (2016: 90–5), on which: Scafoglio (2017b).

[22] The Greek text of the *Posthomerica* follows the critical edition by Vian; the translation is taken from Hopkinson (2018).

And then from the streams of broad Thermodon
there arrived Penthesileia, clothed in godlike beauty.

In both passages, the arrival of the Amazons is announced by the same verb, agreeing with a subject in the singular, since their army is accounted for by their queen, who is called by name by Quintus (Penthesilea), while the Cyclic distich presents her generically as Ἀμαζών, or maybe 'the Amazon' *par excellence*. And this is not the only variation made by Quintus, who replaces the high-sounding epithet concerning military value (Ἄρηος θυγάτηρ μεγαλήτορος ἀνδροφόνοιο) with a more modern one, referring to the beauty of the Amazon: θεῶν ἐπιειμένη εἶδος. Far from disproving the imitation or making it less evident, such variations conversely confirm it and even give literary dignity to it, turning it into an allusion. The incipit of the *Posthomerica* may indeed be seen as an expansion of the Cyclic distich, whose first segment (ὣς οἵ γ' ἀμφίεπον τάφον Ἕκτορος) has been more largely developed by Quintus in lines 1–4, while the remaining part is reflected in lines 18–19.

A closer look at the variation concerning the epithets tells us something interesting about Quintus' (Alexandrian) aesthetics, and provides further confirmation on the allusive reference to the Cyclic distich. The epithet we find in the latter, pointing to Ares not only as Penthesilea's father, but also as a metaphor of military value, stresses one of the two main, inherent features of the Amazons, who are 'warrior women' by definition. The epithet chosen by Quintus, in turn, recalls precisely the other characteristic that distinguishes them: the female nature, which beauty highlights and emphasises. We can therefore say that the two epithets are complementary, each of them presenting one of the two faces that constitute the double nature (warlike and female) of the Amazons. Moreover, both epithets announce the future events, but each of them from a different angle: the one concerning military value anticipates the fight between Achaeans and Amazons and in particular the *aristeia* of their queen, while the other underlines the great beauty of Penthesilea that will arouse the admiration (and maybe something more) of Achilles. Quintus has chosen to sacrifice the paradigmatic value of the epithet in the Cyclic distich, improving instead its allusive strength and focusing on a different, even opposite aspect, which he considered peculiar and attractive.

Besides, another version of the incipit of the *Aethiopis* circulated in antiquity; we find it on a papyrus of the first century CE: Ὀτρήρη<ς> θυγάτηρ εὐειδὴς Πενθεσίλ<ε>ια (P. Lit. Lond. 6.22.43–4).[23] This could be a later reworking of the quoted line, but it may as well be a *varia lectio* circulating from the beginning. Actually, the existence of textual alternatives in some passages of the Cyclic poems should not be surprising, in the light of their

---

[23] Milne (1927: 19).

origin from oral tradition, which is by definition 'fluid' and 'multiform'.[24] If Quintus read this version, in the place of or in addition to the other, we may say that he followed more closely the incipit of the *Aethiopis*, where he could have found the reference to the beauty of Penthesilea he needed as an allusive hint to later events.

The connection with Homeric epics is clearly recognisable not only at the beginning of the *Posthomerica*, but also at the end. A little before the conclusion, in fact, Quintus mentions the concern of Athena for Odysseus, 'who was destined to suffer many troubles from the wrath of Poseidon': ἄχνυτ' Ὀδυσσῆος πινυτόφρονος, οὕνεκ' ἔμελλε / πάσχειν ἄλγεα πολλὰ Ποσειδάωνος ὁμοκλῇ (14.630–1). Actually, switching from the *Posthomerica* to the *Odyssey* could never have been easy and perfectly fluid, due to the specific structure of the latter, with its ὕστερον πρότερον and flashback through Odysseus' first-person narrative. But Quintus has been able to steer around the obstacle, concluding his poem with a vaguer and more flexible transition passage than the incipit. Indeed, at the very end of the *Posthomerica*, after telling the terrible storm unleashed by Poseidon (14.632–55), Quintus mentions generically the returns home of the Achaeans who had escaped death (14.655–8). On the one hand, it must be noted that the last part of the *Posthomerica* does not cover all the matter of the *Nostoi*, which came just before the *Odyssey* in the Epic Cycle (or better, in the big picture of the Epic Cycle constructed a posteriori by later scholars):[25] Quintus does not include in his poem the return home of some of the Achaeans (e.g. Agamemnon), maybe in order not to widen his subject too much. On the other hand, the last two lines of the *Posthomerica* match well with the very beginning of the *Odyssey*, that is lines 11–12 (just after the proem),[26] both passages referring in a generic and collective way to the returns home of Greek survivors. It is true that there is a chronological gap between Quintus' mention of the events and the retrospective reference that recalls them at a distance of time (seven years after!) in the *Odyssey*, but it is still the same matter: the returns home of the Achaeans who left Troy.

It is clear therefore that Quintus conceived his poem as a continuum with the Homeric epics, just as later scholars saw the Epic Cycle. And he organised and developed his subject in the same way as a Cyclic poem, that is through the juxtaposition of episodes following each other in time, within a linear structure. Even if it is no longer possible to read the Epic Cycle, this is precisely

---

[24] Burgess (2002); Scafoglio (2004b).

[25] Cf. Proclus, *Chrest.* 306.

[26] Q.S. 14.657–8, ἄλλη δ' ἄλλος ἵκανεν, ὅπη θεὸς ἦγεν ἕκαστον, / ὅσσοι ὑπὲρ πόντοιο λυγρὰς ὑπάλυξαν ἀέλλας, 'And those who survived the voyage through that dreadful tempest landed wherever they could.' *Od.* 1.11–12, ἔνθ' ἄλλοι μὲν πάντες, ὅσοι φύγον αἰπὺν ὄλεθρον, / οἴκοι ἔσαν, πόλεμόν τε πεφευγότες ἠδὲ θάλασσαν, 'So now all who escaped death in battle or by shipwreck had got safely home.'

the impression given by Proclus' summaries: an orderly succession of events, lacking any underlying theme or common thread (such as Achilles' wrath in the *Iliad*). Of course, one might argue that summaries inevitably give a reductive vision of literary works; and yet the idea of the Epic Cycle shared by later readers, including Quintus himself, was affected by this kind of synthesis, even if the poems were still available. If instead they were already lost, summaries were the only means to know their contents and to get a sense of what they were.

Anyway, the most important source *ad hoc* is the *Poetics* of Aristotle, who praises Homer as the best poet (θεσπέσιος, 'divinely talented'), while criticising and even censuring the authors of the Epic Cycle (that he generically calls οἱ ἄλλοι, 'the others'), with respect to subject choice as well as narrative structure (1459a30–b2):

> διὸ ὥσπερ εἴπομεν ἤδη καὶ ταύτῃ θεσπέσιος ἂν φανείη Ὅμηρος παρὰ τοὺς ἄλλους, τῷ μηδὲ τὸν πόλεμον καίπερ ἔχοντα ἀρχὴν καὶ τέλος ἐπιχειρῆσαι ποιεῖν ὅλον· λίαν γὰρ ἂν μέγας καὶ οὐκ εὐσύνοπτος ἔμελλεν ἔσεσθαι ὁ μῦθος, ἢ τῷ μεγέθει μετριάζοντα καταπεπλεγμένον τῇ ποικιλίᾳ. (. . .) οἱ δ' ἄλλοι περὶ ἕνα ποιοῦσι καὶ περὶ ἕνα χρόνον καὶ μίαν πρᾶξιν πολυμερῆ, οἷον ὁ τὰ Κύπρια ποιήσας καὶ τὴν μικρὰν Ἰλιάδα.

> So in this respect, too, compared with all other poets Homer may seem, as we have already said, divinely inspired, in that even with the Trojan war, which has a beginning and an end, he did not endeavor to dramatize it as a whole, since it would have been either too long to be taken in all at once or, if he had moderated the length, he would have complicated it by the variety of incident. (. . .) The others, on the contrary, all write about a single hero or about a single period or about a single action with a great many parts, the authors for example of the *Cypria* and the *Little Iliad*.[27]

Aristotle appreciates the selective and motivated narrative that Homer realised in the *Iliad*, focusing on a precise theme (*sc.* Achilles' wrath) and pivoting the whole story around it. He stigmatises on the contrary 'the other poets', such as the authors of the *Cypria* and the *Little Iliad* (that is *antehomerica* and *posthomerica*), since they dwell from time to time on different characters and events, drawing a review of autonomous episodes rather than an organic and consistent tale: the plot of these poems is 'formed by many distinct parts' (πολυμερῆ), lacking unity and coherence.[28]

---

[27] Text by Kassel (1966); translation adapted from Fyfe (1932).
[28] Scafoglio (2007).

This is exactly what we find in Quintus' poem, each book focusing on a specific character or event,[29] with a more or less precise parallel in the Epic Cycle, as summarised by Proclus. He seems to imitate the Cyclic poems through the filter of Aristotle's *Poetics* (probably with the mediation of Alexandrian philology), whether he read their texts (as I am inclined to believe) or knew them exclusively by the means of prose compendia; and in the latter case the influence of Aristotelian and Alexandrian criticism must have been even stronger.[30]

Thus, if the *Posthomerica* are in many respects a Homeric poem (and there is no doubt that they are), they are at the same time a Cyclic poem. After all, a Cyclic poem is still a Homeric poem, but a different kind of Homeric poem,[31] that comes after Homer and turns away from this archetypal model for several features, such as subject choice and narrative structure. The *Posthomerica* share those aspects that (at least, according to Aristotle) characterised the Epic Cycle and distinguished it from the Homeric poems.

We may wonder, then, why Quintus chose to write a Cyclic poem, despite the devaluation of the Epic Cycle by Aristotle and the Alexandrians. The answer seems to me intuitive, maybe even mandatory: Homer is only one, that is the author of the *Iliad* and *Odyssey*; there is no other Homer. Nevertheless, the authors of the Epic Cycle followed in the footsteps of Homer, in their own way: they were 'Homeric poets', similar to and different from Homer at the same time. For Quintus (as for any other author coming after Homer), being a 'Cyclic poet' was actually the only way to be a 'Homeric poet'. As for Aristotle's devaluation of the Epic Cycle, I do not think that Quintus saw it in the same light as Aristotle himself, or as a modern scholar. Being inferior to Homer was not a major problem, and certainly not a poetic failure, for any other author who dared to engage with such a great model on his own ground, that is the Trojan epics.

A last question, of a general nature: we may wonder why Quintus chose to fill the gap between the *Iliad* and *Odyssey*, rather than starting from the beginning, i.e. narrating the previous events, the causes of the war. Two different answers can be provided, depending whether we consider the texts of the Epic Cycle lost or still available at Quintus' time. In the first case, the

---

[29] Penthesilea (Book 1), Memnon (Book 2), Achilles' death (Book 3), funeral games for Achilles (Book 4), contest for the arms (Book 5), Eurypylus (Book 6), Neoptolemus (Book 7), Eurypylus' death (Book 8), Philoctetes (Book 9), Paris' death (Book 10), final battles (Book 11), the Wooden Horse (Book 12), the sack of Troy (Book 13), the returns (Book 14).

[30] I agree with Cerri (2015) in recognising the importance of the Aristotelian mediation for Quintus' reception of the Epic Cycle, but I differ from him in believing that Quintus stays consciously closer to the Epic Cycle than to Homer: cf. the *excursus* (below).

[31] Not by chance, the poems of the Epic Cycle are often attributed to Homer and to different authors (e.g. Stasinus for the *Cypria*) at the same time.

answer cannot depend on the Cyclic poems, which no longer existed; it must instead be found in the features of the legend and in Quintus' literary taste and purpose (obviously with a largely subjective assessment): we may think that he preferred the war narrative as a heroic and truly epic theme to the romance narrative of the prequels. If conversely the texts were still available at his time (as seems more likely to me), then the answer rests perhaps in the different setup of the poems concerning respectively the events before and after the matter of the *Iliad*: indeed, the prequels were collected in a sole, wide-ranging poem, the *Cypria*, while the events following the *Iliad* were divided among (at least) three epics, namely the *Aethiopis*, the *Ilioupersis* and the *Little Iliad*, with some overlaps and duplications, as well as some contradictions due to different versions of the legends, in the matter shared by the last two poems.[32] We can imagine that Quintus wanted to rework the subsequent events into a coherent and organic setup, analogous to that of the prequels collected in the *Cypria*, in order to get only two wide-ranging poems, covering respectively the *antehomerica* and the *posthomerica*. In addition, the idea of connecting both Homeric poems would not have been unattractive to Quintus.

EXCURSUS: QUINTUS AS HOMER'S EPIGONE

I have tried to show that Quintus presents himself in the invocation to the Muses as an *alter Homerus*, that is Homer's epigone, from the perspective of Aristotelian and Alexandrian criticism (a perspective shared by Quintus himself). The mistake of contemporary philology, which has branded Quintus precisely as an 'epigone' of Homer,[33] resulted from a 'Homerocentric' prejudice (also coming from Aristotelian and Alexandrian criticism!) that was very widespread until quite recently, and that not incidentally has also weighed heavily on the studies on the Epic Cycle.[34] But this mistake of modern scholars has been partly caused by Quintus' literary posture too, since he stimulates comparison with Homer (through far-reaching imitation of the *Iliad* and even with a metaliteray statement, in the invocation to the Muses), without daring to place himself on the same level of his *auctor princeps*. His Homeric imitation, concerning several episodes and stylistic features, is framed in a wider-ranging imitation of the Epic Cycle that makes his poem much more similar to the latter than to the *Iliad* (and even less to the *Odyssey*).

---

[32] Scafoglio (2004a: 49–53).

[33] E.g. Dihle (1989: 436); Fornaro (2001: 724). According to James (2007: 414, abstract), 'the success with which [Quintus] imitated the language and style of the Homeric epics encouraged the opinion that he lacked sufficient originality to do more than simply reproduce the material from the sources.'

[34] Scafoglio (2014).

The mistake of contemporary philology has been to consider as a serious shortcoming and even a poetic failure the result of a conscious and dignified literary choice. For a late epic poet, it was an honour to be an 'epigone' of Homer (just as the authors of the Epic Cycle were considered) and in any case it was the only way to engage with a giant such as Homer. It is clear that his conception of 'epigone', or better 'Homer's epigone' (which is not the same as the epigone of any other author) does not coincide with ours and does not imply a value judgement diminishing the literary quality of his poetry. We can imagine, in fact, that he admired the poets of the Epic Cycle, that he imitated even more widely than Homer: he admired them precisely as 'Homer's epigones'.

After all, it was not possible for any poet imitating Homer in the imperial period to escape the label of 'epigone', at least in the context of Greek-speaking culture. Some observation on the Homeric imitation carried on in 'the other half of the world', that is the Latin culture, may perhaps help to clarify this point in general (and Quintus' literary posture, too).

The first epic poem and probably the first piece of literature in Latin was a translation of the *Odyssey* by Livius Andronicus: it was precisely a translation, no matter how 'free' or 'artistic' it was; and not by chance it concerned one of the Homeric poems.[35] Naevius followed a different way, that of the historical matter, in order to gain some autonomy, still within the wider domain of the epic genre (headed by Homer, though). Livius remained 'under the wing' of the *auctor princeps*, limiting himself to reproducing Homer's content in Latin (albeit with changes and variations often related to a process of 'Romanisation'); Naevius got as far away as possible from the archetypal model, with a subject coming from Roman history (but not that far away, after all, given that history is connected to myth, just as Roman matter is to Greek, Aeneas being the joining link). Ennius was therefore the first to openly engage with Homer, despite the historical and Roman subject of his *Annals*: if the use of the hexameter (conceived and constructed as the Homeric verse, which is not quite the same as the Hellenistic one)[36] were not enough to prove it, direct imitation of the *Iliad* is still recognisable in some fragments of his *Annals*.[37] Ennius takes the standpoint of Alexandrian criticism, as he defines himself as *dicti studiosus* (corresponding to the Greek φιλόλογος);[38] and we can well understand how hard it was for him, in this spirit, to confront Homer through the practice of *aemulatio*. As an ideal disciple, follower, imitator of Homer, he could not easily escape the label of epigone: if he wanted to be an *alter Homerus*, he could not be other than an epigone. But he found a brilliant expedient, by resorting to Pythagorean theory of metempsychosis as a tool to reinterpret the Alexandrian theme of the

---

[35] von Albrecht (1999: 42–4).
[36] Williams (1968: 684–99).
[37] Elliott (2013: 75–134).
[38] *Ann.* 206–9 Skutsch.

poetic initiation: in the proem of the *Annals*, he described a dream in which Homer appeared to him and explained the nature of the universe and the transmigration of souls; the dream culminates in the revelation that the true soul of Homer now lodged in the breast of Ennius.[39] The latter thus stated himself to be not an *alter Homerus* (an epigone of Homer, according to the Alexandrian mindset, shared by Ennius), but Homer himself: not the second, but the only one, who was reborn through reincarnation in the Roman world: hence, a *Homerus Romanus*.[40]

Later, in the second half of the first century BCE, Virgil would engage with Homer with a much higher grade of self-awareness and a different approach, fully realising the competitive practice of *aemulatio*.[41] This is what Propertius means, when he announces: *nescio quid maius nascitur Iliade* (2.34.66). Nevertheless, the Greek poets of the imperial period neither shared Virgil's emulative attitude nor saw it in a positive light: they continued to regard the author of the *Aeneid* and other Latin epic poets as Homer's epigones. This is why, in my view, late Greek poets such as Quintus (but also Tryphiodorus, Nonnus and Colluthus) ignore, or better pretend to ignore the *Aeneid* and other Latin epics, such as Ovid's *Metamorphoses*: they recognise the dignity of allusive imitation with respect to Homer, but not to his Latin 'epigones'. Even if they imitate Virgil and other Latin poets (and I definitely think they do), their approach with those 'minor' models is never evident, not to say hidden: they do not openly 'declare' the emulative practice through allusive references (as they proudly do, on the contrary, with respect to Homer); they overshadow it, indeed. Hence the harsh difficulty and disagreement among modern scholars in recognising and assessing the relationship of Quintus and other late Greek poets with Latin models.[42]

QUINTUS AND THE Ἀμαζονία

It is now time to take a closer look at Quintus' imitation of the Epic Cycle both in the content and the structure of individual episodes of the *Posthomerica*: I will focus on the first book of the poem as a case study. This belongs to a set of books (notably 1–3) where the Cyclic influence seems to be stronger than in the later ones (maybe depending on the subject, which did not imply overlaps

---

[39] *Ann.* 2–9 Skutsch. Cf. Suerbaum (1968: 94–113); Skutsch (1985: 147–87); Dominik (1993: 38–42).

[40] Brink (1972). But Ennius would not have loved how Horace calls him *alter Homerus* (*Ep.* 2.1.50): Brink (1982: 92–6).

[41] La Penna (2005: 141–51).

[42] Cf. the chapters by Bär, Greensmith, Papaioannou and Scafoglio in Carvounis, Papaioannou and Scafoglio (forthcoming).

and 'competition' with other sources, such as Greek tragedy or Latin epics): the main model followed by Quintus, in this part of the *Posthomerica*, seems to be the *Aethiopis*.[43] This is probably the most ancient piece of the Epic Cycle: it can be assumed, based on its bipartite structure (as seen in Proclus' summary), that it resulted from the fusion of two mythical themes that were originally the subjects of two oral songs concerning the fight of the Achaeans with the Trojans' allies, the Amazons and the Ethiopians, respectively.[44] Achilles was the protagonist, who killed the queen of the former and the king of the latter (although one must be cautious in speaking of a protagonist in such an archaic epic):[45] the poem ended with his death and funeral rites.[46]

The arrival of Penthesilea with her people of warrior women to the rescue of the Trojans is announced in the incipit of the *Posthomerica* (quoted *supra*). Yet, a difference with the *Aethiopis* comes out from the beginning, as Quintus claims that the queen of the Amazons came Θερμώδοντος ἀπ' εὐρυπόροιο ῥεέθρων, 'from the streams of broad Thermodon' (1.18), while she is defined as Θρᾷσσα δὲ τὸ γένος in Proclus' summary of the Cyclic poem (*Chrest.* 176). This has been enough to provoke the mistrust of the scholars on the relationship between the *Posthomerica* and the *Aethiopis*; but the denial of a wide-ranging imitation based on such a detail (however important it may be) is out of the question. Perhaps the *Aethiopis* gave the more ancient version of the legend, locating the Amazons in Thrace, while Quintus follows a relatively recent and much luckier one, referring to a farther and most remote place (*sc.* in Pontus), which was commonly considered as the homeland of the Amazons since the classical period.[47] Quintus may have diverted from the *Aethiopis* not so much to follow the best-known legend, but rather to recall allusively the extended description of the river Thermodon and its estuary given by Apollonius Rhodius (2.962–1001), who covers the ethnography of the local tribes of Amazons too.[48]

Moreover, the two topographic indications are not really in contrast with each other, if one considers the precise meaning of Proclus' phrase, framing it in the whole sentence. Penthesilea is in fact defined as Ἄρεως μὲν θυγάτηρ, Θρᾷσσα δὲ τὸ γένος, 'daughter of Ares' and accordingly 'of Thracian lineage': she is originally from Thrace, like her father, Ares; but this does not mean that she and her people live in that region. Anyway, an incertitude or an oscillation about the homeland of the Amazons, and the consequent attempt to impose order through a distinction between their origin and their actual location, are

---

[43] For an overview of this lost poem, based on fragments and evidence: Davies (2016).
[44] Severyns (1925); Kopff (1983).
[45] Debiasi (2004: 125).
[46] Actually, there was also space for the ὅπλων κρίσις: Scafoglio (2017a: 78–86 and *passim*).
[47] Cf. Herod. 4.110.
[48] Bär (2009: 169–72).

attested in other sources too, e.g. by Virgil and Propertius. The former, in a simile related to Camilla, calls the Amazons *Threiciae*, but he also says that they 'run along the banks of the Thermodon' (*Aen.* 11.659–60).[49] The latter calls one of them *Strymonis* (with reference to the Thracian river Strymon), but he locates her *prope Thermodonta* (4.4.71–2).[50]

In the *Posthomerica* Penthesilea comes to the rescue of the Trojans for two reasons (ἄμφω), as clearly stated by Quintus: first, to indulge and express her warlike nature (στονόεντος ἐελδομένη πολέμοιο, 1.20); second, 'and even more', to expiate the involuntary killing of her sister Hippolyta (1.21–32). Here too, Quintus seems to combine two distinct versions of the legend, which are indeed attested by different sources.[51] Proclus' summary of the *Aethiopis* does not detail the specific reason of her coming: this may be due only to its synthetic outline, but more likely it supports the presence of the former (and easier) version in the lost poem. On the other hand, Quintus could have found the theme of killing and pollution in a later passage of the *Aethiopis* too, as we will see: he chose to exploit it here, as Penthesilea's reason to come to Troy, rather than at a later stage of the story. Nevertheless, though this motivation would have been more than sufficient to explain her participation in the war, he also maintained the original reason that he found in the *Aethiopis* (1.20); he even felt the need to specify that there were two causes for her coming (ἄμφω), implicitly pointing out the *contaminatio*.

In the *Posthomerica*, the *aristeia* of Penthesilea that unfolds in the absence of Achilles and Ajax (1.205–493) culminates with her fight with both them (538–72) and with the final duel with Achilles, who kills her (573–642). Penthesilea's *aristeia*, leading to her slaying at the hands of the son of Peleus, was undoubtedly a major episode of the *Aethiopis*,[52] which Quintus followed at least in its broadest outlines (probably, but not necessarily, reading the text of the poem); but it is equally certain that he made important changes and introduced new elements, such as the failed attempt of the Trojan women to join the battle (1.403–76). After killing Penthesilea without much difficulty, Achilles gives a prideful speech (1.643–53); but soon after, his mood completely changes, since he removes her helmet and sees her outstanding beauty, which deeply affects him, raising sadness and regret in his heart (657–74). Here Quintus inserts a digression on Ares' reaction to the death of his daughter: oppressed by grief and wrath, he rushes earthward to take revenge on Achilles, but he is stopped by the lightning bolts of Zeus, who menaces him, forcing him to give up and

---

[49] *Quales Threiciae cum flumina Thermodontis / pulsant et pictis bellantur Amazones armis.* Cf. Horsfall (2003: 369).

[50] Warden (1978).

[51] For the first reason, e.g. Hellanicus, 4.F.149 Jacoby; for the second, Diodorus Siculus, 2.46, as well as Apollodorus, *Epit.* 5.1.

[52] *Chrest.* 176–7, καὶ κτείνει αὐτὴν ἀριστεύουσαν Ἀχιλλεύς.

turn back (675–715). In Proclus' summary and in other evidence concerning the *Aethiopis*, there is no trace of such a digression, which must be Quintus' invention. Maybe the poet felt the quasi-romantic scene of Achilles 'falling in love' to be not completely appropriate to the heroic spirit of the epic genre: the digression interrupts the description of Achilles' 'love at first sight' and brings back the narrative tone to the epic stature. Just after, the gaze turns again to the strong impression of Penthesilea's beauty on the hero (716–21): a striking simile even compares his reaction of grief and regret to the sorrow he felt for the death of Patroclus (720–1), this being certainly another innovative contribution by Quintus, given that the best friend of Achilles was unknown to the oral tradition and accordingly he was not present in the Cyclic poems.[53] Actually, the son of Peleus had a close friend in the *Aethiopis*, but he was not Patroclus: he was rather the latter's model, Antilochus.[54]

In the *Posthomerica*, Achilles' emotional weakness against Penthesilea's beauty does not go unnoticed: Thersites reproaches and taunts him with an aggressive and sarcastic speech (1.722–40). Achilles hits him with a punch and kills him, arousing the approval of other soldiers, who despised that nasty fellow because of his provocative attitude towards everyone (741–65). Only Diomedes (bound by a family relationship with Thersites)[55] gets angry and is about to attack Achilles; but he is held by his comrades, who succeed in calming him down and preventing a brawl (766–81). The body of Penthesilea with her armour and weapons is returned by the Achaeans to the Trojans, who burn it and bury her remains with great honour in the tomb of Laomedon (782–810).

Now, let us see what happened in the *Aethiopis*, starting from Proclus' summary: after the arrival of Penthesilea, κτείνει αὐτὴν ἀριστεύουσαν Ἀχιλλεύς, οἱ δὲ Τρῶες αὐτὴν θάπτουσι, 'she dominates the battlefield, but Achilles kills her and the Trojans bury her' (*Chrest.* 176–7).[56] There was therefore the *aristeia* of the Amazon, culminating with her slaying at the hands of Achilles, who then returned her body to the Trojans, allowing them to bury her, not unlike in the *Posthomerica*. Proclus continues by saying that 'Achilles kills Thersites after being abused by him and insulted over his alleged love for Penthesilea': Ἀχιλλεὺς Θερσίτην ἀναιρεῖ λοιδορηθεὶς πρὸς αὐτοῦ καὶ ὀνειδισθεὶς τὸν ἐπὶ τῆι Πενθεσιλείαι λεγόμενον ἔρωτα (178–80). It seems that, in the *Aethiopis*, Achilles killed Thersites at a later time, compared to the *Posthomerica*: not soon after the duel and the slaying of Penthesilea, but after her burial. Yet, some scholars question Proclus' summary, suspecting a possible change in the sequence of

[53] Kullmann (1960: 44–5, 193–4); Dihle (1970: 159–60); Erbse (1983).

[54] Scafoglio (2017a: 41–7).

[55] This family relationship is a post-Homeric (and arguably post-Cyclic) invention: the most ancient witness is Pherecydes, 3.F.123 Jacoby (fifth century BCE).

[56] Text by Severyns (1963); translation adapted from West (2003).

events.[57] But this issue is related to another, major problem: what happened to Achilles, and what did he do, after killing Penthesilea?

Achilles defeated and killed her: this is certain. Did he fall in love with her? Love is such a big word: actually, it sounds appropriate for the feeling of the hero in the *Posthomerica* (this is why Quintus needs the digression about Ares' failed revenge to restore the epic tone); but it could hardly be so for the corresponding scene of the *Aethiopis*, which is supposed to be more consistent with the rules of its literary genre: we may rather imagine that Achilles was fascinated by Penthesilea, struck by her beauty as well as by her bravery. Proclus does not specify when this happened, while some of the many iconographic representations of the killing of Penthesilea dating between the sixth and fourth centuries BCE highlight an intense exchange of looks between Achilles and her in the last moments of the duel.[58] I do not think, though, that the hero's emotional reaction happened during the fight: it is well known that artisans and painters tend to concentrate events in space and time; and it is also understandable that they found the duel more interesting *in fieri* than its result (when Penthesilea was already dead), but neither did they want to give up the sentimental side of the story. I think that, in the *Aethiopis*, Achilles was impressed by Penthesilea's beauty just after her death, as he removed her helmet, as it happens in the *Posthomerica*, which follow the Cyclic model in this respect.

In some sources of the imperial age, besides, Achilles is ascribed a perverse attitude towards Penthesilea's dead body (necrophilia):[59] this could well be a further evolution of the legend, due to the morbid sensibility of Hellenism or late antiquity. Nevertheless, some scholars trace it back to the Epic Cycle, and therefore to the *Aethiopis*, based on the witness of Eustathius (*ad Il.* 2.220):

Ἡ δὲ νεωτέρα ἱστορία καὶ ἀναιρεθῆναι τὸν Θερσίτην ὑπ' Ἀχιλλέως λέγει κονδυλισθέντα, ὁπηνίκα τὴν Ἀμαζόνα Πενθεσίλειαν ἐκεῖνος ἀνελὼν οἶκτον ἔσχεν ἐπὶ τῇ κειμένῃ. ὁ μὲν γὰρ ἐθαύμαζε τὸ κάλλος καὶ ὡς καλὴν ἅμα καὶ ἀνδρείαν ἀνδρειότατος καὶ κάλλιστος ἠλέει κειμένην τὸ ὅμοιον οἰκτιζόμενος· ὁ δέ, ὡς εἴρηται, πιθηκόμορφος ἐπὶ λαγνείᾳ σκώπτει τὸν καλὸν ἥρωα. ὁ τοίνυν Ἀχιλλεὺς γογγύλῃ χειρὶ παίσας τὸν αἴσχιστον τῇ καλῇ Πενθεσιλείᾳ συγκατακλίνει.

A more recent tale says that Thersites was killed by Achilles with a punch, that time when the latter, after killing Penthesilea, felt pity for her. He, who was bravest and most handsome, admired her beauty and mourned out of pity for her, lying dead, as beautiful and brave at the

---

[57] E.g.Vian (1959a: 20–1).

[58] *LIMC* s.v. 'Achilleus', 719–44, esp. the neck-amphora by Exekias, 723, pl. 7.

[59] Liban. *Progymn.* 9.1.22; *Serv. auct. ad Aen.* 2.555; Nonn. *D.* 35.27–30; *Schol. ad Soph. Ph.* 445.

same time. But Thersites, resembling an ape, as the story says, taunted the handsome hero charging him with lust. Achilles, then, after hitting him with a punch, lay with the beautiful Penthesilea.

Eustathius is rightly regarded as a reliable author, who provides useful information on the Homeric epics, often going back to Alexandrian philology. In this particular case, in fact, he uses the phrase νεωτέρα ἱστορία, that recalls the definition of νεώτεροι usually attributed by Hellenistic scholars to the poets of the Epic Cycle: this is why this witness is supposed to come from Aristarchus, and so it is taken seriously, as referring to the *Aethiopis*.[60] However, there are some problems preventing me from sharing this position, beginning with the difference between Eustathius' witness and Proclus' summary, which is still the most important evidence on the *Aethiopis*. We might even assume that Proclus passes over in silence Achilles' lust for Penthesilea's dead body because of the very concise setting of his summary (or for any other reason, such as *pudoris causa*); but he puts the killing of Thersites by Achilles at a later time, after the burial of Penthesilea: we should admit an inversion in the order of facts (as some scholars do) in order to make the *Aethiopis* consistent with Eustathius' witness. This witness also presents some internal incongruities, as Achilles' first feelings of pity and admiration for the beauty and bravery of his dead enemy, and even the fact that he 'mourned for her', do not provide any adequate reason for the charge of Thersites: ἐπὶ λαγνείᾳ. In Eustathius' account, paradoxically, such a lust comes only after the killing of Thersites and, even more weirdly, confirms his accusation a posteriori! Furthermore, despite the apparent consequentiality between Achilles' appreciation of Penthesilea's beauty and his subsequent attitude of lust, I see a too serious deterioration and even a substantial opposition between what Eustathius calls 'pity' (οἶκτον, and little later οἰκτιζόμενος) and describes as a feeling of admiration (ἐθαύμαζε) aroused by her beauty and likewise by her courage (ὡς καλὴν ἅμα καὶ ἀνδρείαν), on the one side, and the brutal sexual act practised by the hero on her dead body shortly after, on the other.

For these reasons, I think that Eustathius has juxtaposed two different versions, coming from distinct sources: Achilles' admiration and pity for the dead enemy comes from the *Aethiopis* – this is what Eustathius found in an Alexandrian scholium – while Achilles' perverted sex with the cadaver was known to him from later sources. The common element to both versions that maybe served as a *trait d'union* was Achilles' killing of Thersites after his accusation. He charged Achilles ἐπὶ λαγνείᾳ in both versions, but the meaning of this word was not the same: it does indeed mean 'sex', 'sexual intercourse'[61] and 'sex

---

[60] E.g. Vian (1959a: 20–1).
[61] Hipp. *De nat. puer.* 20; Arist. *HA* 575a21.

excess', 'lust'.[62] In the version of the *Aethiopis*, Thersites misunderstood Achilles' feelings of admiration and pity, and accused him of being *sous le charme*, fascinated by Penthesilea. Nothing more, but this was enough to undermine the honour of the hero and to hurt his pride, pushing him to that violent reaction. Eustathius did not understand such a reaction and searched for the reason for it in a stronger and more sinister meaning of the word λαγνεία: he found it easily in another version of the legend from a different, more recent source, which spoke of the sexual practice on the dead body. In this source, Thersites saw Achilles doing it, and made contemptuous comments, due to which Achilles killed him, and then he completed his dirty work (ὁ τοίνυν Ἀχιλλεὺς γογγύλῃ χειρὶ παίσας τὸν αἴσχιστον τῇ καλῇ Πενθεσιλείᾳ συγκατακλίνει). It is also possible that Eustathius found the two versions already mixed in an intermediate source, that had merged (for the very reason just reconstructed) the Cyclic story transmitted by Aristarchus with the more recent account featuring necrophilia.

The supposed genesis of the double and mixed account transmitted by Eustathius, moreover, allows us to trace the origin of the raunchy version of the legend, or at least to glimpse its possible cause. Thersites' accusations based on Achilles' attitude of admiration and pity for the dead enemy did not provide a proper explanation of the hero's backlash, in the eyes of more 'modern' readers (in the Hellenistic period, but maybe even earlier).[63] The (post-Homeric) fame of Achilles' sexual voracity, exploited in several episodes of his life (from Deidamia to Patroclus, without forgetting Troilus and continuing until the death of the hero, caused by his love for Polyxena),[64] did the rest.

Anyway, Quintus has followed the Cyclic version of the story, which was not the only one available at his time, and which probably was not the more widespread; but it was the cleaner and more streamlined, and the one that saved Achilles' dignity. Whether Quintus read the text of the *Aethiopis* (as I believe), or he knew that version from a summary of the poem, or he took it from an intermediate source without even knowing its origin (but I do not think so), he chose it and followed more or less consciously (in my view, with full awareness) in the wake of the Epic Cycle. Actually, he introduced changes and variations, such as the failed attempt of the Trojan women to join the battle and Ares' unfulfilled revenge (not by chance, two episodes that have an impact on the climate of the tale, increasing the pathos, but have no consequence on the overall development of the action, just like the Patroclus simile). He exploited and enhanced the sentimental side of the story, transforming Achilles' admiration

---

[62] Xen. *Mem.* 2.1.1; Arist. *EE* 1231a20.

[63] One may think, for instance, of the lost tragedy *Achilleus Thersitoktonos* by Chaeremon (fourth century BCE).

[64] Fantuzzi (2012).

and pity into 'love at first sight', with a more modern and 'romantic' appeal[65] (counterbalanced by Ares' very epic incident).

Now we can turn back to another change that we find in the *Posthomerica*, with respect to Proclus' summary of the *Aethiopis*: in the former, Achilles kills Thersites (1.741–3) before the Achaean kings decide to give Penthesilea's body to the Trojans, who burn it and bury her remains (1.782ff.); in the latter, it seems that the killing of Thersites happened after the return of her body and the burial: οἱ δὲ Τρῶες αὐτὴν θάπτουσι. καὶ Ἀχιλλεύς Θερσίτην ἀναιρεῖ (*Chrest.* 177–8). I think that in fact it happened not *after*, but *because of* the return of the cadaver to the Trojans by the decision of Achilles, a decision that gave Thersites the reason and occasion to accuse the hero, who reacted by punching him and causing his death. This would explain why, in Proclus' very succinct summary, the killing of Thersites is placed after the return and burial of Penthesilea's body, which actually happened after, but depended on the decision taken by Achilles just before, a decision that was the cause of the quarrel. Quintus changed this point completely, increasing Achilles' emotional reaction to the dead Penthesilea's beauty and presenting Thersites' accusations as his immediate response to the hero's weird love for the enemy; on the other hand, the decision to return the body to the Trojans is taken by the 'Achaean kings' and not by Achilles alone.

The killing of Thersites unleashed a dispute among the Achaeans, according to Proclus: καὶ ἐκ τούτου στάσις γίνεται τοῖς Ἀχαιοῖς περὶ τοῦ Θερσίτου φόνου (*Chrest.* 180–1). Is this the same dispute between Achilles and Diomedes told by Quintus (1.766–81)? This is what some scholars believe, compelling Proclus' wording (under the pretext of its succinctness) to match the corresponding episode of the *Posthomerica*;[66] but I do not think so. Indeed, the word στάσις (which is not Homeric and that Proclus hardly took from the text of the *Aethiopis*), might indicate a quarrel between two characters, but it mainly means a rebellion, a popular uprising, a brawl involving many people.[67] I would interpret it as a rising by (a part of) the army against Achilles, not so much in solidarity with Thersites or to refuse the violence and abuses of power, but rather to avoid the collective pollution due to the bloodshed.[68] This is why Achilles was forced to leave the army and travel to Lesbos, where he accomplished a rite of purification, offering sacrifices to the gods, with the help of Odysseus: μετὰ δὲ ταῦτα Ἀχιλλεὺς εἰς Λέσβον πλεῖ, καὶ θύσας Ἀπόλλωνι καὶ Ἀρτέμιδι καὶ Λητοῖ καθαίρεται τοῦ φόνου ὑπ' Ὀδυσσέως

---

[65] The same appeal is recognisable in other episodes of the *Posthomerica*, first and foremost that of Oenone in Book 10.

[66] Vian (1959a: 21–2); Kullmann (1960: 86).

[67] Radici Colace and Sergi (2000).

[68] For the relevance of the concepts of pollution and purification in early (non-Homeric) epics: Lloyd-Jones (1971: 73); and for their reflections in the *Iliad*: Davies (2016: 56).

(*Chrest.* 182–4). Quintus has simplified this point and has made it closer to Homer (that is to the *Iliad*), turning it into a dispute between two heroes, and eliminating Achilles' travel and purification ritual, especially since he had already exploited the pollution motif, with regard to Penthesilea's participation to the Trojan War. But that dispute is ultimately a very marginal episode, which has taken the place of a narrative segment that most probably was a major development in the *Aethiopis* (at least judging by the space it occupies in Proclus' summary). Quintus introduced this dispute only to fill a gap: not really a gap in the plot of his poem, which had no need for such an expedient, but a gap in the overall pattern of events that he found in his model (the *Aethiopis*, or at least its content and general structure, as available through a summary) and that he reworked in his *Posthomerica*. Even the differences, therefore, far from disproving a priori Quintus' relationship with the Epic Cycle, can instead help in understanding and properly assessing this relationship.

Book 1 of the *Posthomerica* ends with the funeral rite for Penthesilea and the burial of cadavers of both sides, during a truce (1.782ff.): it presents a compact and consistent structure pointing not so much to a Homeric book, but rather to an individual and independent song: the kind of song that could have been found in Archaic times in the oral tradition and that had been fixed in writing in the Cyclic poems, such as the Ἀμαζονία that converged in the *Aethiopis*.

Finally, I hope I have shown that the *Posthomerica* depend on the Epic Cycle (and/or on the view of the Epic Cycle elaborated in Aristotelian and Alexandrian criticism) for its overall design, literary conception and architecture. My study of Book 1 reveals a 'dialectic approach' with (the first part of) the *Aethiopis*, which Quintus follows in its broader outlines (whether he read its text or not), yet departing from it on some occasions, by turning to other models or even inserting elements that have a good chance of being entirely new. My analysis confirms the (partial and relative) dependence of the *Posthomerica* on the Epic Cycle, which remains a point of reference in the rich and complex framework of Quintus' models and sources, over and above the long-standing and maybe unsolvable problem of direct imitation. But it also demonstrates, I hope, the critical and creative relationship established by Quintus with his models and, more generally, with the cultural tradition. The denial of this creativity, often repeated by scholars until recently, has been the cause of a misunderstanding of many aspects the *Posthomerica* (including its connection with the Epic Cycle) and even of the poem as a whole.

PART V

Re-Readings and Re-Workings

Philological Editor and Protestant Pedagogue: How Lorenz Rhodoman (1545–1606) Worked on the *Posthomerica* of Quintus Smyrnaeus[1]

Thomas Gärtner

The editor of Quintus of Smyrna who made the largest-scale emendations to his *Posthomerica* (*PH*) is doubtless Lorenz Rhodoman,[2] who reflects on his conjectural-critical achievement in ll. 155–6 of the dedicatory poem that we shall study in the present article: αὐτοῦ λύματ᾽ ἀοιδοῦ / πολλὰ μάλ᾽ ἐξεκάθηρα. Rhodoman carried out textual criticism on the *PH* twice. At the beginning of his scholarly career, he published the three concluding books of the *PH* in a special edition at the request of his teacher in Ilfeld, Michael Neander (1577),[3] and at the end of his life, he crowned his academic activity with a complete edition of the *PH*, expanded with a large number of paratexts (1604).[4] His emendatory achievements find echoes everywhere even in a modern *apparatus criticus* to the *PH*, but the context of his life is less well known.[5] He was a Protestant scholar from a modest family in the generation immediately after Luther: in his autobiography,[6] he identifies the year of his

---

[1] English translation: Brian McNeil.
[2] See my survey article: Gärtner (2016); also T. Gärtner (2017).
[3] Partial edition of the *PH* (subscribed in 1573): Neander (1577).
[4] Complete edition of the *PH*: Rhodoman (1604a).
[5] The only monograph on Rhodoman is outdated, but it contains a wealth of material: Lange (1741).
[6] *Bioporikon* (subscribed 1582), in: Crusius (1585); critical edition: Gärtner (forthcoming); German translation with notes and commentary: Ludwig (2014).

birth (1545) with the last year of Luther's life (not with the year of his death).[7] He would doubtless have wished for a synchronism that placed his birth in the year of the Reformer's death.

Luther is the person who determines Rhodoman's understanding of his own self and of history. Rhodoman sees himself as a pedagogue at the service of the Lutheran Reformation, as one who blazes the trail for this salutary movement that embraces the whole of Germany. Other Reformers who took alternative paths, such as Calvin, are clearly downgraded by Rhodoman in his *vita* of Luther; it is the Wittenberg Reformer who ensures that Germany holds the leading position in theology. All the other disciplines are fertilised by theology and follow in its wake, so that Germany is experiencing a golden age with regard to science and education.[8] The classical languages enjoy a particular importance in the academic canon, especially ancient Greek, which makes it possible to penetrate through the mediating stage of the Roman-Latin tradition to the Greek originals both in sacred scripture and in archaeology. In this sense, Rhodoman too plays a significant role in the progress of the Reformation, as a teacher who imparts knowledge of ancient Greek.

Rhodoman is, however, no lone warrior here. In many testimonies about his own life, he locates himself in the Grecist school of Michael Neander in Ilfeld, which produced a number of scholars who composed poems in the classical Greek language as vehicles for Reformation contents. Rhodoman was probably the one who developed the highest measure of linguistic skill. He wrote mythological epyllia that his teacher Neander published anonymously as pseudo-ancient literature,[9] and this learned hoax had considerable success with a part of the academic public (for example, with the Jesuit Denys Petau and the celebrated English author and philologist Joshua Barnes). We may say that the Lutheran Reformation's endeavour to have recourse to the original

---

[7] *Biop.* 43–5 (cf. Ludwig 2014: 152):

ἦν δ' ἔτος ὑστάτιον μεγάλῳ Χριστοῖο προφήτῃ
Λουθήρῳ, Γερμανὶς ὃν ἔξοχον αἶα φύτευσεν,
ᾧ Χριστός μιν ἔμελλεν ἐς αἰθέρα λαμπρὸν ἀείρειν.
Annus erat Christi, quem maximus ille propheta,
quotquot sanctiloquos peperit Germania vates,
Lutherus, coelo iam debitus, ultimum agebat.

It was the last year of the life of Luther, the great prophet of Christ, whom the Germanic land brought forth as its outstanding son. In that year, Christ was on the point of raising him up into the shining aether.

[8] This is the core affirmation of Rhodoman's *Protrepticon* (printed as a paratext in Neander 1582).

[9] Neander (1588). In 2019, Weise published a critical edition of the *Arion*, which is included in this work, with a commentary (Weise 2019).

text of the scriptures, which was uncorrupted by the Roman tradition, cata-
lysed German Philhellenism in a decisive manner, and that its most important
representatives were Neander's and Rhodoman's school of poets who wrote
in classical Greek. It was they who gave the German Philhellenism of the
sixteenth and seventeenth centuries its basic shape.

But let us return to Quintus of Smyrna. In addition to theologically relevant poetry in classical Greek, including a theological didactic poem,[10] a *vita*
of Luther,[11] a dialogical presentation of the Catechism,[12] and an epic history
of Palestine from Adam and Eve down to his own time,[13] Rhodoman also
devoted himself to antiquarian-philological studies, which bore fruit especially
in the important new editions of Diodorus Siculus[14] and Quintus of Smyrna.
Rhodoman's first edition of Quintus is accompanied by a dedicatory text in
hexameters addressed to Eberhard von Holle, Bishop of Lübeck (1531/32-86),
to whom Rhodoman owed the post as rector in Lüneburg that he held at the
time of its publication. Although von Holle was long deceased at the time of
the later, complete edition (1604), and Rhodoman had been appointed in the
meantime to a professorship in Wittenberg, he retained parts of this dedication
in hexameters, namely, the observations about Quintus and his relationship to
Homer (103-37) and about the usefulness of the PH (192b-237). A number of
small textual interventions partially eliminated the linguistic form of a dedicatory address in the second person singular, but the very fact that he retained
a part of this text shows the importance that Rhodoman as editor attached to
such paratexts. Like most of Rhodoman's other works, the poetical dedicatory text of the PH has the characteristic parallel form of interrelated Greek
and Latin hexameters. The Latin is not an exact translation of the Greek; in its
general tendency, it is rather a free parallel rendering.

The present chapter is accompanied by a critical edition based on the two
editions. The text begins with a retelling of the Trojan War, starting *ab ovo* with
the foundation of the city of Troy and thus going far beyond the framework
of the epic cycles themselves. In this mythological compendium, Rhodoman
gives the reader a systematic introduction to the story of Troy. The section in
which he explains the motivation of the expedition to Greece by Paris, the
son of the king of Troy, gives an impression of the sovereign complexity of his
presentation (48-57):

αὐτὰρ ἐϋκτεάνου Πριάμου πάϊς ὕβρεϊ χαίρων
ἤρτισεν εὐσκάρθμων νηῶν στόλον· ᾗσι πέρησεν

---

[10] Extant in the Weimarer MSS fol. 67 and fol. 68.
[11] Rhodoman (1579).
[12] Rhodoman (1596).
[13] Rhodoman (1589).
[14] Rhodoman (1604b).

Ἑλλάδ’ ἐς εὐναέτειραν, ἵν’ ἤθεα καὶ πέδον ἀνδρῶν
ἀλλοδαπῶν σκέψαιτο κακόσχολος, ἢ τίσιν αὐτοῖς
ὁρμαί<ν>ων, ὅτι πατρὸς ἑοῦ νόσφισσεν ἀδελφὴν
Ἡσιόνην χαρίεσσαν ἐὺ σθένος Ἡρακλῆος,
Δαρδανίης ὑπ’ Ἄρηϊ λύσας κρήδεμνα πόληος,
ἢ καὶ θελξινόοισιν ἐφημοσύνῃσι πιθήσας
Κύπριδος, ᾗ νέμε πρῶτα, περιφροσύνην ἀθερίξας
Παλλάδος ἠνορέην τε καὶ Ἥρης ὄλβιον ἀρχήν.

But the high-spirited son of the wealthy Priam made ready a voyage of his swift ships, with which he reached Greece with its fine settlements. His aim was to get to know the characters and the country of the foreigners, on a vacation with dreadful consequences. Or else he aimed at revenge on them, because Heracles the strong had separated the lovely Hesione, Priam's sister, from Paris' father when he broke through the cordon of the Trojan city. Or else he was following the enchanting task given him by the Cypriot (Aphrodite) to whom he gave the first place, paying no heed to the prudence of Pallas and to the strength and the rich rule of Hera.

Only the third of these motivations (55-7) corresponds to the traditional version of the judgement of Paris. The second alternative (51-4, vengeance for the seizing of Hesione at the first destruction of Troy) is the rationalistic motive that is played off against the 'un-rationalistic' judgement of Paris in the Trojan mythography of late antiquity (especially in Dares Phrygius), with which Rhodoman was acquainted.[15] Even before these two literary variants, Rhodoman posits another possible motivation on the part of Paris, namely, that he merely wanted to get to know foreign customs and countries (50–1, ἵν’ ἤθεα καὶ πέδον ἀνδρῶν / ἀλλοδαπῶν σκέψαιτο κακόσχολος). In comparison with the two other alternatives, this possibility is not per se very convincing; it is formulated with an allusion to the prooemium to the *Odyssey* (*Od.* 1.3, πολλῶν δ’ ἀνθρώπων ἴδεν ἄστεα καὶ νόον ἔγνω). The words ἤθεα καὶ πέδον skilfully reproduce the Homeric ἄστεα καὶ νόον in an exact metrical and morphological analogy, but in the reverse sequence. This intertextual allusion allows Rhodoman to make it clear that 'this Paris, whom one might at first sight take for a tolerant traveller like Odysseus, a man who has rather bad luck with his sightseeing (κακόσχολος), is in reality a warmonger who brings ruin, even if (according to the rationalistic

[15] It is clear from Rhodoman's own *Troika*, first printed by Neander as a pseudo-ancient work in 1588 (see note 9 above) and then printed in a slightly altered version in the collected edition of Quintus Smyrnaeus (1604), that Rhodoman knew these rationalisations in late antiquity. Here, he draws especially on the version by Dares Phrygius: Achilles is murdered in a Trojan temple to Apollo when he woos Polyxena.

version of the myths) his only intention originally was to demand the return of Priam's sister, or else (according to the classical version) he was doing the bidding of Aphrodite'. The continuation with ἡ δέ οἱ ἀμφ᾽ Ἑλένης κληηδόνι φίλτρον ἐνῆκεν (58) and the further course of the narrative show that Rhodoman prefers the last version.

In the overall context of the dedicatory poem and of what Rhodoman says about the poet Quintus of Smyrna whom he is editing, however, the mythological compendium does more than introduce the reader to the Trojan material or display Rhodoman's sovereign grasp of all the variants of the tradition. It achieves a total focusing on the myth, that is, on the material aspect of Quintus' work. The work that Rhodoman edits is perceived wholly from the perspective of the mythical material that is its theme.

It is in a certain sense the mythological material itself – which, according to Rhodoman, is dictated to Homer by the god of poetry, Phoebus, in person (111) – that determines its distribution among various poets. When Hector, the strongest son of Priam, falls in battle, Homer's Muse grieves to such an extent that she breaks off her narrative and brings the work (the *Iliad*) to a close (112–15):

ἀλλ᾽ οὐκ εἰς πολέμοιο βαρυκμήτοιο τελευτὴν
ἤγαγεν (*sc.* Ὅμηρος) ἡδυεπῆ Μούσης θρόον, ἀλλὰ σιωπὴν
ἔμβαλεν ἀχνυμένη[16] φόνον Ἕκτορος, ὥς μιν Ἀχιλλεὺς
συμμίξας ἐδάμασσεν ἀμυνόμενον περὶ πάτρης.   115
Sed non funesti dulciflua stamina Musa
texuit ad finem belli, namque Hectoris aegra
funere rupit opus, dum pro patria arma gerentem
sternit Pelides et circum moenia raptat.

But Homer did not conduct the pleasant sound of his Muse down to the end of the war with its heavy sounds. She fell silent because she lamented the death of Hector, when Achilles disfigured him and killed him in his courageous fight for the fatherland.

This simplifying account by Rhodoman disregards the fact that Homer's *Iliad* did not in the least describe the entire course of the Trojan War down to the death of Hector. It also fails to mention that Homer's Muse (if one assumes the identity of this poetic persona) takes up the story at a later point in the mythical chronology, namely, at the *nostos* of Odysseus in the Homeric *Odyssey*. These

---

[16] The change of subject to the Muse is somewhat harsh, and an obvious conjecture would be ἀχνυμένῃ, so that Homer could remain the subject. On the other hand, the Muse is consistently the subject in the parallel Latin version.

simplifications cannot possibly be due to ignorance on Rhodoman's part, since he was thoroughly familiar with the Trojan material in all its details. They can be explained only through his endeavour to present the poet Quintus of Smyrna, whose work he was editing, as the one whose poetic account picked up immediately at the point where Homer's Muse broke off her story.

Rhodoman thus focuses his picture of Quintus entirely on the 'after' that is found in the title *PH* or τὰ μεθ' Ὅμηρον. It must be emphasised that Rhodoman does not intend this to be understood as a reference to the fact that Quintus lived at a much later period than Homer, nor as indicating a qualitative subordination. He has nothing to say in the dedicatory verses about a historical contextualisation of Quintus in the imperial age in which the poet lived, and he underscores that Quintus is not to be thought inferior to Homer with regard to his learning and his linguistic presentation (118–23). By leaving Quintus completely uncontextualised in his biographical data (and we know, in fact, nothing about him except the consecration of the Muses near Smyrna; see below) and by restricting him to two aspects of the aesthetics of reception, εὐμαθίη and ἀρτιέπεια, he is able to present Quintus as an equal pendent to Homer. If, on the other hand, he had given Quintus his historical place as an imperial poet, he would have had to admit that his εὐμαθίη was no longer anything special in that period (unlike the situation in the archaic Homeric age), and that his ἀρτιέπεια merely reproduced the poetic language of an epoch long past. Here too, Rhodoman acts consistently when he depicts Quintus completely against the background of the mythical Trojan material.

Rhodoman thus consistently interprets the μεθ' Ὅμηρον of the work's title in the sense of δεύτερος Ὅμηρος (122–3):

> (. . .) ὡς μεθ' Ὅμηρον
> πάνσοφον ἀτρεκέως ὅ γε δεύτερός ἐστιν Ὅμηρος.
> (. . .) merito censebitur alter Homerus,
> qui tam felici studio succedit Homero.

For after Homer, who was wise in every sphere, he (i.e. Q.S.) is indisputably the second Homer.

This tendency is also confirmed by a special reading of the Latin version in the later edition. In the first edition, he says of Quintus: *qui tam felici studio succedit Homero*. In the second edition, the relative clause refers back to Homer: *cuius felici sequitur vestigia passu*. Rhodoman echoes here the celebrated epilogue of the *Thebais* of Statius, who describes his work as follows (12.816–17):

> (. . .) Nec tu divinam Aeneida tempta,
> Sed longe sequere et vestigia semper adora.

And you (sc. the *Thebais*), do not compete with the divine *Aeneid*, but follow it at a great distance and be content with venerating its footprints.

The words *felici sequitur vestigia passu* assert that Quintus has no need of the humility appropriate to an epigone in relation to Homer. Rather, he is entitled to consider himself Homer's 'happy', that is to say, 'equal', follower.

After these remarks about Quintus' relationship to Homer against the background of the mythological Trojan material, Rhodoman speaks of the few facts about Quintus that can be affirmed (124–30):

τόνδ' οὐ γνήσιον οὔνομ' ἐπηυδάξαντο Κάλαβρον,
οὕνεκα Βησσαρίων ποτ' ἐν ἀγχιάλοισι Καλάβρων   125
εὕρατό μιν δαπέδοισιν ἀϊστωθέντα πάροιθεν
ἐκ μερόπων· ὁ δὲ κλῆσιν ἐτήτυμον ἔσχε Κοΐντου.
Σμύρνη δ' αὐτὸν ἔθρεψεν, ὅθεν καὶ δῖος Ὅμηρος,
ὡς αὐτὸς σήμηνεν ἐνὶ σφετέρης σελίδεσσι
μάρτυρος ἀξιόπιστος. (. . .)   130
Hunc Quintum falso Calabrum cognomine dicunt,
quod fuit in Calabris a Bessarione repertus,
hospes ubi latuit carie confectus in urbe
Hydruntis. verum sed nomen redde Cointo,
quem Smyrnaea aluit tellus, unde ortus Homerus.
haec vero ipse sua, cui fas quoque credere, voce
testatur vates. (. . .)

They give him the incorrect name *Calaber*, because Bessarion once found him in the fields of Calabria, after he had previously disappeared completely from the human world. His correct name was Quintus. He grew up in Smyrna, the city from which Homer too came, as he himself bore witness in his work.

This refers to Quintus' incorrect sobriquet *Calaber*, which goes back to the discovery in Calabria by Cardinal Bessarion of an important manuscript, the Hydruntinus, and to his provenance from Smyrna, which is inferred from his own testimony. This provenance is adduced only in order to create a new parallel between Quintus and Homer, since Smyrna was one of the cities that claimed Homer as its own citizen.

This is followed by an evaluation of Quintus' celebrated testimony to his consecration by the Muses near Smyrna, the only information he gives about himself:

(. . .) ἔπος καὶ τοῦτο χαράξας,   130
ὡς Μοῦσαί μιν ἔθηκαν ἁλιρρόου ἀγχόθεν Ἕρμου

βώτορ' ἐῶν ὀΐων καὶ ἐνὶ φρεσὶ χεῦαν ἀοιδὴν
οὐκ ἔτ' ἰουλίζοντος ἐπήρατον· ἔνθεν ἔοικε
παίδων ἀρτιμαθῶν κοσμήτορα τόνδε γενέσθαι
μουσοπόλοις περίβωτον ἐν ἀνδράσιν· αὐτὰρ ἄϊστον,   135
ὄντινά μιν βίος ἔσχεν ἀνὰ χρόνον, ὧν δ' ἀνέτειλεν
ἐκ πατέρων, οἵην τε τελευτήσας λάχε μοῖραν.

(. . .) *reliquisque hoc insuper addit,*
Musarum quod pavit oves, ubi volvitur Hermus
in mare, et in tenero concepit flore iuventae
munere Pieridum perfectam carminis artem.
hinc patet ingenuas pubem duxisse per artes
et tunc eximios inter fulsisse poetas.
sed latet ignotum, quo tempore traxerit aevum
et qua stirpe satus, qua functus morte quiescat.

And he also said that the Muses had appointed him the shepherd of their sheep near Hermos that flows into the sea, and that they had poured their lovely song into his heart before the down of his beard grew. It seems therefore that he was a teacher of children who are just learning, and that he became celebrated among those who have dealings with the Muses. But it is not known in which epoch he lived, who were his ancestors, or how he came to meet his death.

The underlying text here is *PH* 12.306–13:

τούς μοι νῦν καθ' ἕκαστον ἀνειρομένῳ σάφα, Μοῦσαι,
ἔσπεθ' ὅσοι κατέβησαν ἔσω πολυχανδέος ἵππου·
ὑμεῖς γὰρ πᾶσάν μοι ἐνὶ φρεσὶ θήκατ' ἀοιδήν,
πρίν μοι <ἔτ'>[17] ἀμφὶ παρειὰ κατασκίδνασθαι ἴουλον,
Σμύρνης ἐν δαπέδοισι περικλυτὰ μῆλα νέμοντι   310
τρὶς τόσον Ἕρμου ἄπωθεν ὅσον βοόωντος ἀκοῦσαι,
Ἀρτέμιδος περὶ νηὸν Ἐλευθερίῳ ἐνὶ κήπῳ,
οὔρεϊ οὔτε λίην χθαμαλῷ οὔθ' ὑψόθι πολλῷ.

Name me now these [heroes] clearly, every single one of them, since I ask you, O Muses, who it was that descended into the horse with its heavy paunch. For you have placed every song in my heart even before the down of my beard spread across my cheeks, as I tended splendid sheep in the fields of Smyrna, three times so far away from Hermos that

---

[17] The ἔτι inserted here comes from Hermann Köchly (1815–76) and was thus not known to Rhodoman, who reads πρίν μοι ἀμφί both in the partial edition and in the complete edition of 1604.

I could have heard the roar of its waters, near the temple of Artemis in the Eleutherian garden, on a hill that is neither excessively small nor reaches up far into the heights.

In Rhodoman, Quintus' formulation ὑμεῖς γὰρ πᾶσάν μοι ἐνὶ φρεσὶ θήκατ' ἀοιδήν, / πρίν μοι <ἔτ'> ἀμφὶ παρειὰ κατασκίδνασθαι ἴουλον (12.308–9) is reproduced by ll. 132–3, ἐνὶ φρεσὶ χεῦαν ἀοιδὴν / οὐκ ἔτ' ἰουλίζοντος ἐπήρατον. It is, however, striking that the participial expression Σμύρνης ἐν δαπέδοισι περικλυτὰ μῆλα νέμοντι (12.310), which in fact describes only the setting of the entire scene (Quintus as a shepherd near Smyrna), becomes in Rhodoman ὡς Μοῦσαί μιν ἔθηκαν ἁλιρρόου ἀγχόθεν Ἕρμου / βώτορ' ἑῶν ὀΐων (131–2). In other words, the very conventional setting of the scene for the consecration by the Muses in Quintus is interpreted in Rhodoman as a metaphorical expression for Quintus' activity as a teacher, which enjoyed the favour of the Muses. This is made very clear in the conclusion, which is presented as an interpretative inference (133–5):

> (. . .) ἔνθεν ἔοικε
> παίδων ἀρτιμαθῶν κοσμήτορα τόνδε γενέσθαι
> μουσοπόλοις περίβωτον ἐν ἀνδράσιν. (. . .)   135

It seems therefore that he was a teacher of children who are just learning, and that he became celebrated among those who have dealings with the Muses.

This highly remarkable metaphorisation of the concept of shepherd is not merely an αὐτοσχεδίασμα that Rhodoman invented only for his metrical dedicatory address. We find the same interpretation in the prose preface to his great edition of the whole of the *PH* in 1604 (*praefatio ad lectorem*):

> *Caeterum ex indicio isto, quod de se ipse facit, Musarum oves in liberali Smyrnae horto se pavisse testatus, scholam in Ioniae littore isto nec infrequentem nec incelebrem habuisse poetam nostrum colligere est. nec triviale magisterium id fuisse apparet inde, quod oves suas, id est discipulos, nobiles seu fama illustres* περικλυτὰ *epitheto satis emphatico appellat, unde si divinare licet, id tandem elicimus, Cointum fuisse ex professione illorum, quos sophistas, id est philosophiae et eloquentiae magistros, grammaticos, qui poetarum interpretes erant et iuventutis scholasticae doctores, florens adhuc Graecia indigetabat. quid enim aliud per Musarum hortum et oves praeter quam scholam et discipulos in ea doctrinae studiis et eloquentiae studiis addictos intelligi existimemus?*

Besides this, one can infer from this testimony that he makes about himself – namely, that he tended the sheep of the Muses in the garden of the Liberal Arts in Smyrna[18] – that our poet had a school on this Ionian coast that had not a few pupils and was not uncelebrated. Nor was it an elementary education, as we see from the fact that he calls his sheep, that is to say, his pupils, noble or celebrated for their prestige, using the sufficiently emphatic adjective περικλυτά. If we may be allowed to take this as a basis for speculations, we come finally to the conclusion that Quintus belonged to the professional class of those that Greece in its finest flowering called sophists, that is, teachers in philosophy and oratory, or grammarians, who were interpreters of the poets and teachers of the schoolboys. For what else are we to suppose could be meant by a garden of the Muses and sheep, if not a school and pupils who devote themselves in this school to the study of erudition and eloquence?

Besides this, the dedicatory preface in hexameters speaks in three other passages of the relationship between teacher and pupil. First, Rhodoman speaks about his own time as a pupil in the school at Ilfeld under Michael Neander. It was here that he was first introduced to Quintus of Smyrna (138–43):

τόνδε ποτ' ἀγχίνοον πινυτοῦ μιμήτορ' Ὁμήρου
Ἑρκυνίοις ὑπ' ὄρεσσιν ἑαῖς ξύνωσε Νέανδρος
ποίμναις, τὰς ἀνὰ κῆπον ἐλεύθερον[19] ἄνθεσι Μουσῶν   140
φέρβει. τῇσιν ἐγώ ποτε σύννομος εἶδαρ ἔρεψα
ἄφθονον, ἰδμοσύνης τε καὶ ἤθεος εἶδαρ ἀμώμου,
μυρία δ' ἐσθλὰ πέπονθα φιλοφροσύνῃσι Νεάνδρου.

Once in the past, Neander at the foot of the Harz communicated this clever imitator (Q.S.) of the wise Homer to his flocks, whom he nourished in the garden of the Liberal Arts with the blossoms of the Muses. Together with these flocks, I too browsed and plucked rich fodder for myself, the fodder of knowledge and of an irreproachable character, and I have experienced innumerable benefits thanks to Neander's kindly gifts.

Secondly, he writes about the spiritual pastoral activity of Bishop Eberhard von Holle (170–1):

ἀλλὰ σὺ, τριχθαδίης τιμῆς ἀριδείκετε φωστὴρ,   170
ὃν Θεὸς ὢν προβάτων ἀγανόφρονα ποιμένα θῆκεν.

---

[18] Rhodoman clearly here interprets the Greek Ἐλευθερίῳ ἐνὶ κήπῳ ('in the Eleutherian garden') to mean 'in the garden of the Liberal Arts'.

[19] See the previous footnote. It is very obvious here that Rhodoman equates the (supposed) 'flocks of the Muses' of Quintus of Smyrna with his own education in Ilfeld.

But you, O celebrated beacon of a threefold honour, whom God appointed as the gentle shepherd of his sheep.

Thirdly, Rhodoman says about his own activity as a teacher (175–9):

> ὡς χάριν οἶδα τεῇς εὐεργεσίῃσιν ἑτοίμως,   175
> αἷς μ' ἀγανῶς κόσμησας ἐνηέα ῥάβδον ὀπάσσας
> <u>ποίμνης βοσκομένης</u> ἱεροῖς ἐνὶ τέμπεσι <u>Μουσῶν</u>,
> ἧσι ποθεινὸν ἔδειμας ἐπαύλιον εὔφρονι θυμῷ
> πολλὰ χαριζόμενός σφιν ὀνήσιμα. (. . .)

Because I readily acknowledge my gratitude to your acts of kindness, which you so mildly bestowed upon me when you granted me to wield the gracious pastoral staff over a flock that browses in the sacred valley of the Muses – the acts whereby you established a shelter in your great kindness and gave them (the sheep) much help.

The Muses are always found in the context of the shepherd metaphors. The exception is the case of Bishop Eberhard von Holle; but he too is said in other contexts (179–81; 239–41) to have an affinity to the Muses, since knows that a religious attitude needs a basis in education (183–4, καὶ ὡς λόγος ἔνθεος αἰεὶ / τοιαύτης κρηπῖδος ἐν ἀνθρώποισι χατίζει), and he is a model for the children through his interest in the classical Greek language (239–44).

We must therefore conclude that Rhodoman misunderstood Quintus' consecration by the Muses in the light of a cluster of metaphors that was very familiar to him from his contemporary milieu. This misunderstanding saw Quintus at the time of his consecration not as a shepherd in the traditional sense, but as the teacher of a 'flock' of young pupils that was entrusted to his care. The prose preface even infers from the juncture περικλυτὰ μῆλα that this must have been an especially prominent school.

This reading of his misinterpretation of Quintus' consecration by the Muses finds confirmation in another work by Rhodoman. The *Hymnus scholasticus*, attached as preface to a work by Rhodoman's teacher Neander,[20] praises human education and interprets the entire course of human history, beginning with the Book of Genesis in the Old Testament and ending with the school in Ilfeld, as a sequence of foundations of schools. The dedicatory preface to the *PH* can be understood in a corresponding manner: Quintus himself was the teacher of a celebrated school, and he presumably handed on the Homeric language to his pupils. In the present time, Neander continued this tradition in Ilfeld and handed on the *PH* to his pupil Rhodoman, who in turn handed

---

[20] *Hymnus scholasticus*, in Neander (1585).

it on to his own pupils (Rhodoman insists in many passages of the prooemium to his work that he is writing everything that he writes for the benefit of his pupils). It was the patronage of Bishop Eberhard von Holle, a man likewise well disposed to the Muses and a recipient of their favour, that made it possible for Rhodoman to carry out his teaching activity. Rhodoman thus ultimately integrates Quintus into his image of the world, where intellectual history takes place in the successive foundation of important schools.

After noting that there is no further information about the life of Quintus of Smyrna (136–7) – which also accords with Rhodoman's lack of interest in the historical context of the poet – he relates (144–51) that Neander gave him the task of working on the last three books of the *PH*, and that he gladly did so.

This is followed by the actual dedication to Bishop Eberhard von Holle, in the form of a question: 'To *whom* should I dedicate the present work?'

> ἀλλὰ τίνι πρώτῳ καρπῶν ἀναθήσομ' ἀπαρχὰς
> ἡμετέρων; (. . .)
> *Sed cui primitias nostrae sacravero messis?*

But to whom ought I to dedicate the first fruits of my harvest?

The question in this form reminds the reader who knows classical literature of the introductory poem in which Catullus of Verona dedicates his *libellus* to Cornelius Nepos:

> *Cui dono lepidum novum libellum*
> *Arida modo pumice expolitum?*
> *Corneli, tibi. (. . .)*

To whom ought I to give the pretty little new book that has just been polished with dry pumice stone? To you, Cornelius Nepos.

In the specific form of his question, however, Catullus is following a Greek model, namely, the introductory poem of the *Garland* woven by Meleager, the oldest collection of epigrams that is recognisable in the *Palatine Anthology* (Meleager *Anth. Pal.* 4.1 = *HE* 3926-9):

> Μοῦσα φίλα, τίνι τάνδε φέρεις πάγκαρπον ἀοιδὰν;
>   ἢ τίς ὁ καὶ τεύξας *(an πλέξας ?)* ὑμνοθετῶν στέφανον;
> ἄνυσε μὲν Μελέαγρος· ἀριζάλῳ δὲ Διοκλεῖ
>   μναμόσυνον ταύταν ἐξεπόνησε χάριν.

Dear Muse, to whom do you bring this song full of fruits? Or who was it in fact that created (or 'wove') the garland of the singers of songs?

Meleager did the work, but he brought this gift, created with much labour, to the illustrious Diocles for remembrance.

The comparison of the objects καρπῶν (. . .) ἀπαρχὰς and πάγκαρπον ἀοιδὰν makes it seem likely that Rhodoman has Meleager's introductory poem in mind. He employs the juncture ἀναθήσομ' ἀπαρχάς to add to it the solemn, sacral colouring of a sacrifice of first fruits. Rhodoman presents his partial edition of Quintus of Smyrna to the bishop like a sacred offering.

Rhodoman's train of thought is, nevertheless, closer to Catullus than to Meleager, since the introductory epigram to the *Garland* closes after two distichs without giving any reason for the choice of Diocles as addressee, whereas Catullus supplies an explanation through the clause with *namque* that follows the *tibi*. His choice lies on two levels: first, a personal level (Nepos greatly appreciated Catullus' *nugae*: Cat. *Carm.* 1.3–4), and, secondly, a substantial objective level (Nepos himself was the author of a learned universal history and wrote literature of a high quality: Cat. *Carm.* 1.5–7).

In Rhodoman, the explanation of this dedication to Eberhard is supplied in a section that is longer in comparison (162–94). He begins by drawing a positive picture of Eberhard (170–94) in contrast to the contemporary despisers of the Muses (162–9); this is, in one sense, the aspect of the objective appropriateness of Eberhard as addressee. Besides this, Eberhard has conferred a personal benefit on Rhodoman, and this is much more concrete than Nepos' appreciation of Catullus' poetry: he made him rector of the 'Michaelisgymnasium' in Lüneburg (175–7), the position that Rhodoman still held when he wrote the *praefatio*.

Rhodoman's dedicatory address can thus be understood as an extreme stretching of the argumentative form of Catullus' dedicatory poem. The praise of Eberhard justifies his selection as addressee of the dedication and, as in Catullus, this explanation is followed by a formal act of dedication (*praefatio* 238–9, νῦν δὲ σὺ τόνδε (*sc.* ἀοιδὸν) δέδεξο γαληνιόωντι προσώπῳ, / θυμῷ δ' εὐφρονέοντι; in Latin: *hunc igitur facili complectere mente poetam / et placido aspectu*, cf. Cat. *Carm.* 1.8–9, *quare habe tibi quicquid hoc libelli, / qualecumque*).

Before this, Rhodoman speaks to Bishop Eberhard von Holle about the usefulness that reading the *PH* can have for a contemporary leader (192–4). Here, he has recourse one final time to the key words εὐμαθίη and ἀρτιέπεια (121) as qualities in the aesthetic reception of Quintus. A leader can delight in the ἡδυεπείη of the poet (195–7), and he can also draw practical benefit from the stories of the mythological princes that are recounted in the *PH* (198–237).

The content of this teaching is formulated in anaphoric clauses with ὡς (from l. 207) that depend on διδάξει (206). These begin with moralising-political commonplaces: the end of great dominions, predetermined by God (207–8); then the corrupting effect of moral vice in the people and their leaders (209–10) and the futility of human resistance to God (210–11); a misogynistic reference to the corrupting erotic effect of women (212) has its expected place, as does an affirmation of the decisive impact that the action of one good or evil citizen can have (213–14); and cunning wins the victory over military strength (215).

The teaching unfolded in ll. 216–23 is much more concrete than these commonplaces. Here, we are told:

πολλάκις ὡς μεθύουσι καὶ ἀτρεμέουσιν ἀκαίρως
ἐχθρὸς ὑπὲρ κεφαλῆς ἐπὶ τέρψει πῆμα κορύσσει,
ὡς ἡμεῖς θαλίῃσι μεμηλότες ἠδὲ χορείαις
φιλτροτόκοις τε γυναιξὶ καὶ ἠλεμάτως τρυφόωντες,
πολλὰ δ' ἄωρα τελεῦντες ἀταρβέες εὐδιόωμεν,   220
Τυρκῷ δ' αὖ τὰ μεταξὺ καὶ ἀλλοδαποῖσι τυράννοις
κείρειν Τευτονίην χθόνα λείπομεν, ἄχρι καὶ ἐλθεῖν
εἰς πρόπυλον,[21] φανερῆς δ' οὐδεὶς ἐμπάζεται ἄτης.

That often, against people who are drunk and fearless at the wrong time, the enemy who looms over their head just at the moment when they are enjoying themselves brings a catastrophe upon them. And this is like our situation today. We are concerned about festivities, about dances and women who arouse love, and we devote ourselves foolishly to luxury and do much that is untimely. We live for the moment, and have no fear, while we surrender the German land to the Turk and to foreign tyrants for pillage. Finally, they will stand before our gates, but no one cares about the ruin that stares us in the face.

The passage beginning at l. 224 then offers somewhat general reflections on the vicissitudes of the lives of leaders such as Priam. A concrete political lesson is to be learnt from the fall of Troy. The Trojans, who devoted themselves unsuspectingly in their last night to wine, women and song are compared to the Germans, who carry on with their activities and are not at all impressed by the danger from the Turks, who are almost standing before their gates.

This way of looking at the Trojan War is unusual for a classical philologist, especially for a Latinist, who is accustomed to follow Vergil's apologia for Aeneas in the *Aeneid* by seeing the destruction of Troy as a typical intrigue of the cunning Greeks against the unsuspecting ancestors of the Romans and, in keeping with the well-known dictum of Aeneas, to derive the character of the Greeks in general from the one intrigue of Sinon. Rhodoman takes a very different line, castigating the dreaminess of the Greeks over their wine

---

[21] According to *PH* 13.20, οὐδ' ἄρ' ἐφράσσατ' ἐπὶ προθύροισιν ὄλεθρον ('and they did not notice the ruin that stood before their gates').

and treating this as a paradigm of political-military inattentiveness. The myth is stretched here to the very limit of its flexibility, for the destruction of Troy was not in fact a φανερὴ ἄτη (223) that the Trojans could have recognised, something about which they could have 'cared'.[22] On the contrary, this was simply a ruse of war, as Rhodoman himself explicitly states in l. 215.

There is a close parallel here to the mythological compendium at the beginning of the dedicatory address, where Rhodoman speaks of the guilt that Troy incurred by receiving back Paris, the king's son, who – in accordance with Helen's dream of the burning torch – ought instead to have been killed. We read here that the loving hearts of his parents no longer paid heed to the sign of their doom in the threatening dream of Hecuba (38–41, ἔνθα μιν ἀσπασίως κραδίη πρόσπτυξε τοκήων / οὐκέτι φραζομένη σφετέρης τεκμήριον ἄτης; cf. 223, φανερῆς δ᾽ οὐδεὶς ἐμπάζεται ἄτης). A few lines later, the text states (42–7):

εὖτε γὰρ ἀνθρώποισι κακῶν τεκταίνετ᾽ ἀμοιβὴν
ὕβριος ἐργατίνῃσιν ἔχων Θεὸς ἔκδικον ὄμμα,
φαίνει δῆλα πάροιθεν ἑοῦ σημήϊα θυμοῦ,
εἴ ποθ᾽ ὑποστρέψωσι βροτοί, προφύγωσι δ᾽ ὀϊζύν.   45
παυρίδιοι δ᾽ ἀλέγουσι προάγγελα σήματα ποινῆς
ἐκ κακίης νήψαντες· ὁ δ᾽ εἰς τίσιν ὄρνυτ᾽ ἀνηλῶς.

For when God wreaks vengeance in the form of suffering on the human beings who act arrogantly, turning his avenging eye on them, he shows them beforehand clear signs of his wrath, so that the mortals may perhaps change their conduct and escape their misery. But only a few are concerned about the premonitory signs of the punishments and leave their wickedness to come to sobriety. But then God hastens without compassion to punish them.

Here, using very similar concepts (44, φαίνει δῆλα, cf. 223, φανερῆς; 46, ἀλέγουσι, cf. 223, ἐμπάζεται; 39, οὐκέτι φραζομένη σφετέρης τεκμήριον ἄτης,

---

[22] Rhodoman probably has in mind the omens that, according to Quintus, preceded the fall of Troy – omens that the Trojans ignore (PH 13.519–23):

(. . .) μάλα μυρία δ᾽ ἄλλ᾽ ἐφαάνθη
σήματα Δαρδανίδῃσι καὶ ἄστεϊ πῆμα φέροντα·   520
ἀλλ᾽ οὐ δεῖμ᾽ ἀλεγεινὸν ἐπὶ Τρώων φρένας ἷξε
δερκομένων ἀλεγεινὰ τεράατα πάντα κατ᾽ ἄστυ·
Κῆρες γὰρ πάντων νόον ἔκβαλον. (. . .)

And innumerable other signs manifested themselves to the Trojans, proclaiming destruction to the city; but no painful fear entered the minds of the Trojans, although they saw every possible painful premonitory sign in the city – for the Keres robbed them of their understanding.

cf. 223, φανερῆς δ' οὐδεὶς ἐμπάζεται ἄτης), the signs of the divine wrath that were not perceived are identified as the cause of the fall of Troy. In Rhodoman's eyes, a similar nonchalance is displayed by the leaders of Germany with regard to the danger from the Turks and other foreign races that threaten Germany.

We can sum up as follows: in his poetic dedicatory *praefatio* to the *PH* of Quintus of Smyrna, Rhodoman presses two contemporary ideas on to the text, not without doing it some violence. First, he presses on to Quintus' consecration by the Muses the idea of a shepherd who is active as a teacher, in accordance with his own ideal of academic progress and of a successive spreading of the Reformation. Secondly, he presses on to the fall of Troy a disregard of divine premonitory signs, which he also perceives in the way in which the rulers of his own time deal with the Turkish danger. Rhodoman paints a positive image of Quintus in literary terms, the image that one often finds when Quintus is not contextualised in his own imperial age as a latecomer to Homeric poetry, but is regarded simply as an exponent of his mythological Trojan material: in that case, he is to some extent a second Homer who is in fact equal to the first.

Let us conclude by discussing a poetic reception of Quintus of Smyrna by Rhodoman outside the dedicatory prologue to his edition of the *PH*. In several passages in his poems, Rhodoman links the school of Michael Neander in Ilfeld (which we have mentioned above), where he himself had been a pupil, and its important former pupils, with the Trojan Horse.[23] In two passages, there is also a parallel comparison with a beehive. We read in Rhodoman's autobiographical *Bioporikon*:[24]

παντοδαποὶ δ' ἐπὶ τῷδε λόγων σπόρον ἔνθα καὶ ἔνθα
δασσάμενοι κατὰ γαῖαν ἀγήνορα Τευτονιδάων

---

[23] The comparison (ultimately Ciceronian: see below) between the Trojan Horse and Neander and his school in Ilfeld was made, probably in a secondary manner, by the celebrated school founder Valentin Friedland, known as Trozendorf (1490-1556), who brought Protestant humanism from Wittenberg to Silesia. Neander's Sapphic poem *De miseria, una etiam dignitate et gloria paedagogorum* (Neander 1588: 489–90) says of him:

οὐ σχολή, ὡς δουράτεος Πελάσγων
ἵππος, ἐς πάσας διδαχῇσι χώρας
εὐκλέας, πάσαις μεγάλους τε τέχναις
  ἔκχεεν ἄνδρας.

Like the Wooden Horse of the Pelasgians, his school poured out into every land men who were celebrated for their learning and outstanding in all the arts.

[24] See above, note 6.

Εἰφέλδης προιόντες, ἅτ' ἐκ σίμβλοιο μέλισσαι
Δαρδανίου <θ'> ἵππου λαγόνων ἡρῴος ἑσμός.
(. . .) et illos / (. . .) inter
ex variis missos terris, qui munera spargunt
doctrinae loca per varia in Germanide terra,
quos ut mellificis volucres emittit ab antris
duratei vel equi partum schola docta Neandri.

And after him (sc. Fickelthaus, the pupil of Neander who has just been mentioned by name) came people from everywhere who scattered the seed of the sciences here and there over the soil of the Germans that is so rich in men. They swarmed out from Ilfeld like bees from a hive and the swarm of heroes from the flank of the Trojan horse.

The two similes are treated with even greater differentiation in the *Hymnus scholasticus*, mentioned above.[25] They are interlocked under the rubric *iudicia et testimonia sapientum de Ilfelda*:

μαρτυρίην δέ τε πᾶσα βοᾷ χθών, ὥσπερ ἔοικεν
Εἰλφέλδη γονίμοισι παλαιοῦ κεύθεσιν ἵππου.
ὡς γὰρ τοῦδ' ἔκθρωσκε μενέκλονον ἄνθος Ἀχαιῶν
εὐκλείην Δαναοῖσι φέρον, Τρώεσσι δ' ὄλεθρον,
ὣς θάλος Ἑρκυνίης πεπνυμένον ἔνθεν ὀροῦον
βάρβαρα δυσσεβίης τ' ἀδαημοσύνης τε κραταιῶς
ἤθε' ἀπημάλδυνε καὶ ὑμῖν κῦδος ἀέξει.
σίμβλῳ δ' Εἰλφέλδην μελικευθέϊ φασὶν ὁμοίην,
ἔνθεν μουσοπόλων μάλα ταρφέα φῦλα μελισσῶν
ἐκπέταται σοφίης μελικηρίδας ὠδίνοντα
τῇ καὶ τῇ· φήμης δ' ὑμῖν χάρις ἔνθεν ἱκάνει.
Omnis proclamat regio, ceu Palladis ille
quod sit equus docto praegnans Ilfeldia fetu.
nam velut exsiluit flos armiger inde Pelasgum
ad decus aeternum Danais Troiaeque ruinam,
sic florem Hercyniae mittit sacer ille recessus,
quo cadat impietas et barbarus intereat mos
vestraque laus totum resonet cantata per orbem.
sunt, quibus alveolo similis schola vestra videtur,
ex quo musarum volitent examina, passim
doctrinae dulci stipent quae nectara fetu:
gratia et hinc vobis iucundi spiret honoris.

---

[25] See above, note 20.

The simile is expressed here as follows:

> The whole land bears witness with a loud voice that Ilfeld resembles the womb of the horse of old, the womb that gave birth. For just as the war-hardened flower of the Greeks sprang from the horse, bringing fame to the Greeks but ruin to the Trojans, so from here (*sc.* from Ilfeld) the elite of the Harz, inspired by the spirit, sprang forth and mightily destroyed the barbarous bad habits of godlessness and ignorance, and increased your fame (a reference to the fame of the Lords of Hohnstein, who are the addressees). It is also said that Ilfeld is like a beehive containing honey, from which the very numerous peoples of the bees, solicitous of the Muses, fly out in all directions and produce the honeycomb of wisdom. And for you (*sc.* the Lords of Hohnstein) this leads precisely to the gift of your fame.

The simile of the bees that is constructed separately in the last four verses affirms that the bees that swarm out 'produce the honeycomb of wisdom (σοφίης μελικηρίδας ὠδίνοντα)'.

The separation of the similes of Troy and the bees that we can observe here means that the collective effect of the beings that swarm out is formulated first in negative terms in the Troy metaphor (the destruction of godlessness – that is, of unreformed Christianity – and of ignorance), and then in positive terms in the simile of the bees (the production of the honeycomb of wisdom). The Greek warriors in the Wooden Horse are certainly evaluated positively, as the elite champions of a goal that is useful to the collective, that is to say, the destruction of Troy or (on the level of the simile) the spreading of the Reformation. Once again, as in the association of the capture of Troy with the danger from the Turks in the dedicatory address to the *PH*, which we have discussed above, Rhodoman shows no deference to the pro-Roman or pro-Trojan way of looking at the myth that was customary from Vergil onwards. And one may even wonder whether the pro-Greek and anti-Trojan attitude that he takes is also meant as an expression of his rejection of the genealogical offshoots of the Trojans – that is to say, of Rome as the home of the Roman Catholic pope.

This is linked to an evaluation of the Trojan Horse that is very striking, especially against the background of Vergil; and this too can be traced back to classical models apart from the Vergilian *Aeneid*. The comparison of the Trojan Horse to an important elite school is based on Cicero, *De oratore* 2.94:

> *Ecce tibi est exortus Isocrates (. . .) cuius e ludo tamquam ex equo Troiano meri principes exierunt.*

> See, before your time Isocrates arose, from whose school – as from the Trojan Horse – only leading men came forth.

The description of the men in the Trojan Horse as elite troops (*meri principes*) is much older still: Hom. *Od.* 4.272:

ἵππῳ ἔνι ξεστῷ, ἵν' ἐνήμεθα πάντες ἄριστοι.

In the timbered Wooden Horse where we, *only the best ones*, were cooped up.

There is one other striking aspect to the stereotypical parallel drawn by Rhodoman in both passages between the Trojan simile and an apian simile. This parallel means that the comparison with the Trojan Horse no longer entails a martial threat or destructiveness. It adds to this comparison the connotation of a fruitful intellectual activity, as we see especially in the passage from the *Hymnus scholasticus*.

This stereotypical parallel between the heroes who spring out of the Trojan Horse and insects that swarm out of the hive can be traced back to a passage in the concluding books of Quintus of Smyrna, which Rhodoman edited twice. Here, the poet compares the Greeks who emerge from the Trojan Horse to startled wasps (PH 13.54–9):

οἵ ῥα τότ' ἀμφ' αὐτῇσι (sc. κλίμαξι) κατήιον ἄλλοθεν ἄλλοι,
θαρσαλέοι<ς> σφήκεσσιν ἐοικότες, οὕς τε κλονήσῃ   55
δρυτόμος, οἳ δ' ἄρα πάντες ὀρινόμενοι περὶ θυμῷ
ὄζου ὑπεκπροχέονται, ὅτε κτύπον εἰσαΐουσιν·
ὣς οἵ γ' ἐξ ἵπποιο μεμαότες ἐξεχέοντο
ἐς Τρώων πτολίεθρον ἐΰκτιτον. (. . .)

(. . .) who then climb down the ladders, all of them on different sides, like furious wasps that a worker in the woods has startled; they are all stirred up, full of anger, and pour out of a hole in a branch as soon as they hear the noise. This is how the heroes streamed, full of zeal, out of the horse into the well-constructed city of the Trojans.

Rhodoman replaces the aggressive, destructive wasps in Quintus of Smyrna, probably in view of Triphiodorus' use of an apian simile in regard to the Trojan Horse (where the bees are, in principle, producers of honey, but are a danger to their environment in the situation on which the comparison focuses, like the wasps in Quintus of Smyrna).[26] Instead, his are purely productive

---

[26]Triph. *Iliup.* 533–40:

οἱ δ' ἕτεροι γλαφυρῆς ἀπὸ γαστέρος ἔρρεον ἵππου,
τευχησταὶ βασιλῆες, ἀπὸ δρυὸς οἷα μέλισσαι,
αἵτ' ἐπεὶ οὖν ἔκαμον πολυχανδέος ἔνδοθι σίμβλου   535

bees from the Vergilian *Aeneid*.[27] It thus becomes possible to apply the double simile of the Trojan Horse and the beehive to the constructive intellectual activity of the spreading of the Reformation in Germany through the pupils of Neander, who swarm out of Ilfeld. In Rhodoman's world, the elite Greek warriors who swarm out against Troy like wasps become antipapists with an excellent Grecist education (for ultimately, Rome, the Catholic centre, is the successor to Troy). Their educational activity in accordance with the Reformation can be symbolised by constructive bees that gather honey, better than by aggressive bees, and still less by startled wasps. The change of the insects' character is linked to the change in the evaluation of the image of the Trojan Horse, which now is positive. Here too, Rhodoman's contemporary milieu is channelling his reception of Quintus of Smyrna.

> κηρὸν ὑφαίνουσαι μελιηδέα ποικιλοτέχναι,
> ἐς νομὸν εὐγυάλοιο κατ' ἄγγεος ἀμφιχυθεῖσαι
> νύγμασι πημαίνουσι παραστείχοντας ὁδίτας·
> ὣς Δαναοὶ κρυφίοιο λόχου κληῖδας ἀνέντες
> θρῷσκον ἐπὶ Τρώεσσι. (. . .)   540

But the others streamed out of the belly of the concave horse, armed kings, like bees from an oak that have laboured to produce delicious honey in skilled activity within the spacious hive, and now pour out into the free field in the deep valley around them, and annoy the passing wanderers with their stings. This is how the Greeks opened the bolts of their hidden ambush and sprang against the Trojans.

[27] The words *examina, passim / doctrinae dulci stipent quae nectara fetu* in Rhodoman's Latin version come from Verg. *Aen.* 1.430–3:

> *Qualis apes aestate nova per florea rura*
> *Exercet sub sole labor, cum gentis adultos*
> *Educunt fetus, aut cum liquentia mella*
> *Stipant et dulci distendunt nectare cellas.*

As at the beginning of summers the bees are busy with their work on the blooming land while the sun shines, when they lead out the grown-up progeny of their race, or when they press wet honey together and almost burst the cells (of the beehive) with sweet honey.

Vergil imitates his own poetry here: see *Georg.* 4.158–64, where, however, the adjective that Rhodoman imitates in the text *dulci stipent* (. . .) *nectara fetu* is not *dulci*, but *liquido*, before *distendunt nectare cellas* (*Georg.* 4.164). In Rhodoman, the bees do not take care of their young, but are interested only in the (academic) production of honey. It is thus logical that the concept of *fetus* is transferred from the young bees to the honey. The context of the comparison in the first book of the *Aeneid* is also important: it sheds light on the diligent activity of the Carthaginians at the foundation of their new city. The wasps, which illustrate in Quintus of Smyrna the destruction of an ancient city, are replaced in Rhodoman by the Vergilian bees, which are the image of the foundation of a new city.

BIBLIOGRAPHY: EARLY MODERN EDITIONS

Crusius 1585: M. Crusius, *Germanograeciae libri sex*. Basel: Leonard, 348–55.

Lange 1741: M. *Laurentii Rhodomani* (. . .) *vita et in Graecas cum primis litteras merita* (. . .) *recensuit M. Carolus Henr. Langius*. Lübeck.

Neander 1577: *Opus aureum et scholasticum, in quo continentur* (. . .), *edita omnia studio et cura Michaelis Neandri*. Leipzig.

Neander 1582: *Chronicon sive epitome historiarum* (. . .) *Michaelis Neandri* (. . .). Eisleben.

Neander 1585: *Physice sive potius syllogae physicae rerum eruditarum* (. . .) *Michaelis Neandri* (. . .). Leipzig.

Neander 1588: *Argonautica, Thebaica, Troica, Ilias parva, poematia Graeca auctoris anonymi, sed pereruditi* (. . .) *Michael Neander*. Leipzig.

Rhodoman 1579: *ΛΟΥΘΗΡΟΣ ἤτοι ΑΠΛΗ ΕΚΘΕΣΙΣ ΤΟΥ ΤΕ ΒΙΟΥ ΚΑΙ ΤΗΣ ΚΑΤΗΧΗΤΙΚΗΣ ΔΙΔΑΧΗΣ ΤΟΥ ΛΟΥΘΗΡΟΥ* (. . .) *ὑπὸ ΛΑΥΡΕΝΤΙΟΥ ΤΟΥ ΡΟΔΟΜΑΝΟΥ*. *Lutherus sive expositio simplex vitae, doctrinae catecheticae et certaminum Lutheri* (. . .) *autore M. Laurentio Rhodomanno* (. . .).

Rhodoman 1589: *ΠΟΙΗΣΙΣ ΧΡΙΣΤΙΑΝΗ. ΠΑΛΑΙΣΤΙΝΗΣ ΗΤΟΙ ΑΓΙΑΣ ΙΣΤΟΡΙΑΣ ΒΙΒΛΙΑ ΕΝΝΕΑ. Poesis Christiana. Palaestinae seu historiae sacrae libri novem* (. . .) *autore Laurentio Rhodomano*. Frankfurt.

Rhodoman 1596: *ΘΕΟΛΟΓΙΑΣ ΧΡΙΣΤΙΑΝΙΚΗΣ ΚΑΤΗΧΗΣΙΣ. Theologiae Christianae tirocinia, carmine heroico Graecolatino in V libros digesta* (. . .) *a Laurentio Rhodomano*. Leipzig.

Rhodoman 1604a: Ἰλιὰς Κοίντου Σμυρναίου *seu Quinti Calabri paraleipomena* (. . .) *a Laurentio Rhodomano* (. . .). Hanau.

Rhodoman 1604b: *ΔΙΟΔΩΡΟΥ ΤΟΥ ΣΙΚΕΛΙΩΤΟΥ ΒΙΒΛΙΟΘΗΚΗΣ ΙΣΤΟΡΙΚΗΣ ΒΙΒΛΙΑ ΠΕΝΤΕ ΚΑΙ ΔΕΚΑ ΕΚ ΤΩΝ ΤΕΣΣΑΡΑΚΟΝΤΑ. Diodori Siculi Bibliothecae historicae libri XV de XL* (. . .) *studio et labore Laurentii Rhodomani* (. . .). Hanau.

APPENDIX: EDITION OF RHODOMAN'S DEDICATORY PREFACE TO HIS PARTIAL EDITION OF THE *POSTHOMERICA* OF QUINTUS OF SMYRNA

The sigla **1577** and **1604** denote the two editions by Rhodoman.

τῷ ἐντιμοτάτῳ καὶ ἐπι- φανεῖ ἄρχοντι καὶ κυρίῳ Εὐεράτῳ, τῶν Λουβεκκαίων καὶ Φερεδαίων ἐπισκόπῳ καὶ τῆς οἰκίας ἐν τῇ καλῇ Λουνο- πύργῃ προστάτῃ, τῆς εὐσεβείας καὶ πάσης ὑγιοῦς δι- δασκαλίας κηδεμόνι καὶ εὐεργέτῃ ὑγιαί- νειν τε καὶ εὖ πράττειν	reverendissimo et in- clyto praesuli ac domino, D. Eberhardo, Lubecensium et Verdensium episcopo domusque Lunebergensis domino, pietatis et omnis sanae doctrinae Mecoe- nati, d(omi)n(o) suo clementiss(imo) s(alutem)
	Phrygia
χώρη τις νύμφης Ἀθαμαντίδος ἄγχι θαλάσσης κέκλιται, οὔνομ᾿ ἔχουσα περικλυτὸν εἵνεκεν ἀλκῆς θούριδος, εὐποτίης τε καὶ ἀρχῶν εὐρυμεδόντων· Τρωάδα τὴν καλέουσιν ἐπώνυμον· ἧχι Σκάμανδρος καὶ Σιμόεις προχέουσιν ὕδωρ εἰς γείτονα πόντον	est regio Aeoliae, qua se mare contrahit Helles, cui quondam virtus bene gestis cognita bellis imperiumque et opes vexere ad sidera nomen; hanc Phrygiam dicunt; flavas ubi volvit arenas Xanthus et aequoreis Simois confunditur undis

5

4 ἐσθώνυμον **1577**

	Ida
Ἴδης ἀρχομένω πολυπίδακος· ἔνθα θεαίνας κρῖνε δικαζομένας Πριάμου πάϊς εἵνεκα μορφῆς· ἔνθα ποτ᾽ ὄλβιον ἄστυ, θεῶν ἀριδείκετον ἔργον, ναίετ᾽ ἐϋκτεάνοισιν ὑπ᾽ ἀνδράσιν, οὔνομα Τροίη·	ex Ida geniti: iudex ubi nata diremit Priamides inter divas certamina formae; barbaricis hic clara opibus constructaque divum urbs fuit auspicio, celebrato nomine Troia;
	Troia
10 ἦν καὶ Δαρδανίην τε καὶ Ἴλιον αὐδάζονται, ἕδρανον ἀρχαίων τε καὶ εὐσθενέων βασιλήων.	appellant etiam de nomine Dardani et Ili. haec veterum sedes regum sceptrisque potentum,
	Troia quando condita
τῶν γὰρ ἀνακτορίη μεγαλώνυμος ἔλλαχεν ἀρχήν, δώδεκ᾽ ἔτεσσι πάρος θεοειδέος ἔθνος Ἀβράμου εἰς χθόνα πατρῴην περάαν ἀπ᾽ ἐρημάδος αἴης· 15 χίλια δ᾽ εἰσέτι Φοῖβος ἐτήσιον οἶμον ὀδεύων δίς τε διηκόσι᾽ εἶχε καὶ ὀγδώκοντα τελέσσαι, πρὶν Θεὸς υἱὸν ἔπεμψε λαβεῖν μεροπηΐδα μορφήν. σκήπτρων δ᾽ αὖ κράτος εἶχον ὑπέρβιον, ἔθνεα δ᾽ αὐτοῖς μυρί᾽ ὑπηκούοντο κατ᾽ Ἀσίδα πουλυβότειραν.	qui iecere sui primum fundamina regni, quando bis senis restabant lapsibus anni, ante sacras iniit quam terras Abramidum gens: et sol omnipotens bis septem secula habebat cursibus evolvenda suis et lustra bis octo, ante Dei humanos proles quam sumeret artus. horum etiam late se extendit gloria sceptri innumeras Asiae gentes complexa feracis:
	regni Troiani duratio

20   ἀλλὰ μινυνθάδιον χρόνον ἤλδανε κύδιμος ἀρχή·
      πέρθετο γὰρ μιαρῆσιν ἀτασθαλίῃσιν ἀνάκτων
      οὔτε τριηκοσίων ἐτέων εἰς τέρμα τεθήλει.
      πῆμα κακὸς γὰρ ἄναξ, ὅσσον τ᾽ ἀγαθὸς μέγ᾽ ὄνειαρ.
	sed brevis ille fuit flos et dominatio Troiae:
	nam cadit obscoena prostrata libidine regum,
	cum tria complesset vix saecula tanta potestas,
	ut regni momenta ducum sunt ardua mores.

	somnium Hecubae gravidae cum Paride

ὡς γὰρ κοιρανίης εὐανθέος ἡνία νώμα
25   ἕκτος ἀπὸ πρώτου κοσμήτορος ἠδὲ γενάρχεω
      Δαρδανίδης Πρίαμος, τόθ᾽ ὑπὸ κνέφας εἶδεν ὄνειρον
      ἀγχιτόκος βασίλισσα, φέρειν ἐγκύμονι κόλπῳ
      αἰθόμενον πρηστῆρα καὶ εἰς φάος ὀψὲ λοχεύειν,
      ὃς τάχ᾽ ἀϊστώσειε πατρώϊον οὐδας ἀνάψας
30   πᾶσιν ὁμοῦ κτεάτεσσιν. ὀνειροπόλοι δὲ πίφαυσκον
      πῆμα φέρειν λαοῖσιν ὀλέθριον ἠδὲ καὶ ἀρχῇ
      δαιμονίην Ἑκάβην, Τροίην ὅ τε πᾶσαν ἀμέρσῃ.
	namque ubi florentis tenuit moderamina regni
	latipotens Priamus, qui prima ab origine stirpis
	Dardaniae sextus fuit, uxor regia somnum
	Lucinae propior vidit, ceu lampada vivam
	ventre gerat tumido iamiamque emittat ad auras,
	quae patriam involvat flammis atque omnia perdat.
	consulti vates igitur responsa dederunt
	exitio foetum regno populisque futurum,
	infelix Hecube gravida quem ferret in alvo.

	Paris infans exponitur et alitur ab ursa

τοὔνεκα γεινόμενον βρέφος ἔκβαλε θηρσὶν ἐδωδὴν
αἰνοτοκὴς γενετήρ. κρυφίων δ᾽ ὑπὸ δήνεσι Μοιρέων
35   παῖς ὀλοὸς φύγε κῆρα, δασύτριχα δ᾽ ἄρκτον ἄμελγε
      χείλεσι πειναλέοισι· βοῶν δέ μιν ἤρανος εὗρε
      καὶ τράφεν, εἰσόκεν ἄνθος ἀνέδραμεν εὔχλοον ἥβης·
      ἔνθα μιν ἀσπασίως κραδίη πρόσπτυξε τοκήων
      οὐκέτι φραζομένη σφετέρης τεκμήριον ἄτης·
	ergo feris praedam vix tractum ad lumina vitae
	exponit genitor puerum. sed numine divum
	arcano evitat fatum: sua porrigit ursa
	ubera deserto, dum forte per avia pastor
	suscipit inventum pubesque educit ad annos.
	agnitus hic iterum subiit pia tecta parentum,
	quos monita illa deum nihil amplius abdita tangunt.

13 an *seni[s]* ? cf. *Biop.* 197 *iam duo transibant revolutis mensibus anni*
19 μυρία 1577
19 ὑπηκόουντο 1577
22 οὖτε 1577 : an οὐδὲ ?
32 οἶτε 1577

40 καὶ Πάριν ἐξονόμηναν Ἀλέξανδρόν τε πολῖται.
    ὣς ὀλίγοι ὑπάλυξαν, ἃ δὴ πεπρωμένα κεῖται.
    εὖτε γὰρ ἀνθρώποισι κακῶν τεκταίνετ' ἀμοιβὴν
    ὕβριος ἐργατίνησιν ἔχων Θεὸς ἔκδικον ὄμμα,
    φαίνει δῆλα πάροιθεν ἑοῦ σημήϊα θυμοῦ,
45 εἴ ποθ' ὑποστρέψωσι βροτοί, προφύγωσι δ' ὀϊζύν.
    παυρίδιοι δ' ἀλέγουσι προάγγελα σήματα ποινῆς
    ἐκ κακίης νήψαντες· ὁ δ' εἰς τίσιν ὄρνυτ' ἀνηλῶς.

dictus Alexander prius, ac Paris inde vocatus.
sic pauci effugiunt decretum immobile fati.
namque ubi constituit meritas infligere poenas
vindicis ira Dei et sceleratos perdere cives,
ostendit primum manifesti signa furoris,
si fors convertant animum avertantque ruinam.
sed pauci advertunt divinis pectora monstris
emendantque nefas: ideo vindicta redundat.

causae variae profectionis Paridis in Graeciam

    αὐτὰρ ἐϋκτεάνου Πριάμου πάϊς ὕβρεϊ χαίρων
    ἤρτισεν εὐσκάρθμων νηῶν στόλον· ᾗσι πέρησεν
50 Ἑλλάδ' ἐς εὐναέτειραν, ἵν' ἤθεα καὶ πέδον ἀνδρῶν
    ἀλλοδαπῶν σκέψαιτο κακόσχολος, ἢ τίσιν αὐτοῖς
    ὁρμαί<ν>ων, ὅτι πατρὸς ἑοῦ νόσφισσεν ἀδελφὴν
    Ἡσιόνην χαρίεσσαν ἐϋ σθένος Ἡρακλῆος,
    Δαρδανίης ὑπ' Ἄρηϊ λύσας κρήδεμνα πόληος,
55 ἢ καὶ θελξινόοισιν ἐφημοσύνῃσι πιθήσας
    Κύπριδος, ἣ νέμε πρῶτα, περιφροσύνην ἀθερίξας
    Παλλάδος ἠνορέην τε καὶ Ἥρης ὄλβιον ἀρχήν.
    ἡ δέ οἱ ἀμφ' Ἑλένης κληηδόνι φίλτρον ἐνῆκεν.
    ἔπλεε δ' εἰς κλυτὸν ἄστυ φιλοξείνου Μενελάου,
60 Σπάρτην καλλιγύναικα, φίλην δέ οἱ ἅρπασ' ἄκοιτιν
    κάλλεος ἄκρα λαχοῦσαν, ἐχέφρονος ἄμμορον αἰδοῦς·

hic Paris instructa classi scelerum improbus autor
tristibus auspiciis Graiorum tendit in oras
excultas, ut vel mores et clara virorum
moenia spectaret vacuus vel damna pararet
contra, quod Priami Tyrinthia clava sororem
transtulit ad Graios, lacrymosi praemia belli,
quando solo aequarant domitae munimina Troiae,
improba vel blandae Veneris promissa secutus,
cui formae palmam dederat, Iunonia sceptra
postponens Helenae viresque artesque Minervae,
cuius eum magno Cypris inflammarat amore.
idcirco claras Menelai fertur ad arces,
Sparta ubi pulchra iacet: quem cara coniuge privat,
cui facies praestans forma, mens cassa pudore.

Paris rapit Helenam

    ἣν μάλα κυδιόων εἰς Τρώϊον ἄστυ κόμ[ο]ισσε,
    σπέρμα κακοῦ πολέμοιο καὶ ὀκρυόεντος ὀλέθρου
    λαῶν θ' ἡγεμόνων τε θεοκμήτου τε πόληος.

hanc Paris exsultans delatam ad Pergama iungit
connubio, (heu!) segetem belli fontemque malorum
Troiugenumque simul regno pubique Pelasgum.

Graeci proficiscuntur ad Troiam ulturi raptum Paridis

65 αὐτίκα γὰρ κατὰ γαῖαν Ἀχαιΐδα πρῶτα φέροντες
    τισσόμενοι λυγρὸν ἔργον ἀμύντορες Ἀτρείωνι
    σφὸν κράτος εἰς ἓν ἄγειραν ὁμοφραδέεσσι μενοιναῖς
    καὶ στρατιὴν νήριθμον ἀόλλισαν· ἦν ἐπὶ Τροίην
    τυφομένην νήεσσιν ἀλιπτερύγεσσι κόμιζον.
70 πρῶτα δὲ δηώσαντο πέριξ ὁμοτέρμονα χῶρον
    λαῶν, οἳ Τρώεσσιν ὁμόφρονα θυμὸν ἄεξον,
    ἄστεα μύρι' ἑλόντες ἅμ' ἀνδράσιν α<ἰ>χμητῇσιν.
    ὀψὲ δὲ πᾶσαν ἔτρεψαν Ἄρεος ζηλήμονος ἀλκὴν
    Ἴλιον εἰς εὔπυργον. ἐπ' ἠόσι δ' Ἑλλησπόντου

dedecus hoc etenim commune ardentibus armis
ulturi coiere duces et robore iuncto
Atridam auxilio iuvere indigna ferentem
Aegeumque salum tot millibus arma ferentum
traiiciunt validisque invadunt viribus hostes.
ac primum fidei Troianae iura tuentes
subiiciunt socioque excludunt milite Troas
innumerasque ipsis delent cum civibus urbes.
hinc omnes belli vires ad moenia Troiae
turrigerae vertunt et castra Athamantidos Helles

40 ὀξονόμηναν **1577**
41 ὡς **1577**
42 τεκταίνε τ' **1577**
52 ὁρμαίων **1577**
53 ἡσιόνης **1577**
56 *cui* (cf. Graec. ἣ) : *qui* **1577**
62 κόμοισσε **1577**
71 οἱ **1577**
72 ἀχμητῇσιν **1577**
74 *Turrigenae* **1577**
74 *Adamanthidos* **1577**

75 ἱλαδὸν αὐλίζοντες ἀνὰ Ξάνθοιο ῥέεθρα πολλάκι σὺν Τρώεσσι διεκρίναντο σιδήρῳ, πολλάκι Δαρδανίης ὑπὸ τείχεσι, πολλάκι δ᾽ αὐτῆς ἄγχ᾽ ἁλός· ἀλλήλων δὲ μένος χαλεποῖσι κυδοιμοῖς τρῦχον ἀνηκέστως.	littoribus figunt et ad alta fluenta Scamandri crebro decernunt cum Troum pube feroci, crebro etiam ad Troiae portas et littora crebro obsessi maris: inque vicem se Marte fatigant infractis animis.

	Hector Troianus
80 οὐ γὰρ κράτος ἔλλιπε Τρῶας Ἕκτορος ἡγεσίης εὐθαρσέος, ὅς σφισιν ἦμαρ οὐλοὸν ἠνορέῃσι μενεπτολέμοισιν ἄμυνεν, εἵως ἔμπνοος ἦε, μόνος δ᾽ ἦν πατρίδος ἕρκος. πολλοὶ δ᾽ ἀμφοτέρωθεν ἀριστῆές τε καὶ ἄλλοι, ὧν οὐκ ἔστιν ἀριθμὸς, ἀγήνορα θυμὸν ὄλεσσαν.	nec deerat robur in armis Iliadis magni ductu Hectoris; ille furentes unus sustinuit ceu murus aheneus hostes et patriae avertit casum, dum fata sinebant. utrinque innumeros Mavortius abstulit ensis ductoresque aliosque: quis enumerare valeret?

	Hector, Achilles, Aiax, Paris pereunt ante captam urbem
85 δάμνατ᾽ ἀνικήτου θράσος Ἕκτορος, ὤλετο δ᾽ ἀλκὴ Πηλείδεω Ἀχιλῆος ὑπέρβιος, ἤριπε δ᾽ ἠὺ Αἴαντος μέγεθος κρατερόφρονος, ἔφθιτο δ᾽ αὐτοῦ ἀγλαΐη Πάριδος, φθισήνορος αἴτιος ἄτης.	Hectoris invicti domita est fiducia tandem, frangitur Aeacidae cedendi nescia virtus, sternitur Aiacis robur proprio ense cadentis, forma perit Paridos, quae perniciem attulit omnem

	quamdiu pugnatum sit ad Troiam
90 αὐτὰρ ἐπεὶ δέκ᾽ ἄνυσσεν ἀεξιμόθους ἐνιαυτοὺς ἤματα δ᾽ ἓξ ἐπὶ μησὶ δυώδεκα φέγγεος ἀρχὸς, τέρμα πόνοις ἐπέθηκαν ὑποκνήσαντες Ἀχαιοί,	postquam autem duo lustra infando exercita bello finierat Titan et bis sex ordine luces Lunaque sex menses, tunc fessi Pergama Graeci

	Troia capitur equo
95 εἷλον δ᾽ ἄστυ δόλῳ Πριαμήϊον, ὄρρα δαμάζειν οὐκ ἐδύναντο βίῃ, λόχον ἵππου ἀρτύναντες. καὶ τὸ μὲν Ἡφαίστου μαλερῇ τέφρωσαν αὐτμῇ, κτήματα δ᾽ ἐκτὸς ἕλοντο καὶ ἀργαλέως κτάνον ἄνδρας σὺν σφετέροις τεκέεσσιν, ἐδούλωσαν δὲ γυναῖκας. κοιρανίης δέ τ᾽ ἄνακτα φίλης τ᾽ αἰῶνος ἄμερσαν, δαίμονος ἀσταθέος μέγα θαῦμα βροτοῖσι γεγῶτα.	occulto cepere dolo, quae vincere Marte non poterant, et equo metam invenere laborum. tunc cadit in cineres Vulcani tradita flammis urbs vetus, et praedas abigunt ad castra Pelasgi; masculeam extingunt stirpem abducuntque puellas; imperio regem mulctant et munere vitae, in quo fortunae speculum mutabilis extat.

	reditus Graecorum in patriam
100 οἱ δ᾽ εἰς πατρίδα γαῖαν ἐπεντύνοντο νέεσθαι, ἀλλὰ κακῶς ἀπόλοντο κακοὶ δι᾽ ἀεικέα λώβην, οἱ μὲν ὑποβρύχιοι στυγεροῖς μετὰ κύμασι πόντου, οἱ δ᾽ οἴκοι κύρσαντες ὀλεθροφόροισιν ἀνάγκαις.	hinc patrios repetunt victrici classe penates, at belli poenas expendunt turpiter acti: nam maris absumsit multos cum navibus aestus, in laribus fatum multos excepit acerbum.

80 an ἡγεσίης ?
81 ἠωρέῃσι 1577
81 *seu* 1577
82 εἰὼς 1577
95 *abiguunt* 1577
99 οἵδ᾽ 1577
99 *patrias* 1577
101 ὑπὸ βρύχιοι 1577

	Homerus
τοῦτο πολυχρονίοιο μόθου κλέος, οὗ φάτις ἕπτη πάντα κατὰ τριμεροῦς χθονὸς ἕδρανα, πᾶσιν ἀκούειν. 105 τοῦ γὰρ μνῆστιν ἄεξον ἀριστολόγοις γραφίδεσσι πολλοὶ καὶ λόγιοι· μάλ᾿ ἐνὶ πρώτοισι δ᾿ Ὅμηρος ἀνδρομέης σοφίης πρεσβήϊον οἷον ἀείρων, πάσης δ᾿ εὐμαθίης γένεσιν Δαναοῖσιν ὀπάσσας· ὃς βίβλοις τετόρεσσι καὶ εἴκοσι μῶλον ἄεισε 110 Τρώων τ᾿ Ἀργείων τε, θεόσσυτον ἔργον ὑφαίνων· Φοῖβος γὰρ ποίησεν, ἀπέγραφε δ᾿ ὀξὺς Ὅμηρος. ἀλλ᾿ οὐκ εἰς πολέμοιο βαρυκμήτοιο τελευτὴν ἤγαγεν ἡδυεπῆ Μούσης θρόον, ἀλλὰ σιωπὴν ἔμβαλεν ἀχνυμένη φόνον Ἕκτορος, ὥς μιν Ἀχιλλεὺς 115 συμμίξας ἐδάμασσεν ἀμυνόμενον περὶ πάτρης.	haec tibi prolixi brevis est narratio belli, quod fama triplicis peragravit climata terrae. huius enim calamo mandarunt gesta diserto multi atque eloquio clari, quos inter Homerus, qui summos gerit humanae sapientiae honores, omnis et Argivis doctrinae praebuit ortum: ille ter octo libris lento conserta duello Pergama cum Danais divino carmine narrat: nam Phoebus dictavit, acutus scripsit Homerus. sed non funesti dulciflua stamina Musa texuit ad finem belli, namque Hectoris aegra funere rupit opus, dum pro patria arma gerentem sternit Pelides et circum moenia raptat.
	Cointus Smyrnaeus incipit, ubi Homerus desinit
ἔνθεν δ᾿ ἀρξαμένη Σμυρναίου Μοῦσα Κοίντου Μαιονίδην πλήρωσε καὶ εἰς τέλος ἤνυσεν ἔργον, Δαρδανίης δ᾿ ἐνέπει πύματον κακὸν ἠδέϊ μέτρῳ εὐπίην χαρίτεσσιν Ὁμήρου πάμπαν ὁμοίῳ. 120 τοῦδε γὰρ εὐφυέως μιμήσατο κάλλιμον ἦθος, ἠέ που εὐμαθίην ἢ καὶ φράσιν ἀρτιέπειαν πευκαλίμοις σκέψαιο νοήμασιν· ὡς μεθ᾿ Ὅμηρον πάνσοφον ἀτρεκέως ὅ γε δεύτερός ἐστιν Ὅμηρος.	hinc telam instituens Smyrnaei Musa Cointi Maeonidae pertexit opus partesque tuetur: suaviloquis nam fata modis canit ultima Troiae, eloquio, dignus, dulci qui certet Homero et venam ingenio referat solerte canoram. si doctrinam igitur, si verba utriusque poetae contuleris, merito censebitur alter Homerus, qui tam felici studio succedit Homero.
	Cointus Smyrnaeus cur hactenus non vere Cointus Calaber dicatur
τόνδ᾿ οὐ γνήσιον οὔνομ᾿ ἐπηυδάξαντο Κάλαβρον, 125 οὕνεκα Βησσαρίων ποτ᾿ ἐν ἀγχιάλοισι Καλάβρων εὑρατό μιν δαπέδοισιν ἀϊστωθέντα πάροιθεν ἐκ μερόπων· ὁ δὲ κλῆσιν ἐτήτυμον ἔσχε Κοίντου.	hunc Quintum falso Calabrum cognomine dicunt, quod fuit in Calabris a Bessarione repertus, hospes ubi latuit carie confectus in urbe Hydruntis. verum sed nomen redde Cointo,

106 μάλα δ᾿ ἐν πρώτοισιν Ὅμηρος **1604** (ubi traduntur tantum 103–37 et 192b–237)
107 an οἷος (**1604**) ?
109 τετάρεσσι **1604**
110 τ᾿ om. **1604**
111 δῖος Ὅμηρος **1604**
112 s. *Musa sed ad finem funesti stamina belli / non ita pertexit. namque Hectoris aegra molesto* **1604**
113 ἀλλὰ **1577** : ἡ δὲ **1604**
114 an ἀχνυμένη ? at cf. Lat.
117 καὶ ὡς κολοφῶν᾿ ἐπέθηκεν **1604**
117 *M. complevit opus ceu fine coronans* **1604**
118 ἠδέϊ **1577**
120 τοῦδε **1604** : τοῦ δὲ **1577**
121 εἴτε που εὐμ. εἴτ᾿ αὖ **1604**, melius
123 *cuius felici sequitur vestigia passu* **1604**
124 an τὸν δ᾿ (**1604**) ?
125 Καλαύρων **1604**
126 *confectus* **1577** : *vexatus* **1604**
127 *Cointi* **1604**

Σμύρνη δ' αὐτὸν ἔθρεψεν, ὅθεν καὶ δῖος Ὅμηρος, ὡς αὐτὸς σήμηνεν ἐνὶ σφετέρης σελίδεσσι 130 μάρτυρος ἀξιόπιστος, ἔπος καὶ τοῦτο χαράξας, ὡς Μοῦσαί μιν ἔθηκαν ἁλιρρόου ἀγχόθεν Ἕρμου βώτορ' ἐῶν οἴων καὶ ἐνὶ φρεσὶ χεῦαν ἀοιδὴν οὐκ ἔτ' ἰουλίζοντος ἐπήρατον· ἔνθεν ἔοικε παίδων ἀρτιμαθῶν κοσμήτορα τόνδε γενέσθαι 135 μουσοπόλοις περίβωτον ἐν ἀνδράσιν· αὐτὰρ ἄϊστον, ὅντινά μιν βίος ἔσχεν ἀνὰ χρόνον, ὧν δ' ἀνέτειλεν ἐκ πατέρων, οἵην τε τελευτήσας λάχε μοῖραν.	quem Smyrnaea aluit tellus, unde ortus Homerus. haec vero ipse sua, cui fas quoque credere, voce testatur vates reliquisque hoc insuper addit, Musarum quod pavit oves, ubi volvitur Hermus in mare, et in tenero concepit flore iuventae munere Pieridum perfectam carminis artem. hinc patet ingenuas pubem duxisse per artes et tunc eximios inter fulsisse poetas. sed latet ignotum, quo tempore traxerit aevum et qua stirpe satus, qua functus morte quiescat.
	Neander
τόνδε ποτ' ἀγχίνοον πινυτοῦ μιμήτορ' Ὁμήρου Ἑρκυνίοις ὑπ' ὄρεσσιν ἑαῖς ξύνωσε Νέανδρος 140 ποίμναις, τὰς ἀνὰ κῆπον ἐλεύθερον ἄνθεσι Μουσῶν φέρβει. τῆσιν ἐγώ ποτε σύννομος εἶδαρ ἔρεψα ἄφθονον, ἰδμοσύνης τε καὶ ἤθεος εἶδαρ ἀμώμου, μυρία δ' ἐσθλὰ πέπονθα φιλοφροσύνῃσι Νεάνδρου.	hunc quondam Hercinia florens sub valle Neander praecinuit gregibus Romano suaviter ore, libero in Aonidum quos pascit floribus horto: inter quos etiam me pubescentibus annis doctrinae et sacrae virtutis gramine pavi, cum patrio nudum me fovit amore Neander.
	summa trium librorum Cointhi Smyrnaei
οὗτος ἄρ' Ἑλλήνων βίβλων ἐπιδέξιος Ἑρμῆς 145 ἡμῖν Σμυρναίοιο μετέφρασεν ἐσχατοώσας τρεῖς βίβλους, αἷς εἶπε δολορράφον ἵππον Ἀχαιῶν, μήδεα Σίνωνος πολυκερδέα καὶ θράσος αἰπὺ Τρώων τ' ἀφραδίην κακὸν ἀμφαδὸν οὐκ ἐσορώντων νίκην τ' Ἀργείων ἀπατήλιον, ἔσχατον ἄτην 150 ἄστεος αἰθομένοιο δαϊζομένων τε πολιτῶν ληϊάδων θ' ὕβριν καὶ ἀτερπέα νόστον Ἀχαιῶν.	is veterum pollens Graecorum interprete lingua Ausonio nobis Smyrnaei reddidit ore tres libros, celebravit equum quibus ille Pelasgum Sinonisque dolos et pectus ad omnia promptum et caecos Troum sensus sua fata trahentum, victrices Danaum latebras, lachrymabile Troiae incensae fatum, crudelia funera gentis, captarum sortem, reditus discrimina Achivum.
τῶν μὲν ἐγὼ βίβλων γε μετάφρασιν ἐκ χερὸς αὐτοῦ δεξάμενος ποτὶ χρῆσιν ἐπαρτέα θῆκα φέρεσθαι εἰς χέρας ἐσθλομαθῶν. βίβλον δὲ σύνοψιν ἑκάστης 155 δίγλωσσον μελέτησα καὶ αὐτοῦ λύματ' ἀοιδοῦ πολλὰ μάλ' ἐξεκάθηρα, τά οἱ χρόνος ἀργὸς ἔμιξε.	hos ego conversos, iucundum munus, ab ipso accepi libros discentumque usibus aptos effeci et gemino librorum carmine summas conscripsi ac mendas, quas barbara secula vati miscuerant, dempsi, ne quid bona publica tardet.
τὸν δ' ἄρ' ἄεθλον ἐμοί γε διδάσκαλος ἐσθλὸς ἔταξε. χρὴ γοῦν παιδευτάο παραιφασίῃσι πιθέσθαι· ὁρμαίνω δὲ καὶ αὐτὸς ὀνήσιμα πολλὰ τελέσσαι, 160 κουροτέροις δὲ μάλιστα· τὸ γὰρ γέρας ἐστὶν ἐμεῖο.	hoc mihi praeceptor studium commisit honestum. at decet omnino monitis parere magistri, quamvis ipse etiam vitae prodesse laborem, praecipue pueris, quorum mihi tradita cura est.

128 *tellus* 1604 : om. 1577
129 *voce quod ipse sua liquide, cui credere dignum* 1604
130 μάρτυς γ' ἀξιόπιστος 1604
130 ἔπος δὴ τοῦτο 1604
130 *reliquis ubi talia miscet* 1604
133 οὐκέτ' 1577 1604; exspectes οὔπω
134 κούρων ἐσθλομαθῶν 1604
134 *hinc arteis pubem ingenuas docuisse patescit* 1604
135 *tunc* 1577 : *hunc* 1604
136 *latet* 1577 : *manet* 1604
136 *traxerit* 1577 : *degerit* 1604
137 ἐκ γονέων 1604
137 τελευτῶν ἔλλαχε 1604
156 an *tarde<n>t* ?

	dedicatio
ἀλλὰ τίνι πρώτῳ καρπῶν ἀναθήσομ' ἀπαρχὰς ἡμετέρων· πολλοὶ γὰρ ὑπερφιάλοισι νόεσσιν οὐ μόνον ἡδίσταις Μουσέων χαρίτεσσι θύρετρα ἀφραδέως κλείουσιν ἀδωρήτους τ' ἀφιᾶσιν, 165 ἀλλὰ κακαῖς νύσσουσιν ἐπεσβολίῃσι μολούσας, πάγχυ δ' ἀποστυγέουσιν ἀχρήϊον ἠΰτε παῖγμα, νήπιοι, οὐ νοέοντες, ὅτι Ζεὺς ὤπασε μύθους χρήζοντος βιότου κειμήλιον ὀλβιόκαρπον, οὖ κεν ἄνευθε πέσοιεν ὁμῶς ἀγοραί τε καὶ ἀρχαί.	sed cui primitias nostrae sacravero messis? multi etenim, nostro quos vana superbia tollit tempore, non solum charites a limine pellunt Musarum vacuasque immiti corde remittunt, probra sed in miseras etiam et convicia iactant, prorsus et explodunt, ceu lusus inutilis esset; o stolidi, quos non tangit reverentia dulcis doctrinae, ad nostram quam contulit ipse salutem Iuppiter et sine qua nec sceptra aut concio florent.
ἀλλὰ σύ, τριχθαδίης τιμῆς ἀριδείκετε φωστήρ, 170 ὃν Θεὸς ὢν προβάτων ἀγανόφρονα ποιμένα θῆκεν, ἀμφότερον καὶ σκῆπτρα καὶ ἱερὰ σεμνὰ βραβεύειν, δέχνυσο τοῦτο πόνημα, καὶ εἰ μάλα φαίνετ' ἄτιμον· τοῦτο γὰρ ἡμετέροιο νόου τεκμήριον ἔστω, 175 ὡς χάριν οἶδα τεῆς εὐεργεσίησιν ἑτοίμως, αἷς μ' ἀγανῶς κόσμησας ἐνηέα ῥάβδον ὀπάσσας ποίμνης βοσκομένης ἱεροῖς ἐνὶ τέμπεσι Μουσῶν, ᾗσι ποθεινὸν ἔδειμας ἐπαύλιον εὔφρονι θυμῷ πολλὰ χαριζόμενός σφιν ὀνήσιμα· καὶ γὰρ ἄριστα 180 ἐν πυκινῇσι φρένεσσιν ἐπίστασαι, ὡς βίος οὐδέν, εἰ μὴ Μουσάων σπουδάσματα καλὰ τεθήλῃ, εἰ μὴ παιδείας νόμος ἄρτιος ἤθεα παίδων καὶ νόας εὖ πλάσσῃσι, καὶ ὡς λόγος ἔνθεος αἰεὶ τοιαύτης κρηπῖδος ἐν ἀνθρώποισι χατίζει· 185 ὃν σὺ πόθῳ στέργεις ἀψευδέΐ καί ἑ πρὸ πάντων τιμᾷς, ὅσσ' ἐρίτιμα καὶ ἱμερόεντα πέφανται· <..> οὔτε σ' ὑπ' ἀγχιθύροισι λύκοις βαρὺ δεῖμα ταράσσει. ἔσθλος ἔοις· σὲ δ' ὄπισθεν ἐπάξιος ἵζετ' ἀμοιβή. 190 καὶ τὰ μὲν ἀτρεκίη με λέγειν ἀναφανδὸν ἀνώγει, καί περ ἀναινομένοιο σέθεν. σὺ δὲ με<ί>λιχος εἴης προσπτύξας τὸν ἀοιδὸν εὔκλυτόν. οὐ μὲν ἀεικὲς ἀρχῷ ἐῢ πρήσσοντι διελθεῖν πρήξιας ἀρχῶν, οὓς προτέρων ἀνέδειξε βροτῶν βιοδαίδαλος αἰών.	at tibi, lux patriae, triplicis quem splendor honoris illustrat, curam ipse pii cui Christus ovilis mandat, ut et sacris praesis et sceptra gubernes, exiguum miti, precor, accipe fronte laborem, qui certo gratam declaret pignore mentem, qua colo, qua veneror tanti benefacta favoris, me quibus exornas, dum me gregis esse tenelli custodem facis Aonidum pascentis in agris, templa quibus nuper sacrasti et munera large accumulas tutosque tuis facis esse sub alis. nam certum est animoque sedet, quod corruat omnis vita, nisi studiis teneat se fulta colendis, ni bona deformes iuvenum informatio mentes expoliat moresque regat; quod verba salutis hoc velut insistant miserae fundamine vitae: quae tibi verus amor, quae sunt tibi summa voluptas et cunctis potiora, hominum quae pectora mulcent: haec gregibus syncera tuis das pabula, nec te instantum terrent fremitus et vota luporum. macte animo: tibi parta Dei sunt praemia in arce. atque haec me veri ratio proferre iubebat, te renuente licet; sed tu sis mitis et istum excipias gremio vatem. non dedecet alta conspicua virtute ducem legisse priorum facta ducum et vitae petere hinc exempla probatae.

166 ἀποστυγέωσιν **1577**
170 an *at tu* (cf. Graec.) ?
179 an *tutasque* (sc. *Musas*) ?
187 lacunam indicavi
188 an οὐδὲ ?
189 σὺ δ' **1577**
189 *arte* **1577**
191 μέλιχος **1577**
193 εὖ πρήσσοντι διελθεῖν πρ. ἀρχῶν **1577**: ἐῢπρήσσοντι δαῆναι πρ. ἀνδρῶν **1604**
193 num *conspicuum* (**1604**) ?
193 *legisse* **1577** : *cognosse* **1604**
194 *probata* **1604** ut vid.

e lectione librorum Cointi Smyrnaei quae petenda sin

195 ἔνθα γὰρ οὔ σοι μοῦνον ἐύφρονα θυμὸν ἰαίνει
Τέρψις ἀοιδοπόλοιο μελίφρονος (οὐ γὰρ ἐκείνου
Μούσης ἀντιάει γλυκερώτερον ἡδυεπείης),
ἀλλὰ καὶ ἔσπετ' ὄνειαρ, ὅ σοι θυμάρμενον ἔσται
ὑμετέρου τ' οἴηκος ἐπάξιον· οὐ γὰρ ἔθηκεν
200 ἔργα μικρῶν ἀγελαῖα βροτῶν εἰς μέσσον ἰδέσθαι
ἀλλά, τά θ' ἡγεμόνεσσιν ἀριζήλοισι τελέσθη
εἵνεκα κοιρανίης, τῆς περ κλέος αἰθέρ' ἵκανεν.
ἔνθ' ὑποθημοσυνῶν πολλῶν χρέος ἐστὶ νοῆσαι
πᾶσι μὲν, ἀλλὰ μάλιστα βροτῶν ἡγήτορι λαμπρῷ.
205 Τροίη μὲν πολύολβος, ἀϊστωθεῖσα δ' ὀπίσσω
πρόρριζον τάδε πάντα πολύφρονα φῶτα διδάξει·
ὡς τέλος ἄτρεπτον μεγάλης Θεὸς ὥρισεν ἀρχῆς,
ᾧ πεσέειν χρέος ἐστὶν, ἐπὴν εἰς ἄκρον ἵκωνται·
ὡς δέ τ' ἀτασθαλίῃσιν ὁμῶς λαῶν τε καὶ ἀρχῶν
210 κοιρανιῶν μέγα κάρτος ἀμείβεται· ὡς δέ τ' ἀβληχρὸν
πᾶν κάρτος καὶ μῆχος, ὅταν Θεὸς ἀντία βαίνῃ·
ὡς κακὰ πολλὰ λόχευσεν ἀναίσιμα φίλτρα γυναικῶν·
πολλάκις ὡς σύμπασα πόλις κακοῦ ἀνδρὸς ἐπαυρεῖ,
εἷς δέ τ' ἀνὴρ ἀγαθὸς λαόν τε καὶ ἄστυ σαώζει·

hic tibi non tantum ceu nectare tincta Voluptas
oppressos curis mulcebit carmine sensus,
quo Venus et Charites digitos lavere tenellos,
sed maiora etiam tibi commoda Musa ministrat
nec curis indigna tuis: nec enim obvia passim
cantat et abiecto tractata negocia vulgo,
magnorum sed gesta ducum consultaque narrat
de regno, cuius volitavit ad aethera nomen.
propterea dives monitorum hic copia praesto est
cuilibet inprimisque illi, qui tractat habenas.
en primum florens opibus, mox diruta Troia
exemplo docet ipsa suo, quod Numina regnis
constituant metas, quas non transcendere possunt;
quod plerunque trahant, cum ventum ad summa, ruinas
quod populi rabies et iniqua libido regentum
exitium pariat regni; quod nulla potestas
invitis valeat divis, solertia nulla;
illicitus quod amor clades accersat acerbas;
saepe quod unius totam scelus hauriat urbem,
unius et virtus contra tota agmina servet;

195 ἔνθα **1604** : ἔνθε **1577**
195 ἰαίνε **1604**
196 θέλκτρον ἀοιδοπόλοιο μελισταγὲς **1604**
196 s. parenthesin distinxi
197 *Charite* **1577**
199 κυδαλίμου τ' **1604** (ut allocutio tollatur)
199 *nec sceptris indigna ipsis* **1604** (ut allocutio tollatur)
201 ἡγεμόνεσσιν **1577**
201 *ducum* **1577** : *virum* **1604**
202 πλεὸς **1577**
203 ὑποθυμοσυνῶν **1577**
203 *est* **1604** : *esse* **1577**
205 ἀειστωθεῖσα **1577**
206 βαθύφρονα **1604**
206 διδάσκει **1604**
206 *ipsa* **1577** : *usque* **1604**
207 ἄτρεπτον **1604** : ἄτερπτον **1577** : *vix ἄτερπνον*
207 ἀρχῆς **1577**
207 *possint* **1604**
208 *trahunt* **1577**
208 *ruinam* **1604**
210 ἀμείβεται **1577** : ἐρείπεται **1604**
210 ἀβλαχρὸν **1577**
210 *pariant regnis* **1604** : fort. *pariat regnis* (at cf. Graec.)
212 λόχευσε παραίσιμα **1604**
212 *illicitos* **1577**
213 *totum* **1577**

ὡς κρύφιος δόλος ἤνυσ', ὃ μὴ φανερὴ δύνατ' ἀλκή·
πολλάκις ὡς μεθύουσι καὶ ἀτρεμέουσιν ἀκαίρως
ἐχθρὸς ὑπὲρ κεφαλῆς ἐπὶ τέρψει πῆμα κορύσσει,
ὡς ἡμεῖς θαλίῃσι μεμηλότες ἠδὲ χορείαις
φιλτροτόκοις τε γυναιξὶ καὶ ἠλεμάτως τρυφόωντες,
220 πολλὰ δ' ἄωρα τελεῦντες ἀταρβέες εὐδιόωμεν,
Τυρκῷ δ' αὖ τὰ μεταξὺ καὶ ἀλλοδαποῖσι τυράννοις
κείρειν Τευτονίην χθόνα λείπομεν, ἄχρι καὶ ἐλθεῖν
εἰς πρόπυλον, φανερῆς δ' οὐδεὶς ἐμπάζεται ἄτης.
εἴσιδε καὶ Πριάμου μεγάλου πολυτειρέα μοῖραν,
225 ὃς δὴ πρόσθεν ἔην θνητοῖς πάντεσσιν ἀγητὸς
ὄλβῳ καὶ τεκέεσσι καὶ εὐρυβίῃ βασιλείῃ·
αὐτίκα σὺν τέκνοισιν ὀϊζυρώτατος ἔσκεν,
ὄλλυτο δ' ὀλλυμένοισιν ἐφ' υἱάσιν ἠδὲ πόληϊ.
σκέψεαι ἀτρεκέως ἄρχων βίον, οἷά τε δαίμων
230 ἄστατος ἀλλάσσει μεροπήϊα πάντα καθ' ὥραν,
λυγροῖς ἠδ' ἀγαθοῖσιν ἀμοιβαίοισιν ἀθύρων·
αἶψα γὰρ αὐχήεντα χάμαι βάλεν, αἶψα ταπεινὸν
Ζηνὸς ὑπ' ἐννεσίῃσι πρὸς ὄλβων ὕψος ἀείρε·
τοὔνεκεν οὐ θέμις ἐστὶ Τύχης ἀπάτῃσι πιθέσθαι.
235 καὶ τὰ μὲν ἄλλα τε πολλὰ φέρει σκέψασθαι ἀοιδὸς
ἡμέτερος, μελέεσσι δ' εὐρρύθμοισι κέκευθεν,
ὅσσ' ἐνέπειν μακρόν ἐστι καὶ ὀχληρὸν φρονέοντι.

quod dolus efficiat, quae vis non ulla peregit;
saepe quod incautis et onustis pectora Baccho
perniciem volvat supra caput impiger hostis:
sic, dum nos structaeque dapes laetaeque choreae
foemineique iuvant lusus et splendor inanis
ociaque haud matura, omnis dum cura sepulta est,
interea patrios nobis stertentibus agros
barbarici vastant reges et ad intima ferro
haud segni penetrant – sed quis ea damna moratur?
aspice deinde senis Priami mirabile fatum,
quem prius (heu!) nimium felix ad summa vehebat
sors opibus sceptrisque et multa prole superbum:
mox vice mutata detrusit ad infima, cunctis
ut miser amissis Plutonia regna subiret.
regia vita tibi nonne hic elucet et ipsa
Fortunae facies, subito quae evertere casu
cuncta solet vicibusque alternis invida ludit?
nam mox sublimem solio deturbat ab alto
permissu Iovis et miserum ad fastigia tollit:
non tutum est igitur malefidae fidere Sorti.
talia nempe monet vates et condita Musis
exhibet argutis alia insuper, edere longum
quae foret atque animo sapienti audire molestum.

215 ὁ **1577** : ἃ **1604**, fort. scribendum, cf. Lat.
215 *non vis ulla* **1604**
216 *in cautis* **1577**
217 κυλίνδει **1604**
218 an ὡς ?
218 *laetaeque choreae* **1604** : *chorae laetaeque* **1577**
219 τρυφόωντες **1604** : τροφόωντες **1577**
220 ἀτερβέες **1604**
221 τυρκῷ **1577**
221 αὖ τὰ μεταξὺ **1604** : αὖ τα μεταξὺ **1577** : an αὖ τὸ μεταξὺ vel αὖτε μεταξὺ ?
221 *sterdentibus* **1577**
223 *quisnam ea* **1604**, fort. scribendum
224 *miserabile* **1604**
225 θνντοῖς **1577**
226 *sceptris et* **1604**
227 *mox* **1604** (cf. αὐτίκα) : *mors* **1577** (quod male anticipat *Plutonia regna*)
229 ἄκέψεαι **1577**
230 *subito quae* **1604** : *subitoque* **1577**
232 *sublimen* **1577**
233 αἰνεσίῃσι **1577 1604** (correxi); αἰνεσίῃσι θεοῖο πρὸς ὄλβιον ὕψος ἄειρε **1604**
233 an ὄλβιον (cf. **1604**) ?
233 ἄννειρε **1577** : an ἀνῇρε vel ἀναῖρε vel ἀναίρει?
233 *Iovae* **1604**
234 τοὔνεκ' ἀρισφαλές **1604**
236 πινυτοῖς μουσέων ταμιεύμασι κεύθων **1604**
236 *addere* **1604**
237 ἐστὶ **1577** : ἔνθα **1604**

240	νῦν δὲ σὺ τόνδε δέδεξο γαληνιόωντι προσώπῳ, θυμῷ δ' εὐφρονέοντι· τὸ γὰρ κεχαρισμένον ἔσται Μούσαις, αἵ σε φιλεῦσι καὶ οὐ λίπον ἄμμορον ἀνθῶν οἷς μάλα κυδαίνουσιν, ὅσοι σφίσιν ἄρθμιοί εἰσιν. ὁπλοτέροις δ' ἔμεναι σπουδῆς τόδε κέντρον ἔολπα, μᾶλλον ὅπως ἀγαπῶσιν Ἀχαιΐδος ἤθεα φωνῆς, εἰ κλειτοὺς ὁρόωσιν ἀνάκτορας οὐκ ἀθερίζειν.	hunc igitur facili complectere mente poetam et placido aspectu: nam sic praestabis amicum officium Musis, quae te venerantur et ornant floribus Aoniis, queis pectora amica coronant. sic etiam calcar discentibus addere spero, gnavius ut studeant Graiam cognoscere linguam, quando vident dominos etiam has complectier artes.
245 250	οὐκ ἔτ' ἐρητύσω σε, δαΐφρονος αἷμα γενέθλης, εἰ πάρος εὐχωλῇσι Θεὸν περὶ σεῦ ἱκέτευσα, ὄφρα πολυχρόνιόν σε καὶ ἀρτεμέοντα φυλάξῃ καὶ καθαρὸν λώβης καὶ πήματος αἰὲν ἄθικτον εἰς πάγκοινον ὄνειαρ, ἐμὸν δέ τε καὶ χρέος αὐτοῦ, ὃς χρῄζω πτερύγεσσι τεαῖς ὑπὸ δηρὸν ἀλύξαι λιμὸν ἀεικέλιον καὶ χρήσιμα παισὶν ἀνύσσαι καὶ Θεὸν ὑμνῆσαι καὶ σὸν κλέος, εἰς ὅσον ἥκω.	iam te dimittam, generis decus armipotentis, si prius exorem coeli super axe Parentem, ut sanas longo servet tibi tempore vires et tutum a vitiis praestet sortisque procellis. publica id utilitas et sors mea postulat una, qui vestris exopto diu latitando sub alis evitare famem puerisque impendere curas, quaque datur, cantare Deo et tibi grata, facultas.
	ἐν Σεληνοπόλει, τῇ ἱερᾷ τοῦ Βαρθολομαίου ἀποστόλου ἡμέρᾳ, ἔτει σωτηρίας ά.φ.ο γ.	Luneburgi in festo Bar- tholomaei, anno sal(utis) MDLXXIII
	τῆς χρηστότητός σου ὑπουργὸς Λαυρέντιος Ῥο- δομὰν ἐν Λουνοπύργῃ παρὰ τοῦ ἁγίου Μιχαήλου γυμνασιάρχης	clementiae tuae observantiss(imus) cliens M. Laurent(ius) Rhodom(an) scholae Lunebur- gensis ad d(ivum) Mi- chaelem rector

243 ἀγαποῖσιν 1577
245 an οὐκέτ'?
250 χρῄζῳ 1577
250 an ὕπο?
252 ἥκω 1577 : an ἀρκῶ?
subscriptio ἔτει : ἔτη 1577

Too Homeric to Be True: John Tzetzes' Reception of Quintus of Smyrna and the Importance of Plausibility

Valeria F. Lovato

INTRODUCTION

The desire to fill the gaps left by the Homeric poems was not an exclusive feature of the authors belonging to the so-called Second Sophistic. In twelfth-century Byzantium, an era that witnessed a veritable revival of the study of Homer, many literati endeavoured not only to interpret but also to complement the Homeric narrative of the Trojan War. Interestingly, most Byzantine writers who aimed at 'completing' Homer drew considerably from the works of their Second Sophistic predecessors. Dictys of Crete and Flavius Philostratus are probably the most quoted sources, whereas, rather surprisingly, Quintus of Smyrna does not feature prominently in the Byzantine accounts of the Trojan War. Yet, there is at least one exception to this trend, and it is on this very exception that the present study will focus.

To be sure, Quintus is mentioned quite often in the so-called *Carmina Iliaca*, a short hexametric poem penned by the twelfth-century polymath John Tzetzes. As we learn from the *Carmina Iliaca* itself, Tzetzes composed this work when he was still young and facing a difficult moment of his life. Indeed, he had just lost his position as the secretary of a certain Isaac, the Byzantine *doux* of Berroia (modern Veria in Macedonia) and was now trying to start a new career as a private teacher. The *Carmina Iliaca*, which aim to provide a complete account of the Trojan War, was intended as a demonstration of the talent of its author, in the hope of attracting potential new clients. What better way to advertise one's learning than writing a short but exhaustive compendium of one of the most famous conflicts of all times, finally filling in the lacunae of the Homeric narrative? Tzetzes' desire to complete and summarise Homer emerges both from the initial scholium to the poem and from the tripartite structure of the entire work: the first section covers all the events preceding the Homeric narration, the second one summarises the episodes narrated in the *Iliad*, while the third and last one recounts what happened after Hector's death. Not surprisingly, it is in this last part that Quintus' *Posthomerica* is quoted the most, both in the text of the poem and in the scholia that Tzetzes himself added to his own verses.

However, as I intend to show, Tzetzes' interest in Quintus does not simply stem from a general desire to acquire an accurate knowledge of both the Trojan matter and the – more or less – ancient authors who wrote about it. On the contrary, Quintus seems to attract Tzetzes' attention (and disapproval) for a number of reasons that are deeply connected with the scholar's authorial practices and with the principles informing his literary criticism.

To prove my point, I will start by comparing Tzetzes' treatment of Quintus to that of Triphiodorus, the author of *The Sack of Troy* (*Halōsis Iliou*). Despite featuring quite prominently in the last section of the *Carmina Iliaca*, both poets are strongly criticised by Tzetzes, who, as usual, projects the competitiveness of twelfth-century Byzantine intellectual milieus onto his reception of past literature.[1] This antagonistic attitude emerges most clearly in the last part of the poem, where Tzetzes' authorial voice is increasingly present in the narrative, thus further uncovering his self-advertising strategies.

However, Tzetzes' attitude towards Quintus and Triphiodorus is not exactly the same. In spite of his shortcomings, Triphiodorus is not completely dismissed by Tzetzes, who, in some instances, presents the *Sack of Troy* as a potential forerunner of his *Carmina Iliaca*. Differently from Triphiodorus – and despite being often used as a source – Quintus is never explicitly quoted as a positive example and is seldom even mentioned outside the *Carmina Iliaca,* except for one significant passage that I will discuss in the conclusion of this study. Apart from this exceptional case, Quintus hardly escapes Tzetzes' harsh criticism, which targets especially the ambitious scope of the *Posthomerica*. Indeed, partly anticipating the conclusions reached by modern scholars, Tzetzes suggests that Quintus is trying to pose as a new Homer.[2] However, in the polymath's eyes, the *Posthomerica* is no *Iliad*. Far from being a match for the great Homer, Quintus managed to appropriate only the most censorable aspects of the Homeric poems, composing an implausible and verbose account

---

[1] Much has been written on the competitiveness characterising twelfth-century literary circles. Apart from the now classical study by Garzya (1973), see Cameron (2016: 3–8) with extensive bibliography.

[2] See Bär's characterisation of Quintus as a 'novus Homerus' (Bär 2007: 41–5 and 54; see also Bär 2009: 12–13, 69–74). As shown by Bär, however, Quintus' relationship with the Homeric model cannot be qualified as simple imitation. Moreover, the *Posthomerica* creates a wider network of intertextual allusions, which further enrich Quintus' self-fashioning (see again Bär 2007: 45–51 and 2009: 74–8 on the Hesiodic and Callimachean paradigms).

of the Trojan War. As I argue, in his *Carmina Iliaca* Tzetzes sets out to unmask the preposterousness of Quintus' literary endeavour, while also setting forth an alternative and superior model of rhetorical and literary composition: his own.

TRIPHIODORUS' SUPERFICIAL MISTAKES

To fully appreciate the reasons behind Tzetzes' criticism of Quintus, it will be useful to start by comparing the passages where the polymath criticises Quintus himself with those where it is Triphiodorus who is under attack. Thus, not only will we identify the rhetorical strategies characterising Tzetzes' invectives against his predecessors, but we will also understand what specific features of the *Posthomerica* attracted the scholar's displeasure.

One of the central moments of the last section of the *Carmina Iliaca* is the arrival of Penthesilea and her contingent of Amazons. And it is precisely in connection with the episode of Penthesilea's death that we find the first – slightly disparaging – remark that Tzetzes ever addresses to Triphiodorus, who, together with Quintus, is one of the scholar's principal sources for the events revolving around the queen of the Amazons.

As Tzetzes himself remarks, there are many different accounts of Penthesilea's final moments. In the lines immediately preceding the passage we are now going to examine, the scholar has just presented the version of the story that he deems more reliable: according to his sources, the wounded Amazon was thrown, still alive, in the river Xanthos, where she then drowned.[3] As usual, however, Tzetzes also reports the other variants that he has come across during his readings. This time, the alternative version he quotes is the one transmitted by Triphiodorus and other unnamed writers:

Οὐδ' ἄρα Τρυφιοδώρῳ ἐφανδάνει, οἷα καὶ ἄλλοις,
Ξάνθου ἐνὶ ῥεέθροις ῥιφῆναι Πενθεσίλειαν,   210
Αἰακίδη δ' ἐρέει κτανέειν ἅμα καὶ κτερεΐξαι.[4]

Just as others, Tryphiodorus (*sic*) was not pleased
with Penthesilea being thrown in the currents of the Xanthos;
instead, he says that it was the Aeacid who both killed and buried her.

With this ironic remark, Tzetzes seems to imply that Triphiodorus did not select the most accurate or plausible version of the story, which is the choice

---

[3] Tz. *Carm. Il.* 3.194–208 Leone. This is one of the many instances where, despite drawing from the *Posthomerica* (Q.S. 1.716–49; 767–81), Tzetzes does not acknowledge his debt.

[4] Tz. *Carm. Il.* 3.209–11.

that every writer should always make. On the contrary, the author of the *Sack of Troy* is implicitly accused of having chosen a variant that better suited his personal taste, with no regard for either truthfulness or reliability.

The credibility of Triphiodorus' account is questioned also when it comes to another central detail, namely the date of the fall of Troy. For someone like Tzetzes, who was particularly interested in all sorts of chronological issues, such an oversight cannot be taken lightly. There is no mistaking Tzetzes' indignation at Triphiodorus' blunder:

Τρυφιόδωρος δ' οὐκ εἰδώς, ὅτε πέρθετο Τροίη,   700
πολλοῖς σὺν ἑτέροις κἀμὲ δοκέων ἀπαφίσκειν,
οὕνεκά μ' Ἰσαάκιος ἀτίσατο αἰσχεοτίμας,
ἄνθεσιν ἐστεφάνωσε τὸν ἵππον ἐκ ποταμοῖο,
χειμῶνος μεσάτοιο ἐόντος, ὡς ἐρεείνω·
Ὀρφεὺς γάρ μ' ἐδίδαξεν, ἀπ' ἀνέρος ἄλλου ἀκούσας,   705
ψευδέα μή ποτε μῦθον ἐνίσπειν ἀνθρώποισιν.[5]

Not knowing when Troy was sacked, Tryphiodorus (*sic*)
thought that he could trick me as he had done with many others,
since Isaac, who celebrated shameful individuals, stripped me of the
          honour I was owed.
Thus, he (*sc.* Triphiodorus) crowned the horse with river flowers,
even though it was the middle of winter, as I declare.
Indeed, having learned it from another man, Orpheus
taught me never to lie to mankind.

These few verses deserve a closer analysis, since they display some features that we will encounter also in our discussion of Tzetzes' reception of Quintus. First of all, both this passage and the one quoted above are quite remarkable in that the polymath mentions explicitly in the body of the poem the name of the author whose version he is rectifying. Despite featuring also elsewhere in the *Carmina Iliaca*, the insertion of such direct criticism in the main text remains quite exceptional. Indeed, in most cases, Tzetzes seems to consider the scholia as the most appropriate destination for the harshest invectives.[6] This time, however, the polymath takes special care to point out that, differently from those who fell for Triphiodorus' inaccurate dating, not only he was not fooled by the apparent precision of his predecessor's account, but he was also able to correct his mistake. What is more, the discursive strategy of this extract contributes

---

[5] Tz. *Carm. Il.* 3.700–6.
[6] This applies especially to Homer's faults (on which see also *infra*). Cf. also the scholar's tirade against the arch-liar (ψευδέστατος) Philostratus (schol. in *Carm. Il.* 3.334, p. 225, 1–5).

both to disparaging Triphiodorus' supposed knowledge of the events and to exalting Tzetzes' competence. With a rhetorically effective move, the polymath represents Triphiodorus in the act of crowning the Trojan Horse with a garland of flowers, as if the poet had actually taken part in the events recounted in his *Sack of Troy*. Through this ironic imagery, Tzetzes caustically denounces the unreliability of his predecessor, who misled his readers by providing deceptively detailed information on facts he clearly knew nothing about.

The reference to Orpheus further highlights the centrality of this passage for Tzetzes' self-advertising strategy. As I have shown elsewhere,[7] Orpheus plays a central role in Tzetzes' authorial self-fashioning, being often represented as the scholar's true 'teacher' and as a paradigm of literary excellence, which Tzetzes alone was able to truly appropriate. His presence in this context subtly underscores Tzetzes' scrupulous adherence to the truth, while also emphasising the incompetence of the scholar's rivals, past and present.

This interpretation is strengthened by Tzetzes' bitter reference to his difficult relationship with his former employer, the *doux* Isaac. As we learn from other passages of his works, the polymath was particularly irritated by the fact that Isaac privileged other, incompetent, individuals over his talented secretary, whose superior eloquence he was unable to appreciate.[8] The reference to Isaac's unfairness is aimed at further enhancing Tzetzes' self-advertising: the reader is implicitly invited not to behave like Isaac and to cherish the scholar's exceptional talent instead.

QUINTUS UNDER SCRUTINY

If the aforementioned attacks against Triphiodorus might seem quite disparaging, Tzetzes' criticism of Quintus will prove even harsher. This time, instead of following the order in which the relevant passages appear in the *Carmina Iliaca*, I will start from the less virulent attacks to conclude with the most striking one.

Penthesilea and the Amazons

As mentioned, Tzetzes is particularly interested in the details surrounding the Amazons' arrival at Troy. Along with Triphiodorus, Quintus is one of his main sources for the reconstruction of this event. The scholar is especially interested in identifying the reasons behind Penthesilea's alliance with the

---

[7] Lovato (2017: 194–202).
[8] See e.g. *Carm. Il.* 2.142–5.

Trojans, as well as in determining the size of her army. In both these respects, Tzetzes does not seem to agree with anything Quintus has to say.

Τοῖσι δὲ μυρομένοισιν ἀγαστόνου εἴνεκα πάτρης
ἠοῖ ἐνὶ τριτάτῃ ἀπὸ Θερμώδοντος ἰοῦσα
ἤλυθε Πενθεσίλεια, κόρη μεγάθυμος Ὀτρήρης,
ἠϋγενὴς τελέθουσα Ἀμαζονίδων βασίλεια.
Ἤλυθε δ᾽, ὡς ὁ **Κόϊντος ἑοῖς ἐπέεσσιν ἀείδει,**   10
οὕνεκα ἣν κάσιν ἔκτανεν Ἱππολύτην ἐνὶ θήρῃ,
μύσος ἀλευομένη, δυοκαίδεκα δ᾽ ἄλλαι ἕποντο.
Ταῦτα μὲν ὧδε Κόϊντος ἑοῖς ἐπέεσσιν ἀείδει.
Ἑλλάνικος, Λυσίας δὲ καὶ ἄλλοι ἄνδρες ἀγαυοὶ
φάν, ἕνεκα σφετέρης ἀρετῆς ἐπιήλυθε Τροίη,   15
κῦδος ἀεξήσουσα, ὅπως κε γάμοισι μιγείη.
(. . .)
Τοὶ δ᾽ ὑπὸ δώρων Ἑκτορέων ἐρέουσιν ἰοῦσαν   20
πυθομένην μόρον Ἕκτορος αἶψ᾽ ἐθέλειν ὑποείκειν·
τὴν δ᾽ ὁ γέρων Πρίαμος κατέρυξεν ἑοῖς ἐνὶ δώροις,
πολλοὺς ἄνδρας ἔχουσαν ἀπὸ Σκυθέων κλυτοτόξων,
πεζοὺς ἱππῆάς τε ἀρηϊφίλους τε γυναῖκας.⁹

While they (*sc.* the Trojans) shed tears over their lamentable fatherland,
on the third day, proceeding from the Thermodon,
Penthesilea came to their help: she was the magnanimous daughter of
    Otrera
and the noble queen of the Amazons.
As Quintus sings in his verses, she came
because she had killed her sister Hippolyta during a hunt and
was now seeking to avoid the blame. Twelve others followed.
This is what Quintus sings in his verses.
But Hellanicus, Lysias and other illustrious men
said that she went to Troy for the sake of her own fame,
to increase her glory so as to be able to marry.
(. . .)
Others say that, having come because of Hector's gifts,
when she learned about Hector's death she wanted to depart straight away.
However, the old Priam held her back by offering his own gifts,
since she had with her many men from the ranks of the renowned Scyth-
    ian archers, along with units of infantry, cavalry and warlike women.

Even if Quintus is not yet openly challenged, Tzetzes' opinion of the poet could not be clearer. Let us consider the reasons underlying Penthesilea's decision

⁹ Tz. *Carm. Il.* 3.6–16; 20–4.

to join the Trojans. After summarising Quintus' version of the story, Tzetzes implicitly contrasts it with the variant reported by 'other illustrious men', such as Hellanicus and Lysias. The implication of these lines is self-evident: the reader should not trust what Quintus says, but he should listen to other sources, whom Tzetzes deems to be more reliable. In other words, while Hellanicus and Lysias proved worthy of the fame they enjoy, Quintus' merits (and renown) are subtly questioned.

When it comes to Penthesilea's army, Tzetzes' stance becomes even more explicit. Once again, after reporting the version narrated by Quintus, the *Carmina Iliaca* swiftly and subtly rectifies it. The twelve Amazons who, according to the *Posthomerica*, were the only other warriors to accompany Penthesilea are implicitly opposed to the 'many men' that Tzetzes mentions at the very end of the passage.

This time, however, Tzetzes does not limit himself to indirectly rectifying Quintus' account, but also wants to make sure that his audience will not miss his point. After all, when it comes to chronicling a war, no matter how remote, it is essential to ascertain the magnitude of the forces at play. This is why the polymath feels the need to further expand upon this matter in two related scholia, where his disagreement with Quintus is finally voiced explicitly. In these marginal notes Tzetzes does not hesitate to point out that his mention of the 'many men' (πολλοὺς ἄνδρας) following Penthesilea was deliberately aimed at refuting Quintus, whose account of the events is deemed to be implausible:

> Πολλοὺς ἄνδρας ἔχουσαν· τοῦτο πρὸς Κόϊντον ἀποτεινόμενος εἶπον· ἐκεῖνος γάρ, καθὼς ἔφημεν πρότερον, σὺν δώδεκα μόναις Ἀμαζόσι φησὶν ἐπὶ τὴν Ἴλιον παραγενέσθαι τὴν Πενθεσίλειαν, φεύγουσαν τὸ μῖσος τοῦ φόνου τῆς ἀδελφῆς.[10]

> *She had with her many men*] I said this with reference to Quintus. As I mentioned before, he maintains that Penthesilea went to Troy with twelve Amazons only, so as to avoid the blame caused by the murder of her own sister.

Machaon's Fate

If, when it comes to Penthesilea and her army, Tzetzes' criticism of Quintus is mostly confined to marginal notes, things start to change when the scholar deals with the warrior healer Machaon, son of Asclepius.

---

[10] Schol. in *Carm Il.* 3.23, p. 211, 8–11. See also schol. in *Carm Il.* 3.185, p. 218, 18–20, where Tzetzes makes the exact same point (πλῆθὺς δ' ἄσπετος ἦεν· πρὸς τὸν Κόϊντον ἀποτεινόμενος καὶ **δεικνὺς ὅτι οὐ δώδεκα μόναι ἦσαν ἀλλὰ πολλαὶ**, ἔφην 'πλῆθὺς δ' ἄσπετος ἦεν').

The first mention of Quintus' treatment of Machaon occurs in a rather enigmatic line of the *Carmina Iliaca*. In this passage, Tzetzes is recounting the feats of Eurypylus, the son of the Mysian king Telephus. Specifically, the scholar reports that, according to the *Posthomerica*, Eurypylus slayed many Greek heroes, including the healer Machaon:

> Εὐρύπυλος δ' ἐπίκουρος Τρωσὶν ἐπήλυθεν αὖθις,
> Τηλεφίδης μεγάθυμος, Μυσός, ἐπήρατος ἄναξ.
> Κτεῖνε δὲ πολλοὺς Ἀργείων Ἀσκληπιάδη τε,   520
> ἥρω ἰητῆρα, Μαχάονα, κάλλιμον ἄνδρα,
> ὥς ῥα Κόϊντος ἔφη· ὁ δ' ἄρ' Ὀρφεὺς ἄλλ' ἐπαείδει.[11]

> But a new ally comes to join the Trojans, Eurypylus,
> the magnanimous son of Telephus, the fair Mysian king.
> He killed many Argives, including the son of Asclepius,
> the healing hero Machaon, an excellent man.
> This is what Quintus said. But Orpheus sings otherwise.

At first glance, Tzetzes seems to be simply paraphrasing Quintus' version of the facts, while casually hinting at the existence of alternative variants of the story. However, what we have observed in the paragraph devoted to Triphiodorus should alert us to the potential significance of an explicit reference to Orpheus, no matter how cursory.

Our supposition is confirmed some sixty verses later, when Tzetzes fully reports Orpheus' version of the story, which he clearly deems to be the most reliable of all. This time, the scholar's opinion on the *Posthomerica* is quite explicit:

> Αὐτίκα δ' ἐκ Λήμνοιο Ποιάντιος ἤλυθεν ἥρως,   580
> εὐμήκης, μελανόχροος, εὔθετος ἠδὲ σύνοφρυς,
> τόξα φέρων στονόεντα· πόδας δέ οἱ ἕλκος ἔτειρε.
> Πέτρῃ δ' ἀρτεμέα ἐχιήτιδι τεῦξε Μαχάων.
> Τὸν δ' ὁ Κόϊντος ἔπεφνεν ὑπ' Εὐρυπύλοιο βολῇσιν.[12]

> And soon came from Lemnos the hero son of Poeas,
> he was tall, dark-skinned, with a harmonious frame and meeting eyebrows
> and he brought with him a deadly bow. A festering wound tormented
>   his feet.
> But Machaon cured him with a serpentine stone,
> the very same hero that Quintus killed with Eurypylus' blows.

[11] Tz. *Carm. Il.* 3.518–22.
[12] Tz. *Carm. Il.* 3.580–4.

Tzetzes has waited until this moment to relate the 'authentic' version of the events because Machaon plays an essential role in healing Philoctetes upon the latter's return from Lemnos, as recounted, among others, by Orpheus' *Lithica*.[13] After all, who else could have cured the hero's terrible wound, if not the son of Asclepius himself? Having thus shown the plausibility of Orpheus' account, Tzetzes cannot resist the urge to make a final cutting remark to Quintus, whose version of the story has once again proved to be completely unreliable. To strengthen his point, the scholar employs the same rhetorical strategy we have encountered in the passage concerning Triphiodorus' wrong dating of the fall of Troy. Just like Triphiodorus, Quintus is ironically represented as an actor in the events he pretends to be informed about. This time, however, Tzetzes' irony is even more pungent, since Quintus is depicted in the act of personally dealing the final blow to the hero that he decided to prematurely erase from his version of the story.

The use of this specific rhetorical device is not the result of a casual choice. Nor can it be seen as an especially vivid discursive tool that the scholar reserves for crucial topics, such as the chronology of the war of Troy or the role played by central characters of the story. Rather, as I will show in what follows, the Byzantine scholar employs this vivid imagery especially when dealing with certain – questionable – features of Quintus' authorial strategies.

Nestor and Memnon: an Impossible Conversation

One last extract from the *Carmina Iliaca*, along with the related scholia, will help to clarify my point. In this case, Tzetzes is concerned with an episode that is attested exclusively in the *Posthomerica*, namely the encounter between Nestor and Memnon. According to Quintus' narrative, desiring to avenge the death of his son, Nestor decided to face the fearsome Memnon, who had recently joined the Trojans. However, instead of fighting the old king, Memnon addresses him with touching words, declaring that he could never hurt a man who reminded him of his own father. Tzetzes was certainly struck by this episode, since he decided to mention it in his poem. However, the impression that Quintus made on his Byzantine reader is far from positive:

Μοῦνος ἀπ' ἄλλων Νέστωρ Μέμνονος ἤλυθεν ἄντα   280
υἱέος ἀχνύμενος· μέγα δ' ἔστενεν ἔνδοθι ἦτορ.
Σὺν δ' ἄρα οἱ ὁ Κόϊντος ἔην πέλας, ὃς ἐπάκουεν
Μέμνων ὅσσα ἔειπε γέροντ' Ἀραβηῖδι φωνῇ.
Πεζὸς ἐγὼ τελέθων δέ, Ἰσαακίοιο φραδαῖσιν,

---

[13] [Orph.] *Lithica* 346–54 Halleux and Schamp. It is worth noting that Tzetzes believed the *Lithica* to be an authentic poem by Orpheus.

ὅς μ' ἀπὸ Βερροίης ἐριβώλακος ἠδὲ Σελάων   285
πεζὸν ἔπεμψε νέεσθαι, ἐμεῦ ἵπποιο ἀμέρσας
(. . .)
φεῦγον οὐδ' ἐσάκουσα, τὰ Μέμνων ἐξερέεινεν.[14]   290

The only one who faced Memnon was Nestor
who was grieving his son: in his heart, he let out a mighty wail.
Close to him there was Quintus, who was able to hear
what Memnon told the old man in the Arabic tongue.
As for me, I was on foot, as a consequence of the decisions of Isaac,
who, having deprived me of my horse, made me walk back home
from the fertile Berroia and from Selai
(. . .)
Since I was fleeing, I was unable to hear what Memnon said.

This is probably the most corrosive expression of Tzetzes' opinion on Quintus' poetic skills. Not only does the polymath point out that such a long conversation would have been impossible in the midst of a battle,[15] but he also remarks that the two interlocutors would never have been able to understand each other, since they did not even speak the same language. Unsurprisingly, it is in this passage that we find the most representative example of the very same rhetorical device we have encountered in some of the preceding extracts: once again, when it comes to pointing out the unreliability of an author, Tzetzes ironically represents him as an active participant in the events he writes about. This time, however, the target of Tzetzes' criticism is explicitly contrasted to Tzetzes himself, who, contrary to Quintus, is said to have been unable to eavesdrop on the supposed exchange between the two heroes. Invective and self-advertising are once again strictly intertwined: the attack against Quintus provides another occasion to expand upon Tzetzes' recent past, with special attention to the unfair treatment he received from his former employer Isaac.

If the reader still had some doubts concerning the tone of this extract, Tzetzes dispels any possible uncertainty in two rather explicit scholia. In the first one, the scholar states that his intent was to ridicule (διασύρειν, literally 'pull to pieces') Quintus for the absurd episode he managed to concoct.[16] The second scholium, whose beginning is worth quoting in full, provides further details on the scholar's overall agenda:

πεζὸς ἐγὼ τελέθων· ὅτι μὲν οὐκ **ἤμην ἐγὼ οὔτε τοῖς Τρωϊκοῖς ὁμόχρονος χρόνοις** οὔτε **τῷ Σμυρναίῳ Κοΐντῳ**, ἀλλ' ὅτι οὐδὲ **πέπλακα** τὸν Τρωϊκὸν

---

[14] Tz. Carm. Il. 3.280–6; 290. On this passage, see also Braccini (2009/10: 168–9; 2011: 48).
[15] See also schol. in Carm. Il. 3.282, p. 223, 14–17.
[16] Schol. in Carm. Il. 3.282, p. 223, 14.

πόλεμον, τοῦτο πᾶσι κατάδηλον. ἔστι δὲ τοῦτο τὸ σχῆμα βαρύτης ἐπίκρυπτος τῷ ἀστεϊσμῷ καὶ τραχεῖα καταφορά, ὅτι πεισθεὶς ὁ σεβαστὸς Ἰσαάκιος τῇ τούτου συζύγῳ καὶ ἀφελόμενός μου τοὺς ἵππους, πεζὸν εἴασε πρὸς τὴν πατρίδα παλινδρομεῖν ἔκ τε Βερροίας (. . .)[17]

I was on foot] The fact that I did not live at the time of the Trojan War nor during the era of Quintus is evident to anyone, just as it is evident that I did not compose a fictional account of the Trojan War. This rhetorical scheme is an invective hidden behind a joke as well as a harsh attack, since the sebastos Isaac, trusting his wife[18] and having sequestered my horses, made me return back home on foot from Berroia (. . .)

Tzetzes goes to great lengths to emphasise the ironic and sarcastic tone of his comment on the alleged encounter between Memnon and Nestor. He starts by pointing out that neither he nor Quintus lived at the time of the Trojan conflict: this should be evident to anyone, just as everyone should know that Tzetzes did not compose a fictional account of the Trojan War (πέπλακα, a crucial term that we will encounter again). Tzetzes also adds that these lines are a demonstration of his own rhetorical prowess: specifically, they show his ability to hide a harsh attack behind the appearance of a joke. Once more, the invective against Quintus insensibly gives way to another, bitter, reminiscence of the scholar's falling out with his former employer, who was so petty as to force Tzetzes to go back to Constantinople on foot. Literary criticism, self-representation and rhetorical display are artfully blended in these few lines, which, as we will see, hold the key to a deeper understanding of both Tzetzes' reception of the tradition *and* his authorial agenda.

TRIPHIODORUS AND QUINTUS COMPARED

Based on the texts analysed so far, we can identify some similarities between the passages where Tzetzes attacks Triphiodorus and those where he criticises Quintus. In both cases, the polymath employs sarcastic and ironic tones that allow him to highlight – and scoff at – the unreliability of the two poets. What is more, Tzetzes' criticism of Quintus and Triphiodorus is used as a pretext

---

[17] Schol. in *Carm. Il.* 3.284, pp. 223, 18–224, 3.

[18] In other passages of the *Carmina Iliaca* (see e.g. 2.142–5; 3.287–9; 3.620–3; 3.754), Tzetzes seems to imply that his misfortunes had been mainly caused by Isaac's treacherous wife, who persuaded her husband to fire his young secretary because the latter had rejected her advances (see Braccini 2010: *passim*). This interpretation is now disputed by Agapitos (forthcoming).

to draw the readers' attention to the scholar's situation. Indeed, in most of the extracts here discussed, Tzetzes deliberately inserts direct references to his personal experience, complaining about the unjust treatment he received from his former employer, who was unable to appreciate his talent. By doing so, the polymath further highlights the unfairness of his own predicament, all the while presenting both Quintus and Triphiodorus as unworthy predecessors.

In this respect, I believe that Tzetzes' particularly aggressive stance towards these two authors might also stem from their relative recentness. Indeed, in Tzetzes' own works, both these poets and Tzetzes himself are often qualified as *neoi* ('new, recent'), especially with respect to Homer and other authors such as Orpheus[19] or Dictys, whom Tzetzes considered to be direct witnesses of the Trojan War.[20] This chronological distinction features time and again in Tzetzes' writings, where being *neos* is sometimes presented as a potentially negative trait. In the introduction to his *Exegesis of the Iliad*, the scholar states that his being both young and 'recent' should not be considered as a parameter to gauge the quality of his works.[21] On the contrary, despite being *neos*, Tzetzes should be considered as no less than Homer's very son, since no one else can better understand and interpret the verses of the Poet.[22] Therefore, the relative chronological proximity between Quintus and Triphiodorus, on the one hand, and Tzetzes, on the other, might have contributed to increase the latter's aggressiveness towards the two 'recent' poets, who, despite their incompetence, enjoyed a success that the equally *neos* but considerably more talented Tzetzes was unjustly being denied. Such competitiveness might have been further enhanced by the fact that Tzetzes and his two rivals shared a similar goal, since they all aimed at completing the story that Homer never told in its entirety. Finally, the deliberate comparison between these 'new' poets' mistakes and Tzetzes' superior (albeit underestimated) competence is an essential component of the scholar's self-advertising strategy, which, despite permeating the whole *Carmina Iliaca*, emerges most clearly in its conclusive section. Indeed, it is immediately after his final attack against Triphiodorus that Tzetzes reveals the primary purpose of his composition and explicitly offers his services to the 'children of privileged parents' (τέκνα μοιρηγενέων γενετήρων) who are the target audience of his hexametric poem.[23]

---

[19] Orpheus' παλαιότης is often quoted as a testament to his reliability (see e.g. Tz. schol. in *Carm. Il.* 223a, p. 191, 8–9 and schol. in Lycophronem 1048, 9–12 Scheer).

[20] See e.g. *Chil.* 4 hist. 16.995–6 Leone, where Triphiodorus is labelled as a νέος ποιητής. The same definition must have also applied to Quintus, since the two poets are almost constantly associated with one another in Tzetzes' works: see e.g. the prologue of the *Allegories of the Iliad* (1.483 Boissonnade), along with *Exeg. Il.* 67.18–20.

[21] Tz. *Exeg. Il.* 8.11–12.

[22] Tz. *Exeg. Il.* 19.17–20.6, to be read together with Cullhed (2014: 60).

[23] Tz. *Carm. Il.* 3.753–60.

However, despite these similarities, Tzetzes' attitude towards Triphio-dorus is not entirely comparable to his treatment of Quintus. To be sure, Triphiodorus features also in other works by Tzetzes, who seems to have an overall positive opinion of his poetic skills. For instance, in some passages of the *Exegesis of the Iliad*, Triphiodorus is quoted as a paradigmatic example of the allegorical technique that should be applied to the interpretation of the Homeric poems.[24] Elsewhere, Tzetzes cites a hexameter from the *Sack of Troy* in support of a potentially controversial etymological interpretation of a rare word.[25] Therefore, despite his undeniable shortcomings, Triphiodorus is not completely dismissed by Tzetzes. Notably, the same does not apply to Quintus of Smyrna. If we exclude the sarcastic comments featuring in the *Carmina Iliaca*, the author of the *Posthomerica* is hardly mentioned in Tzetzes' later works.[26]

Since the scholar was clearly familiar with Quintus' poem and since the scope and content of the *Posthomerica* were rather close to his own literary pursuits, it is worth investigating the reasons for such an apparent disinterest in – and negative reception of – the poet from Smyrna.

Let us start by quickly reconsidering the polemical extracts from the *Carmina Iliaca* we have analysed so far. If Triphiodorus' main mistakes are his inaccuracy in the dating of the capture of Troy or the alteration of a minor detail based on (arbitrary) personal preferences, when it comes to Quintus Tzetzes' criticism focuses on other crucial aspects. Differently from Triphiodorus, Quintus is not simply accused of being inaccurate, but his version of the story is presented as *deliberately* implausible, especially when it comes to major episodes that could significantly alter the logical and narrative structure of the events.

The case of the Amazons' troops is a perfect example of Quintus' tendency to insert details that are as specific as they are unrealistic: how could thirteen Amazons keep the whole Greek army in check? Equally unreliable is Quintus' account of Machaon's death, which contradicts the version related by more trustworthy sources and ends up altering the chronological sequence of the events. The same applies to the touching conversation between Memnon and Nestor: had the ridiculous detail on the number of the Amazons not been enough, the impossible conversation between the two heroes cannot but definitively unmask the preposterousness of Quintus' narrative.

[24] See e.g. Tz. *Exeg. Il.* 78.13–17; 385.19–22 and 402.1–5 (reference to *Sack of Troy* 234). For a similar example, see also *Exeg. Il.* 330.14 (*Sack of Troy* 128).

[25] Tz. *Chil.* 6, hist. 85.860–1.

[26] As far as I know, if we exclude the extract from the *Chiliads* discussed *infra*, Quintus features only in Tzetzes' commentary on Lycophron's *Alexandra* (schol. in Lycophronem 61.1–10 and 1048b.1–12 Scheer). In this latter work, the *Posthomerica* is mentioned with reference to Oenone's and Machaon's deaths. However, already in the *Carmina Iliaca*, Tzetzes clearly rejects Quintus' variants. For Machaon, see *supra*; for Oenone, see *Carm. Il.* 3.596–8.

If we look closely at Tzetzes' criticism of the poet, however, we will remark that the charge of deliberate implausibility is strictly connected to another, deeper issue. As noted, in Tzetzes' ironic invectives against Quintus, the latter is repeatedly depicted as an active character of his own poem. Admittedly, the same strategy is once applied also to Triphiodorus, who is equally represented in the act of adorning the Trojan Horse on the day of the city's fall. However, it is only when it comes to Quintus that Tzetzes feels the need to clarify that the representation of the poet as a direct witness of the Trojan conflict is nothing more than a rhetorical expedient. As I argue, this difference stems from a feature of Quintus' *Posthomerica* that Tzetzes was well aware of and that he wants to point out to his readers. Differently from Triphiodorus' 'mistakes', Quintus' unreliable account of the events does not simply stem from an oversight or from the failure to consult the appropriate sources. Rather, it seems to be the consequence of a deliberate pose. Indeed, in the *Posthomerica* Quintus intentionally behaves as if he had been present on the Trojan plain, consciously making up implausible minutiae that only a direct witness could have known about.

HOMER'S SOURCES AND THE LIMITS OF FICTIONALITY

Tzetzes' remarks on Quintus' dubious knowledge of surprisingly specific details are reminiscent of a long tradition of scholarly debates focusing on the extraordinary precision of the Homeric account.[27] How could Homer know about all the heroes that took part in the conflict and go as far as to remember the name and fate of each one of them? Did he live at the time of the Trojan War? Was he able to talk with direct witnesses of the events? Or did he draw this information from other written accounts of the conflict? Like most Homeric exegetes, Tzetzes does not hesitate to participate in this age-old debate. His opinions are detailed in the introduction to his *Exegesis of the Iliad*, which was likely addressed to the same audience as the *Carmina Iliaca*. After discussing the positions of his predecessors, Tzetzes concludes that Homer could not have lived much later than the events he writes about. With all likelihood, even if he did not partake in the war, he must have been able to talk with direct witnesses of the events, such as Orpheus or one of Odysseus' companions, if not Odysseus himself. What is more, he also appears to have drawn from contemporary accounts of the conflict, like those penned by Dictys of Crete or the mysterious Sisyphus of Cos.[28] Whatever the case,

---

[27] On this long-standing debate, see Kim (2010a), with extensive bibliography.

[28] Tz. *Exeg. Il.* 39.11–40.1. Like many Byzantine writers, Tzetzes considered Dictys' *Ephemeris belli Troiani* to be one of the most reliable sources for the events of the Trojan War. Most likely, however, Tzetzes knew the *Ephemeris* through the mediation of the *Chronicle* of John Malalas (see e.g. Jeffreys 1990: 266).

Tzetzes concludes his discussion of Homer's potential sources by reassessing the famous Iliadic verse where the Poet declares that he did not witness the events he sings about:

Τὸ

ἡμεῖς δὲ κλέος οἶον ἀκούομεν οὐδέ τι ἴδμεν (Hom. *Il.* 2.486)
μή τίς μοι προφερέτω. Ἔστι γὰρ αὐτῷ τινα ἐπειπεῖν καὶ ἐπὶ πραγμάτων νυνὶ γινομένων, θεατοῦ δὲ τούτων μὴ καθεστηκότος τοῦ λέγοντος.[29]

And please, no one bring forward the verse where he (*sc.* Homer) says: *we hear but tales of glory, yet we did not see anything* (Hom. *Il.* 2.486).
One could say these words also with regards to events that are happening in present times, but that the speaker was not able to witness personally.

In other words, Tzetzes maintains that, even if Homer could not observe the events directly, this does not necessarily imply that he did not live at the time of the Trojan War. Otherwise, he would not have been able to meet direct witnesses, nor would he have had access to first-hand accounts of the conflict.

However, differently from his (supposed) sources, such as Dictys or Sisyphus of Cos, Homer was not a chronicler or a historian, but a poet. Just like the Roman Virgil, he composed a poetic rewriting (*metaphrasis*) of the oral and/or written accounts he had been able to get hold of.[30] Such a 'translation' of history into poetry allows for the insertion of some fictive elements, which render the narration more palatable also to simpler audiences. However, if fiction (*plasis*) is acceptable in a poetic work, there are some rules to be followed: the inventions must be plausible and they must provide the audience with useful teachings.[31] In other words, even when inserting fictional details, poets need to respect a set of basic principles. Should they fail to do so, they would end up producing a rhetorically flawed work. When it comes to the Trojan conflict, this might prove particularly pernicious, since the audience would be provided with an unreliable account of an event that, even when poetically refashioned, does belong to the realm of history.

---

[29] Tz. *Exeg. Il.* 40.1–5.

[30] Tz. *Exeg. Il.* 31.13–15.

[31] See e.g. schol. in *Carm. Il.* 20a, p. 108, 18–20, where Tzetzes lists the four essential qualities of any narration (*diēgēsis*): clarity, conciseness, plausibility and Attic diction (σαφήνεια, συντομία, πιθανότης καὶ ὁ τῶν ὀνομάτων ἑλληνισμός). The first three 'virtues' of *diēgēsis* quoted by Tzetzes might stem from the so-called Anonymous Seguerianus (see Kustas 1973: 77; on this anonymous treatise, see Dilts and Kennedy 1997: IX–XV).

Engaging with fiction can lead down a slippery path. Indeed, not even the golden Homer was immune to the dangers posed by an improper use of fictionality. His excessive partiality for the wily Odysseus made him alter the true development of the Trojan War, as Tzetzes does not hesitate to remark in a rather aggressive scholium addressed to the Poet. Putting aside the admiration he elsewhere shows for the author of the *Iliad*, the scholar does not hesitate to qualify the Homeric version of the story as an inconsistent and badly conceived 'invention' (ἀνακόλουθα καὶ **κακόπλαστα**).[32]

This said, we can now go back to Tzetzes' aggressive remarks against Quintus and shed further light on the reasons behind his harsh criticism of the poet. Just like Homer, Quintus is accused of inserting details that are implausible and inconsistent. However, differently from Homer, whose unrealistic inventions focus on a specific character of the story and are dictated by a precise (albeit questionable) agenda, Quintus' whole narrative seems to be characterised by the systematic insertion of more or less minute details that are as specific as they are unbelievable. What is more, even if it does not always follow the principles of plausibility and trustworthiness, Homer's detailed narrative is mostly based on first-hand knowledge of the events that he is talking about. If he remembers the names of every single hero, it is because he was able to speak to them directly or to consult reliable written accounts. Quintus' situation is rather different, since not only did he live centuries after the Trojan conflict, but he also seems to ignore the information transmitted by other, trustworthy, sources. Yet, despite his chronological distance from the war of Troy and his evident neglect of the existing records of the conflict, he behaves as if he had personally witnessed the facts he writes about. In other words, by parading a detailed knowledge of the events that he could not have gained unless he had taken part in the war itself, Quintus is deliberately playing the part of a second Homer. However, in Tzetzes' opinion, Quintus' attempt to compose a new *Iliad* is a complete failure. The only Homeric feature that Quintus managed to master is the Poet's improper use of fictionality, along with his unacceptable tendency to modify the 'true' version of the facts in order to fulfil his personal interests.

These considerations will allow us to better appreciate the nuances of meaning of the extracts analysed above. Specifically, it is worth reading again the beginning of the scholium where Tzetzes comments upon the impossible meeting between Nestor and Memnon:

I *was on foot*] The fact that I did not live at the time of the Trojan War nor during the era of Quintus is evident to anyone, just as it is evident

---

[32] Schol. *in Carm. Il.* 241b, pp. 195, 12–17 – 196, 15–16. For Tzetzes' complex reception of Homer, see Lovato (2017: 172–239, along with Lovato 2016: *passim*).

that I did not compose a fictional account of the Trojan War (οὐδὲ **πέπλακα** τὸν Τρωϊκὸν πόλεμον). This rhetorical scheme is an invective hidden behind a joke as well as a harsh attack (. . .)[33]

As noted, in this passage Tzetzes is drawing an explicit comparison between Quintus and himself. He starts by emphasising what he and Quintus have in common: neither of them lived at the time of the Trojan War, which means that, differently from others, they could not benefit from first-hand knowledge of the events. However, contrary to Quintus, Tzetzes did not make up (**πέπλακα**) the story of the Trojan War. Through the consultation of the appropriate sources, and by relying especially on historical records, the Byzantine polymath was able to produce a much more accurate and realistic account of the war than that of Quintus. Despite posing as a new Homer and pretending to have a detailed knowledge of the conflict, the author of the *Posthomerica* only managed to compose a rhetorically flawed narrative, whose implausibility inevitably compromises its usefulness.

As shown by modern scholarship, usefulness (*ōpheleia*) was probably the main (declared) goal of any Byzantine writer.[34] In order to be accepted and acceptable, one's literary production needed to aim first and foremost at the education of its readers. This was all the more true for apparently frivolous genres such as epic poetry, whose mythological and fictional components *needed* to be justified in terms of usefulness.

Plausibility was not the only requisite for a literary work to be considered useful. In order to be profitable to its audience, a literary or rhetorical composition also needed to be concise. This is what the 'poet' Tzetzes clearly states in the introductory scholium to his *Carmina Iliaca*.

Ὁ παρὼν ποιητής, φιλοσύντομος ὤν καὶ τῆς ὠφελείας τῶν νέων φροντίζων, συνοπτικῶς τὴν πᾶσαν Ἰλιάδα ἐν τῇ παρούσῃ βίβλῳ ἐξέθετο.[35]

The present poet, appreciating **brevity** and being concerned with what is **useful** for the young, has expounded in this book a **comprehensive overview** of the whole *Iliad*.

Despite its intrinsic connection with the crucial requisite of usefulness, conciseness (*syntomia*) is another rhetorical virtue that Quintus seems be unaware of. In his attempt to compose a continuation of the *Iliad*, he tries to equal the Homeric model also when it comes to its structure and length, thus producing

---

[33] Schol in *Carm. Il.* 3.284, pp. 223, 18–224, 3.

[34] On ὠφέλεια in Byzantine literature and literary criticism, see now Toth (2018: 42–3) with further bibliography.

[35] Schol. in *Carm. Il.* p. 101, 1–3.

an extensive hexametric poem that takes up a considerable number of books. The ambitious scope of Quintus' poetic endeavour did not elude the attention of other Byzantine scholars, who equally noticed the formal similarities linking the *Posthomerica* to the *Iliad*.[36] At the very beginning of his *Parekbolai on the Iliad*, Eustathius chooses to quote nothing less than Quintus' *Posthomerica* as the most representative example of a lengthy poetic composition that, just like the *Iliad*, needed to be divided into different books.[37]

If we keep in mind the cruciality of *syntomia* for Tzetzes' rhetorical agenda, it does not seem far-fetched to conclude that the Byzantine scholar must have had some reservations about the remarkable length of the *Posthomerica*. Once again, by unsuccessfully trying to imitate Homer, Quintus ends up violating another fundamental principle of the rhetorical art, at least as conceived by Tzetzes.

QUINTUS REDEEMED?

Despite Tzetzes' negative opinion of the *Posthomerica*, there seems to be at least one composition by Quintus that the Byzantine scholar finds worth quoting and remembering. This time, Quintus is not mentioned in the heroic context of the *Carmina Iliaca*. Instead, he appears in a completely different work that Tzetzes composed later in life, namely the so-called *Chiliads* or *Historiai*.

The *Chiliads* is a verse commentary to Tzetzes' own *Epistles*. This extensive work is divided into different 'histories' (*historiai*), each one revolving around a specific topic or character featuring in the polymath's letters. Apart from the desire to clarify the content of Tzetzes' epistolographic collection, the main aim of this self-exegesis is to refine the historical, rhetorical and literary education of its readership, which is sometimes addressed in explicitly pedagogical tones.[38] Given the negative reception of Quintus in the *Carmina Iliaca*, encountering his name in a work like the *Chiliads* is quite surprising, especially since the author of the *Posthomerica* seems to be presented in a rather positive light.

At the end of a long *historia* entirely devoted to the life of Heracles, Tzetzes decides to conclude his account of the hero's adventures with a quotation from what he believes to be a poetic composition by Quintus. After remarking that

---

[36] As for Tzetzes, see e.g. *Exeg. Il.* 67.16–20. Despite not focusing specifically on the length of the *Posthomerica*, the scholar includes Quintus amongst the authors looking to compose 'another *Iliad*'. This extract is reminiscent of the passage from Eustathius' *Parekbolai* mentioned in the following footnote.

[37] Eust. *in Il.* 1.9.5–10 van der Valk.

[38] On the structure and aims of Tzetzes' *Chiliads*, see now Pizzone (2017: *passim*).

all educated people are supposed to remember the details of Heracles' adventures, Tzetzes goes on to cite directly some hexameters where the author of the *Posthomerica* supposedly records the hero's famous labours:

Ὁ Κόϊντος δὲ γέγραφεν οἶμαι τοὺς ἄθλους τούτου
συντετμημένως ἔπεσι, Κόϊντος ὁ Σμυρναῖος.
Οὕτω τὰ ἔπη δ' ἔχουσιν ἅπερ ἰσχύσω φράσαι.
'Πρῶτα μὲν ἐν Νεμέᾳ βριαρὸν κατέπεφνε λέοντα.
Δεύτερον ἐν Λέρνῃ πολυαύχενον ἔκτανεν ὕδραν.   495
Τὸ τρίτον αὖτ' ἐπὶ τοῖς Ἐρυμάνθιον ἔκτανε κάπρον.
Ὑψίκερων δ' ἔλαφον μετὰ ταῦτ' ἤγρευσε τέταρτον.
Πέμπτον δ' ὄρνιθας Στυμφαλίδας ἐξεδίωξεν.
Ἕκτον Ἀμαζονίδος κόμισε ζωστῆρα φαεινόν.
Ἕβδομον Αὐγείου πολλὴν κόπρον ἐξεκάθηρεν.   500
Ὄγδοον ἐκ Κρήτηθε πυρίπνοον ἤλασε ταῦρον.
Εἴνατον ἐκ Θρῄκης Διομήδεος ἤγαγεν ἵππους.
Γηρυόνου δέκατον βοῦς ἤλασεν ἐξ Ἐρυθείης.
Ἑνδέκατον κύνα Κέρβερον ἤγαγεν ἐξ Ἀΐδαο.
Δωδέκατον δ' ἤνεγκεν ἐς Ἑλλάδα χρύσεα μῆλα.   505
Θεστίεω θυγατρῶν τρισκαιδέκατος πέλεν ἄθλος.'[39]

It was Quintus, I think, that recorded his (*sc.* Heracles') labours
in some concise verses – I mean Quintus of Smyrna.
These verses, that I will try to report, read as follows:
'In the first labour, he killed the strong lion of Nemea.
For the second, he slayed the Lernaean Hydra of many necks.
Then, in the third one, he slayed the boar of Erymanthus.
After that, the capture of a high-horned deer was his fourth labour.
For the fifth one, he chased away the Stymphalian birds.
The sixth one consisted in carrying off the shining belt of the Amazon.
For the seventh one, he cleared away Augeas' huge amount of dung.
In the eight labour he drove away from Crete the fire-breathing bull.
For the ninth, he took away from Thrace Diomedes' horses.
In the tenth one, he drove away from Erytheia Geryon's cattle.
For the eleventh one, he brought out of Hades the dog Cerberus.
The twelfth consisted in bringing to Greece the golden apples.
The thirteenth labour were the daughters of Thestius.'[40]

---

[39] Tz. *Chil.* 2 hist. 36.491–506.
[40] This thirteenth labour refers to a *parergon* connected to the killing of the Lion of Nemea. During the hunt, Heracles was hosted by the king of the Thespians, who arranged for his fifty daughters to lie with him. On this episode, see also Bremmer (2017), with extensive bibliography.

These hexameters appear in a significant position of the *historia* devoted to Heracles. Being placed at the very end of the account of the hero's adventures, they play the role of a conclusive summary, meant to recapitulate the detailed narrative of the preceding verses. The few lines introducing the supposed composition by Quintus equally suggest that, in this case at least, the author of the *Posthomerica* is presented as a useful and instructive source. Indeed, the fact that Tzetzes seems to be citing these lines by heart (ἅπερ ἰσχύσω φράσαι) might be a further sign of his appreciation: had they not been worth remembering, why memorise them and then insert them in such a crucial section of his work? Moreover, when introducing Quintus' hexameters, Tzetzes is careful to highlight one of their most distinctive characteristics, namely their conciseness. To be sure, these thirteen verses perfectly epitomise the association between brevity and usefulness that informs Tzetzes' rhetorical and pedagogical agenda. For once, even the overambitious and unreliable Quintus seems to have been able to live up to Tzetzes' standards and to provide his readers with memorable verses, the style of which are strikingly reminiscent of some of Tzetzes' own pedagogical works.

However, it seems that, even in this case, Quintus is not the rightful recipient of Tzetzes' appreciation. As has been noted both by Francis Vian and by Pietro Luigi M. Leone in their critical editions of the *Posthomerica* and the *Chiliads*, the thirteen hexameters that Tzetzes attributes to Quintus did not stem from his pen after all.[41] Instead, they were composed by an anonymous poet and have been preserved, in slightly differing versions, by a disparate number of manuscripts.[42] Among these we can count the codices transmitting the so-called *Appendix Planudea*, which makes up the sixteenth book of the modern edition of the *Greek Anthology*. Here, a version of our epigram on Heracles can be read as poem 92. As shown by this quick overview, the manuscript tradition of this short hexametric composition is quite complex and cannot be addressed here in any detail. There is, however, one factor that might prove relevant to the subject at hand and therefore deserves to be briefly discussed. According to Vian, who has collated most of the codices preserving the epigram on Heracles, all the manuscripts attributing this composition to Quintus depend on Tzetzes' *Chiliads*.[43] Should Vian's conclusions be correct, it would appear not only that the sole verses by Quintus that Tzetzes appreciates were not in fact composed by him, but also that Tzetzes is at least partly

---

[41] Vian (1966: 61–3), Leone (2007: 59–60).

[42] According to Vian (1966: 62), this epigram is a rewriting of the so-called *Tabula Albana* (*IG* 14.1293). Its most ancient witness is the ms. *Laur. gr.* 32.9 (fol. 79ᵛ). Concerning the variants of the poem, Vian has shown that the manuscripts containing the Planudean corpus preserve a different version of the thirteenth hexameter, while also adding a fourteenth verse that jokingly hints at the spicy nature of Heracles' last 'labour'.

[43] See Vian (1966: 61–2 with n2 and n3).

responsible for a tradition wrongly attributing these spurious hexameters to Quintus himself.[44]

How to explain this misunderstanding? The most likely scenario is that, during one of his many encounters with the more or less ancient manuscripts he had access to,[45] the scholar came across these thirteen lines, which he then either memorised or recorded for future use. It is also quite plausible that, like most manuscripts preserving the epigram, Tzetzes' source did not mention the name of its author. However, both the hexametric form and the topic of the short poem may have reminded the scholar of the description of Heracles' labours featuring in a famous passage of the *Posthomerica*, namely the long *ekphrasis* of Eurypylus' shield (Q.S. 6.198–293).[46] Based on these similarities, Tzetzes must have concluded that the anonymous hexameters he found in his source(s) could be quite safely attributed to Quintus. The slightly hesitant tone with which the scholar introduces the epigram in the *Chiliads* – note especially the use of the verb οἶμαι at l. 491 – seems to confirm that the attribution to Quintus is the result of a conjecture by Tzetzes himself.[47] The scholar's notorious preoccupation with issues of authorship and 'copyright' might also have played a role in his desire to associate a name to a composition that he seemed to find rather valuable.

Tzetzes' interest in this epigram, which in turn led to its mistaken attribution to Quintus, might also have stemmed from the fact that the scholar saw in this composition a perfect realisation of the principles informing his own rhetorical and pedagogical methods. Confused by the affinity of the topic with Quintus' *ekphrasis* of Eurypylus' shield and simultaneously attracted by the stylistic similarity between these hexameters and his own writings, the scholar must have decided to insert them at the end of his treatment of Heracles' adventures, thus acknowledging, for once, that even Quintus could sometimes write good and instructive poetry. In other words, by expressing his appreciation of what he believes to be a composition by Quintus, Tzetzes is doing nothing but implicitly reasserting the superiority of his own rhetorical methods.

---

[44] Since Vian's analysis of the manuscript tradition is not exhaustive, some caution is required. To reach a final conclusion, it might be necessary to examine the whole manuscript transmission of the epigram, such as the Hesiod manuscripts that Vian never managed to consult (see Vian 1966: 62, n3). In any case, what matters here is that Tzetzes believed these hexameters to be the work of Quintus, even though we cannot identify with certainty the source of this mistaken attribution.

[45] On the manuscripts consulted by Tzetzes, see Luzzatto (1998; 1999: 156–62).

[46] On this episode, see Baumbach (2007) and Bär (2018a: 111–15).

[47] I wish to thank Prof. Tommaso Braccini for pointing this out to me. The attribution of the Heracles epigram to Quintus sounds less hesitant in a scholium that Tzetzes himself added to the first hexameter of this composition (schol. in *Chil.* 2.494, p. 539).

And yet, if we take a closer look at the final lines of the *historia* on Heracles, we will realise that not even this Tzetzes-like Quintus is truly able to equal his Byzantine counterpart. After quoting the thirteen verses supposedly composed by Quintus, Tzetzes adds a short but rather telling remark, with which he decides to conclude the whole *historia*:

Οὕτω μὲν γέγραφεν αὐτός, συντάξας ἐν τοῖς ἄθλοις
τὸν ψευδοτρισκαιδέκατον ἆθλον οὐκ ὄντα τοῦτον.
Τοὺς ἄθλους ἔχεις γὰρ αὐτὸς πάντας ἐγγεγραμμένους
καὶ τὰ τῶν ἄθλων πάρεργα. Καὶ τί μηκύνω λόγους;[48]   510

Thus he (*sc.* Quintus) wrote, including in the labours
also the fake thirteenth one, which did not exist.[49]
Now you have a written record of all the labours,
as well the other episodes connected to them. Why waste more words?

Once again, the only trustworthy source is none other than Tzetzes himself. Even in his most Tzetzean transfiguration, Quintus cannot but disappoint and reveal his true unreliable self. Those who want to know the authentic story of Heracles' labours must turn to Tzetzes. Why waste more words?

---

[48] Tz. *Chil.* 2 hist. 36.507–10.

[49] In his *historia* on Heracles, Tzetzes does not completely reject the episode of the hero's sexual encounters with the daughters of Thespius (*Chil.* 2, hist. 36.224–8). However, he classifies this episode as one of the many *parerga* connected to Heracles' canonical labours, which, in his opinion, are the only ones deserving of the name.

CHAPTER 20

A Postmodern Quintus? Theories of Fan Fiction and the *Posthomerica*

Stephan Renker

It has become commonplace among cultural critics of various types of academic provenance to observe that fan fiction has moved away from being a rather obscure literary phenomenon – mainly maintained by Internet geeks – towards a widely recognised pop-cultural mass phenomenon.[1] Among the best-known instances of economically successful novel and film adaptations are productions such as the *Gabriel Trilogy*,[2] the *Beautiful Bastard*[3] series, and the most popular *Fifty Shades Trilogy*,[4] all of which originally started out online as *Twilight* fan fiction. Although fan fiction in a broader sense is, as we shall see later on, not a recent phenomenon, the Internet has changed the worldwide availability of and interconnection between authors, readers and works in an unprecedented way. Accordingly, research on the topic has evolved drastically since Henry Jenkins' seminal work *Textual*

I would like to express my gratitude to Silvio Bär and Emma Greensmith for extremely helpful suggestions on this piece, as well as to Arnold Bärtschi and Fiona Macintosh, who allowed me to share my ideas with audiences at Bochum and Oxford.

[1] See Basu (2016: 1.1): 'We are living in an age when fan fiction has come out of the closet.'

[2] The *Gabriel Trilogy* by an anonymous Canadian author who goes by the pen name of Sylvain Reynard consists of the three novels *Gabriel's Inferno*, *Gabriel's Rapture* (both 2012) and *Gabriel's Redemption* (2013).

[3] *Beautiful Bastard* (2013) and its sequels *Beautiful Stranger*, *Beautiful Player* and *Beautiful Secret* were published under the pen name Christina Lauren.

[4] The *Fifty Shades* trilogy by E. L. James consists of the novels *Fifty Shades of Grey* (2011), *Fifty Shades Darker* and *Fifty Shades Freed* (both 2012). Over 100 million copies were sold. An additional fourth book simply titled *Grey* was published in 2015. The distribution companies Focus Feature and Universal Studios hold the rights to the trilogy, turning them into films in 2015, 2017 and 2018 respectively.

Poachers[5] towards diverse and multi-faceted approaches to recent fan fiction and its sociocultural and economic implications. There is also increasing interest in tracing the roots of fan fiction in more distant time periods,[6] such as the classical literary period.[7] In this chapter, I want to elaborate on this trend by focusing on the *Posthomerica* as a paradigmatic example of early fan fiction. Furthermore, I aim to lay theoretical foundations for a more nuanced analysis and understanding of the relationship between various theories of fan fiction and Quintus' poem.

As the concept of fan fiction entails many complexities, in the first part of my chapter, I want to demonstrate the difficulties scholars currently face when trying to define what type of literature fan fiction is from a historical perspective.[8] What is important to me, is the observation that certain theories that aim to explore how fan fiction works are equally applicable to explaining many of Quintus' traits and thus able to access definitional problems from a historical perspective. In the second part, I pay attention to three eminent postmodern philosophers or psychologists whose theories scholars of fan fiction have applied in order to gain an understanding of how this genre works. By applying to the *Posthomerica* Jacques Derrida's concept of the 'archive', Gilles Deleuze's ideas in his magnum opus *Difference and Repetition* and Mihaly Csikszentmihalyi's psychological concept of 'flow', I demonstrate that they

---

[5] See Jenkins (1992) and also the 'Updated Twentieth Anniversary Edition' Jenkins (2012).

[6] See e.g. Jamison (2013) and Hellekson and Busse (2014).

[7] Volume 21 of the online-only publication *Transformative Works and Cultures* with the title *The Classical Canon and/as Transformative Work*, edited by Ika Willis in 2016, represents one such enterprise aiming to unveil traces of fan-fictionesque literature in antiquity. This collection includes chapters on topics such as the reception of the classical world in modern fan fiction and instances of 'early' fan fiction in Philip Sidney's *The Countess of Pembroke's Arcadia*, as well as a chapter by Shannon K. Farley dealing with the *Iliad* and the *Odyssey*. Despite discussing numerous other rewritings of the Homeric epics, Farley does not engage with the *Posthomerica*.

[8] The question remains of how the study of fan fiction enables us to see this relationship in a new light. A look into one of the most intriguing papers on the theory of fan fiction by Veerle Van Steenhuyse gives us an impression of why Quintus indeed can be understood as a fan of Homer. She begins her article with a definition-like statement: 'Fans are fans by virtue of their enthusiasm and commitment. Unlike "mundanes", they are dedicated enough to seek out fellow-fans, to gush over their object of affection, or, indeed, to write about it. (. . .) This writing, known as fan fiction, features characters, settings, concepts, and/or plot elements of the writers' chosen source texts.' See Van Steenhuyse (2011: 2). If we approve of Van Steenhuyse's definition of fan fiction, one might say that Quintus can be seen as a fan of the Homeric epics, especially the *Iliad*. To put it simply and to use Van Steenhuyse's words again: Quintus writes about his 'object of affection', the Homeric epics. More precisely, he writes 'fiction' (the *Posthomerica*) about '[his] chosen source text' (the *Iliad* and the *Odyssey*) by featuring 'characters, settings, concepts, and/or plot elements of [this] source text'.

are all able to foster our understanding of Quintus' relationship to his most influential model, the Homeric epics, both from an author-centered and from a reader-centered approach.[9]

The aim of this chapter is thus twofold: first, it supplies scholarship on the *Posthomerica* with fresh heuristic devices that we can use to describe the relationship between Quintus and Homer.[10] I argue that we should call the *Posthomerica* 'archontic' literature or an 'archontic' text, and that we should call the Homeric epics, especially the *Iliad*, 'archival' texts.[11] Secondly, the theories of the postmodernists allow us to reassess current trends in Quintian scholarship. Whereas past scholarship on Quintus often aimed towards a 'rehabilitation'[12] of the author, thinkers like Deleuze and Derrida enable us to deconstruct such a discourse of power structures, authority and dependence.

---

[9] By doing so, I also help to evaluate the potential strengths and weaknesses of the respective authors when applied to literary text. See Daniel (2001: 22): 'Ein wenig mehr Diskussionsenergie auf die Frage zu verwenden, was passiert, wenn bestimmte Ansätze in der Forschung angewandt werden, könnte m. E. dazu führen, Vorteile und Nachteile von Theorien und Methoden, die dabei erkennbar werden, abzuwägen, statt puristische Scheingefechte zu führen. Und noch etwas anderes könnte die Folge sein: Man könnte an konkreten Beispielen besser als bisher darüber zu diskutieren lernen, was (...) Forscherinnen und Forscher eigentlich tun, wenn sie Theorien und Methoden anwenden, Quellen auswerten, Begriffe benutzen, argumentieren und ihre Ergebnisse in sprachliche Form kleiden. Erst dann hätten wissenschaftliche Grundsatzdebatten die Chance, den Boxring des Theorie- und Methodenstreits bzw. das Ghetto der Vorworte und der Fußnoten zu verlassen und Teil der wissenschaftlichen Praxis zu werden.'

[10] Similarly, Felix Guattari and Gilles Deleuze's answer to the question of 'What is philosophy?' is: 'philosophy is the art of forming, inventing, and fabricating concepts'. See Deleuze and Guattari (1996: 2).

[11] It appears to me that Derecho is not always consistent in her nomenclature. At one point she calls the seemingly 'derivative' or 'appropriative' text 'archontic', see Derecho (2006: 64): 'To label the genre of fiction based on antecedent texts "derivative" or "appropriative", then, throws into question the originality, creativity, and legality of that genre. I prefer to call the genre "archontic" literature because the word *archontic* is not laden with references to property rights or judgments about the relative merits of the antecedent and the descendant works.' Later on, she seems to denote the 'antecedent text' as archontic. See Derecho (2006: 65): 'An archontic text allows, or even invites, writers to enter it, select specific items they find useful, make new artifacts using those found objects, and deposit the newly made work back into the source text's archive.'

[12] E.g. Schenk (1997: 385): 'Künstlerische Vollkommenheit ist es sicher nicht, aber Quintus zeigt uns in seinen *Posthomerica*, daß er die epische Technik beherrscht und so unter Ausnutzung seiner Vorlagen zu einer durchaus eigenständigen Gestaltung findet'; Gärtner (2009: 129): 'Mittlerweile ist eine gewisse Trendwende zu beobachten; neuere Arbeiten zeigen, dass wir es nicht nur mit einem äußerst belesenen Dichter zu tun haben, sondern mit einem Dichter, der seinen Text kunstvoll formt und sich dabei von ganz eigenen Gestaltungskriterien leiten lässt'; Gärtner (2015): 'Durchgehend ist der Wunsch zu spüren, daß dem Gedicht die ihm gebührende Anerkennung erwiesen werde.'

FAN FICTION: A HISTORICAL APPROACH

The concept of fan fiction is not easy to define.[13] One way of approaching the phenomenon is historically. Here we can take a narrow or a broad stance. Narrowly speaking, one can see the beginnings of fan fiction in the creation of the fan cultures that emerged in the 1930s with the beginning of the so-called Sherlock Holmes Societies. The first clubs of these kinds enabled enthusiasts of the fictional private detective to gather and exchange information and hold meetings.[14] Another instance of a narrow approach is represented by the emergence of Star Trek fanzines in the 1960s. It was then that the term fan fiction was used for the first time. A wider concept of fan fiction would entail the idea that fan fiction has always existed, even in antiquity. The classical concept of *imitatio* and *aemulatio* would come close to this broader approach.[15] If we take this stance, Virgil's *Aeneid* or even the *Odyssey* could be seen as fan fiction, plundering the resources of canonical texts, especially the *Iliad*, in so far as they include characters, settings or plot elements of the Homeric source text.[16] A third valuable approach towards what fan fiction entails lies in the middle ground between these two positions. Accordingly, fan fiction is neither the result of a relatively recent trend in audience response nor an always-existing phenomenon of a Bloomian 'revisionary ratio'.[17] This is because interdependences between fan fiction and more traditional types of literature do exist. Thus, fan fiction does not seem to be an entirely new narrative approach that

[13] The noun 'fan' is an abbreviation of the adjective 'fanatic', thus coming from the Latin adjective *fanaticus*, which the *OLD* s.v. 1 translates as 'of or belonging to a temple; (m. or f. as noun) a temple servant, devotee' and s.v. 2b 'of or typical of a devotee, fanatic'. Appearing for the first time in late nineteenth century to describe devoted baseball fans, the noun soon shifted to denote theatregoers who 'had come to admire the actors rather than the plays'.

[14] Both the Sherlock Holmes Society in London and the Baker Street Irregulars in New York were founded in 1934. Though the Sherlock Holmes Society had to stop its activities due to the Second World War, it was newly established in 1951. It publishes the *Sherlock Holmes Journal* biannually. The Baker Street Irregulars' official publication is the *Baker Street Journal*.

[15] For the concept of *imitatio* and *aemulatio*, see West and Woodman (1979).

[16] Van Steenhuyse (2011: 2). An example from antiquity that probably comes closest to our modern understanding of a fan is Pliny the Younger's depiction of Silius Italicus in letter 3.7. Silius (*c*.25–100 CE), author of the epic poem *Punica*, was an avid admirer of Virgil. See 3.7.8, *Multum ubique librorum, multum statuarum, multum imaginum, quas non habebat modo, verum etiam venerabatur, Vergili ante omnes, cuius natalem religiosius quam suum celebrabat, Neapoli maxime, ubi monimentum eius adire ut templum solebat.* The words *religiosius* and *templum* take us close to the semantic range of *fanaticus* as pointed out above. Sherwin-White (1966) *ad loc.* fittingly speaks of 'Silius' cult of Vergil'.

[17] It is debatable which of the six Bloomian categories is most apt to describe the relationship between Quintus and Homer. I would argue that it is either *Clinamen* or *Tessera*. See Bloom (1973: 14, 19–45, 49–73).

emerged in the twentieth century without any predecessor. On the other hand, fan fiction cannot be defined as including most of literature because the phenomenon seems to be more specifically defined, especially with regard to characters, settings etc.[18]

The question of what fan fiction is, therefore, can be answered from a historical perspective. Accordingly, by taking a broader stance, the *Posthomerica* can be viewed as a piece of fan fiction, as Quintus engages with the characters, storylines and plot elements of his source text, the Homeric epics.

THE ARCHIVE: JACQUES DERRIDA

A uniting feature of criticism on Quintus during the nineteenth and early twentieth centuries was a nearly unequivocal agreement on his seemingly unimaginative and dull dependence on Homer and his poetic features.[19] Abigail Derecho observes that fan fiction is also often criticised for being overly imitative and is thus called 'derivative' or 'appropriative' literature.[20] Her description of derivative literature comes close to how Quintus has been judged with regard to his relationship to Homer. Denoting these terms as negative, she opposes them with the concept of 'archontic' literature. She favours this term due to the increased degree of neutrality. Whereas adjectives such as derivative and appropriative point to a hierarchy of antecedent and succeeding text, the term archontic does not bear such remnants of traditional power structures.[21] By coining the term archontic, Derecho refers to Jacques Derrida's idea of an archive, explained in his essay 'Archive Fever: A Freudian Impression'.[22] According to Derrida, an archive can never be closed – even more, it constantly wants to expand itself and thus gain knowledge and authority.[23] If we apply this idea to the relationship

---

[18] See Derecho (2006: 62-3).

[19] See Hugh Lloyd-Jones' (1969: 101) comment, for whom Quintus was 'among the late Greek epic poets (...) by far the worst', and Ernst-Günther Schmidt's (1999) article with the title 'Quintus von Smyrna: Der schlechteste Dichter des Altertums?' For a concise synopsis of both negative and positive judgements, see Baumbach and Bär (2007b: 23-5) and Bär (2009: 33-6).

[20] Derecho (2006: 64): '*Derivative*, when applied to artwork, has a negative connotation in everyday speech; it usually denotes a poor imitation or even a corruption of an original, pure work. Calling a text based on a prior text "derivative" thus signifies a ranking of the two texts according to quality and classifies the secondary text as the lesser one.'

[21] See note 11.

[22] Derrida (1995). Derrida delivered this paper at a conference in London in June 1994. The French title is 'Mal d'archive: Une impression freudienne'. Eric Prenowitz translated it for the Journal *Diacritics*.

[23] Derrida (1995: 45): 'By incorporating the knowledge which is deployed in reference to it, the archive augments itself, engrosses itself, it gains in *auctoritas*. But in the same stroke it loses the absolute and meta-textual authority it might claim to have. (...) The archivist produces more archive, and that is why the archive is never closed. It opens out of the future.'

between the Homeric epics and Quintus' *Posthomerica*, it becomes clear that the archive through which Homer extends itself is the *Posthomerica*.

One might argue that every text can be labelled archontic in as far as every text alludes to prior texts. Literary critics such as Julia Kristeva, for example, claim that the concept of intertextuality is inherent to all literature.[24] However, the difference between intertextual and archontic literature is that the latter places itself deliberately within the horizon of expectations of the source text[25] and thus I argue that this comes close to what Quintus does in the *Posthomerica*. He is the one who allows the archive Homer to gain *auctoritas* by adding to it the events that happened after the end of the *Iliad*. He deliberately places himself in the Homeric archive by stressing the continuative or interstitial[26] character of his work as a sequel to the *Iliad*. This becomes most clear in the absence of a Muse invocation at the beginning of Book 1. Quintus goes *in medias res* and thus starts immediately where the *Iliad* ends (Εὖθ' ὑπὸ Πηλείωνι δάμη θεοείκελος Ἕκτωρ / καί ἑ πυρὴ κατέδαψε καὶ ὀστέα γαῖα κεκεύθει, / δὴ τότε Τρῶες ἔμιμνον ἀνὰ Πριάμοιο πόληα / δειδιότες μένος ἠὺ θρασύφρονος Αἰακίδαο, 'When godlike Hector by Peleides slain / Passed, and the pyre had ravined up his flesh, / And earth had veiled his bones, the Trojans then / Tarried in Priam's city, sore afraid / Before the might of stout-heart Aeacus' son', Q.S. 1.1-4).[27] Coming from a reader-response criticism position, Derecho states that 'readers [of non-fan fiction] do not expect a novel to state outright, in its first few sentences, that it is a revision of, a continuation of, or an insertion into a prior narrative'.[28] Quintus, however, does nothing short of that. He deliberately places himself in the tradition of the Homeric epics, above all the *Iliad*.[29] What's more, towards the end of Book 14, the last book of his epic, he connects his narrative to the *Odyssey* by pointing

---

[24] See Kristeva (1980: 66): 'Any text is constructed as a mosaic of quotations; any text is the absorption and transformation of another.' Roland Barthes goes one step further by claiming that intertextuality is the foundational concept of every text. See Barthes (1981: 39): 'Intertextuality, the condition of any text whatsoever, cannot of course be reduced to a problem of sources or influences; the intertext is a general field of anonymous formulae whose origin can scarcely ever be located; of unconscious or automatic quotations, given without quotation-marks.'

[25] Some fan fiction deliberately breaches the readers' horizon of expectations, for example by mixing genres. See e.g. the mashup *Pride and Prejudice and Zombies* (2009) by Jane Austen and Seth Grahame-Smith.

[26] See below.

[27] See Bär (2007; 2009: 138-44) for a detailed analysis. Translations of the *Posthomerica* follow Way (1913).

[28] Derecho (2006: 66).

[29] Harrison (2011: 27) calls such recognisable features 'explicit metageneric signals'. See Bär (2009: 139) on the first lines of the *Posthomerica*: 'Aus narratologischer Sicht handelt es sich um einen sog. "etischen" Textbeginn, d. h. einen Lektüreeinstieg, der davon ausgeht bzw. suggeriert, dass sich der Leser im Referenzfeld des Textes bereits auskennt, wodurch von Beginn weg ein implizites "wir-Gefühl" zwischen Rezipient und Text (bzw. Erzähler) zustande kommt.' See also Bär (2009: 145): 'Die Anknüpfung an diese Details aus der *Ilias* werden als bekannt

to the hardships that some of the heroes are about to endure on their way back home (ἄλλη δ' ἄλλος ἵκανεν, ὅπη θεὸς ἦγεν ἕκαστον, / ὅσσοι ὑπὲρ πόντοιο λυγρὰς ὑπάλυξαν ἀέλλας, Q.S. 14.657–8). Even more obvious is the intertextual connection to the beginning of the *Odyssey* in Q.S. 14.628–31, Αὐτὰρ Ἀθήνη / ἄλλοτε μὲν θυμῷ μέγ' ἐγήθεεν, ἄλλοτε δ' αὖτε / ἄχνυτ' Ὀδυσσῆος πινυτόφρονος, οὕνεκ' ἔμελλε / πάσχειν ἄλγεα πολλὰ Ποσειδάωνος ὁμοκλῇ ('Athena now rejoiced / Her heart within, and now was racked with fears / For prudent-souled Odysseus; for his weird / Was through Poseidon's wrath to suffer Woes / Full many').[30] In between, Quintus even covers in retrospect many famous events that happened during the Homeric *Iliad* and, by doing so, even fosters the interconnectedness between the *Posthomerica* and the *Iliad*. Notable examples include Achilles' lament over Patroclus' death (Q.S. 1.720–1), his anger over Briseis (Q.S. 14.210–16), and Odysseus' resentment against Thersites (Q.S. 1.758–60).[31] Lastly, Quintus features a notable in-proem[32] in which he presents himself as a *Homerus novus*, or indeed still Homer, by stating that he received his *Dichterweihe* Σμύρνης ἐν δαπέδοισι ('on Smyrna's pasture-lea', Q.S. 12.310). This is noteworthy because, in antiquity, Smyrna was considered the most probable birthplace of Homer.[33] Taking these points into consideration, I propose that the term archontic literature, applied to fan fiction by Abigail Derecho, is worthy of being considered to describe Quintus' *Posthomerica*.[34]

REPETITION WITH A DIFFERENCE: GILLES DELEUZE

Derrida's concept of an archive can be understood as opposing a strict hierarchisation of antecedent and descendent texts. In this section, I demonstrate how some of the ideas of his fellow postmodernist Gilles Deleuze[35] can help us

---

vorausgesetzt – es handelt sich um einen etischen Textbeginn, dem Leser soll suggeriert werden, dass er sich in einem ihm bereits vertrauten Referenzfeld befindet.' For the concept of 'etisch' and 'emisch', see Harweg (1968: 152–70). For further discussions on the beginning of the *Posthomerica*, see U. Gärtner (2017).

[30] For a general discussion of the final scenes in the *Posthomerica*, see Carvounis (2007). On the role of the *Posthomerica* as an Intertext, see U. Gärtner (2017).

[31] See Carvounis (2014: 181).

[32] See Bär (2007; 2009: 69–78); Boyten (2010: 239–46); Tomasso (2010: 25–83); Maciver (2012c: 27–38) and Greensmith (2018).

[33] See Latacz (2011: 22): 'Der Geburtsort war nach aller Wahrscheinlichkeit Smyrna, ein wichtiger Wirkungsort Chios, der Todesort die Insel Ios (. . .).' See also Bär (2007: 52–5).

[34] A similar concept would be that of Irene Peirano Garrison, who deals with a distinct literary group of texts that she calls 'fakes'. According to her definition, these texts 'self-consciously purport (. . .) to be the work of the author to whom they are attributed'. See Peirano (2012: 3).

[35] Gilles Deleuze (1925–75) was a French philosopher, who was interested in literature, cinema and the fine arts. Besides *Difference and Repetition* (1968), his best-received works are *Capitalism and Schizophrenia: Anti-Oedipus* (1972), *A Thousand Plateaus* (1980), both co-authored with Félix Guattari.

further re-evaluate the relationship between the *Posthomerica* and the Homeric epics. Despite the recent interest in postmodern theory within Classics, Deleuze has received comparatively little attention from classical scholarship to date. Whereas the works of his contemporaries Jacques Derrida, Michel Foucault and Jacques Lacan attract lasting interest,[36] the ideas of Deleuze and his colleague Félix Guattari play a lesser role among today's classical scholars.[37] This might come as a surprise, as Deleuze was and still is widely praised as one of the pre-eminent thinkers of the twentieth century.

Deleuze, in his perhaps most influential book, *Différence et Répétition* (1968), puts forth the concept that repetition does not necessarily mean 'repetition of the Same', i.e. 'physical, mechanical or bare repetition', but refers to 'more profound structures of a hidden repetition in which a "differential" is disguised and displaced'.[38] With this claim, he deliberately positions himself as an anti-Hegelian, claiming that the concept of difference and repetition replaces the idea of thesis and antithesis, of positive and negative.[39] According to Deleuze, it is possible that there exists such a thing as repetition containing more than mere repetition. There are, for example, repetitions with differences: repetitions that are at first sight bare repetitions of something old, yet on a second glance contain differences, which make the repetition seem to look different.[40] For Deleuze, this is a widely observable phenomenon – he refers, for example, to the French writer, poet and essayist Charles Péguy's ideas that 'it is not Federation Day which commemorates or represents the fall of the Bastille, but the fall of the Bastille which celebrates and repeats in advance all the Federation Days; or Monet's first water lily which repeats in advance all the others'.[41] Deleuze summarises the paradox of such iterating 'festivals' by claiming that 'they repeat the 'unrepeatable'. They do not add a second and a third time to the first, but carry the first time to the '"nth" power'.[42] If, thus, one reads an archontic text, one, according to Deleuze's thoughts applied to literature, reads two texts. First, while one reads the archontic text at hand, the archival text naturally

---

[36] E.g. Larmour, Miller and Platter (1998); Porter and Buchan (2004); Leonard (2010).

[37] Notable exceptions are Holmes (2012) and a session at the Annual Meeting of the Society for Classical Studies in Boston 2018 with the title 'Deterritorializing Classics: Deleuze, Guattari and their Philological Discontents', organised by Kyle Khellaf.

[38] Deleuze (1994: xvi).

[39] See Deleuze (1994: 1): 'difference and repetition have taken the place of the identical and the negative, of identity and contradiction', and also Deleuze (1994: xvii): 'The task of modern philosophy is to overcome the alternatives temporal/non-temporal, historical/eternal and particular/universal.'

[40] See Deleuze (1994: xvi): 'confronted with the most mechanical, the most stereotypical repetitions, inside and outside ourselves, we endlessly extract from them little differences, variations and modifications.'

[41] Deleuze (1994: 2).

[42] Deleuze (1994: 2).

remains present in the reader's mind. This idea has been put forward by Charles Martindale by means of a musical analogy in his seminal work 'Redeeming the Text: Latin Poetry and the Hermeneutics of Reception', where he, with regard to Derrida's key term of *différance*, states that 'every performance is different from every other performance'.[43] What Deleuze's concept of difference and repetition thus achieves is – just as Derrida does – to liberate us from concepts of hierarchy, of prior and later, of antecedent and descendent. The archontic texts are able to gain a large degree of resonance with archival text and it is this resonance that gives the archontic text importance and significance.[44]

I now want to show how these observations relate to Quintus and the Homeric epics. One example of its intertextual nature appears right in the first line of the *Posthomerica*: the use of the adjective θεοείκελος, 'godlike', in line 1.1 seems to the reader to be a mere repetition of an epithet well known from the Homeric epics. Looking closer, one sees that the word is more than a mere repetition of a Homeric staple. Quintus uses the adjective in an unusual context and Silvio Bär has shown that the epithet is reserved for Achilles in the *Iliad*, thus interpreting Quintus' usage in line 1 with regard to Hector as a subtle way of foreshadowing.[45] However, the context is only unusual for the *lector doctus* who is capable of detecting the difference in the repetition.[46] Likewise, structural elements of the *Iliad*, such as similes and typical scenes, are repeated with a difference in the *Posthomerica*.[47] From a Deleuzian point of view, one could argue that the Quintian scenes too are more than a mere repetition of Homeric ones, but a repetition with a difference, a 'complex repetition'.[48]

Deleuze also puts forth the opinion that one has to distinguish between the 'virtual', the 'actual' and the 'real'. He proclaims that 'the virtual is opposed not to the real but to the actual. The virtual is fully real in so far as it is virtual.'[49] Accordingly, Deleuze is of the opinion that there is a set of virtual realities, possibilities or potentially imaginable situations, which coexist along with the actual conditions. What Deleuze understands as 'virtual' are those situations that *could* happen and as 'actual' those that *do* indeed happen. I argue that these observations are valuable to the concept of archontic literature. Every text entails an infinite set of potentialities or virtualities, which can be actualised by the writer. In our case, the archival text of the *Iliad* features potentialities, which the archontic text of the *Posthomerica* actualises. Derecho employs the term 'interstitial material'[50] with regard to these archival potentialities. With

---

[43] Martindale (1993: 17).
[44] See Derecho (2006: 73–4).
[45] See Bär (2009: 146–7).
[46] See Bär (2010) on the role of a *lector doctus* in the Second Sophistic.
[47] See, for example, Arnold Bärtschi's chapter in this volume.
[48] Deleuze (1994: xvi).
[49] Deleuze (1994: 272).
[50] Derecho (2006: 74).

this concept, she denotes all the events that occur in between the scenes of any given source text. It is up to the author of the archontic text to what extent he wants to fill these narrative gaps. Applying this nomenclature to the Homeric texts, I argue that the entire *Posthomerica* can be seen as such a piece of inter-stitial material, as the virtualities and potentialities of the archival text become, thanks to Quintus, actualised in the archontic text.

FLOW: MIHALY CSIKSZENTMIHALYI

I would like to combine the phenomenon of this 'gap-filling' with a concept hailing from the field of personality psychology. Fan-fiction texts – what I call archontic texts – have been called 'immersive' because they represent 'transformed versions of the universe of and in the primary text'.[51] Accord-ingly, archontic texts take place inside the universe of the archival text, a textual world already familiar to the reader. Thus, a feeling of immersion ensues rather naturally. This phenomenon can be exemplified by explaining that readers of fan fiction of, for example, the TV programme *House M.D.*[52] can easily represent in their mind Dr Gregory House's office in detail, including, for example, the position and shape of its furniture.[53] They are also likely to have a clear vision of what Dr House and his colleagues look like, how they speak etc. This makes it very easy for the readers of *House M.D.* fan fiction to become immersed in the text, as they are already familiar with the characters and surroundings with which they are confronted in the archontic text of fan fiction due to their exposure to the textual universe of the archival literature.[54]

I would like to argue that the same observations which van Steenhuyse makes with regard to *House M.D.* fan fiction can be applied, with certain cave-ats, to Quintus and the *Posthomerica*. From their reading of the archival text, the *Iliad* and the *Odyssey*, the reader is familiar with the world, the time frame, the characters etc. they will face in the archontic text. In addition, it is highly likely that every reader of the *Posthomerica* will already be acquainted with the formal features of the Homeric epics. As already mentioned above, most

---

[51] Van Steenhuyse (2011: 2). For the concept of 'immersion' see Ryan (2001: 89–171). A related concept is that of 'transportation.' See Gerrig (1998).

[52] *House M.D.* (mostly just called *House*) is an American television medical drama on the uncon-ventional medical practitioner Dr Gregory House. Running between 2004 and 2012, it was considered a huge success and won numerous awards, most notably five Emmy Awards and two Golden Globes Awards.

[53] On the problem of forming internal mental images, see Kosslyn, Thompson and Ganis (2006) and Grethlein and Huitink (2017: 3–8).

[54] See Van Steenhuyse (2011: 3).

readers will know the peculiarities of the Homeric language, e.g., the epithets, dialect and metre, as well as other formal elements, such as type-scenes and similes. One important difference from Van Steenhuyse's observations regarding a reader of *House M.D.* fan fiction is that, of course, a reader of the *Posthomerica* is likely to imagine the city of Troy, as well as characters such as Achilles and Helena, just as they had imagined them during their reading of the *Iliad*. They are not predetermined by the visual images from a TV programme, but rather by their own imagination.[55]

These observations give us room to make use of a concept developed in the 1970s by the Hungarian psychologist Mihaly Csikszentmihalyi:[56] the concept of 'flow'. Csikszentmihalyi coined the term after he had conducted interviews with artists describing to him their experiences when they became so immersed in their work that they forgot about basic needs such as sleep, food and even water.[57] According to Csikszentmihalyi, one criterion to reach a state of flow during a certain activity is a delicate balance of 'challenge' and 'skill'.[58] One is in need of an activity characterised by a high level of difficulty, thus posing a challenge. At the same time, it is necessary that the person engaging in that very activity is in possession of an equally high level of skill. If, for example, the skill level of a person ranks high, but the challenge level of the activity at hand ranks considerably low, what follows is either boredom or relaxation. On the contrary, if the skill level of a given person is low, but the challenge level of a task is high, the result is either worry or even anxiety. The ideal is a high level of skill matched with a high level of challenge. The opposite is a low skill level and low challenge level, resulting in a state of apathy.[59] Van Steenhuyse raises awareness

---

[55] The imageability of Homeric scenes, as discussed in Grethlein and Huitink (2017); Grethlein (2017: 32–5) does not concern me. What is important to me is not *how* the reader builds up internal pictures of Troy when reading the *Posthomerica*. What is important to me is *that* they build them up just as they did when reading the *Iliad*.

[56] See Van Steenhuyse (2011: 3–4). Csikszentmihalyi was born in 1934 and taught at colleges and universities in Illinois and California. The concept of flow was applied to many realms such as gaming, music, sports, but also in education and the workplace. There is an abundance of books and articles by Csikszentmihalyi on the flow effect. A concise summary including an ample bibliography of Csikszentmihalyi's ideas on flow is Nakamura and Csikszentmihalyi (2002); perhaps the most popular book is Csikszentmihalyi (1990).

[57] See e.g. Csikszentmihalyi (1975: 36): 'In the flow state, action follows upon action according to an internal logic that seems to need no conscious intervention by the actor. He experiences it as a unified flowing from one moment to the next, in which he is in control of his actions, and in which there is little distinction between self and environment, between stimulus and response, or between past, present, and future.'

[58] See e.g. Csikszentmihalyi (1975: 49–54).

[59] Examples can easily be found in many areas of everyday life. While learning to drive a car, for instance, the skill level of a beginner is considerably low during the first driving lessons. The challenge level, however, is staggeringly high. One has to switch gears, accelerate, hit the brakes, indicate, all while paying attention to the road, street signs, the traffic and so on.

of the point that texts of fan fiction are equally prone to evoke a state of flow in the reader. They are very likely to feel immersed because, on the one hand, their skill level is sufficiently high due to the fact that they have knowledge of the universe of the archival text. On the other hand, the challenge level of the archontic text is also relatively high, as it requires the reader to incorporate new information about characters into their imagined world constantly.[60]

How can we apply this concept to the *Posthomerica*? My assumption is that a reader who has honed his skills by extensive engagement with the Homeric epics and thus in possession of a respectably high skill level is likely to fall into a state of flow when reading Quintus' text. First, as pointed out above, they come across familiar characters, places, storylines and scenes. In addition, the reader is even familiar with the linguistic peculiarities of the Homeric source text. Thus, a speedier and increasingly fluent reading process is more likely to take place than it would if the reader were confronted with a text full of vocabulary, type-scenes, etc. with which they were not as familiar. On the other side, as scholarship on the *Posthomerica* has shown, Quintus manages to deviate playfully from his role model Homer in many ways. Thus, the skilful reader is confronted with an increased challenge level, as they are constantly forced to adapt their horizon of expectations in manifold ways.[61] The occurrence of a state of flow while reading fan-fiction texts can be explained by what Marie-Laure Ryan calls 'prospective orientation'.[62] According to this, the reader of the archontic text gradually learns more about the characters with which they are already familiar due to their reading of the primary (what I call archival) text, e.g., in what other events they are involved, with what other characters they intervene, how they eventually die and so on. It requires

---

Naturally, most beginners are rather nervous or even anxious when facing their first driving lessons and feel relieved when the driving instructor reduces the challenge to a manageable level by conducting the first driving lessons on a practice area or a relatively empty road in the countryside. However, after a while, the beginner becomes more and more accustomed to navigating the car, his skill level increases and the challenge level of an empty road is unable to keep up with his increased skill level. As a result, the possibility of boredom arises. Thus, the instructor is equipped with the option of increasing the challenge level by conducting driving lessons in crowded downtown areas, by night or on multi-lane motorways. This now increased challenge level can match the equally high level of skill on the driver's side and is thus likely to evoke a state of flow.

[60] See Van Steenhuyse (2011: 4–5).

[61] See Van Steenhuyse (2011: 4): 'On the one hand, genre schemas ensure fluent processing as they enable readers to understand the text with a familiar schema. On the other hand, they do not specify "the minutiae of the narrative" (Douglas and Hargadon 2001: 156) forcing the reader to imagine new elements. While the first circumstance encourages us to read in a "steady, unbroken rhythm", the second makes us apply all of "our cognitive capacities" to the text (Douglas and Hargadon 2001: 156). I argue that this situation is likely to induce a state of flow.'

[62] Ryan (2001: 113).

a certain skill-set on the side of the reader to incorporate these events into the set of information they already possess. However, the reader who has read the *Iliad* and the *Odyssey* is most likely sufficiently equipped with the skills necessary to meet the challenges of the archontic text and is thus likely to fall into a state of flow.

QUINTUS AS A FAN?

The goal of this chapter was twofold: first, to re-evaluate the relationship between Quintus of Smyrna and his most prominent role model, the Homeric epics *Iliad* and *Odyssey*, in the light of postmodernist thinkers. I have shown that the reading of Jacques Derrida and Gilles Deleuze can help us when trying to gain a fresh look at the often unnecessarily hostile remarks scholars have made with respect to the *Posthomerica* in the past. They also extend our methodological toolkit when assessing Quintus' artistic dependence on and freedom towards Homer. I argue that the *Posthomerica* is not be scolded for being unimaginative and dull, but rather to be appreciated, or at least liberated from power structures of hierarchisation, for expanding the 'archive Homer' as well as filling manifold interstitial gaps in the Homeric archival text. Second, I have opened the scholarly discussion on Quintus to the vast field of fan fiction. I am, to be sure, far from suggesting that Quintus can be considered as a fan in the modern sense. However, the theory of 'flow' as put forth by Mihaly Csikszentmihalyi, in particular, presents itself as an approach worthy of consideration when it comes to introducing the relatively new field of fan fiction studies to the scholarship on classical literature in general and the *Posthomerica* in particular.

Bibliography

Abbreviations of journals follow the conventions of *L'Année philologique*. Web pages were last accessed on 31 March 2021.

Accorinti, Domenico (ed.). 2016. *Brill's Companion to Nonnus of Panopolis*. Leiden and Boston: Brill.

Adams, James N. 2003. *Bilingualism and The Latin Language*. Cambridge: Cambridge University Press.

Adams, James N. Mark Janse and Simon Swain (eds). 2002. *Bilingualism in Ancient Society: Language Contact and The Written Text*. Oxford: Oxford University Press.

Adkins, Arthur W. H. 1960. *Merit and Responsibility: A Study in Greek Values*. Oxford: Clarendon Press.

Agapitos, Panagiotis. Forthcoming. '"Middle-class" Ideology of Education and Language, and the "Bookish" Identity of John Tzetzes.' In: Yannis Stouraitis (ed.), *Ideologies and Identities in the Medieval Byzantine World*. Edinburgh: Edinburgh University Press.

Agosti, Gianfranco. 1989. 'Alcuni omerismi nella "Visio Dorothei" (P. Bodmer XXIX).' *Orpheus* 10, 101–16.

Agosti, Gianfranco. 1997. 'P. Oxy. 3537r: etopea acrostica su Esiodo.' *ZPE* 119, 1–5.

Agosti, Gianfranco. 2002. '*POxy* 4352, fr. 5.II.18–39 (*Encomio a Diocleziano*) e Menandro Retore.' *ZPE* 140, 51–8.

Agosti, Gianfranco. 2006. 'La voce dei libri: dimensioni performative dell'epica greca tardoantica.' In: Eugenio Amato, Alexandre Roduit and Martin Steinrück (eds), *Approches de la Troisième Sophistique: Hommages à Jacques Schamp*. Brussels: Latomus, 35–62.

Agosti, Gianfranco. 2012. 'Greek Poetry.' In: Scott F. Johnson (ed.), *The Oxford Handbook of Late Antiquity*. Oxford: Oxford University Press, 361–404.

Agosti, Gianfranco. 2014. 'Contextualising Nonnus' Visual World.' In: Spanoudakis (2014), 141–74.

Agosti, Gianfranco. 2015. 'Poesia greca nella (e della?) Biblioteca Bodmer.' *Adamantius* 21, 86–97.

Agosti, Gianfranco. 2017. '(Re)constructing a Christian Community through its Poetry.' In: Joseph Verheyden, Tobias Nicklas and Elisabeth Hernitscheck (eds), *Shadowy Characters and*

Fragmentary Evidence: The Search for Early Christian Groups and Movements. Tübingen: Mohr Siebeck, 233–50.

Allan, William. 2006. 'Divine Justice and Cosmic Order in Early Greek Epic.' *JHS* 126, 1–35.

Allen, Thomas W. (ed.). ²1919 [1909]. *Homeri Odyssea.* 2 vols. 2nd ed. Oxford: Clarendon Press.

Allen, Thomas W. (ed.). ³1920 [1902]. *Homeri Ilias.* 2 vols. 3rd ed. Oxford: Clarendon Press.

Andersen, Øivind. 1978. *Die Diomedesgestalt in der Ilias.* Oslo, Bergen and Tromsø: Universitetsforlaget.

Anderson, William S. 1995. 'Aspects of Love in Ovid's *Metamorphoses.*' *CJ* 90, 265–9.

Antin, Paul. 1961. 'Sur le "rire en pleurs" d'Andromaque.' *BAGB* 3, 340–50.

Appel, Włodzimierz. 1993. *Mimesis i kainotes: Kwestia oryginalności literackiej Kwintusa ze Smyrny na przykładzie IV pieśni 'Posthomerica'.* Toruń: Wydawnictwo Uniwersytetu Mikołaja Kopernika.

Appel, Włodzimierz. 1994a. *Die homerischen hapax legomena in den* Posthomerica *des Quintus Smyrnaeus.* Toruń: Wydawnictwo Uniwersytetu Mikołaja Kopernika.

Appel, Włodzimierz. 1994b. 'Grundsätzliche Bemerkungen zu den *Posthomerica* und Quintus Smyrnaeus.' *Prometheus* 20, 1–13.

Arthur, Marilyn B. 1982. 'Cultural Strategies in Hesiod's *Theogony*: Law, Family, Society.' *Arethusa* 15, 63–82.

Auerbach, Erich. 1953 [1946]. *Mimesis: The Representation of Reality in Western Literature.* Translated by William R. Trask. Princeton: Princeton University Press.

Austin, Norman. 1966. 'The Function of Digressions in the *Iliad.*' *GRBS* 7, 295–312.

Austin, Norman. 1975. *Archery at the Dark of the Moon: Poetic Problems in Homer's* Odyssey. Berkeley, Los Angeles and London: University of California Press.

Avlamis, Pavlos. 2019. 'Contextualizing Quintus: The Fall of Troy and the Cultural Uses of the Paradoxical Cityscape in *Posthomerica* 13.' *TAPhA* 149, 149–208.

Ax, Wolfram. 1984. 'Die pseudovergilische "Mücke" – ein Beispiel römischer Literaturparodie?' *Philologus* 128, 230–49.

Ax, Wolfram. 1991. 'Timons Gang in die Unterwelt: Ein Beitrag zur Geschichte der antiken Literaturparodie.' *Hermes* 119, 177–93.

Ax, Wolfram. 1993. '*Phaselus ille – Sabinus ille* – Ein Beitrag zur neueren Diskussion um die Beziehung zwischen Texten.' In: Ax and Glei (1993), 75–100.

Ax, Wolfram and Reinhold Glei (eds). 1993. *Literaturparodie in Antike und Mittelalter.* Trier: Wissenschaftlicher Verlag Trier.

Bakker, Egbert J. 1999. 'Mimesis as Performance: Rereading Auerbach's First Chapter.' *Poetics Today* 20, 11–26.

Bakker, Egbert J. 2002. '*Khrónos, Kléos*, and Ideology from Herodotus to Homer.' In: Michael Reichel and Antonios Rengakos (eds), *Epea Pteroenta: Beiträge zur Homerforschung. Festschrift für Wolfgang Kullmann zum 75. Geburtstag.* Stuttgart: Franz Steiner, 11–30.

Ballabriga, Alain 2000. 'Approche du burlesque divin dans l'antiquité.' In: Desclos (2000), 123–31.

Bannert, Herbert and Nicole Kröll (eds). 2018. *Nonnus of Panopolis in Context II: Poetry, Religion, and Society.* Leiden and Boston: Brill.

Bär, Silvio. 2007. 'Quintus Smyrnaeus und die Tradition des epischen Musenanrufs.' In: Baumbach and Bär (2007a), 29–64.

Bär, Silvio. 2009. *Quintus Smyrnaeus. 'Posthomerica' 1: Die Wiedergeburt des Epos aus dem Geiste der Amazonomachie. Mit einem Kommentar zu den Versen 1–219.* Göttingen: Vandenhoeck & Ruprecht.

Bär, Silvio. 2010. 'Quintus of Smyrna and the Second Sophistic.' *HSPh* 105, 287–316.

Bär, Silvio. 2016. 'Reading Homer, Writing Troy: Intertextuality and Narrativity of the Gods and the Divine in Quintus of Smyrna's *Posthomerica*.' In: James J. Clauss, Martine P. Cuypers and Ahuvia Kahane (eds), *The Gods of Greek Hexameter Poetry: From the Archaic Age to Late Antiquity and Beyond*. Stuttgart: Franz Steiner, 215–30.

Bär, Silvio. 2018a. *Herakles im griechischen Epos: Studien zur Narrativität und Poetizität eines Helden*. Stuttgart: Franz Steiner.

Bär, Silvio. 2018b. 'Diktys und Dares vor dem Hintergrund des zweitsophistischen Homer-revisionismus.' In: Brescia *et al.* (2018), 151–76.

Bär, Silvio. Forthcoming a. 'Sinon and Laocoon in Quintus of Smyrna's *Posthomerica*: A Rewriting and De-Romanization of Vergil's *Aeneid*?' In: Carvounis, Papaioannou and Scafoglio (forthcoming).

Bär, Silvio. Forthcoming b. 'Quintus Smyrnaeus.' In: Mathieu de Bakker and Irene J. F. de Jong (eds), *Speech in Ancient Greek Literature*. Leiden and Boston: Brill.

Bär, Silvio and Manuel Baumbach. 2015. 'The Epic Cycle and imperial Greek epic.' In: Fantuzzi and Tsagalis (2015), 604–22.

Bär, Silvio and Anastasia Maravela. 2019. 'Narrative, Narratology and Intertextuality: New Perspectives on Greek Epic from Homer to Nonnus.' *SO* 93, 1–11.

Barbaresco, Katia. 2019. 'La terra e il sangue (secondo Quinto Smirneo).' *Lexis* 37, 323–39.

Barbaresco, Katia. 2021. 'Pentesilea e le donne troiane: Sconfinamenti da Omero a Quinto Smirneo.' In: Elena Porciani and Cristina Pepe (eds), *Sconfinamenti di genere: Donne coraggiose che vivono nei testi e nelle immagini*. Santa Maria Capua Vetere: Polygraphia (Quaderni) 2, 25–33.

Barbaresco, Katia. Forthcoming. 'Invisibili e distanti. Dei epici sul campo di battaglia tra Omero e Quinto Smirneo.'

Barchiesi, Alessandro. 1993. 'Future Reflexive: Two Modes of Allusion and Ovid's *Heroides*.' *HSPh* 95, 333–65.

Barringer, Judith M. 1995. *Divine Escorts: Nereids in Archaic and Classical Greek Art*. Ann Arbor: University of Michigan Press.

Barthes, Roland. 1981. 'Theory of the Text.' In: Robert Young (ed.), *Untying the Text: A Post-Structuralist Reader*. Boston, London and Henley-on-Thames: Routledge and Kegan Paul, 31–47.

Bartley, Adam Nicholas. 2003. *Stories from the Mountains, Stories from the Sea: The Digressions and Similes of Oppian's Halieutica and the Cynegetica*. Göttingen: Vandenhoeck & Ruprecht.

Barton, Tamsyn. 1994a. *Ancient Astrology*. London and New York: Routledge.

Barton, Tamsyn. 1994b. *Power and Knowledge: Astrology, Physiognomics, and Medicine under the Roman Empire*. Ann Arbor: University of Michigan Press.

Bärtschi, Arnold 2019. *Titanen, Giganten und Riesen im antiken Epos: Eine literaturtheoretische Neuinterpretation*. Heidelberg: Winter.

Basu, Balaka. 2016. 'Virgilian fandom in the Renaissance.' *Transformative Works and Culture* 21. https://journal.transformativeworks.org/index.php/twc/article/view/683/605.

Battezzato, Luigi (ed.). 2018. *Euripides: Hecuba*. Cambridge: Cambridge University Press.

Baumbach, Manuel. 2007. 'Die Poetik der Schilde: Form und Funktion von Ekphraseis in den *Posthomerica* des Quintus Smyrnaeus.' In: Baumbach and Bär (2007a), 107–42.

Baumbach, Manuel. 2017. 'Poets and Poetry.' In: Richter and Johnson (2017), 493–507.

Baumbach, Manuel and Silvio Bär (eds). 2007a. *Quintus Smyrnaeus: Transforming Homer in Second Sophistic Epic*. Berlin and New York: Walter de Gruyter.

Baumbach, Manuel and Silvio Bär. 2007b. 'An Introduction to Quintus Smyrnaeus' *Posthomerica*.' In: Baumbach and Bär (2007a), 1–26.

Baumbach, Manuel and Silvio Bär. 2010. 'Quintus von Smyrna.' In: Christine Walde (ed.), *Der Neue Pauly*. Suppl. vol. 7: *Die Rezeption der antiken Literatur: Kulturhistorisches Werklexikon*. Stuttgart and Weimar: J. B. Metzler, 783–90.

Beck, Deborah. 2005. *Homeric Conversation*. Cambridge, MA and London: Harvard University Press.

Beck, Deborah. 2012. *Speech Presentation in Homeric Epic*. Austin: University of Texas Press.

Beckby, Hermann (ed.). ²1965 [1957, -58]. *Anthologia Graeca: Griechisch–Deutsch*. 4 vols. 2nd rev. ed. Munich: Ernst Heimeran.

Bednarek, Bartłomiej. 2017. 'Whole and Ground: *krithai* and *alphita*.' In: Bielawski (2017), 145–82.

Bednarek, Bartłomiej. 2019. 'Pelting Pentheus: On the Use of *Oulai* in Sacrificial Ritual.' *CPh* 114, 144–53.

Beekes, Robert. 2010. *Etymological Dictionary of Greek*. 2 vols. Leiden and Boston: Brill.

Belfiore, Stefano. 2009. *Il Periplo del Ponto Eusino di Arriano e altri testi sul Mar Nero e il Bosforo. Spazio geografico, mito e dominio ai confini dell'Impero Romano*. Venice: Istituto veneto di scienze, lettere ed arti.

Berdozzo, Fabio. 2011. *Götter, Mythen, Philosophen: Lukian und die paganen Göttervorstellungen seiner Zeit*. Berlin and Boston: Walter de Gruyter.

Berenson Maclean, Jennifer K. and Ellen Bradshaw Aitken (eds). 2001. *Flavius Philostratus: Heroikos. Translated with an Introduction and Notes*. Atlanta: Society of Biblical Literature.

Bergren, Ann. 1983. 'Odyssean Temporality: Many (Re)turns.' In: Carl A. Rubino and Cynthia W. Shelmerdine (eds), *Approaches to Homer*. Austin: University of Texas Press, 38–73.

Bertone, Simone. 2000. 'I *Posthomerica* di Quinto Smirneo: un'indagine tra espressione e pensiero.' *Koinonia* 24, 67–94.

Beye, Charles R. 1964. 'Homeric Battle Narrative and Catalogues.' *HSPh* 68, 345–73.

Beye, Charles R. 1982. *Epic and Romance in the Argonautica of Apollonius*. Carbondale and Edwardsville: Southern Illinois University Press.

Bezantakos, Nicolas P. 1992. 'Le *Philoctète* de Sophocle et Néoptolème dans les *Posthomerica* de Quintus de Smyrne.' *Parnassos* 34, 151–7.

Bielawski, Krzysztof (ed.). 2017. *Animal Sacrifice in Ancient Greece: Proceedings of the First International Workshops in Kraków*. Warsaw: Global Scientific Platform.

Bielawski, Krzysztof (ed.). 2019. *Animal Sacrifice in Ancient Greece: Proceedings of the Second and Third Workshops*. Warsaw: Global Scientific Platform.

Bloom, Harold. 1973. *The Anxiety of Influence: A Theory of Poetry*. London, Oxford and New York: Oxford University Press.

Boardman, John. 1988. 'Herakles.' [Introduction]. *LIMC* IV.1, 728–31.

Boissonnade, Jean-François (ed.). 1851. *Tzetzae Allegoriae Iliadis. Accedunt Pselli Allegoriae quarum una inedita*. Paris: Dumont.

Bolling, George Melville. 1929. 'The Meaning of που in Homer.' *Language* 5, 100–5.

Bolshakov, Andrej Petrovich. 2016. *Kvint Smyrnsky: Posle Gomera. Κοίντου τὰ μεθ' Ὅμηρον*. Moscow: Russkiy Fond Sodeystviya Obrazovaniyu i Nauke.

Bonnechère, Pierre. 1997. 'La *pompe* sacrificielle des victimes humaines en Grèce ancienne.' *REA* 99, 63–89.

Bonnechère, Pierre. 1999. '"La μάχαιρα était dissimulée dans le κακοῦν": Quelques interrogations.' *REA* 101, 21–35.

Bonnechère, Pierre. 2000. 'Mythes grecs de sacrifice humain en Étrurie: Problèmes iconographiques et socio-historiques.' Review of Steuernagel (1998). *Kernos* 13, 253–64.

Borgna, Elisabetta. 1992. *L'arco e le frecce nel mondo miceneo*. Rome: Bardi.

Bouvier, David. 2005. 'Penthésilée ou l'absence de la muse au début des *Posthomériques* de Quintus de Smyrne.' In: Antje Kolde, Alessandra Lukinovich and André-Louis Rey (eds), *Κορυφαίῳ ἀνδρί: Mélanges offerts à André Hurst*. Geneva: Librairie Droz, 41–52.

Bowie, Angus (ed.). 2013. *Homer: Odyssey Books XIII and XIV*. Cambridge: Cambridge University Press.

Bowie, Ewen L. 1989. 'Poetry and Poets in Asia and Achaia.' In: Walker and Cameron (1989), 198–205.

Bowie, Ewen L. 2019. 'Poetic and Prose Oral Performance in the Greek World of the Roman Empire.' In: Consuelo Ruiz-Montero (ed.), *Aspects of Orality and Greek Literature in the Roman Empire*. Newcastle: Cambridge Scholars Publishing, 49–80.

Boyten, Bellini. 2007. 'More "Parfit Gentil Knyght" than "Hyrcanian Beast": The Reception of Neoptolemos in Quintus Smyrnaeus' *Posthomerica*.' In: Baumbach and Bär (2007a), 307–36.

Boyten, Bellini. 2010. *Epic Journeys: Studies in the Reception of the Hero and Heroism in Quintus Smyrnaeus'* Posthomerica. PhD thesis, University College London. http://discovery.ucl. ac.uk/1310146/1/1310146.pdf.

Braccini, Tommaso. 2009/10. 'Erudita invenzione: riflessioni sulla *Piccola grande Iliade* di Giovanni Tzetze.' *Incontri Triestini di Filologia Classica* 9, 153–73.

Braccini, Tommaso. 2010. 'Mitografia e miturgia femminile a Bisanzio: il caso di Giovanni Tzetze.' *I Quaderni del Ramo d'Oro on-line* 3, 88–105. http://www.qro.unisi.it/frontend/ sites/default/files/Mitografia_e_miturgia_femminile.pdf.

Braccini, Tommaso. 2011. 'Riscrivere l'epica: Giovanni Tzetze di fronte al ciclo troiano.' *CentoPagine* 5, 43–57. https://www.openstarts.units.it/bitstream/10077/9518/1/Braccini.pdf.

Braun, René. 1983. '"*Honeste cadere*": un *topos* d'hagiographie antique.' *Bulletin du Centre de Romanistique et de Latinité Tardive (Nice)* 1, 1–12.

Bremmer, Jan N. 1998. 'The Novel and the Apocryphal Acts: Place, Time and Readership.' In: Heinz Hofmann and Maaike Zimmerman (eds), *Groningen Colloquia on the Novel IX*. Groningen: Egbert Forsten, 157–80.

Bremmer, Jan N. 1999. *Greek Religion*. 2nd rev. ed. Oxford: Oxford University Press.

Bremmer, Jan N. 2017. 'Mythe et rituel dans l'initiation d'Héraclès.' In: Claude Calame and Pierre Ellinger (eds), *Du récit au rituel par la forme esthétique: Poèmes, images et pragmatique culturelle en Grèce ancienne*. Paris: Les Belles Lettres, 269–304.

Bremmer, Jan N. 2018. 'Transformations and Decline of Sacrifice in Imperial Rome and Late Antiquity.' In: Michael Blömer and Benedikt Eckhardt (eds), *Transformationen paganer Religion in der römischen Kaiserzeit: Rahmenbedingungen und Konzepte*. Berlin and Boston: Walter de Gruyter, 215–56.

Bremmer, Jan N. 2019a. *The World of Greek Religion and Mythology: Collected Essays*. Vol. 2. Tübingen: Mohr Siebeck.

Bremmer, Jan N. 2019b. 'The First Columns of the Derveni Papyrus and *Polis* Religion.' *Eirene* 55, 127–41.

Bremmer, Jan N. 2019c. 'Demons: An Epilogue.' In: Eva Elm and Nicole Hartmann (eds), *Demons in Late Antiquity: Their Perception and Transformation in Different Literary Genres*. Berlin and Boston: Walter de Gruyter, 167–73.

Bremmer, Jan N. 2019d. 'Dying for the Community: From Euripides' *Erechtheus* to the Gospel of John.' In: David du Toit, Christine Gerber and Christiane Zimmermann (eds), Sōtēria: *Salvation in Early Christianity and Antiquity. Festschrift in Honour of Cilliers Breytenbach on the Occasion of his 65th Birthday*. Leiden and Boston: Brill, 66–85.

Brescia, Graziana et al. 2018. *Revival and Revision of the Trojan Myth: Studies on Dictys Cretensis and Dares Phrygius*. Hildesheim, Zurich and New York: Georg Olms.

Bretzigheimer, Gerlinde. 1994. 'Diana in Ovids *Metamorphosen*.' *Gymnasium* 101, 506–46.

Brink, Charles O. 1972. 'Ennius and the Hellenistic Worship of Homer.' *AJPh* 93, 547–67.

Brink, Charles O. 1982. *Horace on Poetry: Epistles Book II. The Letters to Augustus and Florus*. Cambridge: Cambridge University Press.

Broich, Ulrich. 1985. 'Formen der Markierung von Intertextualität.' In: Ulrich Broich and Manfred Pfister (eds), *Intertextualität: Formen, Funktionen, anglistische Fallstudien*. Tübingen: Max Niemeyer, 31–47.

Brown, Christopher G. 1989. 'Ares, Aphrodite, and the Laughter of the Gods.' *Phoenix* 43, 283–93.

Brown, Sarah Annes. 2005. *Ovid: Myth and Metamorphosis*. London: Bristol Classical Press.

Brügger, Claude, Magdalene Stoevesandt and Edzard Visser. 2003. *Homers Ilias: Gesamtkommentar (Basler Kommentar/BK)*. Vol. II.2: *Zweiter Gesang (B): Kommentar*. Munich and Leipzig: K. G. Saur.

Brunius-Nilsson, Elisabeth. 1955. *Daimonie: An Inquiry Into a Mode of Apostrophe in Old Greek Literature*. Uppsala: Almqvist and Wiksells.

Buchanan, Ian and John Marks. 2000. 'Introduction: Deleuze and Literature.' In: Ian Buchanan and John Marks (eds), *Deleuze and Literature*. Edinburgh: Edinburgh University Press, 1–13.

Budelmann, Felix. 1999. *The Language of Sophocles. Communality, Communication, and Involvement*. Cambridge: Cambridge University Press.

Bulanda, Edmund. 1913. *Bogen und Pfeil bei den Völkern des Altertums*. Vienna and Leipzig: Alfred Hölder.

Burgess, Jonathan S. 1995. 'Achilles' Heel: The Death of Achilles in Ancient Myth.' *ClAnt* 14, 217–44.

Burgess, Jonathan S. 2001. *The Tradition of the Trojan War in Homer and the Epic Cycle*. Baltimore and London: Johns Hopkins University Press.

Burgess, Jonathan S. 2002. 'Kyprias, the *Kypria*, and Multiformity.' *Phoenix* 56, 234–45.

Burgess, Jonathan S. 2004a. 'Early Images of Achilles and Memnon?' *QUCC* 76: 33–51.

Burgess, Jonathan S. 2004b. 'Untrustworthy Apollo and the Destiny of Achilles: *Iliad* 24.55–63'. *HSPh* 102, 21–40.

Burgess, Jonathan S. 2006. 'Neoanalysis, Orality, and Intertextuality: An Examination of Homeric Motif Transference.' *Oral Tradition* 21, 148–89.

Burgess, Jonathan S. 2009. *The Death and Afterlife of Achilles*. Baltimore: Johns Hopkins University Press.

Burgess, Jonathan S. 2015. 'Coming adrift: The limits of reconstruction of the cyclic poems.' In: Fantuzzi and Tsagalis (2015), 43–58.

Burkert, Walter. 1960. 'Das Lied von Ares und Aphrodite: Zum Verhältnis von Odyssee und Ilias.' *RhM* 103, 130–44.

Burkert, Walter. 1983. 'Götterspiel und Götterburleske in altorientalischen und griechischen Mythen.' In: Rudolf Ritsema (ed.), *Das Spiel der Götter und Menschen*. Frankfurt a.M.: Insel-Verlag, 335–67.

Burkert, Walter. ²2011 [1977]. *Griechische Religion der archaischen und klassischen Epoche*. 2nd rev. ed. Stuttgart: Kohlhammer.

Bussemaker, Ulco Cats. 1849. *Scholia et paraphrases in Nicandrum et Oppianum*. Paris: Didot.

Byre, Calvin S. 2002. *A Reading of Apollonius Rhodius'* Argonautica: *The Poetics of Uncertainty*. Lewiston, Queenston and Lampeter: Edwin Mellen.

Cadau, Cosetta. 2015. *Studies in Colluthus'* Abduction of Helen. Leiden and Boston: Brill.

Cairns, Douglas L. 2012. '*Atê* in the Homeric poems.' *Papers of the Langford Latin Seminar* 15, 1–52.

Cairns, Douglas L. and Laura Fulkerson (eds). 2015. *Emotions between Greece and Rome*. London: Institute of Classical Studies.

Calero Secall, Inés. 1995. 'El tema de la Ilegada y recepción de los héroes en la epopeya de Quinto de Esmirna.' *Faventia* 17, 45–58.

Calero Secall, Inés. 1998a. 'El Áyax de Quinto de Esmirna y sus precendentes literarios.' In: Máximo Brioso and Francisco José González Ponce (eds), *Actitudes literarias en la Grecia romana*. Seville: Libros Pórtico, 77–91.

Calero Secall, Inés. 1998b. 'La figura de Neoptólemo en la epopeya de Quinto de Esmirna.' In: Francisco Rodríguez Adrados and Alfonso Martínez Díez (eds), *Actas del IX congreso español de estudios clásicos*. Vol. 4. Madrid: Ediciones Clásicas, 101–6.

Cameron, Averil. 2016. *Arguing it Out: Discussion in Twelfth-Century Byzantium*. Budapest and New York: Central European University Press.

Camerotto, Alberto. 1998. *Le metamorfosi della parola: Studi sulla parodia in Luciano di Samosata*. Pisa and Rome: Istituti editoriali e poligrafici internazionali.

Camerotto, Alberto. 2009. *Fare gli eroi. Le storie, le imprese, le virtù: composizione e racconto dell'epica greca arcaica*. Padua: Il poligrafo.

Campagnolo, Marco. 2010/11. *Commento al secondo* logos *dei* Posthomerica *di Quinto Smirneo*. PhD thesis, Università Ca' Foscari di Venezia. http://dspace.unive.it/bitstream/handle/10579/1218/Posthomerica%20II.pdf?sequence=1.

Campbell, Malcolm. 1981. *A Commentary on Quintus Smynaeus Posthomerica XII*. Leiden: Brill.

Cannatà Fera, Maria. 2003. 'Pindaro in Trifiodoro.' In: Francesco Benedetti and Simonetta Grandolini (eds), *Studi di filologia e tradizione greca in memoria di Aristide Colonna*. Vol. 1. Perugia and Naples: Edizioni scientifiche italiane, 193–8.

Cantilena, Mario. 2001. 'Cronologia e tecnica compositiva dei *Posthomerica* di Quinto Smirneo.' In: Franco Montanari and Stefano Pittaluga (eds), *Posthomerica. Tradizioni omeriche dall'Antichità al Rinascimento*. Vol. 3. Genoa: Dipartimento di archeologia, filologia classica e loro tradizioni, 51–70.

Carvounis, Katerina. 2007. 'Final Scenes in Quintus of Smyrna, *Posthomerica* 14.' In: Baumbach and Bär (2007a), 241–57.

Carvounis, Katerina. 2008. 'Transforming the Homeric Models: Quintus' Battle among the Gods in the Posthomerica.' *Ramus* 37, 60–78.

Carvounis, Katerina. 2014. 'Landscape Markers and Time in Quintus' *Posthomerica*.' In: Marios Skempis and Ioannis Ziogas (eds), *Geography, Topography, Landscape: Configurations of Space in Greek and Roman Epic*. Berlin and Boston: Walter de Gruyter, 181–208.

Carvounis, Katerina. 2019. *A Commentary on Quintus of Smyrna*, Posthomerica 14. Oxford: Oxford University Press.

Carvounis, Katerina. 2020. 'Through the Epic Tradition: Speech and Assemblies in Quintus' *Posthomerica.' Trends in Classics* 12, 134–53.

Carvounis, Katerina, Sophia Papaioannou and Giampiero Scafoglio (eds). Forthcoming. *The Latin Literary Tradition and Later Greek Poetry: Further Explorations*. Berlin and Boston: Walter de Gruyter.

Casabona, Jean. 1966. *Recherches sur le vocabulaire des sacrifices en Grèce, des origines à la fin de l'époque classique*. Paris: Éditions Ophrys.

Cerri, Giovanni. 2015. 'I poemi ciclici nel giudizio di Aristotele e di Quinto Smirneo.' *Philologia Antiqua: An International Journal of Classics* 8, 129–49.

Chantraine, Pierre. 1952. 'Le divin et les dieux chez Homère.' In: Herbert J. Rose *et al.* (eds), *La Notion du Divin depuis Homère jusqu'à Platon*. Vandœuvres and Geneva: Fondation Hardt, 45–94.

Chantraine, Pierre. 1956. *Études sur le vocabulaire grec*. Paris: Klincksieck.

Chantraine, Pierre. 1968–80. *Dictionnaire étymologique de la langue grecque: Histoire des mots*. 4 vols. Paris: Klincksieck.

Chaudhuri, Pramit. 2014. *The War with God: Theomachy in Roman Imperial Poetry*. Oxford: Oxford University Press.

Chrysafis, Gerasimos. 1985. 'Pedantry and Elegance in Quintus Smyrnaeus, *Posthomerica.' Corolla Londiniensis* 4, 17–42.

Ciampa, Silvana. 2009. 'Laodice: storia di una polemica mitologica dall'ellenismo alla tarda antichità.' *Prometheus* 35, 34–52.

Clark, Matthew. 2007. 'Poulydamas and Hector.' *College Literature* 34.2, 85–106.

Clarke, Howard W. 1969. 'The Humor of Homer.' *CJ* 64, 246–52.

Clarke, Michael. 2001. '"Heart-Cutting Talk": Homeric κερτομέω and Related Words', *CQ* 51, 329–38.

Cohen, Beth (ed.). 1995. *The Distaff Side: Representing the Female in Homer's Odyssey*. New York and Oxford: Oxford University Press.

Colakis, Marianthe. 1986. 'The Laughter of the Suitors in *Odyssey* 20.' *CW* 79, 137–41.

Colish, Marcia L. 1985. *The Stoic Tradition from Antiquity to the Early Middle Ages*. Vol. 1: *Stoicism in Classical Latin Literature*. Leiden: Brill.

Collins, Derek. 2008. 'The Magic of Homeric Verses.' *CPh* 103, 211–36.

Collobert, Catherine. 2000. 'Héphaïstos, l'artisan du rire inextinguible des dieux.' In: Desclos (2000), 133–41.

Combellack, Frederick M. 1968. *The War at Troy: What Homer Didn't Tell. By Quintus of Smyrna. Translated, and with an Introduction and Notes*. Norman: University of Oklahoma Press.

Combellack, Frederick M. 1987. 'The λύσις ἐκ τῆς λέξεως.' *AJPh* 108, 202–19.

Conte, Gian Biagio. 1986. *The Rhetoric of Imitation: Genre and Poetic Memory in Virgil and Other Latin Poets*. Translated by Charles Segal. Ithaca, NY and London: Cornell University Press.

Coray, Marina. 2016. *Homers Ilias: Gesamtkommentar (Basler Kommentar/BK)*. Vol. XI.2: *Achtzehnter Gesang (B): Kommentar*. Berlin and Boston: Walter de Gruyter.

Corfù, Nicolas Assur. 2016. 'Der Polyxena-Sarkophag von Çanakkale – archaisch oder archaistisch?' *Numismatica e Antichità Classiche, Quaderni Ticinesi* 45, 43–66.

Cramer, Frederick H. 1954. *Astrology in Roman Law and Politics*. Philadelphia: American Philosophical Society.

Cribiore, Raffella. 2001. *Gymnastics of the Mind: Greek Education in Hellenistic and Roman Egypt*. Princeton: Princeton University Press.

Crugnola, Annunciata (ed.). 1971. *Scholia in Nicandri theriaka cum glossis*. Milan: Istituto editoriale cisalpino.

Csikszentmihalyi, Mihaly. 1975. *Beyond Boredom and Anxiety: The Experience of Play in Work and Games*. San Francisco: Jossey-Bass.

Csikszentmihalyi, Mihaly. 1990. *Flow: The Psychology of Optimal Experience*. New York: Harper Perennial.

Cullhed, Eric. 2014. 'The blind bard and "I": Homeric biography and authorial personas in the twelfth century.' *Byzantine and Modern Greek Studies* 38, 49–67.

Curran, Leo. 1978. 'Rape and Rape Victims in the Metamorphoses.' *Arethusa* 2, 213–41.

Cuypers, Martijn. 2005. 'Interactional Particles and Narrative Voice in Apollonius and Homer.' In: Harder and Cuypers (2005), 35–69.

Dällenbach, Lucien. 1989 [1977]. *The Mirror in the Text*. Translated by Jeremy Whitely and Emma Hughes. Cambridge and Oxford: Chicago University Press.

Daniel, Ute. 2001. *Kompendium Kulturgeschichte: Theorien, Praxis, Schlüsselwörter*. Frankfurt a.M.: Suhrkamp.

Davies, Malcolm. 2016. *The Aethiopis: Neo-Neoanalysis Reanalyzed*. Cambridge, MA and London: Harvard University Press.

Davies, Malcolm and Patrick J. Finglass (eds). 2014. *Stesichorus: The Poems*. Cambridge: Cambridge University Press.

de Bakker, Mathieu and Irene J. F. de Jong (eds). Forthcoming. *Speech in Ancient Greek Literature*. Leiden and Boston: Brill.

de Jong, Irene J. F. 2001. *A Narratological Commentary on the Odyssey*. Cambridge: Cambridge University Press.

de Jong, Irene J. F. ²2004a [1987]. *Narrators and Focalizers: The Presentation of the Story in the Iliad*. 2nd rev. ed. London: Bristol Classical Press.

de Jong, Irene J. F. 2004b. 'Introduction. Narratological Theory on Narrators, Narratees, and Narrative.' In: Irene J. F. de Jong, René Nünlist and Angus M. Bowie (eds), *Narrators, Narratees, and Narratives in Ancient Greek Literature*. Leiden and Boston: Brill, 1–10.

de Jong, Irene J. F. 2007. 'Homer.' In: de Jong, Irene J. F. and René Nünlist (eds), *Time in Ancient Greek Literature*. Leiden and Boston: Brill, 17–37.

de Jong, Irene J. F. 2014. *Narratology and Classics: A Practical Guide*. Oxford: Oxford University Press.

Debiasi, Andrea. 2004. *L'epica perduta: Eumelo, il Ciclo, l'occidente*. Rome and Padua: 'L'Erma' di Bretschneider.

Degani, Enzo. 1961. *AIΩN da Omero ad Aristotele*. Padua: Cedam.

Deleuze, Gilles. 1994 [1968]. *Difference and Repetition*. Translated by Paul Pattam. New York: Columbia University Press.

Deleuze, Gilles and Félix Guattari. 1996. *What Is Philosophy?* New York: Columbia University Press.

Derecho, Abigail. 2006. 'Archontic Literature: A Definition, a History, and Several Theories of Fan Fiction.' In: Karen Hellekson and Kristina Busse (eds), *Fan Fiction and Fan Communities in the Age of the Internet: New Essays*. Jefferson, NC and London: McFarland and Company, 61–78.

Derrida, Jacques. 1995. 'Archive Fever: A Freudian Impression.' *Diacritics* 25.2, 9–63.

Desclos, Marie-Laurence (ed.). 2000. *Le rire des Grecs: Anthropologie du rire en Grèce ancienne*. Grenoble: Éditions Jérôme Millon.

Desmond, Marilynn. 1994. *Reading Dido: Gender, Textuality, and the Medieval Aeneid*. Minneapolis: University of Minnesota Press.

Dickey, Eleanor. 1996. *Greek Forms of Address: From Herodotus to Homer*. Oxford: Clarendon Press.

Dickson, Keith. 1995. *Nestor: Poetic Memory in Greek Epic*. New York and London: Garland.

Dieu, Éric. 2016. 'Le type accentuel μηρός / μῆρα du grec ancien.' In: Alain Blanc and Daniel Petit (eds), *Nouveaux acquis sur la formation des noms en grec ancien*. Leuven and Paris: Peeters, 37–56.

Diggle, James. 2007. 'Housman's Greek.' In: Patrick J. Finglass, Christopher Collard and Nicholas J. Richardson (eds), *Hesperos: Studies in Ancient Greek Poetry Presented to M.L. West on his Seventieth Birthday*. Oxford: Oxford University Press, 145–69.

Dihle, Albrecht. 1970. *Homer-Probleme*. Opladen: Westdeutscher Verlag.

Dihle, Albrecht. 1989. *Die griechische und lateinische Literatur der Kaiserzeit: Von Augustus bis Justinian*. Munich: C. H. Beck.

Dillery, John. 2005. 'Chresmologues and *Manteis*: Independent Diviners and the Problem of Authority.' In: Sarah Iles Johnston and Peter T. Struck (eds), *Mantikê: Studies in Ancient Divination*. Leiden and Boston: Brill, 167–231.

Dilts, Mervin R. and George A. Kennedy (eds). 1997. *Two Greek Rhetorical Treatises from the Roman Empire: Introduction, Text, and Translation of the Arts of Rhetoric Attributed to Anonymous Seguerianus and to Apsines of Gadara*. Leiden, New York and Cologne: Brill.

Dominik, William J. 1993. 'From Greece to Rome: Ennius' *Annals*.' In: Anthony J. Boyle (ed.), *Roman Epic*. London and New York: Routledge, 37–58.

Donner, Johann Jacob Christian. 1866/67. *Quintus von Smyrna: Die Fortsetzung der Ilias. Deutsch in der Versart der Urschrift*. 5 vols. Stuttgart: Krais and Hoffmann.

Dougherty, Carol. 2001. *The Raft of Odysseus: The Ethnographic Imagination of Homer's Odyssey*. Oxford: Oxford University Press.

Douglas, J. Yellowlees and Andrew Hargadon. 2001. 'The pleasures of immersion and engagement: schemas, scripts and the fifth business.' *Digital Creativity* 12, 153–66.

Draycott, Catherine M. 2018. 'Making Meaning of Myth: On the Interpretation of Mythological Imagery in the Polyxena Sarcophagus and the Kızılbel Tomb and the History of Achaemenid Asia Minor.' In: Lucy Gaynor Audley-Miller and Beate Dignas (eds), *Wandering Myths: Transcultural Uses of Myth in the Ancient World*. Berlin and Boston: Walter de Gruyter, 23–70.

duBois, Page. 1982. *History, Rhetorical Description and the Epic: From Homer to Spenser*. Cambridge: D. S. Brewer.

duBois, Page. 1991. *Centaurs and Amazons: Women and the Pre-History of the Great Chain of Being*. Ann Arbor: University of Michigan Press.

Duckworth, George E. 1933. *Foreshadowing and Suspense in the Epics of Homer, Apollonius and Vergil*. Princeton: Princeton University Press.

Duckworth, George E. 1936. 'Foreshadowing and Suspense in the *Posthomerica* of Quintus of Smyrna.' *AJPh* 57, 58–86.

Durand, Jean-Louis. 1986. *Sacrifice et labour en Grèce ancienne: Essai d'anthropologie religieuse*. Paris and Rome: Éditions La Découverte.

Ebeling, Heinrich. 1880, -85. *Lexicon homericum*. 2 vols. Leipzig: B. G. Teubner.

Ebert, Joachim. 1969. 'Die Gestalt des Thersites in der *Ilias*.' *Philologus* 113, 159–75.

Edwards, Anthony T. 1984. '*Aristos Achaiōn*: Heroic Death and Dramatic Structure in the *Iliad*.' *QUCC* 17, 61–80.

Edwards, Mark W. 1991. *The Iliad: a commentary. Volume V: books 17–20*. Cambridge: Cambridge University Press.

Ehnmark, Erland. 1999. 'The Gods and Fate.' In: Irene J. F. de Jong (ed.), *Homer: Critical Assessments*. Vol. 2: *The Homeric World*. London and New York: Routledge, 359–68.

Ekroth, Gunnel. 2005. 'Blood on the Altars? On the treatment of blood at Greek sacrifices and the iconographical evidence.' *AK* 48, 9–29.

Ekroth, Gunnel. 2018. 'Vernant et les os. Théorie et pratique du sacrifice grec.' In: Stella Georgoudi and François de Polignac (eds), *Relire Vernant*. Paris: Les Belles Lettres, 83–115.

Ekroth, Gunnel and Jenny Wallensten (eds). 2013. *Bones, behaviour and belief: The zooarchaelogical evidence as a source for ritual practice in ancient Greece and beyond*. Stockholm: Svenska Institutet i Athen.

Elderkin, George W. 1906. *Aspects of the Speech in the Later Greek Epic*. Baltimore: J. H. Furst.

Elliott, Jackie. 2013. *Ennius and the Architecture of the Annales*. Cambridge: Cambridge University Press.

Elsner, Jaś. 2002. 'Introduction: The Genres of Ekphrasis.' *Ramus* 31, 1–18.

Erbse, Hartmut. 1983. 'Ilias und "Patroklie".' *Hermes* 111, 1–15.

ETT: Emotions Through Time: From Antiquity to Byzantium. University of Edinburgh. http://emotions.shca.ed.ac.uk/about.

Fantham, Elaine. 1998. 'Allecto's First Victim: A Study of Virgil's Amata.' In: Hans-Peter Stahl (ed.), *Vergil's Aeneid: Augustan Epic and Political Context*. London: Duckworth, 135–93.

Fantuzzi, Marco. 2012. *Achilles in Love: Intertextual Studies*. Oxford: Oxford University Press.

Fantuzzi, Marco and Christos Tsagalis (eds). 2015. *The Greek Epic Cycle and its Ancient Reception: A Companion*. Cambridge: Cambridge University Press.

Farley, Shannon K. 2016. 'Versions of Homer: Translation, fan fiction, and other transformative rewriting.' *Transformative Works and Culture* 21. https://journal.transformativeworks.org/index.php/twc/article/view/673/600.

Farron, Steven. 1993. *Vergil's Aeneid: A Poem of Grief and Love*. Leiden, New York and Cologne: Brill.

Feeney, Denis. 1991. *The Gods in Epic: Poets and Critics of the Classical Tradition*. Oxford: Clarendon Press.

Feldherr, Andrew. 2010. *Playing Gods: Ovid's* Metamorphoses *and the Politics of Fiction*. Princeton: Princeton University Press.

Felson-Rubin, Nancy. 1994. *Regarding Penelope: From Character to Poetics*. Princeton: Princeton University Press.

Fenik, Bernard. 1968. *Typical Battle Scenes in the Iliad: Studies in the Narrative Techniques of Homeric Battle Description*. Wiesbaden: Franz Steiner.

Fenik, Bernard. 1974. *Studies in the Odyssey*. Wiesbaden: Franz Steiner.

Ferrari, Luigi. 1963. *Osservazioni su Quinto Smirneo*. Palermo: Luxograph.

Ferreccio, Alessia. 2011. 'Παιδοφονεύς, "uccisore di figli", nella poesia postomerica tardoantica.' *RFIC* 139, 413–21.

Ferreccio, Alessia. 2014. *Commento al libro II dei* Posthomerica *di Quinto Smirneo*. Rome: Edizioni di Storia e Letteratura.

Ferreccio, Alessia. 2018. *Gli epiteti degli dèi nei* Posthomerica *di Quinto Smirneo*. Rome: Edizioni di Storia e Letteratura.

Finglass, Patrick J. 2006. 'The Hero's Quest in Sophocles' *Philoctetes*.' *Prometheus* 32, 217–24.

Finkelberg, Margalit. 1998. '*Timē* and *Aretē* in Homer.' *CQ* 48, 14–28.

Fisher, Elizabeth A. 1982. 'Greek translations of Latin literature in the fourth century A.D.' *YClS* 27, 173–215.

Flach, Hans (ed.). 1876. *Glossen und Scholien zur hesiodischen Theogonie mit Prolegomena*. Leipzig: B. G. Teubner.

Foley, John Miles. 1995. 'Sixteen Moments of Silence in Homer.' *QUCC* 50, 7–26.

Fornaro, Sotera. 2001. 'Quintus. [3] (Κόιντος) von Smyrna.' *DNP* 10, 722–4.

Foucher, Louis. 1996. 'Aion, le Temps absolu.' *Latomus* 55, 5–30.

Fowler, Don P. 1991. 'Narrate and Describe: the Problem of Ekphrasis.' *JRS* 81, 25–35.

Fowler, Don P. 1997. 'Second Thoughts on Closure.' In: Deborah H. Roberts, Francis M. Dunn and Don P. Fowler (eds), *Classical Closure: Reading the End in Greek and Latin Literature*. Princeton: Princeton University Press, 3–22.

Fowler, Robert L. 2000, 2013. *Early Greek Mythography*. 2 vols. Oxford: Oxford University Press.

Fraenkel, Eduard (ed.). 1950. *Aeschylus: Agamemnon. Edited with a Commentary*. 3 vols. Oxford: Clarendon Press.

Fränkel, Hermann. 1952. 'Apollonius Rhodius as a Narrator in *Argonautica* 2.1–140.' *TAPhA* 83, 144–55.

Fränkel, Hermann. 1960. *Wege und Formen frühgriechischen Denkens*. Edited by Franz Tietze. 2nd rev. ed. Munich: C. H. Beck.

Fratantuono, Lee. 2016. 'The Penthesilead of Quintus Smyrnaeus: A Study in Epic Reversal.' *WS* 129, 207–31.

Freund, Winfried. 1981. *Die literarische Parodie*. Stuttgart: J. B. Metzler.

Friesen, Courtney J. P. 2016. 'Dying like a Woman: Euripides' Polyxena as Exemplum between Philo and Clement of Alexandria.' *GRBS* 56, 623–45.

Frisk, Hjalmar. 1960, -70, -72. *Griechisches etymologisches Wörterbuch*. 3 vols. Heidelberg: Winter.

Fuhrer, Therese and Richard Hunter. 2002. 'Imaginary Gods? Poetic Theology in the *Hymns* of Callimachus.' In: Franco Montanari (ed.), *Callimaco*. Vandœuvres and Geneva: Fondation Hardt, 143–87.

Funke, Hermann. 1981. 'Zu den Vorläufern der Militärgroteske.' In: Hans-Jürgen Horn and Hartmut Laufhütte (eds), *Ares und Dionysos: Das Furchtbare und das Lächerliche in der europäischen Literatur*. Heidelberg: Winter, 239–58.

Fyfe, W. Hamilton (ed.). 1932. *Aristotle: Poetics* [. . .]. *With an English translation*. London: William Heinemann and New York: G. P. Putnam's Sons.

Gaifman, Milette. 2018. *The Art of Libation in Classical Athens*. New Haven and London: Yale University Press.

Gaisser, Julia Haig. 1969. 'A Structural Analysis of the Digressions in the *Iliad* and the *Odyssey*.' *HSPh* 73, 1–43.

Galán Vioque, Guillermo. 2015. 'Joseph Scaliger's Notes on Quintus of Smyrna's *Posthomerica*.' *GRBS* 55, 946–68.

Gangloff, Anne. 2010. 'Rhapsodes et poètes épiques à l'époque impériale.' *REG* 123, 51–70.

García Romero, Francisco Antonio. 1985. 'El *destino* en los *Post Homerica* de Quinto de Esmirna.' *Habis* 16, 101–6.

García Romero, Francisco Antonio. 1986. 'La "intervención psíquica" en los *Post Homerica* de Quinto de Esmirna.' *Habis* 17, 109–16.

García Romero, Francisco Antonio. 1989a. 'Algunas figuras mitológicas en Quinto de Esmirna.' *Emerita* 57, 95–102.

García Romero, Francisco Antonio. 1989b. 'Un estoico en Troya: Nestor en los *Post Homerica* de Quinto de Esmirna.' *Actas del VII congreso español de estudios clásicos*. Vol. 2. Madrid: Sociedad Española de Estudios Clásicos, 197–202.

García Romero, Francisco Antonio. 1990. 'Aportaciones al estoicismo de Quinto de Esmirna. Un comentario a la figura de Anfitrite y a *Posthomerica* XI 106 s.' *Emerita* 58, 119–24.

García Soler, Maria José. 2014. 'Panes y pasteles en el ritual griego.' In: Ángel Martínez Fernández *et al.* (eds), *Ágalma: Ofrenda desde la Filología Clásica a Manuel García Teijeiro*. Valladolid: Ediciones Universidad de Valladolid, 905–10.

Gärtner, Thomas. 1999. 'Zum Geschick der Pleiade Elektra im sogenannten "Mythographus Homericus" (Pap. Ox. 4096) und bei Quintus von Smyrna.' *ZPE* 124, 22–4.

Gärtner, Thomas. 2016. 'Lorenz Rhodoman.' In: Wilhelm Kühlmann *et al.* (eds), *Frühe Neuzeit in Deutschland 1520–1620: Literaturwissenschaftliches Verfasserlexikon*. Vol. 5. Berlin and Boston: Walter de Gruyter, 300–10.

Gärtner, Thomas. 2017. 'Lorenz Rhodoman – ein homerisierender Dichter im Dienste der lutherischen Reformation.' *NLJ* 19, 175–97.

Gärtner, Thomas. Forthcoming. 'Zwei Widmungstexte im Schrifttum des Philhellenen Lorenz Rhodoman.' In: Francesco Furlan, Hartmut Wulfram and Katharina-Maria Schön (eds), *The Tradition of Dedication – La tradizione della dedica – Die Tradition der Widmung*. Pisa and Rome: Fabrizio Serra.

Gärtner, Ursula. 2005. *Quintus Smyrnaeus und die Aeneis: Zur Nachwirkung Vergils in der griechischen Literatur der Kaiserzeit*. Munich: C. H. Beck.

Gärtner, Ursula. 2007. 'Zur Rolle der Personifikationen des Schicksals in den *Posthomerica* des Quintus Smyrnaeus.' In Baumbach and Bär 2007a, 211–40.

Gärtner, Ursula. 2009. 'Laokoon bei Quintus Smyrnaeus.' In: Dorothee Gall and Anja Wolkenhauer (eds), *Laokoon in Literatur und Kunst: Schriften des Symposions 'Laokoon in Literatur und Kunst' vom 30. 11. 2006, Universität Bonn*. Berlin and New York: Walter de Gruyter, 127–45.

Gärtner, Ursula. 2010. *Quintus von Smyrna: Der Untergang Trojas. Griechisch und deutsch*. 2 vols. Darmstadt: Wissenschaftliche Buchgesellschaft.

Gärtner, Ursula. 2013. 'Πιερίδες, τί μοι ἁγνὸν ἐφωπλίσσασθε Μάρωνα; Das griechische Epos der Kaiserzeit und die Bezüge zur lateinischen Literatur.' In: Paul Schubert and Pascale Derron (eds), *Les grecs héritiers des Romains*. Vandœuvres and Geneva: Fondation Hardt, 87–146.

Gärtner, Ursula. 2014. 'Schicksal und Entscheidungsfreiheit bei Quintus Smyrnaeus.' *Philologus* 58, 97–129.

Gärtner, Ursula. 2015. Review of Maciver (2012a). *Gnomon* 87, 493–7.

Gärtner, Ursula. 2017. 'Ohne Anfang und Ende? Die *Posthomerica* des Quintus Smyrnaeus als "Intertext".' In: Christine Schmitz, Jan Telg genannt Kortmann and Angela Jöne (eds), *Anfänge und Enden: Narrative Potentiale des antiken und nachantiken Epos*. Heidelberg: Winter, 313–38.

Garvie, Alex F. (ed.). 1994. *Homer: Odyssey Books VI–VIII*. Cambridge: Cambridge University Press.

Garzya, Antonio. 1973. 'Literarische und rhetorische Polemiken der Komnenenzeit.' *Byzantinoslavica* 34, 1–14.

Gassino, Isabelle. 2012/13. 'De la comédie humaine à la comédie divine: Politique, philosophie et iconographie: Les vecteurs de la satire des dieux chez Lucien.' *Nuntius Antiquus* 8–9, 91–114.

Gebauer, Jörg. 2002. *Pompe und Thysia: Tieropferdarstellungen auf schwarz- und rotfigurigen Vasen*. Münster: Ugarit-Verlag.

Geffcken, Johannes (ed.). 1902. *Die Oracula Sibyllina*. Leipzig: J. C. Heinrich.

Geisz, Camille. 2018. *A Study of the Narrator in Nonnus of Panopolis' Dionysiaca: Storytelling in Late Antiquity*. Leiden and Boston: Brill.

Genette, Gérard. 1997 [1982]. *Palimpsests: Literature in the Second Degree*. Translated by Channa Newman and Claude Doubinsky. Lincoln and London: University of Nebraska Press.

George, Edward V. 1972. 'Poet and Characters in Apollonius Rhodius' Lemnian Episode.' *Hermes* 100, 47–63.

Georgoudi, Stella. 2005a. 'Sacrifice et mise à mort: aperçus sur le statut du cheval dans les pratiques rituelles grecques.' In: Armelle Gardeisen (ed.), *Les équidés dans le monde méditerranéen antique*. Lattes: Édition de l'Association pour le développement de l'archéologie en Languedoc-Roussillon, 137–42.

Georgoudi, Stella. 2005b. 'L'"occultation de la violence" dans le sacrifice grec: donnés anciennes, discours modernes.' In: Georgoudi, Koch Piettre and Schmidt (2005), 115–41.

Georgoudi, Stella. 2008. 'Le consentement de la victime sacrificielle: une question ouverte.' In: Véronique Mehl and Pierre Brulé (eds), *Le sacrifice antique: Vestiges, procédures et strategies*. Rennes: Presses universitaires de Rennes, 139–53.

Georgoudi, Stella. 2017. 'Reflections on Sacrifice and Purification in the Greek World.' In: Hitch and Rutherford (2017), 106–35.

Georgoudi, Stella, Renée Koch Piettre and Francis Schmidt (eds). 2005. *La cuisine et l'autel: Les sacrifices en questions dans les sociétés de la méditerranée ancienne*. Turnhout: Brepols.

Gerbeau, Joëlle and Francis Vian (eds). 1992. *Nonnos de Panopolis: Les Dionysiaques*. Vol. 7: *Chants XVIII–XIX*. Paris: Budé [incl. a French translation].

Gerrig, Richard J. 1998. *Experiencing Narrative Worlds: On the Psychological Activities of Reading*. New Haven and London: Yale University Press.

Giangrande, Giuseppe. 1967. '"Arte Allusiva" and Alexandrian Epic Poetry.' *CQ* 17, 85–97.

Giangrande, Giuseppe. 1986. 'Osservazioni sul testo e sulla lingua di Quinto Smirneo.' *Siculorum Gymnasium* 39, 41–50.

Gibson, Craig A. 2008. *Libanius's Progymnasmata: Model Exercises in Greek Prose Composition and Rhetoric. Translated with an Introduction and Notes*. Atlanta: Society of Biblical Literature.

Gilka, Marcelina. 2017. *'Antehomerica': The Mythical Tradition of the 'Abduction of Helen' and Its Late Antique Reception in Colluthus and Dracontius*. PhD thesis, University of Exeter.

Gillis, Daniel. 1983. *Eros and Death in the Aeneid*. Rome and Padua: 'L'Erma' di Bretschneider.

Glei, Reinhold F. ²2008 [2001]. 'Outlines of Apollonian Scholarship 1955–1999 [with an Addendum: Apollonius 2000 and Beyond].' In: Papanghelis and Rengakos (²2008), 1–28.

Golden, Leon. 1989. 'Διὸς ἀπάτη and the Unity of *Iliad* 14.' *Mnemosyne* 42, 1–11.

Goldhill, Simon. 1991. *The Poet's Voice: Essays on Poetics and Greek Literature*. Cambridge: Cambridge University Press.

Goldhill, Simon. 2002. *The Invention of Prose*. Oxford: Oxford University Press.

Goldhill, Simon. 2007. 'What Is Ekphrasis for?' *CPh* 102, 1–19.

Goldhill, Simon. 2009a. 'Undoing in Sophoclean Drama: *Lusis* and the Analysis of Irony.' *TAPhA* 139, 21–52.

Goldhill, Simon. 2009b. 'The Anecdote: Exploring the Boundaries Between Oral and Literate Performance in the Second Sophistic.' In: William A. Johnson and Holt N. Parker (eds), *Ancient Literacies: The Culture of Reading in Greece and Rome*. Oxford: Oxford University Press, 96–113.

Goldhill, Simon. 2012. 'Forms of Attention: Time and Narrative in Ecphrasis.' *The Cambridge Classical Journal* 58, 88–114.

Goldhill, Simon. 2015. 'Preposterous Poetics and the Erotics of Death.' *Eugesta* 5, 154–77.

Goldhill, Simon. 2020. *Preposterous Poetics: The Politics and Aesthetics of Form in Late Antiquity*. Cambridge: Cambridge University Press.

Goldhill, Simon. Forthcoming. *The Christian Invention of Time: Temporality and the Literature of Late Antiquity*. Cambridge: Cambridge University Press.

Gordon, Richard. 2013. 'Hero-cults, old and new.' Review of Jones, Christopher P. 2010. *New Heroes in Antiquity: From Achilles to Antinoos*. Cambridge, MA and London: Harvard University Press. *JRA* 26, 852–60.

Goția, Andrei. 2007. 'Light and Darkness in Quintus Smyrnaeus' *Posthomerica* 2.' In: Baumbach and Bär (2007a), 85–106.

Gow, Andrew S. F. (ed.). 1952a. *Bucolici Graeci*. Oxford: Clarendon Press.

Gow, Andrew S. F. (ed.). ²1952b. *Theocritus: Edited with a Translation and Commentary*. Vol. 1: *Introduction, Text, and Translation*. Cambridge: Cambridge University Press.

Graf, Fritz. 1980. 'Milch, Honig und Wein. Zum Verständnis der Libation im griechischen Ritual.' In: *Perennitas: Studi in onore di Angelo Brelich*. Rome: Ed. dell'Ateneo, 209–21.

Graf, Fritz. 2012. 'One Generation after Burkert and Girard.' In: Christopher A. Faraone and Fred S. Naiden (eds), *Greek and Roman Animal Sacrifice*. Cambridge: Cambridge University Press, 32–51.

Graziosi, Barbara and Johannes Haubold. 2005. *Homer: The Resonance of Epic*. London: Duckworth.

Graziosi, Barbara and Johannes Haubold (eds). 2010. *Homer: Iliad Book VI*. Cambridge: Cambridge University Press.

Green, Steven J. and Katharina Volk (eds). 2011. *Forgotten Stars: Rediscovering Manilius' Astronomica*. Oxford: Oxford University Press.

Greensmith, Emma. 2018. 'When Homer Quotes Callimachus: Allusive Poetics in the Proem of the *Posthomerica*.' *CQ* 68, 257–74.

Greensmith, Emma. 2020. *The Resurrection of Homer in Imperial Greek Epic: Quintus Smyrnaeus' Posthomerica and the Poetics of Impersonation*. Cambridge: Cambridge University Press.

Grethlein, Jonas. 2017. *Die Odyssee: Homer und die Kunst des Erzählens*. Munich: C. H. Beck.

Grethlein, Jonas and Luuk Huitink. 2017. 'Homer's Vividness: An Enactive Approach.' *JHS* 137, 67–91.

Grethlein, Jonas and Christopher Krebs (eds). 2012. *Time and Narrative in Ancient Historiography: The 'Plupast' from Herodotus to Appian*. Cambridge: Cambridge University Press.

Griffin, Jasper. 2011. 'Helen.' In: Margalit Finkelberg (ed.), *The Homer Encyclopedia*. Vol. 2. Malden, MA, Oxford and Chichester: Wiley-Blackwell, 335–7.

Grossardt, Peter. 2006. *Einführung, Übersetzung und Kommentar zum Heroikos von Flavius Philostrat*. 2 vols. Basel: Schwabe.

Guidorizzi, Giulio. 1997. 'The Laughter of the Suitors: A Case of Collective Madness in the *Odyssey*.' In: Lowell Edmunds and Robert W. Wallace (eds), *Poet, Public, and Performance in Ancient Greece*. Baltimore: Johns Hopkins University Press, 1–7.

Hadjicosti, Ioanna L. 2006. 'Apollo at the wedding of Thetis and Peleus: Four problematic cases.' *AC* 75, 15–22.

Hadjittofi, Fotini. 2007. '*Res Romanae*: Cultural Politics in Quintus Smyrnaeus' *Posthomerica* and Nonnus' *Dionysiaca*.' In: Baumbach and Bär (2007a), 357–78.

Hadjittofi, Fotini. 2008. 'The Death of Love in Nonnus' Dionysiaca: The Rapes of Nicaea and Aura.' *Ramus* 36, 114–35.

Hainsworth, John B. 1993. *The Iliad: a commentary. Volume III: books 9–12.* Cambridge: Cambridge University Press.

Hall, Edith. 2018. 'Why are the Erinyes Female? or, What is so Feminine about Revenge?' In: Lesel Dawson and Fiona McHardy (eds), *Revenge and Gender in Classical, Medieval, and Renaissance Literature.* Edinburgh: Edinburgh University Press, 33–57.

Halliwell, Stephen. 1991. 'The Uses of Laughter in Greek Culture.' *CQ* 41, 279–96.

Halliwell, Stephen. 2004. 'Aischrology, Shame, and Comedy.' In: Ineke Sluiter and Ralph M. Rosen (eds), *Free Speech in Classical Antiquity.* Leiden and Boston: Brill, 115–44.

Halliwell, Stephen. 2008. *Greek Laughter: A Study of Cultural Psychology from Homer to Early Christianity.* Cambridge: Cambridge University Press.

Hammerstaedt, Jürgen, Pierre-Marie Morel and Refik Güremen (eds). 2017. *Diogenes of Oinoanda: Epicureanism and Philosophical Debates / Diogène d'Œnoanda: Épicurisme et Controverses.* Leuven: Leuven University Press.

Harder, Annette (ed.). 2012. *Callimachus: Aetia. Introduction, Text, Translation, and Commentary.* 2 vols. Oxford: Oxford University Press.

Harder, Annette and Martijn Cuypers (eds). 2005. *Beginning from Apollo: Studies in Apollonius Rhodius and the Argonautic Tradition.* Leuven, Paris and Dudley, MA: Peeters.

Hardie, Alex. 1983. *Statius and the Silvae: Poets, Patrons and Epideixis in the Graeco-Roman World.* Liverpool: Francis Cairns.

Hardie, Philip. 1986. *Virgil's Aeneid: Cosmos and Imperium.* Oxford: Clarendon Press.

Hardie, Philip, Alessandro Barchiesi and Stephen Hinds (eds). 1997. *Ovidian Transformations: Essays on Ovid's Metamorphoses and its Reception.* Cambridge: The Cambridge Philological Society.

Harmon, Austin M. (ed.). 1936. *Lucian: With an English Translation.* Vol. 5. London: William Heinemann and Cambridge, MA: Harvard University Press.

Harris, Harold A. 1972. *Sports in Greece and Rome.* London: Thames and Hudson.

Harrison, Stephen J. 2011. *Generic Enrichment in Vergil and Horace.* Oxford: Oxford University Press.

Hartog, François. 2011 [2003]. *Regimes of Historicity: Presentism and Experiences of Time.* Translated by Saskia Brown. New York: Columbia University Press.

Hartog, François. 2020. *Chronos: L'Occident aux prises avec le Temps.* Paris: Gallimard.

Harweg, Roland. 1968. *Pronomina und Textkonstitution.* Munich: Fink.

Hatch, William Henry Paine. 1908. 'The Use of ἀλιτήριος, ἀλιτρός, ἀραῖος, ἐναγής, ἐνθύμιος, παλαμναῖος, and προστρόπαιος: A Study in Greek Lexicography.' *HSPh* 9, 157–86.

Hedén, Erik. 1912. *Homerische Götterstudien.* Uppsala: K. W. Appelberg.

Hedreen, Guy. 2001. *Capturing Troy: The Narrative Functions of Landscape in Archaic and Early Classical Greek Art.* Ann Arbor: University of Michigan Press.

Hegedus, Timothy. 2007. *Early Christianity and Ancient Astrology.* New York et al.: Peter Lang.

Heinze, Richard. 1993 [³1913]. *Virgil's Epic Technique.* Translated by Hazel and David Harvey and Fred Robertson. London: Bristol Classical Press.

Helbig, Jörg. 1996. *Intertextualität und Markierung: Untersuchungen zur Systematik und Funktion der Signalisierung von Intertextualität.* Heidelberg: Winter.

Hellekson, Karen and Kristina Busse (eds). 2014. *The Fan Fiction Studies Reader.* Iowa City: University of Iowa Press.

Henderson, John. 1987. 'Lucan/The Word at War.' *Ramus* 16, 122–64.

Henrichs, Albert. 1991. 'Namenlosigkeit und Euphemismus: Zur Ambivalenz der chthonischen Mächte im attischen Drama.' In: Heinz Hofmann and Annette Harder (eds), *Fragmenta dramatica: Beiträge zur Interpretation der griechischen Tragikerfragmente und ihrer Wirkungsgeschichte*. Göttingen: Vandenhoeck & Ruprecht, 161–201.

Henrichs, Albert. 2019. *Greek Myth and Religion. Collected Papers*. Vol. 2. Edited by Harvey Yunis. Berlin and Boston: Walter de Gruyter.

Heubeck, Alfred and Arie Hoekstra. 1989. *A Commentary on Homer's Odyssey*. Vol. 2: *Books IX–XVI*. Oxford: Clarendon Press.

Heubeck, Alfred, Stephanie West and John B. Hainsworth. 1988. *A Commentary on Homer's Odyssey*. Vol. 1: *Introduction and Books I–VIII*. Oxford: Clarendon Press.

Hewitt, Joseph William. 1928. 'Homeric Laughter.' *CJ* 23, 436–47.

Himmelmann, Nikolaus. 1997. *Tieropfer in der griechischen Kunst*. Opladen: Westdeutscher Verlag.

Hinds, Stephen. 1998. *Allusion and intertext: Dynamics of appropriation in Roman poetry*. Cambridge: Cambridge University Press.

Hitch, Sarah and Ian Rutherford (eds). 2017. *Animal Sacrifice in the Ancient Greek World*. Cambridge: Cambridge University Press.

Hoffer, Stanley E. 1995. 'Telemachus' "Laugh" (*Odyssey* 21.105): Deceit, Authority, and Communication in the Bow Contest.' *AJPh* 116, 515–31.

Hohendahl-Zoetelief, Icky Maria. 1980. *Manners in the Homeric Epic*. Leiden: Brill.

Holmes, Brooke. 2012. 'Deleuze, Lucretius, and the Simulacrum of Naturalism.' In: Brooke Holmes and Wilson Henry Shearin (eds), *Dynamic Readings: Studies in the Reception of Epicureanism*. Oxford: Oxford University Press, 316–42.

Hopkinson, Neil. 1984. 'Callimachus' *Hymn to Zeus*.' *CQ* 34, 139–48.

Hopkinson, Neil. 1994. *Greek Poetry of the Imperial Period: An Anthology*. Cambridge: Cambridge University Press.

Hopkinson, Neil (ed.). 2018. *Quintus Smyrnaeus: Posthomerica. Edited and translated*. Cambridge, MA and London: Harvard University Press.

Horn, Fabian. 2014. *Held und Heldentum bei Homer: Das homerische Heldenkonzept und seine poetische Verwendung*. Tübingen: Gunter Narr.

Hornblower, Simon (ed.). 2015. *Lykophron: Alexandra. Greek Text, Translation, Commentary, and Introduction*. Oxford: Oxford University Press.

Hornblower, Simon and Christopher Pelling (eds). 2017. *Herodotus: Histories Books VI*. Cambridge: Cambridge University Press.

Horowitz, Franklin E. 1975. 'Greek *skhétlios*, Sanskrit *kṣatríyaḥ*, and the Indo-European Image of the Warrior.' *SL* 29, 99–109.

Horsfall, Nicholas M. 2003. *Virgil, Aeneid 11: A Commentary*. Leiden and Boston: Brill.

Horsfall, Nicholas M. 2008. *Virgil, Aeneid 2: A Commentary*. Leiden and Boston: Brill.

Hunter, Richard. 1993. *The Argonautica of Apollonius: Literary Studies*. Cambridge: Cambridge University Press.

Hunter, Richard. 2012. 'The Songs of Demodocus: Compression and Extension in Greek Narrative Poetry.' In: Manuel Baumbach and Silvio Bär (eds), *Brill's Companion to Greek and Latin Epyllion and Its Reception*. Leiden and Boston: Brill, 83–109.

Hunter, Richard (ed.). 2015. *Apollonius of Rhodes: Argonautica Book IV*. Cambridge: Cambridge University Press.

Hunter, Richard. 2018. *The Measure of Homer: The Ancient Reception of the Iliad and the Odyssey*. Cambridge: Cambridge University Press.

Hunter, Richard and Katerina Carvounis (eds). 2008. *Signs of Life? Studies in Later Greek Poetry* (special issue *Ramus* 37).

Hupe, Joachim (ed.). 2006. *Der Achilleus-Kult im nördlichen Schwarzmeerraum vom Beginn der griechischen Kolonisation bis in die römische Kaiserzeit: Beiträge zur Akkulturationsforschung*. Rahden: Leidorf.

Hurst, André, Olivier Reverdin and Jean Rudhardt (eds). 1984. *Papyrus Bodmer XXIX: Vision de Dorothéos. Edité avec une introduction, une traduction et des notes.* Cologny and Geneva: Fondation Martin Bodmer.

Jacquemin, Anne. 2014. 'Le sacrifice dans le monde grec et ses interprétations.' *Archimède: Archéologie et historie ancienne* 1, 107–13.

Jahn, Stefanie. 2009. 'Die Darstellung der Troer und Griechen in den Kampfszenen der Posthomerica des Quintus von Smyrna.' *WS* 122, 87–108.

Jahn, Thomas. 1987. *Zum Wortfeld 'Seele-Geist' in der Sprache Homers.* Munich: C. H. Beck.

James, Alan W. 1978. 'Night and Day in Epic Narrative from Homer to Quintus of Smyrna.' *MPhL* 3, 153–83.

James, Alan W. 2004. *Quintus of Smyrna: The Trojan Epic. Posthomerica. Translated and edited.* Baltimore and London: Johns Hopkins University Press.

James, Alan W. 2005. 'Quintus of Smyrna.' In: Jones Miles Foley (ed.), *A Companion to Ancient Epic*. Malden, Oxford and Victoria: Blackwell, 364–73.

James, Alan W. 2007. 'Quintus of Smyrna and Virgil – A Matter of Prejudice.' In: Baumbach and Bär (2007a), 145–57.

James, Alan W. and Kevin Lee. 2000. *A Commentary on Quintus of Smyrna, Posthomerica V.* Leiden, Boston and Cologne: Brill.

Jameson, Michael H. 2014. *Cults and Rites in Ancient Greece: Essays on Religion and Society.* Cambridge: Cambridge University Press.

Jameson, Michael H., David R. Jordan and Roy David Kotansky. 1993. *A Lex Sacra from Selinous.* Durham, NC: Duke University.

Jamison, Anne. 2013. *Fic: Why Fanfiction Is Taking Over the World.* Dallas: Smart Pop.

Janko, Richard. 1992. *The Iliad: a commentary. Volume IV: books 13–16.* Cambridge: Cambridge University Press.

Jeffreys, Elizabeth. 1990. 'The transmission of Malalas' chronicle: 1: Malalas in Greek.' In: Elizabeth Jeffreys, Brian Croke and Roger Scott (eds), *Studies in John Malalas.* Leiden: Brill, 245–68.

Jenkins, Henry. 1992. *Textual Poachers: Television Fans and Participatory Culture.* Carbondale: Southern Illinois University Press.

Jenkins, Henry. 2012. *Textual Poachers: Television Fans and Participatory Culture.* 2nd rev. ed. Abingdon: Routledge.

Johnson, Aaron P. 2013. *Religion and Identity in Porphyry of Tyre: The Limits of Hellenism in Late Antiquity.* Cambridge: Cambridge University Press.

Johnston, Sarah Iles. 1999. *Restless Dead: Encounters Between the Living and the Dead in Ancient Greece.* Berkeley, Los Angeles and London: University of California Press.

Jouan, François. 1990/91. 'Comment partir en guerre en Grèce antique en ayant les dieux pour soi.' *Revue de la société Ernest Renan* 40, 25–42.

Kahil, Lilly and Pascale Linant de Bellefonds. 1990. 'Iphigeneia.' *LIMC* V.1, 706–29.

Kakridis, Phanis J. 1962. *Κόϊντος Σμυρναῖος: Γενικὴ μελέτη τῶν "Μεθ᾽ Ὅμηρον" καὶ τοῦ ποιητῆ τους.* Athens: Βιβλιοπωλεῖο τῆς Ἑστίας.

Kassel, Rudolf (ed.). 1966. *Aristotelis De arte poetica liber.* Oxford: Clarendon Press.

Kauffman, Nicholas. 2018. 'Slaughter and Spectacle in Quintus Smyrnaeus' *Posthomerica*.' *CQ* 68, 634–48.

Keaney, John J. and Robert Lamberton (eds). 1996. *[Plutarch]: Essay On the Life and Poetry Of Homer.* Atlanta: Scholars Press.

Kearns, Emily. 2011. 'Ὁ λιβανωτὸς εὐσεβές καὶ τὸ πόπανον: the rationale of cakes and bloodless offerings in Greek sacrifice.' In: Pirenne-Delforge and Prescendi (2011), 89–103.

Kehmptzow, Franz. 1891. *De Quinti Smyrnaei fontibus ac mythopoeia.* Kiel: Fiencke.

Keizer, Heleen M. 1999. *Life Time Entirety: A Study of AIΩN in Greek Literature and Philosophy, the Septuagint and Philo*. PhD thesis, Universiteit van Amsterdam.

Kelly, Adrian. 2007. *A Referential Commentary and Lexicon to Homer, Iliad VIII*. Oxford: Oxford University Press.

Kelly, Adrian. 2008. 'Performance and Rivalry: Homer, Odysseus, and Hesiod.' In: Martin Revermann and Peter Wilson (eds), *Performance, Iconography, Reception: Studies in Honour of Oliver Taplin*. Oxford: Oxford University Press, 177–203.

Kelly, Adrian. 2012. 'The Mourning of Thetis: "Allusion" and the Future in the *Iliad*.' In: Franco Montanari, Antonios Rengakos and Christos Tsagalis (eds), *Homeric Contexts: Neoanalysis and the Interpretation of Oral Poetry*. Berlin and Boston: Walter de Gruyter, 221–65.

Kennedy, George A. 2003. *Progymnasmata: Greek Textbooks of Prose Composition and Rhetoric. Translated with Introductions and Notes*. Leiden and Boston: Brill.

Kermode, Frank. 1979. *The Genesis of Secrecy: On the Interpretation of Narrative*. Cambridge, MA and London: Harvard University Press.

Kermode, Frank. 1983. *Essays on Fiction 1971–82*. Abingdon and New York: Routledge.

Keydell, Rudolf. 1949/50. 'Seneca und Cicero bei Quintus von Smyrna.' *WJA* 4, 81–8.

Keydell, Rudolf. 1954. 'Quintus von Smyrna und Vergil.' *Hermes* 82, 254–6.

Keydell, Rudolf. 1961. Review of Vian (1959a). *Gnomon* 33, 278–84.

Keydell, Rudolf. 1963. 'Quintus von Smyrna.' RE XXIV.1, 1271–96.

Kim, Lawrence. 2010a. *Homer Between History and Fiction in Imperial Greek Literature*. Cambridge: Cambridge University Press.

Kim, Lawrence. 2010b. 'The Literary Heritage as Language: Atticism and the Second Sophistic.' In: Egbert J. Bakker (ed.), *A Companion to the Ancient Greek Language*. Malden, MA, Oxford and Chichester: Wiley-Blackwell, 468–82.

Kirk, Geoffrey S. 1985. *The Iliad: a commentary. Volume I: books 1–4*. Cambridge: Cambridge University Press.

Kirk, Geoffrey S. 1990. *The Iliad: a commentary. Volume II: books 5–8*. Cambridge: Cambridge University Press.

Klein, Ludwig. 1931. 'Die Göttertechnik in den Argonautika des Apollonios Rhodios.' *Philologus* 86, 18–51, 215–57.

Kneebone, Emily. 2007. 'Fish in Battle? Quintus of Smyrna and the *Halieutica* of Oppian.' In: Baumbach and Bär (2007a), 285–305.

Knight, Virginia. 1995. *The Renewal of Epic: Responses to Homer in the* Argonautica *of Apollonius*. Leiden, New York and Cologne: Brill.

Knox, Bernard M. W. 1985. 'Epilogue.' In: Patricia E. Easterling and Bernard M. W. Knox (eds), *The Cambridge History of Classical Literature*. Vol. 1: *Greek Literature*. Cambridge: Cambridge University Press, 714–18.

Köchly, Hermann (ed.). 1850. Κοΐντου τὰ μεθ' Ὅμηρον. *Quinti Smyrnaei Posthomericorum libri XIV: Recensuit prolegomenis et adnotatione critica instruxit*. Leipzig: Weidmann.

König, Jason. 2005. *Athletics and Literature in the Roman Empire*. Cambridge: Cambridge University Press.

Konstan, David. 2006. *The Emotions of the Ancient Greeks: Studies in Aristotle and Classical Literature*. Toronto, Buffalo and London: University of Toronto Press.

Kopff, E. Christian. 1983. 'The Structure of the *Amazonia* (*Aethiopis*).' In: Robin Hägg (ed.), *The Greek Renaissance of the Eighth Century B.C.: Tradition and Innovation*. Stockholm: P. Aström, 57–62.

Kosslyn, Stephen M., William L. Thompson and Giorgio Ganis. 2006. *The Case for Mental Imagery*. Oxford: Oxford University Press.

Kristeva, Julia. 1980. *Desire in Language: A Semiotic Approach to Literature and Art*. Edited by Leon S. Roudiez. Translated by Thomas Gora, Alice Jardine and Leon S. Roudiez. New York: Columbia University Press.

Kröll, Nicole (ed.). 2020. *Myth, Religion, Tradition, and Narrative in Late Antique Greek Poetry*. Vienna: Verlag der österreichischen Akademie der Wissenschaften.

Kullmann, Wolfgang. 1960. *Die Quellen der Ilias (Troischer Sagenkreis)*. Wiesbaden: Franz Steiner.

Kullmann, Wolfgang. 1981. 'Zur Methode der Neoanalyse in der Homerforschung.' *WS* 15, 5–42.

Kullmann, Wolfgang. 1991. 'Ergebnisse der motivgeschichtlichen Forschung zu Homer (Neoanalyse).' In: Joachim Latacz (ed.), *Zweihundert Jahre Homer-Forschung: Rückblick und Ausblick*. Stuttgart and Leipzig: B. G. Teubner, 425–55.

Kumpf, Michael M. 1984. *Four Indices of the Homeric Hapax Legomena: Together with Statistical Data*. Hildesheim, Zurich and New York: Georg Olms.

Kustas, George L. 1973. *Studies in Byzantine Rhetoric*. Thessaloniki: Patriarchikon Hidryma Paterikōn.

Kyriakou, Poulheria. 1995. *Homeric Hapax Legomena in the Argonautica of Apollonius Rhodius: A Literary Study*. Stuttgart: Franz Steiner.

Kyriakou, Poulheria. 2001. 'Warrior Vaunts in the *Iliad*.' *RhM* 144, 250–77.

La Penna, Antonio. 2005. *L'impossibile giustificazione della storia: Un'interpretazione di Virgilio*. Rome and Bari: Laterza.

LaCourse Munteanu, Dana (ed.). 2011. *Emotion, Genre and Gender in Classical Antiquity*. London: Bristol Classical Press.

Lamberton, Robert. 1986. *Homer the Theologian: Neoplatonist Allegorical Reading and the Growth of the Epic Tradition*. Berkeley, Los Angeles and London: University of California Press.

Langella, Elena. 2016. 'L'eroe stoico e le similitudini in Quinto Smirneo.' *Koinonia* 40, 555–81.

Langella, Elena. 2017/18. *Commento al libro VII dei* Posthomerica *di Quinto Smirneo*. PhD thesis, Università degli studi di Milano. https://air.unimi.it/retrieve/handle/2434/611610/1126342/phd_unimi_R11203.pdf.

Langella, Elena. 2018. 'Nuovi eroi nell'epica postomerica: il caso di Neottolemo.' In: Brescia *et al.* (2018), 288–309.

Lardinois, André. 1997. 'Modern Paroemiology and the Use of Gnomai in Homer's *Iliad*.' *CPh* 92, 213–34.

Larmour, David H. J., Paul Allen Miller and Charles Platter (eds). 1998. *Rethinking Sexuality: Foucault and Classical Antiquity*. Princeton University Press.

Latacz, Joachim 1966. *Zum Wortfeld 'Freude' in der Sprache Homers*. Heidelberg: Winter.

Latacz, Joachim. 2011. 'Zu Homers Person.' In: Antonios Rengakos and Bernhard Zimmermann (eds), *Homer Handbuch: Leben – Werk – Wirkung*. Stuttgart and Weimar: J. B. Metzler, 1–25.

Lateiner, Donald. 2005. 'Telemachos' One Sneeze and Penelope's Two Laughs (*Odyssey* 17.541–50, 18.158–68).' In: Robert J. Rabel and Jonathan S. Burgess (eds), *Approaches to Homer: Ancient and Modern*. Swansea: Classical Press of Wales, 91–104.

Latte, Kurt. 1920/21. 'Schuld und Sünde in der griechischen Religion.' *Archiv für Religionswissenschaft* 20, 154–98.

Lattimore, Richmond. 1951. *The Iliad of Homer. Translated with an Introduction*. Chicago and London: University of Chicago Press.

Lavigne, Donald E. 2008. 'Bad *Kharma*: A "Fragment" of the *Iliad* and Iambic Laughter.' *Aevum(ant)* 8, 115–38.

Leaf, Walter (ed.). ²1900, ²1902. *The Iliad*. 2 vols. London: Macmillan.

Lelli, Emanuele *et al.* 2013. *Quinto di Smirne: Il seguito dell'*Iliade. *Testo greco a fronte in edizione critica*. Milan: Bompiani.

Lemon, Lee and Marion Reis (eds). 1965. *Russian Formalist Criticism: Four Essays*. Lincoln: University of Nebraska Press.

Leonard, Miriam (ed.). 2010. *Derrida and Antiquity*. Oxford: Oxford University Press.

Leone, Pietro Luigi M. (ed.). 1995. *Ioannis Tzetzae Carmina Iliaca*. Catania: CULC.

Leone, Pietro Luigi M. (ed.). 2007. P. A. M. Leone (ed.), *Ioannis Tzetzae Historiae*. Lecce: Congedo.

Lesky, Albin. 1966 [²1963]. *A History of Greek Literature*. Translated by James Willis and Cornelius de Heer. New York: Crowell.

Levi, Doro. 1944. 'Aion.' *Hesperia* 13, 269–314.

Levine, Daniel B. 1980. *Γέλῳ ἔκθανον: Laughter and the Demise of the Suitors*. PhD thesis, University of Cincinnati.

Levine, Daniel B. 1982a. '*Odyssey* 18: Iros as Paradigm for the Suitors.' *CJ* 77, 200–4.

Levine, Daniel B. 1982b. 'Homeric Laughter and the Unsmiling Suitors.' *CJ* 78, 97–104.

Levine, Daniel B. 1983. 'Penelope's Laugh. *Odyssey* 18.163.' *AJPh* 104, 172–8.

Levine, Daniel B. 1987. 'Flens matrona et meretrices gaudentes: Penelope and Her Maids.' *CW* 81, 23–7.

LfgrE: Snell, Bruno *et al.* (eds). 1955–2010. *Lexikon des frühgriechischen Epos*. 4 vols. Göttingen: Vandenhoeck & Ruprecht.

Lianeri, Alexandra (ed.). 2011. *The Western Time of Ancient History: Historiographical Encounters with the Greek and Roman Past*. Cambridge: Cambridge University Press.

Linant de Bellefonds, Pascale. 2009. 'Polyxene.' *LIMC* Suppl. 1, 430–2.

Littré, Émile (ed.). 1841. *Œuvres complètes d'Hippocrate, traduction nouvelle avec le texte grec en regard*. Vol. 3. Paris: J. B. Baillière.

Lloyd-Jones, Hugh. 1969. Review of Combellack (1968). *CR* 19, 101.

Lloyd-Jones, Hugh. 1971. *The Justice of Zeus*. Berkeley, Los Angeles and London: University of California Press.

Lloyd-Jones, Hugh and Nigel G. Wilson (eds). 1990. *Sophoclis fabulae*. Oxford: Clarendon Press.

Long, Anthony A. 1970. 'Morals and Values in Homer.' *JHS* 90, 121–39.

Lopez Eire, Antonio. 2000. 'À propos des mots pour exprimer l'idée de "rire" en grec ancien.' In: Desclos (2000), 13–43.

Lord, Albert B. 1938. 'Homer and Huso II: Narrative Inconsistencies in Homer and Oral Poetry.' *TAPhA* 69, 439–45.

Lorimer, Hilda L. 1950. *Homer and the Monuments*. London: Macmillan.

Louden, Bruce. 2006. *The* Iliad: *Structure, Myth, and Meaning*. Baltimore: Johns Hopkins University Press.

Lovato, Valeria Flavia. 2016. 'Ulysse, Tzetzès et l'éducation à Byzance.' In: Nicholas S. M. Matheou, Theofili Kampianaki and Lorenzo M. Bondioli (eds), *From Constantinople to the Frontier: The City and the Cities*. Leiden and Boston: Brill, 236–44.

Lovato, Valeria Flavia. 2017. *Ψεύδεα πολλὰ λέγειν ἐτύμοισιν ὁμοῖα: La ricezione di Odisseo e di Omero presso Giovanni Tzetze e Eustazio di Tessalonica*. PhD thesis, Université de Lausanne and Università di Torino.

Lovatt, Helen. 2013. *The Epic Gaze: Vision, Gender and Narrative in Ancient Epic*. Cambridge: Cambridge University Press.

Lowe, Nick. 2000. *The Classical Plot and the Invention of Western Narrative*. Cambridge: Cambridge University Press.

Lowry, Eddie R. 1991. *Thersites: A Study in Comic Shame*. New York and London: Garland.

LSJ: Liddell, Henry George, Robert Scott and Sir Henry Stuart Jones. ¹⁰1996. *A Greek–English Lexicon*. Oxford: Clarendon Press.

Luce, John Victor. 1975. *Homer and the Heroic Age*. London: Harper and Row.

Ludwich, Arthur (ed.). 1909, -11. *Nonni Panopolitani Dionysiaca*. 2 vols. Leipzig: B. G. Teubner.

Ludwig, Walther. 2014. 'Der Humanist Laurentius Rhodomanus als griechischer Dichter: Laurentios Rhodoman und seine Autobiographie von 1582.' *NLJ* 16, 137–71.

Luzzatto, Maria Jagoda. 1998. 'Leggere i classici nella biblioteca imperiale: note tzetziane su antichi codici.' *QS* 48, 69–86.

Luzzatto, Maria Jagoda. 1999. *Tzetzes lettore di Tucidide: Note autografe sul Codice Heidelberg Palatino Greco 252*. Bari: Dedalo.

Lynn-George, Michael. 1988. *Epos: Word, Narrative and the* Iliad. Basingstoke and London: Macmillan.

Maas, Paul. 1951. 'Aeschylus, *Agam.* 231 ff., Illustrated.' *CQ* 1, 94.

McGlew, James F. 1989. 'Royal Power and the Achaean Assembly at *Iliad* 2.84–393.' *ClAnt* 8, 283–95.

Maciver, Calum A. 2007. 'Returning to the Mountain of *Arete*: Reading Ecphrasis, Constructing Ethics in Quintus Smyrnaeus' *Posthomerica*.' In: Baumbach and Bär (2007a), 259–84.

Maciver, Calum A. 2011. 'Reading Helen's Excuses in Quintus Smyrnaeus' *Posthomerica*.' *CQ* 61, 690–703.

Maciver, Calum A. 2012a. *Quintus Smyrnaeus' Posthomerica: Engaging Homer in Late Antiquity*. Leiden and Boston: Brill.

Maciver, Calum A. 2012b. 'Flyte of Odysseus: Allusion and the *Hoplōn Krisis* in Quintus Smyrnaeus *Posthomerica* 5.' *AJPh* 133, 601–28.

Maciver, Calum A. 2012c. 'Representative Bees in Quintus Smyrnaeus' *Posthomerica*.' *CPh* 107, 53–69.

Maciver, Calum A. 2014. Review of Whitmarsh (2013). *Phoenix* 68, 367–70.

Maciver, Calum A. 2016. 'Nonnus and Imperial Greek Poetry.' In: Accorinti (2016), 529–48.

Maciver, Calum A. 2017. 'Netherworld Destinations in Quintus Smyrnaeus' *Posthomerica*: Some (Homeric) Problems.' In: Ilinca Tanaseanu-Döbler et al. (eds), *Reading the Way to the Netherworld: Education and the Representations of the Beyond in Later Antiquity*. Göttingen: Vandenhoeck & Ruprecht, 123–37.

Maciver, Calum A. 2018. 'Program and Poetics in Quintus Smyrnaeus' *Posthomerica*.' In: Robert Simms (ed.), *Brill's Companion to Prequels, Sequels, and Retellings of Classical Epic*. Leiden and Boston: Brill, 71–89.

Maciver, Calum A. 2020. 'Triphiodorus and the Poetics of Imperial Greek Epic.' *CPh* 115, 164–85.

Macleod, Colin W. (ed.). 1982. *Homer: Iliad Book XXIV*. Cambridge: Cambridge University Press.

MacLeod, Matthew D. 1970. 'Humour in *Iliad* Book 23.' In: *International Homeric Symposium 1969: The Communications*. Athens: International Society for Homeric Studies, 53–6.

McLeod, Wallace. 1965. 'The Range of the Ancient Bow.' *Phoenix* 19, 1–14.

MacPhail, John A. (ed.). 2011. *Porphyry's* Homeric Questions on the Iliad: *Text, Translation, Commentary*. Berlin and New York: Walter de Gruyter.

Madigan, Brian C. 1992. *The Temple of Apollo Bassitas*. Vol. 2: *The Sculpture*. Princeton: The American School of Classical Studies at Athens.

Mair, A. W. (ed.). 1928. *Oppian, Colluthus, Tryphiodorus. With an English Translation*. Cambridge, MA and London: Harvard University Press.

Mansur, Melvin White. 1940. *The Treatment of Homeric Characters by Quintus of Smyrna*. PhD thesis, Columbia University, New York.

Mantero, Teresa. 1966. *Ricerche sull'Heroikos di Filostrato*. Genoa: Istituto di filologia classica e medioevale.

Maravela, Anastasia. 2019. 'The Judgemental Narrator: Narratorial *Nepios*-Comments from Homer to Nonnus.' *SO* 93, 58–105.

Marconi, Clemente. 1994. 'Iphigeneia a Selinunte.' *Prospettiva* 75–6, 50–4.

Martin, Catherine Ellen. 2015. *Baring the Breast in Homer and Attic Tragedy: Death, Dunning and Display.* PhD thesis, University of South Africa. http://uir.unisa.ac.za/bitstream/handle/10500/21711/dissertation_martin_ce.pdf?sequence=1&isAllowed=y.

Martin, Richard P. 1989. *The Language of Heroes: Speech and Performance in the* Iliad. Ithaca, NY and London: Cornell University Press.

Martin, Richard P. 1997. 'Similes as Performance.' In: Egbert J. Bakker and Ahuvia Kahane (eds), *Written Voices, Spoken Signs: Tradition, Performance, and the Epic Text.* Cambridge, MA and London: Harvard University Press, 139–66.

Martin, Richard. 2009. 'Epic as Genre.' In: John Miles Foley (ed.), *A Companion to Ancient Epic.* Malden, MA: Blackwell, 9–19.

Martindale, Charles. 1993. *Redeeming the text: Latin poetry and the hermeneutics of reception.* Cambridge: Cambridge University Press.

Martini, Wolfram. 2013. 'Die visuelle Präsenz der Amazonen in Athen im 6. und 5. Jh. v. Chr.' In: Charlotte Schubert and Alexander Weiß (eds), *Amazonen zwischen Griechen und Skythen: Gegenbilder in Mythos und Geschichte.* Berlin and Boston: Walter de Gruyter, 171–84.

Massetti, Laura. 2019. *Phraseologie und indogermanische Dichtersprache in der Sprache der griechischen Chorlyrik: Pindar und Bakchylides.* PhD thesis, Universität zu Köln. https://kups.ub.uni-koeln.de/9627/3/LM_Dissertation.pdf.

Masters, Jamie. 1992. *Poetry and Civil War in Lucan's* Bellum Civile. Cambridge: Cambridge University Press.

Masterson, Mark, Nancy Sorkin Rabinowitz and James Robson (eds). 2015. *Sex in Antiquity: Exploring Gender and Sexuality in the Ancient World.* Abingdon and New York: Routledge.

Mazza, Daniele. 2014. 'Aspects of the Reception of Iliadic ὁπλοποιία in Later Greek Epic Poetry (Quintus and Nonnus).' *Atlantide* 2, 1–22. http://atlantide.univ-nantes.fr/IMG/pdf/atlantide-2-mazza.pdf.

Meirano, Valeria. 2017. 'Offerte incruente in Magna Grecia. Un approccio iconografico per lo studio di dolci e pani in contesto rituale.' *Scienze dell'Antichità* 23.3, 351–71.

Mengelkoch, Dustin. 2010. 'The Mutability of Poetics: Poliziano, Statius, and the *Silvae*.' *MLN* 125, 84–116.

Mestre, Francesca. 2004. 'Refuting Homer in the *Heroikos* of Philostratus.' In: Ellen Bradshaw Aitken and Jennifer K. Berenson Maclean (eds), *Philostratus's* Heroikos: *Religion and Cultural Identity in the Third Century* C.E. Atlanta: Society of Biblical Literature, 129–41.

Meuli, Karl. 1946. 'Griechische Opferbräuche.' In: Olof Gigon *et al.* (eds), *Phyllobolia: Für Peter von der Mühll zum 60. Geburtstag am 1. August 1945.* Basel: Schwabe, 185–288 (reprint in: *Gesammelte Schriften.* Vol. 2. Basel: Schwabe, 907–1022).

Meyer, Susan Sauvé. 2009. 'Chain of Causes: What is Stoic Fate?' In: Salles (2009), 71–90.

Middleton, Fran. 2018. 'The Poetics of Later Greek Ecphrasis: Christodorus Coptus, the *Palatine Anthology* and the *Periochae* of Nonnus' *Dionysiaca*.' *Ramus* 47, 216–38.

Miguélez-Cavero, Laura. 2008. *Poems in Context: Greek Poetry in the Egyptian Thebaid 200–600 AD.* Berlin and New York: Walter de Gruyter.

Miguélez-Cavero, Laura. 2013. *Triphiodorus, The Sack of Troy: A General Introduction and a Commentary.* Berlin and Boston: Walter de Gruyter.

Mikalson, Jon D. 1983. *Athenian Popular Religion.* Chapel Hill and London: University of North Carolina Press.

Miller, John F. 1993. 'Ovidian Allusion and the Vocabulary of Memory.' *MD* 30, 153–64.

Milne, H. J. M. 1927. *Catalogue of the Literary Papyri in the British Museum.* London: Trustees.

Miltner, Helene. 1937. 'Τόξον.' RE VI.A2, 1847–53.

Mondino, Marialuisa. 1957. 'Di alcune fonti di Quinto Smirneo: IV – Quinto Smirneo e i poeti alessandrini.' *RSC* 5, 133–44.

Montanari, Franco. 2015. *The Brill Dictionary of Ancient Greek*. Leiden and Boston: Brill.

Morales, Helen. 2016. 'Rape, Violence, Complicity: Colluthus's *Abduction of Helen*.' *Arethusa* 49, 61–92.

Morgan, Teresa. 1998. *Literate education in the Hellenistic and Roman worlds*. Cambridge: Cambridge University Press.

Morrison, James V. 1997. 'Kerostasia, the Dictates of Fate, and the Will of Zeus in the *Iliad*.' *Arethusa* 30, 273–96.

Morton, Jacob. 2015. 'The Experience of Greek Sacrifice: Investigating Fat-Wrapped Thigh Bones.' In: Margaret M. Miles (ed.), *Autopsy in Athens: Recent Archaeological Research on Athens and Attica*. Oxford and Havertown: Oxbow Books, 66–75.

Most, Glenn W. 1993. 'Die Batrachomyomachia als ernste Parodie.' In: Ax and Glei (1993), 27–40.

Most, Glenn W. (ed.). 2006. *Hesiod: Theogony, Works and Days, Testimonia. Edited and translated*. Cambridge, MA and London: Harvard University Press.

Mullen, Alex and Olivia Elder (eds). 2019. *The Language of Letters: Bilingual Roman Epistolography from Cicero to Fronto*. Cambridge: Cambridge University Press.

Mullen, Alex and Patrick James (eds). 2012. *Multilingualism in the Graeco-Roman Worlds*. Cambridge: Cambridge University Press.

Murray, Augustus T. and George E. Dimock (eds). ²1999 [1919]. *Homer: Odyssey. With an English translation*. 2 vols. 2nd rev. ed. Cambridge, MA and London: Harvard University Press.

Murray, Augustus T. and William F. Wyatt (eds). ²1999 [1924]. *Homer: Iliad. With an English translation*. 2 vols. 2nd rev. ed. Cambridge, MA and London: Harvard University Press.

Muth, Robert. 1992. *Die Götterburleske in der griechischen Literatur*. Darmstadt: Wissenschaftliche Buchgesellschaft.

Myers, Tobias. 2019. *Homer's Divine Audience: The* Iliad's *Reception on Mount Olympus*. Oxford: Oxford University Press.

Mylonopoulos, Ioannis. 2013. 'Gory Details? The Iconography of Human Sacrifice in Ancient Greek Art.' In: Pierre Bonnechère and Renaud Gagné (eds), *Sacrifices humains / Human sacrifice*. Liège: Presses universitaires de Liège, 61–85.

Nagy, Gregory. 1979. *The Best of the Achaeans: Concepts of the Hero in Archaic Greek Poetry*. Baltimore and London: Johns Hopkins University Press.

Nagy, Gregory. 1990. *Pindar's Homer: The Lyric Possession of an Epic Past*. Baltimore: Johns Hopkins University Press.

Nagy, Gregory. 2009. *Homer the Classic*. Cambridge, MA and London: Harvard University Press.

Naiden, Fred. 2006. 'Rejected Sacrifice in Greek and Hebrew Religion.' *Journal of Ancient Near-Eastern Religions* 6, 189–223.

Naiden, Fred. 2013. *Smoke Signals for the Gods: Ancient Greek Sacrifice from the Archaic through Roman Periods*. Oxford: Oxford University Press.

Nakamura, Jeanne and Mihaly Csikszentmihalyi. 2002. 'The Concept of Flow.' In: Shane J. Lopez and Charles R. Snyder (eds), *Oxford Handbook of Positive Psychology*. Oxford: Oxford University Press, 89–105.

Napolitano, M. Luisa. 2002. *Philoktetes e l'arco: Dalla Magnesia all'Oeta*. Rome: Accademia Nazionale dei Lincei.

Nesselrath, Heinz-Günther. 1992. *Ungeschehenes Geschehen: 'Beinahe-Episoden' im griechischen und römischen Epos von Homer bis zur Spätantike*. Stuttgart: B. G. Teubner.

Nesselrath, Heinz-Günther. 2019. '"Almost-episodes" in Greek and Roman epic.' In: Reitz and Finkmann (2019), 565–608.

Newby, Zahra. 2009. 'Absorption and Erudition in Philostratus' *Imagines*.' In: Ewen Bowie and Jaś Elsner (eds), *Philostratus: Greek Culture in the Roman World*. Cambridge: Cambridge University Press, 322–42.

Nisbet, Gideon. 2003. *Greek Epigram in the Roman Empire: Martial's Forgotten Rivals*. Oxford: Oxford University Press.

Nisbet, Robin G. M. and Niall Rudd. 2004. *A Commentary on Horace, Odes, Book III*. Oxford: Oxford University Press.

Noack, Ferdinand. 1892. Review of Kehmptzow (1891). *Göttingische Gelehrte Anzeigen* 20, 769–812.

Nock, Arthur Darby. 1934. 'A Vision of Mandulis Aion.' *HThR* 27, 53–104.

Notopoulos, James A. 1964. 'Studies in Early Greek Oral Poetry.' *HSPh* 68, 1–77.

Nünlist, René. 2009. *The Ancient Critic at Work: Terms and Concepts of Literary Criticism in Greek Scholia*. Cambridge: Cambridge University Press.

Nussbaum, Alan J. 2018a. 'A Dedicatory Thigh: Greek μηρός and μῆρα Once Again.' In: Lucien van Beek *et al.* (eds), *Farnah: Indo-Iranian and Indo-European Studies in Honor of Sasha Lubotsky*. Ann Arbor and New York: Beach Stave Press, 232–47.

Nussbaum, Alan J. 2018b. 'Limning Some Limbs: A Note on Greek μηρός 'thigh' and Its Relatives.' In: Dieter Gunkel *et al.* (eds), *Vina Diem Celebrent: Studies in Linguistics and Philology in Honor of Brent Vine*. Ann Arbor and New York: Beach Stave Press, 288–98.

O'Keefe, Tim. 2010. *Epicureanism*. Abingdon and New York: Routledge.

Oguibénine, Boris. 1998. *Essays on Vedic and Indo-European Culture*. New Delhi: Motilal Banarsidass Publishers.

Oikonomopoulou, Polytimi. 2004. 'To Kill or not to Kill? Human Sacrifices in Greece according to Euripidean Thought.' In: Danai-Christina Naoum, Georgina Muskett and Mercourios Georgiadas (eds), *Cult and Death:* Proceedings of the Third Annual Meeting of Postgraduate Researchers. The University of Liverpool, May 2002. Oxford: BAR Publishing, 63–7.

Ortony, Andrew, Gerald L. Clore and Allan Collins (eds). 1988. *The Cognitive Structure of Emotions*. Cambridge: Cambridge University Press.

Ozbek, Leyla. 2007. 'Ripresa della tradizione e innovazione compositiva: la medicina nei *Posthomerica* di Quinto Smirneo.' In: Baumbach and Bär (2007a), 159–83.

Ozbek, Leyla. 2011. 'L'eccidio degli uomini a Lemno: il modello delle *Argonautiche* di Apollonio Rodio e la sua rifunzionalizzazione in Quinto Smirneo *Posthomerica* 9, 338–352.' *Philologus* 155, 292–306.

Ozbek, Leyla. 2018. '(Almost) Like a God: Depicting Aeneas in Quintus Smyrnaeus' *Posthomerica*.' *SIFC* 16, 133–56.

Ozbek, Leyla (ed.). Forthcoming. *Filottete in Quinto di Smirne*. Posthomerica *9.333–546: Introduzione, testo e commento*. Pisa: Edizioni della Normale.

Paley, Frederick A. ²1879 [1876]. *Quintus Smyrnaeus and the 'Homer' of the Tragic Poets*. London: F. Nobgate.

Pallone, Maria R. 1984. 'L'epica agonale in età ellenistica.' *Orpheus* 5, 156–66.

Pantelia, Maria C. 1993. 'Spinning and Weaving: Ideas of Domestic Order in Homer.' *AJPh* 114, 493–501.

Papanghelis, Theodore D. and Antonios Rengakos (eds). ²2008 [2001]. *Brill's Companion to Apollonius Rhodius*. 2nd rev. ed. Leiden and Boston: Brill.

Papathomopoulos, Manolis. 2002. *Concordantia in Quinti Smyrnaei Posthomerica*. 2 vols. Hildesheim, Zurich and New York: Georg Olms.

Papathomopoulos, Manolis (ed.). 2007. *Εξήγησις Ιωάννου Γραμματικού του Τζέτζου εις την Ομήρου Ιλιάδα*. Athens: Ακαδημία Αθηνών, Κέντρον Ερεύνης της Ελληνικής και Λατινικής Γραμματείας.

Parca, Maryline. 1991. *Ptocheia or Odysseus in Disguise at Troy (P Köln VI 245)*. Atlanta: Scholars Press.

Parker, L. P. E. 2007. *Euripides: Alcestis. Edited with Introduction and Commentary*. Oxford: Oxford University Press.

Parker, Robert. 1983. *Miasma: Pollution and Purification in Early Greek Religion*. Oxford: Clarendon Press.

Parker, Robert. 2005. 'ὡς ἥρωι ἐναγίζειν.' In: Robin Hägg and Brita Alroth (eds), *Greek Sacrificial Ritual: Olympian and Chthonian: Proceedings of the Sixth International Seminar on Ancient Greek Cult*, Göteborg University, 25–27 April 1997. Stockholm: Svenska Institutet i Athen, 37–45.

Parker, Robert. 2009. 'Sacrifice and Battle.' In: Hans van Wees (ed.), *War and Violence in Ancient Greece*. Swansea: Classical Press of Wales, 299–314.

Parker, Robert. 2011. *On Greek Religion*. Ithaca, NY and London: Cornell University Press.

Parks, Wards. 1990. *Verbal Dueling in Heroic Narrative: The Homeric and Old English Traditions*. Princeton: Princeton University Press.

Parsons, Peter J. 1983. '3537. Hexameter Verse: Ethopoea and Encomium.' *The Oxyrhynchus Papyri* 50, 59–66.

Paschal, George Washington. 1904. *A Study of Quintus of Smyrna*. Chicago: University of Chicago Press.

Paton, William R., Max Pohlenz and Wilhelm Sieveking (eds). 1929. *Plutarchi Moralia*. Vol. 3. Leipzig: B. G. Teubner.

Paul, Stephanie. 2018. 'Les grains du sacrifice. Le lancer d'orges dans la pratique sacrificielle en Grèce ancienne.' *Kernos* 31, 59–72.

Peirano, Irene. 2012. *The Rhetoric of the Roman Fake: Latin* Pseudepigrapha *in Context*. Cambridge: Cambridge University Press.

Pellizer, Ezio. 2000. 'Formes du rire en Grèce antique.' In: Desclos (2000), 45–55.

Pépin, Jean. 1965. 'Porphyre, exégète d'Homère.' In: Heinrich Dörrie *et al.* (eds), *Porphyre*. Vandœuvres and Geneva: Fondation Hardt, 229–72.

Peradotto, John. 1990. *Man in the Middle Voice: Name and Narration in the* Odyssey. Princeton: Princeton University Press.

Pernot, Laurent. 2005. 'Le sacrifice dans la littérature grecque de l'époque impériale.' In: Georgoudi, Koch Piettre and Schmidt (2005), 317–28.

Person, Raymond F. 1995. 'The "Became Silent to Silence" Formula in Homer.' *GRBS* 36, 327–39.

Petropoulou, Maria-Zoe. 2008. *Animal Sacrifice in Ancient Greek Religion, Judaism, and Christianity, 100 BC to AD 200*. Oxford: Oxford University Press.

Pfeiffer, Rudolf (ed.). 1953. *Callimachus*. Vol. 2: *Hymni et epigrammata*. Oxford: Clarendon Press.

Pilz, Oliver. 2011. 'Achilleus und Penthesileia auf einem kretischen Tonrelief aus Phanes auf Rhodos.' In: Oliver Pilz and Mirko Vonderstein (eds), *Keraunia: Beiträge zu Mythos, Kult und Heiligtum*. Berlin and Boston: Walter de Gruyter, 195–213.

Pirenne-Delforge, Vinciane and Gabriella Pironti. 2011. 'Les Moires entre la naissance et la mort: de la représentation au culte.' *Études de lettres* 3–4, 93–114.

Pirenne-Delforge, Vinciane and Francesca Prescendi (eds). 2011. *'Nourrir les dieux?': Sacrifice et représentation du divin*. Liège: Presses universitaires de Liège.

Pisanello, Patrizia. 1999. 'Il comico e il serio-comico nei poemi omerici.' *Rudiae* 11: 91–102.

Pizzone, Aglae. 2017. 'Tzetzes' *Historiai*: a Byzantine "Book of Memory"?' *Byzantine and Modern Greek Studies* 41, 182–207.

Platz, Christian Friedrich. 1857/58. *Quintus von Smyrna. Uebersetzt*. 2 vols. Stuttgart: J. B. Metzler.

Pompella, Giuseppe (ed.). 1979, -87, -93. *Le Postomeriche*. 3 vols. Naples: Loffredo and Cassino: Garigliano [incl. an Italian translation].

Pompella, Giuseppe (ed.). 2002. *Quinti Smyrnaei Posthomerica*. Hildesheim, Zurich and New York: Georg Olms.

Porter, Andrew. 2011. '"Stricken to Silence": Authoritative Response, Homeric Irony, and the Peril of a Missed Language Cue.' *Oral Tradition* 26, 493–520.

Porter, James I. and Mark Buchan (eds). 2004. *Before Subjectivity? Lacan and the Classics.* Lubbock: Texas Tech University Press.

Posner, Donald. 1991. 'Pietro da Cortona, Pittoni, and the Plight of Polyxena.' *The Art Bulletin* 73, 399–414.

Postlethwaite, Norman. 2000. *Homer's Iliad: A Commentary on the Translation of Richmond Lattimore.* Exeter: University of Exeter Press.

Potter, Amanda. 2016. 'Classical monsters in new *Doctor Who* fan fiction.' *Transformative Works and Culture* 21. https://journal.transformativeworks.org/index.php/twc/article/view/676/588.

Prendergast, Christopher. 2019. *Counterfactuals: Paths of the Might Have Been.* London and New York: Bloomsbury.

Prosperi, Valentina. 2013. *Omero sconfitto: ricerche sul mito di Troia dall'antichità al Rinascimento.* Rome: Edizioni di storia e letteratura.

Pulleyn, Simon. 2000. *Homer: Iliad Book 1. Edited with an Introduction, Translation, and Commentary.* Oxford: Oxford University Press.

Purves, Alex C. 2010. *Space and Time in Ancient Greek Narrative.* Cambridge: Cambridge University Press.

Purves, Alex C. 2019. *Homer and the Poetics of Gesture.* Oxford: Oxford University Press.

Quint, David. 1993. *Epic and Empire: Politics and Generic Form from Virgil to Milton.* Princeton: Princeton University Press.

Rabel, Robert J. 1997. *Plot and Point of View in the* Iliad. Ann Arbor: University of Michigan Press.

Radici Colace, Paola and Emilia Sergi. 2000. 'Στάσις nel lessico politico greco.' *ASNP* 5, 223–36.

Radt, Stefan. 1973. 'Zu Aischylos' *Agamemnon*.' *Mnemosyne* 26, 113–26.

Ratinaud-Lachkar, Isabelle. 2010. 'Hephaestus in Homer's Epics: God of Fire, God of Life.' In: Menelaos Christopoulos, Efimia D. Karakantza and Olga Levaniouk (eds), *Light and Darkness in Ancient Greek Myth and Religion.* Lanham *et al.*: Rowman and Littlefield, 153–64.

Rausing, Gad. 1967. *The Bow: Some Notes on Its Origin and Development.* Lund: Habelt.

Rea, John R. 1996. '4352. Hexameter Verses.' *The Oxyrhynchus Papyri* 63, 1–17.

Redfield, James M. 1975. *Nature and Culture in the* Iliad: *The Tragedy of Hector.* Chicago and London: University of Chicago Press.

Reece, Steve. 1995. 'The Three Circuits of the Suitors: A Ring Composition in *Odyssey* 17–22.' *Oral Tradition* 10, 207–29.

Reed, Joseph D. 2007. *Virgil's Gaze: Nation and Poetry in the* Aeneid. Princeton: Princeton University Press.

Reinsberg, Carola. 2003. 'Wilde Mädchen, schöne Braut. Der Polyxena-Sarkophag in Çanakkale.' *AA* 2003, 124–6.

Reinsberg, Carola. 2004. 'Der Polyxena-Sarkophag in Çanakkale.' In: Renate Bol and Detlev Kreikenbom (eds), *Sepulkral- und Votivdenkmäler östlicher Mittelmeergebiete (7. Jh. v. Chr. – 1. Jh. n. Chr.): Kulturbegegnungen im Spannungsfeld von Akzeptanz und Resistenz.* Möhnesee-Wamel: Bibliopolis, 199–217.

Reitz, Christiane and Simone Finkmann (eds). 2019. *Structures of Epic Poetry.* 4 vols. Berlin and Boston: Walter de Gruyter.

Remijsen, Sophie. 2014. 'Appendix: Games, Competitors, and Performers in Roman Egypt.' *The Oxyrhynchus Papyri* 79, 190–206.

Remijsen, Sophie. 2015. *The End of Athletics in Late Antiquity: Greek Culture in the Roman World*. Cambridge: Cambridge University Press.

Rengakos, Antonios. 1999. 'Spannungsstrategien in den homerischen Epen.' In: J. N. Kazazis and Antonios Rengakos (eds), *Euphrosyne: Studies in Ancient Epic and its Legacy in honor of Dimitris N. Maronitis*. Stuttgart: Franz Steiner, 308–38.

Renker, Stephan. 2020. *A Commentary on Quintus of Smyrna, Posthomerica 13*. Bamberg: University of Bamberg Press.

Richardson, Nicholas J. 1993. *The Iliad: a commentary. Volume VI: books 21–24*. Cambridge: Cambridge University Press.

Richardson, Scott. 1990. *The Homeric Narrator*. Nashville: Vanderbilt University Press.

Richlin, Amy. 1992. 'Reading Ovid's Rapes.' In: Amy Richlin (ed.), *Pornography and Representation in Greece and Rome*. New York: Oxford University Press, 158–79.

Richter, Daniel S. and William A. Johnson (eds). 2017. *The Oxford Handbook of the Second Sophistic*. Oxford: Oxford University Press.

Ridgway, Brunilde Sismondo. 1974. 'A Story of Five Amazons.' *AJA* 78, 1–17.

Rieu, Emile Victor. 2003. *Homer: The Iliad*. Revised and updated by Peter Jones with D. C. H. Rieu. Edited with an Introduction and Notes by Peter Jones. London: Penguin.

Robbins, Hollis. 2015. '*Django Unchained*: Repurposing Western Film Music.' *Safundi: The Journal of South African and American Studies* 16, 280–90.

Robertson, Martin. 1970. 'Ibycus: Polycrates, Troilus, Polyxena.' *BICS* 17, 11–15.

Robinson, Matthew. 1999. 'Salmacis and Hermaphroditus: When Two Become One (Ovid, Met. 4.285–388).' *CQ* 49.1, 212–23.

Roccos, Linda Jones. 1995. 'The Kanephoros and Her Festival Mantle in Greek Art.' *AJA* 99, 641–66.

Roettig, Katharina. 2010. *Die Träume des Xerxes: Zum Handeln der Götter bei Herodot*. Nordhausen: Traugott Bautz.

Roselli, David K. 2007. 'Gender, Class and Ideology: The Social Function of Virgin Sacrifice in Euripides' *Children of Herakles*.' *ClAnt* 26, 81–169.

Ross, William D. (ed.). 1959. *Aristotelis Ars rhetorica*. Oxford: Clarendon Press.

Roueché, Charlotte. 1993. *Performers and Partisans at Aphrodisias in the Roman and Late Roman Periods*. London: Society for the Promotion of Roman Studies.

Rousseau, Philippe. 2013. 'L'usage du laid: la scène de Thersite dans le Chant II de l'*Iliade*.' In: Philippe Rousseau and Rossella Saetta Cottone (eds), *Diego Lanza, lecteur des œuvres de l'Antiquité: poésie, philosophie, histoire de la philologie*. Villeneuve-d'Ascq: Presse universitaires du Septentrion, 23–50.

Rudhardt, Jean. ²1992 [1958]. *Notions fondamentales de la pensée religieuse et actes constitutifs du culte dans la Grèce classique*. Geneva: Librairie Droz.

Russell, Donald A. (ed.). 1964. *Longinus: On the Sublime. Edited with Introduction and Commentary*. Oxford: Clarendon Press.

Russell, Donald A. and Nigel G. Wilson (eds). 1981. *Menander Rhetor*. Oxford: Clarendon Press.

Russo, Joseph, Manuel Fernández-Galiano and Alfred Heubeck. 1992. *A Commentary on Homer's Odyssey*. Vol. 3: *Books XVII–XXIV*. Oxford: Clarendon Press.

Ryan, Marie-Laure. 2001. *Narrative as Virtual Reality: Immersion and Interactivity in Literature and Electronic Media*. Baltimore: Johns Hopkins University Press.

Sale, William. 1995. Review of Foley, John Miles. 1995. *The Singer of Tales in Performance: Voices in Performance and Text*. Bloomington: Indiana University Press. *BMCR* 95.12.20. https://bmcr.brynmawr.edu/1995/1995.12.20.

Salles, Ricardo (ed.). 2009. *God and Cosmos in Stoicism*. Oxford: Oxford University Press.

Sánchez Barragán, Ernesto Gabriel. 2001. 'Pentesilea: héroe y mujer. El rostro de la amazona arcaica.' *Nova Tellus* 19, 69–107.

Sanders, Ed and Matthew Johncock (eds). 2016. *Emotion and Persuasion in Classical Antiquity.* Stuttgart: Franz Steiner.

Santos, Maria Joã. 2008. 'The Triple Animal Sacrifice and the Religious Practice of the Indigenous Western Hispania.' *Acme* 103, 253–76.

Sarischoulis, Efstrations. 2016. 'Fate, Divine Will and Narrative Concept in the Homeric Epics.' *Mythos* 10, 81–105.

Satterfield, Brian. 2011. 'The Beginning of the *Iliad*: The "Contradictions" of the Proem and the Burial of Hektor.' *Mnemosyne* 64, 1–20.

Scafoglio, Giampiero. 2004a. 'Proclo e il ciclo epico.' *GFA* 7, 39–57.

Scafoglio, Giampiero. 2004b. 'La questione ciclica.' *RPh* 78, 289–310.

Scafoglio, Giampiero. 2007. 'Aristotele e il ciclo epico. Una nota a *Poet.* 1459a37–b7.' *RHT* 2, 287–98.

Scafoglio, Giampiero. 2014. 'Introduction: An Epic Cycle revival.' *Philologia Antiqua: An International Journal of Classics* 7, 11–15.

Scafoglio, Giampiero. 2016. 'Il riuso del testo omerico e del ciclo epico nel *Troiano* di Dione. Osservazioni metodologiche ed esemplificazione.' In: Eugenio Amato *et al.* (eds), *Dion de Pruse: l'homme, son œuvre et sa postérité. Actes du Colloque international de Nantes (21–23 mai 2015).* Hildesheim, Zurich and New York: Georg Olms, 435–63.

Scafoglio, Giampiero. 2017a. *Ajax: Un héros qui vient de loin.* Amsterdam: Adolf M. Hakkert.

Scafoglio, Giampiero. 2017b. Review of Davies (2016). *BMCR* 2017.04.43. https://bmcr.brynmawr.edu/2017/2017.04.43.

Schaumberg, Anton. 1910. *Bogen und Bogenschütze bei den Griechen mit besonderer Rücksicht auf die Denkmäler bis zum Ausgang des archaischen Stils.* Nürnberg: B. Hilz.

Scheer, Eduard (ed.). 1908. *Lycophronis Alexandra.* Vol. 2: *Tzetzae exegesis in Lycophronis Alexandra.* Berlin: Weidmann.

Scheijnen, Tine. 2015. '"Always the Foremost Argive Champion"? The Representation of Neoptolemus in Quintus of Smyrna's *Posthomerica*.' *Rosetta* 17.5, 93–110.

Scheijnen, Tine. 2016a. 'Facing Achilles in Two Lessons: Heroic characterization in Quintus of Smyrna, *Posthomerica* 1 and 2.' *LEC* 84, 81–104.

Scheijnen, Tine. 2016b. 'De kracht van het verleden. De invloed van de Ilias op de karakterisering van Achilles en Ajax in de Posthomerica van Quintus van Smyrna.' *Koninklijke Zuid-Nederlandse Maatschappij voor Taal- en Letterkunde en Geschiedenis* 69, 185–200.

Scheijnen, Tine. 2017. 'Ways to die for Warriors: Death Similes in Homer and Quintus of Smyrna.' *Hermes* 145, 2–24.

Scheijnen, Tine. 2018. *Quintus of Smyrna's* Posthomerica: *A Study of Heroic Characterization and Heroism.* Leiden and Boston: Brill.

Schein, Seth L. 1984. *The Mortal Hero: An Introduction to Homer's Iliad.* Berkeley, Los Angeles and London: University of California Press.

Schein, Seth L. (ed.). 2013. *Sophocles: Philoctetes.* Cambridge: Cambridge University Press.

Schenk, Peter. 1997. 'Handlungsstruktur und Komposition in den *Posthomerica* des Quintus Smyrnaeus.' *RhM* 140, 363–85.

Schlatter, Emrys. 2018. *Der Tod auf der Bühne: Jenseitsmächte in der antiken Tragödie.* Berlin and Boston: Walter de Gruyter.

Schmid, Wilhelm and Otto Stählin. ⁶1924 [1889]. *Geschichte der griechischen Literatur.* Vol. II.2. Munich: C. H. Beck.

Schmidt, Ernst Günther. 1999. 'Quintus von Smyrna – der schlechteste Dichter des Altertums?' *Phasis* 1, 139–50.

Schmiel, Robert. 1986. 'The Amazon Queen: Quintus of Smyrna, Book 1.' *Phoenix* 40, 185–94.

Schmitt Pantel, Pauline. 1985. 'Banquet et cité grecque: Quelques questions suscités par les recherches récentes.' *MEFRA* 97, 135–58.

Schmitz, Thomas A. 2005. 'Vorhersagen als narratives Mittel in der griechischen Epik von Homer bis Quintus von Smyrna.' In: Wolfram Hogrebe (ed.), *Mantik: Profile prognostischen Wissens in Wissenschaft und Kultur*. Würzburg: Königshausen and Neumann, 111–32.

Schmitz, Thomas A. 2007a [2002]. *Modern Literary Theory and Ancient Texts: An Introduction*. Translated by Thomas A. Schmitz. Malden, MA, Oxford and Victoria: Blackwell.

Schmitz, Thomas A. 2007b. 'The Use of Analepses and Prolepses in Quintus Smyrnaeus' *Posthomerica*.' In: Baumbach and Bär (2007a), 65–84.

Schoess, A. Sophie. Forthcoming. 'Objects of the Lusting Gaze: Viewing Women as Works of Art in Late Antique Poetry.' In: Verhelst and Scheijnen (forthcoming).

Schofield, Malcolm. 1986. '*Euboulia* in the *Iliad*.' *CQ* 36, 6–31.

Scholz, Peter. 2017. 'Gute und in jeder Hinsicht vortreffliche Männer: Überlegungen zur Funktion und Bedeutung der *paideia* für die städtischen Führungsschichten im kaiserzeitlichen Kleinasien.' In: Werner Eck and Matthäus Heil (eds), *Prosopographie des Römischen Kaiserreichs: Ertrag und Perspektiven*. Berlin and Boston: Walter de Gruyter, 155–85.

Schubert, Paul. 1996. 'Thersite et Penthésilée dans la *Suite d'Homère* de Quintus de Smyrne.' *Phoenix* 50: 111–17.

Schubert, Paul. 2007. 'From the Epics to the Second Sophistic, from Hecuba to Aethra, and finally from Troy to Athens: Defining the Position of Quintus Smyrnaeus in his *Posthomerica*.' In: Baumbach and Bär (2007a), 339–55.

Schürr, Diether. *Sine anno*. 'Mit Quintus durch Lykien I–VII (provisorisch).' https://www.academia.edu/36140998/Mit_Quintus_durch_Lykien_I-VII_provisorisch_.

Schwarz, Gerda. 2001. 'Der Tod und das Mädchen: Frühe Polyxena-Bilder.' *MDAI(A)* 116, 35–50.

Scodel, Ruth. 2008. *Epic Facework: Self-presentation and social interaction in Homer*. Swansea: Classical Press of Wales.

Seale, David. 1972. 'The Element of Surprise in Sophocles' *Philoctetes*.' *BICS* 19, 94–102.

Seale, David. 1982. *Vision and Stagecraft in Sophocles*. London: Croom Helm.

Segal, Charles. 1994. *Singers, Heroes, and Gods in the Odyssey*. Ithaca, NY and London: Cornell University Press.

Severyns, Albert. 1925. 'L'*Éthiopide* d'Arctinos et la question du Cycle Épique.' *RPh* 49, 153–83.

Severyns, Albert. 1926. 'La patrie de Penthésilée.' *Musée belge* 30, 5–16.

Severyns, Albert. 1928. *Le Cycle Épique dans l'école d'Aristarque*. Liège: Vaillant-Carmanne and Paris: Édouard Champion.

Severyns, Albert. 1963. *Recherches sur la Chrestomathie de Proclos*. Vol. 4: *La* Vita Homeri *et les sommaires du Cycle*. Paris: Les Belles Lettres.

Shaw, Pamela-Jane. 2001. 'Lords of Hellas, Old Men of the Sea: The Occasion of Simonides' Elegy on Plataea.' In: Deborah Boedeker and David Sider (eds), *The New Simonides: Contexts of Praise and Desire*. Oxford: Oxford University Press, 164–81.

Sherwin-White, Adrian Nicolas. 1966. *The Letters of Pliny: A Historical and Social Commentary*. Oxford: Clarendon Press.

Shorrock, Robert. 2001. *The Challenge of Epic: Allusive Engagement in the* Dionysiaca *of Nonnus*. Leiden, Boston and Cologne: Brill.

Shorrock, Robert. 2011. *The Myth of Paganism: Nonnus, Dionysus and the World of Late Antiquity*. London: Bristol Classical Press.

Sicking, Christiaan Marie Jan. 1993. 'Devices for Text Articulation in Lysias I and XII.' In: Christiaan Marie Jan Sicking and Johannes Max van Ophuijsen (eds), *Two Studies in Attic Particle Usage: Lysias and Plato*. Leiden, New York and Cologne: Brill, 3–66.

Sider, David (ed.). 2020. *Simonides: Epigrams and Elegies. Edited with Introduction, Translation, and Commentary*. Oxford: Oxford University Press.

Skiadas, Aristoxenos D. 1965. *Homer im Griechischen Epigramm*. Athens: Griechische Humanistische Gesellschaft, Zentrum für Klassische Studien.

Skinner, Marilyn B. 2005. *Sexuality in Greek and Roman Culture*. Malden MA, Oxford and Chichester: Wiley-Blackwell.

Skutsch, Otto (ed.). 1985. *The Annals of Quintus Ennius. Edited with Introduction and Commentary*. Oxford: Clarendon Press.

Snodgrass, Anthony M. 1967. *Arms and Armour of the Greeks*. Ithaca, NY and New York: Cornell University Press.

Snodgrass, Anthony M. 1998. *Homer and the Artists: Text and picture in early Greek art*. Cambridge: Cambridge University Press.

Sodano, Angelo Raffaele. 1947. 'Le fonti del mito di Achille nel terzo libro dei μεθ' Ὅμηρον di Quinto Smirneo.' *Antiquitas* 2, 53–78.

Sodano, Angelo Raffaele. 1951. 'Il mito di Pentesilea nel I libro dei μεθ' Ὅμηρον di Quinto Smirneo.' *AFLN* 1, 55–73.

Sommerstein, Alan H. (ed.). 1989. *Aeschylus: Eumenides*. Cambridge: Cambridge University Press.

Spanoudakis, Konstantinos (ed.). 2014. *Nonnus of Panopolis in Context: Poetry and Cultural Milieu in Late Antiquity with a Section on Nonnus and the Modern World*. Berlin and Boston: Walter de Gruyter.

Spawforth, A. J. S. 1989. 'Agonistic Festivals in Roman Greece.' In: Walker and Cameron (1989), 193–7.

Spinoula, Barbara. 2000. *Animal-Similes and Creativity in the* Posthomerica *of Quintus of Smyrna*. PhD thesis, University of St Andrews. https://research-repository.st-andrews.ac.uk/handle/10023/2780.

Squire, Michael. 2011. *The Iliad in a Nutshell: Visualizing Epic on the Tabulae Iliacae*. Oxford: Oxford University Press.

Squire, Michael and Jaś Elsner. 2016. 'Homer and the Ekphrasists: Text and Picture in the Elder Philostratus' "Scamander" (*Imagines* I.1).' In: John Bintliff and Keith Rutter (eds), *The Archaeology of Greece and Rome: Studies In Honour of Anthony Snodgrass*. Edinburgh: Edinburgh University Press, 57–99.

Stanford, William B. (ed.). ²1971 [1947, -48]. *The Odyssey of Homer. Edited with General and Grammatical Introduction, Commentary, and Indexes*. 2 vols. 2nd rev. ed. London: St Martin's Press.

Stanley, Keith. 1993. *The Shield of Homer: Narrative Structure in the Iliad*. Princeton: Princeton University Press.

Steiner, Deborah (ed.). 2010. *Homer: Odyssey Books XVII–XVIII*. Cambridge: Cambridge University Press.

Steiner, George. 1989. *Real Presences: Is There Anything in What We Say?* London: Faber.

Steiner, Peter. 2016. *Russian Formalism: A Metapoetics*. Ithaca, NY and London: Cornell University Press.

Stengel, Paul. 1910. *Opferbräuche der Griechen*. Leipzig and Berlin: B. G. Teubner.

Steuernagel, Dirk. 1998. *Menschenopfer und Mord am Altar: Griechische Mythen in etruskischen Gräbern*. Wiesbaden: Ludwig Reichert.

Stewart, Andrew. 1995. 'Imag(in)ing the Other: Amazons and Ethnicity in Fifth-Century Athens.' *Poetics Today* 16: 571–97.

Stivale, Charles J. 1999. 'Comment peut-on être deleuzien? Pursuing a Two-Fold Thought.' In: Ian Buchanan (ed.), *A Deleuzian Century?* Durham: Duke University Press, 135–44.

Stocking, Charles. 2011. 'Language about Achilles: Linguistic Frame Theory and the Formula in Homeric Poetics.' In: Timothy Pepper (ed.), *A Californian Hymn to Homer*. https://chs.harvard.edu/chapter/5-language-about-achilles-linguistic-frame-theory-and-the-formula-in-homeric-poetics-charles-stocking/.

Stoevesandt, Magdalene. 2004. *Feinde – Gegner – Opfer: Zur Darstellung der Troianer in den Kriegsszenen der Ilias*. Basel: Schwabe.

Strauss Clay, Jenny. 2003. *Hesiod's Cosmos*. Cambridge: Cambridge University Press.

Suerbaum, Werner. 1968. *Untersuchungen zur Selbstdarstellung älterer römischer Dichter: Livius Andronicus, Naevius, Ennius*. Hildesheim, Zurich and New York: Georg Olms.

Taplin, Oliver. 2007. *Pots and Plays: Interactions between Tragedy and Greek Vase-painting of the Fourth Century B.C.* Los Angeles: J. Paul Getty Museum.

TLG: *Thesaurus Linguae Graecae: A Digital Library of Greek Literature*. http://stephanus.tlg.uci.edu.

Toledano Vargas, Mario. 2002. 'El personaje de Neóptolemo en las "Posthoméricas" de Quinto de Esmirna.' *Epos* 17, 19–42.

Tomasso, Vincent. 2010. *'Cast in Later Grecian Mould': Quintus of Smyrna's Reception of Homer in the Posthomerica*. PhD thesis, Stanford University. http://purl.stanford.edu/hn098nn5393.

Tomasso, Vincent. 2019. Review of Hopkinson (2018). *NECJ* 47, 25–7.

Toth, Ida. 2018. 'Modern Encounters with Byzantine Texts and their Reading Publics.' In: Teresa Shawcross and Ida Toth (eds), *Reading in the Byzantine Empire and Beyond*. Cambridge: Cambridge University Press, 37–50.

Touchefeu-Meynier, Odette. 1994. 'Polyxene.' *LIMC* VII.1, 431–5.

Trypanis, Constantine A. 1970. 'The Word ἀνούατον.' *CPh* 65, 51.

Tsagalis, Christos. 2004. 'The Poetics of Sorrow: Thetis' Lament in *Iliad* 18, 52–64.' *QUCC* 76, 9–32.

Tsomis, Georgios P. 2007. 'Vorbild und *aemulatio*: An der Kreuzung von intertextuellen Bezügen in den Totenklagen dreier Frauen in Quintus Smyrnaeus' *Posthomerica*: Briseis, Tekmessa und Oinone.' In: Baumbach and Bär (2007a), 185–207.

Tsomis, Georgios P. 2018a. *Quintus Smyrnaeus. Kommentar zum siebten Buch der Posthomerica*. Stuttgart: Franz Steiner.

Tsomis, Georgios P. 2018b. *Quintus Smyrnaeus: Originalität und Rezeption im zehnten Buch der Posthomerica*. Trier: Wissenschaftlicher Verlag Trier.

Tuna-Norling, Yasemin. 2001. 'Polyxena bei Hektors Lösung: Zu einem attisch-rotfigurigen Krater aus Tekirdag (Bisanthe/Rhaidestos).' *AA* 2001, 27–44.

Tychsen, Thomas Christian (ed.). 1807. *Κοΐντου τὰ μεθ' Ὅμηρον. Quinti Smyrnaei Posthomericorum libri XIV. Nunc primum ad librorum manuscriptorum fidem et virorum doctorum coniecturas recensuit, restituit et supplevit Thom. Christ. Tychsen. Accesserunt observationes Chr. Gottl. Heynii*. Straßburg: Societas Bipontina.

Ullucci, Daniel C. 2012. *The Christian Rejection of Animal Sacrifice*. Oxford: Oxford University Press.

Usener, Knut. 2007. 'Wege und Formen, Umwege und Umformungen: Quintus Smyrnaeus und die Rezeption der Trojasage in Kaiserzeit und Spätantike.' In: Baumbach and Bär (2007a), 393–409.

van den Berg, Baukje. 2017. 'Eustathios on Homer's Narrative Art: the Homeric Gods and the Plot of the *Iliad*.' In: Filippomaria Pontani, Vassilis Katsaros and Vassilis Sarris (eds), *Reading Eustathios of Thessalonike*. Berlin and Boston: Walter de Gruyter, 129–48.

van der Valk, Marchinus. 1952. 'Ajax and Diomede in the *Iliad*.' *Mnemosyne* 5, 269–81.

van der Valk, Marchinus (ed.). 1971. *Eustathii archiepiscopi Thessalonicensis Commentarii ad Homeri Iliadem pertinentes*. Vol. 1. Leiden: Brill.

Van Hook, LaRue. 1916. 'On the Degradation in Meaning of Certain Greek Words.' *CJ* 11, 495–502.

van Minnen, Peter. 2016. 'Nonnus' Panopolis.' In: Accorinti (2016), 54–74.

Van Steenhuyse, Veerle. 2011. 'The Writing and Reading of Fan Fiction and Transformation Theory.' *CLCWeb: Comparative Literature and Culture* 13.4, 1–9.

van Straten, Folkert T. 1995. *Hierà kalá: Images of Animal Sacrifice in Archaic and Classical Greece.* Leiden, New York and Cologne: Brill.

van Thiel, Helmut. 1982. *Iliaden und Ilias.* Basel and Stuttgart: Schwabe.

van Thiel, Helmut (ed.). 1991. *Homeri Odyssea.* Hildesheim, Zurich and New York: Georg Olms.

Vanséveren, Sylvie. 1996. 'L'image du guerrier indo-européen: linguistique et idéologie.' *IF* 101, 89–93.

Vanséveren, Sylvie. 1998. 'Σχέτλιος dans l'épopée homérique.' In: Lambert Isebaert and René Lebrun (eds), *Quaestiones Homericae: Acta Colloquii Namurcensis 7–9/9/1995.* Louvain: Peeters, 253–73.

Verhelst, Berenice. 2017. *Direct Speech in Nonnus' Dionysiaca: Narrative and Rhetorical Functions of the Characters' 'Varied' and 'Many-Faceted' Words.* Leiden and Boston: Brill.

Verhelst, Berenice and Tine Scheijnen (eds). Forthcoming. *Latin and Greek Poetry of Late Antiquity: Form, Tradition and Context.* Cambridge: Cambridge University Press.

Verity, Anthony. 2011. *Homer: The Iliad. A new translation.* Oxford: Oxford University Press.

Vernant, Jean-Pierre. 1974. *Mythe et société en Grece ancienne.* Paris: François Maspero.

Vernant, Jean-Pierre. 1985. *Mythe et pensée chez les Grecs.* Paris: François Maspero.

Verweyen, Theodor and Günther Witting. 1979. *Die Parodie in der neueren deutschen Literatur: Eine systematische Einführung.* Darmstadt: Wissenschaftliche Buchgesellschaft.

Vian, Francis. 1954. 'Les comparaisons de Quintus de Smyrne.' *RPh* 28, 30–51, 235–43.

Vian, Francis. 1959a. *Recherches sur les Posthomerica de Quintus de Smyrne.* Paris: Klincksieck.

Vian, Francis. 1959b. *Histoire de la tradition manuscrite de Quintus de Smyrne.* Paris: Presses universitaires de France.

Vian, Francis (ed.). 1963, -66, -69. *Quintus de Smyrne: La Suite d'Homère.* 3 vols. Paris: Budé [incl. a French translation].

Vian, Francis. 1985. 'À propos de la "Vision de Dorothéos".' *ZPE* 60, 45–9.

Vian, Francis. 1988. 'La théomachie de Nonnos et ses antécédents.' *REG* 101, 275–92.

Vian, Francis. 1997. 'Ange Politien lecteur des poètes grecs.' In: Ugo Criscuolo and Riccardo Maisano (eds), *Synodia: Studia humanitatis Antonio Garzya.* Naples: M. D'Auria, 981–92.

Vian, Francis. ²2008 [2001]. 'Echoes and Imitations of Apollonius Rhodius in Late Greek Epic.' In: Papanghelis and Rengakos (²2008), 387–411.

Vian, Francis and Élie Battegay. 1984. *Lexique de Quintus de Smyrne.* Paris: Les Belles Lettres.

Vian, Francis and Émile Delage (eds). 1974, -80, -81. *Apollonios de Rhodes: Argonautiques.* Paris: Budé [incl. a French translation].

Volk, Katharina. 2009. *Manilius and his Intellectual Background.* Oxford: Oxford University Press.

von Albrecht, Michael. 1999. *Roman Epic: An Interpretative Introduction.* Leiden, Boston and Cologne: Leiden.

von Bothmer, Dietrich. 1957. *Amazons in Greek Art.* Oxford: Clarendon Press.

von der Mühll, Peter (ed.). 1962. *Homeri Odyssea.* Basel: Helbing and Lichtenhahn.

Wagner, Richard. 1894. *Mythographi Graeci.* Vol. 1: *Apollodori bibliotheca: Pediasimi libellus de duodecim Herculis laboribus.* Leipzig: B. G. Teubner.

Walker, Susan and Averil Cameron (eds). 1989. *The Greek Renaissance in the Roman Empire.* London: Institute of Classical Studies.

Wallies, Max (ed.). 1909. *Philoponi in Aristotelis analytica posteriora commentaria.* Berlin: Georg Reimer.

Walsh, Thomas R. 2005. *Fighting Words and Feuding Words: Anger and the Homeric Poems.* Lanham et al.: Rowman and Littlefield.

Warden, John. 1978. 'Another Would-Be Amazon: Propertius 4, 4, 71–2.' *Hermes* 106, 177–87.

Watkins, Calvert. 1995. *How to Kill a Dragon: Aspects of Indo-European Poetics.* Oxford: Oxford University Press.

Way, Arthur S. (ed.). 1913. *Quintus Smyrnaeus: The Fall of Troy. With an English Translation*. Cambridge, MA and London: Harvard University Press.

Webb, Ruth. 2009. *Ekphrasis, Imagination and Persuasion in Ancient Rhetorical Theory and Practice*. Farnham and Burlington: Ashgate.

Webb, Ruth. 2017. 'Schools and Paideia.' In: Richter and Johnson (2017), 139–53.

Weise, Stefan (ed.). 2019. *Der Arion des Lorenz Rhodomann: Ein altgriechisches Epyllion der Renaissance. Einleitung, Text, Übersetzung, Wortindex*. Stuttgart: Franz Steiner.

Wenglinsky, Maria Henderson. 1999. 'Response to Philosophical Criticism of the Portrayal of the Gods: The *Posthomerica* of Quintus of Smyrna.' *AncPhil* 19, 77–86.

Wenglinsky, Maria Henderson. 2002. *The Representation of the Divine in the* Posthomerica *of Quintus of Smyrna*. PhD thesis, Columbia University, New York.

West, David and Tony Woodman (eds). 1979. *Creative Imitation and Latin Literature*. Cambridge: Cambridge University Press.

West, Martin L. (ed.). 1966. *Hesiod: Theogony. Edited with Prolegomena and Commentary*. Oxford: Clarendon Press.

West, Martin L. (ed.). 1978. *Hesiod: Works and Days. Edited with Prolegomena and Commentary*. Oxford: Clarendon Press.

West, Martin L. (ed.). 1998, 2000. *Homerus: Ilias*. 2 vols. Munich and Leipzig: K. G. Saur.

West, Martin L. (ed.). 2003. *Greek Epic Fragments from the Seventh to the Fifth Centuries* BC. *Edited and translated*. Cambridge, MA and London: Harvard University Press.

West, Martin L. 2013. *The Epic Cycle: A Commentary on the Lost Troy Epics*. Oxford: Oxford University Press.

West, Martin L. (ed.). 2017. *Homerus: Odyssea*. Berlin and Boston: Walter de Gruyter.

Westra, Haijo Jan. 2010. 'Irony, Ambiguity, and Laughter in Greek and Latin Texts.' In: Hans-Georg Moeller and Günter Wohlfart (eds), *Laughter in Eastern and Western Philosophies: Proceedings of the Académie du Midi*. Freiburg im Breisgau: Alber, 140–51.

Whitman, Cedric H. 1958. *Homer and the Heroic Tradition*. Cambridge, MA: Harvard University Press.

Whitmarsh, Tim. 2013. *Beyond the Second Sophistic: Adventures in Greek Postclassicism*. Berkeley, Los Angeles and London: University of California Press.

Wifstrand, Albert. 1933. *Von Kallimachos zu Nonnos: Metrisch-stilistische Untersuchungen zur späteren griechischen Epik und zu verwandten Gedichtgattungen*. Lund: C. W. K. Gleerup.

Willcock, M. M. (ed.). 1978, -84. *Homer: Iliad. Edited with Introduction and Commentary*. 2 vols. London: St. Martin's Press.

Williams, Gordon W. 1968. *Tradition and Originality in Roman Poetry*. Oxford: Clarendon Press.

Willis, William Hailey. 1941. 'Athletic Contests in the Epic.' *TAPhA* 72, 392–417.

Wilson, Emily. 2018. *Homer: The Odyssey. Translated*. New York and London: W. W. Norton.

Wilson, John R. 1971. 'Τόλμα and the Meaning of τάλας.' *AJPh* 92, 292–300.

Wilson, Nigel G. (ed.). 2007. *Aristophanis fabulae*. Oxford: Clarendon Press.

Wilson, Nigel G. (ed.). 2015. *Herodoti Historiae*. 2 vols. Oxford: Clarendon Press.

Wolff, Gustav (ed.). 1856. *Porphyrii de philosophia ex oraculis haurienda librorum reliquiae*. Berlin: Julius Springer.

Wong, Edwin. 2002. 'The Harmony of Fixed Fate and Free Will in the *Iliad*.' *Antichthon* 36, 1–18.

Yamagata, Naoko. 1994. *Homeric Morality*. Leiden, New York and Cologne: Brill.

Zanusso, Valentina. 2013. 'Quinto e la tradizione letteraria: fonti e modelli.' In: Lelli *et al.* (2013), XXII–LVI.

Zanusso, Valentina. 2014. 'Quinto di Smirne e la tradizione mitica di argomento troiano: *imitatio, variatio*, allusività.' *Atlantide* 2, 1–17. http://atlantide.univ-nantes.fr/IMG/pdf/atlantide-2-zanusso.pdf.

Zecher, Jonathan L. 2015. *The Role of Death in the Ladder of Divine Ascent and the Greek Ascetic Tradition*. Oxford: Oxford University Press.

Zeitlin, Froma I. 1996. *Playing the Other: Gender and Society in Classical Greek Literature*. Chicago and London: University of Chicago Press.

Zerhoch, Sebastian. 2016. *Erinys in Epos, Tragödie und Kult: Fluchbegriff und personale Fluchmacht*. Berlin and Boston: Walter de Gruyter.

Zogg, Fabian. 2014. *Lust am Lesen: Literarische Anspielungen im* Frieden *des Aristophanes*. Munich: C. H. Beck.

Zuenelli, Simon. 2016. 'Die *Perioche* der *Dionysiaka* als Mittel der Selbstinszenierung.' *Mnemosyne* 69, 572–96.

Zuntz, Günther. 1992. *Αἰών in der Literatur der Kaiserzeit*. Vienna: Verlag der Osterreichischen Akademie der Wissenschaften.

Index of Passages Cited

Aeschylus
  Agamemnon
    232: 155
    236–7: 153
    1299: 236
  Choephoroe 88: 221
  Fr. 350 Radt: 47, 134
  Seven Against Thebes 423–56:
    132
  Suppliants
    636: 239
Aethiopis
  Arg. 4b West: 140
Alcaeus
  Fr. 354 Voigt: 140
Aphthonius
  22 Rabe: 53
Apollodorus
  2.4.11: 291
  Epitome 3.32: 52
Apollonius of Rhodes
  Argonautica
    1.461: 225
    1.996–7: 124
    1.1140: 124
    2.75: 222
    2.210: 224
    2.246: 239
    2.546: 225
    2.601: 238
    2.718: 220
    2.727–45: 131
    2.727–51: 29
    2.962–1001: 311

  2.1179–80: 219
  3.23: 225
  3.390: 224
  3.397: 225
  3.456: 225
  3.891: 239
  3.1161: 225
  3.1406: 225
  4.557–8: 124
  4.738: 199
  4.739: 197
  4.745–8: 199
  4.1411: 221
Aristophanes
  Clouds 407: 236
  Lysistrata 155–6: 67
Aristotle
  Poetics
    1455b24–1456a32: 249
    1459a30–b2: 306

Bacchylides
  Odes 17.87: 231

Callimachus
  Aitia Fr. 75.68–9:
    145
  In Dianam 53: 238
Catullus
  Carmina
    1.1–3: 332
    1.3–4: 333
    1.5–7: 333
    1.8–9: 333

Cicero
  De oratore 2.94: 338
Clement of Alexandria
  Stromateis 2.144.1:
    155
Cypria
  F 34 Bernabé = 27
    Davies: 151

Derveni Papyrus
  § 17 Kotwick = VI.7
    Kouremenos: 145
Dio Chrysostom
  36.14: 140
Diodorus Siculus
  4.15.1: 140

Ennius
  Annales 206–9 Skutsch:
    309n38
Euripides
  Alcestis 428: 236
  Andromache
    52–3: 134
    627–31: 67
    655: 134
  Hecuba
    94–5: 151
    387–8: 134
    398: 71
    524–6: 154
    534–41: 155
    567–70: 155
  Helen 1567: 236

Iphigeneia at Aulis
  10: 152
  88: 152
  352: 152
  765: 236
  1036–80ff.: 46
  1574: 155
  1596: 152
Iphigenia in Tauris 1165–7:
  147
Orestes 38: 144
Suppliants
  586: 236
  680: 236
  985–1072: 132
Eustathius
  ad Iliadem 2.220: 314
  in Iliadem B 450–2 (van der
    Valk 252.27–8): 122n20
  in Iliadem Ω 615–18 (van der
    Valk 1367.55–1368.28): 131

Hecataeus
  FGrH 1 F 300: 140
Hellanicus
  FGrH 4 F 149 = F 149
    Fowler: 144
Hermogenes
  15.18–17.1 Rabe: 53
Herodotus
  1.132: 150
  2.2.9–11: 237
  2.145: 140
  5.1.3: 125
  6.98.1: 125
  7.12.1: 125
  7.214.2: 125
  8.135: 237
Hesiod
  Fr. 33a.29 M–W:
    291
  Scutum 455–6: 124
  Theogony
    140: 231
    511: 224
    521: 224
    546: 224
    636: 235
    657: 224
    678: 234
    690: 235
    832: 244
  Works and Days
    48: 224
    153: 224

195: 231
654–9: 42
Homer
Iliad
  1.198–222: 188
  1.206: 215
  1.353: 227
  1.371: 225
  1.477: 227
  1.483: 257
  1.488–92: 258
  1.571: 226
  1.595–9: 267, 270
  1.599: 242
  2.35–40: 70
  2.38: 70
  2.72–5: 69
  2.117–18: 251
  2.211–77: 280–2
  2.271–278a: 282
  2.486: 365
  3.228: 227
  3.246: 220
  3.380–2: 89
  3.413: 199
  3.413–17: 206
  3.414: 197
  3.416–17: 201
  4.47: 218
  4.104: 292
  4.105–11: 292–3
  4.127–39: 124
  4.248: 236
  4.305: 227
  4.540: 221
  5.97: 295
  5.209: 295
  5.302: 242
  5.311–46: 89
  5.412: 216
  5.424: 227
  5.672: 215
  6.38–41: 283
  6.270: 145
  6.372: 227
  6.378: 227
  6.383: 227
  6.410–30: 91
  6.414–20: 51
  6.438–9: 129
  6.441–65: 251
  6.484: 277
  7.267: 234
  8.1: 227
  8.309–12: 124

  8.361: 202
  8.409: 226
  9.186ff.: 43
  9.432–9: 91
  9.443: 176
  9.447–95: 91
  9.557: 227
  9.560: 227
  9.628–33: 200
  10.102–76: 219
  10.163–7: 205
  10.169–71: 205
  10.553: 215
  11.1–2: 226
  11.69: 242
  11.783–4: 180
  12.60: 218
  12.68: 227
  13.48: 224
  13.383–91: 251–2
  13.554–5: 124
  14.54: 227
  14.132: 142
  14.231–360: 130
  14.319: 227
  14.323–4: 140
  15.27: 216
  15.99: 220
  15.122: 237
  15.310: 226
  15.458–65: 124
  15.521–3: 124
  16.46–7: 251
  16.97–100: 251–2
  16.313–25: 219
  16.320: 218
  16.431–8: 163
  16.431–61: 85
  16.433–4: 163
  16.439–49: 163
  16.599a–601: 274
  17.140–68: 207
  17.149–51: 207
  17.195–6: 46
  17.514: 111
  17.685: 217
  18.84–5: 46
  18.143: 226
  18.349: 224
  18.382: 227
  18.385: 227
  18.391: 226
  18.424: 227
  18.533–7: 169
  18.552: 242

Homer (*cont.*)
18.555: 242
19.1–2: 226–7
19.86–7: 107
19.238–9: 219
19.381–2: 34
19.416–17: 133
20.3–74: 270, 278–9
20.407–10: 51
20.419–54: 51
20.435: 111
21.34–135: 52
21.118–20: 51
21.136–8: 51
21.140–210: 52
21.211–382: 52
21.277–8: 134
21.362–5: 224–5
21.367: 226
21.385–513: 270, 278–9
21.551: 225
22.15: 216
22.37–76: 209
22.41: 202
22.78: 210
22.81–9: 209
22.91: 210
22.98–130: 82
22.139–44: 82
22.209–13: 162
22.335: 251
22.359–60: 133
22.367–75: 62
22.367–404: 91
22.370–1: 65
22.469: 236
22.477–514: 251
23.166–83: 150
23.184–91: 65
23.277: 227
23.570: 217
23.581: 217
23.586: 217
23.618–23: 41
23.773–84: 283
23.798–825: 40
23.886: 41
23.891: 41
24.32–54: 209, 217
24.55–63: 47, 211
24.60–1: 48
24.64–76: 210
24.77: 226
24.159: 226
24.255–9: 52

24.257: 52
24.409: 28
24.506: 218
24.524: 103, 224
24.527–33: 111
24.614–17: 131
24.696: 227
24.769: 227
26.121: 227
Odyssey
1.3: 324
1.8–9: 258
1.11–12: 305
1.11–21: 258
1.206–9: 258
1.329: 216
2.212–13: 257–8
2.420–1: 257, 259
2.429: 257
3.123–5: 258
3.164: 142
3.359–60: 142
3.447: 150
4.1–289: 68
4.103: 224
4.141–50: 258
4.272: 339
4.427: 225
4.572: 225
4.623: 227
4.721: 199
4.721–34: 206
4.727–4: 199
4.729: 197
5.4: 227
5.333: 227
6.13–14: 224
6.49: 227; 21.160: 227
6.57: 234
6.96–113: 256
6.121: 219
6.156: 221
7.169–75: 256
8.43–5: 45
8.62–4: 45
8.67: 44
8.73: 43–5
8.83: 44
8.105: 44
8.254: 44
8.261: 44
8.266: 44
8.266–366: 132
8.266–369: 271
8.286: 226

8.297: 226
8.326: 242
8.327: 226
8.367: 44
8.487–91: 45
8.489: 45
8.500: 44
8.514: 44
8.516: 44
8.521: 44
8.576: 219
9.3: 221
9.6: 221
9.156: 295
9.176: 219
9.291: 28
9.345–52: 205
9.355–6: 205
10.309: 225
10.360: 224
10.465: 221
11.38: 221
11.117: 218
11.121–31: 262
11.130: 151
11.212: 224
11.345: 216
11.558–60: 100
11.603: 227
12.375: 227
13.102–12: 131, 263
13.202: 219
13.378: 218
14.212–13: 234
14.392: 237
15.171: 227
15.363: 227
15.405: 241
16.356–7: 129
17.531: 220
18.158–303: 64
18.212–13: 65
18.250–80: 64
19.109–11: 219–20
19.357: 216
19.363–4: 219
19.367: 221
19.445: 237
19.491: 216
20.8: 221
20.134: 216
21.11: 295
21.59: 295
21.124: 295
21.149: 295

21.178–85: 295
21.243: 295
21.246: 295
21.264: 295
21.359: 295
21.362: 295
21.381: 216
21.393–5: 295
21.405–9: 295
21.419–23: 295
22.409–12: 272
23.52: 221
23.59: 272
23.248–53: 72
23.267–77: 262
23.295–309: 70
23.310–43: 43
23.331: 227
24.47–9: 134, 136
24.50–7: 135
24.60–2: 134
24.65–70: 150
24.85–92: 39
Homeric Hymn to Apollo
115–18: 131
Homeric Hymn to Ares
2: 231
Horace
Carmina 4.6.3–12: 134
Hyginus
Fabulae
107: 134
113: 134
Ibycus
F 258: 151
Iliou Persis
Arg. 10 Bernabé = Arg. 2a
West: 149
p. 89 Bernabé = Arg 4c
West: 151
Inscriptions
Roueche 52 I: 55
Roueche 52 II: 55
Isocrates
Evagoras
9.1: 42
9.8: 42
9.11: 42
Little Iliad
F 12 West: 149
Lucian
Lexiphanes 5.6:
242
True Histories 2.22:
42

Lycophron
Alexandra
273–4: 134
999–1001: 63
Meleager
Anthologia Palatina 4.1 = HE
3926–9: 332
Moschus
Europa 120–1: 239
Nonnus
Dionysiaca
19.74: 43
19.80–99: 43
19.81: 43
19.104–5: 43
19.106–15: 43
35.21–36: 64
37: 43
On Fractures
33.3: 238
Oppian
Halieutica
1.112: 241
2.348: 241
4.397: 241
4.500: 241
5.6: 224
[Orpheus]
Lithica 346–54 Halleux and
Schamp: 359n13
Ovid
Ars amatoria 3.21–2: 132
Epistulae ex Ponto 3.1.111: 132
Fasti 2.833–4: 155
Metamorphoses
1.2: 18
1.4: 18
12.580–609: 134
13.479–80: 155
13.501: 134
Tristia 5.14.38: 132
Palatine Anthology
4.1: 332
16.110.7–8: 243
16.150: 155
Passio Perpetuae et Felicitatis
20.4: 155
Pausanias
1.21.3: 131
Philostratus
Heroicus
47: 137
48.11–13: 137
50.1–3: 137
51.7: 136

51.8–11: 136
54.5–6: 136
Palatine Anthology 16.110.7–8:
243
Pindar
Isthmian Odes 8.56a–60: 134
Paeans 6.79–82: 134
Pythian Odes 3.101: 134
Plato
Phaedo 67d: 266
Republic 391b: 51
Pliny the Younger
Epistulae 4.11.9: 155
P. Lit. Lond.
6.22.43–4: 304
Plutarch
Moralia 674d–675d: 41
Against the Stoics on
Common Conceptions
1081B.4: 241
On the Failure of Oracles
418E5: 242
Parallel Lives
Cicero 32.7.2: 241
Polybius
6.53–4: 42
Porphyry
On the Cave of the Nymphs
9: 263–4
11: 264
18: 265
25: 265
POxy 3537r: 55
Proclus
Chrestomathy
176: 311
176–7: 313
178–80: 313
177–8: 317
180–1: 317
182–4: 318
Propertius
2.34.66: 310
3.115–16: 63
4.4.71–2: 312
Quintus of Smyrna
Posthomerica
1.1: 20
1.1–4: 303, 378
1.1–17: 77, 90, 276
1.3: 21
1.4–8: 21
1.9–10: 20, 52
1.12–14: 20
1.15: 21

Quintus of Smyrna (*cont.*)
1.18: 311
1.18–19: 21, 304
1.19: 77
1.20: 312
1.20–32: 77
1.21–32: 312
1.28–32: 144, 156
1.29: 32
1.37–40: 77
1.48–51: 77
1.53–83: 78
1.62: 277
1.62–83: 77
1.63–5: 219
1.63–73: 277
1.74–85: 78
1.75–85a: 277
1.89: 78
1.93–7: 85, 184
1.96–7: 33
1.98–117: 85
1.100–6: 179
1.100–13: 276
1.100–14: 33
1.103–4: 79
1.104: 32
1.124–31: 276
1.132: 276
1.133: 240
1.134: 32
1.134–7: 276
1.135: 221
1.138–56: 84
1.138–81: 86
1.153–6: 262
1.163–5: 80
1.172: 104
1.179–81: 132
1.182: 221
1.186–97: 78
1.198–204: 78, 277
1.205–10: 80
1.205–493: 312
1.208: 215
1.212–16: 80
1.220–5: 80
1.225–308: 81
1.227–9: 80
1.235: 218
1.250: 218
1.291–306: 131
1.299: 131
1.314–24: 80
1.316: 243

1.331–4: 179
1.345–9: 80
1.350–3: 80
1.360–1: 125
1.363–6: 83
1.373–5: 276
1.380: 128
1.383–93: 80
1.403–424: 79
1.406–35: 202, 208
1.425–35: 79
1.436–7: 208
1.440–6: 79
1.447–50: 79, 199
1.447–74: 197
1.451–5: 200–1
1.451–69: 199
1.452–4: 202
1.453: 221
1.454–60: 202
1.470–4: 198–9
1.475–6: 79, 198
1.476–93: 80
1.478: 236
1.487: 224
1.487–91: 262
1.533–7: 80
1.538–72: 312
1.538–656: 76
1.571–2: 81, 90
1.573–642: 312
1.575–91: 79
1.577: 179
1.578: 215
1.593: 231
1.594–629: 82
1.607–8: 216
1.625: 224
1.630–42: 85
1.643–53: 312
1.649–50: 179
1.657–74: 63–5, 208, 312
1.657–8: 83
1.659–68: 83
1.659–74: 253
1.661: 64
1.669–74: 82
1.673–4: 64
1.675–715: 253, 313
1.675–88: 120
1.689–90: 123
1.694: 215
1.699: 236
1.706: 225
1.716: 225

1.716–21: 313
1.718–21: 82, 281
1.719: 65, 68
1.720–1: 65, 379
1.722–40: 208–9, 313
1.722–66: 280–2
1.723: 128
1.725: 65
1.727: 65
1.735–6: 65
1.736–40: 212
1.740: 65, 234
1.741–3: 317
1.741–7: 205
1.741–65: 313
1.748–9: 282
1.750–4: 205
1.755–61: 65
1.757–65: 282
1.758–60: 379
1.766–81: 313, 317
1.767–74: 281
1.767–81: 178
1.775–81: 281
1.782–810: 84, 313
1.782ff.: 317–18
1.824: 236
1.825–7: 282
2.10–25: 79, 84–5
2.18–20: 276
2.45: 22
2.52: 22
2.68: 234
2.73: 23
2.85: 225
2.87: 216
2.97: 218
2.102–7: 85
2.112: 221
2.131–2: 85
2.138–9: 216
2.146–56: 85
2.148–55: 184
2.164–82: 86, 118, 120–1
2.172: 112
2.177: 215
2.183–201: 86
2.186: 226
2.193–214: 86
2.198–9: 262
2.207–11: 90
2.208: 217
2.243–4: 217
2.252: 255

2.256: 225
2.268: 217
2.289–90: 120, 122, 124
2.290: 125
2.292: 219
2.294: 218
2.298: 218
2.322: 218
2.341: 221
2.342: 217–18
2.345–52: 262
2.395–548: 76
2.410–29: 209
2.411–29: 207
2.412–51: 89
2.426–9: 212
2.430: 218
2.433: 181
2.437: 216
2.440: 220, 226
2.458: 87
2.459–60: 87
2.466–7: 87
2.470: 87
2.481: 128
2.481–9: 87
2.490–4: 22, 87
2.495–500: 87
2.502: 87
2.507–11: 88, 123
2.507–13: 113, 121–2
2.508: 227
2.511–16: 88
2.518–19: 88, 90
2.520–6: 88
2.530: 222
2.538–50: 88
2.549–69: 253
2.550–69: 88–9
2.570–82: 88
2.580–3 253
2.582–5: 89
2.593–627: 88–9
2.593–8: 113
2.601: 224
2.601–9: 82
2.605: 234
2.616–22: 89, 93
2.625–7: 89, 93
2.628–33: 88
2.634–9: 93
2.635–41: 88
2.640–3: 89
2.643: 217
2.643–50: 89

2.650–1: 89
2.650–2: 125
2.652: 89
2.656: 226
2.661–4: 114
3.1–9: 273
3.7–9: 102
3.8–9: 33
3.11–17: 166
3.26–62: 121
3.26–89: 76
3.26–90: 134
3.26–92: 118
3.42: 128
3.61–2: 222
3.62–82: 222
3.63–5: 262
3.68–82: 185
3.83–5: 222
3.96–127: 198, 209, 212
3.98–127: 47–9, 217
3.99–109: 212
3.104: 243
3.129–33: 198, 212
3.140–1: 222, 225
3.141–8: 90
3.142–5: 222
3.147–8: 222
3.149–63: 222
3.163: 225
3.167–75: 90
3.169–75: 222
3.171: 244
3.174–9: 274
3.178: 90
3.179–85: 253
3.180: 90
3.186–211: 253
3.196–9: 91
3.210–11: 91
3.399–400: 274
3.401–513: 91
3.435–58: 185
3.465–9: 91
3.470–9: 91
3.474: 233
3.494: 243
3.508–11: 262
3.514–25: 273
3.517: 217, 220
3.527: 224
3.533–40: 68
3.540–1: 162
3.544–81: 91
3.549: 220

3.582–94: 134
3.582–631: 92
3.594–6: 134
3.595–7: 135
3.608: 226
3.608–10: 93
3.611–26: 47–9
3.633–48: 93
3.665–6: 93
3.668–70: 93
3.678–82: 150
3.681–2: 158
3.694–718: 262
3.723–5: 92
3.738: 220
3.766–83: 135
3.767–8: 137
3.771–8: 156
3.771–80: 139
3.775–6: 219
3.787: 220
4.11–12: 125–6
4.17–18: 44
4.29: 236
4.49–55: 47–8
4.56–61: 114
4.80: 226
4.95–7: 118
4.110–17: 118
4.115: 227
4.117–70: 25
4.118–80: 40
4.119–21: 41
4.123–4: 46
4.124: 46
4.126: 46
4.128: 220
4.128–43: 46–9
4.129: 44
4.129–30: 43, 221
4.130–1: 53
4.131: 44
4.131–3: 48
4.141–3: 49
4.144–5: 44
4.144–61: 49–53
4.145: 45
4.147–8: 44
4.148–9: 53
4.149: 54
4.151: 51
4.154: 51
4.156–9: 51
4.161: 51
4.162: 45

Quintus of Smyrna (*cont.*)
4.163: 44
4.171–2: 43, 53
4.179–80: 53
4.199–214: 283
4.200–2: 125
4.283: 236
4.349–52: 262
4.381: 227
4.385: 217
4.401: 126
4.416–29: 60
4.418–35: 52
4.465–71: 40
4.479–99: 40
4.545: 236
4.545–88: 40
5.5: 241
5.45: 221
5.49–56: 101
5.69: 221
5.73–9: 45
5.98: 226
5.121: 227
5.125: 208
5.134–5: 223
5.157: 220
5.180–236: 207
5.181: 128
5.181–236: 185
5.188: 244
5.198–9: 181
5.292–305: 185
5.324: 225
5.330: 236
5.338: 223
5.338–40: 47–8, 223
5.355: 225
5.358: 28
5.360–4: 118
5.360–92: 28
5.361: 221
5.366: 224
5.372: 243
5.379: 225
5.385: 225
5.395–403: 130
5.422: 128
5.428–9a: 223
5.504: 239
5.571: 223
5.577–81: 103
5.579–82: 100
5.587: 220
5.594–7: 101–2
5.599–612: 273

5.610–14: 173
6.14: 221
6.33: 225
6.37: 231
6.38–41: 283
6.44–50: 238
6.68: 220
6.98: 258
6.100–1: 258
6.102–9: 103
6.107–11: 258
6.117–20: 118
6.149–52: 103
6.152: 218
6.198–293: 371
6.224: 235
6.234–55: 237
6.246–7: 240
6.309–14: 184
6.331–2: 104
6.384–9: 206
6.455–67: 130
6.461: 225
6.465: 29
6.470: 29
6.471: 29, 131
6.471–2: 130
6.476–82: 29
6.477–82: 131
6.482–3: 131
6.484–91: 29
6.491–3: 29
6.505: 220
6.540: 217
6.547: 238
7.16–95: 273
7.44–55: 103
7.71–84: 110
7.87: 112
7.134: 224
7.176–7: 258
7.184: 220
7.185–6: 185
7.394–417: 259
7.403–6: 186
7.422–30: 178
7.433–4: 185
7.445–51: 185
7.537–8: 185
7.543: 224
7.569–75: 240
7.619–727: 278
7.631–6: 278
7.665: 182
7.668–9: 182, 186
7.689–91: 185

7.715–22: 185
7.762: 253
8.5–12: 167
8.10–40: 121
8.11: 32
8.113: 220
8.125–6: 26
8.127: 125–6
8.133–220: 288
8.173–4: 225
8.205: 224
8.217–20: 170
8.340–3: 121
8.341–3: 123, 135
8.411: 221
8.458–60: 115
8.461–9: 45
8.464: 225
8.480: 26, 45
9.23: 22
9.25: 22
9.29: 220
9.58: 186
9.72: 224
9.80–2: 128
9.172–7: 240
9.107: 237
9.115–20: 107
9.189: 44
9.229: 128
9.246: 225
9.250: 182
9.262: 128
9.283: 24, 187
9.309–23: 121
9.326–9: 288–9
9.333–52: 259
9.333–546: 35
9.344: 231
9.353: 265
9.353–60: 260–1
9.353–75: 290
9.355–91: 60
9.355–97: 109
9.359–60: 265
9.364–6: 261
9.375–91: 290
9.378–91: 260–1
9.385: 241
9.385–7: 265
9.389–91: 265
9.392–7: 290–1
9.396–7: 293
9.398–403: 259
9.410–22: 259
9.414–22: 32

9.414–25: 105
9.425: 109
9.426: 259
9.426–7: 240
9.457: 221
9.460–88: 265
9.461–6: 259
9.491–511: 107–9
9.518–24: 106–7
9.537–9: 250
9.538–9: 265
10.12: 22
10.14: 22
10.16: 22
10.31–40: 23
10.43–4: 23
10.70: 236
10.97–109: 171
10.125–37: 131
10.147–66: 29
10.189: 226
10.209: 32
10.220: 32, 126
10.220–1: 125
10.221: 220
10.223–38: 254–5
10.265–7: 32
10.269: 32
10.298: 231
10.305: 239
10.307–27: 198, 204–5
10.328: 198
10.329–30: 32
10.329–31: 115
10.331: 32
10.332–3: 198
10.342: 32
10.343–60: 122
10.353: 220
10.369: 221
10.415–22: 265
10.420: 224
10.434: 265
10.437: 253
10.464–78: 132
10.479: 265
10.479–82: 132
10.484: 265
10.489: 231
11.20–6: 131
11.25: 221
11.59: 23
11.62–5: 240
11.67–72: 23
11.84: 253
11.91–8: 131

11.97–8: 126
11.159: 23
11.184–92: 165
11.191–200: 60
11.219–20: 187
11.234: 217
11.236: 23
11.240: 227
11.272–3: 112
11.272–5: 32
11.274–7: 100
11.298: 23
11.307–15: 253
11.382: 234
11.415–19: 132
11.445: 243
11.489: 253
11.499–501: 250
11.500–1: 253
11.501: 23
11.504–37: 189
11.784: 218
12.1–159: 280
12.32–8: 148
12.35: 158
12.70–2: 187
12.77–8: 187
12.84–6: 289
12.84–103: 188
12.154: 215
12.160–216: 118, 130
12.160–218a: 278
12.162–89a: 279
12.184–5: 130
12.185–9: 130
12.189b–218a: 279
12.194–5: 31
12.212: 236
12.218b–585: 280
12.254–5: 128
12.264–73: 188
12.275: 182
12.279–80: 188
12.301–2: 188
12.306–11: 35
12.306–13: 300, 328–9
12.310: 379
12.313: 35
12.319: 217
12.379–80: 158
12.379–84: 148
12.382: 158
12.383: 157
12.386: 215
12.395–415: 118
12.404: 237

12.417: 239
12.427–32: 262
12.436–43: 252–3
12.443: 255
12.447: 215
12.447–8: 126
12.447–80: 118
12.449–51: 126
12.500–9: 146, 156
12.519–24: 170
12.539–51: 198, 209
12.543: 210
12.552–61: 198, 210
12.559–60: 206
12.569: 239
13.14–18: 209
13.15: 211
13.19–20: 210
13.24–5: 225
13.27: 44
13.54–9: 339
13.124–32: 168
13.143: 222
13.147: 239
13.187: 129
13.181–207: 178
13.234–5: 125
13.315: 220
13.319: 221
13.326–32: 118
13.374: 210
13.374–84: 209
13.385–402: 66–8
13.403–415: 69
13.420: 220
13.445: 137
13.472: 128
13.473–7: 32
13.477: 221
13.503: 218
13.525: 218
13.544: 221
13.544–51: 126–7
13.551: 137
13.552–3: 126
13.556–7: 126
13.558–60: 112
13.560–1: 126
14.26: 239
14.41–2: 225
14.47: 225
14.47–57: 132
14.62: 24
14.97–100: 116
14.100: 114
14.101–10: 141, 156

Quintus of Smyrna (*cont.*)
  14.115: 252
  14.117: 252
  14.121–42: 25, 50
  14.124: 221
  14.131: 51
  14.135: 51
  14.149–79: 70–1
  14.179–227: 34
  14.180: 217
  14.183: 73
  14.187–91: 189
  14.191: 220
  14.201–3: 34
  14.201–6: 107
  14.204: 34
  14.209: 34
  14.209–22: 151
  14.210–16: 379
  14.214: 153
  14.216–17: 158
  14.241: 153
  14.246–52: 191
  14.254–6: 191
  14.257–62: 152
  14.257–370: 71
  14.267: 221
  14.267–9: 152–3
  14.272–303: 153
  14.290: 240
  14.305–17: 153
  14.308–12: 191
  14.319: 225
  14.331–5: 143, 156
  14.332: 141
  14.416: 234
  14.419–42: 224
  14.419–631: 272
  14.421: 215
  14.427–50: 275
  14.474–7: 261
  14.483: 234
  14.487–658: 261
  14.517: 235
  14.534: 234
  14.557: 221
  14.582–7: 132
  14.627–8: 128
  14.628–31: 379
  14.630–1: 305
  14.632–55: 272, 305
  14.646–55: 127
  14.655–8: 305
  14.657: 127
  14.657–8: 259, 379

Rhodoman, Lorenz
  39: 336
  42–7: 335
  48–57: 323–5
  111–15: 325
  122–3: 326
  124–30: 327
  130–7: 328–9, 332
  138–43: 330
  144–51: 332
  155–6: 321
  162–94: 333
  170–1: 330
  175–9: 331
  179–81: 331
  183–4: 331
  192–4: 333
  195–7: 333
  198–237: 333
  206: 333
  209–14: 334
  215: 334–5
  216–23: 334
  223: 335
  224: 334
  239–44: 331
  1604 edition of *Posthomerica*
    103–37: 323
    192b–237: 323
Scholia
  Schol. ATV on *Il.* 24.257: 52
  Schol. in *Carm. Il.* 3.23, p. 211, 8–11: 357n10.
  Schol. in *Carm. Il.* 241b, pp. 195, 12–17 – 196, 15–16: 366n32
  Schol. in *Carm. Il.* 3.284, p. 223, 18–224, 3: 367n33.
  Schol. in *Carm. Il.* 3.284: 361n17
  Schol. in *Carm. Il.* p. 101, 1–3: 367n35
  Schol. Eur. *Or.* 1287 = fr. 106 F: 67
  Schol. *Od.* 6.121a–d Pontani: 220
  Schol. T *ad Il.* 24.804a: 302–3
Sibylline Oracles
  11.161–89: 240
  11.290–1: 240
Simonides
  Fr. 557: 151

Sophocles
  Antigone
    47: 197
    1004: 236
  Philoctetes 334–6: 134
  Fr. 522–8 Radt: 151
Statius
  Thebais
    12.777–809: 132
    12.816–17: 326
Stesichorus
  S 135–6 Davies = F 118 Finglass: 151
Suetonius
  Caesar 84: 42
  Vespasianus 19: 42
Theocritus
  Idylls
    17.53: 231
    24.48: 239
Theophrastus
  Fr. 584A Fortenbaugh: 142
Triphiodorus
  The Sack of Troy 39: 63
Tzetzes, John
  Carmina Iliaca
    3.6–16: 356n9
    3.20–4: 356n9
    3.209–11: 353n4
    3.280–6: 360n14
    3.290: 360n14
    3.518–22: 358n11
    3.580–4: 358n12
    3.700–6: 353n5
  Chiliads
    2 hist. 36.491–506: 369n39
    2 hist. 36.507–10: 372n48
  Exegesis of the Iliad 40.1–5: 365n29
  Posthomerica
    435–6: 135
    452–8: 135
Virgil
  Aeneid
    1.278–9: 18
    1.474–8: 52
    2.116–19: 149
    2.171–5: 147
    3.518–22: 358n11
    3.580–4: 358n12
    6.57–8: 134
    11.197–9: 151
    11.659–60: 312

General Index

Achilleid, 76
Achilles, 18–21, 25, 32–5, 43–54, 59, 101, 103, 111,
    120, 128, 162, 211–12, 258
  armour of, 28, 90, 137, 220, 251
  death of, 19, 23, 89–93, 133–4, 166, 217, 222–3,
    262, 274
  deification of, 139–40, 143, 157, 190–2
  funeral of, 38–9, 125, 135–6, 150, 158
  Memnon and, 86–9, 206–7, 234
  Penthesileia and, 1, 61–6, 75–7, 79–84, 94, 179,
    276, 311–17
  sacrifice and, 151–3, 155, 157
  speeches of, 176–8, 180–6, 189
  Thersites and, 205, 208–9, 280–2, 313, 317
  wrath of, 151, 188, 200, 258, 306, 379
  see also ecphrasis; shield of Achilles
Aelius Herodian, 234
aemulatio see imitation
Aeneas, 18, 23–4, 31, 37, 73, 118, 132, 165, 238, 242,
    309, 334
Aeolia, 261
Aeschylus, 47
  Agamemnon, 152–5, 236
  Philoctetes, 35
  Seven Against Thebes, 132
  Suppliants, 239
Aesepus, 89, 292
Aethiopis, 39, 63, 134, 140, 144, 302–5, 308, 311–18
Agamemnon, 39–41, 69–70, 99, 107–9, 134, 153,
    155, 177, 183–4, 223, 280
agency, 19, 27, 37, 68, 101–2, 111–12
agonistic culture, 55–6
agriculture, 17
aiōn, 31–2; *see also* temporality

Aisa see Fates; *Kēres*; *Moirai*
Ajax (Locrian or lesser), 29, 40, 60, 224, 234, 282–3
Ajax (Telamonian or greater), 23, 81, 177–8, 200,
    207, 244
  death of, 100, 103–6
  heroic code of, 181–2, 184–5
  madness of, 28, 33, 102
Alcaeus, 140
Alexander the Great, 18, 37
Alexandria, 55
  library of, 232
Alexandrian poetry, 20, 300–1, 304
Alexandrian scholarship, 301, 307–10, 315, 318
Alkathoos, 122
allusion, 71, 100, 153, 217, 221, 226, 228, 275,
    304, 324; *see also* intertextuality
alter Homerus, 228, 301, 308–10, 326, 345
alternative endings, 302–3
Amazons, 1, 80–1, 218, 262, 302–4, 311, 353, 355,
    357, 363; *see also* Hippolyta; Penthesileia
  origins of, 312
ambivalence, 267, 277, 280
Andromache, 33, 51, 79, 85, 91, 179, 236, 251, 276–7
anger, 51, 67, 99–101, 105, 107–9, 129, 218, 259; *see also*
    Achilles, wrath of; Poseidon, wrath of
Antenor, 22–3
Antilochus, 40, 90, 102, 217–20, 255, 313
Antiphus, 26
Aphrodisias, 55
Aphrodite, 44, 129, 132, 233
  anger with Helen, 197, 199, 201, 206
  intervention in relationship of Helen and
    Menelaus, 66–71
  Penthesileia and, 62, 83, 88, 92

Aphthonius, 53
Apollo, 43, 47–9, 125, 210–11, 257, 291
    Achilles and, 33, 121, 133–4, 162, 198, 209, 212,
        216–17, 222, 262
    temple of Apollo Thymbraeus, 52
Apollonius
    Homeric Lexicon, 233
Apollonius Dyscolus, 235
Apollonius of Rhodes, 29, 58, 125, 143, 311
    Argonautica, 38, 124, 128–9, 131–2, 195–6, 219–20,
        231–3, 238
archery, 41, 217, 287–9, 292, 294, 297
archive (Derridean concept), 374, 377–9, 385
'archontic' literature, 375, 377–82, 384–5
Ares, 86, 120–3, 231, 236–7, 253, 304, 311–12, 314,
        316–17
aretē see virtue
Arete (queen of Scheria), 215
Argus, 31
Argyrouli, Eirini, 11
Aristarchus, 70, 73, 315–16
aristeia, 23, 25, 31, 256, 288, 304, 312–13
Aristophanes, 12, 70
    Clouds, 236
    Lysistrata, 67
Aristotle, 26
    Poetics, 249, 300–1, 306–7
Artemis, 63, 65, 83, 103, 147, 155, 329
Asteropaeus, 40, 51–2
atē, 104, 107
Athena, 132, 147, 215, 224, 237, 251–2
    intervention of, 28, 35–6, 92, 99, 121, 126, 188,
        259, 292
Athenaeus, 232–3
athletic games, 42–3, 55
audience reaction, 43, 53–4
    intra- and extradiegetic audiences, 194, 196
    to the Posthomerica, 232–3
Auerbach, Erich, 249, 254
authorial voice, 103, 126–9, 137, 352

Bacchylides, 231
banquets, 45–50, 85, 142–3, 168, 267
Barbaresco, Katia, 10
bards, 44, 46; see also Demodocus; Nestor
Bär, Silvio, 4–5, 8, 20, 134, 145, 167, 195, 299, 381
Bärtschi, Arnold, 6, 11
battlefield speeches, 176, 180, 186, 206, 209
Baumbach, Manuel, 4, 299
beauty
    of Helen, 67–8
    of Penthesileia, 62–5, 68, 77–9, 83–4, 92, 208,
        304–5, 312–17
bees, 79, 337–40
Bessarion, Basilius, 3, 327, 345

birds, 89, 121, 236, 277
blindness, 78, 171–4, 277
body (depictions of), 86, 89–92, 94
bows, 30, 254–5, 287–8, 290–7, 358
Bremmer, Jan N. 10, 12
brightness, 77–8, 80, 86
Briseis, 34, 58, 91, 278, 379
burial, 27, 84, 89, 92, 313, 315, 317–18
Byzantine writers, 3, 11, 300, 302, 351–2, 359,
        367–8

Cadau, Cosetta, 7
Calchas, 23–4, 183, 187, 288–9
Callimachus, 230
    Aitia, 24, 145
    Hymn to Artemis, 238
Callinus, 235
Calliope, 93–4
Calvin, John, 322
Calypso, 18, 58
Capaneus, 132
Carvounis, Katerina, 7, 10, 12, 142, 189, 279
Cassandra, 60, 198, 203–5, 209–10, 224, 236, 239
Catholicism, 338, 340
Catullus, 332–3
causality, 19, 99–100
caves, 25, 29, 126, 130–1, 240, 259–61, 263–5, 290–1
chance see fate
Cheiron, 25, 46, 49
Christianity, 37, 59, 338
Chryseis, 248, 251, 257
Chthonic divinities, 141
Cicero, 241
    De oratore, 338
Circe, 58, 197, 199
Claudian
    Gigantomachia, 55
Cleodorus, 125, 254
Cleomenes, 147
closure, narrative, 24, 27, 58, 61–2, 66, 73–4
Colluthus, 38, 59–60, 310
    Rapture of Helen, 7
Commodus, 240
Constantinople, 361
Cornelius Nepos, 332
counterfactuals, 28, 35–6, 58
Crete, 294, 369
Csikszentmihalyi, Mihaly, 374, 382–3, 385, see also
        flow (state of)
Cyclops, 26, 28, 125, 205, 238
Cycnus, 50–1
Cypria, 50–2, 63, 67, 148, 151, 306, 308

Dares Phrygius, 137, 193, 324
Deidamia, 183, 220, 316

Deiphobus, 66, 122, 128, 182, 183, 187, 237
de Jong, Irene, 161
delay, narrative, 18–23, 27, 29–30, 65–6, 84, 248–9, 255–6; *see also* excursuses
Deleuze, Gilles, 374–5, 379–81, 385
Delphic oracle, 149
Demodocus, 43–6
Derecho, Abigail, 377–9, 381
derision, 267–8, 270–5, 278–80, 282–5
Derrida, Jacques, 12, 374–5, 377, 379–81, 385
Derveni Papyrus, 145
destiny *see* fate; Fates
determinism, 36, 164
    double determinism, 99, 105, 108, 117
Dictys of Crete, 137, 193, 351, 362, 364–5
didactic poetry, 240, 323
Dido, 18, 58
diēgēsis, 28
Dio Chrysostom, 5, 35, 136
Diodorus Siculus, 140, 323
Diomedes, 23, 39, 177–9, 183, 205, 242
    journeys with Odysseus, 35, 105–6, 240, 256–9, 287–90
    quarrel with Achilles, 281, 313, 317
Dionysus, 43, 57
divine councils, 118, 120, 129
divine revelation, 1
Donner, Johann Jacob Christian, 6
Dorotheus (Quintus of Smyrna's son), 1–2
dreams, 70, 73, 188, 190, 276, 310, 335
Duckworth, George, 247

ecphrasis, 27–9, 76, 78, 243, 254
    mountain of virtue, 30, 101, 117
    shield of Achilles, 30, 38, 107, 169
    shield of Eurypylus, 31, 235, 237, 240, 371
education, 331, 340
    of Quintus' audience, 233
Eetion, 50–1
Elektra, 126, 137
emotion, 34–7, 267–9, 272–8, 284, 286
Empedocles, 149, 242
encomium *see* praise
endings (literary), 24, 70, 72–3, 302–3
Ennius, 309–10
Enyo, 83, 88, 169, 252
Eos, 85, 87–9, 93, 120, 122, 124–5, 130, 226–7
Epeius, 40, 262
Epic Cycle, 11–12, 90, 133, 157, 281–2, 298–302, 305–11, 314–18
epic poetry, 7, 54, 161, 169, 367
    modern adaptations of, 59
Epicureanism, 157
epitaphs, 29–30

epithets, 11, 194–7, 270, 304, 381
    Homeric, 214–25
    non-Homeric, 225–7
epyllia, 7, 38, 59, 322
Erechtheus, 43
Erinyes, 32, 77, 107, 144–5, 156–7; *see also* Eumenides; Furies
Eris, 25, 33, 83, 86–7, 127, 169
erōs, 58–9, 62, 65–6, 68, 71, 74, 208
eroticism, 10, 57–62, 65, 73–4, 334
    anti-eroticism, 70–1
Ethiopia, 88–9, 253, 311
Eumenides, 145; *see also* Erinyes; Furies
Euripides, 35, 153
    Alcestis, 236
    Andromache, 67, 134
    Hecuba, 71, 134, 151, 154–5
    Helen, 236
    Iphigeneia at Aulis, 46, 152, 155, 236
    Orestes, 144
    Suppliants, 132, 236
    Trojan Women, 23
Eurycleia, 216, 219, 272
Eurypylus, 26, 30, 168, 170, 183–4, 190, 206, 253, 278, 358
    aristeia of, 256, 288
    see also ecphrasis; shield of Eurypylus
Eustathius, 64, 122, 314–16, 368
Evadne, 132
excursuses, 130–1, 249, 253, 259, 308

fan fiction, 12, 373–4, 376–9, 382–5
fate, 10–11, 32, 37, 97, 99–102, 104–5, 110–17, 119, 172, 182
    endurance and, 98–103, 106, 108–9
    on the battlefield, 167, 169, 173–4, 197, 272
    relationship with gods, 133, 136
Fates, 36, 88, 108, 161–74; *see also Kēres; Moirai*
Ferreccio, Alessia, 11, 124
film soundtracks, 229, 244
flow, state of, 382–5
focalisation, 161
    embedded focalisation, 169–72, 174, 209–10
foreshadowing, 143, 167, 247–8, 254–5, 381
Foucault, Michel, 380
frustration, 61–2, 73–4, 77
funeral games, 23, 25, 33, 38–40, 42, 236, 262, 273, 278, 282

García Romero, Francisco Antonio, 164
Gärtner, Thomas, 11
Gärtner, Ursula, 6, 98–102, 104–9, 112–13, 115–17, 164
gender, 17, 76, 197

Germany, 322–3, 334, 336–7, 340
Gesner, Conrad, 3
ghosts, 34, 39, 73, 100, 107, 134, 151, 192
Giants, 88, 92, 132
gifts, 45–6, 53, 140, 205, 220, 291
Glaucus, 34, 125, 207, 274
glory, 18, 25, 32, 34, 191, 365; see also kleos
Goldhill, Simon, 10–13, 59
Greensmith, Emma, 6–8, 10–12, 20, 26, 30, 230
grief, 33–4, 65, 100–6, 110, 274, 276–8; see also
    burial; mourning

hapax legomena, 4, 41, 230–4, 237, 243
Hecataeus, 140
Hector, 79, 82, 133, 162, 207, 209–12, 177, 254, 381
    death of, 20–2, 27, 47, 65, 91, 217–18, 251–2, 325
Hecuba, 71, 153–4, 209–12, 240, 335, 342
Helen, 22, 24, 59, 73, 122, 132, 201, 218, 225, 335
    Menelaus and, 61, 66–71
Helenos, 122
Hellanicus, 144, 356–7
Hephaestus, 30, 131–2, 216, 220, 224–6, 267, 270–1
Hera, 47–9, 130, 163–4, 177, 198, 211–12, 216–17, 267
Heracles, 139–40, 216, 237, 239, 324, 368–72
    bow of, 30, 287–8, 290–1, 293, 297
    labours of, 31, 369, 371–2
    shield of, 30–1, 235
Hermione, 59
heroic characterisation, 175, 182, 193
Herodotus, 125, 140, 150, 237
heroism, 5, 20, 23, 34, 36, 98, 103, 175, 184, 213;
    see also speech, heroic
Hesiod, 6, 12, 35, 42, 55–6, 118, 224, 230, 275, 300–1
    Theogony, 17, 224, 231, 234–5, 244
    Works and Days, 17, 42, 195, 224, 231
    see also pseudo-Hesiod
Hesione, 324
Hippolyta, 77, 312, 356
Homer see epithets; imitation, literary; intertextuality;
    oral tradition; revisionism
Homeric Hymns
    Homeric Hymn to Ares, 231
    Homeric Hymn to Hermes, 232
Homeric tradition, 11, 269, 284
honey, 131, 338–40
honour, 30, 42, 135, 183, 316, 354
hope, 77–9, 84, 167, 276–7
horses, 20–1, 53, 60, 133, 137, 150, 236, 240, 360–1
hubris, 85, 272–3
Hunter, Richard, 7
hunting, 28, 30, 63, 83, 222, 290, 293, 356
Hyacinth, 43
Hydra, 290, 369
Hypnos, 130
Hypsipyle, 129

Ibycus, 67, 151
Idomeneus, 40, 223
Iliou Persis, 149, 151, 308
imitation, literary, 11–13, 318, 376–7
    Homeric, 3, 97, 209, 214, 219, 228, 308–10
    relationship between Posthomerica and Epic
        Cycle, 298–301, 304, 311
immortality, 18, 25, 43, 89
'in-between' space, 19, 21, 35, 62
innovation (literary), 13, 196, 213, 223, 224, 268,
    297, 313
intertextuality, 9, 30, 195, 233–4, 282, 299, 378
    polychronic, 230–2, 242, 244
    polyphonic, 230
Iphigeneia, 46, 148, 151–5, 157; see also sacrifice,
    human
Iris, 219, 226, 261
Isocrates, 42, 338
Italy, 3, 18
Ithaca, 18, 131, 224, 251, 257, 262, 295

James, Alan W., 4, 65, 117, 142, 145, 241, 299
Jason, 58, 73
joy, 54, 220–1, 267–79, 283–5; see also laughter;
    Schadenfreude
Julius Caesar, 18–19, 42

Kēres, 32, 88, 97, 104, 113, 119, 121, 166–8; see also
    Fates; Moirai
Keydell, Rudolf, 4
kleos, 18, 22–3, 26–7, 30, 35, 37, 58, 93, 176,
Köchly, Hermann, 3, 118–19, 298
Kom el-Dikka auditorium, 55
Kristeva, Julia, 378

Lacan, Jacques, 380
lament see mourning
landscape, 49, 77
Laodike, 126–7, 137
Laokoon, 118, 126, 146, 206, 237
Laomedon, 84, 218, 313
Lascaris, Constantine, 230
laughter, 242, 267–73, 275, 277–9, 284, 285
Lee, Kevin, 4, 241
Lemnos, 35, 105, 240, 259–60, 287–90
Leone, P. A. M., 370
Lesbos, 63, 317
Leuke, 135, 140
lions, 21, 63, 83, 185, 222, 240, 244,
    369
Little Iliad, 67, 122, 149, 306, 308
Livius Andronicus, 309
locusts, 86, 262
Lovato, Valeria F., 11–12
Lucan, 18–19, 110

Lucian, 233
  Dialogues of the Gods, 136
  Lexiphanes, 242
  True Histories, 42
  Zeus catechised, 136
lusis, 11, 65, 248, 253–5, 262–3
  Aristotelian, 249–51
  Platonic, 265–6
Luther, Martin, 321–3; *see also* Reformation
Lycaon, 25, 41, 51–2
Lycia, 29, 125, 131, 138–9, 157, 163
Lycophron, 63–4
lyre, 43–4, 47, 49, 211, 217
Lysias, 356–7

Machaon, 29, 130, 238, 357–9, 263
Maciver, Calum A., 5, 10–11, 20, 30, 35–6, 164, 299
madness, 28, 102, 104, 129–30
Maly-Preuss, Jordan, 11–12
Maravela, Anastasia, 195, 213
Marcus Aurelius, 240
Mark Antony, 240
marriage, 64–5, 71, 73; *see also* wedding of
  Peleus and Thetis
Martin, Richard, 230
Martindale, Charles, 61, 381
marvels, 131, 265
masculinity, 27, 37, 64–5, 199
Medea, 58, 197, 199, 239
medical texts, 237
Medusa, 31
Meleager, 19, 332–3
  Garland, 322–3
Memnon, 22, 33, 124–5, 184, 206–7, 218
  encounter with Nestor, 359–61, 363, 366
  fight with Achilles, 50–1, 75–6, 84–94, 120
memory, 20–1, 27, 71–2
Menander Rhetor, 53
Menelaus, 61, 66–71, 73, 132, 209–10, 223, 343
Mestor, 52
Middleton, Fran, 11
Miguélez-Cavero, Laura, 7, 63
Milton, John, 19
Moirai, 32, 97, 104–7, 111–12, 119, 125–6, 172;
  see also Fates; *Kēres*
Morales, Helen, 59
morality, 35–6, 60, 98–9, 101, 132, 198–9, 333
Moschus, 239–40
mourning, 27, 76, 88, 91–3, 189, 262
Musaeus, 38, 59–60
Muses, 2, 20–1, 25, 35, 49, 93, 134–6, 300–1, 308,
  326–33
music, 43–4, 49, 55, 229
Myrmidons, 120, 122, 183, 186
mythic tradition, 26, 62, 287

Naevius, 309
Naiden, Fred, 138, 146
narrative structure, 4, 11, 13, 306–7
narratology, 11, 18–19, 161, 170–1, 173–4, 247, 263
  diachronic, 5–6, 8–9, 38, 195, 213
  see also focalisation
narrators
  primary, 98–100, 102–3, 106, 166, 171–4
  secondary, 99, 107, 169–70
Neander, Michael, 321–3, 330–2, 336–7, 340, 346
necrophilia, 59, 62, 64–6, 314, 316
Neoplatonism, 11, 266
Neoptolemus, 22–3, 34, 73, 121, 170, 175–9, 181–93,
  278, 288–9
  Polyxena and, 151, 154–5
Neopythagoreanism, 11
Nereids, 45, 47–8, 87, 92, 134–6, 221, 223
Nestor, 25–6, 33, 134–5, 177, 183, 188–90, 205,
  217–19, 273
  encounter with Memnon, 359–61, 363, 366
  on grief, 102–3, 105–15
  poetic performance, 40–1, 43–54, 56
Nicolaus of Myra, 53
Noack, Ferdinand, 298–9
Nonnus, 6, 12, 31, 60, 64–5, 74, 222, 310
  Dionysiaca, 7, 10, 38, 42–3, 59
nostos, 24, 58, 66, 72–3, 248, 305, 325
novels, Greek, 12, 59, 73, 138, 156
nymphs, 29, 130–2, 263, 265

Odysseus, 18, 43–6, 151, 177, 183, 205, 207, 223–4,
  251, 256–8, 262–3, 305
  beating of Thersites, 33, 280
  bow of, 288, 292, 295–7
  Neoptolemus and, 186–7, 189–90, 192
  nostos of, 325
  Philoctetes and, 35–6, 105–6, 109, 240, 248, 259
  reunion with Penelope, 72–3
  speech to Ajax, 99–104
  trickery, 23, 147–8, 215, 234, 289
Oeagrus, 43
Oenone, 32–3, 132, 198, 204–5, 239, 253, 261,
  265
Olympian gods, 115, 233–6, 271, 278
  intervention in narrative, 120–30, 132, 137,
  169
omens, 78–81, 121, 146–7, 236, 277
Oppian, 240–1
oracles, 149, 240, 242
oral tradition, 228, 301, 303, 305, 313, 318
Orpheus, 43, 354–5, 358–9, 362, 364
Orphic *Argonautica*, 38
Ovid, 155
  Metamorphoses, 10, 18, 24, 58, 134, 310
Ozbek, Leyla, 7–8, 11–12, 237

Pacuvius, 42
Palatine Anthology, 155, 332
Paley, Frederick, 298
Pandarus, 292–5
Paneia games, 55
Panopolis, 55
pantomime, 42–3
Papathomopoulos, Manolis, 4
Paris, 22, 91, 125, 216–17, 335
    Achilles and, 133–6
    death of, 31–3, 254–5, 289, 323–4
    judgement of, 324
    relationship with Oenone, 32, 132, 198, 204–5, 239, 253
Paschal, George W., 231–2, 235, 244
Patroclus, 34, 58–9, 65, 163, 251, 254
    death of, 90, 92, 313
    funeral of, 33, 39, 41, 150, 157, 278, 282
Pausanias, 138
Péguy, Charles, 380
Peleus, 67, 180; *see also* wedding of Peleus and Thetis
Pelion, 45–6, 48
Penelope, 43, 58, 64, 70, 72–3, 194, 199, 206, 216, 218, 262, 272
Penthesileia, 11, 21, 104, 179, 253, 353
    Achilles and, 1, 61–5, 75–6, 81–8, 94, 208, 281–2, 312–17, 179
    at Troy, 33, 77–80, 144–5, 262, 275–7, 311, 318, 355–7
    see also Amazons; Hippolyta
performing arts contests, 55
Perseus, 31
Philoctetes, 11, 30–1, 250, 259, 261, 263, 265, 359
    bow of Heracles, 290–3, 297
    encounter with Paris, 239, 254–65
    interaction with Odysseus and Diomedes, 35–6, 99, 104–9, 240, 287
philology, 307–9, 315, 321–3, 334
Philostratus, 233, 243, 351
    Heroicus, 5, 136, 138, 140–1
    Life of Apollonius, 138
Phoenix, 19, 40, 91, 176, 182–3, 186, 233, 278
Phrygia, 131, 341
Pindar, 134
plague, 257
Plato
    Phaedo, 266
    Republic, 51
Platz, Christian Friedrich, 6
plausibility, 359, 364, 366–7
Pliny the Younger, 155
plot, 10, 24, 123, 306
    Homeric, 123, 161, 252, 254–5, 376–7
    tragic, 249, 251

Plutarch, 41, 138, 241–2
Podaleirius, 29, 100, 102–3, 105–6, 110, 113, 265
poetic contests, 10, 42–3, 55
poetic performance, 38, 56
Poliziano, Angelo, 3
Polydamas, 22–4, 216, 220, 234
Polydorus, 51–2
Polyphemos, 205
Polyxena, 34, 52, 71, 143, 148, 151–7, 190–1, 316
Pompella, Giuseppe, 4, 6
Porphyry, 141, 242–3, 263–5
Poseidon, 127, 139–40, 143, 217, 239, 271–2
    intervention of, 121, 135–6
    wrath of, 127, 258–9, 263, 305
Posthomerica
    as cyclic poem, 300–8
    scholarship on, 3–9
postmodernist theory, 375, 379, 385
praise, 42–6, 53–5, 187, 216, 230
prayer, 37, 142, 150, 155, 191
prequels, 301, 306, 308
Priam, 28, 78–81, 85, 177, 183, 209–12, 288–9
    Achilles and, 103, 111, 218
    grief of, 52, 277
    Neoptolemus' killing of, 34, 179
prizes, 39–41, 55
Proclus, 301–2, 306–7, 311
    Aethiopis, 63, 89, 312–15, 317–18
    Cypria, 52
    Iliou Persis, 151
progymnasmata, 53, 233
Prometheus, 31, 48, 223–4
Pronoe, 29, 130
Propertius, 63, 310, 312
Protestantism, 321; *see also* Christianity; Luther, Martin
pseudo-Hesiod
    Aspis, 196
Ptocheia, 235
purification, 63, 145, 317–18
Pythagoreanism, 309

quaestio Latina, 4, 12
Quintus of Smyrna
    as epigone of Homer, 308–10, 327
    biography of, 1–2, 332

rainbows, 219, 277
ransoms, 41, 210, 248, 251
Reformation, 322, 336, 338, 340
Renker, Stephan, 11–12
repetition, 22, 25, 31, 40, 72, 211, 222, 379–81
re-reading, 11, 61
'revisionary ratio', 376
revisionism, 5, 61, 136, 193, 233, 378

rewriting, 19, 112, 365
rhetoric, 1–2, 200, 353, 359–61, 367–8, 370–1
Rhodoman, Lorenz, 3, 321–41
ridicule, 267, 270–2, 360
Rome, 12, 18, 23, 338, 340

sacrifice, 11, 17, 156–8
    animal, 138–47, 151
    human, 33, 147–56, 190–1
sailors, 24, 28, 85
Sarpedon, 40, 113, 116, 163–4, 207, 254
Scafoglio, Giampiero, 11–12
Scaliger, Joseph, 3
Scamander, 20, 137, 225
Schadenfreude, 268–75, 278–9, 281, 283–5
Scheijnen, Tine, 5, 11, 143
schetliasts, 194–6, 205–13
    female, 197–204
Schoess, A. Sophie, 10–11
scholiasts, 235, 238, 241, 244, 301
Scylaeus, 29–30
Scyros, 48, 54, 189, 256–9, 288
Scythia, 140, 356
sea routes, 257
Second Sophistic, 2, 4–5, 8, 76, 137, 242, 351
Selene, 77, 131
sequels, 40, 61, 161, 247, 378
sexuality, 10, 57
shades see ghosts
shepherds, 237, 328–9, 331, 336
shipwrecks, 24, 73, 127–8
Sibylline Oracles, 240
similes, 65, 85–6, 89–90, 275
    creatures, 20–2, 185, 290, 337–40
    natural world, 71, 236, 261–2, 277
    Penthesileia and, 77, 80–2, 94, 313
    use in the Posthomerica, 6, 27–8, 30–1, 75, 132–3,
        137, 381, 383
Simonides, 151
singing, 42, 43–6, 49, 54
Sinon, 142–3, 148–9, 157, 334, 346
Sisyphus of Cos, 364–5
smiles, 267–71, 285
Smyrna, 1–2, 35, 300, 326–30, 379
sophists, 4–5, 233, 243, 329–30
Sophocles, 151
    Antigone, 197, 236
    Philoctetes, 35–6, 109
Sparta, 44, 68, 73, 343
speech
    character-, 127, 129, 180, 185, 196, 198
    direct, 178, 180, 186
    heroic, 11, 179, 182
    indirect, 26, 43, 98, 259
    see also narrators

Staphylus, 43
Statius
    Achilleid, 76
    Silvae, 3
    Thebais, 326
Stesichorus, 68, 151
    Sack of Troy, 67
Stoicism, 5, 8, 11, 33, 37, 98–9, 110, 119, 164, 176,
        192, 230
    apatheia, 74, 103, 109
    gnōmai, 68, 100–2, 106–7, 117, 184–5, 187–8, 277
    see also aretē; determinism
storms, 24, 28, 73, 151–2, 191, 248, 261–3
Strabo, 138
    Geography, 31, 240
supplementarity (deconstruction), 61–2
suspense, 123, 247–9, 253–5, 280, 291
symbolism, 84, 263–4, 291, 340

Telemachus, 129, 199, 257–9, 295–6
Telephus, 50–1, 53, 182, 243, 358
temporality, 10–11, 17–19, 21, 26–7, 37, 66; see also
    delay
Teucer, 40, 125, 238, 283
Theano, 79, 197–204, 208
Theatre of Aphrodisias, 55
Themis, 17, 279
themis, 196
Theocritus, 231, 239
Theognis, 231, 235
theomachy, 38, 130, 270, 278–80
Theophrastus, 142
Thermodon, 21, 304, 311–12, 356
Thersites, 203, 211–12, 280, 282
    death of, 33, 63, 65, 178, 281, 313–5, 317
    rebuke of Achilles, 178, 205, 208–9, 234, 316
Thetis, 39, 43, 53, 89, 216, 227
    mourning of Achilles, 92–3, 134–6, 139–40
    see also wedding of Peleus and Thetis
time see aiōn; temporality
Tiresias, 236
Titans, 45, 88, 115, 225, 234–5
Tithonus, 51, 85, 226
Tomasso, Vincent, 5, 11–12
translation, 147, 309, 323
    of the Posthomerica, 3, 6
Triphiodorus, 7, 38, 63, 310, 339, 352–5, 358–9,
    361–4
Troilus, 51–2, 316
Trojan Horse, 23, 44–5, 148, 170–1, 187, 252, 255,
    336–40, 355
Trojan War, narrative of, 26, 50, 75, 127, 136–7,
    323, 351
Troy, fall of, 10–11, 24, 247–56, 259, 336, 354
Tsomis, Georgios P., 192

Tychsen, Thomas Christian, 3, 118
Tzetzes, John
    discussion of Homer's sources, 364–8
    on Machaon, 357–9
    on Nestor and Memnon, 359–61
    on Penthesileia, 355–7
    response to Triphiodorus, 351–5
    treatment of Quintus, 361–4, 368–72

urgency, narrative, 248, 255–7, 259, 266, 289
usefulness (of literature), 303, 323, 333, 367, 370

Vian, Francis, 3–4, 40, 117, 164, 175, 183, 232, 259,
    298, 370
Virgil, 312, 338, 365
    Aeneid, 18–19, 147, 149, 151, 334, 340, 376
    as Homeric imitator, 310
    Quintus and, 4, 12, 147, 247
Visio Dorothei, 2
visual art, 10, 67, 76, 80–3, 88–94
virtue, 23, 34–5, 42, 54, 101, 107, 117, 367
von Holle, Eberhard (bishop of Lübeck), 323,
    330–3

wasps, 339–40
weaving, 79, 214
wedding of Peleus and Thetis, 25, 44–9, 52, 54, 211,
    217, 223
weighing scales, 162
Welare, Joost, 3
Wenglinsky, Maria, 164
western films, 229, 244
Whitmarsh, Tim, 5, 7
Wooden Horse *see* Trojan Horse

Xenophanes, 60
Xanthos (horse), 133
Xanthos (river), 51–2, 131, 224, 341, 353

Zeus, 17, 22, 47–8, 157, 163–4, 177, 226
    Fate(s) and, 32, 88, 97, 99–101, 109–16
    intervention of, 34, 87, 89, 135, 253
    prevention of divine intervention, 85, 120–3,
        278–9
    scales of, 162
    thunder and lightning of, 45, 84, 86, 132, 188,
        227, 262, 275, 312

Printed in the USA
CPSIA information can be obtained
at www.ICGtesting.com
JSHW052030231023
50693JS00005B/33